Contents

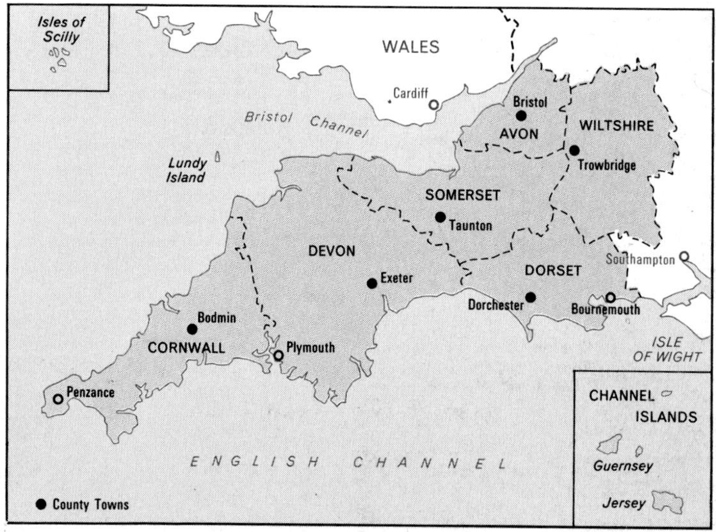
Isles of Scilly
WALES
Cardiff
Bristol Channel
Bristol
AVON
WILTSHIRE
Trowbridge
Lundy Island
SOMERSET
Taunton
DEVON
Southampton
DORSET
Exeter
Dorchester
Bournemouth
Bodmin
CORNWALL
Plymouth
ISLE OF WIGHT
Penzance
CHANNEL ISLANDS
ENGLISH CHANNEL
Guernsey
Jersey
County Towns

PRINCIPAL SIGHTS

Worth a journey ★★★

Worth a detour ★★

Interesting ★

The names of towns or sights described in the guide appear in black on the maps. See the index for the page number.

0 — 30 km — 20 miles

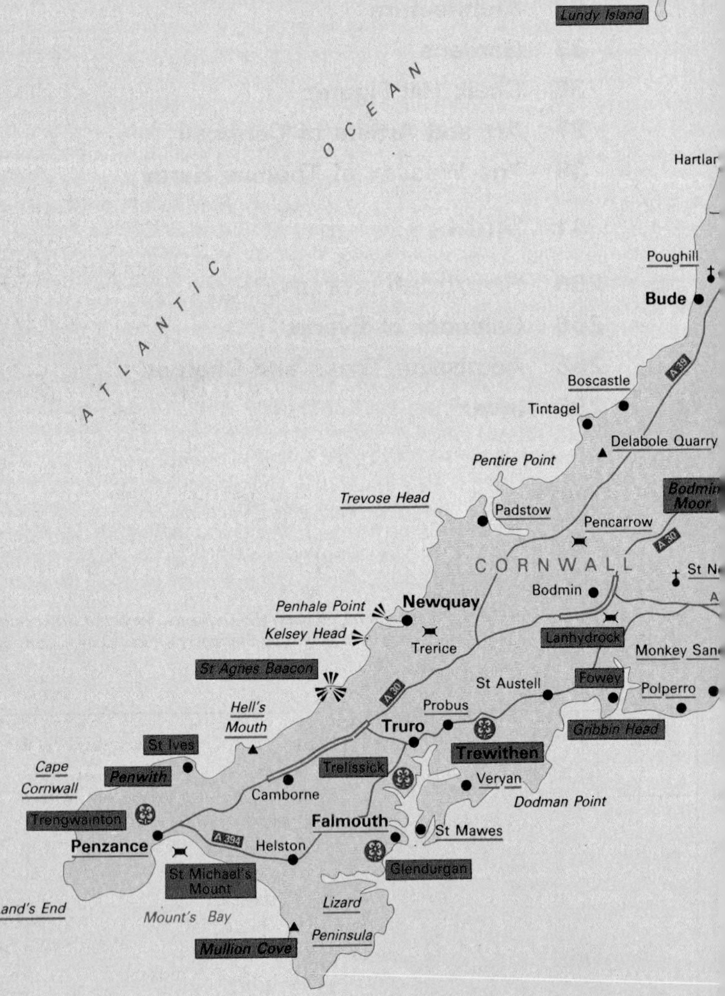

Isles of Scilly

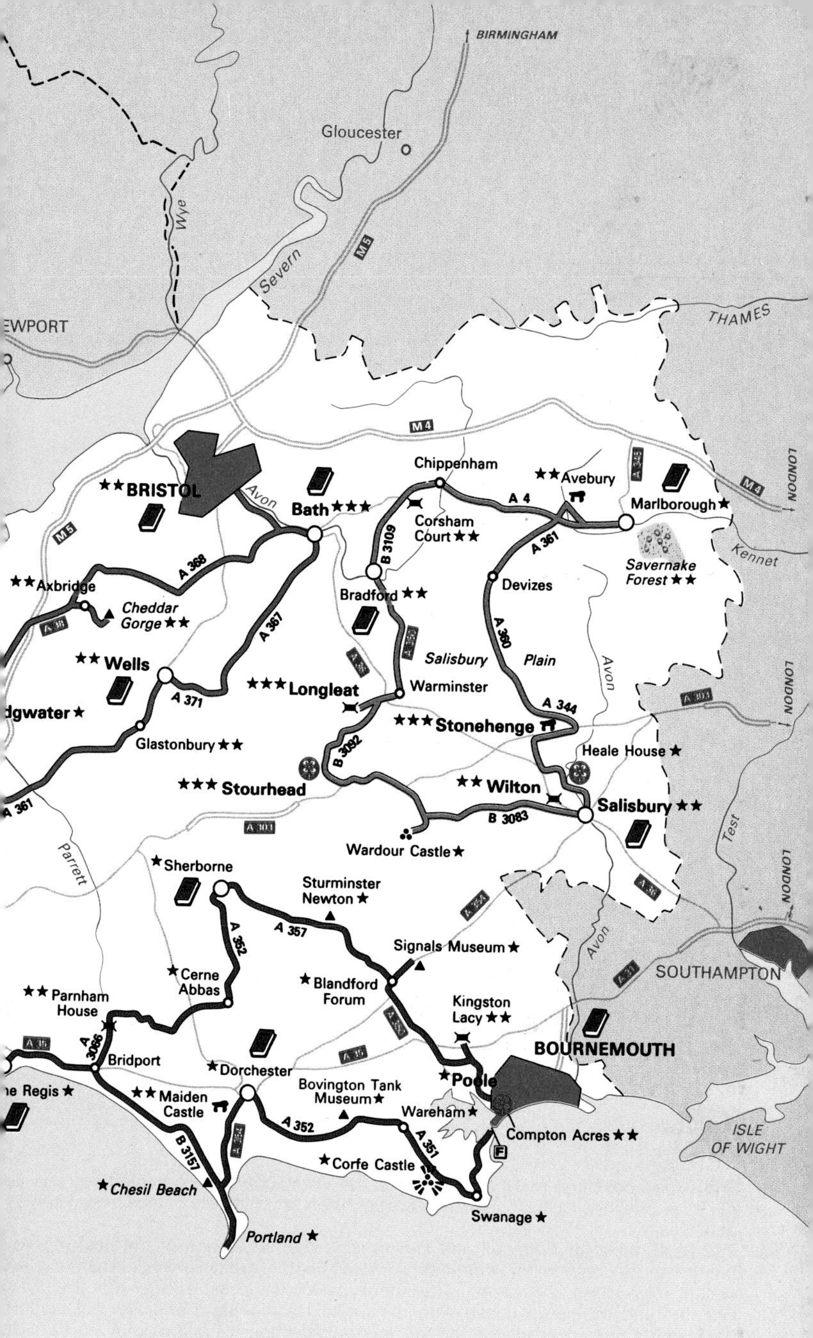

TOUR : Wiltshire (100 miles)

TOUR : Somerset (200 miles)

TOUR : Devon (250 miles)

TOUR : Cornwall (300 miles)

TOUR : Dorset (150 miles)

PLACES TO STAY

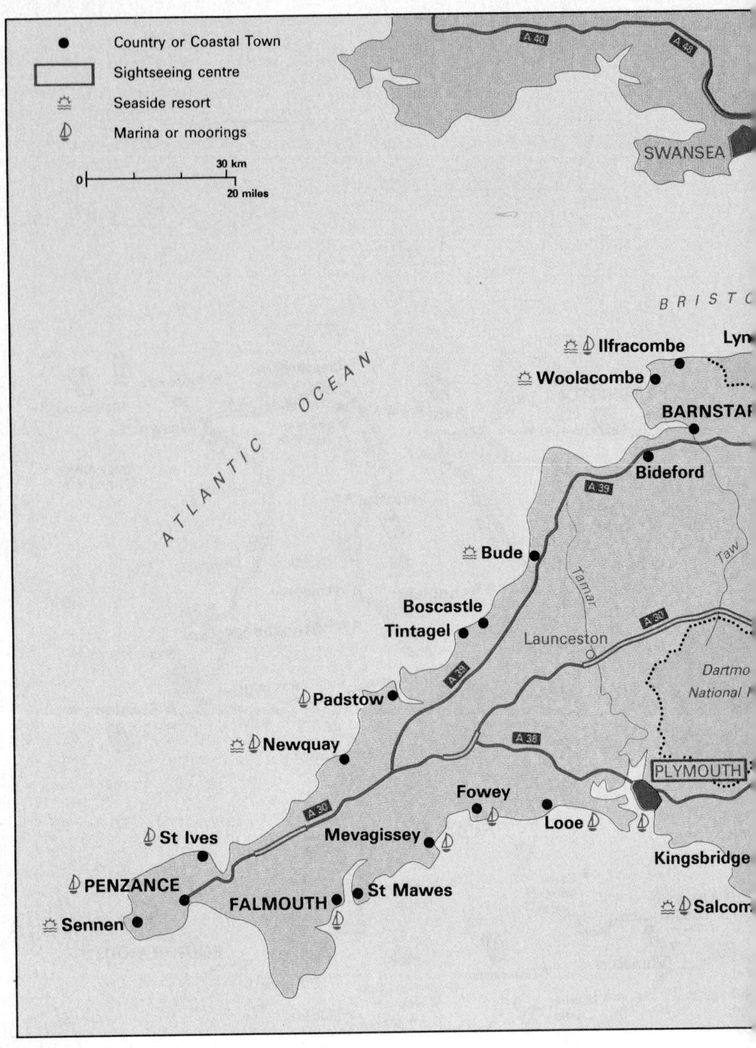

The varied coastline and countryside of the West Country, combined with its la of heavy industry, make it a perfect location for a great variety of leisure and sportir activities.

The north coast of Cornwall and Devon is renowned as one of the best places the south of England for windsurfing owing to the great swell of Atlantic wav which rolls along the shore. The more protected coast further up the Bris Channel and the south coast, with their miles of fine sand and rows of colour beach huts, are ideal places for the archetypal English holiday with buckets a spades, sand castles, ice creams, donkey rides... Between the beaches lie seclud coves and inlets with rock pools in which to delve for pebbles, fossils or mari life.

Water sports, for which there are excellent facilities alongside the pict resque harbours and bustling marinas throughout the region, include yachtir dinghy sailing, motor boating, jet-skiing and water-skiing; among the regular nautic events are regatttas and powerboat races. The inland waterways prese opportunities for canal barging or leisurely cruises along enchanting rivers a estuaries.

The West Country is a favoured location for birdwatchers who can observe t fascinating resident and migrant birdlife *(illustration p 25)*. Animal lovers can al view a wide range of species in the numerous local nature reserves, wildlife pa and animal sanctuaries (which nurture otters, seals, puffins, donkeys, monke parrots...).

Inland, the great moors provide ample acres for rambling, orienteering and po trekking while enthusiasts go pot-holing and caving underground.

Romantics can trace the literary heritage of Hardy's Wessex or King Arthur's real or explore the more ancient mysteries of prehistoric man. Botanists a horticulturalists have a wide choice of fine gardens to visit, and lovers of architectu or history may tour some of the many historic houses and fine churches in t region.

The map above highlights the main seaside resorts and other picturesque tow and villages in which to stay, together with the main boating centres. For deta on sporting and other organisations to contact, refer to the chapter on **Practi Information** at the end of this guide.

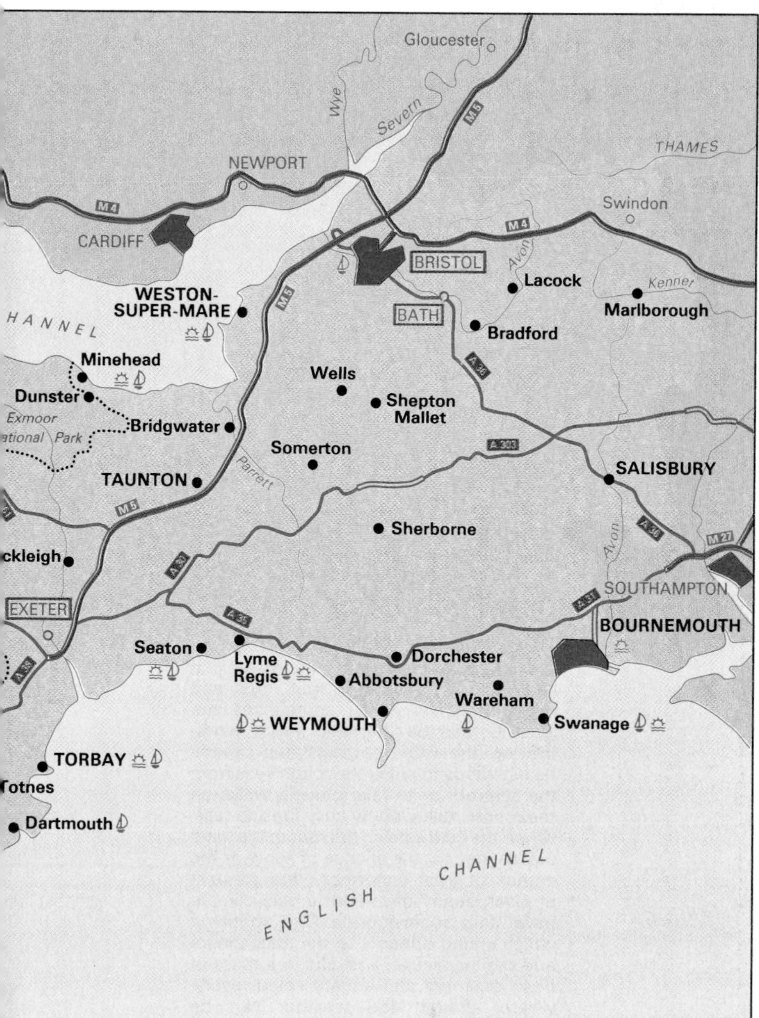

STEAM RAILWAYS

Until the advent of the railway in the 19C the West Country was relatively inaccessible except by stage coach, a dangerous mode of travel in the days when coaches were vulnerable to attack by highwaymen.

The Great Western Railway, which was formed in the 1830s with Isambard Kingdom Brunel as its Engineer, operated its first steam locomotives, between London and Bristol, in 1843. By 1878 the company had incorporated into its network the Bristol and Exeter Railway, the South Devon Railway and the Cornwall Railway, thereby giving it control of all the broad-gauge tracks west of Bristol.

Today the many steam railways operating in the West Country have a nostalgic appeal.

The smart livery of the locomotives and passenger carriages, together with the smell of the steam and the distinctive noise of the train, recaptures the spirit of a more romantic age of travel.

The dozen or so engines running on broad-gauge tracks throughout the region (there are also numerous narrow-gauge railways in the area) include the following :

Avon Valley Railway	Willsbridge, Avon
Bodmin and Wenford Railway	Bodmin, Cornwall
East Somerset Railway	Cranmore, Somerset
Lappa Valley Steam Railway	St Newlyn East, Cornwall
Launceston Steam Railway	Lauceston, Cornwall
Paignton and Dartmouth Steam Railway	Paignton, Devon
Plym Valley Railway	Plymouth, Devon
South Devon Railway	Buckfastleigh, Devon
Swindon and Cricklade Railway	Blunsden, Wiltshire
West Somerset Railway	Minehead, Somerset

Owing to the southwesterly position of the West Country, the hot days of summer fade into warm autumnal months tempered by chilly mornings and evenings - weather for strolls along the uncrowded beaches, or in the russet and gold forests to harvest fruit, nuts and mushrooms. As winter approaches, the weather can be dramatic : it is worth braving the wild tempests and breathtaking winds to enjoy the rough seas from the seafront or to take bracing walks on the moors, followed by cosy fireside teas. When the cold sets in, the roar of the wind makes way for the silence of snow or the crunch of frost underfoot : the contrast of clear, sunny days with a cold climate never fails to invigorate. The softening which spring brings - to the atmosphere and the landscape - results in a mass of fresh greenery and vibrant colour everywhere, though the weather can be changeable, alternating between blustery showers and glorious sunshine. As the days lengthen and then become hotter, so the West Country draws the crowds; its spectacular coastlines and unspoilt countryside make it one of Britain's most popular holiday destinations.

Introduction

THE COUNTIES OF THE WEST COUNTRY

WILTSHIRE

Area 1344 sq m

Wiltshire is a fertile, undulating county, bounded along its eastern border by the distinctive Marlborough Downs; south and west lies open country watered by the Wylye and other rivers. The many stretches of woodland include the small but soaring Savernake Forest. Great houses and manor houses with their gardens enhance the landscape's natural beauty. Important monuments and what many consider to be England's finest cathedral contrast with small and friendly market towns, picture-postcard villages, tithe barns and village greens.

At the centre of Wiltshire rises the great Salisbury Plain (some of it used for army training and consequently out of bounds), part of the range of chalk hills which run southwest into Dorset, and which rise as the North Downs south of the Thames Valley into Surrey, as the South Downs in Sussex. Throughout the ages the downlands have supplied pasture for large flocks of sheep, and, more recently, arable land for farming.

The chalk downlands have their own particular legacy : the enormous chalk figures *(qv)* which have been carved out of the turf and are almost unique to this area, and an abundance of prehistoric monuments – Wiltshire has the greatest concentration of large-scale prehistoric monuments in England – including the three finest in Europe (Stonehenge, Avebury and Silbury). Many of the prehistoric monuments are near the end of the ancient Ridgeway Path, the upland trail which provided access across five counties for contemporary tribesmen.

The network of roads has developed from the Ridgeway Path, through Roman, Saxon and medieval highways and post roads, turnpikes and coaching roads, to the modern trunk roads and the motorway (M4); the canal was dug early in the 19C; later in the same century came the Great Western Railway.

AVON

Area 520 sq m

The county, created under the Local Government Act of 1972, comprises the city of Bristol which had been granted county status in its own right as far back as 1373 by Edward III and a area of north Somerset including the city of Bath, but not Wells. Its existence is currently under review.

The Bristol Channel, or Severn Estuary, forms the county's northwesterly shoreline from which the view extends across the water to the hills of South Wales. The gentle rise and fall of the wooded countryside perfectly shields and reveals some fine country houses (Clevedon Court, Dyrham Park, Claverton Manor).

The two cities – Bristol and Bath afford infinite variety to the visitor through their contrasting backgrounds and their current atmosphere. The former was a port made prosperous through the sea and merchant trading, the venturers closely allied and always generous to their city. The latter city was built for recreation and leisure in the Roman age, rebuilt and fashionable in Stuart times and rebuilt again as the supreme example in England of urban planning in the 18C.

Each city has its "great man" : Bath in the 18C was transformed by **Beau Nash**; Bristol will always bear the imprint of **Isambard Kingdom Brunel** (1806-59). In 1830 Brunel's design for the Clifton Suspension Bridge was accepted; in 1833 his plans for improvement of the city docks were agreed; in the same year he was appointed Engineer to the newly formed Great Western Railway with the specific task of opening the line between London and Bristol. As a result he supervised the laying of 118 miles of track (Stephenson's 11 mile Stockton-Darlington line : 1826) and the excavation of the nearly 2 miles long Box Tunnel; he designed Temple Meads Station and collaborated with the architects of Paddington Station. By 1841 he was engaged on what he saw as an "extension" to the London-Bristol railway, namely ships to provide a regular trans-Atlantic service : the *SS Great Western*, a paddlesteamer launched out of Bristol in 1837, the *SS Great Britain* and finally, the colossal *SS Great Eastern.*

SOMERSET

Area 1332 sq m

Somerset derives its name from "summer land" or "land of the summer-farm dwellers" as it was once largely marshland out of which rose, like islands, the numerous hills of the region : only in summer could the livestock be brought down from the hills to graze on the rich pasture of the "levels" which in winter were flooded over. The region ranked fourth in the production of wool *(qv)* when England was the premier wool producing country in the world.

The county, which lies on a limestone base, has a generous number of hills : the Mendips, the Poldens, the Quantocks, the Brendons and the Blackdowns, not forgetting the sharp mount from which Montacute's name originates. It also boasts the open heathland and wooded valleys of Exmoor, fine caves (Cheddar Gorge, Wookey Hole) and excellent agricultural land – the Vale of Taunton is one of the great farming areas of England; as long ago as the 12C Henry II was buying Cheddar Cheese.

Church Building in Somerset – In this county where some claimed that Glastonbury had been founded by Joseph of Arimathea, the medieval wool prosperity coincided with the 13C-16C period of church renewal and rebuilding, the Gothic Perpendicular period, which was aided by the abundance of fine, workable, building stone *(qv)* in the region. The local lord of the manor or squire funded the church chancel and family chapels; the parishioners, the nave, the aisles and transepts. Construction, furnishings and embellishment were executed by bands of travelling masons, stone-cutters, carpenters and skilled carvers in stone and wood.

Towers, which in Norman churches rose above the crossing and were crowned with spires, were shifted to the west end and ceased to support often dangerous, tapering cones. They were the last part of the church to be built and marked the triumphant culmination of local enterprise – they became objects of considerable local rivalry.

The requirement of a west tower to include a belfry was universal but it became evident over time that there was a seemingly infinite number of ways of combining in the upper parts blank lights, bell lights, buttresses, pinnacles, castellations, friezes and panelling, rising tier upon tier, ever higher...

A unique ornament was the filling of the upper lights with **Somerset tracery,** uniformly carved screens of the tractable stone.

Bishop's Lydeard

Batcombe

Evercreech

Bristol

Taunton

The travelling masons must have carried ideas from site to site; villagers undoubtedly went to see and report back what was being erected in the neighbouring parish. Today, 400-500 years on, partisanship is still strong.

Church roofs – The church interiors demonstrate the skill of the woodmen : the carpenters in the wagon, hammer-beam, tie-beam, king and queen post roofs; the carvers in the moulding, the cresting, the wall plates, the infinitely varied bosses, the panelling and tracery, and most notably, the life-size angels.

Earlier than the parish churches had come the great glory that is Wells Cathedral.

DORSET

Area 1 025 sq m

The beauty and charm of Dorset lies in its variety, the contrast between the coast and the hinterland which, even a few miles inland, seems remote from the sea.

Between the North and low-lying South Dorset Downs, so close to the sea that the Osmington White Horse with George III upon it is best seen from offshore, the countryside extends east and north in a series of barren heath-covered moors. The whole area, from Blackmoor Vale in the west to the part-forested, part-cleared Cranborne Chase in the east, is drained by gentle rivers flowing north-south to the sea.

Southeast of Wareham, the so-called "isle" of Purbeck is separated from the mainland" by a line of hills, the only gap on the skyline being filled by the gaunt outlines of Corfe Castle.

The landscape, which incorporates rock which has been quarried for centuries to build houses and cathedrals, is windswept on the headlands, steeply undulating and wooded just inland. The heather often gives the hills a blue-purple aspect.
Dorset's cliff-lined coast is marked by arches or "doors" in primeval rocks (eg Durdle Door), the off-shore chalk stacks known as the Old Harry Rocks, by golden sand beaches, the unique Chesil Beach, towering headlands and the long Isle of Portland. Lyme Regis and the Cobb provide excellent sites for fossil-hunting. Further inland, Dorset boasts Maiden Castle – considered to be the finest earthwork in Britain – the beautiful small abbey at Sherborne, and some fine country towns (Dorchester, Wimborne, Wareham, Blandford Forum...).

Thomas Hardy statue, Dorchester.

Dorset Worthies – The classic Dorset Worthies, including Thomas Hardy *(qv)*, were men of the 17C-19C and first quarter of the 20C; more recent local luminaries include the glass engraver Laurence Whistler *(qv)*; Reynolds Stone, the letterer on wood and stone who designed the monograms and "logos" which gave a distinctive style to print, trade-marks, bookplates, programmes and name plates for a generation; John Fowles, the novelist; John Makepiece, the furniture designer...

DEVON

Area 2 591sq m (3rd largest county in England after N Yorkshire and Cumbria)

Devon became popular from the mid-19C when the advent of the railway made the county much more accessible; the fine sand or shingle beaches along both its northern and southern borders, the verdant valleys of its many rivers and the wildness offered by the Dartmoor National Park with its free-roaming ponies have ensured that it has remained a perennial favourite.
The spectacular cliffs and headlands along the north coast (interspersed with the miles of sand beaches at Wesward Ho!, Croyde and Woolacombe) are in contrast with the more gentle coves, headlands and estuaries of the south coast, which are accessible at every point by the South Devon Coast Path.
At Devon's centre is the granite boss of Dartmoor, tilted southwards with the highest tors and widest horizons to the north, the network of narrow, wooded lanes and villages to the south.
Numerous rivers and streams keep the area lush.

The American Connection – The early history of the United States, it has been claimed, owes more to Devon than to any other English county; more emigrant ships left Devon bound for North America, more expeditions sailed westward from Plymouth than from all other English ports put together. Probably the most famous expedition was that of the Pilgrim Fathers who finally sailed from Plymouth in the *Mayflower* on 6 September 1620. After three months of sailing through ever-shortening days, they finally landed at New Plymouth, now Plymouth Massachusetts, on 21 December.

The 17C-19C colonists – Jamestown, Virginia, established on 14 May 1620, was the first permanent English settlement in the New World.
In the early 17C fishermen were not only landing in America to dry their catches and re-supply their boats but had set up trading posts with the Indians for furs. Numbers increased : it has been estimated that between 1600 and 1770, 750 000 people crossed the Atlantic. The passage cost £10; the ships, some of only ten tons were not adapted to passenger transport at all, returning home with timber and fish.
By the 19C the traffic divided into bulk traffic through the larger ports for the poorer people – it is estimated that half a million emigrants sailed out of Plymouth alone – and individual passages on ships using the smaller ports such as Bideford and Torquay.
The middle of the century saw a further transformation with the development of steam-driven transport, the increase in the size of ships, the inauguration of regular trans-Atlantic services with ships such as the *SS Great Western* and *SS Great Britain (qv)*.

Place-names – Although English immigrants were not the most numerous to colonize America, a large number of place-names in the United States do derive from the towns, villages and counties of England; around 120-150 of them are from Devon alone.

CORNWALL

Area 1376 sq m

Cornwall is a county of "diversified pleasings" as Richard Carew *(qv)* phrased it : of wonderful coastal scenery, jagged headlands, sheer cliffs and offshore needles, of golden sand beaches and picturesque harbours; of rock outcrops and standing stones on the windswept, open moorland; of lush, heron-haunted river valleys with banks densely fringed with oak trees, of glorious gardens contrasting with the stark chimneys of derelict copper and tin mines.

It is a land of Celtic legend and the saints, of King Arthur and fairy tale giants, of the 'Obby 'Oss and the famous Furry Dance.

The Cornish economy, which was for so long dependent on copper and tin mining *(qv)*, now relies on the mining of china clay. Farming has changed from the vast sheep flocks of the Middle Ages, 16C and 17C which provided so much wool *(qv)* to cattle and crops together with, since the coming of the railway in the 19C, the production of early vegetables and, in the far west and Isles of Scilly, flowers.

The Duchy of Cornwall – William of Normandy created his half-brother, Roger of Mortain, first Earl of Cornwall soon after the Conquest. Roger's lands extended far beyond the bounds of Cornwall into Devon, Somerset and even Gloucestershire.

In 1337 the Duchy of Cornwall was created by Edward III from the former earldom, for his son Edward, the Black Prince (1330-76). Since 1503 the monarch's eldest son as heir apparent has always succeeded to the title. The lands still extend beyond the confines of Cornwall into Devon (including much of Dartmoor) and Somerset and today number 130 000 acres in the West Country alone.

Until the 19C the Duchy gained its wealth from the "coinage" dues or stamp with the duchy seal which was required on every smelted block of tin before it could be sold, a duty performed in the Stannary Towns of both Cornwall and Devon. In 1838 the dues were abolished by parliament and compensation paid. Today the Duchy leases estates, farms and individual houses to tenants, farms land and manages great tracts of woodland on its own behalf. Work on the Duchy estates is displayed each year in exhibits at the Royal Cornwall Agricultural Show.

Christianity – According to tradition, Cornwall was converted by saintly men who sailed the sea on millstones and lilypads. In fact Christianity was probably introduced, before the Roman invasion of Britain, by missionaries from Gaul who followed the ancient trade routes established in the 6C BC by Phoenicians buying copper and Irish gold.

The earliest inscriptions, using the oldest form of the XP monogram, have been found along the main road running north-south across Cornwall, and there are similarities with the sculptures on Irish crosses and those in southern Gaul.

Several of the early Celtic priests were deeply venerated in their lifetime and were canonised by the early church. Neither the departure of the Romans nor the Saxon invasion in the second half of the 5C influenced this church, which continued in the old Celtic practice in religious matters until the 10C when King Athelstan conquered Cornwall, established the English diocese of Cornwall and introduced the latest Roman practice.

In the early days the missionary monks preached in the open. As certain sites became recognised places of assembly and worship, they were marked by a cross. Later the people built small wooden chapels or, in west Cornwall where wood is scarce, stone cairns. As the Saxon invasion of Cornwall proceeded (9C-10C), these primitive chapels were gradually replaced by stone structures, which were themselves replaced in the 12C-13C by churches in the Norman-Romanesque style.

The fervour of the people whose lives on the land had always been so poor, and at sea so perilous, the ardour of the church itself, brought about a new wave of rebuilding, in the Perpendicular style, during the 15C-17C when there was a wave of prosperity among the tin-miners. Thereafter came a period, lasting 200-300 years, of almost total neglect followed, in the 19C, by vigorous restoration which, at least, saved the fabric. Work undertaken today has tended to bring out again the local character of the buildings.

Churches – Outside, the towers are all different, most noticeably those on the coast which served as important landmarks to mariners; slate, to be seen on the roofs, serves also as louvres in belfry openings, as biscuit-thin tombstones in churchyards and memorial tablets against church walls outside and in, and is often beautifully lettered and incised.

Inside, note the oak wagon roofs, sometimes with carved wall plates; the massive fonts, circular with bold geometric moulding, and the powerful, square-cut, granite vessels with bearded heads, once coloured, at the angles. Finally, look out for 15C-16C bench-ends, carved in oak with Biblical and local scenes and personalities.

Celtic crosses – There are some 300 crosses scattered in the county marking sacred sites (see above), in churchyards *(usually east of the south porch)*, by the wayside or in fields, indicating the route followed by pall bearers bringing a corpse for burial. They are usually incised on the shaft with typical Celtic-Irish interlacings and knots, and carved with signs of the Cross, the Chi-Rho (XP) monogram, the figure of Christ, sometimes in a tunic *(illustration p 231)*.

The See of Cornwall – Historically the Cornish church remained independent of the Saxon Christian church established by St Augustine until AD 926 when King Athelstan, having completed the political and religious conquest of Cornwall, created a Cornish See on the Saxon model. The bishopric endured until 1043 when it was transferred first to Crediton then to Exeter. Only in 1876 did Cornwall once again become independent, a new cathedral being erected in Truro in celebration.

THE LAND

TENURE

Dating from the time when kingdoms were considered to be the personal property of a king or chieftain, grants of land were the rewards made to favourites both secular and episcopal. When Edward the Confessor came to the throne in 1042, however, he decreed that all royal lands that had been assigned by his forerunners to the Saxon nobility should be returned to the crown.

William I, therefore, took over extensive crown lands. He retained very considerable territories, notably the royal chases or forests; he gave great swathes, particularly on the borders of the kingdom, to his half-brothers including **Robert of Mortain,** first Earl of Cornwall, and his barons including the de Redvers, appointed sheriffs and subsequently created the first Earls of Devon. The barons built motte and bailey castles to defend their, and the Conqueror's, land against the Celts and continental invaders.

William I also gave extensive property to the Church for the foundation of new monasteries which, by their preaching and care of the poor, would further the pacification of the kingdom and by their clearance of scrubland, draining of marshlands, farming and animal husbandry, would increase its wealth.

Many of the monasteries and convents founded by the king and by his barons were dependent houses of existing communities in France (eg St Michael's Mount and the Benedictines).

By the 14C, however, Edward III considered that the Church should be restrained and passed a statute of mortmain. The Hundred Years War had begun (1327-1453) and although Henry IV rejected a parliamentary petition to disendow the Church, he fined monasteries with overseas connections; his heir, Henry V, under the Alienation Act forced all religious houses to sever overseas connections.

The Church, which had reached a peak of learning and husbandry in the 13C-14C, was in decline; the number of religious, reduced by between one half and a third like the population as a whole by the Black Death in 1348-50, never regained its size or its energy; establishments were run by an abbot or prior, a handful of religious and numerous lay servants. The land remained in the Church's possession but fell into neglect.

Dissolution of the Monasteries – Henry VIII, urged on by Wolsey in the early years of his reign, began by dis-establishing the monastic houses with less than five religious; Thomas Cromwell made his inventory. The ambitious and the land-hungry urged the king on to further action and Henry, who was by this time (1535) in dispute with the pope (over his divorce from Catherine of Aragon and subsequent marriage to Anne Boleyn in 1533), demanded that all churchmen take the Oath of Supremacy, acknowledging him as head of the Church in place of the pope; finally he decreed the Dissolution.

Over 800 of them were dissolved in 1536-39, which not only enriched the monarch's own coffers with their treasure but also brought about a major redistribution of land throughout the realm.

Land previously held in mortmain or in perpetuity as a possession of the Church returned to the hazards of private ownership, of division, exchange, sale and, for many centuries, royal attainder. Prosperous Tudor merchants, venturers, the newly ennobled, second sons, were able to purchase tracts of land; those with estates extended them or purchased property in other parts of the country.

So much was available – one third of the total acreage of the kingdom, it has been estimated – that prices were not exorbitant. Commissioners were appointed for each area and sales continued into the latter part of Elizabeth's reign.

A condition of sale was that if the abbey church was not required by the parish (as at Sherborne or Stogursey) it should be razed (as at Glastonbury and Abbotsbury) if the church remained, monastic buildings must be obliterated. Whatsoever the

Wilton House, Wiltshire.

alternative, the new owner, therefore, frequently found himself the possessor not only of his land but of a quantity of ready dressed stone. With this he built a house to rival those already in existence which went back to Domesday and the Conquest. These, both the 16C and the medieval, together make up, in greater part, England's unique heritage of historic houses.

Post 16C Landholders – The character of the houses erected after the Dissolution varied in different parts of the country, reflecting confidence in a peaceful future or the probability of border wars. In the West Country the houses were built as residences without fortifications – even where towers, crenellations and gatehouses were included there were also large Perpendicular-style windows. Estates were let to tenant farmers who constructed the manor houses still to be seen in Wiltshire, north Dorset and Somerset.

Four areas only in the region were "different" : the estates of the Duchy of Cornwall where, by definition, there are no "big" houses although there are many farmhouses; Bodmin Moor; Dartmoor and Exmoor National Parks.

WOOL

"The history of the change from medieval to modern England" G M Trevelyan wrote, "might well be written in the form of a social history of the cloth trade". The starting point of that trade was the Black Death.

There had been sheep in Britain since prehistoric times and Stone and Iron Age men had woven wool into cloth. The Normans improved the breeds and while wool was spun and woven for the home market, trade was almost entirely in raw wool.

In the 1350s, after the plague had so reduced the population that there was insufficient manpower to till the fields, harvest the crops and tend cattle, and those freemen who survived had put a premium on their labour and villeins demanded their freedom, the farmers turned to the labour-saving practice of sheep-farming. Soon every village in the West Country, especially in Wiltshire, Dorset and Somerset, appeared to have its regular sheep market and annual wool fair when the fleeces would be sold. Among the early successful farmers were the Cistercian monks of Norton-St-Philip priory which, like many others, developed long-term trade arrangements for the export of fleeces to sister houses on the Continent.

Although by comparison with today's breeds the sheep were small and many died or were killed for want of winter feed, flocks numbered many hundreds and the national total many million. The fleeces, more abundant but coarser on the large, valley stock, were lighter and finer on the upland sheep; they probably weighed between 3-6lbs as against today's 8-20lbs and even 40lbs.

English native cloth remained coarse-woven until the 14C when Edward III brought in Flemish Huguenot weavers, fullers and dyers who gave a new impetus to the industry. Every cottage came to have its spinning wheel, most also had handlooms; evidence of the weavers remains in the wide windows in their former cottages. Fulling mills became common wherever there was water, village greens and fields became quartered with the hooked tenter frames on which cloth was stretched and dried.

By the end of the 14C 5 000 pieces of cloth were being exported annually from England to the Continent in addition to raw wool; by the late 16C the number was 100 000 pieces. Wool had replaced corn as the most important crop in farming; raw wool was prohibited from export in order to maintain supplies for home weavers – a prohibition that gave rise to smuggling on a vast scale and was repealed only in 1824; the government alone could negotiate the sale of wool abroad as in the **Methuen Treaty** of 1703 with Portugal. As a further protection of the industry in the 17C, parliament passed acts to lessen the import of linen and decreed that no material (ie a shroud) unless made entirely of sheep's wool be allowed to be put in a coffin" under penalty of a £5 fine.

By the 15C-16C the wool industry had grown to such an extent that new merchant guilds were formed to control the raw wool and cloth-weaving traders – the staplers and clothiers.

Proof of this long period of considerable prosperity in the West Country appears in the great and small houses, and in Somerset especially in the parish churches with their exterior and interior decoration and, most individually, in their rival west towers. The industry that Daniel Defoe in the 18C constantly refers to in his *Tour through the Whole Island of Great Britain* and describes as "the richest and most valuable manufacture in the world" continued as the mainstay of the West Country until textile fashions changed and processes were altered by the coming of the Industrial Revolution in the 19C.

MINING

Diodorus Siculus, the 1C BC Greek historian, wrote that the Cornish "work the tin into pieces the form of knuckle-bones and convey it to an island which lies off Britain and is called Ictis... the merchants purchase the tin of the natives and carry it from there across the Straits of Gaul" to Greece, Rome or Egypt.

An ingot of that period, shaped in an H form and weighing nearly 160lbs, was found in the River Fal and is now in Truro Museum. The alluvial tin from which it was made was "clean" or nearly pure and could be smelted with charcoal obtained from the dense woods then covering much of the county.

Production was local and with tin so important, by the early Middle Ages the "streamers" or miners had acquired rights and privileges including special courts and a local parliament in four **stannary or coinage towns** chartered by King John – Truro, Helston, Liskeard and Lostwithiel (to which Penzance was added in 1663). There the courts sat, the ingots were assayed and stamped *(see below)* or "coined" with the Duchy seal – hence Coinagehall Street in Helston.

Between 1770 and 1870 copper took precedence over tin as gun manufacture was changing and the Royal Navy became supreme; there was, however, always war, either at sea, in Europe, in the Crimea or in America.
In Cornwall there were 340 mines employing 50 000 men, women and children, one in five of the population. The children's job was to crush the mined ore with stamping machines and pick it over. It has been estimated that, in the 19C, Cornish mining was the unhealthiest occupation in Britain : deaths from accidents and lung diseases were three times higher than among coal miners. 30 million tons of ore were mined in the period of a hundred years, producing 1½ million tons (5%) of pure copper (smelted with coal in Wales). The peak price reached was £100 a ton. In the 19C England became the greatest single producer of copper in the world. British men o' war were "copper bottomed" to prevent parasites and barnacles attacking the hulls and to increase their speed.
At the end of the 19C, the tide turned again : recession spread from America to Europe; new and more accessible deposits were discovered in every continent; prices fell; the mines closed; more than 30% of the miners and their families emigrated until it was said that at the bottom of every hole the world over you would find a Cornish miner. In the 20C tin mining revived until the collapse of the market in 1986; now South Crofty, near Camborne, is the only mine still operating. Relics of the old mines, in the form of disused engine houses and sentinel stacks romantically mark the hills along the north coast and even Cape Cornwall.
China-clay mining around St Austell, by comparison, is a modern industry. Hugely profitable, it has marked the local landscape with green-white slag pyramids and is now Cornwall's economic mainstay.

TRADE

Trade through itinerant merchants walking the Ridgeway Path, Phoenicians and Mediterranean peoples shipping tin and copper from Cornwall, the Romans transporting lead from the Mendips to Pompeii, was transformed in the 16C-17C by the discoveries of the navigators, the spirit of commercial adventure "our chiefe desire, " Richard Hakluyt the geographer (1552?-1616) declared, is "to find out ample vent of our wollen cloth, the naturall comoditie of this our Realme". He went on to propose the opening of new markets in Japan, north China and Tartary.
In the early days boats were small and had only a shallow draft enabling coaster and cross-Channel craft to go far upriver to Exeter, Topsham, Bridgwater; as ship increased in size estuary harbours came into their own and finally the deepwate harbours of Plymouth and Fowey, and Bristol where a constant water level wa ensured by the construction of the Floating Harbour in the 19C.
Bristol became the second city in England after London but even so handled onl 10% of the national trade (the figure for London until the second half of the 20 was always over 50%). Hampered by the smallness of the local population and th lack of local communications – transport was by pack-horse and cart – the Wes Country sought to improve facilities by the construction of canals.
These were almost immediately overtaken by the steam railway, but meanwhile th woollen cloth industry had been first mechanized and then removed to the Midland and North, for which the local port was Liverpool.

THE SEA

THE NAVIGATORS

In the 16C Britain "shifted" from being on the outer edge of navigational char to being at the centre. When the caravan routes to the Orient, opened up by Marc Polo in the 13C, were suddenly closed, the Venetian Empire and the Mediterranea powers ceased to be at the hub of east-west trade.
The navigators of the Atlantic seaboard, particularly the Portuguese, who we encouraged and guided by Prince Henry the Navigator, and the Genoese, who we financed by Venice and Spain, set out to find a route to the east round Africa; th prize was gold, jewels, silks and the costly spices so much in demand at home give flavour to poorly preserved or even rotten meat.
Ports on the **Atlantic seaboard,** Lisbon especially, and later Bristol and Plymout assumed importance; Madeira and the Azores were discovered; the Portugues Bartolemea Dias rounded the Cape of Good Hope (1488) and Vasco da Gam reached Calicut in southern India (1498); in 1492 Christopher Columbus, a Genoe under the patronage of Ferdinand and Isabella of Castile, set out westwards ar discovered **America.**
The following year in 1493, under the Treaty of Tordesillas, the pope divided th discovered and the yet to be discovered world between Spain and Portugal alor a meridian which, in the event, cuts through eastern Brazil.
John Cabot, a Genoese settled in Bristol, set out westward with his sons in 149 under letters of patent from Henry VII – all voyages were licensed by the monarc Cabot sailed in search of the Northwest Passage and discovered Nova Scotia a Newfoundland.
In the 16C Magellan threaded the strait which bears his name (1520) and his ship he died on the voyage – circumnavigated the world. In the same age, rivalry betwe the European nations – England and Spain in particular – grew and explode The great exploring, trading, warring **English mariners** were mostly Devon men John Hawkins, Martin Frobisher (*c*1535-94), Humphrey Gilbert, Francis Drak Richard Grenville (1541?-1591), Walter Raleigh. Two centuries later came th Yorkshireman, James Cook, circumnavigator, surveyor and Pacific cartograph (1728-79).

The Golden Hinde.

Funds to support the quest of the unknown, the driving force of every navigator, were obtained by patronage and trade – the first often based on the promise of the latter. Christopher Columbus sought financial support for years before he was able to set sail; Queen Elizabeth was far from open-handed in support of Drake's ventures; Raleigh was executed for not finding El Dorado.
Already by the 17C the **East India Company** (chartered in 1600), the earlier **Muscovy** and **Turkey** or **Levant Companies** (mid-16C) were in being, and the **Merchant Venturers of Bristol** incorporated (1552); the Hudson's Bay Company was chartered by Charles II in 1670. First raw wool was exported, then cloth; hides, tallow and linen were imported from Ireland, salt from Brittany, wine and brandy from Gascony, also wax, wood, iron and honey, and from Spain and Portugal, olive oil, figs, iron and wine.
After the discovery of the New World, Africa and the Orient, sugar, tobacco, fish, cotton, cocoa (for drinking chocolate), tea and coffee revolutionized trade. Trading posts were established in distant lands – the maxim being "trade follows the flag".

PRIVATEERS AND LETTERS OF MARQUE

A code of practice dating back to the 13C, operated on broadly similar lines by England, France, Spain, Portugal and Holland and with each country supreme in turn, licensed privately-owned merchant ships under **letters of marque** to "annoy" the sovereign's enemies of a named nationality in time of war. If war had not been officially declared, ships attacked in recompense for or on the pretext of previously suffered injury and loss under **letters of reprisal.**
Letters in England were originally issued by the monarch, later they were sold to ships' owners by the lord high admiral. Under this system Queen Elizabeth, without acknowledgment or expense, was able to ensure almost perpetual harassment of Spanish shipping.
The rules of this licensed piracy were strict and £3 000 bond had to be left as surety that they would be obeyed. The Admiralty, which judged the value, took 10% of every prize; customs duty (5%) was paid on all cargo captured which, in theory, had to be brought in as captured; two thirds of the remainder was then divided among the ship's promoters and the final third amongst the crew who relied on this "purchase" or booty together with "pillage" of the valuables not forming part of the cargo, as their pay.
The Spanish galleons were tall and clumsy; the British merchant ships or barques were at first between 50 and 100 tons with crews of 40 to furnish boarding parties and men to sail prizes home. By an Order in Council of 1695 the ships were required to be of not less than 200 tons and 20 guns; half the crew had to be "landmen" so as not to attract sailors, often then impressed, from the navy.
Many owners, masters who sailed the ships, captains who controlled the crews including the lawless boarders, lost all, even their lives in this adventuring; others made sufficient; many turned to cut-throat piracy, for which the penalty, if caught, was death. Drake and several of his contemporaries made fortunes on the Spanish Main and off the shores of Spain capturing the treasure ships which returned home each summer from South America, laden with the treasure of the Incas, gold, silver, precious stones and rich cargoes. Queen Elizabeth's coffers were filled.
Prizes from those times still to be seen in the region include the rose-silk damask furnishings in the drawing room at Pencarrow, the head of Christ in Golant Church, the pillars in the manor house at Bickleigh Castle in Devon, Sharpham House overlooking the River Dart, Tregothnan House overlooking the River Fal built with prize money in the 18C...
On a more modest scale are the half-timbered merchants' houses near the quayside in the Barbican in Plymouth – the Elizabethan House and its neighbour – and the district to the rear, erected by speculative builders of the time for returned sea-captains.

PIRATES AND PIRACY

Pirates, 15C-18C highway robbers of the sea, owed allegiance to no one. All men's hands were against them and they were against all men.
The crewmen would sign on and, in lieu of wages, receive a specified share of any prize captured. Hard and brutal, each was in it for the adventure and the loot. They plundered any ship they could overcome in home waters and, when these were too well patrolled, they sailed to the waters around the West Indies and off the North American coast.

Booty was sold to Spanish, French and English colonists, who, in theory, were obliged to trade only with their countries of origin; countless island and mainland creeks became pirates' lairs.
The 15C-16C **Fowey Gallants,** with their raids on the coasts of France and Spain, although sometimes referred to as pirates, were of an altogether different breed, as were the men of Devon who set out to avenge the Plymouth raid by Bretons in 1403, the Cornishmen who sought vengeance on the Spaniards who had burned Marazion – all were land-based groups, pirates for a day or a week only.

WRECKERS AND WRECKING

Wrecking, as every Cornishman, Devonian and coastal dweller will tell you hotly, has nothing to do with decoy lights and leading ships to their doom on the saw-toothed coastal rocks – nature alone has always seen to that. It has been estimated that, over the centuries, as many as 250 ships have been wrecked along each mile of cliff and cove of the British Isles : Lyme Bay was known as the Bay of 1 000 Wrecks; not for nothing are the Manacles so called...
What would happen, and happens even now, is that a ship, seeking shelter from gale-force winds, would come too close in and get caught on underwater rocks or in a race or current, and break up.
Warned by the watch, the villagers of old would gather in wait, all too often not to rescue the crew, but to seize the ship and her cargo, to loot everything and finally break up the hull until not a spar was left. The cargo of treasure and coin, timber, coal, satins and finery, the provisions, china and glass, the anchors, cordage and sails were regarded by all as a legitimate harvest of the sea, a bumper beach-combing.

SMUGGLERS AND SMUGGLING

In 1784 William Pitt the Younger calculated that 13 million pounds in weight of tea were consumed in Britain annually, 7½ million pounds of which were smuggled. The "trade", as smuggling was known along the length of England's south coast, began when customs dues were first levied in the early Middle Ages on incoming and outgoing goods; it flourished from the 16C to the mid-19C, particularly in times of war, and ended when ships of the Royal Navy, freed from the centuries of intermittent war and coastal blockades against France, Spain and America, could patrol the coast in support of the coastguard cutters and small boats of the revenue or "preventive" men. Although everyone, particularly in Cornwall, was against the revenue men, it has been estimated that they succeeded in seizing the contraband of one in three venturers. Where the boat was captured and the captain convicted – rarely in Devon or Cornwall – the hull would be sawn in three and sold for firewood together with her equipment and cargo.
The early "free traders" slipped across the Channel in 10-ton fishing smacks to take out raw wool and "bring in" brandy, wine, spices, fine silk and lace for local consumption; by the 19C 300-ton armed cutters were making 7 or 8 voyages a year carrying as much as 11 tons of tea and some 3 000 half-ankers of spirits a time (an anker or keg = 9½ gallon cask; the spirits were usually over proof and diluted on shore by the smugglers' wives). Goods were bespoke, and handling and distribution by pack-horse from the landing place in cove or harbour was conducted by a waiting team. Where necessary kegs would be weighted and dumped overboard to be collected when the coast was clear if not previously discovered by the preventive men. Contraband also came in through cargo ships, including the great tea-clippers. When a trading ship was sighted, pilot gigs manned by 8 oarsmen would race to her, the leading boat gaining the right to pilot her into harbour and handle her cargo, not all of which would pass through the custom house.
With the abolition of many duties and the lowering of many more – a policy instigated by the Younger Pitt as the best means of knocking the bottom out of the illicit trade – with the revolution in official, retail distribution and the different style of living, smuggling (apart from drugs) is now on a small scale : tobacco is imported not by the ton but in cartons, whiskey is trans-shipped in bottles, wine and brandy comes in perhaps by the case but no longer by the cask.

LIGHTHOUSES

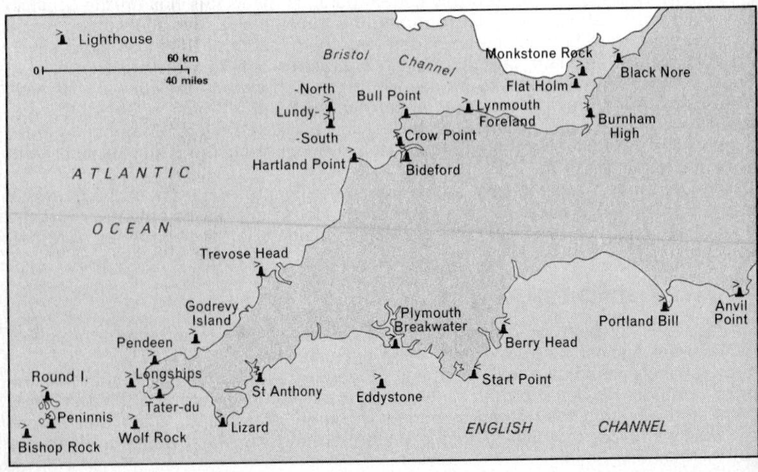

NAME	FIRST CONSTRUCTED	LIGHT CHARACTER
ANVIL POINT	1881	1 wh flash : 10 secs
BERRY HEAD	1906	2 wh gp flashes : 15 secs
BIDEFORD (Instow Front and Rear)	1820	occulting wh lights, 5 in 6 secs, 8 in 10 secs
BISHOP ROCK	1858	2 wh gp flashes : 15 secs
BLACK NORE	1894	2 wh gp flashes : 10 secs
BULL POINT	1879	3 wh gp flashes : 10 secs
BURNHAM HIGH	1801	1 wh flash : 7.5 secs
CROW POINT	1954	1 red flash : 5 secs
EDDYSTONE	1698	2 wh gp flashes : 10 secs
FLAT HOLM	1737	Wh + red gp flashes Z 3 : 10 secs
GODREVY ISLAND	1859	1 wh + 1 red flash : 10 secs
HARTLAND POINT	1874	6 wh gp flashes : 15 secs
LIZARD	1751	1 wh flash : 3 secs
LONGSHIPS	1795	1 equal wh & red : 10 secs
LUNDY	1897	South : 1 wh fl : 5 secs North : 2 wh gp fl : 20 secs
LYNMOUTH FORELAND	1900	4 wh gp flashes : 15 secs
MONKSTONE BEACON	1839	1 wh flash : 5 secs
PENDEEN	1900	4 wh gp flashes : 15 secs
PENINNIS	1911	1 wh flash : 20 secs
PLYMOUTH BREAKWATER	1844	1 wh & red flash : 10 secs
PORTLAND BILL	1720	4 wh gp flashes : 20 secs
ROUND ISLAND	1887	1 red flash : 10 secs
ST ANTHONY	1835	wh & red light for 11.25 secs : 15 secs
START POINT	1836	3 wh gp flashes : 10 secs
TATER DU	1965	3 wh gp flashes : 15 secs
TREVOSE HEAD	1847	1 red flash : 5 secs
WOLF ROCK	1870	1 wh flash : 15 secs

Key : wh = white; gp = grouped

At the discretion of the principal keeper, whose jurisdiction is final, a few lighthouses are open to the public.
The times of opening are usually, in summer only, Monday-Saturday, 1300hrs to one hour before sunset. Enquire locally.

There are around 80 lighthouses around the coast of England and Wales, 29 of hem in the West Country. Since 1836, by Act of Parliament, lighthouses have been under the jurisdiction of **Trinity House,** a corporation of shipmen or mariners ncorporated in 1514 as the regulating authority for pilots in British waters. In 1594 he Corporation acquired the rights of beaconage under which it marked navigational channels and erected waymarks.

.ighthouses, however, were constructed by individual venturers under patents granted by the Crown. The licensee, who was required to pay rent to the Crown, ecouped his expenditure at the custom house by levying tolls on passing shipping. **lat Holm,** built for £900 in the 18C with a nominal annual rent of £5 – £10, charged ½*d* per ton to all Bristol ships; 3*d* to all foreign ships; 1*d* to coasters to or from reland; 1*s* to vessels from St David's Head or Land's End (market and fishing boats xcepted). Shipping increased so colossally in the 18C and 19C that when Trinity House bought out the owners under the 19C Act, the lighthouse had become so rofitable that the remaining 12-year lease cost the corporation £15 838 18*s* 10*d.*

n some cases the necessity for a light and, therefore, toll rates was hotly contested y Merchant Venturers, shipmasters and Trinity House, and the granting of a building atent was delayed for years.

)ther lights came into existence modestly and personally : the first **Burnham** light s said to have been a candle set in her window by a fisherman's wife; the sexton ventually took over with a light in St Andrew's church tower and in the 19C, the urate, when dues were fixed at 5*s* for British vessels, 10*s* for foreign and 3*s* for oasters. The short remainder lease was purchased in 1829 for £16 000.

)elays in construction were also due to vested interests. For many the ships, which vere driven onto the rocks by the winter gales, were a source of rich plunder. Local pposition caused a 50 year delay before the first lighthouse was built on the **Lizard** 1 1619. Its existence was brief : shipmasters claimed that it was a wrecker's decoy nd refused to pay the tolls. In 1752 a second lighthouse was built which had four owers each burning a coal fire; in 1812 the building was altered to its present utline; first an oil lamp and then an electric light was installed.

he patent for the **Portland Bill** lighthouse overlooking the Portland Race, the neeting of tides between the Bill and the Shambles sandbank, was delayed nearly 0 years before finally, in 1720, two lighthouses with enclosed coal fire lanterns vere constructed. In 1789 a new building was erected which nine years later was ortified against possible Napoleonic invasion by the installation of two 18lb cannon. he lighthouse has since been twice replaced, the present 133ft tower dating from 906.

Lighthouses were, at first, built upon clifftops and headlands until it was appreciated that although the height made the beam carry further in fine weather, the summit might well be hidden in sea fog just when a bearing was most urgent : the **Lundy** light was at first on Chapel Hill.
Eddystone, the Wolf, Longships and the Bishop, standing out to sea, pinned to rocks surrounded by the Atlantic swell, each signal a triumph of engineering construction. The many gales resulted in the first **Bishop Rock** tower being washed away incomplete after two years' work and the second tower taking seven years to construct inside a coffer dam. The feat was accomplished finally by dressing, dovetailing and numbering each of the 1-2 ton blocks of granite before transporting it to the site; the foundations were re-secured, the base re-cased and the light raised to its present position of nearly 160ft above the waves in 1881. It was within a short distance of Bishop Rock that the British squadron returning from the Mediterranean under Admiral Sir Cloudesley Shovel in the *Association* was wrecked with the loss of 1 800 men on 22 October 1707 (the admiral, washed ashore alive, was murdered for his gold ring).
Construction of the **Wolf Rock** began in 1791 with the erection of a 20ft wrought-iron mast held by six stays and topped by a metal model of a wolf. It was immediately swept away. In 1835-39 an iron beacon was erected – on average only 60 hours work could be accomplished in any year; finally in 1861-70 the present 116ft granite tower with walls 7ft 9in thick at the base was constructed and the light shown.

The Eddystone Lighthouse.

The **Eddystone** light stands 14 miles off Plymouth. It originated as a wooden structure erected by Henry Winstanley, showman and shipowner, who had lost a vessel on the rocks. Problems with the site, the elements, labour, were capped when in 1697 a French privateer kidnapped Winstanley himself and took him across the Channel to Versailles. Louis XIV, however, ordered Winstanley's immediate return to Eddystone, with the words "France is at war with England, not humanity".
In November 1698 the Eddystone light was lit for the first time and survived, with improvements, until the worst gale ever recorded in Britain swept away the tower and its designer in November 1703.
By 1709 a new wooden tower with a lead roof and massive candelabrum was in operation. It endured for 49 years before it caught fire and burned for 5 days. The third builder was **John Smeaton,** a Yorkshireman, who constructed a tower of dressed granite blocks, dovetailed on all four sides and secured by quick drying cement; the tower stood for 123 years before cracks appeared and it was replaced in 1882 by the present stalwart 167ft lighthouse. (The Smeaton Tower was subsequently re-erected by public subscription on Plymouth Hoe.)
Many lighthouses, including the Eddystone, have now been automated.
The Trinity House Lighthouse Service is funded, as were the individual lighthouses originally, from dues levied on all shipping sailing to and from United Kingdom ports.

BIRD LIFE

Oystercatcher (1)

Grey heron (2)

Razorbill (3)

Gannet (4)

Common sandpiper (5)

Shag (6)

Guillemot (7)

Avocet (8)

Curlew (9)

Coot (10)

Common tern (11)

HISTORICAL TABLE AND NOTES

EARLY INVASIONS AND SETTLEMENTS

Prehistoric and Celtic periods

600 000-	Stone Age invasions on foot from the Continent
10 000 BC	Opening of the Irish Channel Ridgeway Path in being
6 000 BC	Opening of the English Channel
2800-1550 BC	Stonehenge
1800 BC	Avebury
2500 BC-AD 43	First sea-faring invasions; Bronze and Iron Ages; Iberian and Mediterranean sea trading; Iberian invasions, early Celtic invasions, 600-33 BC; each wave pushing predecessors further west Cornwall and Devon settled by the Dumnonii tribe; Dorset by the Durotriges, Wiltshire by the Belgae

The Romans

55 BC	Invasion of Britain by Julius Caesar
AD 43-407	Roman conquest, occupation and withdrawal
AD 300	Coastal raids by Saxons begun and increased
432	Conversion of Ireland undertaken by St Patrick (*c*389-461), a Romano-Briton; Irish missionary monks journeyed to Cornwall

The Anglo-Saxon Kingdoms; the Danish Kings

500-600	Kingdoms of Northumbria, Mercia and Wessex established
639-709	St Aldhelm
688-726	Ine, King of Wessex
871-901	Wars against the Danes waged by Alfred the Great, King
973	Edgar crowned first King of all England
979	King Edward murdered at Corfe Castle
1016-1035	Canute the Dane, King

THE NORMANS AND PLANTAGENETS

1066-1087	King Harold defeated by Duke William of Normandy (crowned William I of England; Conquest completed 1072 with submission of Exeter) Saxon land-holdings given to Norman barons, William's brothers and the church
1086	Domesday Book – national survey for taxation purposes of land holdings, buildings and population (total : 1 000 000 of whom approximately 8 000 were Norman)
1215	Magna Carta signed between King John and the barons
1220-1266	Building of Salisbury Cathedral
1337-1485	The Hundred Years War
1337	Edward the Black Prince, 1st Duke of Cornwall
1348-1350	Black Death – population reduced by half
1362	French replaced by English as the official language in courts of law (cf 1549)

THE TUDORS

1485-1509	Henry VII
1492	Discovery of America by Christopher Columbus
1496	Discovery of Nova Scotia and Newfoundland by John Cabot wh sailed from Bristol
1498	Advance by Perkin Warbeck, accepted by Yorkists as the rea Richard IV, brother of the murdered Edward V, on Exeter and Taunto (executed 1499)
1509-1547	Henry VIII
1535	Inventory by Thomas Cromwell of all monastic property
1536-1539	Dissolution of the Monasteries Construction of forts along the south coast
1547-1553	Edward VI : the "reign" of Edward Seymour, Protector Somerse (executed 1552)
1549	Cranmer's Book of Common Prayer published in English; Prayer Boo Revolt in Cornwall
1558-1603	Elizabeth I. The Age of the Navigators : Sir John Hawkins (1532-1595 Sir Humphrey Gilbert (1537-1583), Sir Francis Drake (*c*1540-1596 Sir Walter Raleigh (1552-1618)
1577-1580	Circumnavigation of the Globe by Drake in the *Golden Hinde*
1588	Defeat of the Spanish Armada
1600	Foundation of the East India Company (monopoly ended 1813)

THE STUARTS AND THE COMMONWEALTH

1603-1625	James I
1611	Authorised Version of the Bible
1620	Pilgrim Fathers set sail for America
1625-1649	Charles I
1642-1645	Civil War. Escape of the future Charles II through the West Country to the Isles of Scilly, and eventually to the Continent, following Cromwell's victory at Naseby (1645).
1649-1660	Trial and execution of Charles I; abolition of the monarchy, establishment of the Commonwealth
1651	Escape by Charles II, again via the West Country, to France, following defeat at the Battle of Worcester
1660-1685	Restoration of the monarchy : Charles II
1673	Test Act passed : exclusion of Nonconformists and Catholics from civil office (repealed 1828)
1685-1688	James II
1685	Monmouth Rebellion : Battle of Sedgemoor; Bloody Assizes
1688	Landing of William of Orange (future William III, 1689-1702) at Brixham
1702-1714	Queen Anne
1707	Union of England and Scotland

Charles I at his trial.

THE HOUSES OF HANOVER AND WINDSOR

18C	Wars in Europe (Austrian Succession; Seven Years) at sea, in North America and India
1714-1727	George I
1727-1760	George II
1760-1820	George III. Conquest of Canada completed 1760
1769	First voyage to Australia by Captain Cook
1775-1783	War of American Independence
1793-1815	French Revolutionary and Napoleonic Wars Blockades at sea of France, England and America by England and France
1800	Union of England and Ireland
1805	Battle of Trafalgar
1807	Abolition of the slave trade in British possessions (effectively ended 1833)
19C	The Industrial Revolution. Migration of industry to the coal-rich areas of the North and Midlands; decline of wool and fishing industries and of tin-mining in the West Country
1810	Construction of Kennet and Avon Canal : 1st Transport Revolution
1812-1814	Anglo-American War (US revolt against sea-blockade)
1820-1830	George IV
1832	Reform Act (final act 1928)
1833	Isambard Kingdom Brunel appointed engineer to the Great Western Railway; 2nd Transport Revolution
1834	Grand National Consolidated Trades Union launched by Robert Owen; Tolpuddle Martyrs
1837-1901	Queen Victoria
20C	The advent of the internal combustion engine : coaches and cars; 3rd Transport Revolution. Growth of tourism
1914-1919	First World War
1939-1945	Second World War
1952	Accession of Queen Elizabeth II

ARCHITECTURE

LOCAL BUILDING STONE

The rocks and strata of stone below ground in each region are to be seen everywhere above ground in the local buildings. While special types of stone were hauled hundreds of miles for great cathedrals and public buildings – Preseli mountain stone from South Wales for Stonehenge, Portland from Dorset for St Paul's, London – houses, tithe barns and parish churches were built of local materials from moor or outcrop stone, wood and cob, flint, limestone, slate and granite.
The transport of stone and other materials from earliest times was by water and, where there was no water course, by packhorse; only in the 19C with the construction of canals and, soon after, the railway, did bulk transport over long distances become feasible : bricks manufactured as far away as East Anglia penetrated the West Country blurring the local idiom...

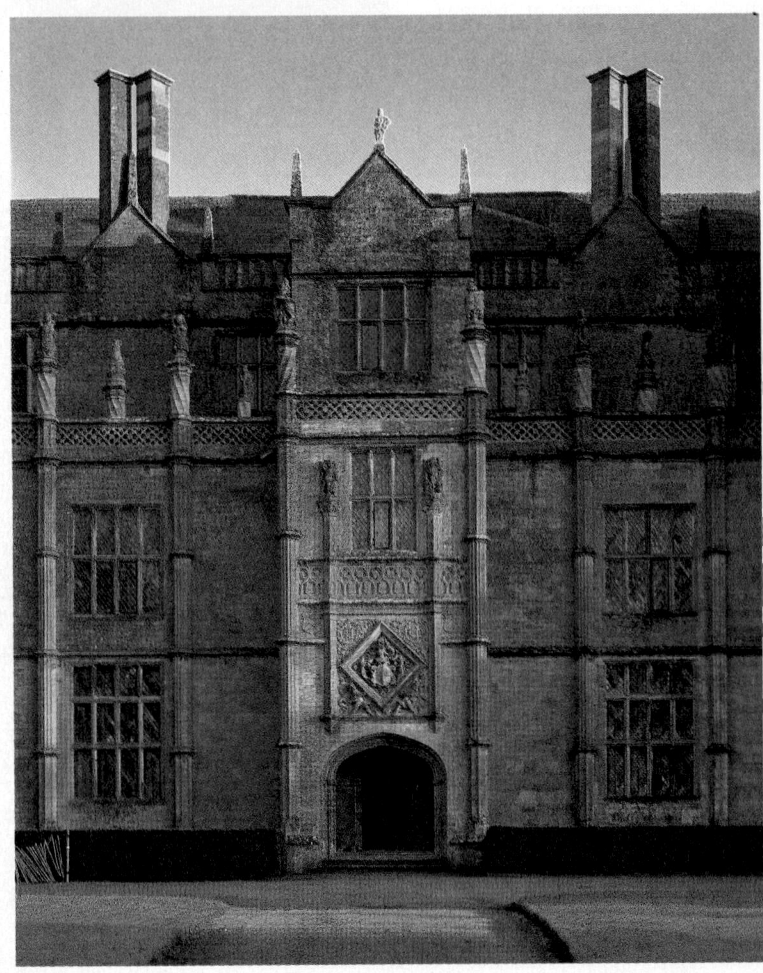

Montacute House, Somerset.

Wiltshire

Wiltshire has used local stone since the time of Stonehenge and Avebury when **sarsen stones** were brought to the sites from the Marlborough Downs. By the 13C the silver-grey limestone to be found at **Chilmark** was being quarried, dressed and transported down the Avon to build the new cathedral at Salisbury.
Throughout the county delightful houses in the villages and small manor houses are built of the local stone which varies in hue from light to dark grey. The roofs are of stone or terracotta tiles and a few still of thatch.
The Ham Hill quarries of Somerset exceptionally provided the stone for Longleat; sandstone, cob and brick furnished more modest houses.

Somerset and Avon

Dundry stone, a pink conglomerate or puddingstone from the hills on the far side of the Avon Gorge, is Bristol's native stone which can still be seen in the little old houses and church northwest of Broadmead. Much of the other stone used in building the old city was, of course, brought in by water.
Today the new buildings are of poured concrete or, newest of all, dark red brick.

he north Somerset landscape is dominated by the lines of the Mendips, which re of porous limestone, as is demonstrated by the caves at Cheddar and Wookey ole.
he Quantocks, the Brendon and the Blackdown Hills are formations of very hard, **d Sandstone,** the stone of the Quantocks being true in its pink to dark red colour the generic name of **Old Red Sandstone.** A sedimentary rock formed by the ementing together of grains of quartz or detritus resulting from the denudation f granite, it dates from the Devonian period, 350-400 million years ago and proved be the perfect building material for the area, notably in Taunton Deane, where it ppears rough hewn for cottage and church walls, dressed for trimming house and hurch windows and tractable for the decoration and carving of the west towers. the southern part of the county the **Ham Hill** quarry provided a superb golden-chre limestone from Roman and Norman times until recently. Whole villages vere built of the second-quality stone while the first grade was reserved for the onstruction of the parish church towers, with their unique Somerset tracery in ie bell lights, or was despatched to build the several great houses in the locality. he city of Bath is built almost entirely of creamy-yellow **Bath Stone,** quarried from earby Combe Down.

)orset

orset is the source of **Portland** and **Purbeck** stone, some of the hardest fine-grained uilding stone in the country; both Portland and Purbeck are limestones of the urassic period of some 150 million years ago.
n Portland Bill everything from the prison to keepers' cottages and garden walls built of the stone dug out of the quarries which pockmark the island; in Purbeck, ouses, large and small, and churches have dressed stone walls; within the churches re polished stone or marble pillars and fonts.

)evon

ranite bosses, the bone structure and bulwark against the entire peninsula being ashed away by the sea, rise up first on Dartmoor in Devon.
outh of the granite tors lie **Old Devonian Sandstones;** to the north ancient sedimentary tone known as metamorphic rocks which, under intense heat and pressure 500-00 million years ago, became transformed into **shale, slate** and **schist.**
he dense woods maintained **half timber** construction longer than in many areas; hen the wood became exhausted timber frames were retained and dense **cob walls** n moorstone foundations became widespread; finally in the mid-19C **bricks** were rought in by water and by rail. Plymouth, Exeter and Taunton all have fine large lizabethan half-timbered houses.
Vhere stone is used, as at Tiverton, it is for the most part rough hewn into blocks f approximately the same small size and laid in courses with quoins at the ngles. In Exeter and Crediton, particularly, note the use of red sandstone and pink ıfa.

;ornwall

he **granite** which forms the peninsula's backbone appears in the tors on Bodmin loor, in outcrops north of St Austell Bay, northwest of Falmouth and throughout enwith. In all these areas, small workers' cottages, solitary inns like Jamaica Inn, olated farmhouses and outbuildings, and the churches are built of granite with late roofs.
o the north, around **Delabole** where slate was quarried to furnish not only Cornwall ut the whole of the south of England, the houses, boundary walls and everything built of **slate schist,** a laterally grained rust-grey stone.
ranite, proverbially so hard, is sometimes carved; slate can be clean-cut and cised – note the beautifully lettered street name plates.
lineral-bearing rock lies below the surface in north and west Cornwall, as witness ie ancient minehouses and chimneys.
he Lizard is unique with its **serpentine rock.** Cottages and churches alike were built f the blackish rock which when dressed begins to show its colour and when polished eveals the veining and tones which have given it its name.

Old Post Office, Tintagel.

CHURCHES

Stonehenge, Salisbury Cathedral and the Roman Catholic Cathedral of St Peter an St Paul in Bristol, each all of a piece or in a single architectural style, are the ra exceptions to what is almost the rule in England, namely that churches, of whatev size, evolve during their building. Most churches stand, therefore, as examples two or even three styles : walls, windows, pillars and arcades, chancel arches, towe and tower bases, were incorporated in rebuildings; until the 19C-20C and the Goth revival, remodellings and additions were made proudly in the contemporary styl

Celtic and Saxon : 5C – 11C

Incredibly, the sites of most of the 10 000 and more cathedrals and parish church in England were hallowed before the Conquest. Churches originated often as regul preaching stands which, in time, would be marked by a cross, an oratory an eventually a small church built of wood or stone. The most obvious relics of thes early times are, in the case of the Celts, the up-standing Celtic Crosses with the individual shape, sculptured figures of Christ and carved interlacing. They stand the churchyards in Cornwall *(usually east of south door)* and by the waysid *(illustration p 263).*

Of Saxon work, there remain St Lawrence's Church in Bradford-on-Avon, the altere St Martin's at Wareham, typical "long and short" stonework at the base of sever towers and inside St James' Church, Avebury, an area of solid wall with taperin windows.

Except in a very few cases, both Celtic and Saxon churches, and those built lat on their foundations, have always been oriented due east, unlike elsewhere Europe.

Norman or Romanesque : mid-11C – mid-12C

Romanesque or Norman architecture came to England before William, Duk of Normandy, arrived, travel and close ties in the Church having already made familiar.

The style, characterized by weight and mass, has great, thick, flat walls pierced small **round-headed windows** and **doors,** these last decorated with carved zig-za dog-tooth or beaked surrounds; filling the upper doorway might be a carved sto tympanum.

Inside, **cylindrical columns,** topped by plain cushion capitals were superseded, in tim by clustered columns surrounding cruciform pillars and carved capitals.

The **arcade arches** were circular, as was the **roof vault** which was built of heavy mason Where two lengths of barrel (wagon or tunnel) vaulting crossed, diagonal ribs we formed at the intersection. Complications arose where communicating arcades different height had to be roofed over; to get the inter-pillar arches to the sam height the pointed arch, which allows any degree of sharp or wide curve, wa invented. It came into general use at the end of the 12C when it virtually solve all vaulting problems.

Gothic : mid-11C – late 16C

The period divides into three parts : **Early English** from 1150-1290, **Decorated** fro 1290-1350 and **Perpendicular** from 1350-1550.

During these centuries church builders took advantage of the pointed arch and th new knowledge that weight could be channelled through supporting ribs to fixe points which could be buttressed or supported by flying buttresses, a furth evolution. Windows were enlarged and elaborated. Churches were built ever high and were more finely decorated with pinnacles, castellations, pierced stonewor niches and figures.

In Early English times the **lancet windows,** which were sometimes stepped to for an east window, were eventually widened, the dividing mullion splitting at the to to leave a diamond; the apex diamond was then pierced by circles which containe **quatrefoil tracery.**

In the Decorated age the taller, **transomed windows** with ever more pointed apex contained an increasingly **flowing tracery.** Ornament everywhere was elaborated.

In the Perpendicular period the window peaks flattened to produce a wider ape over vast areas of glass; above 5, 7, 9 lights the infilling was simplified to a **geometric tracery.** Attention became focused on the vaulting, which reached its climax the **fan vaulting** to be seen in Sherborne Abbey and the chapter-house of Wel Cathedral.

The country was prosperous from wool and weaving in the Perpendicular perio faith was strong and the church, mindful of Henry VIII's constant need of treasur invested in non-removable buildings. **Parish churches** soared on the old sites techniques were taken over from the cathedrals and larger churches; towers move to the west end, spires ceased to be built; Somerset led the way in beautiful tower While vaulting ribs were spun in fine webs to support cathedral roofs, most We Country parish **church roofs** continued to be made of wood. The barrel frames we boarded in or ceiled; the beams were carved and chamfered; tie-beam roo developed centre king-posts or lateral queen-posts, with braces and bracket all able to be decorated with carving, cresting and tracery. Joints were hidde beneath small leaf mouchettes, foliate and flowered blocks, heraldic device and bosses, carved with the patron's head; against the wall were carved **wa plates** and **corbels** – in both Dorset and Somerset figures often took the form flying angels : the unique roof of Bere Regis has the apostles "oyled" and ove hanging in the manner of a hammer-beam roof; at Martock there is an ang roof.

Many of the roofs are coloured, some are gilded, every one is different.

The Georgian Period : 1710 – 1810

In the 18C a small number of late medieval churches were rebuilt in the new Classical style with pillars and often a portico, pedimented doors and windows in which the tracery had been replaced by glazing bars.
Inside, tall, single pillars divided the nave from the aisles, frequently supporting wide tribunes or galleries extending along the north, south and west walls.

Furnishings

Fonts – Saxon fonts, small, circular and plain, are rare but Celtic fonts are still to be found in many churches in Cornwall. Huge, square blocks of granite, they stand often on five pillars (the five wounds of Christ), carved with bearded heads at the angles and foliate designs on the sides; they would originally have been coloured.
They date from the end of the Celtic-early Norman period.

Tombstones and memorials – The *Harrowing of Hell* in Bristol Cathedral, carved c1050, is a rare example of Saxon carving.
The representation of a person either by engraving or with an effigy became general in the Middle Ages. There are stone recumbents of knights in full armour, sometimes accompanied by their wives, of bishops, robed and as cadavers. Many had the monuments which were to adorn their tombs carved in their own lifetime. Others, more modest, are commemorated in fine brasses.
The Renaissance taste of the Elizabethans and Jacobeans is mirrored in their tombs : the earlier, dignified stone effigies were superseded as the century wore on by ruffed and robed figures presented with their spouses and their children aligned as weepers on the chest below; above were canopies or screens decorated with scrolls and strapwork, eulogies, heraldic devices, achievements, helms and obelisks. Brilliant colours heightened the effect. One of the finest examples is to be seen in the church at Lacock.
The Classical influence of the late 17C-18C introduced tombs with figures carved by the fashionable and famous sculptors of the day including Rysbrack, Westmacott and Nost.

Woodwork – Lively **bench-ends** in Cornwall, and **rood screens** (the carved and often painted open screen which stands across the entrance to the chancel of a church) in Devon dating from the 15C-16C for the most part, embellish many parish churches; in the cathedrals are **misericords** (the carved bracket under a hinged seat in the chair stalls, which provided support during a long period of standing), **bishops' thrones,** and canopied stalls.
Following Archbishop Laud's (1573-1645) injunction to keep animals away from the altar and to prevent the theft of holy water, splendid **font covers** and **altar rails** were carved in the Jacobean period, also pulpit stair bannisters.

Chandeliers – Cathedrals and parish churches alike in the region are often lit by beautiful brass chandeliers suspended, in a few cases, on wrought-iron hangers. With the exception of two 16C Flemish lamps, all are 18C.

HOUSES

Houses, as they pass from owner to owner by inheritance or sale, as fortunes ebb and flow and fashions alter and because they are lived in, are in a constant state of change. It must also be remembered that the cob, bricks and timber and thatched roofs used for the smaller houses were not substantial and, if neglected, soon fell into decay; that labour for building was readily available and, therefore, when occupants died or streets were re-aligned, houses would be knocked down and rebuilt elsewhere; many were also destroyed by the repeated fires of past eras. Few of the general run of houses to be seen in towns and villages, therefore, are more than 350-400 years old. Many appear older, local builders preferring tried ways of construction to new styles and choosing to follow fashion more in superficial decoration than in structure.

Thatched cottage, Avebury.

The rich merchants and landowners who bought the former monastic properties at the Dissolution were the trend-setters in house building. They commissioned architect-surveyors and craftsmen who travelled from property to property; they were also often in the sovereign's employ and would have travelled on the Continent, seeing the Renaissance style in Italy and France. These new owners returned with a fund of architectural ideas which they wished to use and be able to display to all, in particular to the monarch in the days of Elizabethan and Stuart royal progresses, but also to relations and neighbours at all periods.

Tudor, Jacobean Periods, 15C – 17C

The houses have timber frames with exposed and cruck beams; the timbers, closer together in early work, have plaster or brick infilling. Oversailing upper floors were discontinued in Jacobean times as they were considered a fire-hazard. Great pointed **gables** characterize the roofs.

Chimney stacks appear for the newly introduced fireplaces; in Elizabethan times they were grouped, set symmetrically, often of brick and fancifully decorated.

The **windows** of the period are small, sometimes single casements, but on occasion extend right across a front; the frames have flat-arched heads beneath a hood. Windows in the big houses, illuminating great halls and often the **long galleries** characteristic of the Elizabethan age, followed Perpendicular church architecture in comprising great expanses of glass.

Inside, the walls (except where clad with tapestries) were **oak panelled.**

Plasterwork came into its own with ceilings decorated with formal and imaginative patterning and great pendants; friezes and overmantels were full of interest incorporating the favourite Jacobean strapwork and the display of arms.

The **stairs,** whether of monolithic blocks of stone or single timbers, mounted as spirals in the Elizabethan age and as splendid wide staircases, cantilevered and turning in straight flights around open, square wells in the Jacobean period; the **bannisters** of wood inches thick, were often deeply carved, the **newels** heraldic.

The Classical Period, 17C – 18C

The achievement of the 17C was the remarkable development in English architecture which led, by the end of the century, to the style of domestic architecture which subsequently became known as **Queen Anne,** whereby palatial, Classical proportion and style were attuned to smaller country and town houses. The precepts, as laid down by Palladio and imparted by Inigo Jones (1573-1652), were advanced by Sir Christopher Wren (1632-1723) and others.

House **fronts** became plain with centre **doorways** and symmetrically placed **sash windows,** the latter introduced in the early 18C. As the period progressed window frames and glazing bars, at first thick and cumbersome, became ever more slender.

The houses stood four-square beneath **hipped roofs** (roofs sloping up on all four sides to a flat top). Where more rooms (and windows) were required than there was space for within the Classical limits governing the height according to the frontage, those rooms would be built into the roof and lit by means of **dormer windows.**

The eaves were given a plain cornice-style decoration, the angles were often quoined with dressed stone – but the secret of their charm was the apparent simplicity of perfect proportion.

The **doorways** were almost invariably crested with pediments and broken pediments shell canopies and other light fantasies supported on brackets or, more elaborately on pilasters. Where the owners were wealthy, the **fireplaces** inside would be decorated after the manner of the front doors with framing pillars and a pediment; **ceilings** were ornamented with garlands of fruit and flowers carved realistically and almost in the round.

The **Georgian period** developed as a refinement of the Queen Anne style and marked its adaptation to the new requirements of crowded urban living.

The 18C prided itself on being "the age of reason"; precepts in architecture were formulated and adhered to : the Palladian-Classical origin became more evident a doorways, for example, were less exuberantly decorated. Windows, proportioned and set as before, were pedimented, wrought-ironwork was used to decorate balconies, railings and front gates.

In the middle of this stylised world there appeared the **Georgian terrace.** Following the obligatory rules of proportion, it could rise through several floors because the extent of the terrace gave it width, and each house, as a section of the whole, could therefore, be provided with sufficient rooms. **Squares** and terraces, designed as single façades, became 18C versions of Classical palaces, complete with central pediments columns, porticoes and arcades. Some were planned as single fashionable streets ending in a focal point such as St Mary Magdalene, Taunton; some, such as the squares, crescents and the **Circus** at Bath, were designed as elements in the most dignified city plan ever devised in England. Inside, houses were greatly influenced by the **Classical style decoration** of Robert Adam (1728-92), which can be seen much as he designed it at Saltram.

The 19C

The **Regency architecture** of the early part of the century continued the Georgian tradition, adding touches such as the prominent bow window, and in town, a great use of stucco.

As Regency gave way to the **Victorian style,** long rows of bay-windowed, steeply roofed, solidly built houses appeared, still to be seen in many seaside towns. In the late 18C Horace Walpole announced that he was going "to build a little Gothic structure at Strawberry Hill", Twickenham. Walpole's house was a pastiche, a mixture of the genuine, which he bought at sales in England and on the Continent, and what he had built and decorated in an increasingly extreme manner, so developing what came to be known as the **Gothick** style. Decoration, ornament, furniture and furnishings in the style became fashionable and were to be seen at one time in many houses.

At the same time many architects concerned with designing churches (or restoring them) and public buildings punctiliously followed traditional Gothic precepts.

Two 19C "big houses" of particular interest in the West Country are Lanhydrock which, because of the fire which nearly destroyed it, was rebuilt within its 16C granite walls by 19C craftsmen to late 19C standards of taste and comfort (central heating) and Knightshayes Court which was constructed for a cotton-lace magnate by two temperamental architects and could only be of its time.

GARDENS

No holiday in the West Country would be complete without a visit to one or more of the great gardens where spring begins earlier, autumn continues longer than in many regions. A bonus is that several of the gardens are sited amid beautiful valleyed parkland, overlooking river estuaries or the sea.

GARDEN DESIGN

Although there were forerunners, the English genius in garden design dates from the 18C.

The earliest gardens were the formal Elizabethan **knot gardens,** with little beds containing herbs or small-flowered plants outlined by miniature, clipped box hedges – the whole an intricate pattern of almost unrelieved evergreen.

A later variation, still almost entirely green in aspect, was the Jacobean **Mount garden.**

The 17C

As Renaissance ideas spread from Europe, the garden forms of Italy and France were adapted to England. Design remained geometrical but on a large scale : gardens were divided into separate "rooms" each surrounded by a tall hedge; flower-beds, symmetrically arranged and still edged with clipped box, were made larger and were brilliantly, if identically, planted as carpets or parterres; openings in the hedges afforded vistas, often onto water stylized into a circular basin and fountain or a "canal".

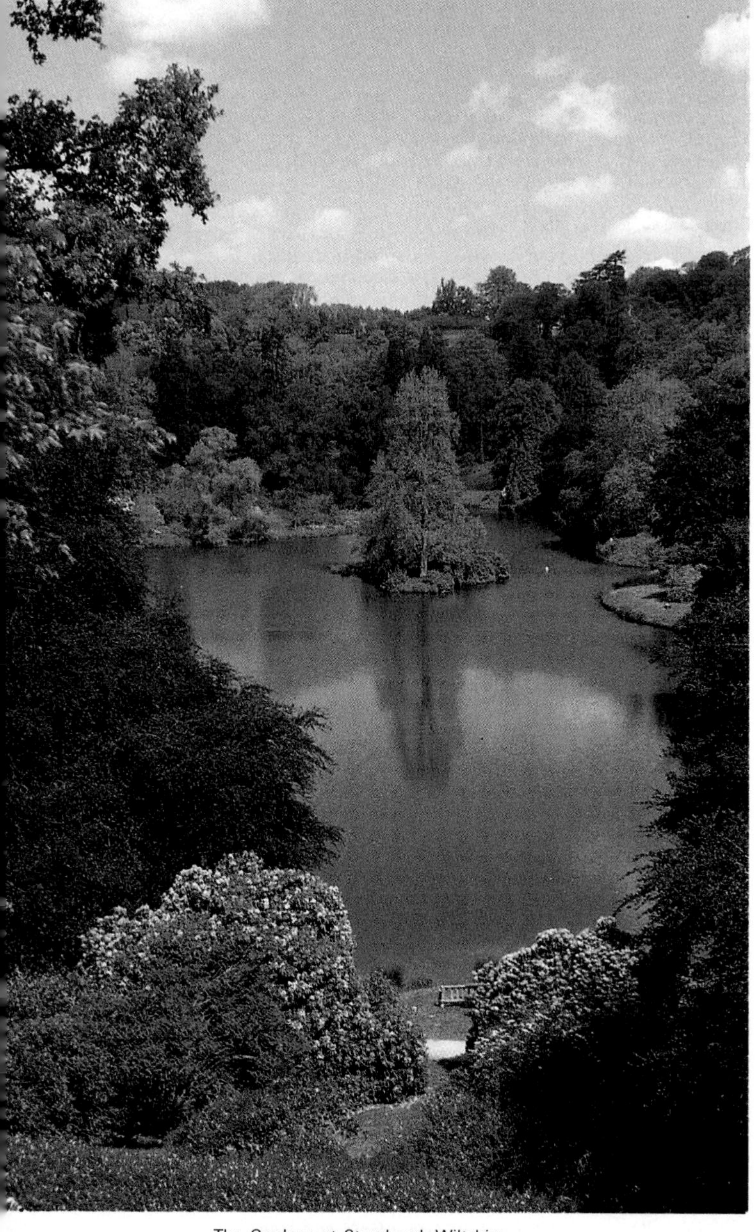

The Gardens at Stourhead, Wiltshire.

The 18C

The Romantic Movement swept into garden design as a search to find "the genius of the place" which being interpreted meant enhancing the natural beauty of the site – **Lancelot Brown** (1715-1783) described the task as improving the "capability" of a site.

Formal patterning and bedding were abandoned; enclosed spaces were opened out – **William Kent** (1684-1748) invented the ha-ha, an open ditch which enabled the garden to merge visually with the adjoining parkland landscape, at the same time keeping deer and cattle at a distance. Canals became serpentine ponds and lakes; hillsides were planted with trees selected for their leaf colours, their size and shape as clumps or as specimens; cedars of Lebanon, introduced to England in 1676, oaks, ashes and beeches were sited to focus a view, counterpoint a house front.

Poetry and painting were almost literally translated in some cases : landscapes were transformed, lakes excavated, temples, grottoes, follies constructed and situated after the manner of pictures, as may be seen at Stourhead.

Humphry Repton (1752-1818), the next in the line of designers, followed the landscaping precepts of Capability Brown, his famous Red Books giving his clients a detailed idea of how his plans would materialise. His advance on Brown was to re-introduce flowers in beds and on terraces in close proximity to his clients houses.

The 19C

Plant hunting, inaugurated in the 16C-17C by the **Tradescants,** father and son was undertaken on an ever-increasing scale in the 19C-early 20C. Expeditions were financed by several members of a family or owners in a county specimens would be parcelled out and enthusiasts set about improving and hybridising the plants before seeking registration with the Royal Horticultural Society.

To accommodate the new ranges of plants, garden design changed again to a labour-intensive formula with flowers overwintered or raised in greenhouses and conservatories and bedded out each summer; herbaceous borders were crowded with plants; dense shrubberies were allowed to grow; terraces were draped and decorated with climbers and plants in pots. Collections of trees were planted as pinetums and arboretums.

The 20C

Reaction produced a less crowded appearance, and, with **Gertrude Jekyll** (1843-1932 and **Vita Sackville-West** (1892-1962), a discrimination appeared that gives value to each plant for its flowers, its foliage and as a whole, to produce the plantsmen's and plantswomen's gardens of today.

Another "innovation" of the 20C is the return to gardens divided into "rooms" sometimes by colour, more often by season.

Listed below are 36 gardens described in this guide.

AVON
Claverton Manor
Clevedon Court

CORNWALL
Cotehele
Glendurgan
Lanhydrock
Mount Edgcumbe
Pencarrow
Trelissick
Trengwainton
Trerice
Tresco
Trewithen

DEVON
Bicton
Cadhay
Killerton
Knightshayes Court
Sharpitor
Tapeley Park
Ugbrooke

DORSET
Abbotsbury
Athelhampton
Compton Acres
Cranborne Manor
Parnham House

SOMERSET
Barrington Court
Clapton Court
East Lambrook Manor
Forde Abbey
Gaulden Manor
Tintinhull House

WILTSHIRE
Bowood
Heale House
Littlecote
Longleat
Stourhead
Wilton House

Walkers, campers, smokers...
please be careful!
Fire is the worst threat to woodland

Respect the life of the countryside
Drive carefully on country roads
Protect wildlife, plants and trees

:HALK HILL FIGURES

ill figures cut into chalk escarpments are an idiosyncratic feature of the region though they are not unique to it. They largely date from the 18C and 19C though ›me have their origins in earlier times.

ıe greatest number are in Wiltshire – 7 horses still visible plus other figures although the oldest are outside the county : the Uffington Horse on the Berkshire owns (Oxon), Dorset's Cerne Giant *(qv)*, and the Long Man of Wilmington in East ussex.

ll the figures, because of their size and consequent foreshortening, can only be ewed from a distance, therefore viewpoints as well as the location are listed below. ecause it is interesting to see a figure close to, if only once, where there is easy ccess this is also mentioned.

3 : several figures are on private land, others may be enclosed because of erosion; addition some figures may be difficult to see if overgrown with grass and awaiting ouring, but the majority, most of the time, are white, clearly defined and visible om afar.

ffington White Horse – White Horse Hill (856ft), Berkshire Downs. Location :)0ft up overlooking the Vale of the White Horse.

ewpoints : Ashbury/Wantage rd (B4507), Swindon/Faringdon rd (A420) and the ale rd (B4508), also the railway between Swindon and Reading.

ccess : by car – B4507 (signpost); on foot – from the Ridgeway Path *(qv)*.

3 : the horse is not visible from the Ridgeway.

is possible that both the Uffington Horse and the Cerne Giant originally had a ligious significance; the date the horse is unknown but has been put at 100 BC to D 100. The sculpture is 55ft long and, with Osming-n *(qv)*, is alone in facing ht.

'estbury White Horse Bratton Down. Location : cing west.

ewpoint : 1½ miles along 3098 from Westbury.

ccess : continue along 3098 almost to Bratton lage, turn right (signpost) a steep track to Brat-n Castle *(qv)* and the orse.

ıe horse, near the end of the eep west-facing chalk down, easures 166ft x 163ft high d is Wiltshire's oldest, ving been cut in 1778 by connoisseur of horseflesh ho had been irritated for any years by an earlier figure the same site. The earlier imal, smaller, dachshund-e in form and facing the her way, might possibly ve been Saxon, but was ore probably of 17C-18C te. The 1778 figure, now secured by stones and concrete, has sired a long e.

Westbury White Horse.

ıerhill Horse – Cherhill, Calne. Location : facing north.

ewpoints : Calne/Marlborough rd (A4) just east of Cherhill, Calne/Melksham rd 3102) just out of Calne.

ccess : a path from A4 leads to Oldbury Castle hillfort (¾ mile) and the chalk ure.

ıe horse, which measures 131ft by 123ft from nose to tail, dates from 1780. ıe obelisk on the skyline beyond its tail was erected by Lord Lansdowne, of Bowood *v)*, in 1845.

arlborough Horse

ewpoint : 200yds beyond the College, on the south side of the Bath rd (A4); look t across the field to the low escarpment.

e horse was designed and cut in 1804 by boys from the local town school. It 62ft long, 47ft high and perky with a docked tail and round eye.

ton Barnes Horse – Old Adam Hill, Pewsey.

ewpoints : the horse looks south over the Vale of Pewsey and can best be seen om the small road running west from Alton Barnes to Allington or the parallel oodborough-Beechingstoke rd.

ıe figure was cut on a gradual slope in 1812 and its general outline follows that the Cherhill horse. This horse measures 166ft by 160ft long; its dominant feature, obably due to weathering and scouring, is its enormous eye which is 11ft long 8ft deep.

Hackpen Horse – Hackpen Hill, Marlborough. Location : the far side of th Ridgeway Path from Marlborough.

Viewpoint : B4041 between Broad Hinton and junction with A361 and again on A36 Devizes-Swindon rd before the Wootton Bassett turning.
Access from the Ridgeway Path *(qv)*.
The horse is said to have been cut in celebration of Queen Victoria's coronatio in 1838. Its dimensions, 90ft x 90ft, may be an attempt to overcome the lack hillside incline; the slenderness of the neck and legs is unusual, the round eye possibly after Alton Barnes.

Broad Town Horse – Wootton Bassett.

Viewpoint : from Wootton Bassett take the Broad Town rd (B4041).
The horse is said to have been cut in 1864 by a farmer, which perhaps explain its proportions (78ft long by 57ft) and more naturalistic appearance except for th eye.

Pewsey Horse

Viewpoint : Pewsey-Salisbury rd (A345) just out of the town, and, closer t Pewsey-Everleigh side road.
The trotting horse was commissioned by the town council to celebrate the coronatio of King George VI in 1937.
It replaced an almost obliterated, late 18C horse and, after being pegged out b the designer, was excavated and chalk-filled by the local fire brigade. It measure 45ft x 66ft long.

Regimental Badges – Fovant Down. Location : on the escarpment behind th military camp south of Wilton-Shaftesbury rd, A30.

Viewpoint : off the road east of Fovant, a signpost on A30 indicates a footpath whic gives a closer view of the badges.
The frieze of military crests was cut by successive companies of soldiers in cam in Fovant in 1916. As a sign of changing times, they and all other hill figures we covered over in 1939 to prevent their use as navigational bearings.
Among the figures, from east to west, are : a map of Australia, and about 4 alon a rising sun and a kangaroo (all Australian), RAMC badge, YMCA triangle, 6th Ci of London Rifles, London Rifle Brigade, the Rifle Brigade, Devonshire Regime (towered castle), 7th Royal Fusiliers, Royal Warwickshire Regiment (a deer).

Bulford Kiwi – Beacon Hill, Bulford Barracks, Amesbury. Location : on th escarpment.

Viewpoint : the kiwi faces northwest and is best viewed from the Bulford-Tidwor side road off A303 (Amesbury-Andover rd).
The bird is vast, being 420ft long and covering 1½ acres of ground; the lette NZ below the bill are 65ft high and the bill itself 130ft long. It was designed b a New Zealand engineer to commemorate the troops' stay in the barracks and wa cut in 1918. Note especially the brilliant foreshortening which makes the bi instantly recognisable from a great distance and many angles.

In earlier times, when the monarch was personally responsible for the nation's finances, sources of revenue included the sale of royal forests ; rents from the royal estates ; customs dues ; fees, fines, forfeits from the administration of justice ; monies extracted on the basis of a vassal's duty to his overlord ; and finally the system of licences, patents and charters, all of which had to be granted and purchased from the king or his appointed officer.
Licensing in the Middle Ages became a science : permits, often costly, were required to graze hogs and cattle in the royal forests ; to fish, to hunt even the smallest game ; to gather fallen branches for fuel ; to cut coppice wood ; crenellate a house, to keep a dog or hound ; to transfer property ; charters were needed to hold fairs and markets...
Tax-farmers or collectors took their tithe. Others purchased or were granted – usually in return for a gift – export or import licences as was Sir Walter Raleigh (qv) for commodities such as wool and woollen cloth.
Even the Elizabethan navigators had to obtain a licence – for instance a letter of marque (qv) – or had to present as tribute a proportion of their often hard-won treasure.

ART AND ARTISTS OF CORNWALL

Although the West Country has been birthplace and home of many artists, the area is most famous for the two schools of art which emerged in the far west of Cornwall in the late 19C.

Cornwall's clear light, in particular around the coast and especially after a storm, had always attracted painters but it was only in the late 19C that the area became widely-known, when the advent of the railway meant that previously inaccessible areas now became more easily reachable for the intrepid traveller.

Newlyn School – The Newlyn School of painting began to form in the 1880s when many painters started to settle in the fishing village south of Penzance, overlooking Mount's Bay. The attraction of the area around Newlyn was partly due to the extraordinary light there, and to its similarities with the landscapes of Brittany, which had become a fashionable place for artists to paint. The artists at Newlyn also owed a stylistic debt to the French Impressionists of the mid-19C who, in an effort to bring a more naturalistic approach to their work and to capture the very essence of the light around them, had taken to *"plein air"* (outdoor) painting. The mild Cornish climate was favourable to these modern working practices.

The Newlyn painters chose unassuming subjects – the modest lives of local inhabitants, the fishermen and their families – with which the artists familiarized themselves by living in the community, in order to be able to paint them with honesty. The results are quiet, dignified pictures full of charm or pathos which avoid the sentimental excesses of much Victorian genre painting.

The artistic community was led partly by **Stanhope Forbes** (1857-1947; *Fish Sale on a Cornish Beach,* 1884), who was dedicated to the idea of working in the open air, and his wife Elizabeth (1859-1912), also a painter : in 1889 they opened a school of painting in Newlyn which attracted students from all over the world. Other painters there included **Frank Bramley** (1867-1943; *A Hopeless Dawn,* 1888), **Norman Garstin** (1847-1926; *The Rain it Raineth Every Day,* 1889), Percy Craft, Walter Langley, Harold Knight and his wife Dame Laura, Dod Shaw, Ernest Procter and **Henry Scott Tuke** (1858-1929), who began painting in the Newlyn manner but whose use of colour became more vibrant after a trip to the Mediterranean in 1892.

Heva Heva by Percy Craft.

St Ives School – The other major, though less clearly-defined, school was based at St Ives on the north coast of the Penwith peninsula; the town is still a magnet for artists today. The rugged scenery and clear light around St Ives attracted artists who were more interested in landscapes and seascapes than in figure painting. The town and its surroundings were first brought to prominence by **Whistler** and **Sickert** who spent the winter of 1883-84 there; others soon followed. The conversion of sail lofts along Porthmeor beach into studios provided the perfect environment for the artists, and the old fishing quarter soon became the centre of the group. **Julius Olsson** (1864-1942), famous for his nocturnal seascapes, ran a school for marine painting in the area. The local artistic community thrived with the result that, in 1926, the **St Ives Society of Artists** was founded.

The Advent of Abstract Art – A new wave of artists, linked by nothing more than a less traditional approach to their art, also began to appear in St Ives after the war; these included the potter **Bernard Leach** (1887-1979), who came to St Ives in 1920 after studying in Japan and whose decorative stoneware pieces masterfully reinterpreted Japanese designs, and the naive artist **Alfred Wallis** (1855-1942), who began painting at the age of seventy following the death of his wife. Wallis painted ships, some from childhood memory, in simplified blocks of colour but with an instinctive feel for abstract design, using decorators' paint on pieces of board given to him by a local shopkeeper. He was "discovered" in 1928 by Ben Nicholson and Christopher Wood but his apparently crude works only ever attracted a small following. His tomb in St Ives cemetery has a plaque by Leach.

Wallis' flat shapes may, nonetheless, have had a substantial impact on the younger, more dynamic artists in the area who were striving to describe the world in a new, modern way, and whose challenging works soon put them at the forefront of abstract art in this country.

In the late 1930s **Adrian Stokes** (1902-72), the inspired writer on art and painter of subtle, light-filled landscapes, still lifes and nudes, had moved to St Ives with his wife; they invited the couple Ben Nicholson and Barbara Hepworth - later two of the biggest names in British abstract art – to stay, and were joined by the Constructivist sculptor **Naum Gabo** (1890-1977) who remained in Cornwall until the end of the war. Gabo believed that artists had no need to copy the external world as they could work with "absolute forms" to produce pure art works; he was influenced by and in turn influenced both Hepworth and Henry Moore.

Barbara Hepworth (1903-75) had a love of organic shapes and was one of the first artists to work in totally abstract form. Her assured, lyrical sculptures echo nature's generous, sensual shapes and have profound associations with landscape, the coastline, and vegetal forms.

Hepworth's house in St Ives is now a museum.

Ben Nicholson (1894-1982) was already known, by the time he joined the Stokes', as a painter of still lifes and abstracted landscapes full of space, light and colour, and subsquently as an abstract sculptor who had developed a still-purer aesthetic through the use of light and shade alone *(White Reliefs* series, 1930s). In Cornwall he returned to painting still lifes and landscapes but no longer made distinctions between figurative and non-figurative forms.

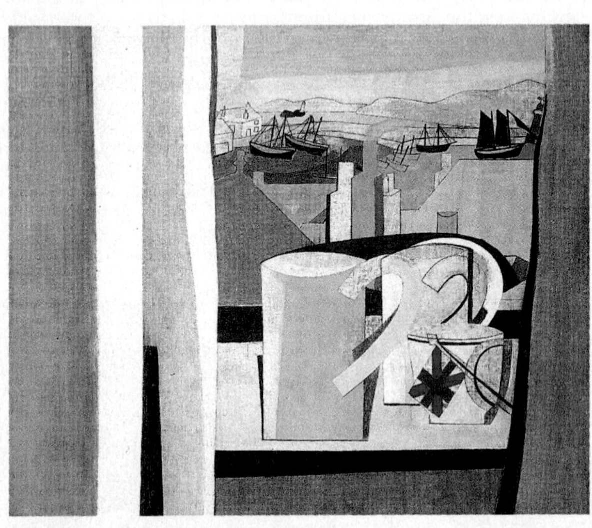

St Ives, Cornwall by Ben Nicholson.

Penwith Society of Arts – After the Second World War another generation of artists developed around St Ives, many of whom had begun as figurative painters but whose work had become progressively more influenced by the modern movement; shackled by the reactionary views of the president of the St Ives Society of Artists, Sir Alfred Munnings (1878-1968), they broke away to form, in 1949, the Penwith Society of Arts, with **Herbert Read** (1893-1968), the critic, philosopher and champion of modern art, as its president.

As the 1950s progressed, this group began to fuse abstract ideas and figurative elements more freely, so that the artists of St Ives became less obviously followers of either strictly abstract or strictly figurative tenets.

These artists included **Bryan Wynter** (1915-75) who lived in Cornwall from 1946 to his death : an abstract painter, his romantic and expressive works (usually landscapes) embraced pure colour.

The simplified forms in primary or earth colours with black and white, which typified the abstract works of **Roger Hilton** (1911-75) during the early 1950s, often hinted at landscapes or female figures. From the mid '50s, when Hilton visited St Ives, shallow pictorial space returned to his work and motifs of floating figures or boats were suggested more strongly.

Though the sculptor **Dennis Mitchell** (1912-93) worked exclusively in the abstract idiom – he was Hepworth's assistant for over 10 years – his woodcarvings, and later bronze and slate sculptures, many of which make references to the landscape, were some of the more accessible pieces of the modern movement.

Peter Lanyon (1918-64) was the only Cornishman of the St Ives School. From the 1950s his paintings, heavily influenced by Cubism and by the work of Gabo and Nicholson, were largely abstract but made references to the Cornish landscape and way of life (tin-mining, fishing, farming), as did his reliefs and free-standing pieces. By the later 1950s Lanyon's brushwork had become looser and his paintings included more direct allusions to the sky and weather.

The painter **Terry Frost** (b 1915) worked originally in a style reminiscent of Van Gogh but turned to abstract painting in 1949 : gently bobbing boats in harbour are often suggested in his works.

Patrick Heron (b 1920) is also a respected critic of Post-War British Art. Heron admired and was influenced by the works of Braque, and his own works bear some stylistic similarities in their colourful, abstract nature. The new **Tate Gallery at St Ives** (overlooking Porthmeor beach), highlighting works by artists of the St Ives School, features a stained-glass window by Heron, who still lives and works in Cornwall.

'HE WESSEX OF THOMAS HARDY

'LACE-NAMES IN THOMAS HARDY'S WESSEX

homas Hardy (1840-1928), who was born at Higher Bockhampton and whose heart es in Stinsford churchyard, took as his literary arena an area approximately that f King Alfred's Wessex. Indeed Hardy popularised the revival of the name of Wessex; e knew its countryside in minute detail : the heaths and vales, towns, villages, the ews, lanes and fields, individual houses, the churches... At times his descriptions vere "straight", at times combined with place-names disguised to a greater or lesser xtent : a few, such as Bath, Bristol, Falmouth, Plymouth, Chippenham, Stonehenge nd Wardour Castle and some geographical features, appear under their real names; thers use an old form as in Shaston for Shaftesbury.

'ardy's Wessex extended beyond the borders of this guide : listed below, for those olidaying in Dorset and the surrounding counties, are the geographical name and e disguised place-name, together with the prose works in which these occur. The xicon below has been compiled with the learned assistance of the Secretary of e Thomas Hardy Society, J C Pentney.

.EY TO TITLES

ovels in order of publication

R	*Desperate Remedies*
GT	*Under the Greenwood Tree*
3E	*A Pair of Blue Eyes*
MC	*Far from the Madding Crowd*
E	*The Hand of Ethelberta*
N	*The Return of the Native*
M	*The Trumpet-Major*
	A Laodicean
T	*Two on a Tower*
C	*The Mayor of Casterbridge*
	The Woodlanders
TD	*Tess of the d'Urbervilles*
JO	*Jude the Obscure*
WB	*The Well-Beloved*

Short Story volumes

WT	*Wessex Tales*
GND	*A Group of Noble Dames*
LLI	*Life's Little Ironies*
CM	*A Changed Man*
+	old form of place-name
?	doubtful identification

'ORSET – Hardy's South Wessex

lace-name	Hardy's name	Novel
Affpuddle	East Egdon	RN
Athelhampton	Athelhall	CM
Beaminster	Emminster	FMC TD
Bere Regis	Kingsbere (sub-Greenhill)	FMC RN TM TD WT
Blandford Forum	Shottsford (Forum)	FMC TM MC W JO WT GND LLI CM
Bournemouth	Sandbourne	HE TD JO WB LLI
Brickyard Cottages, Brianstspuddle	Alderworth	RN
Bridport	Port-Brady	MC W TD WT LLI
Blackmoor Vale	Vale of Little Dairies	TD
Buckland Newton	Newland Buckton	W
Canford Manor	Chene Manor	GND
Cerne Abbas	Abbot's Cernel	W TD LLI
Chesil Beach or Bank	The Pebble Bank	WB
Church Ope-Cove, Portland	Hope Cove	WB
Corfe Castle	Corvsgate Castle	DR HE
Cranborne	Chaseborough	TD
Cranborne Chase	The Chase	TD GND
Dole's Ash ?	Flintcomb-Ash	TD
Dorchester	Casterbridge	DR UGT FMC RN TM MC W TD JO WT GND LLI CM
Duck Dairy Farm, nr Lwr Bockhampton	The Quiet Woman Inn	RN LLI
East Holme & East Stoke	Holmstoke	WT
Easton, Portland	East Quarries	WB
Eggardon Hill	Haggardon Hill	TM
Encombe House, nr Corfe Castle	Enckworth Court	HE
Evershot	Evershead	TD WT GND CM
Farrs House, nr Wimborne	Yewsholt Lodge	GND
Fordington	Durnover	UGT FMC MC CM
Fortuneswell, Portland	The Street of Wells	TM WB
Frampton	Scrimpton	LLI
River Frome	Froom or Var	UGT MC TD CM
Frome Valley	Valley of the Great Dairies	TD
Gillingham	Leddenton	JO
Hardy's Cottage, Higher Bockhampton	Tranter Dewy's	UGT
Hartfoot Lane	Stagfoot Lane	TD
Hazelbury Bryan	Nuttlebury	TD
Higher Bockhampton	Upper Mellstock	UGT
Horton Inn	Lornton Inn	TT GND
Kingston, nr Corfe Castle	Little Enckworth	HE
Kingston Maurward House	Knapwater House	DR UGT (the Manor)
Lower Bockhampton	Lower or East Mellstock	UGT
	Carriford	DR
Lulworth Cove	Lulwind Cove; Bay	DR FMC; LLI
Lyme or West Bay	Deadman's Bay	WB
Lytchett Minster	Flychett	HE
Maiden Castle	Mai-Dun (Castle)	TM MC CM
Maiden Newton	Chalk Newton	UGT FMC TD GM
Marnhull	Marlott	TD UGT
Maumbury Rings, Dorchester	The Ring	MC
Melbury Osmond	Little/King's Hintock	W; GND
Melbury House	King's Hintock Court	GND
Middlemarsh	Marshwood	W
Milborne St Andrew	Millpond (St Jude's)	FMC TD

Milton Abbey	Middleton Abbey +	W TD
Minterne Magna ?	Great Hintock	W TD
Moreton	Moreford	LLI
Norris Hill Farm ?	Talbothays	TD
Okeford Fitzpaine ?	Oakbury Fitzpiers	W
Owermoigne	Nether-Moynton/Mynton	TN WT; DR
Pennsylvania Castle, Portland	Sylvania Castle	WB
Pentridge (also Tarrant Hinton)	Trantridge	TD
Piddlehinton	+ (Lower) Longpuddle	UGT TM LLI
Piddletrenthide	+ Upper Longpuddle (not wholly consistent)	FMC
Poole	Havenpool	HE MC LLI CM
Portesham	Po'sham	TM
Portland	Isle of Slingers, Vindilia	WB
Portland Bill	The Beal	TM
Poundbury Camp, Dorchester	Pummery +	MC
Poxwell	Oxwell	TM
Preston	Creston	DR CM
Puddletown	Weatherbury or Lower Longpuddle	UGT FMC
Puddletown Forest	Egdon Heath	UGT FMC RN TD
Ringstead	Ringsworth	DR WT
Sandsfoot Castle, Weymouth	Henry VIII Castle	WB
Shaftesbury	Shaston +	TD JO
Sherborne	Sherton Abbas	W TD GND
Stafford House, West Stafford	Froom Everard House	CM
Stalbridge	Stapleford	GND
Stinsford	Mellstock	UGT RN TD
Sturminster Newton	Stourcastle	TD
Sutton Poyntz	Overcombe	TM
Swanage	Knollsea	HE
Tarrant Hinton (also Pentridge)	Trantridge	LLI
Tincleton	Stickleford	RN TD WT LLI
Tolpuddle	Tolchurch	DR
Troy Town	Roy-Town	FMC
Wareham	Anglebury	DR HE RN MC TD WT
Waterston Manor, Puddletown	Weatherbury Upper Farm	FMC
Weymouth (and Melcombe Regis)	Budmouth (Regis)	DR UGT FMC RN TM L TT MC W WT GND LLI CM
Wimborne (Minster)	Warborne	TT GND
Woodbury Hill	Greenhill	FMC RN TM TT TD LLI
Wool	Wellbridge +	TD
Woolbridge Manor	Wellbridge Manor +	TD
Yellowham Hill, Wood, nr Higher Bockhampton	Yalbury Hill, Wood	UGT FMC LLI

CORNWALL – Lyonesse – Hardy's Off Wessex

Beeny Cliff	Windy Beak	PBE
Boscastle	Castle Boterel	PBE
Bude	Stratleigh	PBE
Camelford	Camelton	PBE
Lanhydrock House	Endelstow House	PBE
Launceston	St Launce's	PBE
Lesnewith	East Endelstow	PBE
Pentargon Bay,	Targon	PBE
Cliff	Cliff without a Name	PBE
Penzance	Penzephyr	CM
Redruth	Redrutin	CM
St Juliot	West Endelstow	PBE
Tintagel	Dundagel	PBE
Trebarwith Strand	Barwith Strand	PBE
Truro	Trufal	CM

DEVON – Hardy's Lower Wessex

Barnstaple	Downstaple	GND
Coombe Martin	Cliff-Martin	GND
Exeter	Exonbury	PBE TM W LLI CM
Sidmouth	Idmouth	CM
Silverton	Silverthorn	CM
Tiverton	Tivworthy	CM
Torquay	Tor-upon-Sea	CM

SOMERSET & AVON – Hardy's Outer or Nether Wessex

Dunster	Markton	L
Dunster Castle	Staney Castle	L
East Coker	Narrobourne	LLI
Mells Park	Falls Park	GND
Montacute House	Montislope House	CM
Taunton	Toneborough	L GND LLI
Wells	Fountall	LLI CM
Yeovil	Ivell +	W GND LLI

WILTSHIRE – Hardy's Mid Wessex

Marlborough Downs	Marlbury Downs	GM
Old Sarum	Old Melchester	LLI
Salisbury	Melchester	FMC HE TT MC TD JO GND LLI CM
Salisbury Plain	The Great Plain	TD LLI

Sights

★★ ABBOTSBURY Dorset Pop 401

Michelin Atlas p 8 or Map 403 – M32 – Facilities

Abbotsbury, which derives its name from a Benedictine abbey suppressed 1541, lies at the western end of the Fleet, the lagoon formed by Chesil Bea *(see below)*. Its village street is lined with reed-thatched stone cottages.

★ SWANNERY ⏲

The lush bamboo and flower-filled **gardens**, and the **duck decoy** with 4 "pipes" (no a ringing station), lead to the **Swannery** where an enormous number of **Mute Swa** cluster on the open waters of the **Fleet.** This, the only managed colony of swar was founded over 650 years ago by the monks; it numbers over 400 birds pl their cygnets. The swans are ringed (rather than pinioned) from which it h been discovered that they live some 20 years and return regularly to the san nesting sites on the two-acre meadow, where they are prepared to do batt against upstarts.

★★ CHESIL BEACH

The fine sliver of **shingle** forms a unique, ten mile beach between Abbotsbu and the Isle of Portland to the southeast, joining the isle to Weymouth. Th pea-gravel at Abbotsbury increases to cannonball-sized stones at Portland whi the ridge itself rises to 50ft in places. Throughout the year the sea rolls ar crashes against the pebbles but never tears the bank apart. In the lee lies **Fle Lagoon,** a shallow tidal waterway which is the habitat of the Abbotsbury swar together with herons and cormorants, also tern and overwintering and migra waterfowl. Parts of the beach, a Nature Reserve, are closed during the nesti season.

★ SUB-TROPICAL GARDENS ⏲

The woodland gardens lie in a hollow, a geological fault, protected from th salt-laden winds by bands of holm-oak. Within the 20 acres is a semi-form walled garden, laid out in the 18C adjoining a now vanished castle. The garde are famous for their Mediterranean climate in which sub-tropical plants such oleanders thrive out of doors. There are also camellias and rhododendror specimen **trees** and modern plantings : oaks, palms, myrtles, a 70ft tall tulip tre trees from Chile and Australia, a beautiful golden false acacia, a rare Caucasi wing nut of record height...

ADDITIONAL SIGHTS

Tithe Barn Country Museum ⏲ – The magnificent thatched barn dates fro the early 15C and is one of the largest of its kind in England (272ft by 30 it has close standing buttresses, a west gable and wide porch. The barn no houses a collection of curios, artefacts, tools and gadgets relating to rural li A 17C dovecote stands in the barnyard.

Abbey ruins – In 1541, after the Dissolution *(qv)*, the abbey lands were leas on condition that all "edifices being within the site and precinct of the la Monastry.... be hereafter thrown down and removed"; the church was reduc to mere footings, the monastic buildings converted into a private residen (burned down in 1644).

St Nicholas' Church – The parish church, in local buff stone with Portla stone dressings, was built between the late 14C and the 17C. Note the plas vault of 1638 above the two east bays; the 18C pedimented and Corinthia columned **altarpiece** with a vineleaf frieze; the 15C-16C **stained-glass panel** of t Virgin; the 18C **chandelier** and the plain Jacobean testered **pulpit** with a back par punctured by two bullet holes from a skirmish in 1644, after which the Royal Sir John Strangways, owner of the abbey lands, was imprisoned in the Tow A 14C stone figure of a monk stands in the porch.

★ **St Catherine's Chapel** ⏲ – *½ mile uphill; 30min Rtn on foot.*
The small chapel, rugged and windblown on its 250ft downland crest, is t only 14C monastic building to remain. It has thick walls, an octagonal stair tur with lancet windows, and flat-topped buttresses which are surprisingly stout f such a small building : they support the stone tunnel vault. The Perpendicu windows were added later.
The church probably served as a seamen's lantern.

EXCURSION

Hardy Monument – *4 miles northeast on B3157 and a by-road.*
The strange 70ft tall stone tower which stands on Blackdown and is visible f miles commemorates **Admiral Hardy** (1769-1839), Nelson's flag-captain, who spe his boyhood in the village of Portesham. It was erected in 1844. There a panoramic **views** from the foot of the tower *(not open)*.

Mead, which was drunk in pre-Roman times in Britain, is made by fermentin honey with hops or yeast; it was sometimes flavoured with spices or wil flowers. Metheglin, a speciality of the West of England, was a type of mea flavoured with herbs and spices which was said to have aphrodisiac properties.

★ A LA RONDE Devon

Michelin Atlas p 4 or Map 403 - J32 - 2 miles north of Exmouth

The unique 16-sided **house** ⓥ *(undergoing restoration)* with sweeping views of the Exe estuary was built in 1798 by two unmarried cousins, Jane and Mary Parminter, to designs said to have been by Jane herself. The original thatch roof was replaced with tiles in the Victorian era and dormer windows added.

Jane Parminter was the daughter of a Devon merchant; she spent her early years in London where, under the influence of Mrs Delany, she learnt many of the genteel arts of the period using such mediums as shells, feathers, paper, paint and needlework to create decorative effects. In the 1780s she set out with companions on a Grand Tour of Europe which was to last 10 years, and on her return she incorporated many ideas she noted abroad into the design of the house; she used the skills learnt in London to decorate its interior. The result is a remarkable **period piece.**

The 16-sided house.

The **interior** comprises eight rooms, each of different shape and connected by wedge-shaped anterooms, all radiating from a central octagon 45ft in height surmounted by a shell gallery reached through Gothick grottoes. The drawing room is decorated with a feather frieze and examples of the ladies' needlework, cut paper, and seaweed and sand pictures.

Consult the index to find an individual town or sight.

AMESBURY Wiltshire

Pop 5 519

Michelin Atlas p 9 or Map 403 - O30

The town and its church, which stand at a major road crossing beside the Avon, are descendants of a centuries-old market and an abbey. According to legend it was to a nunnery at Amesbury that, in the 5C-6C, **Guinevere** *(qv)* fled from the court of King Arthur and remained until she died.

In 979 **Queen Aelfryth** *(qv)*, in expiation of the murder of Edward the Martyr, founded a Benedictine abbey in Amesbury dedicated to St Mary and St Melor, the Breton boy saint murdered by his uncle. In 1501 the abbey lodged Catherine of Aragon on her way to London but, like the queen, the abbey suffered Henry's displeasure and in 1539 it was suppressed and the church presented to the parish.

St Mary's Church - The largely flint building is Early English in appearance with traces of Norman and Perpendicular work; a low tower sits squarely over the crossing. Inside, note the small two-tier piscina *(south aisle)*, the two fonts, one Norman the other octagonal and even older, the nave's 16C oak roof beams which were carved when in place, the Early English vaulting in the Jesus Chapel and the plain oak rood screen with a 16C door.

EXCURSION

Bulford Kiwi - *4 miles east by A303. See Bulford Kiwi.*

★ ANTONY HOUSE Cornwall

Michelin Atlas p 3 or Map 403 - H32

Visitors cross the park and turn into the forecourt to face the Classical grey stone house, extended through short colonnades to red brick wings. The building was completed in 1721 and houses a collection of portraits and mementoes.

TOUR ⓥ *45min*

Halls - The halls are dominated by one of the four memorable portraits by Edward Bower of **Charles I** *(qv)* at his trial. In addition there hang on the walls the likenesses of Sir William Carew, ardent Jacobite and builder of the house, and **Richard Carew** *(by the staircase)*, high sheriff, colonel of the troops guarding the estuary at the time of the Armada and author of the fascinating *Survey of Cornwall* of 1602.

Staircase - Note the three turned balusters to each tread and the original bubble lights.

Dining Room – The **chairs** outside the door are covered by still-bright 17C-18C Soho tapestry; those inside are by Chippendale. Against the panelled walls hang early sporting paintings, and a lovely Queen Anne pier-glass between the windows.

Saloon – The panelled room contains three portraits by Reynolds.
The Queen Anne **furniture** includes a pair of mirrors, each above a gesso table made especially for the exact position in which they still stand.
The George I period chandelier is Waterford glass; the china includes Dr Wall (1752-76) Worcester vases, Chelsea vases and late 18C Staffordshire cockerels.

Tapestry Room – The carved gilt wood, eight branch **chandelier** is William and Mary, the Diogenes tapestries are 18C Soho; the mirror in the chimneypiece was fitted when the house was built in 1721. The **tables** are William and Mary with seaweed marquetry, George I with satyrs' masks and Queen Anne with carved Red Indians' heads. The **armchairs** are by Chippendale.

Library – The library, which contains a copy of the *Survey of Cornwall*, is hung with Carew family **portraits** and a likeness of Sarah Jennings, Duchess of Marlborough.

Upstairs – The sporting paintings on the west staircase walls are by Francis Sartorius (1734-1804); in the bedrooms, among the four-posters, lie rare 18C single beds.

EXCURSION

Mount Edgcumbe ⊙ – *8 miles southeast : from Antony go south, then east on B3247; from Plymouth by Torpoint Car Ferry or Cremyll passenger ferry from Admiral's Hard, Stonehouse.*
Walks through the 800-acre park and gardens and along 10 miles of coastline paths afford extensive **views★** across the Sound.
In 1353 William Edgcumbe of Edgcumbe, Milton Abbot, Devon married Hilaria de Cotele whose dowry was Cotehele House *(qv)*; in 1493 their descendant Piers Edgcumbe married Jean Durnford, heiress to considerable estates on both sides of the Tamar and the important **Cremyll Ferry**; in 1539, just before he died, Piers received a royal licence to enclose grounds for the park in which his son, Sir Richard, built Mount Edgcumbe House in 1547-54.
Richard Carew in his *Survey (see above)* described Mount Edgcumbe as "building square, with a round turret at each end, garretted on the top, and the hall rising in the mids above the rest, which yealdeth a stately sound as you enter the same (and) the parlour and dining chamber (which) give you a large and diversified prospect of land and sea". This house with later additions was gutted by incendiary bombs in 1941. It was rebuilt to the original square plan and the additional 18C octagonal corner towers so that it now looks much as in Carew's description.
The interior includes a family **portrait** by Reynolds, a **longcase clock** of 1610 (John Matchett, Covent Garden), 17C and 18C furniture (two fine Boulle desks) and a pair of **Bronze Age hunting horns.**
The **higher gardens,** near the house, feature a wooded Amphitheatre, formal Italian and French gardens, a New Zealand garden and an English garden with specimen shrubs and trees.

St Germans – *9 miles northwest on A374; after 7 miles turn right.*
At the centre of the old village stand the attractive and practically-designed Sir William Moyle **Almshouses** of 1583 (restored 1967), surrounded by neatly kept stone cottages set in gardens of roses and clematis.

★ **St Germans Church** – *½ mile east.* The church possesses a majestic **west front** of dissimilar towers framing a Norman doorway, encircled by seven decorated orders carved in the local, dark blue-grey-green, Elvan stone. It stands on the site of Cornwall's Saxon Cathedral.
The doorway was begun before 1185, the towers *c*1200 but abandoned until the 13C and 15C when the north tower was completed to an octagonal plan with Early English lancet windows and the 72ft south tower in the Perpendicular style. Simultaneously work progressed on the attached monastery, for St Germans was a priory church. In 930 Athelstan appointed its abbot Bishop of Cornwall; in 1043 the see passed to Crediton *(qv)*.
Inside, note the Norman capitals, the East window with glass by William Morris, the battered Purbeck stone font and the 15C porch with a groined moorstone roof.

★ APPLEDORE Devon — Pop 2 135

Michelin Atlas p 6 or Map 403 – H30

Over the centuries Appledore has evolved into a network of narrow streets. In 1845 the quay was constructed (rebuilt 1941); until then it was an irregular tide-covered strand lined by a straggle of cottages.
It was in an Appledore shipyard that, in 1973, a replica of Drake's *Golden Hinde* was built. The same yard builds pleasure-craft and fishing vessels while at the other end of the scale, one of Europe's largest covered yards, Appledore Shipbuilders Bidna complex, produces container ships, sand-dredgers, coasters...

Streets – Follow the line of the point along the Quay, with its views across the Torridge to Instow *(irregular passenger ferry in season)* and north to Braunton Burrows *(qv)*; wander back along the long **Irsha Street** with its older, vividly painted cottages (one named Smugglers' Run is dated 1664), centre gully and minute courts. In the narrow **Market Street** note the white-painted bow-windowed houses.

North Devon Maritime Museum ⊙ – *Odun House.*
The house (1834) is named after a Saxon chieftain who defeated Hubba the Dane in battle in 878 just outside Appledore. It traces ship development from the building of wooden ships on open beaches to the construction of steel vessels by flow-line production : girthing chains, traverse boards, gammon corners, fiddleheads and carpenter's tools.

★ ARLINGTON COURT Devon

Michelin Atlas p 6 or Map 403 – I30 – 8 miles northeast of Barnstaple

The model ships alone – 36 made by French Napoleonic prisoners of war, 10 Dunkirk Little Ships and some 70 others – would make the Court unique but the ships comprise only one of the collections made by the house's former owner, Miss Rosalie Chichester.
Miss Chichester was a Victorian-Edwardian lady who was born in 1865, the year her father enlarged the Classically-styled house (built 1820-23), creating the grandiose staircase and hall as a background to the glittering social life he enjoyed with his wife.
When she was three and again at twelve, Rosalie Chichester went on long Mediterranean cruises with her father aboard his 276 ton yacht and became imbued with a lifelong interest in ships; when she was 16, however, her father died, leaving the estate heavily mortgaged; it took 47 years to clear all the debts. Meanwhile, modestly at first, she began the collections which were to furnish and characterize her home. Miss Chichester died in 1949, 16 years before her step-nephew, Sir Francis Chichester, made his epic voyage round the world in *Gipsy Moth* (1966-67).

HOUSE ⊙ *1 hour*

Entrance Hall – Among the photographs is one of the young Miss Chichester in 1885 in a straw hat.

State Rooms – The 70ft long south front was designed with *scagliola* marble columns to form one long gallery or be divided into three rooms.
The **Morning Room** contains a typical 19C collection of shells, several ships and a Portuguese pottery bull; the **Ante Room** features a notable collection of silver, English and Irish glass, a Chinese rock crystal cat and small jade, soapstone and crystal animals and scent bottles, a Bristol glass ship of 1851 and the **William Blake** painting *Cycle of the Life of Man* (1821).
The **White Drawing Room,** the end room, has a late 18C Donegal glass chandelier, a carpet with the Chichester herons in the corners, English, French and Chinese porcelain, precious snuff-boxes and a unique red amber elephant.

Small Boudoir – The enriched plaster ceiling, faded rose and gold silk hangings, Chinese porcelain and 19C *papier maché* furniture are reflected in the obliquely set mirrors. A display case contains more small animals, snuff boxes and vinaigrettes.

Corridor – The cabinets contain **commemorative mugs** of the years 1887-1937 and an important collection of English pewter from platters to spoons, dominoes and chessmen.

Staircase hall, gallery and lobby – The fleet of ships can be seen assembled in these rooms, including the Little Ships that went to Dunkirk and *Gipsy Moth,* made as a centrepiece to the collection.
The **Napoleonic prisoners' ships** date largely from 1814; 122 000 men were taken between 1794-1815. Almost immediately they were set to constructing prisons and public works – Princetown on Dartmoor *(qv),* the Floating Harbour in Bristol... Among the men in the south of England were a number of Flemish ivory carvers who, from making and selling small ornaments out of beef and mutton bones, had graduated by 1814 to carving ships which they produced to scale in every detail and embellished with figureheads; the only inaccuracies are the British names and colours given to French vessels for reasons of salesmanship. The distinction of the Chichester collection is that it contains examples of almost every class of ship of the Napoleonic period, from three-deckers to sailing frigates.

GROUNDS ⊙

Paths *(about 1¼ miles)* through the grounds lead down to the lake where an urn marks where Miss Chichester's ashes are buried; in the church a memorial by **John Piper** (1903-92) also commemorates her.

★ CARRIAGE COLLECTION

The handsome 19C stable block, its clock tower dome crowned by a Chichester heron, contains the National Trust collection of 19C-early 20C horsedrawn carriages. They range from Queen Victoria's **pony bath chair** to a hooded buggy, a royal "canoe" landau, hansoms, gigs, phaetons, wagonettes, an omnibus.

★ ATHELHAMPTON Dorset

Michelin Atlas p 8 or Map 403 – M, N31

The house dates from early Tudor times when Sir William Martyn, Lord of Athelhampton and Lord Mayor of London, whose family came originally from Tours in France and claimed descent from St Martin, was given permission to enclose 160 acres of deer park and build himself a towered and battlemented mansion. To this house with its porch, upper room and great hall were added a gabled parlour wing in the same creamy limestone, new fronts and gables and, as a final embellishment, the gardens – the *magnolia grandiflora* at the front of the house is believed to be about 200 years old.

TOUR ⏲ *45min*

Great Hall – The hall is remarkable for its roof, its **oriel** and its linenfold panelling: the roof is built up on braces and collar-beams, the whole given character by the pointed cusps; the oriel is vaulted with cusped ribs and illumined by tall two-light, two-transom windows on each side again with the cusp motif – among the medieval painted glass note the Martyn crest : a chained ape, from the traditional French name for a monkey, *Martin*. The ape, now with a Saxon crown and carrying a mace, has been adopted by the present owner as his heraldic badge – the crown being a reference to the manor's situation in the realms of Athelhelm and Athelstan, the mace to the family service in Parliament.
The **brass chandelier** with the Virgin is 15C; the **tapestry** is Flemish; the chests are from the 14C and 15C and from 1681 (dated), the **love-seat** from the time of William and Mary.

Additional rooms – Note the oak **panelling,** the Pugin and William Morris **wallpaper** and silk wall hangings and among the medley of treasure, which ranges from 17C furniture to examples of metalwork and manufactures from the 1851 Exhibition, a Henry VIII period **credence cupboard,** a painting on glass, *The Miser* by the Flemish artist **Quentin Matsys** (1465-1530), a collection of wine glasses, Chinese and Chinese-style cabinets and mirrors, 200 **19C china jugs** and Westminster mementoes.

GARDENS

Around the house individual gardens have been planned to lead from one to another, often through graceful iron gates, and all so that the focal point of every **vista** is a fountain or statue fountain.
They include a **Great Court Garden** with twin pavilions and giant pyramidal yews, a **Private Garden** with lawns and a fishpond, and a **White Garden.**
Rarest of all is the **Corona,** an Elizabethan-style circular garden, distinguished by an undulating stone wall topped by slender obelisks and banked with flowers; at the centre an urn gently brims over into a small basin.
On the far side of the house are the **Octagon,** a pleached lime cloister and a circular 15C **dovecote** with a renewed hammerbeam roof and lantern and 15C nest-holes.

★★ AVEBURY Wiltshire

Michelin Atlas p 17 or Map 403 – O29

Avebury and its surrounding area is extremely rich in prehistoric monuments and earthworks, the earliest dating from *c*2500-2800 BC; even today, discoveries continue to be made around the valley of the River Kennet. All around Avebury itself, a village of small houses, shops, a 17C pub, a square-towered church, a Tudor-Elizabethan manor house and a 17C thatched tithe barn, thirty to forty-two **sarsen stones** stand silently in the fields.

SIGHTS

★ **The Stones** – The plan of the stones is difficult to decipher, the only vantage points being on the circular earthen bank which, reinforced by an outer ditch, enclose the 28 acre site. The early "rampart", broken at the cardinal points of the compass to provide access to the centre (now the Devizes-Swindon (A361) and the High St-Downs roads), encloses a **Circle** of 100 Iron Age sarsens from the Marlborough Downs and two inner rings. From the south exit an **Avenue** of approximately 100 pairs of stones, square "male" and slender "female" stones

The Avenue, Avebury.

ternating in each file, leads to the burial site known as the Sanctuary *(1½ miles)* on Overton Hill (excavated 1930). It has been estimated that Avebury henge took some 1½ million hours to construct – 200 men working 60 hours a week for 3 years?

The 4500-year old site, after perhaps 1000 years' service, fell into disuse; eventually it became a quarry – John Aubrey, exultant discoverer and designator of the site as a prehistoric monument in the 17C, was able to show Charles II many more stones in position than there are today. One would-be quarryman, a 13C barber-surgeon, was crushed as he toppled one of the huge sarsens; when he was discovered centuries later, he was found to be carrying some Edward I coins in his pouch and what have become the oldest known scissors in Britain.

Alexander Keiller Museum ⊙ – Models of the site, aerial photographs and excavated finds from Avebury, the West Kennet Long Barrow, Windmill Hill and Silbury Hill are displayed to advantage in the museum named after the pre-Second World War excavator.

★ **Church** – St James' appears, at first glance, to be a Perpendicular church with an embattled and pinnacled west tower but the doorway with colonnettes and zig-zag decoration is Norman and inside, at the west end, the two solid walls which extend forwards were the outer walls of the original Saxon church. Aisles were added in the 12C.

In the 19C a local builder removed the Norman columns and substituted Tuscan-style pillars, but left the possibly medieval arches and the circular clerestory windows which are believed to be Anglo-Saxon. The chancel arch is 13C, the chancel 19C rebuilding.

Among the furnishings, the **tub font,** with an intricate carving of two serpents and a bishop, is Norman if not Saxon; the rood-screen is topped by its original 15C loft and crocketed parapet of vine leaves.

Avebury Manor ⊙ – *Undergoing restoration.* The manor house has been regularly altered since its origins, linked to a monastery. It now consists of buildings dating from the early 16C with fine late 17C alterations. The garden boasts topiary, ancient box and medieval walls framing the flower garden.

Museum of Wiltshire Rural Life ⊙ – *Great Barn.* Beneath the thatched timber roof of the late 17C barn, exhibitions on local history and traditional rural crafts are accompanied by displays on cheesemaking, shepherding and thatching.

EXCURSIONS

★ **Silbury Hill** – *2 miles south on north side of A4; lay-by car park; no direct access.* Silbury, which covers 5¼ acres, was built in four stages beginning *c*2500 BC; only human muscle, reindeer antler picks and oxen shoulder-blade shovels were used to pile up its million cubic yards of chalk. The final grassy mound (130ft high), with its distinctive flat top (100ft wide), is one of the largest man-made hills in Europe. Despite shafts sunk to its centre in the 18C and tunnels excavated in the 20C, the reason for its construction remains a mystery.

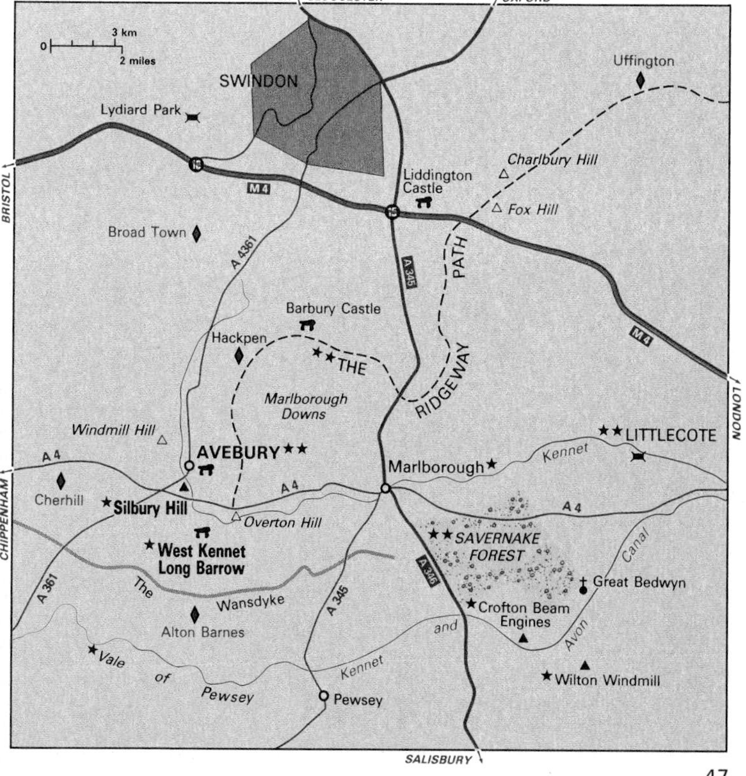

★ **West Kennet Long Barrow** – *3 miles south on south side of A4, plus ¾ mile field footpath – signposted from lay-by car park; take a torch and boots in wet weather.*
No mystery surrounds the earth-covered mound **(view)**; it is England's finest burial barrow (340ft long x 75ft wide) and dates from 3500-3000 BC.
The entrance at the east end is flanked by giant sarsens; on either side are dependent burial vaults and, at the far end, a hall, roofed with massive capstones supported on upright sarsens and drystone walling. Some 50 skeletons of the late Mesolithic builders, farmers and their families were discovered in the vaults.

The Wansdyke – *Access : 4 miles southwest by A361, Devizes road; there is no public right of way along the Wansdyke though many stretches are open.*
The frontier earthwork runs for some 14 miles from east to west. It was built possibly in the 5C or 6C by the Romano-Britons or Saxons of south Wiltshire to protect themselves from incursions by Saxon settlers in the Thames Valley.

Windmill Hill – *4 miles northwest on foot Rtn from the church by a lane and a path.*
The hill is famous, archeologically, as the causewayed camp after which the earliest Neolithic culture in Britain is named. It comprises three concentric ditches and embankments in which the livestock were gathered before the annual autumn slaughter.

★★ AXBRIDGE Somerset — Pop 1 724

Michelin Atlas p 16 or Map 403 – L30

The Cheddar road leads directly into the irregular Square, used since Saxon times as the market place and now ringed by tall 17C-18C houses, the pedimented early 19C town hall, several 18C refronted pubs of earlier vintage and, on the far corner, two half-timbered houses with oversailing upper floors – the legacy of highly prosperous medieval wool and cloth merchants who specialized in knitting stockings.
More recently the town's prosperity has been linked, in part, to strawberries – the surrounding area is known for the quality of the fruits it produces.

★ **King John's Hunting Lodge** ⓥ – The house, an example of a timber framed building, dates from the late 15C but the name is purely notional; it derives from the fact that the Mendip Forest was once a royal hunt and the town's first royal charter was granted by King John. The king's head carving outside, at the angle probably dates from the 17C-18C when the building was the King's Head Alehouse. The lodge is now a **museum** with exhibits including a "nail" *(p 73)* and two early mayoral maces.
The house is most interesting, however, for the revelation inside of its structure. It stands on a stone sill from which it rises through a ground floor, once an open arcade of shops, to upper living and bedroom floors and, finally, an open timber roof of collar beams, wind braces and rafters made from trees from the onetime royal forests.
Note the all-important **corner post,** the wall plates, peg-holes and slots, wattle and daub partition walls, panelling, the original windows and doorways and the 15C staircase with oak stairtreads round a slim, one-piece **newel,** where the 500 year-old carpenters' adze marks remain visible on the beams.

★ **St John the Baptist** – The church, on a mound on the north side of the square, was rebuilt in the Perpendicular style at the height of the town's prosperity in the early 15C : aisles, nave and transepts were built tall with wide windows, the crossing tower was raised to three stages and crowned with a pierced parapet and pinnacles.
Inside, through the notable **south porch,** the eye is immediately attracted to the nave **ceiling** – a rare example in a church of the moulded plasterwork which decorates the great houses of the early 17C : George Drayton, a local craftsman, was paid ten guineas for the roof in 1636. In contrast to the snowflake pattern, the crossing is fan vaulted; the enamelled wrought-ironwork was bought in Bristol in 1729 at a cost of 21 guineas.
Also of interest are the mid-15C **font** with its circle of carved angels, hidden during the Commonwealth in a plaster casing and only rediscovered centuries later when a sexton, waiting for a baptism, idly picked away some of the cracked plaster; the charity **bread cupboard** where loaves are placed every Saturday in accordance with the 1688 Will of William Spearing *(west of south door);* the brass to Roger Harper (d 1493) and his wife *(south chapel);* the **altar frontal** of 1710 embroidered with contemporary altar furnishings.

Town Hall – The building dates from 1833. Inside, artefacts relating to bull-baiting, which occurred here right up to the 19C, are on show.

A number of Touring Programmes is given at the beginning of the guide.
Plan a trip with the help of the preceding Map of Principal Sights.

AXMINSTER Devon

Pop 4 457

Michelin Atlas p 7 or Map 403 - L31

The carpet weaving which was to make the 2 000 year old town's name a household word in Britain was introduced in 1755 by the Axminster clothier Thomas Whitty. During a visit to London he had seen a very large (36ft x 24ft) and beautiful Turkey carpet. He promptly erected an upright loom in his own factory, which still stands in Silver Street (now the Conservative Club), trained his five young daughters, charged his sister as overseer and on midsummer's day began weaving his first large carpet.

Church - By the Middle Ages Axminster was a community of sufficient prosperity to rebuild its Saxon Church in the 12C Norman style, and to add a tower in the 13C (recased in the 19C); it was again rebuilt in the 14C and 15C in the Decorated and Perpendicular styles. The tower was repaired after being damaged in an affray against the Parliamentarians in 1644 and the church was enlarged and remodelled in the 18C-20C.
Inside, note the cut-down Jacobean **pulpit** and **reading desk**, the charity boards, the royal arms painted in 1767 at a cost of £9 14*s* and, in the chancel, the tomb with the lovely recumbent **effigy** with steepled hands of Lady Alicia de Mohun (d *c*1257).

Streets and Squares - The two squares, Trinity and Victoria Place, and the streets between are marked by occasional Georgian houses, rounded shop-fronts and a coaching inn with a Venetian window above the wide yard entrance.

Carpet Factory ⊙ - *Off King Edward Rd, by the station.*
Visitors see the looms being threaded with hundreds of bobbins of different coloured wool yarn; automatic weaving from jacquard cards; shearing. There is inspection at every stage.

★ BARNSTAPLE Devon

Pop 24 490

Michelin Atlas p 6 or Map 403 - H30 - Facilities

In Alfred's reign Barnstaple became a burgh with defences; in 930 it received a charter. Its 1 000 year history as the regional agricultural centre, trade and cattle market is recalled in **Butchers' Row** and the 17C cast-iron, glass-roofed **Pannier Market** where smallholders and farmers' wives pack in each Tuesday and Friday to sell their produce : Devon cream, vegetables, fruit and preserves.

SIGHTS

★ **Long Bridge** - The bridge (520ft by 10ft) was first constructed in stone in *c*1273. In 1539 the drawbridge connection, which until then had existed at the town end, was replaced by three arches making a total of 13. The bridge was widened in 1796, the year a regular coach service to Exeter was inaugurated, and again in 1834.

Parish Church - The church was rebuilt in 1318 adjoining the older tower, which in 1636 was overlapped with a lead-covered broach spire. Inside, the 17C **memorial monuments** *(south aisle)* and the large **mayoral pew** with a lion and unicorn are of particular interest.

Horwood Almshouses and Alice Horwood School - The almshouses and school, which were endowed to take "20 poor children for ever", were built in the 17C in the quiet, cobbled and bollarded Church Lane *(courtyard through the arch)*.

Guildhall ⊙ - *High St end of Butcher's Row.*
The hall, a 19C replacement, contains the **Dodderidge Parlour,** a room panelled in 17C oak from a wealthy merchant's house, in which the town's famous collection of **corporation plate** is displayed. There are three silver-gilt steeple cups of 1620 - a replica was presented to Barnstaple, Massachusets in 1939 on the tercentenary of its foundation - maces, lidded tankards and a vast **punch-bowl** used at the proclamation of the annual fair (Wednesday prior to 20 September).

Queen Anne's Walk - *Downriver from the bridge.*
The walk was built as the merchants' exchange in 1609, enlarged 20 years later and rebuilt in 1708 to comprise a single colonnade beneath a statue of Queen Anne bearing a gilded crown, sceptre and orb. Note the **Tome stone** on which bargains were struck, and wall tablets about the Armada.

Museum of North Devon ⊙ - *The Square.*
The old 19C Atheneum Library and Museum beside the river bridge again houses items and artefacts from the local heritage : 19C and 20C Devon **art pottery;** uniforms and silver belonging to the Royal Devon Yeomanry (1794-1971); pewterware; collections of pressed plants, fossils, shells, **beetles and bugs, stuffed animals;** flint hand axes, Roman gaming counters, 17C armour...

St Anne's Chapel Museum ⊙ - *High Street.*
The 14C chapel, which was used as the local grammar school from 1549 to 1910, now displays the original school furniture and houses a museum on education and the history of the building. John Gay (1685-1732) was a pupil under the schoolmaster Robert Luck.

EXCURSIONS

★★ **Arlington Court** – *8 miles northeast on A39. See Arlington Court.*

★ **Braunton** – *6 miles northwest by A361. See Braunton.*

★★ **Mortehoe** – *15 miles northwest by A361, B3231 and by-roads. See Mortehoe.*

★ BARRINGTON COURT GARDENS Somerset

Michelin Atlas p 8 or Map 403 – L31 – 3½ miles northeast of Ilminster

Nothing certain is known about the origins of this beautiful 16C house of golden Ham Hill stone, surrounded by delightful gardens. It was constructed (1550-60) to the usual Elizabethan E-plan with a porch flanked by two projecting wings enclosing a south facing forecourt; the **roofline** is embellished with gables, finials and spiral chimney stacks. The **Strode block** (1674), originally open on the north side, was built as stabling.

The property changed hands several times, eventually being leased as a farm. It was restored from a mere shell in the 1920s by Col A A Lyle, whose hobby was collecting oak panelling and interior fittings.

The charming gardens bear the imprint of **Gertrude Jekyll** (*qv;* 1843-1932) who advised on the planting.

GARDENS ⊙

Kitchen Garden – High brick walls provide shelter for the vegetables and fruit trees *(plants and produce for sale);* the lead water tanks are dated 1782.

A long herbaceous border is planted against the south face of the south wall.

Maple Garden – Fine autumn colour is provided by the maples in the tennis court garden which is enclosed by a great hedge of Lawson's cypress.

Walled Flower Gardens – The old cattleyards now enclose the **Iris Garden,** a harmony of purples, pinks and blues; the **White Garden,** consisting of geometric beds round a central statue; the lovely brick **Beef Stalls,** built in the 16C for rearing oxen but now planted with climbers and roses; the **Lily Garden,** a display of vivid colours.

Arboretum – The pleached lime walk, east of the south lawn and the sundial, is flanked by an orchard and an arboretum of unusual trees and shrubs – pines, conifers and wych hazels – planted in the 1930s.

HOUSE ⊙

Several features of the original building have survived. Over the library door are the **arms** of William Strode, who owned the house in the 17C. The door to the **garde-robe** of the best bedchamber is visible in the north wall of the stair hall. West of the south door in the screens passage is a **lavabo** where people washed their hands before entering the Great Hall. The huge kitchen **fireplace** in the west wing is disguised by blind windows on the exterior; the lintel is composed of two massive pieces of Ham Hill stone. Beneath the window sill *(left)* are the original charcoal **braziers.** Two **overmantels** (1625), originally brightly painted, survive on the upper floor; they show *(east wing)* the Strode family arms and *(west wing)* the Judgement of Solomon. The **Great Hall** is furnished with a specially designed Ham stone fireplace, Italianate beams and English screens doors and 16C linenfold panelling. An inner wall of early **16C latticed lights** divides the Dining Room, which has a wooden ceiling composed of a deep honeycomb of star patterns, from the Buttery, which is panelled with **Jacobean wainscotting.** The staircase, of which only the lowest newel post is original (early 17C), rises under a **15C timber ceiling.** There is more Jacobean wainscotting in the dressing room where the radiators are covered by **wooden lattices** from the ventilator shafts of old sailing ships.

★★★ BATH Avon — Pop 84 283

Michelin Atlas p 17 or Map 403 – M29 – Facilities

The unparalleled harmony and elegance of Bath's 18C architecture and urban planning combined with its ancient past and its lively present – as the seat of a university, the home of a wealth of museums and a smart shopping centre – makes the city popular with visitors throughout the year.

Legend and history – Britain's only hot springs probably broke through the earth's crust in the time of Neanderthal Man *c*100 000 years ago. According to legend, in 500 BC the leprosy-afflicted **Prince Bladud** had become a wandering swineherd; when his swine appeared cured of their skin ailments after wallowing in the mud, he plunged in himself – and emerged cured. He returned to court, succeeded to the crown, fathered the future King Lear and established his seat at Bath.

However that may be, by the 1C AD, when the Romans had advanced west and were mining lead in the Mendip Hills, the village of Bath was already known for its warm springs.

The **Romans** transformed Bath into England's first spa resort, naming it after a native Celtic goddess, **Aquae Sulis.** They built baths, a temple, possibly a gymnasium or theatre – it was purely a pleasure centre, there were no military interests.

Following the departure of the Romans in the 5C, the city declined; in the 6C Bath was taken by the **Saxons** who built a town within the Roman walls and an abbey not far from the Roman temple site; in the 9C Alfred is said to have made Bath into a fortress; in 973 **Edgar,** the first King of all England, was re-crowned in the Saxon abbey.

The squabbles of pillaging Norman barons so reduced the city that **John de Villula** of Tours, Bishop of Somerset and Physician, was able to purchase it for £500. He began the creation of a vast Benedictine cathedral priory – the church today occupies only the site of the nave – built a palace, a guesthouse, a new suite of baths, founded a school of science and mathematics and encouraged the treatment of the sick (the Hospital of St John was founded in his name in the 12C). His cathedral was never completed. Only in 1499 did building of the present minster begin; Bath was by then a prosperous wool town.

At the Dissolution the monks lost their jurisdiction over the baths and sold off lead from the minster's roof, the bells, glass and ironwork. In 1574 Queen Elizabeth ordered that a fund be set up to restore the abbey and St John's Hospital and ensure that "an unsavoury town... become a most sweet town".

By 1668 Pepys, on a visit, considered it had "many good streets and very fair stone houses". Although he "stayed above two hours in the water" he had reservations about the baths : "Methinks it cannot be clean to go so many bodies together in the same water". Others were less fastidious : where royalty went – Charles II and Catherine of Braganza, Queen Mary of Modena, Queen Anne – crowds followed, until by the early 18C Bath was becoming a place to attend not only for a cure but to be in fashion. From the visitor's point of view, however, the city was dull and unorganised.

Beau Nash – "The Beau" arrived in 1704 (d 1762); he was 31 and came to Bath in the wake of the fashionable fraternity. He had a flair for organisation and on his appointment as Master of Ceremonies he laid down a programme for the highflyers to follow, from early morning bathing to evening assemblies; he ordered that the streets be lit and made safe to walk in; that swords be not worn in the town and sedan chairmen charge the authorized tariff... Within a year he opened the first Pump Room where people might take the waters and meet in civilised society; he organised concerts, balls, cards, the gambling; he laid down eleven rules, which for fear of ostracism and public ridicule were implicitly obeyed. The town prospered, charities benefited, he grew rich and Bath became the most fashionable city in England.

Ralph Allen and John Wood – While Nash refashioned Bath society, Ralph Allen and John Wood undertook the transformation of the city's architecture and entire urban plan.

Allen (1694-1764), a Cornish postmaster, came to Bath in 1710 where he offered the government £2 000 a year for a seven-year concession to make the region's highly unreliable postal service both efficient and profitable; it became a model and with the fortune he made out of it Allen bought stone quarries at Claverton *(qv)* and on Combe Down, with the idea of building a new city with the honey-coloured stone. John Wood (1700-54) was a Yorkshireman who, by 1728, had settled in the city. A Classicist inspired by Bath's Roman past, he sought to build principally in the Palladian style using the stone from Combe Down, now known as **Bath Stone.**

SIGHTSEEING IN BATH

Because of its architectural design, the city is best seen on foot; each of the three walks suggested starts from the Abbey and requires approximately ½ day.

If time is short see : the **Abbey★** (exterior), go into the **Pump Room★** (view the King's Bath – a full visit to the Roman Baths takes an hour), walk up Milsom and Gay Streets to the **Circus★★★**; bear right to the **Assembly Rooms★** and the **Museum of Costume★★★** or left to see the **Royal Crescent★★★**; return down Gay Street.

Note the many fine **street vistas** closed by perfectly sited houses, often pedimented, and the wealth of individual touches and attractive details : iron railings, lamps, forecourt grass...

★★ ABBEY, PUMP ROOM and ROMAN BATHS (BZ) *½ day*

★ **Bath Abbey** ⏲ – The present sanctuary was begun in 1499 by Bishop Oliver King following a dream in which he saw angels climbing to heaven and heard voices commanding that a king, which he took to be himself from his surname, restore the church. From the pillars of the Norman church there eventually arose the pure, late Perpendicular abbey.

Inside, the nave, chancel and narrow transepts all soar to **fan vaulting** designed by Robert and William Vertue (designers of the vaulting in the Henry VII Chapel, Westminster Abbey). Outside, five-light windows are framed by flying buttresses, crocketed pinnacles and a castellated, pierced parapet.

The fine **west front** *(undergoing restoration)* which overlooks the Church Yard presents a Perpendicular window, a 17C door and, in the stone, tall **ladders** with angels ascending as in Bishop King's dream.

★ **Pump Room** ⏲ – The pump room was built from 1789 to 1799, after Nash's death, but with his **statue** presiding over the assembled company it remains forever redolent of "this omnipotent Lord". The interiors of these tearooms feature pilasters, gilded capitals, a coved ceiling, apsed ends, a rounded bay containing the former drinking fountain and from which there is a view of the King's Bath, Chippendale-style chairs, a Tompion long-case clock, a trio, a glass chandelier... altogether the perfect meeting place for Catherine and Mr Tilney in Jane Austen's *Northanger Abbey*.

★★ **Roman Baths** ⏲ – The baths are fed by a spring which pours out approximately 280 000 gallons of water a day at a temperature of 116°F (46.5°C). The Roman complex originally consisted of the Great Bath, a large, warm, swimming pool, once covered but now open to the sky, and two baths of decreasing heat to the east; the second building phase installed a *frigidarium*, or cold room, on the west side, with windows at the north end overlooking the sacred spring or reservoir and further west, two heated chambers (the *tepidarium* and *caldarium*). Later alterations enlarged the east end, elaborated the baths at the west end and transformed the *frigidarium* into a cold plunge Circular Bath.

Due north, beyond the reservoir, was an altar and west of that the temple. A circular temple *(tholos)* was probably added in the 2C AD to the east on the present site of the Abbey.

After the Romans had left, the drains soon clogged through lack of attention and mud covered the site. The temple precinct now lies under Stall Street, and the altar and its court beneath the Pump Room. In the early Middle Ages the Normans constructed the King's Bath, a tank lined with Mendip lead.

In 1727 workmen digging a sewer in Stall Street found a gilded bronze head of **Minerva,** who was known to have been the presiding goddess of the spring. Since then continuing excavations have revealed that the bath

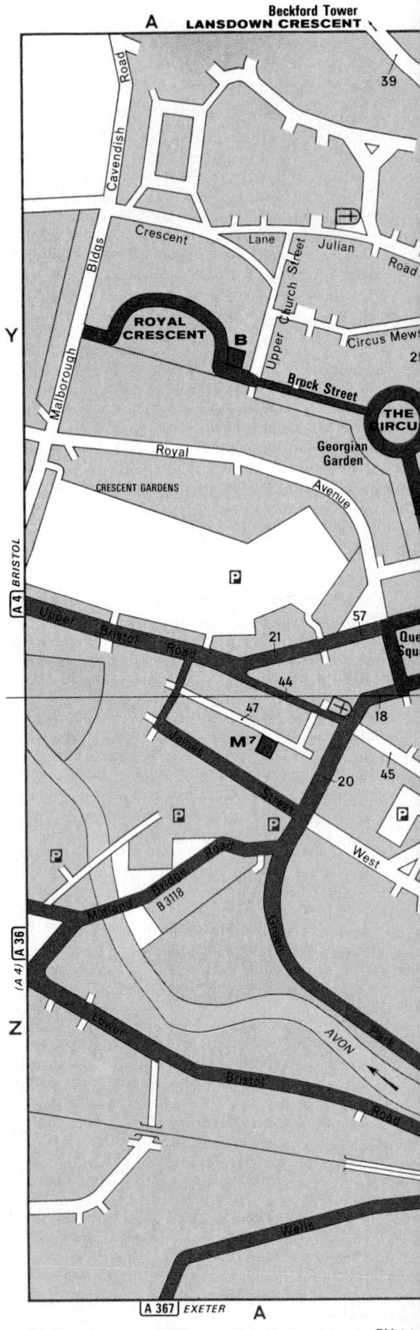

Gay Street	ABY	Bennett Street	BY 11
Green Street	BY 32	Bridge Street	BYZ 13
Milson Street	BY	Broad Quay	BZ 14
New Bond Street	BY 46	Broad Street	BY 16
		Chapel Row	AYZ 18
Abbey Church Yard	BZ 2	Charles Street	AZ 20
Alfred Street	BY 3	Charlotte Street	AY 21
Ambury	BZ 4	Cheap Street	BZ 23
Argyle Street	BY 6	Churchill Bridge	BZ 24
Bath Street	BZ 7	Circus Place	AY 25
Beckford Road	CY 9	Cleveland Place	CY 26
Belvedere	BY 10	Corn Street	BZ 27

complex was repeatedly remodelled; items discovered during the excavations are on display in the **museum** : a lead curse, altars, coins, vessels, carvings including a **gorgon's head** *(illustration p 42)* from the temple façade.

A 1791 colonnade flanks the uneven line of 17C-18C houses and delightful 18C-19C shopfronts facing the Pump Room.

★★ ASSEMBLY ROOMS, MUSEUM OF COSTUME, CIRCUS, ROYAL CRESCENT *½ day*

Before crossing Upper Borough Walls, note the **Royal Mineral Water Hospital** (BZ A) built by John Wood in 1738 and the **castellated medieval wall** opposite, over which cadavers from the hospital used to be thrown.

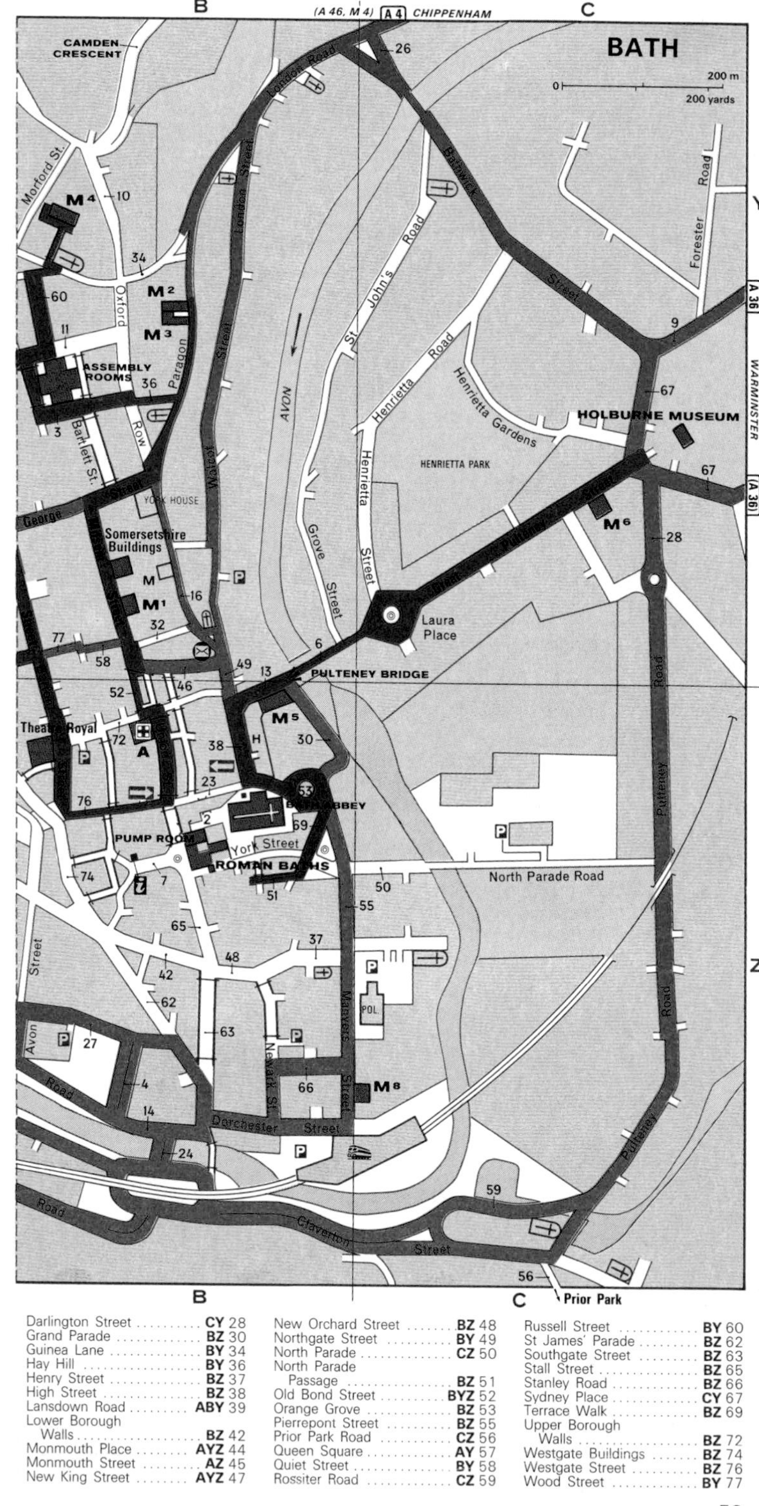

Darlington Street ... CY 28
Grand Parade ... BZ 30
Guinea Lane ... BY 34
Hay Hill ... BY 36
Henry Street ... BZ 37
High Street ... BZ 38
Lansdown Road ... ABY 39
Lower Borough Walls ... BZ 42
Monmouth Place ... AYZ 44
Monmouth Street ... AZ 45
New King Street ... AYZ 47

New Orchard Street ... BZ 48
Northgate Street ... BY 49
North Parade ... CZ 50
North Parade Passage ... BZ 51
Old Bond Street ... BYZ 52
Orange Grove ... BZ 53
Pierrepont Street ... BZ 55
Prior Park Road ... CZ 56
Queen Square ... AY 57
Quiet Street ... BY 58
Rossiter Road ... CZ 59

Russell Street ... BY 60
St James' Parade ... BZ 62
Southgate Street ... BZ 63
Stall Street ... BZ 65
Stanley Road ... BZ 66
Sydney Place ... CY 67
Terrace Walk ... BZ 69
Upper Borough Walls ... BZ 72
Westgate Buildings ... BZ 74
Westgate Street ... BZ 76
Wood Street ... BY 77

Continue up Old Bond Street (1760-70) (**BYZ 52**) into **Milsom Street** (BY), the wide shopping street begun by John Wood, which epitomises the carriage, bonneted and beribboned age of the 1770s.

★★ **Royal Photographic Society National Centre of Photography** (BY M[1]) ⊙ – The octagonal room that houses the centre was a former private chapel (1767) and features a gallery supported on Ionic columns. Beneath the 18C chandelier the story of photography unfolds through every stage : from trapping the light, waxed paper and wet plates to the single reflex lens; elsewhere are a large collection of Leicas and, in three separate galleries, changing exhibitions of contemporary artistic, scientific and experimental photography.
Beyond the arcade next to the Octagon, note the grand curved 18C **Somersetshire Buildings** (now a bank); closing the vista is a range of houses along a raised pavement in **George Street,** which also contains York House *(right),* an old 18C posting inn.

At the east end of George St bear left into the Paragon.

Building of Bath Museum (BY M[2]) ⊙ – The exhibition explains and illustrates the architectural design and construction of Bath through Georgian tools and artefacts and a large-scale model of the city described in 7 languages. The Centre is housed in an old chapel (1765) founded by the Countess of Huntingdon for a Methodist sect.

Museum of English Naive Art (BY M[3]) ⊙ – The Crane Kalman Collection is hung in an old schoolroom and presents a delightful assortment of naive paintings from the mid 18C to *c*1900, depicting the everyday pleasures and concerns of ordinary people : prize pigs and rams, champion fighters and favourite ratcatchers, charming townscapes and seascapes, fearsome barbers and dentists... The friendly and informal museum also includes an assortment of period shopsigns, whirligigs, furniture and other artefacts.

Return south; turn right into Hay Hill and Alfred St.

★ **Assembly Rooms** (BY) ⊙ – The rooms, built in 1769-71, were declared in the 1772 Bath Guide to be "the most noble and elegant of any in the Kingdom". 18C assemblies were evening entertainments at which several activities – dancing, gossip and scandalmongering by the spectators, card-playing and tea-drinking – took place.

Ball Room – The pale green-blue room – 100ft 6in long, 43ft 6in wide and 43ft 6in high – was designed so that the dancers in their finery provided the colour below, while the decoration was concentrated above on the columns, the entablature and the deep Naples-yellow coved ceiling from which are suspended five magnificent crystal **chandeliers.**

Octagon – The small room was intended as the card room.

Tea Room – Wood planned a rich and dignified 18C interior for the room where gossip would be rife. At one end stands a screen of superimposed pillars which continue round the sides to support the coved ceiling, compartmented by enriched flat ribs.

★★★ **Museum of Costume** ⊙ – *In the Assembly Rooms building.*
This enormous collection of clothes, dating largely from the 18C onwards, reveals how previous generations adorned the streets of Bath during its heyday.
Presented within room-sets containing period furniture, groups of figures show the fascinating changes in dress for men, women and children which have evolved to the present day – in shape, texture, colour and adornment. Spitalfields silks, the fabulous embroidery of court attire, the literally breathtaking bodices, the changing length of hemlines and trouser legs are all included, together with countless accessories, continuing right up to the Modern section with its annual inclusion of a new Dress of the Year.

Go up Russel St and bear right into Julian Rd.

★ **Bath Industrial Heritage Centre** (BY M[4]) ⊙ – J B Bowler was a turn-of-the-century **brass founder** by trade, but also an engineer-craftsman, businessman and cordial manufacturer, and he never threw anything away : his small, dark, Victorian shop which houses the heritage centre contains a wealth of tools, machines, ledgers....

Return to Bennet St.

★★★ **The Circus** (AY) – The Circus, originally the King's Circus, was built only in 1754 although it was one of John Wood's earliest concepts. It comprises a tight circle of identical houses pierced by three equidistant access roads. The houses of pale Bath stone, decorated with coupled columns, rise through three floors to a frieze and acorn-topped balustrade.
No 4 houses the Fashion Research Centre, a satellite of the Museum of Costume; it contains the Study Collection and a wide-ranging library.

Brock Street (AY) – The street runs between the Circus and the Crescent, and was built by John Wood II in 1767 with houses of differing design. It is named after Thomas Brock, the first man to lease no 1 Royal Crescent.
It is only from the very end of the street that the unexpected and stunning sweep of the crescent is finally revealed.

★★★ **Royal Crescent** (AY) – The great arc of 30 terrace houses, in which the horizontal lines are counterbalanced by 114 giant Ionic columns rising from the first floor to the pierced parapet, was the great achievement of John Wood II in 1767-74.

★★ **No 1 Royal Crescent** (B) ⊙ – The Georgian house has been authentically restored showing how wealthy residents of the city would have lived. Inside, the wall coverings and furnishings based on contemporary printing blocks and drawings provide the setting for Chippendale, Sheraton and Hepplewhite **furniture,** porcelain and 18C **glassware.** The basement houses the fascinating Kitchen Museum.

Cross the road and enter Royal Victoria Park; follow Gravel Walk down and turn left at the bottom to join Gay St.

Gay Street (ABY) – The long street (1734-60) was the work of the two Woods; no 41, on the corner of Old King Street, was designed by the father and lived in by the son and is the Baroque exception to the Classical style of the street. Next to the recessed bow window on the corner a small, Delft-tiled **powder-cabinet** with a shell niche can be seen inside, where gentlemen could powder their wigs before entering the reception rooms.
This was the period of *The School for Scandal* by Richard Sheridan who in 1772 eloped with Elizabeth Linley from no 11 Royal Crescent.

Queen Square (ABY) – The square was Wood's first example of urban planning. Note the **north side** with its pedimented centre and advanced ends : Wood himself lived at no 24, **Dr William Oliver,** inventor of the Bath Oliver biscuit, at nos 16-18.

Continue by Barton St to Beaufort Square.

Theatre Royal (BZ) – The square of modest 18C houses has been dominated since the early 19C by the Theatre Royal, resplendent inside in an appropriate finery of dark red Regency stripe, with gilding and plum coloured plush for the horseshoe-shaped auditorium.
Adjoining are two houses once occupied by **Beau Nash.**

★ ORANGE GROVE, PULTENEY BRIDGE, HOLBURNE MUSEUM *½ day*

From Orange Grove, with its 18C houses, go south into Terrace Walk; note Bath's oldest **shopfront** (Messrs Eldridge Pope, now a pub).
Turn right into North Parade Passage, the former Lilliput Alley, where Sally Lunn's teashop at **no 3** is a medieval house which now displays Roman and medieval artefacts in the kitchen museum in the basement, and **no 2,** next door, was Ralph Allen's town house.
It was while living here that Allen had the folly **Sham Castle** built to complete the landscape on Combe Down.

Return to Orange Grove; bear northwest into the High St; turn right into Bridge St.

Victoria Art Gallery (BZ M5) ⊙ – The gallery, housed behind the Guildhall buildings, displays a permanent collection of fine art in its Victorian gallery, and also temporary exhibitions.

★ **Pulteney Bridge** (BCY) – The bridge, apparently based on the Ponte Vecchio in Florence with a central Venetian window, domed end pavilions and small shops, was designed in 1769-74 by **Robert Adam** for his friend Sir William Pulteney who hoped to develop a new city area beyond the Avon. (**River boat moorings :** above and below the weir.)

Pulteney Bridge, Bath.

Great Pulteney Street (CY) – The city's longest vista, framed by the classically proportioned terrace houses, extends some 600yds from the end of the bridge. The eye travels along Argyle Street, across the diagonally set Laura Place and down the length of Great Pulteney Street, to rest finally on the Holburne Museum.

Bath Postal Museum (M⁶) ⊙ – This small museum centres on the postal service in the Royal Mail coach period and on more recent developments such as Air Mail.

★★ **Holburne Museum and Crafts Study Centre** (CY) ⊙ – The museum contains the collection of decorative and fine art made by **Sir Thomas William Holburne** (1793-1874), who served in the *Orion* at Trafalgar. The **Crafts Study Centre** possesses a unique archive of books, documents, working notes and photos; its examples of work by 20C British artist-craftworkers in textiles, pottery, ceramics, furniture and calligraphy are displayed for comparison in the museum among the earlier exhibits.
Of especial note are : *(first floor)* porcelain, fine **furniture,** a silver-gilt **rosewater dish** (1616), **silver** and **silver-gilt plate,** particularly Georgian, apostle and sealtop spoons, table silver and snuff boxes; *(staircase)* **18C Wedgwood,** and Roman and *art nouveau* glass; *(top floor)* Italian majolica; Flemish, Dutch and English 16C and 17C paintings including a portrait of Holburne's physician by **Gainsborough** who lived at no 17 The Circus from 1759-74.

ADDITIONAL CITY MUSEUMS

Herschel House Museum (AZ M⁷) ⊙ – The house of the influential Sir William Herschel (1738-1822), King's Astronomer, discoverer of the planet Uranus and of infra-red radiation, contains telescopes, mirrors, prisms, thermometers...

Book Museum (CZ M⁸) ⊙ – The history of the book-making craft from the 16C-20C is explained with examples of beautiful old and new bindings; some important 1st editions included.

CITY OUTSKIRTS

Go north up Broad St; fork left into Oxford Row; at the 5-road junction bear centre right.

★ **Camden Crescent** (BY) – The modest crescent, with its wide **view,** was built by John Eveleigh in 1786-92. It was never completed owing to subsidence at the east end, so the pediment above five giant columns is off-centre.

Return to the junction; take Lansdown Rd northwest; after 150 yds turn left into Lansdown Place East and the Crescent.

★★ **Lansdown Crescent** – The serpentine crescent and the continuing, more ornamented, **Somerset Place**★ were built on this site overlooking the abbey and the city centre in 1789-93.
The crescent consists of three-storeyed houses with a rusticated ground floor and pierced balustrade; it is accented at the centre with pilasters and pediment and at either end by bow windows, and the ensemble completed by area railings and graceful lampholders.
Note the **bridge** between no 20 the Crescent and no 1 Lansdown Place West, built by William Beckford.

Return to Lansdown Rd and continue north to the tower (left).

Beckford Tower and Museum ⊙ – William Beckford (1760-1844), millionaire inheritor with a true 18C collector's taste in books, pictures and art objects, Grand Tour traveller, diarist and MP, was the builder of the fantastic **Fonthill Abbey** (demolished). In 1882 he left Wiltshire for Bath where he purchased Lansdown Hill and two houses in the crescent. On the hill he erected an Italianate tower (154ft) in local stone, crowned by a lantern of eight cast-iron columns and a domed roof, all gilded. The tower, intended as a library retreat, contains the museum and, at the top, a belvedere which affords a **prospect**★ of Bath, the Severn Estuary and Wales, the Cotswolds, Wiltshire...

Prior Park – *Cross the Avon at North Parade Bridge; turn right into Pulteney Rd, left at the major junction into Prior Park Rd (A3062).*
In the 1730s, when Bath had become fashionable, **Ralph Allen** decided to build himself a seat away from the crowds. He believed that the superbly sited mansion (now a school), which was designed by John Wood in the Palladian style with giant columns supporting a pedimented portico, would also serve to demonstrate to sceptical London architects that Bath stone from his quarries was supreme for fine construction work.
Allen kept open house at Prior Park and among his visitors were Alexander Pope, Henry Fielding and Samuel Johnson, Gainsborough, David Garrick and Samuel Richardson.

Henge monuments, which are unique to Britain, are a type of sanctuary. Originally fairly simple, they consisted of a bank and ditch, nearly always circular, which enclosed a sacred area sometimes containing a ring of ritual pits, or rings of standing stones or posts. The Beaker Folk* (qv) *were largely responsible for subsequent, more refined henges, such as Avebury. They also raised monuments to the dead: individual burial under a circular mound replaced the old communal burials in long barrows.

★ BERE REGIS CHURCH Dorset — Pop 1 449

Michelin Atlas p 8 or Map 403 - N31

The church, but little else, was saved in 1788 when the last in a series of fires devastated the village – the communal iron hooks of *c*1600, which were used to pull away burning thatch from cottages on fire, still hang above the church door.

★ **St John the Baptist** – Inside the Perpendicular church is the finest wooden **parish church roof** in Dorset. It was the climax in the then 500-year old church's rebuilding, made possible by the gift in 1475 of a huge sum by the locally born Cardinal Morton (1425-1500), Archbishop of Canterbury and Lord Chancellor to Henry VII.

The apostle roof, Bere Regis.

Roof – The roof is a structure of oak tie beams and braces, crown posts and queen posts, outlined by cresting, filled with tracery, decorated in gold and rich reds, browns, blues, the meeting points masked with bosses, the not-in-fact hammers disguised by almost life-size carved figures of the **apostles.** Easily recognisable are John (holding a book or gospel), Judas (with a money bag), Matthew (holding a book), Philip (with a staff) and Peter (with mitre and keys). In 1738 the entry appears in the churchwardens' accounts "Paid Benjamin Moores for Cleaning and Oyling the Apostles 4*s* 0*d*".

In the roof also are four **bosses** celebrating Cardinal Morton : the head at the east end is said to be a portrait; the arms are of Canterbury of which he was archbishop; the Tudor rose is in honour of Henry VII; the fourth symbolises the marriage Morton arranged between the king and Elizabeth of York. Note the **capitals** in the late 12C arcade with carved figures in an agony of toothache, sore throat...

Since the 14C the south aisle has been the Chapel of the Turbervilles *(qv)* – after whom Hardy modelled the family in *Tess of the d'Urbervilles.*

★★ BICKLEIGH Devon — Pop 205

Michelin Atlas p 7 or Map 403 - J31 - Facilities

Bickleigh looks as a Devon village should : from the old stone bridge over the Exe there is a view across to thatched houses and cottages with whitened cob walls and gardens running down to the water's edge, against a backdrop of rising fields and trees.

SIGHTS

★★ **Bickleigh Mill Craft Centre and Farms** ⊙ – *South side of the bridge.*
The mill with its water-wheel and machinery has been restored to working order.

The 19C farm displays rare and traditional breeds, uses Shire horses and oxen for power, and milks its cows and goats by hand. Old fashioned pigs, ornamental bantams and hens scratching in the farmyard add to the atmosphere. A farming life museum depicts the everyday round at the turn of the century.

Craftworkers – potters, painters, spinners – can be seen at work in individual log cabins.

There is also a fish farm where trout and carp may be fed or fished, a narrow-gauge railway, crazy golf, table tennis...

★ **Bickleigh Castle** ⊙ – *Turn right (A3072) before the bridge, then follow the signs.*

Pink and white water lilies and irises transform the moat; wistaria decks the 14C tufa-stone gatehouse walls; thatched buildings add to the overall charm; 17C Italian and 18C English wrought-iron gates grace the approaches.

Norman Chapel – The thatched chapel was built between 1090 and 1110. The nave and chancel masonry and the doorway arch are original; so also are two windows, the others being 15C when the chancel was barrel roofed.
Note the **sanctuary ring** *(qv),* the Early English font, the medieval glass, the 15C poppy-head **benches** and the hour-long sand-glass sermon **timer.**

Castle – Only the gatehouse remains of the castle itself, Fairfax having ordered all to be slighted so that the Royalist Sir Henry Carew was compelled to construct an adjoining farmhouse of cob and thatch.
Pass through the vaulted **Gatehouse,** which is flanked by an Armoury (Cromwellian arms and armour; display on the siege of the castle in 1646) and the former Guard Room which now contains Tudor furniture.
Climb the early Tudor wooden staircase to the **Great Hall,** which extends across the full width of the gateway, contains two stone fireplaces and is over 50ft in length. The panelled minstrels' gallery is Tudor, the furniture Carolean-Queen Anne.
The rooms in the **Farmhouse Wing** are notable for their ingle-nook fireplaces : the first has a 1588 fireplate and a bread oven to one side, the second a large vaulted oven and an aperture to control the smoke in the adjoining bacon-curing store; the third, in the Garden Chamber, a 17C carved overmantel which depicts crowded, possibly historic, scenes from the lives of the 14C-17C castle owners.
Note also the wooden Ionic pillars in the first room, believed to have furnished the stateroom of a Spanish man o' war, and the very old French china in the Garden Room.
The thatched barn houses the most complete collection in existence of Second World War **spy** and **escape gadgets** and an exhibition about the **Titanic** and the **Mary Rose,** which was commanded by Vice-Admiral Sir George Carew when she sank in 1545.

★ BICTON Devon

Michelin Atlas p 4 or Map 403 – K31, 32

The grounds and gardens of Bicton House, which is now an Agricultural College, have been progressively designed and planted with specimen trees over the last 200 years.

★ GARDENS ⊙

In the 1730s Baron Rolle, the first in a line of keen horticulturalists, rebuilt the house and had the formal **Italian Gardens** laid out after a design by the 17C French landscape gardener, André Le Nôtre.
To these gardens have been added the Palm House (1839), conservatories, an **American Garden** (started in the 1830s), a secluded **Hermitage Garden** with its small summerhouse and lake, heather and dwarf conifer plantations, a pinetum and acres of close-mown lawns banked by rhododendrons, azaleas and magnolias.

Woodland Railway – The 18in gauge railway, originally from the Royal Arsenal, Woolwich, extends over 1¼ miles through the grounds, running close beside the lake and through the woodlands and plantations.

MUSEUM ⊙

James Countryside Collection – The collection shows the tools and implements that were in use on the land almost unaltered for centuries, and the revolution in the same equipment over the last 50 years : there are horse-drawn harrows and a blacksmith's forge, a regal gipsy caravan (1902), a steam traction engine (1894), a Fordson tractor (1917), a cider press (1800).

BIDEFORD Devon Pop 13 826

Michelin Atlas p 6 or Map 403 – H30 – Facilities

Bideford (pronounced "Biddyford") derives its name from its site at the foot of a hillside "by the ford" across the River Torridge. It achieved fame as a port in the 16C-18C and is always recalled as the town with one of the most "beautiful and stately" **bridges** in the kingdom.
As a port it gained early prosperity from having been given by William Rufus to the **Grenvilles** who held it until 1744, by which time they had obtained borough, market and fair charters for it. Through Sir Richard Grenville's colonisation of Virginia and Carolina, Bideford developed a trans-Atlantic trade by the 16C which was greatly increased in the mid-17C by Newfoundland codfishing and, at the turn of the century, by tobacco imports from Maryland and Virginia. In addition there developed a trade in wool from Spain for the local textile industry, and a general commerce with the Mediterranean. The mile-long quay was built by the town corporation in 1663.
Prosperity declined, except for coastal shipping, until the arrival of the railway in the 19C brought the town into the tourist network. Since then local activity has centred on farming, tourism and light industry.

★ BRIDGE

Bideford Bridge.

The first bridge was built of **oak** in the last quarter of the 13C. A **stone bridge** was constructed *c*1460, using the timber as scaffolding and following its line exactly, even to the width of the arches which had varied according to the length of the original timbers ! It is 557ft long, and numbers 24 arches which are between 12ft and 25ft wide and spring from piers of correspondingly different size. It has been repaired and widened many times without losing its individuality.

ADDITIONAL SIGHT

★ **Burton Art Gallery** ⊙ – The modern gallery stands in the extensive and brilliantly flowered Victoria Park at the end of the quay, beyond the statue of Charles Kingsley who wrote a great part of *Westward Ho !* while staying at the Royal Hotel here in 1855.
On display are fine 17C-18C **English pewter** (chargers, platters, jugs and tankards), Bideford and Fremington pottery, notably large, late 18C slipware **harvest jugs,** English domestic silverware, 17C-19C English porcelain including small figurines and paintings. The museum's speciality derives from a rare bequest of 800 **card-cases** : English, French, Oriental in origin and made of ivory, silver, tooled leather, silk, wood marquetry, lacquer, Scottish silk tartan, *papier mâché,* needlework, mother-of-pearl, tortoise-shell... About 100 cases are on display at any one time.

EXCURSIONS

★ **Clovelly** – *11 miles west by A39 and B3237 north. See Clovelly.*

★ **Appledore** – *3 miles north on A386. See Appledore.*

Tapeley Park, Instow ⊙ – *2 miles north on A39, right turn beyond Westleigh.* A long drive banked high with trees and rhododendrons leads to the house which stands in a spectacular **setting** overlooking the Taw and Torridge estuary and a beautiful terraced, Italian garden.
Built of brick with stone dressings, the mansion is 17C, much altered and enlarged but still retaining 18C plasterwork ceilings. Interest inside ranges from 18C-19C service memorabilia to fine porcelain and glass and William Morris furniture.

Westward Ho ! – *3 miles northwest by A386 and a by-road.*
The golden sands beside the village (renamed in the 19C after Kingsley's book) extend for three miles; the Atlantic rollers bring the surf-riders thunderously towards the shallows then subside harmlessly to wash around the ankles of paddling, squatting toddlers – Westward Ho ! is one of Devon's safest beaches. Backing the sands is a ridge of pebbles and behind these the grass-covered **Northam Burrows;** at the west end of the beach the pebbles end in rocks and pools. Above rise the **Kipling Tors** from which there are views towards Hartland Point *(qv).*
Rudyard Kipling (1865-1936) spent his schooldays here at the United Services College, "twelve bleak houses by the shore", about which he wrote a highly fictionalised account in *Stalky & Co.*

★ BLANDFORD FORUM Dorset — Pop 7 249

Michelin Atlas p 8 or Map 403 – N31

The town rose within 30 years of a disastrous fire in 1731 "like the Phoenix from its ashes, to its present beautiful and flourishing state". Houses were rebuilt along the old street courses in the latest 18C style; the church, in new guise, rose on its early site...

SIGHTS

Market Place – The square, the wide juncture of West and East Streets with Salisbury Street coming in at the northwest end, is the town centre.

Town Hall – The 18C hall (north side) stands over a three-bay arcade, filled with iron gates and lanterns and crowned by stone urns matching those on the church.

St Peter and St Paul – The large stone church dating from 1733-39 has a west tower rising squarely to a pierced balustrade, stone urns and an open, domed turret.

The interior, which is filled with light from the tall, rounded, typically Georgian windows, has Portland stone columns with Ionic capitals which soar to a moulded entablature and groined vault. Note, amidst the box pews, the canopied, carved and plush lined **Mayoral Chair** (1748), the **17C pulpit** and the **memorial** to the Bastard family who were responsible for much of the rebuilding.

Old Greyhound – The former inn of vast size (now a bank) has an ornate front comprising giant pilasters, a pediment, decorated window frames, plasterwork grapes and a greyhound.

Red Lion – Note the wide central carriage entrance between the pilasters.

No 26 Market Place – The house on the corner was built by John Bastard for himself and given an integrated façade with the house next door (no 75 East St) which he also built. (East Street itself escaped the fire and contains several older houses.)

Town Houses – North of the main road lies a network of winding streets and alleys with several attractive houses. In Church Lane are **Old Bank House, Lime Tree House,** of unusual purple brick with red brick dressings and vertical decoration between the windows, and **Coupar House,** "The finest post-fire building in Blandford", built of purple bricks laid as headers, relieved by a full complement of stone dressings.

Bear right.

The Plocks – The street was the gathering place for sheep to be sold in the market.

Continue through the triangular, oak planted, Tabernacle.

Old House – *The Close.* The house, which dates from 1660, stands high, rambling and disjointed. The red brick has been ingeniously cut and moulded to ornament the round-arched entrance, to form balusters and colonnettes and fill every space with a decorative motif...

Ryves Almshouses – *Salisbury St, east side.* The range of 1682 is distinguished by a small centre gable, dominant chimneys and an ornate shield of arms.

Bridge – The stone bridge at the west entrance to the town (A354), which spans the River Stour with six arches, dates from 1783.

EXCURSIONS

★ **Royal Signals Museum** ⓥ – *Blandford Camp. 2 miles northeast off B3082.* Less than 150 years separate the invention of the Morse code (1835), the first electric, single needle telegraph (1837), and micro-circuit transmitters and receivers. Chronologically there have been smoke and water signals, beacons, heliographs of metal and mirrorglass, messengers, pigeons, flags and lanterns and despatch riders on horseback and motor cycles. Field telephones date from Ladysmith in 1899; now radio keeps contact with units in the field, guerrilla forces and in 1939-45 with POWs who, against all the odds, made wireless sets in camps in Europe and Asia. This history and a fascinating assortment of equipment is clearly displayed in the museum.

Chettle House ⓥ – *5 miles northeast by A354; turn left beyond Tarrant Hinton.* Chettle comes from the Old English word *Cietal* – a deep valley between hills – which describes the tranquil setting of this **English Baroque house** and its surrounding village (described in Domesday as a town).
In 1710 the Elizabethan house on the site was replaced by this small country house designed by Thomas Archer (*c*1680-1743), a pupil of Vanbrugh. The red brick façade has an entablature and capitals of Chilmark stone (Ham stone at the ends) and has rounded corners in the Archer style. In 1846 the house was bought and altered by the Castleman family – note the castles on the skyline – though later returned to its original shape (hence the replacement Ham stone). The interior boasts an impressive Oak Hall with a double staircase and a gallery and a fine spiral stone staircase down to the basement where pillars support barrel vaulting.
The semi-formal **gardens,** bordered by a vineyard and woodland, are graced by stone urns, lily ponds and a stately cedar.
The banded flint and stone **church** was entirely refurbished in the Decorated style in 1849, apart from the early 16C **tower** with trefoil-headed lights; its 3 old bells (*c*1350) are from a former church here. Inside, the two chairs and kneelers *(chancel)* are Victorian, made from decorative panels of the Jacobean 3-decker pulpit. The south transept, which houses the dainty pipe organ (*c*1870), was originally the Castleman family pew (note the stained-glass windows).

Milton Abbas – *9 miles southwest by A354; turn right in Winterbourne Whitechurch. See Milton Abbas.*

Admission times and charges for the sights described are listed at the end of the guide.

Every sight for which there are times and charges is identified by the symbol ⓥ in the middle section of the guide.

BODMIN Cornwall — Pop 11 992

Michelin Atlas p 3 or Map 403 – F32

Bodmin, named as Cornwall's only town in the Domesday Book, described as the "greatest Markett town in the Shere" with a population of 2 000 in Henry VIII's reign, was for centuries the centre of activity in the county. It was too active perhaps: in 1496 its citizens were among the leaders of a protest march on London against an excessive levy on tin – they were massacred; in 1497 they supported the unsuccessful Perkin Warbeck *(qv)*; in 1549, with Helston, Bodmin took part in the vain Cornish uprising against the imposition of the English Prayer Book. In the 19C it replaced Launceston as the seat of the County, now the Crown Court... but in the 1870s it refused access to the Great Western Railway and Bodmin Road Station was built 4½ miles away. It was thus spared commercialisation, but county offices, the library, museum, the cathedral and businesses established themselves in Truro and as a result Bodmin can seem a little barren.
During the Second World War the crown jewels and the Domesday Book were housed in Bodmin Prison for safe keeping.

★ **St Petroc** – In 1469 the parishioners determined to rebuild their Norman church in the new Perpendicular style. It was completed in 1472, was 151ft long by 65ft wide and cost £196 7*s* 4*d* (half a million pounds in today's money). Everyone contributed : the 40 guilds, the vicar who presented a year's salary, the others who gave materials and labour.

Interior – Beneath the slim pillars with their small capitals are the free-standing tomb of Prior Thomas Vivian (d 1533) carved in grey marble and black Catacleuse stone, the 12C **font,** fantastically carved with winged heads (note the eyes : shut before, open after baptism) and deeply undercut foliage, trees of life and weird beasts, and 12C **ivory casket** *(south wall),* richly decorated and once a reliquary containing the bones of St Petroc (d 564), a Welsh prince who became the master-builder of the Celtic Church in the West Country. In the churchyard is the holy well of St Goran, Petroc's forerunner.

Museum ⊙ – Set on the site of an old Franciscan Friary, the museum concentrates on local history, in particular items relating to cattle and corn markets (weights and measures, the Winchester Bushel, vets' instruments) and items from the old Cornwall County constabulary – the town stocks, a cell door from the old gaol...

★★ BODMIN MOOR Cornwall

Michelin Atlas p 3 or Map 403 – F, G32

Bodmin moor, an elevation of 800-1 400ft covering an area of less than 150 sq miles, is the smallest of the three West Country moors; it is gaunt and wild with rock outcrops, heather, high tors – a savage bleakness in winter and a beauty all its own in summer.
Guarding the moor to east and west are two historic castles, Launceston and Restormel and encircling it, either just on the moor or in the deep wooded valleys which surround it, a number of small villages with attractive churches. The rivers Inny, Lynher, Fowey, St Neot and De Lank flow north – south; the only main road, the A30, runs northeast – its staging post for the last 300 years has been the Jamaica Inn.

LANDMARKS, TOWNS, VILLAGES on the Moor

Altarnun – The village, sheltered in a wooded valley high on the moor, derives its name from St Nona, the mother of St David, who came from Wales in *c*527 – the period of the **Celtic cross** in the churchyard.
The present **church**★ of weathered moorstone (outcrop granite) with a 108ft, embattled and pinnacled tower is 15C. Of especial note are the superb Norman **font** with deeply carved rosettes between once-coloured bearded faces at each angle, the monolithic pillars, capitals and bases, the wagon roofs, rood-screen, full width Jacobean **altar-rail** and the **bench-ends,** 79 in all, carved by Robert Daye (bench nearest the font) in 1510-30 with the Instruments of the Passion, St Michael, local worthies, a fiddler, bagpipe player, jester...

★ **Blisland** – Church and village stand high on the moor, round a tree-planted green. The 11C **church**★ has a tower which abuts the north transept and a staircase turret which overtops 15C pinnacles. Note the 18C slate sundial, the faces among the **bosses** on the 1420 south porch wagon roof and the fonts – one Norman, circular with herringbone moulding, one 15C, octagonal with shields in quatrefoils – the brass of 1410 *(chancel)* and **slate memorial** (1624) with six kneeling figures.

Bolventor – At the centre of the moor stands **Jamaica Inn,** named after the West Indian island where a onetime owner had grown rich on his sugar plantations. This staging post for those making the crossing in the 16C-19C was built of granite and roofed and hung with slate, and in the summer its low beamed rooms are usually crowded; out of season it is worth a visit for its **views.** It is, of course, the setting for Daphne du Maurier's novel, *Jamaica Inn.*

Brown Willy – At 1 375ft, Brown Willy is the highest tor on the moor.

★ **Camelford** – The town, beside the River Camel, centres on a small square lined by 18C-19C houses and the old town hall sporting a gilded camel as weathervane. The **North Cornwall Museum of Rural Life** ⊙, in a onetime coach and wagon building, displays the full ranges of tools required by blacksmiths, cobblers, printers, doctors... and domestic exhibits (bonnets, pottery etc).

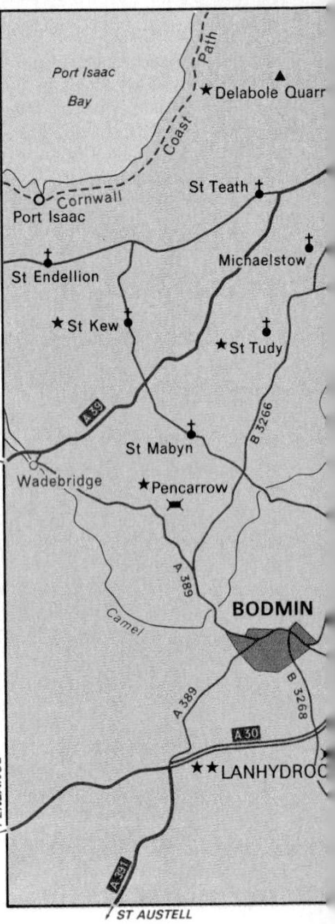

Cardinham – The village, close to the wooded Glynn Valley, has a late 15C **church★** with a three-stage granite tower. Of earlier sanctuaries there remain 9C-10C Celtic Crosses, a Norman font, inscribed stones *(by the sedilia)* and 14C brass *(beneath carpet, south of altar);* the wagon roofs above the aisles and porch and the 71 robustly carved bench-ends date from the 15C. Note also the plaster strapwork **royal arms** of 1661.

The Cheesewring – The stone pile is a natural formation which, according to legend, was the dwelling of a druid who offered water to travellers from a cup of gold.

Dozmary Pool – The pool, 1 000ft above sea-level, is associated with Excalibur *(qv)* and by tradition is bottomless, although it has been known to dry up.

The Hurlers – The Hurlers, the only standing stones on the moor, comprise three circles numbering 9, 17 and 13 stones, in line but of unequal diameter.

Laneast – **St Sidwell's★** is an early 15C rebuilding of a Norman church, with a 14C-15C embattled and pinnacled granite tower; a tall Celtic cross stands nearby. Inside are a robust Norman **font** with three corner heads, slate memorials, a rood-screen, early 16C pulpit and 38 **bench-ends** carved in the 16C.

★ **Launceston** – *See Launceston.*

Liskeard – The town rises on two facing hillsides with late Georgian (The Parade) and early Victorian houses and a portentous, Italianate town hall (1859). The **church★**, high on the hill, was described by Leland as a "fair large thing". Despite repeated restoration there remain a Norman font bowl *(stoup in north porch),* a **chancel arch** (rare in Cornwall), a 16C font, a Jacobean oak pulpit dated 1636, the royal arms of George II, a notice about ladies' pattens, a sundial of 1779 *(south porch),* a number of consecration crosses *(north and south walls)* and a small **leper's window** *(west end)* of three equal lights divided by stone mullions (there was a leper hospital for 200 years at Maudlin, ½ mile away).
Modern glass is made in a mill in the main street (Merlin Glass ⊙).

Michaelstow – The 15C **church★**, with a 9ft Celtic cross in the churchyard, is known for its furnishings : the wagon roofs rest on granite arcades, the benches are 15C-16C, the octagonal font 15C; the beautifully lettered **slate memorial plates** are embellished with running line engravings of winged heads of cherubim, of young girls or even full-length figures in costume – Jane Merifield 1663.

★ **Restormel Castle** ⊙ – *1½ miles north of Lostwithiel.* The 12C-13C shell keep of local slate shale rock stands on a spur above the River Fowey. Walk through the gate-house and circle the walls to overlook the inner courtyard, the kitchen with its great fireplace, the hall and chapel, and to admire the circular **panorama★**.

Rough Tor – The granite boss (pronounced Rowtor to rhyme with now tor) stands out at 1 311ft as the second highest point on the moor.

St Breward – Pop 1 422. On the edge of the moor and at 600ft the highest **church★** in Cornwall, St Breward stands on a site hallowed since Norman times – 5 fat round columns of uneven height with scalloped capitals remain as testimony inside the present 15C rebuilding.
Note the copy of a watercolour by Rowlandson (*c*1800), the royal arms, the figured 17C **slate memorial plates** and, outside, the neat granite blocks of the **tower**. The sundial dates from 1792.
Nearby is the stone-built, wind-buffeted Old Inn, all beams and fireplaces inside.

St Endellion – The village's Perpendicular **church★★** is well known as the setting for the major work of the sculptor, the **Master of St Endellion.** Anonymous in all other respects, he lives on through a tomb chest superbly carved in sleek, black Catacleuse stone with small columns and cusped arches. By the door is a stoup also by the Master.

★ **St Kew** – The **church★** stands tall with a buttressed and battlemented west tower where the road turns between wooded hillsides.
The only neighbours are the late Georgian vicarage, the St Kew Inn, which is Elizabethan, and the Craftsmen's Barn (studios, workshops).
St Kew church is light inside with slender-columned granite arcades beneath wagon roofs and wall plate angels. There are an Elizabethan **pulpit,** royal arms of 1661, **slate monuments** from 1601 – "All is vanity but vertue" – and 15C **stained glass** in clear colours depicting the Passion from the *Entry into Jerusalem* to the *Harrowing of Hell.*

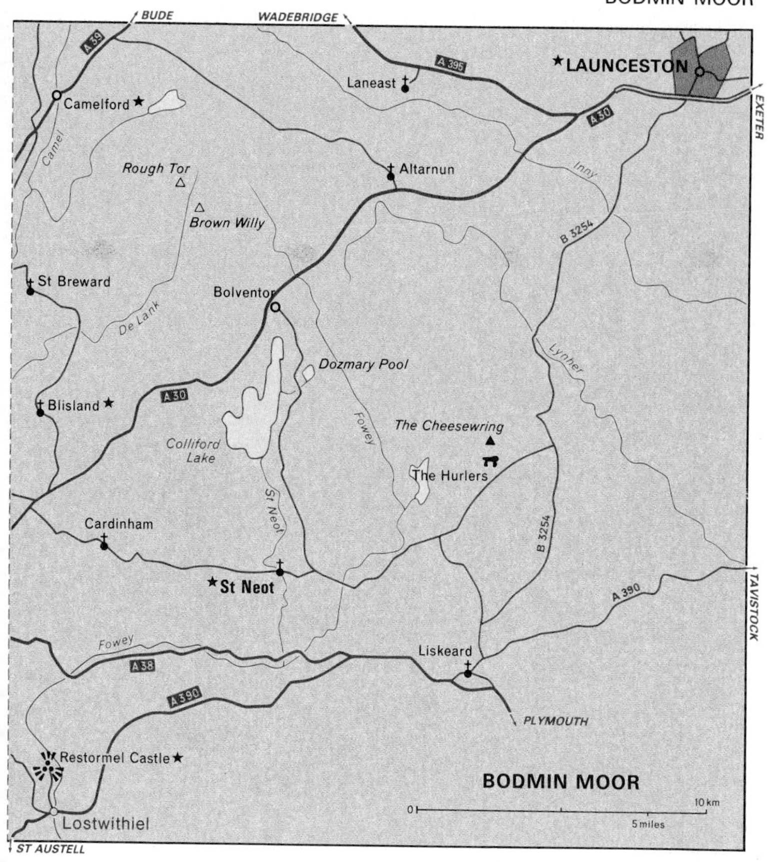

St Mabyn – The **church★** is chiefly notable for its 15C **three stage tower,** abutted partway by a stair turret and unusually decorated with carved figures.

★ **St Neot** – *See St Neot.*

St Teath – The 15C **church★** is a rebuilding around a Norman foundation. Wagon roofs and font are complemented by a Jacobean **pulpit,** figure painted **almsbox** and a **slate memorial** of 1636 with carved figures *(west end, near porch door).*

★ **St Tudy** – The **church** in this attractive village was built on Saxon-Norman foundations in the 15C; it has a tall, pinnacled tower. Perpendicular windows, granite **arcades** and **wagon roofs** with foliated wall plates provide the setting for the square Norman font, an earlier carved head *(facing south door)* and a 5C-6C Celtic gravestone *(in porch).*

BOURNEMOUTH Dorset — Pop 142 829

Michelin Atlas p 9 or Map 403 – O31 – Facilities
Town plan in the current Michelin Red Guide Great Britain and Ireland

Bournemouth lies at the mouth of the River Bourne between two pine-covered hills. It began to develop as a summer and winter resort in the mid-19C, when the arrival of the railway made it easily accessible. Its popularity increased with the laying out of the **public gardens** and the construction of **two piers,** the pavilion, wintergarden and theatre. By the 1890s Bournemouth had become fashionable – Queen Victoria recommended it to Disraeli – and the population had reached 37 781. Since then the population has multiplied fivefold and the hotels now number several hundred.

★ MUSEUMS

Russell-Cotes Art Gallery and Museum ⏱ – *Russell-Cotes Rd.*
East Cliff Hall was the museum-home of Sir Merton Russell-Cotes, hotelier, theatre-goer, JP, mayor and intrepid traveller. Each room, with its massive Victorian furniture, palms, painted ceiling, wallpapers of the period, is filled with pictures (**William Frith's** *Ramsgate Sands, Venus* by **Rossetti**), English fine china (part of a Rockingham tea-service once owned by the Prince Regent, Coalport and Worcester, Wedgwood plaques, Parian ware), silver and gold ware, mementoes of Napoleon (a death-mask) and of Sir Henry Irving, a personal friend. From abroad there are Dresden miniatures, finds from Egyptian tombs, swords, oriental armour, Japanese Noh theatre masks, bronzes, Buddhas, a bronze incense-burner in the style of a cock, a silver and gold elephant with a crystal ball, inlay and lacquerwork, ceramics and lanterns...

The collections formerly housed in the **Rothesay Museum** are now on display here : majolica and delftware, 19C Whitby mourning jet, toby jugs and Staffordshire figures, 17C English furniture, a 16C polygonal virginal, Victorian bygones, African spears, Ghurka kukris, Limoges enamels, hand guns from the 16C-20C, early Italian religious paintings (Sienese school) and a Maori Collection including paintings by C F Goldie (1870-1947), hardstone clubs, carving and a model war canoe.

Shelley Rooms ⊙ – *Shelley Park, Beechwood Av, Boscombe.*
The evocative collection, in part from Casa Magni, home of Percy Bysshe Shelley (1792-1822) at the time he drowned, includes letters, the revolutionary leaflets, poems, notebooks, portraits and miniatures.

EXCURSIONS

★★ **Kingston Lacy** – *5 miles northwest. See Kingston Lacy.*

★ **Wimborne Minster** – *4 miles northwest. See Wimborne Minster.*

★ **Poole** – *2 miles west. See Poole.*

★ **Hengistbury Head** – *7 miles east by the panoramic road. See Hengistbury Head.*

BOVEY TRACEY Devon

Pop 3 434

Michelin Atlas p 4 or Map 403 – I, J32 – Local map p 91

The small town is a gateway to Dartmoor *(qv)*. Many of the cottages are built of moor granite but in typical Devon fashion are mellowed by thatched roofs.

★ **St Peter, St Paul and St Thomas of Canterbury** – The church was founded, it is said, in repentance for his part in St Thomas Becket's murder in 1170 by Sir William de Tracey *(qv)* whose family had long been owners of the village.
The slender tower is 14C, the church, comprising Beer stone arcades with well-carved capitals, is 15C and considerably restored. Of especial interest are the **Jacobean tombs,** the 15C brass **eagle lectern** with three small lions at the base, the pre-Reformation stone **pulpit,** carved with ten still-perfect figures all coloured and gilt, and a remarkably carved 15C **rood-screen** of 11 bays with figures of the saints in the lower panels.

Devon Guild of Craftsmen ⊙ – *Riverside Mill. Across the river from the lower car park.*
A constantly changing series of exhibitions throughout the year celebrates the work of the Guild's craftsmen : batik printers, potters and ceramicists, embroiderers, enamellers, furniture makers, carvers, glassworkers, weavers, lacemakers, metalworkers, silversmiths and jewellers.

Parke ⊙ – *½ mile west on north side of B3344.*
At the heart of a 200-acre woodland estate on the edge of Dartmoor, a rare breeds farm has been established in traditional stone buildings. Among the breeds on view are Long Horned cattle, sheep, ponies, old fashioned pigs and brightly coloured poultry.

House of Marbles and Teign Valley Glass ⊙ – *Pottery Road, ¼ mile west off B382.*
The buildings, an old pottery with listed muffle kilns, now house a glassworks where glassblowing may be viewed, and a small museum section on both the history of the pottery and on glassmaking : tools, powders and pigments used for colouring, chunks of cullet used for marble making, Roman bottles, Georgian glasses...

★ BOWOOD HOUSE Wiltshire

Michelin Atlas p 17 or Map 403 – N29

The house was still under construction in 1757 when **Lancelot Brown** was summoned to Bowood and, for a fee of 30 guineas, gave his opinion of the "capability" of the park; during the period 1762-68 he returned to execute his plans which centred on the creation of the idiosyncratic lake and woodland and the planting of specimen trees including the cedar of Lebanon (now 140ft tall). As the park matured, the house evolved under a succession of famous architects; it was begun in 1725 and sold, still incomplete, in 1754 to the first Earl of Shelburne, father of the future Marquess of Lansdowne.
The Marquesses of Lansdowne were political men holding high office in government at home and appointed as governors, viceroys and diplomats abroad; the marquisate was created in 1784 for negotiating peace with America at the end of the War of Independence. Although Bowood was their principal residence in England, they were often away, sometimes at Lansdowne House in London.
In 1955 the "big house" at Bowood was demolished; the Orangery and its attendant pavilions were retained as a residence and sculpture gallery.

GROUNDS ⊙

Three paths radiate from Temple Gate *(50yds from the car park)* : ahead to the front of the house; left, through glades of trees, across lawns characterized by specimen beeches, cedars, elms, to the timber-built adventure play area; and right, to the far end of the lake (cascade, 18C Doric temple), circling through woods and coppices in a 2 mile arc.

Terraces – The 100yd long terraces, enclosed by low balustrades and punctuated by clipped yews, are bedecked throughout the summer with red and white roses.

Woodland Garden – *Entrance off A432, nearer Sandy Lane.*
In May and June visit the garden to stroll through the acres of bluebells, rhododendrons and azaleas.

HOUSE ⊙ *45min*

Entrance to the house is now through the Orangery, classically designed by **Robert Adam** in 1769 with an important pedimented and giant-columned centre doorway. Inside, the briefest Ionic colonnade leads across the gallery to the chapel.

Laboratory – *Right.* The small room is where **Joseph Priestley** discovered oxygen in 1774 and Jan Ingenhouse (d 1799) the process of plant photosynthesis.

Library – The end room was designed by C R Cockerell after Robert Adam; the warm decor includes a gilded, coved and coffered ceiling and portrait medallions of Greek writers; it is furnished with Etruscan vases by Josiah Wedgwood, a white marble fireplace (1755) from the old house, handsome bookcases and shield-back chairs. From the windows there is a **view★** of the park.

Sculpture Gallery – The gallery, which extends the length of the Orangery, is the setting for chosen pictures, statuary and tapestries from Lansdowne collections past and still in the making – the head of Hermes, the Florentine sleeping cupid, the Diskobolos, portraits by Reynolds, a Gainsborough landscape, gilded, marble-topped console tables, porcelain, a gilded French clock with a blue face framed by a mirror and torchères.

Exhibition Galleries – *Far left end of Sculpture Gallery.*
Surprises in the upper galleries range from the **Albanian costume** in which **Byron** was painted in 1814 (given by the poet to the mother of the 4th marchioness as fancy dress), 18C-19C furniture and small possessions, an immensely rich and colourful assembly of objects collected by 5th Lord Lansdowne when Viceroy of India (1888-94) and a glittering display of family honours, orders, swords, insignia, fabulous jewels...

BRADFORD-ON-AVON Wiltshire — Pop 8 921

Michelin Atlas p 17 or Map 403 – N29

It is the houses rising tier upon tier up the hillside from the river and the old medieval bridge with its weather-vaned chapel which give the town its character. The larger houses were built in the local creamy-yellow ochre limestone by 17C-18C clothiers, by **Paul Methwin** (d 1667) and his contemporaries, some of whom, Daniel Defoe estimated early in the 18C, were worth between ten and forty thousand pounds a man. In the same streets are terraces of weavers' cottages and, in the shopping streets, alleys and shambles, 17C-18C houses above 18C-19C shopfronts.

SIGHTS

Saxon Church of St Lawrence ⊙ – The church may date from the 7C-8C, the time of St Aldhelm *(qv)*, who is known to have founded a convent on the site between AD 672 and 705. In 1001 church and convent were given to the abbey at Shaftesbury *(qv)* but by Domesday the convent had disappeared. From the 12C-19C the church was used as a cottage, a school, a charnel house. The minute stone building, tall and narrow with steeply pitched roofs and a blind **arcading decoration** on the walls, is believed to have been erected in a single phase. It has not been enlarged or altered since, apart from three windows pierced at the west end in the 19C. The chancel is slightly "skewed", a feature made more obvious because the arch at the end of the 25ft x 13ft nave is only 9ft 8in x 3ft 6in. The "floating" angels and assembled altar-stones are Saxon.

Bridge – The town developed around the regular passage across the river at the broad ford.

Bradford-on-Avon Bridge.

The first pack-bridge was built in the 12C. In 1610 when the wool and clc trades were booming a wider bridge was erected with round arches a incorporating a small, square, domed **chapel** ⊙ topped by an Avon gudge **weather-vane.**

Tithe Barn ⊙ – *South bank.* The vast stone barn, which was probably built ea in the 14C by a tenant of Shaftesbury Abbey, has twin gabled doorways a oak doors to which the long iron hinges are most likely attached by the origir **nails.** The robust **timber roof** now shelters the Croker Collection of obsolete 1 farm implements and machinery from the dairy, farmyard, fields, game reserv and sheep walks. The neighbouring granary is later.

Holy Trinity – The church was consecrated in 1150 having been built possi because St Lawrence was too small, more probably because the 12C was great period for church building and Bradford was prosperous : Domesday recor show that there were 126 burgesses – with their families, labourers and servan this would mean a township of, possibly, 1 000 inhabitants. In the early 1 the chancel was extended; in the 15C and 19C the entire church was remodel and embellished. There are, therefore, Norman features (chancel windows, arca piers), a medieval **wall painting** of the Virgin being taught to write *(north of e window),* possibly the longest **squint** in England, cut in the 13C when the chan was lengthened, Flemish glass *(south window in the nave)* presented by an 1 clothier, memorials and brasses to clothiers and, at the west end, a 13C **sculpt** of a young girl in a wimple.

WALK to the TOP OF THE TOWN

Start from the Bridge.

Silver Street – The road crosses the Bridge to become the main shopp street.

Market Street – *Wide, centre left fork.* The street, which is lined with 17C-1 houses with later shopfronts, goes straight up the hill.

Church Street – *Sharp left.* The road, which leads circuitously uphill, ope with two Georgian frontages with Venetian windows : the one is Church Hou the other is a fashionable refacing in black and white of a 16C inn. The 1 converted mill is one of 32 once at work in the town. Old Church House (n a hall) was built in the 17C by the clothier Thomas Horton (brass in the churc Dutch Barton has an 18C front on a 17C foundation. Hill House was the ho of the Druces, early 18C Quaker clothiers. Abbey House with its profusion pediments is 18C, so too is **Orpin House** *(north of the church);* midway betwe the church and the house lies the tomb of Mr Orpin who was parish clerk 40 years. The two Chantry Houses are 16C; Barton Orchard and the terrace **weavers' houses** are 18C.

Newtown – The so-called Newtown is 17C-18C.

Middle Rank – The street is marked by a chapel and gabled terrace hous

Top Rank Tory – The road runs along the crest, past 18C houses and terra and a very special row of 17C **weavers' houses,** to the town's highest point a the **hermit chapel** of St Mary Tory (12C rebuilt in 1877).
At the foot of the hill is the tithe barn and the town dissected by the River Av the Kennet and Avon Canal and the railway. The **view**★ embraces the Marlboro Downs (northeast), Bath, Bristol and the Severn Estuary (northwest) and Somer (southwest).

It is possible to reach St Mary Tory by car by taking the road at the ri (east) end of Newtown, Conigre Hill, and bearing second left into Tory.

★ BRAUNTON Devon — Pop 9 00

Michelin Atlas p 6 or Map 403 – H30

The older, prettier part of Braunton lies at its northeast end, by the church wh overlooks thatched cottages and houses with elegant balconies. The Ri Caen gently splashes beside the churchyard and through the small town to marshes and estuary at Velator. In the 1850s a channel and quay were b at Velator; prior to this only smaller vessels could sail up the estuary but new cut allowed ketches of up to 100 tons and as a result up to 100 vess at a time were using the area up until the First World War. Trade consiste imports of coal, bricks, salt, flour, grain, fertilizers and limestone, and exp of potatoes, apples and cider. The importance of the quay declined with advent of the railway.

★ **St Brannock's Church** – The largely 13C building with its solid Norman **to** surmounted by a 15C lead covered **spire,** was originally cruciform in shape. Ins the **bosses** on the wagon roof (restored 1850) include a litter of piglets, an an a pelican... The **font** is 13C or earlier, with later carvings; the faces at the corr are probably the Evangelists. Note the 16C carved chestnut **bench ends** and the p themselves, great uneven timbers worn smooth and glossy over the centur The Lady Chapel *(right of chancel),* a later addition, contains a late Portuguese **chest** which was probably made for the wedding of the couple its front. Note, on the south wall, the copies of a **palimpsest** (two-sided bras the knight's head side is said to be the oldest brass in Devon. The origina fixed to a tombstone.

The small **chapel** with tiny windows under the tower is the oldest part of the church; the slab of pale carved stone above a window dates from before the Norman Conquest and was probably a tombstone.

Great Field ⊙ – The Great Field, southwest of the town, is one of the very few examples remaining in Britain of **open field cultivation** – the unenclosed strips have their origins in medieval communal farming.
The land was reclaimed from salt marshes, many of which still exist beyond the field, and benefits from a rich, fertile soil. Saxon settlers originally cleared and ploughed the land and divided it into sections. At that time, every village in England was surrounded by three large fields, two of them cultivated while the third lay fallow, being grazed and manured by cattle. The sections were then subdivided into strips based on the amount of land which a man with two oxen could plough in a day.
Each landowner had several strips which were scattered over the field so that fertile and infertile land was allocated fairly. The villagers shared implements and common land was set aside for grazing (here it was mainly on the tidal salt marshes). The division between the land of different owners was formed by one furrow being left unploughed so that it showed as a line of grass and weeds (many strips have now been amalgamated and ploughed as one); these strip divisions are known locally as landsherds. Bondstones – usually large smooth stones from the beach – at the end of the landsherds serve as boundary markers; today few remain.

EXCURSION

Braunton Burrows ⊙ – *2 miles southwest by B3231 and a by-road, signposted.*
The burrows comprise one of the largest **sand dune systems** in Britain, covering an area of *c*2 400 acres (over 3½ miles north to south and about 1½ miles wide); 2/3rds of the area is now a **National Nature Reserve** (some of it leased to the MoD – red flags and sentries during training exercises) supporting a wide variety of plant and animal life.
The dunes are made of windblown sand largely formed by crushed shells. They form because marram – a grass which grows more quickly when stimulated by moving sand – traps the sand until it stabilises; the grass then grows less vigorously, allowing other plants to colonise the area. The dunes are never entirely stable, however, and the sands are constantly shifting. As the wind cannot dislodge wet sand from below the water level, ponds have been dug; these add to the wildlife as many of the low-lying areas which flood in the winter dry out in the summer.
Animal life ranges from lizards, frogs and newts, shrews, hedgehogs, weasels and foxes, to beetles, butterflies and moths. The occasional buzzard may be seen as well as kestrels, magpies and the many waders *(qv)* which congregate on the adjacent estuary, and the migratory birds which stop at the reserve to rest and feed.
Prickly saltwort, sea-holly, biting stonecrop, rest-harrow, wild thyme, marsh orchids and the rarer sand toadflax are among the 400 different species of flowering plants which have been recorded here.
On the coastal side the burrows are bordered by the 3 miles of fine beach known as **Saunton Sands.**

BRIDGWATER Somerset — Pop 30 782

Michelin Atlas p 7 or Map 403 – L30 – Facilities

During the Civil War Bridgwater Castle, which was commanded by a Royalist governor with a garrison of 2 000 men, was besieged, captured and slighted and the surrounding area was set on fire. Otherwise the town has grown steadily from a settlement by the first crossing point on the River Parrett to be Somerset's second most important town.
In earlier centuries Bridgwater was surrounded on all sides by marshes, known locally as "levels", which were drained by open ditches known as "rhines" and traversed by tracks surfaced with logs and brushwood. By 1200 the town had a charter, by 1350 a population of 850, a castle, a church rebuilt on older foundations and a flourishing river port trade in saltfish, wine, iron, barley, wheat, peas and wood for dyeing cloth. In the 18C-19C the Bridgwater-Taunton Canal with its dock and quays was constructed but soon superseded by the railway.

Battle of Sedgemoor – James, Duke of **Monmouth,** the natural, illegitimate son of Charles II born in the Netherlands in 1649, returned four months after the death of his father in 1685, landing at Lyme Regis on 11 June with 82 followers. He proceeded to Taunton where he was proclaimed king and advanced, gathering 5-6 000 followers, to Bristol, only to find the royal forces encamped before the city; he turned, fought a rearguard action at Norton-St-Philip *(qv),* where he stayed at the George, and, with his army reduced to 3 500, confronted the king's force less than three miles from Bridgwater in a night attack on Sedgemoor (6 July 1685).
The aftermath was more cruel than the two-hour battle in which 300 of Monmouth's men and 25 king's men died : summary execution was carried out on the rebels on the field and in the surrounding villages, and within a week James II had despatched **Judge Jeffreys** (1648-89) on the notorious **Bloody Assizes** *(qv).* Monmouth himself was captured two days after the battle and executed on Tower Hill on 15 July 1685.

SIGHTS

West Quay – The quay is overlooked by warehouses, a pub and 18C-19C hous

★ **Castle Street** – *Off West Quay.* The town's most attractive street is lined 18C houses built of brick with stone trims, segment-headed windows, pillar and pilastered doorways and parapets rising to the street's incline.

King Square – The Square, still incomplete, consists of two ranges of 1 houses and a much-altered farmhouse, built on the site of the slighted 13C cas

★ **St Mary's** – The day before the battle the **Duke of Monmouth** climbed the r sandstone tower (60ft) with his spyglass (in the museum) to survey t disposition of the Royalist troops camped on Sedgemoor. The embattled to belonged to an Early English church (*c*1200). The distinctive octagonal sp (113ft) of Ham Hill stone was added in 1367 with monies subscribed by t grateful people who had survived the Black Death; it took a year to build a cost £143 13*s* 5½*d*. The weathercock on the summit (2ft 3in) served for centur as a landmark to shipping on the Parrett.

Interior – A late 17C Bolognese painting of the *Descent from the Cross* provide striking altarpiece. Also of interest are the octagonal, rose decorated **font** of 14 the Queen Anne royal arms of 1712 *(west wall)*, the 15C **oak pulpit**, the former ro screen of 1420 now behind the choirstalls, the Jacobean **altar-table**, the mar monument in the chancel of Sir Francis Kingsmill (d 1620) leaning on one elbo

★ **Admiral Blake Museum** ⏲ – *Blake St.* The **Commonwealth Jack**, flown by Admi Blake and adopted by the Commonwealth, often flies above the museum, the hou where he was born in 1599. On entering parliament in 1640 **Robert Blake** joined Commonwealth cause and played an active part in the Civil War. As General-at-S he embarked on a campaign against the Dutch admirals Tromp, De Ruyter and Witt, and fought with pirates off North Africa. In 1657 he sailed his fleet of 12 sh into Santa Cruz harbour in Tenerife, sank 16 Spanish galleons and sacked the p he died entering Plymouth Sound on 7 August. An audio-visual display of the Ba of Santa Cruz and some of Blake's effects are displayed in the museum. The Shipp Room displays models of 19C and early 20C sailing rigs.
Other rooms are devoted to local history, families, drawings and water colo The **Monmouth Room** illustrates the **Battle of Sedgemoor** : weapons, armour a cannon balls, the spyglass and an offer by James II of £5 000 to anyone "W shall bring in the person of the James, Duke of Monmouth, alive or dead"

EXCURSIONS

★★ **Stogursey Priory Church** – *14 miles northwest by A39 and by-roads.*

Coleridge Cottage, Nether Stowey ⏲ – Pop 1 133. Coleridge lived from 1797-18 with his wife, Robert Southey's sister, and small son in a cottage at the end the village. It was then a pretty thatched cottage with "a clear brook" running bef the door. The former kitchen is now furnished as the parlour contain mementoes, photographs and early editions of the poems and prose works. W at Stowey, Coleridge wrote *The Rime of the Ancient Mariner* and *Kubla Khan (*

Take a by-road north for 3 miles from the far end of Nether Stowey.

★★ **Stogursey Priory Church** – *See Stogursey Priory Church.*

Barford Park – *5 miles west by by-roads.*

Durleigh Reservoir – The 80-acre lake is the haunt of waterfowl and migratory bi

Barford Park ⏲ – The Queen Anne house, low-lying by comparison with the tr all round, is extended by wings on either side curving out from the centre. interior contains earlier kitchens, a modern garden room, and panelled a corniced 18C rooms : hall, dining and big music room, highlighted contemporary furniture, porcelain and silver.
In the garden the informality of a woodland walk contrasts with a semicirc walled garden enlivened by peacocks.

Athelney Marshes – *10 miles southeast by A372 and southwest on A3*

Westonzoyland – Pop 1 548. St Mary's, the Perpendicular parish **church**★★, v the prison after Sedgemoor *(see above)* for 500 of Monmouth's men, "of whi according to the parish register, "there was 79 wounded and five of them d of their wounds in our church". The splendid 15C **tower** rises by four stages 100ft through a west doorway and window, two traceried bays and a triple-li bell stage, to a crest of pierced battlements, pinnacles and sub-pinnacles. Inside, the dark oak **roof**, a construction of braces and king-posts on cres beams, dressed overall with panelled tracery, mouchette bosses, pendant p on bone thin beams, is adorned with **angels** and **half-angels**...

Bear right at Othery into A361.

Burrow Mump – The hillock (250ft) is a major landmark in the flat marshland. A castle stood on the mump in the 12C and before that possibly an Alfredian f Today what remains is a church tower, medieval in origin but altered in the early 1

Athelney Marshes – **King Alfred's** first encounter with the Danes consisted c successful skirmish in December 870, a defeat in 871, a victory at Ashdo in Sussex and then further defeats. In 876 and 877 Wareham and Exeter w attacked by the Danes but liberated by Alfred. In 878 he was surprised at palace in Chippenham and retreated to the marshes near Athelney, where is supposed to have burned a cottager's cakes while planning his next m In May 878 he emerged from hiding, defeated the Danes at Edington *(qv)* signed the Peace of Wedmore which required the Danes to retreat east of Watling Street and obliged Guthrum and 29 of his chief men to accept bapt

In 884 the Danes invaded again and those who had settled in East Anglia rose in revolt; Alfred moved east. In 885 he recaptured London and signed a second treaty with Guthrum. The Danes returned in 890 and 894; Exeter was again invested and again freed by Alfred. It was his last major battle; he died in 901 at the age of 53 and is buried at Winchester.

West of Athelney turn left to Stoke St Gregory and right to North Curry.

Willow and Wetlands ⊙ – The willow industry, the wetlands, their flora and fauna are described in the Visitors' Centre which displays a withy boat and old and new examples of willow craft – baskets and artists' charcoal.
The tour shows how the willow rods are harvested, bundled and bound, sorted into sizes, boiled, stripped and dried to produce buff or white or brown willow, which is used by the basket-makers in the workshop.

Broomfield – *10 miles south and west by A38 and by-roads.*

North Petherton – Pop 3 177. The silver-grey stone **tower★★** of the church is outstanding even for Somerset. It rises to 109ft in three stages : a west door surmounted by a frieze and a large window with tracery at the transom as well as the apex; a three-light, decorated window; paired bell openings and a panelled wall area. Finally, there is an embattled parapet from which pinnacles and sub-pinnacles fountain skywards.

Fyne Court – The manor house was the residence of Andrew Crosse (1784-1855), a scientific investigator into the electricity of the atmosphere, who was known locally as the "Thunder and Lightning Man". The house, largely destroyed in a fire in 1898, is now the office of the Somerset Trust for Nature Conservation.

Broomfield – Pop 202. The **Church of All Saints,** which has a grin of gargoyles and a modest three-stage tower, was built *c*1440 before the great tower rivalry began. Inside are yellow Ham stone columns and the original **wagon roofs,** supported by 47 angels. Note the 16C bench-ends, Queen Anne's royal arms, and, in the porch, a list of charities which includes the provision of free tools to honest workmen who had not pawned previous gifts. The kitchen-type table *(by south door)* with a copper band across it was Andrew Crosse's workbench; his obelisk memorial stands in the churchyard.

BRIDPORT Dorset — Pop 10 615

Michelin Atlas p 8 or Map 403 – L31

Bridport is a name recalled because, as was said as early as 1505, it has been making ships' ropes and cordage "for time out of mind". In the 15C Henry VII decreed that all hemp grown within a five-mile radius of the then river port should be reserved for the king's ships. Changes in rigging, the development of a fish and submarine netting industry, the substitution of nylon for hemp have brought reorganisation; nevertheless the trade remains the town's mainstay.

TOWN

Bridport is T-shaped, the early, walled Saxon river port (where South Street now runs) expanding north and then east-west in Georgian times along the Dorchester-Exeter road.

South Street – The town's original street is lined by the oldest houses, seamen's cottages and inns and the Perpendicular St Mary's church with its many 19C additions.

Museum ⊙ – The museum is in a 16C stone-fronted house with a prominent porch, known as the Castle.
Exhibits include items on local history, old agricultural tools and stuffed animals. The first floor gallery has changing displays of fine art, decorative arts, costume...

West Street – The Georgian street and its continuation, East Street, are overlooked by imposing houses built for merchants and professional men and former coaching inns.
Note **Granville House,** built in the mid-18C *(north side)* opposite a Venetian windowed house, and, at the bottom end of the street, the late 18C stone **Rope and Net Factory.**

East Street – The **chemist's,** no 9, with bow-fronted shop windows and a centre door, smaller, domestic bow windows above and a proud fascia, is late 18C; the **Unitarian Chapel,** with Ionic columns supporting a semicircular porch, is also 18C; the classically columned Literary and Scientific Institute, now the **Library,** is 19C.

EXCURSIONS

Parnham House – *6 miles north on A3066. See Parnham House.*

Beaminster – Pop 2 338. *1 mile north of Parnham House.*
An undulating countryside of woods and trees surrounds Beaminster (pronounced Bemminster) which, at its centre, presents a triangular square with an old-style, pyramid roofed **market cross** (1906) and a number of thriving old family **shops.** All were rebuilt after fires in 1644, 1684 and 1781 had reduced the town to the "pityfullest spectacle".
The **church,** to the southwest, is distinguished by its very tall, castellated **west tower,** built in 1503 in a local ochre stone with a rare number of canopied niches, statuettes and carvings and a spectacular thrust of crocketed pinnacles. Inside, the **arcades** have narrower bays to the east and foliated capitals to the west; the Purbeck marble **font** is 12C-13C, the **pulpit** Jacobean. Note the monuments to members of the Strode family, owners of Parnham House *(qv).*

★★ BRISTOL Avon Pop 374 30(

Michelin Atlas p 16 or Map 403 – M29 – Facilities
Map of conurbation in the current Michelin Red Guide Great Britain and Irela

Bristol is a lively trading city which originated in the 10C as a settlement the bridge across the Avon, at the western limit of the Saxon invasion. By t Middle Ages, as a flourishing port, it had grown to become England's seco city after London. Prosperity increased until the Industrial Revolution dr interests north; recent and ongoing development, the influx of high technolo industries and British Aerospace, and the city's excellent communication lir have resulted in Bristol being once more in ascendance.
This affluence is reflected in the city's architectural heritage : from the Norm through the Gothic – particularly the Perpendicular – to the Jacobean a Palladian periods. For the most part it was spared 19C restoration to its medie churches, while profiting from the engineering architecture of Brunel. In the 2(following heavy bombing in 1940-42, Bristol was replanned and rebuilt.

Bristol from Redcliffe Bridge.

"Shipshape and Bristol fashion" – Bristol's port has undergone three ma transformations in its progress from riparian sailship harbour to tanker a container terminal : in 1240-48, the **Frome Trench** was dug to redirect the cou of the River Frome, improve landing facilities and the water depth; in 1804 the River Avon was diverted into the New Cut, and the **Floating Harbour,** 2½ m in extent, was created to provide a constant water level and an immense quays in the heart of the city; in 1877-79 the **Avonmouth** and **Portishead Docks,** and 1977, the **Royal Portbury Docks,** were opened on the Severn Estuary.
The Floating Harbour has become a pleasure boat harbour with floa restaurants, and quaysides and warehouses converted into an exhibition s clubs and museums. A ship in the Floating Harbour was liable to touch bott at low tide : cargo had to be well stowed or "shipshape and Bristol fashio

Trade and Venturing – Bristol trade in the 10C was concerned with Irela by the 17C it had expanded to the Canaries, the Spanish American colon North America, Africa, the West Indies. In the 18C-19C new industries develo locally : iron, brass, copper, tin, porcelain and glass, chocolate, tobacco.
The merchants, several of whom were Quakers, were incorporated in 1522 the **Society of Merchant Venturers.** They built and endowed churches – **Wil Canynges** even paid for the entire rebuilding of the most magnificent of th St Mary Redcliffe *(see below).* They bought land freed by the Dissolution a erected great houses; they enabled the corporation to buy the Mayoral Cha and presented the city with schools and hospitals. By the 18C many w abandoning their houses in the city centre and moving out to Queen Squ Brandon Hill and Clifton *(qv)* where they built great houses, some now Univer halls of residence.

★ CATHEDRAL DISTRICT *2 hours*

★ **Bristol Cathedral** (AZ) ⊙ – The cathedral is a 14C-15C Perpendicular Go church with a crenellated and pinnacled central tower, twin west towers a tall pointed windows, framed by finialled buttresses and pinnacled parap Although the foundation is ancient the church was completed only in the 1 when the nave and west towers were built. It was an Augustinian abbey a already 400 years old when dissolved by Henry VIII in 1539; three years la it was reconstituted as the Cathedral Church.

Interior – *Walk directly up the nave.* From the crossing look through the scr and carved and canopied choirstalls (lively **15C misericords**) at the high altar be the 19C reconstructed reredos, then up and obliquely to either side to apprec the fascination of the **roof.**

The sight is unique in English cathedrals, a feat of early 14C construction : the east end is a **hall church** with chancel and chancel aisles rising to an equal 50ft. Over the choir, the ribbed vaulting sweeps up directly from the pillars to meet a central row of irregular diamond shapes lined with cusps; above the aisles it has been optically lowered for the sake of proportion, by taking the arching to a cross-beam which also serves to spring the roof ribs. Vaults and spandrels are pierced to add a rare perspective.

Lady Chapels – There are two chapels : the **Elder Lady Chapel** *(off north transept)* dating from c1215 with vaulting of 1270 is notable for its sobriety, its foliated capitals on slender Purbeck columns and small carved figures – St Michael and the dragon, a fox and goose, a lizard, and the monkeys which suggest the mason might also have been responsible for carvings at Wells Cathedral; the **East Lady Chapel,** a 100ft extension added when the Norman chancel was rebuilt in 1298-1330, is memorable for its riot of medieval colour highlighting stone carved into cusped arches, gabled niches, friezes, fleurons, heads, crests... This chapel contains one of the cathedral's special features : the 14C **stellate tomb recess,** an interplay of curving lines and gilded ornament, surrounding a 15C gabled tomb chest.

Sacristy – *Off south chancel aisle.* The small, dark chamber has bossaged flying ribs with foliated corbels and three niches, one of them formerly a bread oven.

Berkeley Chapel – *Down the steps.* The chapel contains a Flemish brass **chandelier** (similar to that in St Michael's Mount church, *qv*) of 1450, transferred from the Temple Church *(see below)* : at the heart stand St George and the Virgin and Child, above a host of golden squares.

Newton Chapel – Note the fine **marble memorial** to Elizabeth Stanhope by Richard Westmacott, together with the 15C, 16C and 17C Newton family tombs.

Harrowing of Hell – *South transept.* The remarkable carving is a 1 000 year-old Saxon stone coffin-lid.

A door on the far side of the transept leads to the cloister and chapter-house.

Chapter-House – A lovely Norman columned vestibule leads to the chapter-house (1150-70), considered one of the finest in the country, where the golden brown stone walls are patterned with interlacing and the roof is intersected by great, zig-zag ornamented ribs.

Norman Arch (AZ) – The abbey precincts, rebuilt in the late 15C, retain the original, robust Norman gateway arch, framed by a collar of zig-zag decoration.

Council House (AZ C) – The curved, modern building, the city administration office, is distinguished by high-stepping golden unicorns, supporters of the city arms.

Lord Mayor's Chapel (AZ)⊙ – The chapel, part of the medieval Hospital of the Gaunts, was purchased at the Dissolution for £1 000 by the City Corporation. A bird's-eye view from inside the door reveals a narrow 13C nave (orientation north-south) and, to the right, a Perpendicular chapel with **15C-17C tombs,** a large window of English and early Renaissance **glass** and the 16C flat, black wooden roof highlighted in gold. Note the mayors' hatchments, a fine gilded swordrest, wrought, like the **iron gates** *(south aisle chapel),* by William Edney in 1702 and formerly in the Temple Church.

Hatchet Inn (AY) – The old gabled farmhouse was first licensed in 1606.

Harveys Wine Museum (AY)⊙ – The museum is in medieval cellars owned since the late 18C by Harveys of Bristol. Highlights of the visit are the collection of 500 silver decanter labels or **bottle tickets,** old **corkscrews,** 17C wine bottles, **18C glasses** and decanters and a pair of silver-gilt **coaster wagons.**

CABOT TOWER AREA (AY) *½ day*

Georgian House⊙ – No 7 Great George Street was built for John Pinney, a sugar planter, on his return from St Kitts to Bristol where as a merchant he made a second, even larger fortune. The house is one now of the best-preserved museums of its kind.

The Bristol architects **Thomas** and **William Paty** produced for him a typical late 18C design in Bath stone with a pedimented front door and rooms with Adam-style decoration, while Pinney himself attended to every detail : "I desire you send me by the waggon a sufficient quantity of Glass for 4 Chinese doors for Book cases... Let it be the best glass as it is intended for handsome Cases".

Office and Hall – The built-in "handsome cases" in the office successfully complement Pinney's original rich mahogany **bureau-bookcase** of 1750. The plain mahogany **standing desk** with brass ledger rails and candle brackets was brought back from the West Indies; the fine walnut-veneered moonphase **long-case clock** is by John Jordan of Bristol and dates from c1740.

Breakfast Parlour and Dining Room – The arch between the two rooms could originally be closed with folding doors. Mahogany is everywhere : the table, sideboard, chairs, Stilton cheese box, dumb waiter and knife urn. The blue and white Chinese porcelain dinner service bears the Pinney coat of arms.

Upstairs – Note the fine pair of gilded **girandoles** (1775) in the pale drawing room, and the enormous Sheraton-style **double secretaire bookcase** (c1800) and the walnut-veneered collector's cabinet with ormolu mounts in the rich green library hung with Piranesi prints. The bedrooms continue the elegant, understated theme.

Basement – The basement contains the service rooms necessary for the smooth running of a wealthy 18C household : the pantry, for dirty chores such as cleaning silver; the housekeeper's room *(left)* containing old or unfashionable pieces of the family's furniture, from where an eye could be kept on anyone approaching the front door; the cold-water plunge-bath which Pinney used every morning, finding it to be "of great service"; the large kitchen with an iron cage-spit in the fireplace, turned by weights as for a clock, a bread oven to its left, and the speaking tubes which were later supplemented by a bell system *(in the hallway);* the laundry, containing two coppers for boiling washing and a wooden rocker-washer (*c*1850) but dominated by a late 18C box mangle; the drying room with a large copper warming pan for the floor of a coach.

Cabot Tower ⓥ – The slim red tower with a square balcony **(view)** and a white cap was built high upon the hill in 1897 to celebrate the 400th anniversary of the sailing, financed by Bristol merchants, of the navigator **John Cabot** *(qv)* across the Atlantic.

Berkeley Square – The handsome square is framed by late 18C terrace houses of ochre stone. John Loudon **McAdam,** Surveyor to the Bristol Turnpike Trust, was living at no 23 when he devised his new method of road surfacing in 1816. The **Cross** at the corner of the green is a 19C replica of the upper section of the former Civic High Cross given to Sir Henry Hoare II and used in the gardens at Stourhead *(qv).*

BRISTOL

Broadmead .... BY 2
Fairfax Street .... BY 26
Galleries (The) Shopping Centre ... BY
Horse Fair (The) ...... BY
Merchant Street ...... BY 40
Nelson Street .... BY
Park Street .... AY

Bedminster .... BZ
Berkeley Avenue .... AY
Berkeley Place ...... AY
Bridgehead .... BZ
Bristol Bridge .... BY
Broad Quay .... BYZ
Broad Street .... BY
Broad Weir .... BY
Charlotte Street ..... AY
Clare Street .... BY
College Green ...... AZ

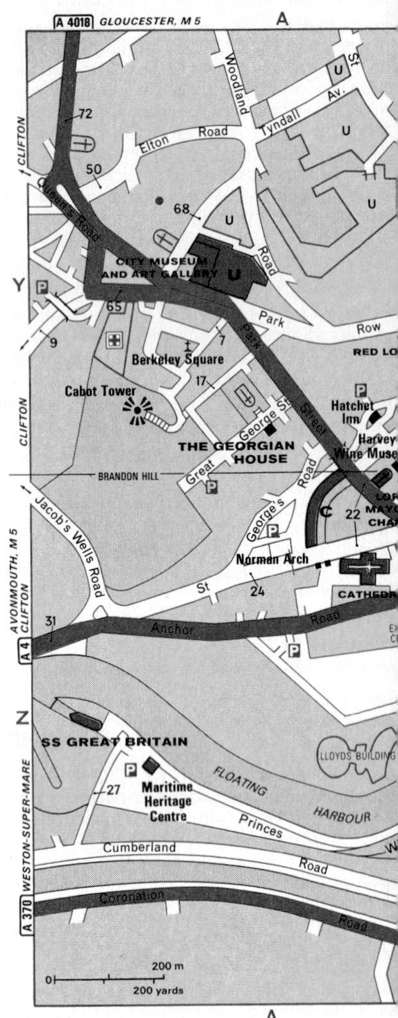

★ **City Museum and Art Gallery** ⓥ – Glass is of particular interest in well-appointed late 19C building, with its airy *Art Nouveau* entrance hall : Bris Nailsea, Roman, pre-Roman and Chinese glass and 18C English drinking glass The earliest Bristol Clear of 1650, used for decanters and glasses, was follov by Bristol White (made to resemble porcelain and sometimes painted) the fam. **Bristol Blue** (1760-1820), Bristol Green with its gold decoration, and ameth – two decanters of 1789, 1790. **Nailsea** is distinguished by trailed or splas white on blue and green.

Pottery and porcelain is another speciality : galleries display hard and soft pa porcelain and tin glazed earthenware, all produced locally. Further galle contain paintings, silver, watches and clocks, railway and ship models, jewell minerals and gemstones, pianos, stuffed animals...

Bristol University (U) – On the hill stands the University **tower,** a biscuit colou stone octagon ending in a circlet of low pinnacles, officially known as the V Memorial Building, which has been a city landmark since its completion in 19 There are about 7 000 students.

Red Lodge ⓥ – The small entrance gives no indication of the splendours wit The magnificent **Great Oak Room** features its original late 16C **carved panelling** v Italian Renaissance motifs (the American Indians on the **porch** are a remin of Bristol's trade with America); the imposing fireplace which complements porch includes alabaster panels personifying Hope, Justice, Charity and Pruder The pomegranate on the plaster ceiling alludes to the Resurrection : in class literature the fruit was associated with Proserpine who returned from the d Other rooms – which include a print room, parlour, reception room – fea later styles of decoration and furnishing. Outside, the design for the Tudor **garden** was taken from the bedroom ceiling.

Colston Avenue .... BY 23
Deanery Road .... AZ 24
Denmark Street .... AYZ 25
Gasferry Road .... AZ 27
Haymarket .... BY 29
High Street .... BY 30
Hotwell Road .... AZ 31
Lawford Street .... BY 36
Lower Castle Street .... BY 37
Lower Park Row .... BY 38
North Street .... BY 43
Penn Street .... BY 44
Perry Road .... BY 45
Quay Street .... BY 47
Queen Charlotte Street .... BZ 48
Queen's Avenue .... AY 50
Redcliffe Bridge .... BZ 51
Redcliffe Way .... BZ 52
St Augustine's Parade .... BYZ 55
St James Barton .... BY 57
St Nicholas Street .... BY 58
St Stephen's Street .... BY 59
Small Street .... BY 62
Temple Gate .... BZ 64
Triangle Street .... AY 65
Union Street .... BY 66
University Road .... AY 68
Wapping Road .... BZ 70
West Street .... BY 71
Whiteladies Road .... AY 72

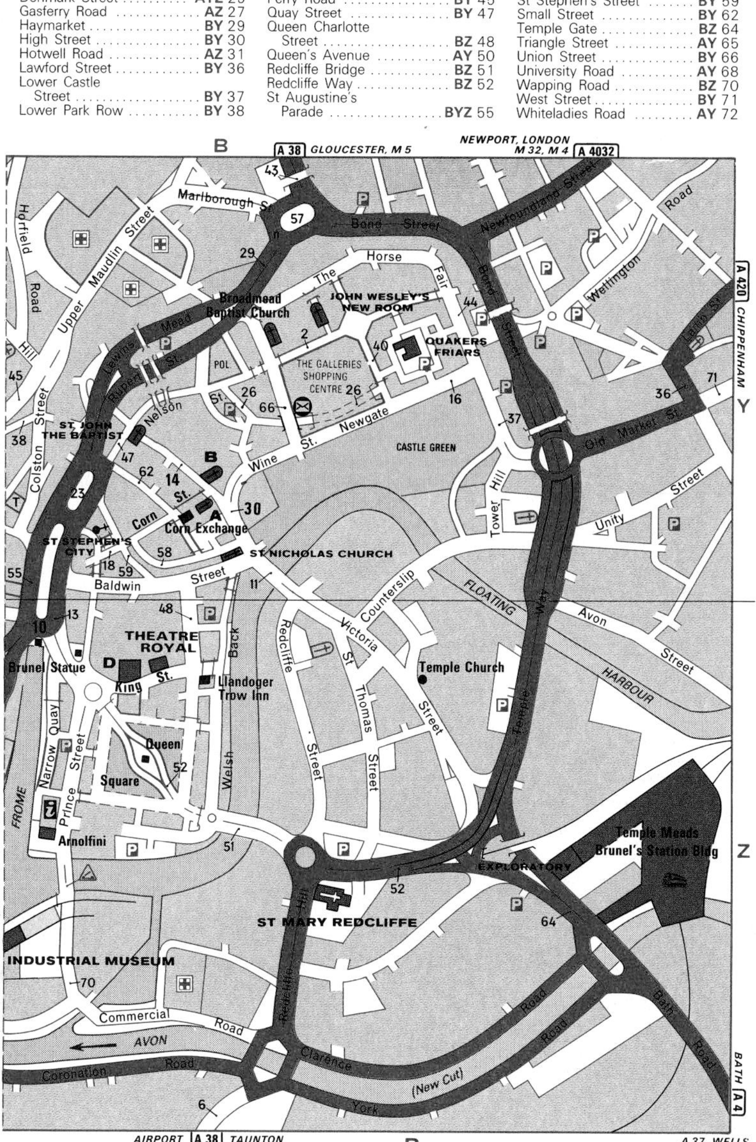

★ OLD CITY *2½ hours*

Bridgehead (BZ 10) – The lead statue of Neptune dates from 1723. The Watershed *(below right)* is a media centre and shopping gallery.

Cross Broad Quay; go north up Colston Av and turn right into Clare St.

★ **St Stephen's City** (BY) ⊙ – The city parish church has a **west tower** which rises 130ft by stages of ogee arched bays to a distinctive crown and two-tier pierced balustrade linking 20ft corner turrets which culminate in fountains of close-standing pinnacles. The tower *(illustration p 149)* was funded entirely by John Shipward, merchant, mayor and MP, and dates from the 1470s when the church was rebuilt on the 13C site.

In the irregularly shaped interior, supported on shafted piers with gilded demi-angel capitals, are memorials to **Edmund Blanket** *(north aisle)*, a wealthy cloth weaver (d 1371), and **Martin Pring** (1580-1627), merchant venturer and general of the East India Company, who discovered Cape Cod in 1603, explored Guiana in 1604, the Virginia coast in 1606 and surveyed the Bristol Channel for a fee of £11 1*s* in 1610 – the oval plaque was embellished in the 18C with symbolic figures including the mermaid and merman. Note also the 17C wrought-iron **gates** *(north aisle)* and **swordrest** *(south chancel pillar)* by William Edney, and the medieval **eagle lectern.**

Corn Street (BY) – The phrase "to pay on the nail" derives from these four **brass nails** on which Bristol corn merchants struck deals and paid in cash. The first nail was cast in 1594.

Corn Exchange – The giant-pilastered and pedimented exchange, before which the nails stand, was built in the mid-18C by John Wood the Elder of Bath.

Lloyds Bank – The bank, designed in Venetian Cinquecento style with columns coats of arms and exuberant figures along the frieze and in every spandrel, dates from 1854.

Old Council House – The sober Greek-style building is early 19C.

Coffee House – The house with a hanging sign on an iron bracket is 18C.

All Saints and Christchurch (BY) – Churches have stood here since Saxon times.

All Saints (A) – *(No longer used for regular services).* Although the tower is 18C parts of the church are Norman – note the two great circular pillars supporting single stepped arches – and others early 15C, such as the slim shafted piers with foliated capitals beneath the open timberwork roofs. Note the **memorial** carved by Rysbrack to the considerable local philanthropist **Edward Colston** (d 1721; *south aisle*).

Christchurch (B) – The austere Georgian church dating from 1791 is known for its painted wood clock **quarter-jacks,** helmeted, moustachioed, kilted and armed with axes.

Broad Street (BY 14) – The wide street, which leads to the old city wall, is partly lined by 17C timber-framed houses and shops.

★ **St John the Baptist** (BY) – The church, including a battlemented tower with a spire, stands over a triple arch, one of the six medieval gateways in the city walls. It was founded in the 14C by William Frampton (tomb in the canopied recess, *north chancel wall*), three times mayor, on the foundations of an earlier chapel, the site determining the narrowness of the nave and chancel.
The woodwork and furnishings are nearly all early 17C : the wooden lectern, **communion table,** the big **hour-glass** intended to curtail sermons. Much earlier is the **brass** *(chancel)* of Thomas Rowley, merchant and burgess (d 1478) and his wife.

The Conduit – *Through the arch, in Nelson St.* The conduit (right), which brought water from Brandon Hill to the old priory and the city in the 14C, is still flowing.

Return up Broad St.

High Street (BY 30) – The street crosses an area of alleys, lanes and small courts. To its west lies the market with, at its centre, **The Rummer,** an inn of 1743 and holder of no 1 public house licence in Bristol.

St Nicholas Church (BY) – The proud Georgian church was gutted by fire in 1941 and rebuilt with a soaring white stone spire.

Cross Baldwin St and skirt the Floating Harbour.

King Street (BZ) – The cobbled street has a unique character with the Floating Harbour at one end, 18C and 19C warehouses, the theatre, pubs and 17C almshouses. The **Llandoger Trow Inn,** named after the flat-bottomed barges which unloaded coal on the adjoining Welsh Back quayside and the original Old Anchor Inn in *Treasure Island,* was built as three stout, half-timbered merchants' houses in 1663; The Old Duke is an aged inn renamed after Duke Ellington; the Bunch of Grapes, Jolly Cobblers, Admiral Benbow, Naval Volunteer were all originally private houses.

★★ **Theatre Royal** – The oldest playhouse in the country still in use opened to a prologue composed by **David Garrick** in 1766 and was granted a royal licence by George III in 1778.
Outside, the rusticated golden stone ground floor is superimposed by giant Corinthian columns, a cornice and pediment bearing the George III royal arms. Inside, the wide foyers and staircase beneath a decorated ceiling are modern; the small, horseshoe **auditorium** on three levels with boxes on either side of the proscenium stage, 18C; the colour is dull green and gold with deep pink lining the walls.

★ **Merchant Seamen's Almshouses** (D) – *Northwest end.* The almshouses bear the coloured arms of the **Merchant Venturers** on the outside wall of the pink-washed former quadrangle. The houses were first built in 1544 and enlarged with funds from **Edward Colston** *(see above)* in 1696. The life story of one of the almsmen of the Spanish Main was used by Edgar Allen Poe as the basis for *The Golden Bug.* Opposite, in the distance, Cabot Tower is visible.

Brunel statue – Beyond the almshouses, on the other side of the road, stands a more than lifesize, top-hatted bronze of Isambard Kingdom Brunel.

BROADMEAD (BY) *45min*

Within the vast new shopping precinct are three buildings of contrasting periods.

Broadmead Baptist Church – The church of 1967-69 has an austere simplicity.

John Wesley's New Room – The chapel (1739) is the oldest Methodist chapel in the world. The two entrances are heralded by statues, of John Wesley on his horse and Charles Wesley preaching.
Note the two decker **pulpit,** the **parliament clock,** mahogany communion table, box pews, graceful **gallery stairs** and former living accommodation (history of Methodism).
It was at the 1771 Bristol Conference, held here, that Francis Asbury was chosen to go to America where he became the first Methodist bishop.

Quakers Friars – The 13C building derives its name from the Dominicans (Black Friars) who occupied it until the 16C, and from the Society of Friends (Quakers) who used it for worship from the 17C to the mid-20C. It now houses local council offices.

★★ SS GREAT BRITAIN and ST MARY REDCLIFFE *½ day*

★ **SS Great Britain** (AZ) ⊙ – Ongoing work to restore the ship to the former glory of her launch in 1843 will continue for a while. Meanwhile this first iron-built, propeller-driven Atlantic liner lies in her original dry dock, a vast 322ft long and 51ft across, with forecastle deck renewed, 43ft bowsprit, reproduction figurehead and gilded trailboards in place, her keel plates exposed inside, her masts shipped once more, the gleaming Dining Saloon ready... Museum and guide describe the innovations of **Brunel's** design, the saga of the ship's history until its return in 1970. Also shown are mementoes of all kinds from both *Great Britain* and *Great Western* and Bristol's maritime history.

Maritime Heritage Centre (AZ) ⊙ – The centre was opened in 1985 to display the collection of ship models and drawings accumulated by the shipbuilders, Hilhouse and his successor, Charles Hill. It illustrates the transition from sail via steam to diesel and from wood via wrought-iron to steel, from 1773 to 1976 when the site was an active shipyard. At the centre is a mock-up of the dredger designed by Brunel to keep the Floating Dock free of mud.

★★ **Industrial Museum** (BZ) ⊙ – Industry, in the context of this museum in a 1950s warehouse overlooking the Floating Harbour, comprises local manufacturing processes from brick moulding to pin-making, transport from penny-farthing bicycles to the world's first purpose-built, horse-drawn caravan (1880), a 1948 Bristol car and historic gauge 1 working railway models.
There is also the definitive collection of Rolls Royce aero engines, made in Bristol, from the Lucifer of 1918 to jet engines in current production.
The museum steams its engine *Henbury* (1937) regularly and is restoring the 1861 **Mayflower Steam Tug** ⊙.

The pale, crescent-shaped and columned modern building across the water is one of many recent developments and restoration projects in the city centre.

★★ **St Mary Redcliffe** (BZ) ⊙ – The church is known, in the words of Queen Elizabeth, as the "fairest, goodliest and most famous parish church in England"; Thomas Chatterton, the young poet born in Redcliffe Way in 1752, named it, more simply "the pride of Bristowe". The construction on an older site began in 1280; the edifice, in pale Dundry stone, represents the Perpendicular style at its most perfect.

Exterior – The **spire** rises 292ft; crocketed pinnacles mark the west end, transepts, porches, the angles of the tower; finialled buttresses separate the wide, pointed windows of the nave and chancel before flying to support the immense clerestory windows. The **north porch** highlights the 270ft front's perfect regularity being hexagonal and set, like a jewel, off-centre. It stands with two tiers of decorated gables, saintly figures and a door with a triple, stellate surround as the antechamber to the shrine of Our Lady, situated in an inner, more modest porch. The **iron grids** once protected relics.

Interior – Slender shafted pillars sweep up to break into **lierne vaulting** in which every one of the 1 200 and more intersections is masked by a different **boss**, each covered in gold leaf except those beneath the tower. Such variety and richness – the bosses were gilded in 1740 – is reflected everywhere in the monuments and furnishings.

American or St John the Baptist Chapel – *northwest end.* Abutting the pillars is a contemporary, painted wooden effigy of **Queen Elizabeth I**, probably a ship's figurehead. On the nave side of the pillar hangs the full armour of **Admiral Sir William Penn** (d 1670; *tombstone at entrance to south transept*), father of the founder of Pennsylvania. Note also the fine medieval stained glass.

South Aisle – Note the medieval octagonal **font** with an angel on the pillar and a gilded dove; the richly coloured **arms** of Charles II *(over the porch);* the **stellate tomb recesses.**

South Transept – The transept serves in part as a chapel to **William Canynges** (1400-74), shipbuilder, merchant prince, mayor, MP and benefactor, who paid for much of the rebuilding of the church; in one tomb effigy he lies beside his wife in full colour, in the second in the vestments of the holy order which he joined on his wife's death.

Ambulatory – The ambulatory passes before the Lady Chapel, for 100 years a school screened from the chancel by a Hogarth triptych and now embellished with contemporary stained glass. Note the 18C brass **candelabra.**
In the chancel, **brasses** commemorate two churchwardens : John Jay (d 1480), merchant, and John Brooke (d 1512), servant-at-law to Henry VIII; at the crossing stands the **lectern**, a fierce 17C eagle, given by James Wathen, "pin Maker".

★ **Bristol "Exploratory"** (BZ) ⊙ – The many moving displays in this "hands-on" science centre make it fun to explore the laws of light, heat, sound, electricity, friction, magnetism, structures and earth science. They are housed in part of **Temple Meads Station,** built by Brunel in 1841.

ADDITIONAL CITY SIGHTS

Queen Square (BZ) – The square, dating from the time of Queen Anne, is framed by houses which merchants had built when leaving the ever more noisome city centre and dockside area; the large bronze equestrian **statue of William III** is by Rysbrack.

Arnolfini (BZ) ⊙ – This centre of the visual arts, music, cinema and dance is in a skilfully-converted 1830s tea warehouse overlooking the Floating Harbour.

Temple Church (BZ) – Bristol's "leaning tower", a monumental stone belfry dating back to 1300, stands proudly, despite bombing and fire, as a reminder of the medieval Knights Templar. The 144ft structure began to lean at an early stage in its construction and is 5ft out of true (Pisa : 180ft with 15ft "lean").

Clifton Suspension Bridge.

★★ CLIFTON ½ day

Take the Hotwell Rd through the Avon Gorge for the best view of the bridge.

★★ Clifton Suspension Bridge – The 702ft long bridge is amazing, spanning the Avon Gorge like a spider's thread, 245ft above high-water level. It won Brunel *(qv)* the designer's prize in open competition in 1829-31 when he was in his early twenties. (Signed drawings submitted by Brunel for the bridge competition though not that of the actual bridge as built, may be seen at the GWR Museum in Swindon, *qv*).
His "first child", "his darling", as he called it, despite "going on glorious" in 1836 suffered long delays and was only completed in 1864, five years after his death. Of countless bridge stories, Sarah Ann Henley's is the happiest : in 1885 a lover's quarrel induced a lover's leap but Sarah Ann's petticoats opened and she parachuted gently down to the mud below – she subsequently married and lived to be 85...

Continue beside the gorge, under the bridge; bear right up Bridge Valley Rd.

Clifton Down – The steep down was populated by sheep farmers until prosperous merchants came to build substantial residences overlooking the gorge, speculative builders to construct Georgian crescents, Regency squares and terraces and Victorian streets.
In the 18C the area became known through the short-lived Hotwells Spa; in the 19C it acquired fame with the opening of the Suspension Bridge.

★★ Bristol Zoological Gardens ⏲ – The famous zoo (opened 1836) features a large selection of rare and wonderful animals – white tigers, okapi, pink flamingos, elephants, tamarins, gorillas – and some interesting new architecture, especially the modern Reptile and Ape Houses.

★★ Clifton R C Cathedral of SS Peter and Paul ⏲ – After three years of construction, the imposing cathedral was consecrated on 29 June 1973 (in place of the 19C pro-cathedral).
A white, 165ft, three plane steeple marks the new church : trees, gardens, a moat provide a natural contrast to the harsh-sounding materials : white concrete, pink granite agglomerate, black fibreglass, lead and glass.

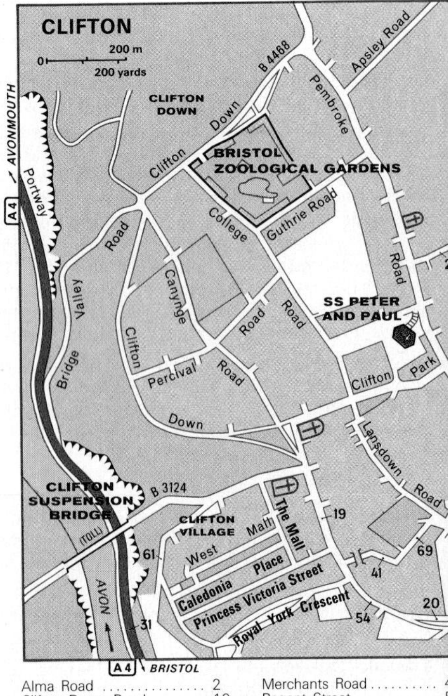

Alma Road	2	Merchants Road	4
Clifton Down Road	19	Regent Street	5
Clifton Hill	20	Sion Hill	6
Hotwell Road	31	Victoria Square	6

Interior – The design motif is the hexagon – elongated to afford a direct view from all sides of the white marble high altar, regular in the flooring, the lanterns, the lights on high, the outline of the organ bay, reduced to a chevron for the flowing stream at the foot of the carved Portland and Purbeck stone font... Warmth and colour are provided by the brown ochre furnishings and wood, and by the limpid blue, greens, greys and jewel reds and yellows in the long, symbolic **windows** of massive glass.

★ **Clifton Village** – The charm of the delightful village, set apart from the bustle of the city, lies in its late 18C and early 19C terrace houses and small shops situated in The Mall, Caledonia Place, Princess Victoria Street, Royal York Crescent – begun by William Paty *(qv)* in 1791 and reputedly the longest crescent in Europe – and several other streets.

EXCURSION

★ **Blaise Castle House Museum** ⏲ – *5 miles northwest up A4018 (AY) and B4055.*
The museum is housed in an 18C mansion designed by William Paty of Bristol; Repton was commissioned to lay out the grounds. The conservatory was added by John Nash and the south portico by Charles Cockerell. The collection illustrates English domestic life in town and country between 1750 and 1900 by way of embroidered waistcoats and Victoriana, dolls, quilted bedcovers, children's and adults' games, bronze wool weights bearing George I's cypher, "dissected" (ie jigsaw) puzzles, a case of Bristol watchmakers' timepieces.

★ **Blaise Hamlet** – *north side of B4057, Weston Rd.*
The nine cottages, which originally had thatched roofs, were designed by John Nash in the cottage *orné* style. Each one is different and stands in its own garden facing the central green; no front door is overlooked by its neighbour.
The hamlet was built (1810-12) to house the older servants and tenants of the Blaise Castle estate.

★ BROWNSEA ISLAND Dorset

Michelin Atlas p 9 or Map 403 – O31 – Poole Harbour

The island ⏲ (1½ miles long, ½ mile wide) is covered with heath and woodland and fringed by inviting beaches along its south shore. Its 500 acres might be considered as two nature reserves ⏲, one on either side of **Middle Street,** the island's central spine.
The **north reserve** is a sanctuary for waterfowl and other birds *(qv)* and supports a heronry, blackheaded gullery and a colony of common tern.
In the open reserve south of Middle Street, visitors may wander at will (and picnic) by the 19C church with its painted angels and memorial tablets, in the **Peacock Field,** habitat of an enormous number of birds, in the **Daffodil Field** *(steps to the beach from paths at the east and west ends of the field),* westwards to the **Baden-Powell Stone,** commemorating the first experimental Boy Scout Camp in 1907. The stone is also the island's principal viewpoint, affording a **panorama**★★ from Poole Bay to the Purbeck Hills with Corfe Castle *(qv)* just visible in the Gap. When walking or sitting still, look out for **red squirrels.**
The island's "castle" was built in the 18C on the site of one of Henry VIII's forts.

BUCKFAST ABBEY Devon

Michelin Atlas p 4 or Map 403 – I32 – Local map p 91

The present abbey church was consecrated in 1932, some 900 years after the original foundation made under King Canute. The new church and monastery, built by members of a community of French monks who had fled to England in the 19C, followed in plan the rediscovered foundation of the Cistercian house dissolved by Henry VIII in 1535.

TOUR ⏲ *½ hour*

The style is Norman in grey limestone relieved with yellow Ham Hill stone; at the centre is the 158ft crossing tower.

Interior – The church of pure white Bath stone rises above the arcades, triforium and clerestory to a plainly vaulted rib roof, 49ft above the nave floor. There is no pulpitum or screen and the eye is immediately drawn the 220ft length of the church to the **high altar,** rich in gold, enamelwork and jewels. Suspended above the altar is a 48-light gilded **corona.**

Continue round behind the altar and east up the steps from the ambulatory.

Blessed Sacrament Chapel – The modern chapel, dedicated in 1966, features **walls of stained glass.** The chapel was designed by the monks who also built it and made and set the glass in all its shades of blue, purple, red and pale yellow.

Crypt – The exhibition traces the history of the Abbey from 1018 to the present with models and photographs.

Audio-Visual Show – The film presents the history of the Abbey and the life of the Buckfast community.

★★ BUCKLAND ABBEY Devon

Michelin Atlas p 3 or Map 403 – H32

Sir Francis **Drake** purchased the house, for £3 400, through nominees in 158
the seller was his lifelong rival, **Sir Richard Grenville,** who had inherited the manc from his grandfather, a property owner in North Devon who had bought the 13 Cistercian abbey after the Dissolution in 1541. Sir Richard (cousin of Sir Walte Raleigh), naval commander and privateer who was to die off the Azores aboar the *Revenge* in 1591, had completed the conversion of the abbey church in a house before he sold it.

In 1581 Drake was forty; he had sailed to West Africa and the Spanish Mai in 1577-80 he had circumnavigated the globe. He was famous, newly knighte and rich : the house was intended to provide a suitable setting should he retir from the sea – but of course he didn't. In the next few years he made expeditior to Vigo (1585) and Cadiz (1587), where he "singed the King of Spain's beard captured a Spanish vessel off the Azores with cargo worth £114 000 an confronted the Armada.

TOUR ⏲ *1 hour*

The house is arranged as three domestic rooms and a kitchen and three museu galleries, two rooms and one gallery being specifically devoted to Drake.

Great Banqueting Hall – The great room with its pink and white paving panelled in oak decorated with fluted pilasters and a holly and boxwood inla above is a moulded ceiling with pendants and, on one side, an allegorical friez Furnishing the hall are a 16C oak table, chests, the patent with the royal se for the Cadiz raid, a replica **medallion** engraved with the circumnavigation rout and two paintings – contemporary **portraits** of Drake by Marc Gheeraerts, an his second wife, Elizabeth Sydenham (of Combe Sydenham, *qv*). At the centr silent, is **Drake's Drum.**

Chapel – The simple chapel stands on the site of the abbey church high alta

Traditional Devon Crafts Gallery – Among the crafts and artefacts displaye are shipbuilding and sailmaking, lacemaking, Plymouth porcelain, pewter, hors brasses, cider-jugs and village Friendly Society pole-heads.

Drake Gallery – The gallery, on the first floor, has murals of the circumnavigatio and displays the **Armada accounts** and the silk banner made to dress the *Golde Hinde* when the queen knighted Drake at Deptford in 1581.

Drawing Room – The oak panelled room is furnished with finely carve 16C-17C pieces and hung on the walls with contemporary **portraits** of the quee and Drake's cousin, Sir John Hawkins (by Hieronymo Custodis).

Georgian Staircase, Georgian Room – The staircase and Georgianised roor were installed in the 18C. The stairs rise 60ft in four flights from two impressiv **dog gates.**

Naval Gallery – The long gallery under the roof is filled with scale models (ships from ancient times to today's warships.

Tower Room – Drake's coat of arms fills the overmantel; note the 14C tracerie window.

Tithe Barn – The great barn in the grounds, buttressed, gabled and onc thatched, dates back to the 14C abbey.

BUDE Cornwall

Pop 2 679

Michelin Atlas p 6 or Map 403 – G31 – Facilities

Bude, a haven in the cliffs standing tall against the incoming Atlantic, offers popular beach of pale gold sand sheltered by the grass-topped headlands an braided by a long line of beach huts sprucely painted purple, mauve, blue, green

★★ **The Breakwater** – At high tide, the breakwater beyond the 19C Bude Can provides a good view and a close feel of the sea.

Compass Point – *Access by footpath (30min Rtn) from the end of Breakwat Rd.* From the point, named after the octagonal waymark tower (with out-of-tru bearings), there are spectacular **views★** along the line of 200-450ft cliffs, marke by offshore reefs. To the south the vista stretches right round the white-sande Widemouth Bay.

EXCURSIONS

This corner of north Cornwall has many villages with compact granite churche containing robustly carved medieval bench-ends, Norman fonts and brass an slate memorials. Two groups, one to the north, one to the south of Bude, a listed below.

1 Round tour starting from Bude *22 miles – local map p 5*

Leave Bude by A3072.

Stratton – Pop 1 288. Stratton is an old market town which was once a por The **church★** was built by stages. The north arcade of sea-green-grey Polyphar stone (1348) was followed by the pinnacled **tower** (90ft) – once a landmark – ar by the granite south arcade in the mid-15C. The chancel dates from 154

The font bowl is Norman, the pulpit Jacobean, the bench-ends medieval, the **royal arms** restyled Stuart-Hanoverian; the east window is by **Burne-Jones.** In the porch is the old door to Stratton prison (the clink).

Continue along A3072; bear left at the first turning.

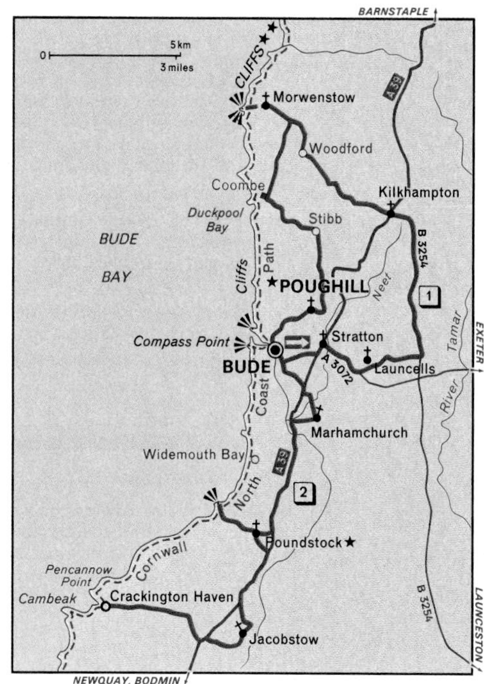

Launcells – Pop 421. The 15C **church★** stands in a wooded valley, the tall pinnacles of its 54ft tower surpassing the trees. Inside, the arcades are of Polyphant stone and granite, the **chancel** is paved with rare 15C Barnstaple encaustic tiles designed with fleurs-de-lis, Tudor roses, lions, pelicans, flowers. Note especially the 15C **bench-ends,** 60 in all carved with the Crown of Thorns, the *Harrowing of Hell,* the empty tomb...

Continue along the by-road; bear left into B3254.

Kilkhampton – Pop 896. The **church★** with its 90ft embattled and pinnacled granite **tower** was rebuilt on a Norman site in 1485. Note the Norman **south door** with three orders, zig-zag and beaked bird decoration and, inside, the 157 carved **bench-ends,** of 1567. The remarkable **monuments** sculpted in wood, stone and slate are by **Michael Chuke** (1679-1742), a Kilkhampton boy sent to London as a pupil to Grinling Gibbons.

By way of cross-country by-roads (Burridge, Woodford) make for the coast.

Morwenstow – Pop 619. Morwenstow was the parish of **Parson Hawker,** poet and preacher, who "lived a life made up of eccentricities", travelling this corner of his beloved Cornwall from 1834-75 in purple frock coat, white cravat, fisherman's jersey and boots, rescuing shipwrecked sailors and giving Christian burial to the drowned. The **church★**, which stands in a dell, the pinnacled and embattled tower a landmark to those at sea, was referred to as "ancient" in a document of 1296. It has a Norman **south door** with zig-zag moulding on small columns, two interior **arcades,** one with Norman and Early English piers supporting an arch with chevron, ball and headed orders and at the base an antelope and other animal masks. Beneath the original bossaged wagon roofs are a Saxon **font** with cable moulding of *c*800 and mid-16C bench-ends.

The spectacular **cliffs★★** (450ft high) reach out to offshore rocks.

Take the by-road south to Coombe; turn inland to Stibb then right.

★ **Poughill** – For centuries the kernel of Poughill (pronounced Poffil) has been St Olaf's Church and Church House (opposite) which dates from 1525.

The **church★★**, a Norman foundation, has a 14C Perpendicular granite tower, square and embattled with crocket pinnacles. Inside, two arcades, one 14C sandstone and tall, the other 15C, granite and short, march beneath late 15C wagon roofs with carved bosses. On the walls two medieval St Christopher frescoes were graphically repainted by Frank Salisbury in the 1920s; the **royal arms,** incorrectly dated 1655, are of Charles II. The deeply carved, oak **bench-ends** (nearly all late 15C) are polished each Epiphany to dark translucence with elbow grease, linseed oil and melted down candle-ends from Christmas – note Jonah and the Whale, Biblical and local characters.

Continue south to Bude.

2 Bude to Crackington Haven *12 miles – local map below*

Leave Bude by A3073 going south.

Marhamchurch – Pop 475. Stone houses with slate or thatched roofs stand round St Morwenne's **church★** (14C-15C) with its square tower abutted by a staircase turret. Of interest in the single arcade interior beneath the old wagon roofs are the oak door with its **sanctuary knocker** *(qv),* the Jacobean **pulpit** with a sounding board, the **royal arms** by Michael Chuke *(see above)* and, in the west wall, the window of a 15C anchorite's cell.

Join A39 and drive south.

★ **Poundstock** – Pop 665. Church, lychgate and unique guildhouse form a secluded group in a wooded dell. The 13C-15C **church★** with a square unbuttressed tower was restored in the 19C. It retains a nail-studded **south door,** a square granite **font** (1300), an early 16C oak chest, a Jacobean **communion table** *(back of nave)* and pulpit, 17C **slate memorials,** wall paintings, the Trebarfoote **wall monument** *(north aisle)* depicting a dapper man in Stuart dress with flowing moustaches.

The **guildhouse★**, sturdily built in the 14C, probably as quarters for the masons constructing the church, passed to the parish guilds as a place of meeting and festivity until such revelries were suppressed by the Puritans. It became a poorhouse, a school... Of cob and stone on two floors with buttresses, wooden mullions and a slate roof over stout timbers, the guildhouse stands as an example of once-common, non-secular building.
One mile west is the Atlantic, pounding the 400ft high cliffs from which the **view★★** extends south to Trevose Head and north even to Lundy.

Return to A39; continue south for 1 mile; bear left.

Jacobstow – Pop 301. The 15C **church★** stands in a hollow, its pinnacled granite tower emerging from the trees. A granite **porch** leads to the earlier nave and aisles. The 12C **font** is carved with faces at the angles; the pulpit was made from bench-ends.

Rejoin A39, immediately bearing right into the by-road to the coast.

Crackington Haven – A wide, lush valley leads down to the resort village and dark sand beach. On either side the headlands rise hundreds of feet out of the sea.

BUDLEIGH SALTERTON Devon — Pop 4 456

Michelin Atlas p 4, 5 or Map 403 – K32

The small town maintains to some degree the atmosphere of a mid-19C watering place. An old sea wall lines the short parade above the beach of steeply shelving shingle – Sir John Millais was living in the town in the 1860s and used both wall and shingle as the setting for his famous painting *The Boyhood of Raleigh*. Salt pans in the marshes beside the River Otter gave Budleigh Salterton its name.

EXCURSIONS

East Budleigh – Pop 859. *2 miles north on A376.*
The small, one-time wool town and birthplace of Sir Walter Raleigh has a 15C **church★** where Raleigh's father was churchwarden. Note especially the carved and coloured **bosses** and 16C **bench-ends**, carved with a sailing ship, craftsmen's tools, dolphins and portrait heads.

Hayes Barton – *2 miles north by A376 through East Budleigh then left (1 mile).*
Sir Walter Raleigh was born in the long, thatched farmhouse in 1552.

★ **Bicton** – *3 miles north by A376. See Bicton.*

Otterton Mill ⏲ – *2½ miles by A376 and right at main crossroads beyond East Budleigh.*
The early 19C mill *(tour)* produces stoneground wholewheat flour which is baked on the premises. There are also craft workshops : pottery, quilting, tie-dyeing, knitwear, wood-turning and table mats. The stream running the length of the village street is spanned by individual **stone bridges** to the houses.

BURNHAM-ON-SEA Somerset — Pop 10 976

Michelin Atlas p 7 or Map 403 – L30

Two special recollections remain after a visit to the seaside resort on the Bristol Channel : the lighthouses *(qv)* on stilts and the Grinling Gibbons carvings.

Lighthouses – In the shallows on the seven mile beach, beyond the sunbathers, sand-castle builders and donkeys, there stands a lighthouse on stilts – a pair with one behind on the sand dunes; in line, they serve as a navigation bearing for ships in the channel; both are vertically striped red and white, the upper one shows a light.

Parish Church – St Andrew's stands just back from the beach, its 14C-15C **tower** noticeably "leaning" out of the vertical. Inside are a delightful gathering of **cherubs** and two expressive **angels** carved by **Grinling Gibbons** (1648-1700) and Arnold Quellin for the Whitehall Palace chapel. After the palace fire of 1698 the altarpiece found its way to Westminster Abbey before being transferred, in part, to Burnham in 1820.

EXCURSION

Wedmore – Pop 2 758. *9 miles east on B3139 to Wells.*
The village, with its lantern-headed market cross, is historic as the signing place of the treaty between King Alfred *(qv)* and the Danes in AD 878.
The crossing **tower** of the Perpendicular **Church of St Mary Magdalene** was inspired by that of Wells Cathedral. Inside, the tower **roof** is fan vaulted, the pulpit Jacobean, the **wall painting** of St Christopher 16C and the **chandelier** 18C.

The Southwest is the traditional home of cider-making in England; Somerset in particular is noted for its cider-apple orchards. Dry (« champagne ») cider is more alcoholic than the sweet variety.

CADHAY Devon

Michelin Atlas p 4, 5 or Map 403 – K31 – 1 mile northwest of Ottery St Mary

"John Haydon esquire, sometime bencher of Lincoln's Inn, builded at Cadhay a fair new house and enlarged his demesne". Haydon was a successful Exeter lawyer who had married Joan Cadhay in 1527 and become rich as one of the local commissioners responsible for selling the dissolved priories in and around Exeter.

Construction – The house, incorporating the earlier Great Hall, was built round three sides of an oblong courtyard, probably in the early 1540s.
John Haydon's heir, Robert Haydon, installed massive Tudor fireplaces with ornamental emblazoned tracery inside and, in a second building phase, enclosed the open side of the courtyard known as the **Court of Sovereigns.**
The 18C owner included among his alterations the horizontal division of the Great Hall and the "Georgianising" of several rooms.
The furniture includes a 16C oak refectory table, 18C mahogany tables and chairs, chests, a secretaire... The owners' taste is reflected everywhere : in the collection in the Long Gallery and Roof Chamber and in the garden, enclosed by tall hedges and white clematis-draped walls, which slopes down to the 15C canons' fish-ponds.

TOUR ⏲ *½ hour*

Court of Sovereigns – The court, the house's unique feature, was enclosed at the end of the 16C and further transformed by the refacing of the **walls** with dark knapped flints and small sandstone blocks in an irregular chequed pattern, and the setting of four elaborate Renaissance-style **niches** above the doors at the centre of each range. In the niches, in full robes of state, stand Henry VIII, Edward VI, Mary Tudor and Elizabeth I – hence the court's name; it was completed in 1617.

Dining Hall – The hall, part of the original Great Hall, has a high coved ceiling, an arcade – formerly open at one end – and one of the giant Tudor fireplaces.

Drawing Room – The room is one of those Georgianised in the 18C.

Roof Chamber – This chamber is the upper part of the Great Hall and, although the timbers have been much cut about, many are the original 15C beams.

Long Gallery – The gallery runs the length of the Court of Sovereigns.

CAMBORNE and REDRUTH Cornwall Pop 34 262

Michelin Atlas p 2 or Map 403 – E33

The continuous conurbation which lines the main road (A3047) comprises three towns, Camborne, Pool and Redruth.

Redruth – The most easterly of the three is the only industrial town in Cornwall; its main street is punctuated by Nonconformist chapels and a granite clock tower.

Pool – The middle town is distinguished by past and present mining landmarks.

Camborne School of Mines – The tall granite and glass buildings of the world-famous school date from the 1970s. Inside is a **museum of minerals** ⏲, labelled and sparkling, and a small art gallery.

Cornish Pumping Engines and East Pool Whim ⏲ – The engines, one with a cylinder 7½ft in diameter, were used for pumping water from mines 2 000 and more feet deep and for bringing men and ore to the surface. The engines, one in motion (electricity-driven), exemplify the use of high pressure steam, patented in 1802 by Richard Trevithick (1771-1883), engineer at the Ding Dong mine *(qv)* and "father of the locomotive engine".
Just beyond, in Tuckingmill, a **plaque** on a factory wall *(south side of the road)*, commemorates **William Beckford** *(qv)*, inventor of the miners' safety fuse (1830).

Camborne – The oldest of the three towns aligned along the main road is marked by 18C-19C houses and a rambling half-timbered inn, once a posting house. The 15C granite church with its distinctive west tower contains a 10C Saxon stone altar slab, an 18C marble altarpiece and chandeliers. There is a 6C holy well and a Celtic Cross in the churchyard.

EXCURSIONS

★ **Poldark Mine, Wendron** – *7 miles south of Redruth on B3297. See Wendron.*

Carn Brea – *1½ miles southwest of Redruth and 500yds south of Carnbrea or Brea village – last 150yds up a field track.*
Crowning the 740ft, boulder-strewn hilltop is a 90ft granite **monument.** A landmark for miles around, it affords a **view★★** over the length and breadth of Cornwall.

Gwennap Pit – *1 mile southeast of Redruth, off A393.*
The Pit is a natural amphitheatre formed by the subsidence of an old mine-shaft. In the mid-18C, when Revivalism was strong in the West Country, it was the setting for meetings numbering as many as 30 000 miners and their families on the 17 occasions when **John Wesley** *(qv)* came to preach between 1762-86. In 1805-06 the amphitheatre was remodelled to its present 12 grass tiers; each summer it is the scene of a Wesleyan revival meeting *(see also Carn Brea chapel, qv)*.

CASTLE DROGO Devon

Michelin Atlas p 4 or Map 403 - I31 - 2 miles northeast of Chagford - Local map pp 90-91

Castle Drogo is the romantic dream of **Julius Drewe** (b 1856), the son of a clergyman. On leaving school Drewe was sent as a tea-buyer to China; on his return he started the Home and Colonial Stores and within ten years had made a fortune. At 33 he retired from active business. He bought himself a country house in Kent, married and bought a larger house, Wadhurst Hall in Sussex, which he took over complete with its tapestries and Spanish furniture.
Drewe's elder brother consulted a genealogist who "proved" that the family was descended from Dru or Drogo, a Norman noble who came over with the Conqueror; his descendant in the 12C, Drogo de Teigne, had settled in Devon and given his name to the village of **Drewsteignton** *(qv)*. On discovering the family history, Julius Drewe began to buy land and a quarry in the area as a first step towards materialising his dream. The second step was his introduction to an imaginative architect at the peak of his career, **Edwin Lutyens** (1869-1944).

Construction - The foundation stone of Castle Drogo was laid in 1911 on a bluff overlooking the Teign Gorge and vast tracts of Dartmoor; the plans were still being evolved, and continued to be so throughout the next 19 years of building.
Constructed of rough-hewn and dressed granite from Drewe's own quarry, the castle presents two three-storey ranges each approximately 130ft long, on different levels, meeting in a wide angle of 160°. Towers mark either end and the centre; windows, in the form of giant canted bays with stone mullions and transoms, pierce the east and southeast fronts overlooking the moor.

TOUR ⏲ *1 hour*

The characteristic **features** throughout are the interplay of heights and levels between the ranges, marked where there are changes in direction by saucer domes; the use of bare white **granite;** the beautiful **views** from the windows.

Walk through the front door.

Hall - *Ground floor.* The first of several tapestries brought from Wadhurst hangs in the hall. Also on view are a 17C Spanish chest, 18C English dummy board figures by the hearth and 16C Limoges enamel roundels.

Library - *Ground floor.* The lustre dishes above the Lutyens oak bookshelves are Spanish; the marquetry bureau is Dutch, the lacquer screens Chinese.

Drawing Room - *Ground floor.* The room features windows lining three sides of the room offering lovely **views.** The chandeliers are Venetian. Among the exotic furniture and furnishings, note the lacquer cabinets and 18C *famille verte* vases from China, and a French Empire clock (*c*1810).

Main Staircase - On the walls hang portraits of Mrs Drewe in her Sussex garden and Mr Drewe in full fishing regalia in Scotland - about which Lutyens commented that "At least he (the artist) could paint boots".

Dining Room - *Lower ground floor.* The room serves as a family portrait gallery.

Service Corridor, Pantry, Kitchen, Scullery - *Basement.* The dolls' house of 1906 in the vaulted corridor was made for one of Mr Drewe's daughters. The fascinating kitchen and scullery are equipped with oak cupboards and a round table designed by Lutyens.

North Staircase - The stone staircase, which rises through five floors, is cantilevered out from the wall, while the oak balustrade is constructed independently round a cage.
The Green Corridor, one of three similarly designed, overlooks the Teign Gorge.

Chapel - *Access from outside.* The chapel lies beneath the south range.

Gunroom - The adjoining vaulted room is now used to display a number of Lutyens drawings and plans for this extraordinary house.

Gardens - The formal gardens have been planted with colourful herbaceous borders and rose beds. Visitors may use the large circular croquet lawn.

CHARD Somerset

Pop 9 357

Michelin Atlas p 7 or Map 403 - L31

The town has long been known as a market centre : for tanning in the 13C wool cloth in the 15C, coarse linens, cloths and serges for the East India Co in the 17C-18C, lace early in the 19C and now engineering, food processing textiles and animal feed.

Fore Street and High Street - The town's prosperity in the 17C-19C is reflected in several substantial buildings : the town hall (1834) with a two-storey portico, the **George Hotel,** the Elizabethan **Manor Court House,** Waterloo House and the Grammar School *(east end, north side)*, founded in 1671 in a house built in 1583.

★ **Museum** ⏲ – *Godworthy House, High St.* Local history centres on lacemaking and the "lace workers riot" of 1842; on **John Stringfellow** (1799-1883), who in 1848 pioneered powered flight following experiments on gliding models and light steam engines with inventor William S Henson (1812-88); on **artificial limbs** which were the creation of local man James Gillingham. Treasures include a facsimile of the Gough map of England and Wales (*c*1360), 17C **embroidery** (*petit point* and stumpwork), a cider mill and press, a **costume gallery** (19C dresses), an old kitchen, toys and puppet theatres. **Net-making machines** and farm machinery are housed in the modern annexe, and a recreated early garage.

St Mary the Virgin – The church stands in the oldest part of town; local wealth in the 15C-16C is reflected in the Somerset tracery, battlements and pinnacles of the tower.

EXCURSIONS

Cricket St Thomas Wildlife Park – *3 miles east by A30. See Cricket St Thomas.*

★ **Clapton Court Gardens** – *11 miles east by A30 and B3165.*

Crewkerne – Pop 6 018. The town centres on the wide Market Street and the **Market Square**, overlooked by the Jacobean-style Victorian Hall and Georgian houses.
The **parish church**★ is a Perpendicular rebuilding with immense windows of an older church. At the time of rebuilding, the substantial piers at the crossing were kept to support a new 80ft tower which includes Somerset traceried bell openings extending through two stages to gargoyles, pinnacles and a pinnacled stair-turret. Battlements and gargoyles appear along the main rooflines and gargoyles in close frills around the twin **octagonal turrets** which mark the west front.
Inside, the piers are tall and slim beneath a wagon roof on angel figures while the north transept and chapel have rich panelled ceilings. Beneath the tower there is a fan vault. Note at the west end the early 19C galleries, the square Purbeck marble font which is Norman and in the chancel *(south wall)*, a brass to Thomas Golde, a knight of 1525, at prayer.

★ **Clapton Court Gardens** ⏲ – The ten acre garden comprises formal terraces, spacious lawns, a rockery, rose and water gardens and a woodland garden with natural streams and glades. Clapton Court is a garden for all seasons, providing blooms throughout the spring and summer and rich autumn colour.

★ **Forde Abbey** – *4 miles southeast on south bank of the River Axe. See Forde Abbey.*

★★ CHEDDAR GORGE Somerset

Michelin Atlas p 16 or Map 403 – L30

The "deep, frightful chasm in the mountain, in the hollow of which the road goes", as Defoe described it in the 18C, has been a tourist sight since the 17C.

★★ GORGE *2 miles – 1:6 gradient – car and coach parks near the bottom*

The gorge, which is best approached from the east end, descends from the Mendip Hills, twisting and turning between limestone cliffs which are lush with greenery or gaunt and grey where the fissured walls and pinnacles rise vertically (350-400ft). The rift is probably a dry river-bed; the Romans seem to have exported lead from the Mendip Hills, transporting it by barge from quays in Cheddar down the Yeo and the Axe to Uphill on Severn and from there to Italy.

Jacob's Ladder ⏲ – From almost the foot of the gorge a staircase *(274 steps; rest benches)* leads up to the plateau level from which there is a panoramic **view**★ of the Mendips, the Somerset moors and the Quantocks.

★ CAVES ⏲ *2 hours*

The caves are near the gorge bottom on the south side *(left going down)*. Cox's Cave was discovered in 1837 by George Cox when quarrying limestone, Gough's Cave in 1890 by Richard Cox Gough. Both caves were opened to the public soon after their discovery.
The series of chambers follows the course of underground streams through the porous limestone; the formations increase by 1 cubic inch in every 400 years.

Gough's Cave – The stalagmites and stalactites, the lace curtains, frozen falls and pillars coloured by the minerals in the limestone are each a different, glistening hue from white to alabaster, amber, rust-red (iron), green (manganese) and grey (lead).
Among the fancifully named, but nonetheless beautiful formations are the nine-tier Fonts, the Swiss Village and Aladdin's Cave, both with mirror pools, King Solomon's Temple with its stalagmite cascade and the blue-spotlighted Black Cat – the only feature in the caves not lit with a white light.

Cox's Cave – Among the formations note the Transformation Scene, the Marble Curtain, the ringing stalactites known as the Peal of Bells, and the Speaker's Mace.

Fantasy Grotto – This cave contains an assortment of fountains, coloured lights, melodramatic moving models and a hologram display.

Adventure Caving – These expeditions explore beyond the limit of the show caves.

Museum – Weapons, utensils in flint, bone and antler horn, iron and bronze, pottery and the skull of Cheddar Man indicate that the caves were inhabited intermittently from the Paleolithic to the Iron Age – 20 000-500 BC – and even in Roman times.

VILLAGE

The village (pop 3 761), which extends from the foot of the gorge to the parish church at the south end of the main street, gave its name to the English national cheese. In 1170 Henry II bought 80cwt of cheddar declaring it the "best cheese in England".
Hannah More (1745-1835), writer and philanthropist who spent her later life improving the physical and mental welfare of the people of the Mendips, opened her first school in a cottage in Venns Close in the centre of the village.

Market Cross – The cross was originally a preacher's cross round which a hexagonal colonnade was built in the 16C converting it into a small covered market; travelling merchants paid rent to sit under cover.

★ **St Andrew's** – The Perpendicular church, the fourth on the site, dates from 1380-1450. The typical Somerset **tower** rises 110ft through four stages from a west door and window, flanked by carved heads believed to be those of Henry V and Queen Catherine, to a pierced and pinnacled parapet and a staircase turret with a spirelet roof.
Inside, the coffered **oak roofs** on arch braces are supported on **corbels** carved with kings' and bishops' heads – possibly an allusion to Mendip Forest having been a royal manor until sold by King John in 1204.
Among the furnishings are an early 14C **font** with a Jacobean cover, a 15C stone **pulpit** coloured as in medieval times, an **altar-table** of 1631, the tombchest and large brasses of Sir Thomas Cheddar and his wife (dd 1443, 1460) and, in the 15C Fitzwalter Chantry *(off south aisle)*, a pre-Reformation **altar-stone** and a painting of *The Last Supper* by Jan Erasmus Quellinns of Antwerp (1629-1715).

EXCURSION

★★ **Axbridge** – *3 miles east; bear left off the by-pass (A371).* *See Axbridge.*

Chewton Cheese Dairy, Chewton Mendip ⊙ – *8 miles east by B3135 and north by A39.*
From the corner of the dairy or from the restaurant above, visitors can watch the cheese-making process : filling the vat with milk, starter and rennet, curd cutting, pressing and bandaging the cheese truckles.

The length of time given in this guide
– for touring allows time to enjoy the views and the scenery
– for sightseeing is the average time required for a visit.

★ CHEW MAGNA Avon — Pop 1 411

Michelin Atlas p 16 or Map 403 – M29

Chew Magna was well established by Domesday. In 1546 John Leland, antiquary to Henry VIII, described it as "a praty clowthing towne" but since then the wool market has moved elsewhere.
The straggling main street opens out into a square, which is triangular in shape and bordered by **Harford House** (a pink stone Georgian building), by a small Georgian town house and a range of cottages, some with white rendering and some of random pink stone.
The 13C-16C church stands back from the road, its pinnacled and gargoyled west tower a proud 99½ft tall. Inside, the **arcades** have 13C, Early English hexagonal columns *(south)* and 15C Perpendicular columns *(north)*. Note also the fluted Norman **font;** the restored medieval **rood screen;** 15C and 16C recumbents on the tomb chests and, in a niche, a 14C coloured wooden effigy of a knight, smiling benignly as he plants one foot on a surprised, sitting lion (the inscription is Victorian and inaccurate).
At the gate stands **Church House,** a long, early 16C building.

EXCURSIONS

★ **Stanton Drew Stone Circles** ⊙ – *3 miles east; south of B3130. Just before the village bear left down a lane and left again for Court Farm.*
Walk through to the field, where the age-old stones stand among cows and chestnut trees. The scattered, Bronze Age site consists of **three circles** : the Great Circle, 370ft in diameter with 27 stones in place, 3 of them upright; the Northeast Circle, 100ft in diameter, 8 stones, 4 upright; and the Southwest Circle (on private ground).

Return to the village and bear left, past the church to the Druid's Arms.

Behind the inn, a group of stones (one fallen and two upright) is known as the **Cove.**

Local legend – Legends connected with the stones abound, the most popular being that "it's a company that assisted at a nuptial ceremony thus petrify'd" : the Cove is the parson, the bride and groom, the circles are the company who danced through Saturday and, from midnight, to the tune of a stranger who played ever faster until at dawn the hypnotised dancers turned to stone. The fiddler, the devil in disguise, said he would play again one day to release them but the dancers wait...

Chew Valley Lake – *4 miles south by B3114.*
The 1 200 acre (4 500 million gallons) reservoir lake lies in a beautiful, drowned valley.

CHIPPENHAM Wiltshire — Pop 21 325

Michelin Atlas p 17 or Map 403 – N29

People have come to Chippenham, the first settlement at the bend in the River Avon, since Saxon times to trade; initially by packhorse and then from 1474 along Maud Heath's Causeway; since 1837 by the railway steaming west along the high striding viaduct, and nowadays by way of main roads and the M4 motorway. At the top end of the town stand the church, a street of houses of every degree and age, and the half-timbered town hall.

SIGHTS

★ **Yelde Hall** ⏲ – The 15C half-timbered hall, on an island site beside the former location of the local gallows, pillory, stocks and whipping post, served as the office of the bailiff and burgesses of the Hundred. Inside are a panelled courtroom over a blind-house or lock-up and adjoining, beneath an open timber roof, the old town hall.

St Andrew's – The many times remodelled Perpendicular church stands on the site of the Saxon church in which Alfred's sister, Aethelswitha, married the King of Mercia in AD 853. Inside, note the flatly **carved effigy** of a beautiful, mysterious 13C woman *(south chapel),* the 13C **vestment chest** with bird and animal carved panels and the outstanding 1730s oak **organ case,** pedimented, turreted, intricately carved and surmounted by trumpet-blowing angels.

St Mary's Street – The long street behind the church is lined with cottages, terrace and large town houses, timber-framed, small windowed and low-lying, or tall and ashlar-faced with graceful doors and windows, pediments and parapets.

Maud Heath's Causeway – Maud Heath, 15C widow, farmer's wife or spinster property owner, no one knows, left houses and land in the town for the construction and, most importantly, the maintenance of a causeway so that local producers could come to market dryshod. The 4½ mile long pathway still exists, running from Wick Hill, where an inscribed stone and 19C pillar crowned by a statue of Maud Heath mark the start, through East Tytherton, Kellaways and Langley Burrell to the former outskirts of the town. A 1698 end stone is now in Barclays Bank in the Market Place; a film-strip about the causeway may be seen in the Yelde Hall *(see above).*

EXCURSION

Round tour – *14 miles; leave Chippenham west by A420; bear right onto B4039; turn left.*

★★ **Castle Combe** – Pop 347. The picture postcard village is approached along a wooded valley, the road coming out from beneath the trees straight into **The Street,** as it is known. Punctuating its length, and contrasting with the stone cottages on either side, are the Upper Manor House of *c*1700 with a shell hood above the door, **mounting blocks** and a **market cross** with a solid pyramid roof. The **church,** with a tall pinnacled tower, was built during the 13C-15C when the village was a rich wool market. Inside are a 15C font with an integral lectern, a 16C pulpit, a royal coat of arms with seated lion and unicorn supporters, a wall tablet of 1588 in mixed Latin and English, and a medieval knight.
Still further along The Street are the **pack bridge** and, opposite, **Water Lane** circling a widening out of the stream into a pool which mirrors the former weavers' cottages bordering the lane. Gardens, trees, flowers and the stream complete the picture.

Continue along the by-road to Ford; turn left into the A420 and right at Giddeahall.

★ **Biddestone** – Pop 479. The village centre is a large green complete with a duck pond; all around, 16C-18C houses and cottages, many with stone mullioned windows, are set in spacious array. One, behind 18C wrought-iron gate and railings, stands in a modest perfection of two storeys with angle quoins, segmented bays and, above the door, an open pediment framing the date, 1730. The manor house just off the green is 17C, with stone walls and roof, gables ending in ball finials, mullioned windows and a brick gazebo poised upon the garden wall.

Continue 2 miles east along the by-road towards Chippenham.

★ **Sheldon Manor** – *See Sheldon Manor.*

Return to Chippenham.

★ CHRISTCHURCH Dorset Pop 32 854

Michelin Atlas p 9 or Map 403 - O31

Christchurch is an attractive town boasting many interesting features : a wide, shallow harbour with a narrow outlet to the sea, pleasure-craft, water meadows, old streets, bridge and ferries, the rivers Stour and Avon flowing into the harbour, a Norman priory which Henry VIII dissolved and a Norman castle which Cromwell slighted.

Early history – Excavations have uncovered a gravel landing and slipway built on the marshes over 2 000 years ago by Iron Age men for beaching and landing their boats; also Roman amphorae for importing wine (100 BC) and wheel pottery from Brittany.
Ten years after Domesday the village was given by William Rufus to his chief minister, Ranulf Flambard, the builder of Durham Cathedral. He pulled down the existing Saxon church and was about to start the construction of a great Norman church when William II died (1100) and he, Flambard, was put in the Tower. Henry I gave the patronage to his cousin Richard de Redvers, Earl of Devon, who, after Flambard had been pardoned in 1107, encouraged him to complete the church.

★ PRIORY *½ hour*

Augustine canons worshipped in the choir, allocated the nave to the parish and erected monastic buildings abutting the north wall. In the early 13C the crossing tower collapsed leaving only the nave and the west and end walls of the transepts; rebuilding proceeded slowly until the 16C by which time the church presented a sequence of architectural styles : Norman in the **turret** and the **nave** – note the fish-scale decoration; Early English in the **clerestory;** 14C Decorated for the **choirscreen,** Perpendicular at the east end in the **choir** and **Lady Chapels** – note the cusped and pinnacled arcading in the chapel and the canopied reredos with the *Tree of Jesse.*
The **choirstalls** are late 15C with an excellent set of **misericords** (one, 13C), depicting everything from a jester to a salmon's head, an angel to Richard III.

Chantry Chapels – The finest, again Perpendicular, is the **Salisbury chantry** *(north chancel aisle)* carved in Caen stone by the Renaissance sculptor, **Torregiano,** with tiers of enriched canopies and fan vaulting but empty because Margaret, Countess of Salisbury, was executed in the Tower by order of Henry VIII in 1541. The traces of paint to be seen on the stonework throughout the interior would once have been a blaze of colour, highlighting every decoration.

Priory legends – It was originally intended that the priory be built on a hill about a mile away but every morning materials taken up the hill the previous day would be discovered mysteriously brought down to the sacred Saxon site until, finally, the builders decided that this was divine intervention. When building began on the town site, the masons and carpenters were joined by an extra, unknown, workman who received no pay and was not seen at meals. One evening it was discovered that a beam had been cut too short and the men went home disconsolate; when they returned in the morning, however, they discovered that it had "grown" in the night; the stranger had vanished. All were convinced it must have been the Carpenter from Nazareth and so the church, and then the town, were renamed Christ's Church.

ADDITIONAL SIGHTS

Castle – The castle keep, built to dominate the countryside from its artificial mound, was originally of wood but by the late 13C had walls of stone 30ft high and 10ft thick. The fort was contested in the Civil War and was razed in 1650.

Constable's House – The ruined house at the castle's foot is late 12C.

Town Bridge – The old stone bridge with its pointed cutwaters dates back to the 12C.

Red House Museum ⊙ – *Quay Rd.* Among the 18C houses round the priory stands the 19C Red House, long and solid in red brick; it has been made into a **local museum** which displays, among many items, the **seine fishing nets** once used to catch salmon in the harbour, fine 19C **chains** for which the town was famous, and archeological finds.

EXCURSION

★ **Hengistbury Head** – *4 miles by B3059; bear left at Tuckton for Southborne.* From the head there is a wide **view★★** over Poole Bay and east to The Needles and the Isle of Wight (less extensive panorama along the **panoramic road** from Bournemouth).

To plan a special itinerary:

- ***consult the map of touring programmes which indicates the recommended routes, the tourist regions, the principal towns and main sights.***
- ***read the descriptions in the Sights section which include Excursions from the main tourist centres.***

Michelin Map no 403 indicates scenic routes, interesting sights, viewpoints, rivers, forests...

CLAVERTON Avon — Pop 109

Michelin Atlas p 17 or Map 403 - N29 - 3 miles east of Bath

The village extends in name from the River Avon and the Kennet and Avon Canal, up a steep hill to the traditional manor house and beyond, on the down, to the new buildings of Bath University created in 1966 from Bristol College of Advanced Technology.

SIGHTS

★★ **American Museum** ⊙ – Housed in a Classical mansion (1820) built of Bath stone on the site of an Elizabethan manor, the museum reveals the interiors of wealthy homes of the white settlers from the late 17C-late 18C, complete with original furnishings; treasures, artefacts and influences from a wider cross-section of people (Indians, cowboys, Mexicans) are also displayed.

Keeping Room – The late 17C room from Massachusetts, with stout beams, massive fireplace and solid turned and polished furniture, shows the developments made from the modest homes (cabins, wigwams) of the first settlers.

Four 18C Rooms – The rooms present regional differences and changing fashions : the charming Lee Room from New Hampshire is encased in blue-green wall boarding, the more formal Perley and Deming Parlors from Massachusetts and Connecticut have pine panelling and painted walls, curving early Queen Anne and later Chippendale-style furniture; the Deer Park Parlor, from Maryland, reveals the influence of Hepplewhite and Sheraton.

Greek Revival Room – The early 19C New York room with Classical themes shows the continuing influence of European tastes on furnishing fashions.

Two Bedrooms – The freshness of the first room, from an 1830 **Connecticut** house, with its painted and stencilled decoration contrasts sharply with the opulence of the second, from **New Orleans** on the eve of the Civil War, and its large-scale furniture adapted from the Louis XV style.

Spicing the exhibition are displays of silver, pewter, glass and **textiles** including quilts, hooked rugs and patchwork. There are dioramas and set pieces on opening up the west, cowboys, Indians; rooms on the Spanish-influenced New Mexico, the Pennsylvania-Germans, the **Shakers**... Gingerbread is baked in the 18C tavern and goods sold in the 19C country store.

New Gallery – The display cases contain an extensive collection of old and rare maps, donated by Dallas Pratt; a hall holds temporary exhibitions.

Gardens – Within the gardens overlooking the wooded valley of the River Avon lurk a covered Conestoga Wagon, a copy of a Northern Cheyenne Indian tepee, a 19C milliner's shop with a delightful collection of band-boxes, a splendid arboretum containing native American species, a fernery and a waterfall, George Washington's Mount Vernon garden and a folk art gallery with a collection ranging from naive portraits to weathervanes, cigar store to carousel figures, an Indian brave figurehead, tin marriage gifts...

★ **Claverton Pumping Station** ⊙ – *On the east side of A36. Take Ferry Lane across the canal; cross the railway line.*
The pump of 1813 has been restored to raise water from the River Avon into the canal (87 miles) which from 1810 linked the River Kennet *(qv)* (navigable from Reading to Newbury) and the Avon (Bath to Bristol).
The pair of elm paddled, breast shot wheels (each 12ft wide and 17½ft in diameter) driven by the headrace, turn the pitwheel, flywheel, crankshaft, working beams and the pumps, which lift 50 gallons a stroke or 87 000 gallons an hour.

★★ CLEEVE ABBEY Somerset

Michelin Atlas p 7 and Map 403 - J30

The red sandstone abbey ruins in a pretty setting are particularly interesting since they comprise the buildings most often destroyed, the monks' quarters.
Cleeve was colonised by an abbot and 12 monks in 1198 when building began on the church. Construction was in two main phases : 1198-1297 and 1455-1537. In the first phase the community increased to nearly 30 monks, a pilgrimage chapel was built at Blue Anchor *(qv)* and land in the area was brought under cultivation; the second phase was a period of renewal and improvement verging on the luxurious, with the provision of sets of rooms decorated with wall paintings for the monks. All was abrogated at the Dissolution.

TOUR ⊙ *½ hour*

The two-storeyed gatehouse leads into a 3-acre outer court and to what was the west end of the priory church (now only footings); walk up the nave and through the arch just before the south transept.

Cloister – Despite the destruction of all but one arcaded wall along part of the west gallery, the enclosed feel of the cloister remains, with the church occupying one side and the high dorter and frater ranges still standing on the east and south sides. Note the **collation seat** in the centre of the church wall, from where the abbot presided over the reading before Compline.

Dorter range – The doorways led, respectively, to the **library**, the **chapter-house**, the parlour and the slype or passageway to the commonroom *(sharp right)*.

Climb the stairs to the vast dormitory or **dorter** (25ft by 137ft), built to accommodate 36 monks. It had a lime and mortar floor supported on the vaulting of the ground-floor rooms and was lit by lancets. Note the night stair into the church *(left of the two doorways in north wall).*

Frater range – The range is a 15C rebuilding of an earlier construction.
The original refectory, of which the splendid **tiled pavement** remains, lay on the far side of the range *(through the barrel vaulted passage at the corner).* The tiles, which from their heraldry date from 1272-1300, show in still-bright red, yellow, black and white the **three leopards** of England borne by Henry III (1216-72), the **lion** of Poitou and **border** of Cornwall of Richard, Earl of Cornwall (1209-72, second son of King John) and his son, Edmund – both abbey benefactors – the **double-headed** eagle of Richard who also held the title King of the Romans, the central **diamond** of Cornwall flanked by those of England...

Return to the cloister.

The later **frater,** through the wide 13C doorway and up the stairs, is a hall (51ft by 22ft) lit by 9 transomed windows with traceried heads – note how the north windows are blank below, where the cloister roof once abutted the wall.
The outstanding feature of the hall is the **roof,** a great timber construction supported on stone corbels, with archbraced collars, trusses, purlins, richly moulded and further decorated with 50 deeply undercut, foliated bosses and crowned angels. The roof is unfinished, being intended as a boarded-in barrel; also it was never painted.
The lobby at the top of the stairs opens on to an office while the gallery alongside the cloister wall leads to small rooms decorated with still visible wall paintings.

★ CLEVEDON COURT Avon

Michelin Atlas p 16 or Map 403 fold 35 – L29

The mellow stone house, begun in the 14C, had achieved its present appearance by 1570; the interior, which reflects every period, has all the attraction and comfort of an Edwardian country house.

TOUR ⏲ *45min*

Great Hall – The 14C hall with Tudor windows and fireplace is hung with family portraits; among them is **Abraham Elton,** purchaser of the house in 1709, Master of the Bristol Merchant Venturers, mayor and MP. The chairs are Stuart, the **drawer table** late 16C, the Dutch **chandelier** 17C.

State Bedroom – The bedroom, 14C solar with an inserted Elizabethan window, reflects the family taste through ten generations. Among the contents are a portrait of the merchant Nicholas Elton, a Hepplewhite **tester bed,** Queen Anne **spoonback chairs,** Cromwellian chairs and chests, late Georgian and Regency pieces and small 18C-19C children's chairs.

Hanging Chapel – The chapel has unique reticulated **window tracery.** The prayer desks are 17C, the Biblical carvings 15C and 16C, the glass 19C.
Note in the smaller bedrooms portraits of and drawings by **Thackeray** including Jane Octavia Brookfield, model for Lady Castlewood in *Henry Esmond,* and of Arthur Hallam, nephew of the then owner of Clevedon Court, in whose memory **Tennyson** wrote *In Memoriam.*

Justice Room – The small room and walls of an adjoining staircase display a fascinating collection of the local **Nailsea glass** made between 1788 and 1873. There are bottles and jars and "friggers" or craftsmen's spare-time mouldings including green glass hats, trailed, blotched and colour-striped perfume bellows, rolling pins and a unique set of brilliantly coloured walking sticks.

Old Kitchen – The kitchen contains a rare collection of **Eltonware,** the remarkable experimental pottery of Sir Edmund Elton, man of many parts, designer of Clevedon Clock Tower *(see below),* who essayed new shapes, decoration on coloured slips and metal lustrework.

Garden – The outlook is over Clevedon Moor to the Bristol Channel and Wales; immediately behind, the hillside rises sharply, covered in dense woods. Between is a long, steeply terraced garden on three levels comprising wide borders at the feet of precipitous stone walls.

EXCURSION

★ **Clevedon** – Pop 17 875. *1½ miles.*
The Victorian resort, which grew out of a fishing village, retains its wide 19C roads bordered by substantial villas, Tuscan, Gothic or Italianate in style, rows of cottages built in local stone and unhurried shops.
The promenade is bordered by gardens with flowers, closely mown lawns, and trees, especially windbent pines.
Characteristic of the time also are the **bandstand** (Green Beach Gardens), the **Clock Tower** and the pagoda-roofed **pier** (1869).
From the park benches the **view★★** extends across the mouth of the Severn to the Welsh hills.

CLOUDS HILL Dorset

Michelin Atlas p 8 or Map 403 - N31 - 9 miles east of Dorchester

T E Lawrence, Lawrence of Arabia, rented then bought **Clouds Hill** ⊙ for his own, "a ruined cottage in a wood near camp". In 1923-25 he was a private in the Royal Tank Corps at Bovington *(qv)* and from 1925-35, in the RAF; throughout this time and in the few weeks before his death in May 1935 in a motorcycling accident, he described in letters to his friends how the cottage became "the centre of my world".

"I put the (Greek) jape, « Why worry » upon the architrave. It means that nothing in Clouds Hill is to be a care upon its inhabitant. While I have it there shall be nothing exquisite or unique in it. Nothing to anchor me" (18/X/32). "I look forward to settling there in a year's time, for good" (26/III/33). "The whole place is designed for just a single inhabitant. Panelling; bookshelves; bare wood and undyed leather. A queer place, but great fun. No pictures and no ornaments" (5/III/34). "Two rooms; one upstairs for music (a gramophone and records) and one downstairs" (23/XI/34). "I think everything, inside and outside my place, approaches perfection" (23/XI/34). "Wild mares would not at present take me away from Clouds Hill. It is an earthly paradise" (8/V/35). (*The Letters of T E Lawrence,* edited by David Garnett; Jonathan Cape, 1938).

EXCURSION

★★ **Moreton Church** - *3½ miles southwest by B3390 and by-roads left.*
T E Lawrence is buried under the cedar in the cemetery entered through the lychgate. St Nicholas itself is a graceful, small Georgian Gothick church with sparkling windows; it dates largely from 1950. Ten years earlier it lay in ruins, destroyed by a bomb jettisoned by a German aircraft. The new church discarded much done in accordance with Victorian taste and reverted to the 18C church plan.

The entrance is beneath the pinnacled tower, trimmed, like the apse and aisle rooflines, with a narrow, lacelike balustrade. Inside, the wide nave beneath a coloured vault leads the eye to the altar standing at the centre of the semicircular apse. The walls are pierced on all sides so that the church is an ethereal lantern.

The engraved **windows** - the first, it is believed, in the outside walls of any church - were executed by **Laurence Whistler** between 1958 and 1980. The design is a celebration, in festive style, of spiritual light and the church's dedication to the patron saint of children and Christmas : St Nicholas. Within the design are candles, ribbons, the emblems of the Passion, trees, a Christmas tree, the church in ruins and rebuilt, the Cross...

★ CLOVELLY Devon Pop 419

Michelin Atlas p 6 or Map 403 - G30, 31

The ever-popular picture postcard village, which was mentioned in the Domesday Book, is reached via a **visitor centre** ⊙ (audio-visual show on local history, and numerous amenities).

Clovelly itself consists of a very steep, stepped and cobbled **High Street** which is known, depending on the direction being faced, as **Down-a-long** or **Up-a-long.** Lining it are whitewashed 18C and 19C houses - decked with bright fuchsias, geraniums and hydrangeas - which seem to tumble down to the tiny harbour, Quay Pool, at the bottom. Donkeys and mules, which are still today the only form of transport up and down the high street, are available for rides.

In season, the village is best visited early in the morning.

SIGHTS

Quay Pool - Overlooking the restored 14C harbour, which is protected from the open sea by a curving breakwater offering **views** extending from Lundy to Baggy Point, are stone-built fishermen's cottages and balconied houses, the old harbour lime kiln, boats drawn up on the pebble beach (short coastal trips in season) and the inn, home of the mounted head of the large (478lb) **porbeagle shark**, caught from the waters off Hartland Point *(qv)* in June 1992; ten men helped bring the shark ashore.

A short walk along the beach *(15min Rtn over the pebbles),* beyond the lifeboat store, leads to a cascading waterfall.

Down-a-long, Clovelly.

Clovelly Church – The church, a Perpendicular rebuilding, is a haven of peace on the outskirts of the village itself. The imposing church gates lead through to a lush, shaded graveyard overlooked by the square, unadorned tower which rises in three parts to a gently-crenellated skyline. The church was mentioned in the Domesday Book.
Inside, note the Norman font, Jacobean pulpit (1634) and contemporary benches. The church is, however, remarkable for its **monuments** which include a brass o 1540, 17C epitaphs and 18C sculptures.

Hobby Drive ⏲ – *3 miles from the car park to A39.*
The private toll road meanders 500ft above sea-level through the woods affording sudden, open **views** of the coast and cliffs. It was laid in the 19C by the owner of Clovelly Court *(private)* and so named because its constructio became his hobby.

★★ COMPTON ACRES Dorset

Michelin Atlas p 9 or Map 403 – O31 – 3 miles southeast of Poole

The 15-acre garden, or series of **gardens** ⏲, set in a rift or *chine* in the sandstone cliffs, is famous for having flowers brilliantly in bloom in all seasons.

Italian Garden – The classical canal and fountain, statues and vases, are highlighted by quantities of flowers, carpets of bedding plants, roses, rhododendrons clematis...

Rock and Water Garden and Woodland Glen – The informal gardens inlcude cascades, pools, iris, agapanthus, eucalyptus, mimosa, palms, jacarandas, a Juda tree.

English Garden – The garden lies open to sunsets and a westerly **view★★★** of Poole Harbour, Brownsea Island and the Purbeck Hills.

Heather Dell – The dell presents a mottled carpet of purple shades.

Japanese Garden – The very big garden is lavishly endowed with garden ornaments animal and bird statuary, and brilliant with flowers and ornamental trees reflected in the waterfall and pools traversed by stepping stones and bridges.

The Michelin Maps for this region are shown in the diagram below the table of contents on page 3.
The text refers to the maps which, owing to their scale or coverage, are the clearest and most appropriate in each case.

COMPTON CASTLE Devon

Michelin Atlas p 4 or Map 403 – J32 – 2 miles west of Torbay

The massively fortified manor house stands on land granted in the 12C to the de Comptons who married into the Gilbert family which, except between 1800 and 1930, has held the manor ever since.
Among the family were **Sir Humphrey Gilbert** (1539-83), navigator, founder o the colony of Newfoundland (1583), his brother **Adrian,** navigator, colonis and seeker after the North West Passage (both half-brothers of Sir Walter Raleigh and **Raleigh Gilbert,** founder of Sagadahoc Colony in the State of Maine (1607).

Castle ⏲ – The castle was built in three phases. In the 1320s the **Great Ha** (42ft x 21ft x 33ft) rose on its east-west axis; in 1450 a west range, including the north-south oriented chapel, was rebuilt on a larger scale; in 1520 a simila structure was raised on the east side as well as the **fortifications** – the curtai wall and gateway with its machicolations and portcullis, the towers, once si in number, and the massive surrounding wall. These defences were required a protection against raids by French and, since the Armada, more especiall Spanish marauders and pirates *(qv).* A high wall at the back encloses a sma garden.

★ CORFE CASTLE Dorset

Michelin Atlas p 8 or Map 403 – N32

Corfe Castle ⏲ has dominated the landscape since the 11C, for its first 500 year as a towering stronghold and since 1646 as a gaunt but enthralling ruin. It stand on a high mound in the single break in the line of the Purbeck Hills, the **Corf Gap.** The **views★★** are spectacular.

History – In 978 the 17 year-old King Edward, the son of Edgar, went to visi his half-brother at the castle. Still mounted, he stopped at the inner gate-hous to greet his stepmother, **Queen Aelfryth** *(qv)* who handed him a cup of wine. A he drank the poisoned wine, the boy king was stabbed to death. The body wa removed to Wareham and, in 980, to Shaftesbury; in 1001 the king wa canonised as **St Edward, King and Martyr.** Aethelred the Unready, Queen Aelfryth' son, took his place as monarch.

Corfe Castle.

In 1635 the castle was purchased by **Sir John Bankes** whose wife was alone in residence when it was twice besieged by the Parliamentarians. Lady Mary resisted the first siege but in 1646 she surrendered; the castle was slighted. At the Restoration, Lady Bankes recovered the family estates; in 1663-65, her son, Sir Ralph Bankes, built a new house at Kingston Lacy *(qv)*.
Today archeological finds from the castle and a tapestry, housed in the **visitor centre**⊙, recall its rich history.

★ CORSHAM COURT Wiltshire

Michelin Atlas p 17 or Map 403 - N29

Corsham Court, an Elizabethan house of 1582, was bought by Paul Methuen in the mid-18C to house, in due grandeur, a collection he was to inherit of 16C and 17C Italian and 17C Flemish **master paintings and statuary.** At the end of the 19C the house was enlarged to receive a second collection, purchased in Florence at the end of the Napoleonic Empire, principally of fashionable Italian masters, rare Italian primitives and stone-inlaid furniture.
Paul Methuen (1732-95) was a great-grandson of Paul Methwin (d 1667) of Bradford-on-Avon *(qv)* and a grandson of John Methuen (1650-1706), ambassador and negotiator of the **Methuen Treaty** of 1703 with Portugal - a treaty which gave the United Kingdom its "oldest ally", permitted the export (formerly prohibited) of British woollens to Portugal and allowed a preferential 33 1/3 % duty discount on imported Portuguese wines - so bringing about a major change in English drinking habits. Field Marshal Lord Methuen (1845-1932), who became famous in the wars in Africa against the Ashanti and the Boers, was the father of 4th baron, Paul Methuen (1886-1974) the painter.
The architects involved in the alterations to the house and park were successively **Lancelot "Capability" Brown** in the 1760s, **John Nash** in 1800 and Thomas Bellamy in 1845-49.
Brown set the style by retaining the Elizabethan stables and riding school (now occupied by the Bath Academy of Art) but rebuilding the gateway, retaining the great, gabled, Elizabethan stone front and doubling the gabled wings at either end and, inside, by designing the east wing as stateroom-picture galleries... He planned the park to include a lake, avenues and specimen trees such as the Oriental Plane, now with a 200yd circumference.
Nash's work, apart from embellishments such as the octagonal corner towers and pinnacles, has largely disappeared; Bellamy's stands fast, notably in the hall and staircase.

TOUR ⊙ *1½ hours*

Four state rooms, music and dining rooms provide the setting for the outstanding collection of over 150 **paintings, statuary, bronzes** and **furniture.**

Picture Gallery - The triple cube of 72 x 24 x 24ft with a white coved ceiling is hung with crimson Spitalfields damask, which was also used to upholster the Chippendale furniture. Note the pier-glasses and tables by the **Adam brothers,** the girandoles attributed to **Chippendale** and the white marble fireplace.
The gallery is hung with the **classic paintings** in the collection by Fra Bartolomeo, Caravaggio *(Tobias and the Angel)*, Guido Reni, Strozzi, Salvator Rosa, Tintoretto *(Adoration of the Shepherds)*, Veronese *(Annunciation)*, Rubens *(Wolf Hunt)*, Van Dyck *(Christ's Betrayal)* and by Sofonisba - a portrait of the *Three Caddi Children*.

Cabinet Room – Among the pictures are **Fra Filippo Lippi's** *Annunciation* (1463) and Cesari's cartoon of a *Flying Cherub.*
The side tables with porphyry tops are attributed to Chippendale, the pier-glasses are by Adam and the inlaid commode and torchères by the cabinet maker **James Cobb.**

State Bedroom – The four-poster and serpentine mahogany chests are by Chippendale; the oval mirrors framed with vines and bushy-tailed squirrels are by **Thomas Johnson.** The 18C bracket clock is Italian. Note also the games table and two pictures : the *Infant Christ* by Guercino and the *Duke of Monmouth* by Lely.

Octagon Room – The highlight of the room designed by Nash in 1800 is **Michelangelo's** *Sleeping Cupid* (1496). Among the paintings are a Claude, a Breughel the Elder flower piece, a Caracci self-portrait and an extraordinary allegorical portrait of *Queen Elizabeth* as a seated old woman with death close by and cherubs bearing off the emblems of sovereignty.

Music Room – The pianoforte of 1807 is by **Clementi.** Note also the aeolian organ and harps and, among the furniture, the Regency mahogany chairs and matching horseshoe-shaped **wine-table** with a hinged coaster. On the showcase are 19C medicine chests and inside are Derby, Rockingham and Minton ware and a big "tea-pot" which is, in fact, a rare 18C Liverpool or Derby creamware **punchpot.**

Dining Room – The room is hung with the finest family portraits : *Paul Methuen,* the purchaser of the house, by **Reynolds** and two delightful children's portraits by the same artist, also one of the girl twenty years later by **Romney.**

CREDITON Devon — Pop 6 054

Michelin Atlas p 7 or Map 403 – J31

"When Exeter was a fuzzy town", the old rhyme goes, "Kirton (Crediton) was a market town" and such it remains with a long wide main street of mostly 18C-19C houses with shops at pavement level and, in some of the taller, three storey houses, traces of weaving lofts from when the town was known for its woollen serges (1800-50).
At the lower, east end of the main street stands the vast church built on the site of the earliest cathedral of the See of Devon.

St Boniface – The Apostle of Germany, a Benedictine who took the name Boniface, was born in Crediton *c*680 to Anglo-Saxon parents who christened him Wynfrith. In 722 he was summoned to Rome by Gregory II and made Bishop of all Germany east of the Rhine for his missionary work among the Germans. He organised the German and Frankish churches, founded the abbey of Fulda (*c*743) and became Archbishop of Mainz (*c*747). As archbishop, he was responsible for crowning Pepin, the father of Charlemagne, king of France. In old age he returned to Frisia, where he was murdered in 754.
A statue of the saint was erected in 1960.

★ HOLY CROSS CHURCH

In 739 Aethelheard, King of Wessex, founded a monastery in Crediton, which in the 10C became the seat of the new bishopric of Devon and Cornwall. In 1050 the see passed to Bishop Leofric who transferred it to Exeter *(qv),* and the church at Crediton became a college of secular canons.
In 1539, when the college was dissolved, the town raised £300 to "purchase" the former collegiate church and annex the rich Exminster living. The transaction was confirmed in 1547 under a charter granted by Edward VI which incorporated 12 "governors" to supervise the church's temporal affairs including the collection of tithes, providing for the poor and establishing a Free Grammar School (in the Lady Chapel, 1572-1876).
The Boniface Centre next to the church provides further information on the church, its work and its patron saint.

TOUR *½ hour*

The church is constructed in the local pink volcanic stone, with creamy Bee stone used to highlight the Perpendicular window tracery and crossing tower pinnacles.

Nave – The pink tufa stone interior (1415), illuminated by clerestory windows (rare in Devon) and covered by a 19C tie-beam roof, is dominated by a "period" memorial (1911) in an extraordinary assortment of marble and mosaic. Note the stone benches, the Norman font bowl *(left of the porch),* the modern wooden statue of St Boniface *(north aisle)* and the lively carving of the 19C wooden eagle lectern.

Crossing – The crossing is the earliest part of the church, dating from *c*1150; among the capitals carved with snakes, scallops and zig-zag decoration, note the pair of solemnly perched birds with spread wings.

South Transept – Note the 15C human head corbels and 20C armorial window.

Former Chapter House and Governors' Room – The three-storey Early English building dating from *c*1300 contains the former chapter-house (now the vestry), a museum with a large model of the High Street in 1743 and, in the Governor's Room on the second floor, 17C armour, a buffcoat, a musket and pair of boots from the Civil War, a 15C **angel boss,** charity boards and an ingenious vote-casting **box.**

Chancel – The chancel and aisles contain a number of **monuments** : Sir John and Lady Sully (full length effigies), he a Knight of the Garter, warrior of Crécy and Poitiers, who is said to have died aged 105 in 1387; Sir William Perryam (d 1650), a judge at Mary, Queen of Scots' trial, leaning on one elbow in his judicial robes above his weeping family; and the 17C Elizabeth Tuckfield, between her be-ruffed husband and father-in-law. In the St Boniface Chapel is a 15C Flemish merchant's **chest.**

CRICKET ST THOMAS WILDLIFE PARK Somerset

Michelin Atlas p 7 or Map 403 – L31

Cricket St Thomas wildlife and leisure park ⏲ lies amid the rolling south Somerset countryside, extending along the banks of a tributary of the River Axe and up towards Windwhistle Hill. Its popularity can make it crowded in season.

House, church and gardens – The handsome early 19C colonnaded house *(private)* and the small church are fronted on the river side by trees, tall dark hedges and colourful flower gardens.

Birds and animals – The animals – elephants, big cats, monkeys, deer, wallabies, llamas (the females produce 6½-9lbs of wool a year), sheep, camels, wapiti and performing sea-lions, otters, birds and reptiles are in enclosures in the house and church area, in the old walled vegetable garden and in large paddocks on either side of the stream. Cows from the home farm are milked each afternoon in the **milking parlour** off the walled garden *(enquire as to time).* There is also a **Heavy Horse Centre** with working shires, a **miniature railway,** a tropical aviary, a Craft Centre with working blacksmith, woodturner and potter, a rare breeds farm, an adventure trail, jungle safari rides, a children's playground, a "Victorian" Shopping Arcade with an original merry-go-round, restaurants, a pub... Special events are held throughout the year.

DARTINGTON Devon

Michelin Atlas p 4 or Map 403 – I32

Fifty years after its foundation Dartington flourishes, expanding further the concepts of the founders, the Elmhirsts, who believed in the encouragement of personal talent and responsibility through education and rural regeneration which, in practical terms, meant the establishment of a working community where people would find scope for their personal development and a sense of fulfilment while earning a living.
Within relatively few years of the Elmhirsts' purchase of the long-desolate, 14C house and 800 acre rump of its estate, the name Dartington had become a synonym for "advanced" co-education, summer schools, art courses, exhibitions and concerts... The school closed in 1987 but the college of art today numbers 370 and the summer schools, concerts and courses are well attended; the estate has been increased to 2 500 acres and includes new hamlets and farms; there are a dozen local enterprises, from Dartington Crystal at Great Torrington *(qv),* to the development at Morwellham *(qv)* on the Tamar, to the Beaford Centre which takes programmes of music, theatre, dance and film to towns and villages in North Devon. About 750 people are employed by the Trust.

Dartington Hall and Gardens ⏲ – The **gardens,** courtyard and, when not in use, the 14C Great Hall with its hammerbeam roof *(through arch beneath clock tower)* are open to visitors.

Cider Press Centre ⏲ – *Shinners Bridge.*
The centre, housed partly in the 16C and 17C stone buildings of an old cider house, provides a permanent exhibition and sales centre for goods produced by the trust's local enterprises and by other craft workers in the southwest. Products include wines, cheeses, gifts, plants, oils, kitchenware, crystal, stationery, fashion, furniture...
During the summer months street entertainers, exhibitions and demonstrations provide further interest.

Join us in our constant task of keeping up-to-date.
Please send us your comments and suggestions.

Michelin Tyre PLC
Tourism Department
Davy House
Lyon Road
HARROW – Middlesex HA1 2DQ
Tel: 081 861 2121
Fax: 081 863 0680

★★ DARTMOOR NATIONAL PARK Devon

Michelin Atlas p 4 or Map 403 - H, I32

Dartmoor is the largest of the five granite masses which form the core of southwest England; it covers 365 sq miles and offers a marvellous sense of space. The centre is **open moorland** at a height of approximately 1 000ft; to the north and west are the **tors,** with another small group in the south, the highest rising to 2 000ft; to the east and southeast lies a pattern of **wooded valleys,** with hanging oakwoods above cascading streams, fields, farms and small villages.

The moor is traversed by two roads - the Ashburton-Tavistock road (B3357) running east-west and the Moretonhampstead-Yelverton road (B3212) running northeast-southwest. Both developed from ancient **trackways** intersecting at Two Bridges *(see below),* the site of the famous **clapper bridge** similar to the one at Postbridge nearby.

Dartmoor is a **National Park** which means that it belongs to the nation as a heritage and cannot be despoiled; it does not mean that the public have a right of access any and everywhere - on enclosed land, access is by public footpaths and bridleways; *it is an offence to drive or park more than 15yds off a road.*

The land is not common ground : much, about 70 000 acres, is owned by the Duchy of Cornwall *(qv),* the rest by farmers and other landowners including Devon County Council, the Forestry Commission, the Water Authority and the Ministry of Defence. A **Commoner,** the occupier of land in a parish or manor which possesses Common Rights, may graze cattle, ponies and sheep, dig for peat, take heather for thatching and stone and sand to repair his house. All **livestock** on the open moor is owned by farmers; animals are rounded up once a year, branded or tagged and culled, with young stock being sold at the famous Widecombe *(qv)* and other fairs.

The number of visitors annually to the moor has been calculated at 8 million; the number of people who live and work in the villages and towns on the moor's edge and the few small villages upon it, 30 000.

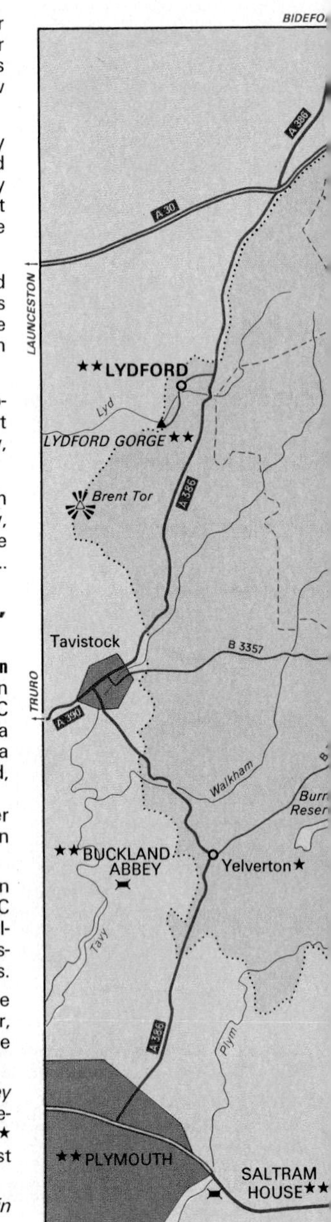

The ponies - The ponies are probably descended from domesticated stock turned out to graze on the moor perhaps as early as the Iron Age. Do NOT feed them - it encourages them to approach cars and the roads where they get run down.

The sheep - The original White Face breed has been replaced by the Cheviot with its prick ears and cumbersome dignity and the Blackfaced Scotch, which was introduced in the 1880s for its hardiness and agility.

The cattle - Galloways and Belted Galloways, black, stocky and hornless, are most often seen, also occasional groups of shaggy, long horned Highland Cattle.

The birds - Buzzards can be sighted high above the moor, and, more commonly, kestrels. There are also ravens and, beside streams, woodpeckers, wagtails, dippers...

LANDMARKS, TOWNS, VILLAGES on the Moor

Moretonhampstead - Known locally as **Moreton** (Moor Town), this was an old market town on the edge of the moor in the 14C-15C when its granite **church** was erected with a commanding **tower.** It also possesses a remarkable row of thatched and colonnaded, granite **almshouses** dating from 1637.

The early 19C **White Hart Inn** is a reminder of when Moreton was a coaching stage on the Exeter–Bodmin road.

Manaton - The village is centred on the green which is overlooked by a typical 15C moorland **church,** notable inside for its full-width **rood screen** depicting the Twelve Apostles and other saints on the lower panels.

Becky Falls ⓥ - Except in dry weather the Becky Brook cascades down from the moor, circling boulders in its rush to descend some 70ft into a wooded glade.

Haytor Rocks - 1 490ft. *5 miles west of Bovey Tracey.* The by-road from Bovey to Widecombe runs close to the rocks. The **view★** extends to the coast at Teignmouth and west towards Widecombe.

Widecombe in the Moor - *See Widecombe in the Moor.*

Buckland in the Moor – The village epitomizes the idyllic Devon village with thatched, stone cottages set in a wooded dell. The late 15C, early 16C moorstone church on older foundations is known for its clockface inscribed MY DEAR MOTHER in place of the usual numerals. Inside is a 16C painted rood screen.

Ashburton – The former stannary town *(qv)* stands on a tributary of the River Dart. When the church with its tall Perpendicular granite tower was built in the 15C, Ashburton was a wool town; the many slate-hung houses date from the 16C-18C when it was a slate mining centre.

Buckfastleigh – The market town on the southeastern edge of the moor, which inspired the Sherlock Holmes mystery *The Hound of the Baskervilles,* was once an important wool and cloth centre.
It is also the northern terminus of the **South Devon Railway** ⊙, a former GWR line, known as one of the most picturesque in England. The centre comprises engine sheds with locomotives and stock, 7¼in gauge miniature steam railway, steam traction engines and a museum.
The GWR standard gauge line has been re-opened over 7 miles, crossing the river at Staverton Bridge, where the station has been restored, and terminating at Totnes Riverside station *(connection with British Rail).*

Buckfast Abbey – *See Buckfast Abbey.*

Dartmeet – The West and East Dart Rivers descend from the open uplands to join forces and flow on through an almost gorge-like valley between wooded hillsides. Footpaths follow the course of the river for some distance.
The swift-flowing streams and the fields and woods on either bank are alive with birds including larks, dippers, green woodpeckers and the occasional heron.

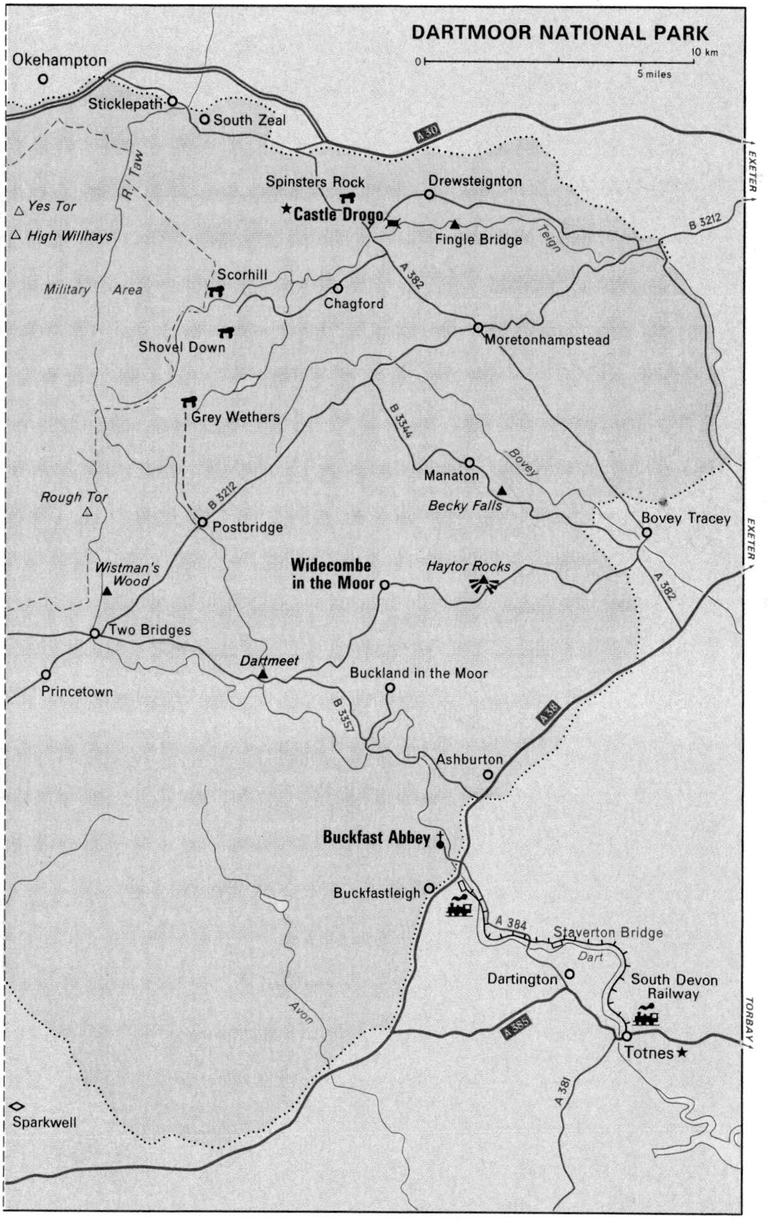

Dartmoor Ponies.

Postbridge – The **clapper bridge,** doubled by a road bridge in the 1780s, is the largest and most upstanding on the moor, with granite slabs weighing up to 8 tons apiece set on tall piles above the waters of the East Dart River. It is believed to have been constructed when tin-mining and farming were being developed in the centre of the moor in the 13C.

Grey Wethers – *6 miles Rtn on foot, northwest from Postbridge via Hartland Tor and White Ridge.* The Wethers comprise two large circles of medium-sized stones.

Two Bridges – The two bridges, one a medieval **clapper bridge,** mark the crossing of the West Dart River by the two tracks which since time immemorial have traversed the moor. Nearby was the meeting place of the old Tinners' Parliament on Crockern Tor *(northeast).*

Wistman's Wood – *3 miles Rtn from Two Bridges along a marked path from the car park.* The path leads over the moor parallel to the West Dart, a swift stream frequented by dippers. The oak trees of the wood are stunted, primeval; their living trunks, growing out of the boulder-strewn slopes, are draped in grey-green lichen. The trees appear to be self-perpetuating yet there are no saplings.

Rough Tor – 1 791ft. The tor stands out to the north of Two Bridges and Wistman's Wood at the centre of the moor.

Princetown – The town, the highest (1 400ft alt) in England, is dominated by the prison built in 1806-08 to hold Napoleonic prisoners of war – in 1809 some 5 000 men were confined in the then much smaller buildings; by 1813 with the addition of some 2 000 American sailors who refused to join the British against their own countrymen the number had increased to 9 000. After a period as a factory it was reopened as a convict prison in the 1840s (when the practice of deportation ceased).

Burrator Reservoir – The reservoir, an artificial lake ringed by wooded banks against a background of granite tors, was originally constructed in 1891 to supply Plymouth with water. It now has a capacity of 1 026 million gallons.

Brent Tor – The volcanic hill (1 130ft) which rises on the western edge of Dartmoor is distinctively crowned by **St Michael's,** a small stone church with a low stalwart tower which commands a good **view★★**.

★★ **Lydford** and **Lydford Gorge** – *See Lydford.*

Yes Tor – 2 030ft. *Within the military zone. Enquire at Okehampton.*

High Willhays – 2 038ft. The highest of the tors stands within the military zone and is not often accessible. *Enquire at Okehampton.*

Chagford – The market town, which in the Middle Ages was one of Devon's four stannary towns *(qv)* and a wool and cloth centre, stands on high ground above the Teign Valley with good **views** of the high tors and Castle Drogo.
A far-seeing vicar in the 19C recognised the town's advantages as a "headquarters for excursions" and encouraged the local people to create the moor's first tourist centre.
Old inns, one built in the 13C-16C as the manor house, and substantial small houses of ashlar granite or whitewashed cob surround the **market square** and its quaint market house known as the Pepperpot.
Overlooking all is the tall, 15C, pinnacled **church tower.** Inside are monolithic granite pillars, carved roof bosses, the tomb of Judge Sir John Whyddon (d 1575).

Scorhill Circle – *4 miles west from Chagford along Teigncombe rd to Batworthy then 1 mile Rtn over Teign footbridge.* A rare stone circle on the moor.

Shovel Down – *4 miles southwest of Chagford along Teigncombe rd to Batworthy then 1 mile south on foot Rtn.* A single stone and five stone files stand on the down from which there is a wide view.

★ **Castle Drogo** – *See Castle Drogo.*

Drewsteignton – The village, to which the nearby Castle Drogo is linked, stands high above the **Fingle Gorge** and has thatched granite and white cob houses around a central square. Overlooking the square are an early Perpendicular granite **church** and the mid-16C **Church House,** which when built served the community as a village hall.

Fingle Bridge – The three-arched granite bridge, which spans the most picturesque reach of the Fingle Gorge, was built in the 16C and has been a famous beauty spot since the early 19C. The hills rise up all round, the highest (700ft) to the north crowned by the ruins of an Iron Age hillfort (Prestonbury Castle). Riverside paths lead through the water meadows and hanging oakwoods beside the Teign.

★ DARTMOUTH Devon Pop 5 282

Michelin Atlas p 4 or Map 403 – J32 – Facilities

Dartmouth, synonymous with the **Britannia Royal Naval College** – the long, turn-of-the-century pink building on the hill – presents visitors with short and winding streets, narrow slypes, steeply stepped alleys, a Butterwalk, a pannier market, pubs, stores and antique shops rather than fine architecture, and of course the river itself.
There are ferries (one passenger, two car) to Kingswear, the Paignton Steam Railway *(qv),* boat trips and the **view★** across the estuary in which Defoe declared that 500 ships of any size could "ride with the greatest safety".
Closely encircled by hills and surrounded by the sea, the town has never grown to unwieldy size. It originated half a mile inland on either side of a creek; as it grew, first the inlet then ever more of the river bank was reclaimed, the final undertaking being the extensive gardens and embankment completed in 1930. A deepwater haven almost invisible from the sea, the town grew wealthy on sea trade – land communications even now are tenuous, the railway has never come closer than Kingswear on the opposite bank. It was an embarkation port for the Mediterranean; in the Middle Ages it traded particularly with Brittany, Gascony and Spain.
When venturing turned to the Spanish Main and the Americas, Dartmouth became the port from which the navigators Sir Humphrey Gilbert *(qv)* and John Davis *(see below)* set out and to which prize Spanish galleons were brought after capture on the high seas.
In the 17C trade concentrated in Bristol and London; Dartmouth became purely a naval port as the presence of the College testifies.

SIGHTS

Between the Embankment and the Church

Embankment – The pontoon landing stage with Victorian cast-ironwork, now the passenger **ferry embarkation point,** was built in hopeful anticipation of the railway coming to the town in the 19C.

Boatfloat – The pool, until the building of the Embankment, was the town's inner harbour.

Newcomen Engine ⊙ – In the garden just upstream, one of Thomas Newcomen's (1663-1729) atmospheric steam engines, model for 75 years for pumping-engines in many mines, can be seen impressively at work.

Quay – The Quay, fronting the Boatfloat, was constructed in 1548 when it served as the centre of the town's activity. Merchants' houses were built in the 17C along its length, four being combined and refronted in the early 19C to form the still-standing coaching inn.

Butterwalk – *Duke St.* The Butterwalk has protected shoppers in Duke Street, at the end of the Quay, since 1635 when a terrace of four shops was built with oversailing upper floors supported on eleven granite pillars. Note the **woodwork** and carved corbels.
There is an impressive **plaster ceiling** of the *Tree of Jesse* at no 12 *(ask in the shop for permission to view).*

Dartmouth Museum ⊙ – *No 6 The Butterwalk.* The panelling and the **plaster overmantel** with the arms of Charles II are 17C. The exhibits comprise principally model ships.

Pannier Market – *Victoria St – continuation of Duke St.*
The market "shops" are now occupied by craftsmen – leatherworkers, silversmiths, copper enamellers... On Fridays fresh produce is brought in by growers and sold on the stones.

St Saviour's Church – *Anzac St.* The tall, square pinnacled tower has been a landmark for those sailing upriver since it was constructed in 1372.
The **chancel** was built by **John Hawley** (d 1408; *see below*) who may be seen in a brass between his two wives *(chancel floor).* MP and mayor, merchant venturer, buccaneer, property speculator in the town, churchgoer, he was typical of the leading citizens who in the 15C brought prosperity to the town.
His fellow townsmen continued to support the church so that it was largely rebuilt in the 1630s.
Note especially the **south door** with its two ironwork lions and rooted tree of life, the medieval altar with legs carved like ships' figureheads, the pre-Reformation carved and coloured pulpit, the 16C **rood screen.**

Downstream from the Embankment

Turn up one of the alleys just below the Ferry Pontoon and, after crossin the wide Newcomen St, bear left.

High Street – The street was the shambles *(qv)* or main street of the mediev town and is still lined by houses of the period, some half-timbered, some refronte in the 18C and 19C; most notable are the early 17C, four-storey **Tudor House** (Dep of Social Security) and, on the corner, complete with its coloured and carve emblem, **The Cherub,** a late 14C, half-timbered merchant's house now an inn, wit oversailing upper floors.

Continue along Higher St and, via Newcomen Rd, into Lower St.

Agincourt House – *Lower St.* The four-storey house around a spaciou courtyard was built, as the name suggests, in the early 15C for a rich merchan it was restored in the 17C and again this century when the courtyard was glaze over.

Continue down to the water's edge.

Bayard's Cove – The "cove", a short cobbled quay, is lined by 18C town house the most attractive being the pedimented **Old Custom House** of 1739 with shell-hooded porch.

Mayflower Stone – The 180 ton *Mayflower,* accompanied by the *Speedwell,* p into Dartmouth for repairs to the *Speedwell,* which was finally abandoned, leavin the pilgrims to sail on in the *Mayflower (qv)* only.

Bearscove Castle – The now-ruined circular fort was constructed in 1537 t supplement the Castle *(see below)* as part of Henry VIII's coastal defences.

DARTMOUTH CASTLE ⊙

1 mile by Newcomen Rd, South Town and (left) Castle Rd.

The fort commands excellent **views★★★** of the estuary.
It was built in the late Middle Ages by the merchants of Dartmouth to prote their homes, warehouses and deepwater anchorage from foreign raiders.
Although their ships traded in the regular fashion, it was also the custom the day for all vessels on the high seas to turn privateer and plunder or captu any prize they might overcome. In addition raids were organised on forei coastal towns and other English ports. Booty was seized and buildings set c fire. The damage from such raids was often long-lasting. The raiders or pirat *(qv)* might number a single ship's company or several thousand men.
Dartmouth suffered two major retaliatory French raids in 1377 and 1400. 1404 the town was "invaded" by 6 000 Bretons on the rampage.
In 1336 Edward III had ordered the estuary to be protected; in 1374 John Hawl *(see above)* and others were commanded "in consideration of the damage ar reproach which might befal the town of Dartemouth through hostile invasion to fortify the same, array the men of the town and do all other things that m be necessary". By the end of the century "a fortalice" or **small fortress** had bee constructed which was reinforced in 1462 by stretching a chain across th harbour mouth to a fort at Kingswear (visible on the far bank). Twenty yea later the townsfolk, still described as "warlike", began to build the fort standi today. Edward IV and Henry VII both contributed to the cost.
The most interesting architectural fact about the castle, begun in 1481 (alter and added to in the 16C and 18C), is that it was the first in England to be design to have **guns** as its **main armament.** Gunpowder had been in use in warfare sin the mid-14C but gunports were generally inserted in old buildings and took th form of enlarged arrow slits; in Dartmouth the **ports** were splayed internally allow a wide traverse without an enlarged opening. The guns were strapp to flat wooden beds; 50 years later, in Henry VIII's forts, they would be mount on wheeled carriages and mobile. Once the castle was built, Dartmouth w never again attacked from the sea.

St Petrox – The Gothic-style church almost abutting the castle dates from 16 when it was rebuilt on a 12C site. It is believed that in its earliest days it bo a light to guide mariners navigating the narrow estuary entrance.
Of interest inside are two large and outstanding 17C **brasses** *(east end),* anoth small brass, the **pulpit** dated 1641, funeral **hatchments,** charity boards a Charles II's arms.

RIVER DART BOAT TRIPS ⊙

An exceptional number of **waterfowl** and other birds *(qv)* are to be seen on th river banks. Note also how the salt water has cut back the lower branches the trees.

West bank landmarks

Britannia Royal Naval College – *See above.*

Anchor Stone – It is said that Sir Walter Raleigh occasionally came here.

Dittisham Village – The creek, Bow Creek, is the longest on the river.

Sharpham House – The house was built on an older site in 1770 in a park design by Capability Brown. The money for the house's building came from explo such as the capture of the Spanish ship *Hermione* off Cadiz, worth £65 0 in prize money.

Home Reach – The long and narrow reach leads to Totnes *(qv).*

East bank landmarks

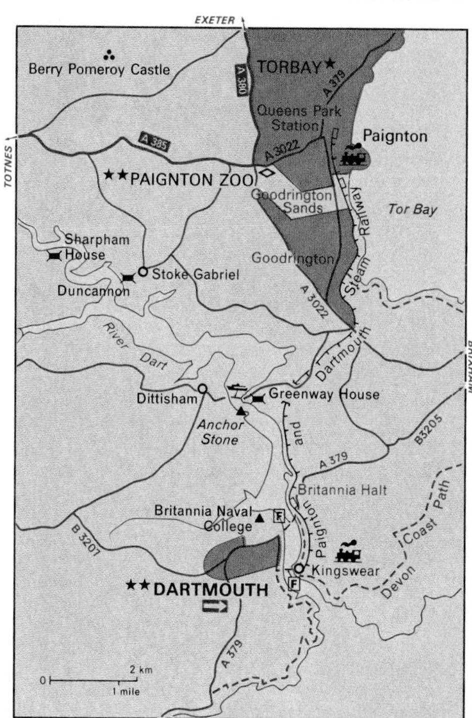

Kingswear – The 13C church tower is a prominent landmark.

Paignton and Dartmouth Steam Railway ⓥ – The train of the Paignton and Dartmouth Steam Railway *(qv)* may be seen puffing in or out of the tunnel.

Greenway House – The house, formely Greenway Court, was the birthplace of the navigator Sir Humphrey Gilbert *(qv)*, and for several years the home of Dame Agatha Christie, the murder-mystery novelist.

Stoke Gabriel – Beside the 15C church is a yew tree estimated to be 1 200 to 1 500 years old. **John Davis,** who discovered the strait between Greenland and Baffin Island while searching for the North West Passage, was baptised and married in the church.

Duncannon – The hamlet was once known for its red sandstone quarries; the tower of St Mary's Church, Totnes *(qv)* is of Duncannon stone.

EXCURSION

Start Point – *14 miles plus 1 mile Rtn on foot; south by B3205 and A379 to Torcross; west to Stokenham and south by-roads to Kellaton, Hollowcombe Head Start Farm and the track to the lighthouse car park.*
The road follows the curve of the bay fringed by long fine sand beaches and at Slapton rides the low ridge separating the lagoon and the sea. The final few miles inland are typical wooded, undulating farmland. The walk to the point and lighthouse *(qv)* is across open country with an ever increasing **view**★.

DEVIZES Wiltshire — Pop 12 430

Michelin Atlas p 17 or Map 403 O29

Devizes nowadays suggests the army – or more precisely the red brick barracks on the outskirts of the town – but from medieval times until the 19C it was an important cloth market which specialized in the narrow woollen suiting known as "drugget" – hence the number of well disposed 18C town houses, many on 17C timber framed foundations : there are more than 500 listed buildings in the ¼ square mile of the town centre.
In the early Middle Ages it was a flourishing sheep market, from which it gained its broad Market Place and evolved the medieval **street plan** which, uniquely, has been neither added to nor reduced over the past 800 years. Before even these times the spur west of the present Market Place was selected by the Normans as a strongpoint on which to build a castle which, in the early 12C, was rebuilt by Bishop Roger of Old Sarum *(qv)*. This fortification eventually became "ruinated" and was finally demolished by Cromwell's forces in 1645. The castle now on the site is a 19C fantasy *(private)*.

SIGHTS

★ **Market Place** – The long, half moon shaped Market Place with its 19C cross and fountain is overlooked almost entirely by 18C houses and a rare number of old inns – the town stands on an old coaching road.

Bear Inn – The inn, part 16C, part 18C, was known in the 18C for the portrait sketches of customers drawn by the landlord's young son, **Thomas Lawrence** (1769-1830), later President of the Royal Academy of Arts.

Northgate House – The brick house with a handsome porch (Council Offices) was the King's Arms coaching inn before becoming the house of the family for which George Eliot worked as a governess while living next door at the giant-pilastered "Sandcliff".

Black Swan Inn – The three-storey, pilastered inn, on the curving east side of the Market Place, is 18C.

Parnella House – *No 23.* The house was built *c*1740 by a doctor who decorate the front with a somewhat odd, roughly carved statue of Asklepios, the Gree god of medicine (modern copy).

No 32 – The house was the White Hart.

No 40 – The 19C Victorian-Florentine style bank was formerly the White Swa

Corn Exchange – The giantly-arcaded and balustraded building, crowned wit the gilded figure of Ceres, is 19C.

Old Town Hall – The hall, facing the Market Place from the far end, dates fro *c*1750 when it was built with an open ground floor to serve as a butter, chees and poultry market beneath Ionic columned and pedimented upper halls an offices.

Town Hall – The "new" hall of 1806, on an island site at the end of St John Street, is an elegant building with a rusticated ground floor with arched wi dows, a rounded back and a wide bow to the front, dignified by tall Ioni columns.

★★ **St John's** – The parish church, through the churchyard, is robustly Norma with a mighty oblong **crossing tower,** which inside has round arches towards th nave and chancel and pointed ones towards the transepts. The broad moulding sharp with zig-zag decoration, the spandrels and walls covered with fish-sca patterning are enhanced by the local golden stone. The chancel has low ri vaulting and walls densely patterned with intersecting arches. The Norma corbels in the chapels are carved with human faces and monster masks.
Later additions include the Perpendicular aisles, the tracery panelled ceiling ov the nave, the acanthus leaf-carved organ case.

★ **Devizes Museum** ⊙ – *41 Long St.* The delightful, esteemed museum includ a local history gallery, geology and natural history collections, an art gallery wi a stained glass window by **John Piper** (1982) and a long-famous **archeologic department** which includes clear, progressive models of nearby Stoneheng and Avebury. Among the finds on display are axe and arrowheads, dagger jewellery, pots, urns, glassware, the Stourhead Collection of gold ornaments, a outstanding bronze collection, small sculptures and a round, smiling Celtic Jan head.

Kennet and Avon Canal Centre ⊙ – *The Wharf.* The exhibition housed an old granary (1810) describes the construction (1794-1810) of the waterw which linked Bristol and London and was engineered by John Rennie, who als designed the bridges and aqueducts. Two pumping stations *(qv)* supplied wat to the locks. The impressive **flight of 29 locks** at Caen Hill is accessible by th **tow path** *(2 miles or 3½ miles or 4½ miles on foot Rtn).* Boat trips on the can are also available.

The Brittox – The shopping street with modern fronts on older houses exist in 1386 when it served as the palisaded entrance to the castle (the meani of the Norman-French *bretasche* from which the name derives).

The Shambles – The old dark street known as the Shambles *(qv)* still serv as a thrice-weekly market.

St John's Alley – *Obliquely across from the Town Hall.*
The alley is lined by a complete range of half-timbered, compact Elizabeth houses with jettied upper floors.

EXCURSION

Potterne – *2 miles south on A360.*
The village of 18C-19C houses of all shapes and sizes with shops below is align along a main street.
The **Porch House**★★ *(private),* at the south end has black and white half-timberin the beams all vertical, gables with neat ball finials, stone tiles, a two-tier h window, an oversailing upper floor and the porch itself, well advanced with oriel window beneath its independent gable. It was built when Henry VIII w on the throne.
Adjoining is a second house, gabled, stone-tiled and with the later 16 "cross-gartered" half-timbering.

★ DORCHESTER Dorset — Pop 13 734

Michelin Atlas p 8 or Map 403 - M31 - Facilities

The small county town, Hardy's home town, possesses still the house lived in by the Mayor of Casterbridge, the Old Crown Court where the Tolpuddle Martyrs were tried and the half-timbered house known as Judge Jeffreys' Lodgings, where the judge stayed during the Bloody Assizes *(qv)* when he came to "try" 290 of Monmouth's local supporters.
It also bears the imprint of the Romans, who in the 3C AD built the hilltop town they named Durnovaria either side of the London-Exeter highway, of the 16C-17C when new houses were erected along the High Street, and of the 18C-19C when those houses were refaced or rebuilt. Every owner decided his own style, producing façades of infinite variety.
Today Dorchester is a popular destination for tourists and shoppers alike, providing good amenities within an attractive setting.

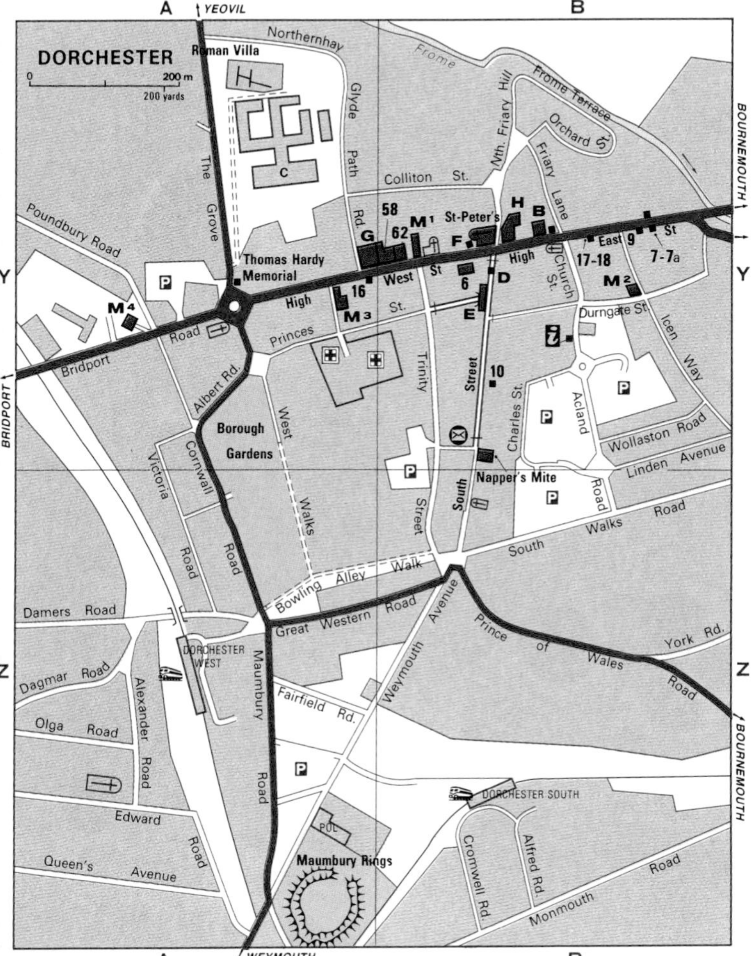

MAIN STREETS

High East Street (BY) – The brick and stone **town hall (H)** with a steepled **clock tower** is 19C.

King's Arms (B) – The inn is 17C, re-faced with Doric columns during the 19C Classical revival; the house and shop opposite, **no 24,** is of the same date.

Nos 31-33 and no 9 – The shopfronts are 19C.

Borough Arms, nos 45 and 7-7a – The inn and houses are all 17C.

Nos 36 and 17-18 – The houses, much altered, date back to the 16C.

South Street (BY) – The street is marked at its opening by **Cornhill,** a pedestrian precinct characterized by a stone **obelisk (D)** (town pump) and the 16C-19C **Antelope Inn (E)** *(see below).*

No 10 – The three-storey, late 18C house (now a bank) of lustered brick headers with redbrick dressings is where the Mayor of Casterbridge lived in the novel of that name by **Thomas Hardy** who, when he left school, worked at no 62, an architect's office, before he went to London.

Napper's Mite – The bell-gabled almshouse was founded by Sir Robert Napper in 1615.

High West Street (ABY) – The street opens with the much restored **St Peter Church,** with its 12C doorway and multi-pinnacled tower and, inside, 14C **milita monuments** and 17C **pulpit** and communion table.
Before the church is a statue of **William Barnes (F)** (1800-86), schoolmaster, lingui and pastoral poet in English – *Linden Lea* – and the Dorsetshire dialect; burie in the porch is the Puritan rector **John White** (1575-1648) who organised a refug for North Atlantic Dorset fishermen which led to many settling in the futur Massachusetts.

No 6, Judge Jeffreys' Lodgings – The judge made his way from the house to th assizes at the Antelope by a secret passage, it is said, for fear of the mob. Th house with its gabled roofline and jettied upper floor is the town's onl half-timbered building.

Old Crown Court (G) ⊙ – Inside the Classical Shire Hall of 1797 is the old Crow Court with the dock in which the six **Tolpuddle Martyrs** *(qv)* stood on 19 Marc 1834. The benches, judge's chair and George III royal arms are 18C.
Outside, note the distances incised on the pale stone.

Old Ship – The inn was built as a coaching inn in 1600.

No 62 – The shopfront is mid-19C, the original bay window above fifty yea older.

No 16 – The house is similar to no 62 but with two upper bays.

No 58 – The house with a rounded doorway is early 19C.

Thomas Hardy Memorial (AY) – Right of the West Gate roundabout at th top of the street sits the figure of Thomas Hardy, a posthumous portrait bronz (1931) by **Eric Kennington** *(illustration p 121).*

MUSEUMS

★ **Dorset County Museum** (BY M1) ⊙ – *High West St.* Three collections combir to make the museum outstanding : the Thomas Hardy Memorial, the Maide Castle Gallery and the fossils.

Thomas Hardy Memorial – The Thomas Hardy (1840-1928) archive is house in a splendid **Victorian gallery** with slim, cast-iron painted pillars supportin a balcony and high glass roof, and Roman mosaics paving the floor. The colle tion includes original drawings for his novels, furniture and pictures fro his house and his study at **Max Gate,** the house he designed for himself o the Dorchester-Wareham road, where he died on 11 January 1928. Oth **Dorset Worthies** celebrated here are William Barnes *(see above),* Admiral S Thomas Hardy (1769-1838) who is also commemorated near Abbotsbu *(qv),* and the painters James Thornhill (1675-1734) and Alfred Steve (1818-75).

Maiden Castle Gallery – The history of Maiden Castle *(qv)* and the artefac discovered when it was excavated in the 1930s and 1980s are displayed i the context of other sites in the county of the same active period.

Fossils – Lyme Regis *(qv)* is the great fossil area of England : on display are fos outlines of leaves and fish imprinted on rocks, ammonites, ichthyosaurus an plesiosaurus, the footprints of a dinosaur, also maps and diagrams of curre prospecting and **oil exploitation** in the county.

Rural Craft Collection – An extensive collection of implements used in Dorset f three centuries to the end of the horse age.

Dinosaur Museum (BY M2) ⊙ – *Icen Way.* This small but lively museum revea all sorts of information on dinosaurs using fossils, skeletons and models; amor the array of display panels and videos stand full-size reconstructions of th enormous creatures. A musical video *(upstairs)* traces their evolution and eventu extinction.

Tutankhamun Exhibition (AY M3) ⊙ – Dorset's connection with ancient Egy lies primarily with the eccentric collector William Bankes of **Kingston Lacy** *(q* this exhibition, however, tries to clarify the mystery of Tutankhamun's identi and houses replicas of some of the treasures found in his grave.

Dorset Military Museum (AY M4) ⊙ – *Bridport Rd.* Combining the histori the heroic and the personal, this regimental museum includes battle honour log-books, despatches and diaries telling of campaigns fought under Clive in Indi in the Napoleonic wars, in the War of Independence, in 1914-18, 1939-45, Ireland, Korea... Colour is provided in the old barracks gatehouse by dress ar battle uniforms – extraordinary headgear – kettledrums and cartouche boxe regimental silver, swords, arms, insignia, trophies. The proud record runs fro the raising of 39th Foot in 1702 to the formation of the **Devonshire and Dors Regiment** in 1958 to the present.

ROMAN REMAINS

Roman Villa (AY) – *North of High West St, behind the County Hall.*
A rich man's town villa has been excavated to reveal the walls and a numb of mosaics.

Maumbury Rings (AZ) – *Weymouth Avenue (A354) – Maumbury Rd cro roads.*
The rings, a Neolithic henge, were remodelled by the Romans to provide seatin pens for wild animals and an arena. In the 17C the Parliamentarians convert the rings into a gun emplacement.

EXCURSIONS

★ **Maiden Castle** – *2 miles southwest off Weymouth Rd (A354). See Maiden Castle.*

Hardy's Cottage, Higher Bockhampton ⊙ – *2½ miles northeast along A35 and ½ mile south up a minor road, then 10min walk from car park.*
The "small low cottage with a thatched pyramidal roof, and having dormer windows breaking up into the eaves, a single chimney standing in the midst" was built by Hardy's great-grandfather early in the 19C. Downstairs are the modest living rooms and the office from which the elder Hardy conducted his business as local builder and smallholder; upstairs is the bedroom where Thomas Hardy was born and given up for dead until rescued by the midwife. The garden is pleasant with herbs and simples.

★ **Athelhampton** – *6 miles northeast on A35.*

Puddletown – Pop 946. The village lies back in an oasis of calm : the "square" of small houses, neatly white-painted or colour-washed, the grey stone Perpendicular **church★** with a pinnacled and crocketed tower a few yards away. The interior of the church is remarkable for its **17C furnishings** and its **monuments :** the oak box pews, three-decker pulpit and prayer-desk, Norman beaker-shaped font, the west gallery with the arms of England and France and 16C black-letter texts on the walls.
From 1485, when Sir William Martyn came to Athelhampton *(qv)*, part of the church became a family chantry for which Sir William had his own, very fine, **funeral effigy** carved in alabaster some twenty years before his death in 1503.

★ **Athelhampton** – *See Athelhampton.*

The A35 continues east to Tolpuddle (qv) and Bere Regis (qv).

★ **Cerne Abbas** – *8 miles north by the Sherborne road (A352).*

Godmanstone – Pop 117. The village has what is reputedly the **smallest inn** in the kingdom, the Smith's Arms, a 17C flint and stone building of one room, snug and warmly thatched.

Cerne Giant – The figure outlined in the turf stands 180ft tall and carries a club 120ft long; his head and eye are respectively 23ft 6in and 2ft 6in across; his feet are in profile. Although he is thought, for obvious reasons, to be associated with ancient fertility rites, the giant's origin and date remain unclear *(see also Chalk Hill Figures, qv).*

Turn around and take the first turning on the left.

★ **Cerne Abbas** – Pop 573. The village main street, bordered by shops and a couple of very old inns, intersects with Abbey Street where there stands a beautiful **range of 16C houses,** timber framed upon brick-coursed flint; carved corbels support jettied upper floors.
The Benedictine abbey, after which the street is named, was founded in 987 and dissolved in 1539. The house (*private;* much rebuilt after a fire) aligned to the street, with a centre gable and angle buttresses, was built as the main gateway to the abbey. The ruined porch to the abbot's hall remains in the undergrowth in the wood to the right.
In *c*1300 the monks gave the village a **church,** St Mary's, the Early English chancel of which was retained when the nave and aisles were rebuilt in the 15C. The spectacular Ham Hill stone **tower** with its statue of the Virgin and Child is 16C.
Of note inside are the **arcades** of attached columns with ring capitals, the **table altar** of 1638 *(south aisle)*, the **testered pulpit** of 1640 and Jacobean **communion rail,** 18C **chandelier,** 14C wall paintings *(chancel)* and the **stone screen** (15C).

16C houses, Cerne Abbas.

Charminster – *1½ miles northwest by A37 and first turning right.*

Charminster Church – St Mary's has a splendid **west tower** of three stages rising to battlements and crocketed pinnacles, presented by Thomas Trenchard of Wolfeton House *(see below)*. The excellent carving properties of Ham stone were relished to the full by the sculptors who created a profusion of gargoyles, grotesques, corbels, angels and the double T monogram of Thomas Trenchard.

The body of the church with its round **chancel arch** and massive circular pillar dates back to the 11C-12C; note the **nail-head decoration** and, at the northeas end of the nave, the purple-pink **pomegranates** which, being similar to thos in Seville Cathedral, are said to have been stencilled by craftsmen sent ove after Philip of Hapsburg and his wife, Joanna, daughter of Ferdinand an Isabella of Spain, had sheltered from a storm at sea in Wolfeton House i 1506.

Wolfeton House ⊙ – A **gatehouse** of massive, but dissimilar, round towers guard the entrance to the former Elizabethan manor house, built by Trenchard in th 16C.

In the house, the **screens passage** with a stone-groin **vault** above linenfol panelling is embellished by a **stone staircase** (*c*1580) with a pierced balustrad and stone caryatid, also by two Jacobean **porch doorways,** robustly carved wit moustachioed Romans in sandals carrying cutlasses and a club-carrying ancier Briton.

The stairs lead through the 16C pedimented doorway to the **Great Chamber** wher a floor-to-ceiling stone fireplace of *c*1600, exotically carved with Red Indians an Orientals, remains from a once fine room.

The Jacobean porches open into the plaster-decorated parlour and dinin room.

The garden offers a good view of the early 16C **south front** with its candle-snuffe buttress, stair-turrets, transomed windows...

A number of Touring Programmes is given at the beginning of the guide.
Plan a trip with the help of the preceding Map of Principal Sights.

★ DOWNSIDE ABBEY Somerset

Michelin Atlas p 16, 17 or Map 403 – M30 Stratton-on-the-Fosse

Downside is the senior Benedictine monastery in England.

The Community of St Gregory the Great was founded in 1605-07 at Douai i northern France by English and Welsh Benedictine monks who had been traine abroad since the Reformation. Among their number were priests who travelle to England on missionary work.

In 1793 Douai University was suppressed by the French Revolution, th Benedictines were put under guard and the monastery was ransacked. Althoug Catholicism was still officially proscribed in England, the penal laws were n being enforced and in 1794 the Community crossed the Channel and, after brief interval, settled at Stratton-on-the-Fosse in 1814.

The community today numbers 45 members; the school about 500 boys. Th buildings *(private),* which include a 17C-18C mansion known as Old House, hav multiplied in every architectural style current in the last 150 years.

★ ABBEY CHURCH ⊙ *½ hour*

The abbey church was built in the neo-Gothic style between 1870 and 193 only the tower (166ft) acknowledges the Somerset tower tradition; the ri vaulting is in the 13C French style. The internal proportions are cathedral-lik (330ft long and 74ft high). Colour is provided by the windows, pictures an statuary.

Nave – The austere nave – very tall, narrow and of white stone – is by Gile Gilbert Scott.

North Transept – The transept contains the altar and shrine (a gilt oa casket) of **St Oliver Plunkett,** hanged in 1681, the last Roman Catholic to die Tyburn. Note the windows with St Aldhelm and St Dunstan.

Holy Angels Chapel – The Flemish school triptych of the *Adoration of th Magi* is 16C.

St Placid Chapel – Note the old oak **statue** of the Madonna, a Spanish 16 **reliquary** and a very old oak **statue,** a copy of Notre Dame de Foy near Dinan Belgium.

St Sebastian Chapel – A 15C Italian painting of a bishop hangs in the chap by Sir Ninian Comper (1864-1960).

St Sylvia's Chapel and Sacred Heart Chapel – One chapel contair a modern relief of the Crucifixion while the other has modern ceram panels.

Lady Chapel – The all-gold chapel was decorated by Sir Ninian Comper.

St Benedict's Chapel – The **bosses** on the groined vault depict the arms the 54 Benedictine abbeys and priories dissolved by Henry VIII.

South Aisle – Both the **Virgin and Child,** from the Upper Rhineland, and the statu of **St Peter** *(west end)* are believed to date from the 15C.

⋆ DUNSTER Somerset

Pop 793

Michelin Atlas p 7 or Map 403 - J30 - Facilities

Dunster is an exceptional small town in a beautiful setting on the northern edge of Exmoor. Its name derives from *dun* or *dune*, a ridge of hills, and *torre*, a fortified tower; its landmark is the Conygar Tower, an 18C embattled folly high on a hilltop, and its symbol the dormered Yarn Market in the centre of the High Street.
By 1197 Dunster had developed into a chartered borough with a flourishing coastal and continental trade exchanging beans and barley for Welsh wool and Bordeaux, Spanish and Italian wine; by the 15C-16C the sea had retreated - it is now two miles distant - and the town had become a wool market and weaving centre. Today, in season, the town is a popular tourist destination.

⋆ CASTLE

The red sandstone castle high on its tor dominates the town, its rugged appearance of towers and battlements belying its age but not its history : a fortification has stood on the site for over 1 000 years. In Saxon times the hilltop probably served as a frontier fortress against the Celts and Northmen. The present castle, however, is largely 19C.

The de Mohuns and the Luttrells - Two families only have owned the castle throughout the centuries : William de Mohun (d 1155), who accompanied the Conqueror and was rewarded with the office of Sheriff of Somerset, built a Norman-style fortress upon the tor and a priory in the town. By 1374, however, the de Mohun line was dying out and the castle, three manors and a Hundred were sold for 5 000 marks (£3 333) to Lady Elizabeth Luttrell. After possession by successive Luttrells who preferred action on the field and in politics to husbandry in Somerset, the castle came in the late 16C to George Luttrell who reconstructed the residential quarters within the medieval walls and in the town rebuilt the Yarn Market and remodelled the Luttrell Arms.

17C to 19C - The castle defences were put to the test in the Civil War : first Thomas Luttrell, a Parliamentary sympathiser, capitulated, paid a fine and allowed the Royalists to occupy the stronghold; then, in 1645 Robert Blake *(qv)* laid siege to it until, after 160 days, peace was negotiated. Parliament gave orders that Dunster was to be slighted : the curtain walls fell but destruction of the house and gateways was stayed - the owner paid a hefty fine and swore allegiance to Cromwell.
A new phase opened in the late 17C when **Col Francis Luttrell** and his rich bride, Mary Tregonwell of Milton Abbas *(qv)*, inherited the castle. They spent extravagantly on clothes and on the decoration of the house but in 1690 the colonel died and all work ceased.
Apart from construction of the **Conygar Tower** folly in 1765, little was done until 1867 when **George Fownes Luttrell** inherited the 15 374-acre property. He promptly called in the architect **Anthony Salvin** to enlarge and reconstruct the castle to its present appearance of a fortified Jacobean mansion.

TOUR ⏲ *45min*

Gatehouse - Walk through the 15C gatehouse, which was part of the medieval castle, and the forecourt, formerly the castle lower ward.

Halls - The various periods of construction are evident throughout the castle. The first hall was created in the 19C; the portrait of **Oliver Cromwell** is contemporary but the wooden overmantel is a Jacobean pastiche.
The second, **inner hall,** is a 16C-17C adaptation of the medieval castle's great hall, complete with the original Jacobean spider-web **plaster ceiling** and **overmantel,** decorated with the Luttrell arms. On the wall between the hall archways hangs an **allegorical portrait** (1550) by **Hans Eworth** of *Sir John Luttrell,* in which, like a triton, he dominates the Scottish storm or forces who had opposed Henry VIII.

Dining Room - The panelled room displays one of the most beautiful moulded **plaster ceilings** in southwest England. It was installed in 1681 by Col Francis and Mary Luttrell *(see above)* whose portraits hang over the fireplace and whose arms are displayed in the frieze. Adjoining is a small panelled **serving room** with another remarkable **ceiling.** The black lacquer long-case clock has a 1730 movement.

Grand Staircase - The staircase with another great **ceiling** forms the climax of Francis and

Luttrell Staircase, Dunster Castle.

Mary Luttrell's alterations : the stairs rise in three shallow flights around a square well; a carved flower-filled vase stands on each newel post, a handrail frames the 4in-thick elm **balustrade,** carved and pierced to illustrate a swirling pattern of acanthus leaves and flowers, inhabited by cherubs and hounds at the chase; a pile of Charles II silver shillings dates the carving as 1683-84. The portrait of an unknown *Young Cavalier* is by Edward Bower *(qv).*

Upper rooms – After the stair-hall, the upper rooms are an anti-climax except for the **views★** from the windows. Among the furnishings, nevertheless, are late 18C **mahogany seat furniture** reputed to be by Thomas Chippendale (Morning Room), hand tooled and coloured **leather wall hangings** depicting the meeting of Antony and Cleopatra, the former moustachioed and both ringleted and costumed in 17C fashion (Gallery), a 1620 overmantel illustrating the *Judgement of Paris* (King Charles' Room), a great arched fireplace in the Billiard Room and late 18C satinwood tables and painted seat furniture (Drawing Room).

Circle the castle and walk down through the gardens beside the River Avill or, if the castle is closed, along Church St, West St and Mill Lane to the mill.

★ **Dunster Water Mill** ⊙ – The mill stands in an idyllic setting beside the River Avill; its machinery runs throughout the open hours. The intregral museum displays traditional agricultural machinery and tools.

The mill, rebuilt and improved at intervals since Domesday, ground corn until the late 19C when it was abandoned. In 1939-45 it came back into temporary wartime use; in 1979-80 the present tenants rebuilt and restored it – a task involving re-roofing with 20 000 random Delabole slates *(qv),* copper nails and roof lead, re-making the overshot water-wheels, rebalancing the phosphor-bronze bearings, re-dressing the stones...

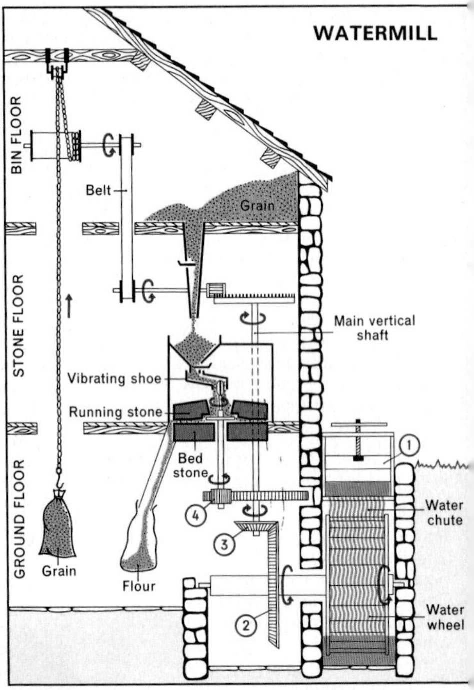

Water power – The diagram is applicable to all water-wheels and to windmills with the obvious difference that in the latter the main vertical shaft is powered from above. At Dunster the two overshot water-wheels, both fed by the one chute controlled by a sluice gate (1), are 12ft in diameter by 3ft 6in wide, with oak spokes and shrouds and 40 elm-wood buckets each holding about 10 gallons of water (100lb approximately); 16 buckets are full at any one time which means that each wheel carries just under 1 ton of water; both wheels turn 4-6 times a minute. The **pit wheel** (2) turns the wallower (3) and main vertical shaft 4 times to the water-wheel's once; the **spur wheel** (4) with applewood cogs, drives the stones gear 7 times faster – the running stone, therefore, turns 4 x 4 x 7 or 112 times a minute to produce 1cwt of flour in 15-20 min or 1½ tons a day per pair. Mills often used one pair of stones for flour, a second for animal feed.

The **stones,** 4ft across, each have an "eye" and one also a "swallow", to receive the grain from the runner; both are "dressed" or "feathered" and "furrowed" – highly skilled incising to reduce, grind and finally expel the flour. These incisions could take up to a week to do.

Mill-stones were made of one piece or of many lumps or burrs of particularly hard rock, principally from quarries in Derbyshire. The burrs would be fitted together and bound with a number of white-hot iron hoops. As the hoops cooled they cinched the rock into a solid mass; as the stones wore down the hoops would be removed – old mill-stones, sometimes seen in farmyards, are often quite thin.

Note how quietly the mill runs.

Before returning to the town, turn left off Mill Lane to go through the car park.

The twin arched **packhorse bridge** over the River Avill leads to the open Exmoor countryside.

TOWN

High Street – The long, very wide street, characterized by the unique yarn market, is bordered on either side by 17C-19C houses with shops at ground level.

Yarn Market – The octagonal, dormered market was most recently rebuilt in the 17C.

Luttrell Arms – The inn dates back to *c*1500. Inside, all still centres on the **Great Hall** with its hammerbeam roof, twelve-light window and huge fireplace with 17C overmantel.

Molly Hardwick Doll Collection ⊙ – *Memorial Hall, right side.* Among the 700 dolls, some date back two centuries.

Church Street – The street is marked by buildings related to the priory founded in 1090 *(see above)* and dissolved in 1539.

Nunnery – The so-called building, slate roofed with slate-hung floors above a stone ground floor, dates in part from the 14C when it was built as the priory guest-house.

Priest's House – The half-timbered house of the same date was over-restored in the 19C.

★ **Dovecote** – The dovecote, which stands beyond the gate in the end wall of the Priory Garden behind the church, is a 20ft high, early medieval pigeon house, round in shape with a conical slate roof.
Inside are over 500 L-shaped **nest holes** set in 4ft-thick stone walls. They are reached by a **ladder** attached to two arms fixed to a central, 400 year old **pole** made of ash. A 3in-long, solid metal cone has been lodged at the pole base enabling it to revolve upon a 7in, dome-headed pin set in the oak floor beam. At the top a pin protrudes from the pole to revolve in a replaceable oak shoe fastened to the exact centre of the cross-beam.
Pigeons pair for life and have a breeding life of 7 years; for most of the year, the breed kept for food laid and hatched two eggs every 6 weeks; the squabs were removed at 6 weeks when they weighed 16oz. Meat production, in a good year, could have amounted to 3 tons.

★ **St George's Church** – The red sandstone parish church, which was built by the Normans in 1120 on an early Christian site, was rebuilt by the monks in the Early English style (1333-55) and extensively rebuilt (1842-76) by the Luttrell family. The **tower** (110ft) was erected in accordance with a contract (1443) which stipulated that it should have a "batylment and pynacles... three french botras (buttresses) and gargoyles". It contains a clock (1876) and a separate carillon which plays a different tune each day of the week at 0900, 1300, 1700 and 2100hrs.

Interior – Beneath the **wagon roof** the nave and aisles are divided from the chancel by a wide **screen** (54ft), an example of local carving with blank panels below cusped and traceried openings separated by slender columns, which branch out into a strongly sinewed fan vault and richly carved friezes. It survived both the Parliamentarians and the Puritans as it was built not as a rood screen, although it carried the three figures of the Holy Rood until 1548, but on the orders of the Bishop of Bath in 1498 to settle a long running dispute between the priory and the parish.
Note also the 16C Perpendicular **font** with quatrefoils carved with Christ's wounds and the instruments of the Passion; two iron-bound chests (12C-13C) and one in the form of a desk (15C) *(south aisle, east end);* Charles II's coat of arms *(nave north wall);* the 19C bench-ends; the 20C ambo. Among the **funerary monuments** are a lady of *c*1300 in a wimple beneath a canopy *(chancel),* the gravestone, bearing a foliated cross, of Adam de Cheddar, Prior of Dunster (*c*1345-55) *(south transept),* a brass of John Wyther (d 1497) and his wife *(nave, west end),* a Jacobean tomb of 1621, the Luttrell tombs, particularly one dated 1428, and a selection of Luttrell **hatchments** (17C-18C) hanging on the walls.

EXCURSIONS

★ **Cleeve Abbey** – *5 miles southeast on A39. See Cleeve Abbey.*

Combe Sydenham Hall ⊙ – *10 miles southeast on A39 and B3188.*
The house, beyond the gatehouse which incorporates a stone arch believed to be of *c*1450, was built to a typical Elizabethan E shape by Sir George Sydenham, father of Elizabeth (*qv,* d 1598), whom Sir Francis Drake married as his second wife in 1585.
Expansion, demolition, rebuilding and further neglect sum up the history of the hall until its rescue by the present owners who have been restoring the house, gardens and grounds, the mill, trout stream, fishponds, creating a birds of prey care centre, nature trails...
Among the rooms completed are the **Great Hall,** the 18C staircase and panelled sitting room and the Restoration banqueting room. On the stone flags in the Great Hall is a cannon-ball which weighs over 100lbs and may be a meteorite but is known locally as **Drake's cannon-ball.** Legend has it that, although Drake had wooed her before going to sea, Elizabeth Sydenham was at the church door when the ball hurtled through the air to fall between the would-be bride and stranger groom. Drake sailed into Plymouth on the next tide...
The cornmill is again in working condition and new trails have also been marked out.

★ DYRHAM PARK Avon

Michelin Atlas p 17 or Map 403 – M29 – 8 miles north of Bath

The building of the house – Dyrham Park presents a rare contrast in its two 17C-18C fronts. One is an example of formality and symmetry; the other, equally Classical, is lightened by touches of Baroque ornament. Both were built within ten years for the same man, William Blathwayt who inherited Dyrham through his marriage.

William Blathwayt (1649-1717) was an efficient administrator and diplomat in the service of the Stuart kings and of William III. His taste had been formed by his uncle, Thomas Povey of Lincoln's Inn, who was a connoisseur, man of fashion, *bon vivant* and friend of Samuel Pepys and John Evelyn. Although he married an heiress and became rich through his appointments, Blathwayt maintained that he "never pretended to any fortune".

Blathwayt's first architect took back the existing Tudor house to the Great Hall and built instead a formal, perfectly regular entrance front of loca stone.

In 1698 the second building phase began. Blathwayt chose as architect this time "the ingenious **Mr Talman**", Comptroller of the Royal Works, second to Sir Christopher Wren, a travelled squire, collector and maverick architect Talman's façade of Cotswold stone, 130ft long with two storeys and an attic the same balustrade and urns as on the other side, is mellowed by such touches as rustication of the ground floor, quoins, alternate pediments and carved panels above the first-floor windows, Tuscan pillars framing the door...

An additional "dressing" is the orangery with round-arched windows, added in 1701.

Inside, the contents of the rooms have barely changed since they were recorded in an inventory by Blathwayt's housekeeper.

Garden and park – To complete the house, Talman and the garden designer George Wise, laid out formal gardens of parterres, fountains and waterworks including a stepped cascade.

By the turn of the 18C-19C there had been developments in the design of garden *(qv)* and the Bath – Gloucester road had been improved, exactly reversing the best approach to the house : the fronts were accordingly inverted and **Humphre Repton** was called upon to replan the park.

TOUR ⏲ *45 min*

East Entrance Hall – The walls are hung with richly embossed **leather,** purchased at 3*s* a skin when Blathwayt was in the Hague, where he may also have obtained the blue and white **delftware.**

Great Hall – The hall is all that remains, and that only in name, of the Tudo house. The sash windows – though the sills have been raised – and the **boo presses** (to the design of Samuel Pepys) were there in Blathwayt's time, as wer the pictures of the monarchs he served and **portraits** by Michael Dahl of himse and Mary Wynter, his wife. The fine set of Dutch walnut "parade" chairs date from *c*1700.

West Hall – Note the **delft tile pictures** of exotic scenes and fruits by the fireplace 17C **muskets** and Blathwayt's own "under and over" holster **pistols,** the firesid companion "pareing of an apple", the **Cromwellian chairs** re-covered in Dutch leathe in *c*1700.

White Stair – By the staircase are **licences** of 1511 and 1620 to enclos 500 acres as parkland, a **Kyp engraving** (1712) and a drawing of the grounds afte the Repton replanting.

The virtuosity of the *Great Perspective* painting at the top of the stairs was muc admired by 17C London society, notably Pepys, when it hung in Thomas Povey' rooms.

Other rooms – Among the furniture and furnishings note especially the perio **blackamoor torchères** and delft flowerpot still standing in the chimney as recorde in 1710 (Balcony Room); the early 18C **Flemish tapestries,** bed and its hanging and **tortoise-shell chest** (Tapestry Room); the two **Rococo mirrors** by John Linnel gilded side-table, Murillo's *Peasant Woman and Boy* and the most un-Spanis copy by the young Gainsborough (Drawing Room).

The **Cedar Staircase** is cantilevered.

The gilt **Leather Closet** was especially designed to further increase the pers pective in the illusionist *View down a Corridor* painted in 1662 by Hoog traeten.

The **Mortlake tapestries** belonged to Povey who was a director of the factor (Diogenes Room); the **state bed** was ordered for a proposed state visit by Quee Anne in 1704 when the Carolean stools were re-covered in the same materi as the bed hangings.

ADDITIONAL SIGHTS

Dyrham Church – *Access by road through the village or up from the garde* The church with an embattled tower, a porch with quatrefoil parapets an Perpendicular windows was rebuilt at different periods in the 15C. The **Flemis triptych** is 15C.

Dyrham Village – Pop 260. The village of 17C-18C stone houses and cottage is named in the *Anglo-Saxon Chronicle* as the site of the key battle of 577 aft which the West Saxons advanced to the Severn Estuary, dividing the Briton in Cornwall from those in Wales.

EDINGTON Wiltshire — Pop 686

Michelin Atlas p 17 or Map 403 – N30

Edington is where, in 879, **King Alfred** *(qv)* finally defeated the Danes. It is also where William of Edington, Bishop of Winchester (1345-66), Treasurer and Chancellor to Edward III, was born and decided in 1351 to rebuild the existing church as a chantry, soon afterwards enlarged into an Augustinian monastery. The monastery was later dissolved, the church given to the village.

★ **St Mary, St Katherine and All Saints** – The church (150ft long) was built in the transitional period between the Decorated (reticulated tracery) and Perpendicular periods (upright, straight-sided panel tracery).
A massive, low, crossing **tower,** a three-storey porch and a twin turreted west gable, framing a wide Perpendicular window over a processional door, are the striking exterior features.
Inside are great clustered columns in golden stone, 17C and 18C pink-and-white and all-white plaster **ceilings,** and a double **chancel screen** or monastic pulpitum of *c*1500 with seats between the trellises and a gallery above. The **chancel,** the Decorated part of the church, has a combined Decorated-Perpendicular window and 14C canopied niches with lively figures. In the north transept, the Crucifixion window is 14C.
The furnishings are principally Jacobean : the testered pulpit (with 18C stairs), the font cover, the **communion rail** with alternating flat and turned balusters and a row of points possibly following Archbishop Laud's injunction to keep "dogs and cows" away from the altar. The monuments are older : three early 14C-15C knights, one with his lady, and a partly coloured tomb *(south transept)* of a blue-robed monk; the barrel or tun at his feet and the sprigs of bay suggest a rebus of his name – Bayton.

★★ EXETER Devon — Pop 103 000

Michelin Atlas p 4 or Map 403 – J31 – Facilities

The skyline of Exeter has been dominated by the twin towers of its cathedral since the 12C. The city's history began some 1300 years earlier when a settlement was established by the local **Dunmoniorum** tribe on the westward-sloping hillside at the limit of the navigable waters of the River Exe. In the 1C AD the Romans captured the settlement, built it up as their most westerly strongpoint and brought it out of isolation by extending the London-Silchester-Dorchester road to it.
A monastery was founded in what is now the cathedral precinct during the early peaceful **Saxon** period, which lasted until 876 when, despite the efforts of **King Alfred** *(qv)*, **Danish invaders** began a series of raids. After the final devastation in 1003 the city was rebuilt and in 1050 Edward the Confessor authorised the translation of the metropolitan see to Exeter from Crediton *(qv)*.
Further tribulations followed. The citizens defied William the Conqueror until 1068 when he marched upon them with 500 horsemen; after 18 days they capitulated. During the **Wars of the Roses** the city changed sides more than once. In 1497 it resisted **Perkin Warbeck's** assault with 600 men; in 1549 it was unsuccessfully besieged by the rebels against the imposition of the English prayer book. In the Civil War Exeter fell first to the Royalists; it was then captured and ransacked by the Parliamentarians and became a minor centre of royalist plots; royal toasts were drunk at an inn in the Blackboy Road. In 1671 the **Black Boy** himself, Charles II, came to Exeter to acknowledge the support he had received. His brother James II, however, was not popular; the citizens gave their support to the **Duke of Monmouth** *(qv)* – 80 local men were condemned at the Bloody Assizes – and later turned out into the streets to welcome the future William III.
Guided tours ⊙ of the city are available.

Exeter Cathedral.

★★ CATHEDRAL (Z) ⏲ *1 hour*

Edward the Confessor appointed Leofric as the first bishop in 1050 (d 1072). The builder of the cathedral's distinctive **transept towers** was Bishop William Warelast (1107-37), nephew of the Conqueror; the builder of the cathedral church much as we know it today was **Bishop Walter Bronescombe** (1257-80) who, while retaining the transept towers, remodelled the major part of the 12C building. The work was finally completed a century later under **Bishop John Grandisson** (*qv;* 1327-69) who was buried in a chapel built within the thickness of the wall of the final achievement, the Decorated west front image screen.

Exterior – On the Green in front of the Cathedral sits the figure of **Richard Hooker,** priest and scholar (1553-1600). The cathedral itself, of grey-white Beer stone, rises through buttresses and flying buttresses, windows of five lights and Decorated tracery, to crocketed pinnacles and castellated parapets. The long lines are massively interrupted by the twin but not identical towers which mount solidly through tiers of rounded blind arcading and intersecting arches to castellations and the angle turrets with pepperpot roofs, substituted in the 15C for the traditional Norman pyramids.
At the west end, one good idea was obviously superimposed upon another : the upper gable window is half-hidden by the main window which, in turn, is masked at the base by the pierced parapet edging the splendid late 14C – early 15C **image screen.** This bears 3 rows of fine stone figures : God the Father; Apostles and Evangelists *(top row)*; King Richard II and many unidentified figures.

Nave – The striking **vaulting** extends 300ft from west to east in an uninterrupted line of meeting ribs with huge gilded and coloured bosses studding the junctures. The ribs fan out from shafts which descend through the triforium stage to important gilded and coloured **corbels** between the pointed arches of the arcade, in turn supported on **piers** of sixteen clustered columns with plain ring capitals.
Note also in the nave the **minstrels' gallery** *(north side)* with 14 angels playing contemporary musical instruments – bagpipes, a recorder, viol, harp; the west **rose window** with its reticulated tracery (20C glass); the great **corbels,** each illustrating as many as three biblical themes.
Except at the crest, the view east is blocked by the pulpitum, a pierced stone screen of 1320, surmounted by a top-heavy organ.

Chancel – The high altar stands before the **Exeter pillar,** the prototype of all the pillars in the cathedral with sixteen shafts and ring capitals.
Through the just pointed arches on either side can be seen the clustered pillars of the ambulatory and the Lady Chapel and, above, the late 14C **east window** containing much original glass.
The 19C canopied choirstalls incorporate the oldest complete set of **misericords** in the country – 49 in number, carved in 1260-80.
The **bishop's throne** (1312) is a fountain of Gothic wood carving in oak, entirely held by pegs – which has enabled it to be twice dismantled in times of danger : during the Commonwealth (17C) and in 1939-45.
The double-canopied, Decorated **sedilia** are 13C.
The 13C effigy in black basalt, on a later gilded and canopied tomb, is **Bishop Bronescombe** *(see above).*

North Transept – Note the Bishop Grandisson **15C astronomical clock** with the sun and moon revolving round the earth.

CATHEDRAL CLOSE (Z)

The close is diamond shaped with the cathedral at the centre almost abutted to the southeast by the gabled, red sandstone bishop's palace. Marking the limits are the old **city wall,** a small spired church, a school and some houses, and a curving line of tall 17C-19C shops and houses ending in a white, Georgian four-storey hotel.

St Martin's Church (Y) – Pinched into the northern corner of the close is the minute red sandstone church, dedicated in 1065 and rebuilt in the 15C.

St Martin's Lane (Y 19) – The alley cuts through between the church and the hotel to the street.
On one side is the **Ship Inn,** half-timbered, heavily beamed, dark and brightly lit and as crowded as in the days when Drake, Hawkins and the queen's admirals used to meet inside.

Cathedral Close Walk (YZ 6) – The northeast side of the close begins at the black and white painted **Mol's Coffee House,** a four-storey house of 1596 beneath an ornate gable with windows extending across its full width. It is also reputed to be one of Drake's onetime haunts.
Small shops with bay windows below, oriels above, merge into Tudor beamed houses with oversailing upper floors over possibly older red sandstone ground floors, and beyond, neat, porched, 18C houses of brick with stone trims.

New Cut – At the east end, New Cut leads out of the close beneath a 19C **cast-iron footbridge** complete with the donors' names.

Southernhay (YZ) – The double terrace of 18C three-storey houses in brick with stone trims, iron railings and tall, rounded ground-floor windows and doorways encloses a broad central garden of trees, lawns and vivid flower-borders.

EXETER

Street	Grid	Street	Grid	Street	Grid
Bedford Street	Y 5	Alphington Road	Z 2	New Bridge Street	Z 13
Fore Street	Z	Barnfield Road	YZ 3	Paris Street	Y 14
Guidhall Shopping Centre	Y	Cathedral Close	YZ 6	Princesshay	Y 16
High Street	Y	Coombe Street	Z 7	Quay Hill	Z 17
		Cowick Street	Z 9	St Martin's Lane	Y 19
		Edmund Street	Z 10	Sidwell Street	Y 23
		King Street	Z 12	Stepcote Hill	Z 24

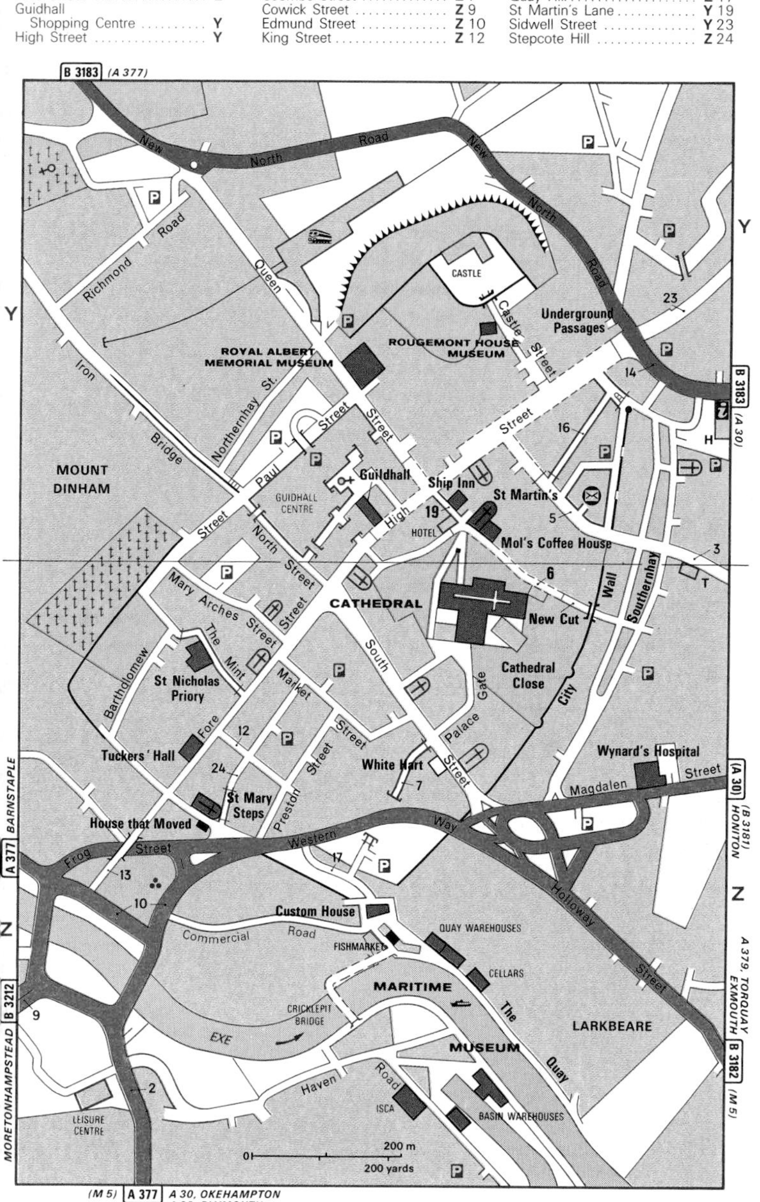

MARITIME MUSEUM (Z) ⏲ *1½ hours*

The unique collection of over 100 fascinating and extraordinary boats from all over the world is accommodated in four period buildings around the canal basin, where the floating craft can be boarded.

Grouped largely according to use (fishing, racing, exploration, living on, transport, feats of courage) the selection reveals similarities and differences in method and materials : wood, reed, straw, bamboo, fibreglass, sheathed in birch bark or seal skin, sails made from sections of flat reeds, beautifully woven together like cloth... Their shapes are long and thin, deep and wide, round : an Italian gondola, a Hong Kong junk, a Fijian proa, a Shetland fourern, a skiff from the Orkneys, rafts, kayaks, curraghs and coracles, fishing luggas, guffas from Iraq, Arabian dhows, sampans from the Far East, the boats of lone Atlantic oarsmen, *Bertha*, Brunel's Drag Boat (1844), *St Canute* – a Danish steam tug, once the ice-breaker and fire-fighter in Odense harbour – and the evocative *Argo*, a modern replica of a classical Greek galley, which retraced the journey of Jason and the Argonauts. Conservation work is carried out by a shipwright and volunteers in the ISCA building (1903) *(stairs to the first floor; through the double doors to the balcony; stairs down to the shop floor at the left-hand end).*

The exhibits in the entrance building (1835) illustrate the five main methods of boat building with craft from every continent.

Quayside – *Access by the Butts ferry or the Cricklepit Footbridge.* The quay dates from earlier days when Exeter was a tidal river port. The period of prosperity was brought to an abrupt end in the 13C *(see Topsham, below).* When after

300 years of litigation, which Exeter won, the corporation sought to re-open th port in the 16C, the river was no longer navigable so the first **ship canal** in Englan was dug (1563-66). The cliffside cellars, which contain a collection of Portugues fishing boats, are flanked by two **warehouses** (1835). At the north end of the qua opposite the old fishmarket, stands the **Custom House** (1680), a symbol of th canal trade at the time and one of the first buildings in Exeter to be constructe of **brick** which was probably imported as ballast from Holland. The **Quay Hous Interpretation Centre** ⊙ is housed in another 17C building, on the site of the origin 1574 Tudor dock; its projecting roof sheltered goods during loading ar unloading. The centre presents models, paintings and artefacts and a video o the history of Exeter.

ADDITIONAL SIGHTS

★ **Royal Albert Memorial Museum** (Y) ⊙ – The Exeter-made **watches and clock gallery** and the unique gallery of 16C-19C **Exeter Silverware** provide the high poin of the general interest museum, housed in a fine Victorian building.
Exeter was for long an assay town with a large number of gold and silversmith jewellers and clockmakers working in the city. On display are communion cup alms dishes, tankards and flagons, Apostle spoons, a baby's sucking bottl Georgian coffee and chocolate pots, cream jugs and tea pots... The work wa little influenced either by the Baroque style of the Huguenots, who did not trav this far west, or by the French Rococo favoured in George II's reign, but retaine its purity of line almost until the 19C. A separate case holds a beautiful beque of 60 **West Country spoons** (16C-17C).
The Devon Gallery in the Natural History section presents the geological featur of the county together with its flora and fauna.
Several well-known artists with local connections are represented in the A Gallery.

Guildhall (Y) ⊙ – The Tudor portico was added in 1593 to, it is believed, th oldest municipal building in the country, erected in 1330 on a possibly Saxo site.

Chamber – The hall has a timber roof of 1468-70 and outstanding oak **panelli** with no two panels carved alike. Note the bear and ragged staff supporters Warwick the Kingmaker and the Yorkist cause, the Caroline chairs, the mayor regalia of several periods, the great 18C brass **chandelier** and the **portraits** Princess Henrietta daughter of Charles I, born in the city, and of the Devoni General Monck first Duke of Albemarle (1608-70), Parliamentary and lat Restoration land and sea general.

Rougemont House Museum (Y) ⊙ – This elegant Regency house (176 standing in its garden beside the old castle gate, houses major tempora exhibitions.
The history of the house is described in a video.

St Nicholas Priory (Z) ⊙ – *Brass rubbing.* The red stone building is the form domestic and guest wing of a small Benedictine priory founded in 1087 ar suppressed in 1536.
The **entrance hall, undercroft-crypt** with massive round columns supporting low, sto ribbed vaulting, the kitchen and, upstairs, the large **guest hall** with an arch brac roof, also the adjoining solar and bedrooms, are furnished with 16C-17C table chairs, chests, a painted **virginal** of 1697 and a tester bed and cradle.

Tucker's Hall (Z) ⊙ – The hall of the Weavers, Fullers (Tuckers) and Shearme created in 1638 when a 15C chapel was divided horizontally, is an examp of Devon high craftsmanship in oak with its **barrel roof** and carved **panelling.** No the **royal arms,** the **boards of benefactors,** also the items discovered when the fal plaster ceiling was removed – halberds, pikes...

Underground Passages (Y) ⊙ – *1 hour.* The cut rock or stone built passag were part of an aqueduct system; a video in the Interpretation Centre and a to explain their history.

Stepcote Hill (Z 24) – The hill with shallow cobbled steps and a centre runr is lined on either side by small, adjoined stone and half-timbered 16C house

St Mary Steps (Z) – The 16C, red sandstone church at the bottom of the h is known for its clock which has **striking jacks.**

House that Moved (Z) – The tall Tudor merchant's house (now a shop) wi oversailing upper floors was so named in 1964 when it was transport 75yds.

White Hart (Z) – The 14C-15C inn, which has massive beams, flagged floo dark panelled rooms and a courtyard, was the house of William Wynard, Record of Exeter.

Wynard's Hospital (Z) – The almshouses *(private),* an attractive group cottages surrounding a cobbled courtyard containing a well, were founded Wynard *(see above)* in 1435 to house 12 poor and infirm citizens and a chapla

Exeter University (Y) – *2 miles north of the city centre via Queen St and Ne North Rd.*
The University, numbering 5 000 students, is mostly situated in new buildin including the Northcott Theatre, on the undulating 350-acre Streatham esta the grounds are recognised as the most beautiful and botanically interesting any British university.

EXCURSIONS

★ **Killerton** – *7 miles northeast by B3181. See Killerton.*

★ **Cullompton** – Pop 4 478. *14 miles northeast by B3181.*
The market town comprises a long main street punctuated by shops, a Tudor manor house (now a hotel), the Walronds of the same date, small courts and alleys and the occasional Georgian house.
Over-riding all is the 120ft red sandstone tower of **St Andrew's Church★**, vast and Perpendicular throughout on a much older site. Inside are a richly painted and gilded **barrel roof**, an equally magnificent **rood screen**, aisles with diamond-patterned roofs and the 1528 Lane aisle with pendented fan vaulting. At the west end note the Jacobean oak gallery on wooden Ionic columns and the medieval **Calvary** or Golgotha carved from a single oak trunk. The external carvings depict 16C cloth machinery.

Topsham – Pop 3 499. *4 miles south on B3182.*
The small port on the point of land between where the Rivers Exe and Clyst flow into the long Exe Estuary reached the height of its importance in the 13C when Isabella, Countess of Devon, built a weir across the river and successfully diverted all trade from Exeter to Topsham *(see Quayside, above)*. Boat-builders set up yards, craftsmen, dockers and sailors appeared on the waterfront and, in the 17C, merchants built the Dutch gabled houses still to be seen along the Strand.
Its heyday has passed but Topsham retains an old-fashioned charm; it is pleasant to stroll along the High Street into Fore Street and the **Strand** to look at the old, half-timbered pubs, the **Shell House** with its hooded doorway, the sailing dinghies on the river and the birds *(qv)* on the mud flats.

Topsham Museum ⏲ – Housed in a late 17C merchant's house, the museum includes period rooms, a sail loft and estuary gardens; it recounts the history of the Exe Estuary, local shipbuilding and maritime trade and includes exhibits on **Honiton lace and lacemaking.**

★ EXMOOR NATIONAL PARK Somerset and Devon

Michelin Atlas p 6, 7 or Map 403 – I, J30

Exmoor is the smallest (265 square miles) of the National Parks, extending into Devon along its western limits but lying largely in Somerset as a 1 200-1 700ft ridged plateau west of the Brendon Hills.
The moor offers a wide range of beautiful scenery from bare upland ridges covered in blue moor-grass, bracken, deer sedge or heather, to great hollows, wide valleys enlivened by streams trickling over stones, or wooded ravines, silent except for birdsong and a rushing torrent.
Three of the moor's rivers, descending 1 500ft in 4 miles, drain into the Bristol Channel.

Exmoor.

Exmoor Forest – In the early Middle Ages the forest was one of many unenclosed, uncultivated tracts of land where game, notably red deer, was preserved for the royal hunt; by 1300 the Royal Forest had been reduced to 20 000 acres around the headwaters of the principal rivers; since 1508 much of the land has been leased out to pasture – as many as 30 000 sheep and additional cattle now graze it between March and October, and ponies all the year round. The stock has always belonged to local farmers, for the moor has been settled since prehistoric times.
In 1818 the last 10 000 acres of the Royal Forest were sold at £5 an acre to **John Knight,** a Midlands ironmaster, who set about revolutionizing farming on the moor : by the end of the century a pattern had been set of isolated farmsteads breeding beef and sheep on the uplands for finishing in the valleys. Between 1800 and 1940, when agriculture everywhere in England sank into decline, the moor looked as though it would take over once more; since 1945 however, the pattern has resumed, with owner-occupiers and tenants farming 50-300 acres with flocks of breeding ewes and small herds of cattle.

The ponies – Exmoor ponies, brown, bay or dun in colour, have a characteristic **mealy-coloured muzzle** and inside ear. The quick intelligence and distinctive head show clearly the Exmoor pony's direct descent from the horses of prehistory.

The red deer – The deer on Exmoor are also descendants of the animals c prehistoric Britain. It is estimated that there are now 500-600 on the moor. The live in the woodlands close to the deeper river valleys and are wild, elusive an seldom seen.

The cattle – The cattle, usually in herds of 25-30, are horned Devon Reds, know as the "Red Rubies" of the West Country.

The sheep – The flocks of 200-250 sheep a time are for the most part th traditional Exmoor Horn breed or the Devon Closewool.

LANDMARKS, TOWNS, VILLAGES on the Moor

★★ **Dunster** – *See Dunster.*

Timberscombe – The village of reddish stone houses with slate roofs, straddlin the A396 just south of Dunster, has a Perpendicular **church★** with an early 18 castellated west tower which was crowned in the 19C with a pyramid roof. Insid beneath the wagon roofs, note the **rood-screen** with carved dado, coving an cornice.

Combe Sydenham Hall – *See Combe Sydenham Hall.*

Wheddon Cross – The crossroads and minute village which stand at 1 200ft, th highest point reached by roads on the moor, are a good **vantage point★** from whic to view Dunkery Beacon *(3 miles west)*, the Brendon Hills and deep, woode valleys.

★★★ **Dunkery Beacon** – *Access from A396 : turn west into B3224 at Wheddon Cros take the second turn right to Dunkery Gate, then follow the path, 3 miles Rt* The 1 706ft beacon, the highest point on the moor, is visible for miles arour and from its summit commands **views★★★** of sixteen counties, so it is sai

★ **Winsford** – Streams run on all sides through the village with the result that with yards there are **seven bridges,** the oldest being the **packhorse bridge** over the Riv Exe *(by the vicarage).*
The **green,** shaded by huge trees, is marked by old thatched houses and cottag and the Royal Oak which has a thatched roof which folds and turns as it tuc up the corners of the rambling old inn.

★ **Dulverton** – Sited 450ft above sea level amid beautiful scenery, the "capital" villa of the area is characterised by a solid **church** with a plain 13C west **tower** (re of the church rebuilt in the 19C) on a hillock at one end and by an old sto bridge with five arches between cutwater piers above the River Barle at th other.
Between, the **main street** and **market square** are appointed with shops, a 19 market-house, stone terrace houses and colour-washed cottages, som thatched, others with broad chimneys built up from ground level. Along back path to the church is a terrace of small Georgian houses.

★★ **Tarr Steps** – *Access from B3223; parking in car park only, then 6 minute walk down steep path – car turning point only at the bottom or continue through the ford.*
The finest **clapper bridge** in the country crosses the River Barle at the centre of an open, wooded valley. The 180ft causeway of 15 "arches", built of flat stones laid upon uprights in the stream bed with many of the stones weighing 2 tons or more and not local in origin, dates certainly from the early Middle Ages and probably centuries earlier. It has often been swept away by floodwaters and as often been rebuilt.

Withypool – The village, which stands beside one of the only two commons on the moor, boasts an ancient Norman font in the church (largely rebuilt 1901) and an old **bridge,** one of only four across the Barle.

Exford – The central green is the heart of the village, with the occasional farmstead and cottage on surrounding hillsides. Exford is the home of the Devon and Somerset Staghounds and at the centre of the hunting country. The **church★**, to which the blacksmith in 1532 left £3 towards "the makying of an yled" – now the only ancient part of the building – contains a 14C octagonal **font** with quatrefoils and a 15C oak **rood screen** with panelled coving and a cornice of richly carved friezes.
The choirstalls were presented by Queens' College, Cambridge.

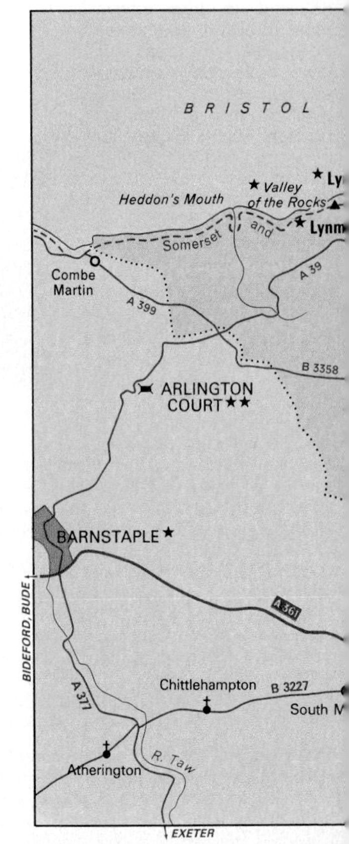

Simonsbath – The village, the centre of John Knight's *(see above)* and his son's operations in the 19C, stands on the River Barle where the Lynton road meets the main east-west road across the moor. The church, with its slate-hung west wall, the school, many of the houses, even the east windbreak of mature beech trees, owe much of their form to the Knights. The **hotel** was built as a royal hunting lodge.

Combe Martin – *See Combe Martin.*

Heddon's Mouth – *See Heddon's Mouth.*

★ **Valley of the Rocks** – *See Valley of the Rocks.*

★ **Lynmouth and Lynton** – *See Lynmouth and Lynton.*

★ **Watersmeet** – *See Watersmeet.*

Oare – Oare, mentioned in the Domesday Book, lies in a green valley only a couple of miles from the sea and owes its fame entirely to *Lorna Doone (see below)* by R D Blackmore. The 14C-15C **church,** with a tower rebuilt in the mid-19C when much else was restored, is the one in which John Ridd and Lorna Doone were married and the north window the one through which Carver shot at Lorna. Note the 18C painting of Moses and the 18C-19C **box pews, pulpit** and desk.
Blackmore's grandfather was a typical, mostly absent, rector of the village in the 19C.

★ **Doone Valley** – *Access from Oare : 6 miles on foot Rtn, 1½ hours.*
The valley came to fame in 1869 with the publication of R D Blackmore's novel *Lorna Doone,* based on tales of a group of outlaws and cut-throats who settled in the Badgworthy Valley in the 1620s and were not expelled until the 1690s.
The path from Oare *(see above)* to the coomb via **Badgworthy Water** and **John Ridd's Waterfall** attracts some 30 000 visitors each year.

★ **Culbone** – *See Culbone.*

★ **Porlock** – *See Porlock.*

★ **Luccombe** – The village is an attractive cluster of cottages, post office and shops, set on the hills southeast of Porlock. A tall embattled tower rises above the 16C Perpendicular **church**★ which has a barrel **roof** decorated with large bosses carved with solemn faces.
Luccombe is a good centre for walking : to the Dunkery Beacon *(6 miles Rtn; see above),* and by woodland paths to Webber's Post, a well known local viewpoint *(7 miles Rtn).*

Allerford – *Page 171.*

★ **Selworthy** – *Page 171.*

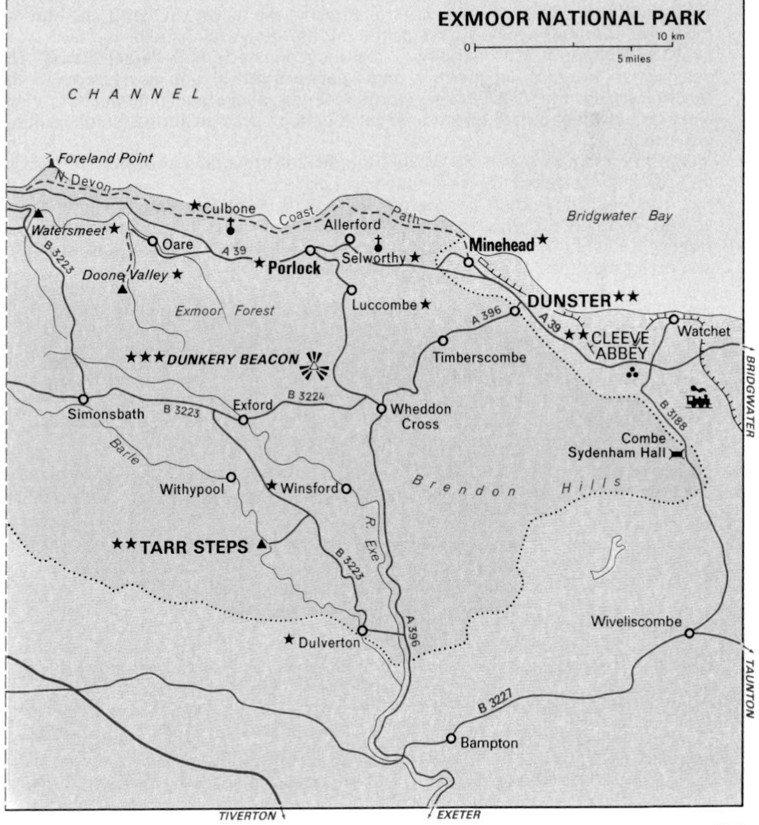

EXMOUTH Devon

Pop 28 037

Michelin Atlas p 4 and Map 403 – J32

Exmouth was a port in pre-Roman times; in the Middle Ages it was subject to North African and other pirate raids and was supplying ships and men for English return ventures.
In the 18C it went with the fashion and determined to become Devon's first watering place : Georgian terraces were built such as those in Bicton Place and on the **Beacon,** where among the early tenants were the sad wives of Lords Nelson (no 6) and Byron (no 19).
The **beach** of fine sand is two miles long.

Littleham Church – *1 mile east along Maer Lane (Sandy Bay Rd).*
The church, which stands on an older site and serves as Exmouth parish church, was begun in 1234; Drakes's aisle (north) was added in 1528.
The **hammerbeam roof** was rebuilt in the 19C using the original 15C carved oak **bosses** and **angels.** The piers with unusually carved **capitals** are of Beer stone. The lectern (13C) was made from an old oak beam. The **rood screen** is early 16C. The late 15C **glass** *(north aisle, 3rd window)* depicts Christ with a reed and crown of thorns.
Lady Nelson, who is buried in the churchyard, is commemorated on a memorial in the chantry chapel.

St John in the Wilderness – *1½ miles northeast; north off A376, Budleigh Salterton Rd.*
The church with its unique **boss** has had a chequered history. After rebuilding in the 15C it was first abandoned then demolished except for the tower and north aisle. In 1936, as restoration work was nearing completion, King George V died and, in anticipation of the coronation of the new king, a boss with the cypher **ER VIII** – the only one ever to be carved – was set in the chancel roof.
In the churchyard *(southeast corner)* is the grave of the Romantic artist, **Francis Danby.**

★ **A la Ronde** – *2 miles north by Exeter Rd, A376 and Summer Lane. See A la Ronde.*

★ FALMOUTH Cornwall

Pop 17 810

Michelin Atlas p 2 or Map 403 – E33 – Facilities
Town plan in the current Michelin Red Guide Great Britain and Ireland

From Pendennis Castle on the point a low ridge runs inland dividing the town in two; the hotel-residential district looks south over Falmouth Bay while the old town with its waterfront faces north up the Fal Estuary, which is always known by its Cornish name of the **Carrick Roads**. It is in fact a drowned river mouth which drains the waters of the Fal and its two tributaries the Tresillian and the Truro. The hotels and tourism began with the arrival of the railway in 1863; the harbour town, by contrast, evolved over centuries, the quay being built in 1670.
In 1688 Falmouth was appointed the most westerly **Mail Packet Station.** The designation brought prosperity : ships called making regular passage to the Mediterranean, the West Indies, North America; docks and boat-building yards were established; a mail coach service to London was instituted; ships required provisioning.
It was to Falmouth that HMS Pickle brought Collingwood's despatch on **Trafalgar** *(qv)* for it to be taken by mail coach to London.
For 150 years Falmouth prospered; then ships turned to steam and the port waned. Today the town's economy relies largely on tourism, cargo handling and **yachting** – Falmouth is a major sailing centre and plays host to important annual summer races (see Calendar of Events, *qv*).

OLD TOWN

The Waterfront – The frontage which extends for over half a mile from Greenbank Quay to the pier is paralleled inland by the shop-lined Market and High Streets. Note the white, porticoed Custom House of 1814. There is no continuous path along the waterfront; access to different quays and slips is through the alleys and opes descending from the main street.

Greenbank Quay – The quay and 19C hotel stand on Penny-come-Quick or more properly Pen y Cwn Gwic which is Cornish for Headland in the Valley of the Creek.

Prince of Wales Pier – *The embarkation point for river cruises.* The river, between Greenbank Quay and the pier, is overlooked by 18C houses and warehouses standing on the 17C harbour wall which was built after the Dutch fashion with large stone slabs set endways on to the sea and piled without mortar to allow slight play.

North and Custom House Quays – The quays, which enclose the inner basin, date back to *c*1670. At the landward end of the Custom House Quay stands a strange, square brick chimney, known as the King's Pipe, which was built to burn contraband tobacco.

Maritime Museum ⊙ – *Bell's Court, off Market St.* The small local museum focuses on the history of the packet ships in particular and has, among its many and varied exhibits, a fine collection of model boats and ships.

The Moor – The main "square" occupies the site of a former creek; the large, cream coloured building at the bottom of the square *(northeast side)* was built on wooden piles and straw.

Packet Memorial – The monument commemorates the long-standing importance of the Packet Service to the town: the first of the Falmouth Packets sailed in 1689.

Art Gallery ⏱ – The town gallery, housed in the **Municipal Buildings,** has an interesting collection of maritime, Victorian and early 20C paintings (Dame Laura Knight, Henry Scott Tuke, Alfred Munnings, J W Waterhouse's study for the *The Lady of Shallot*) and a painting of the *Reconstruction of the Pyramid, Arwenack* (1830; *see below*).

High Street – The street, lined by the older shops and buildings in the town, leads up to the former Town Hall (now an antiques market) where the last case of cannibalism in England was tried.

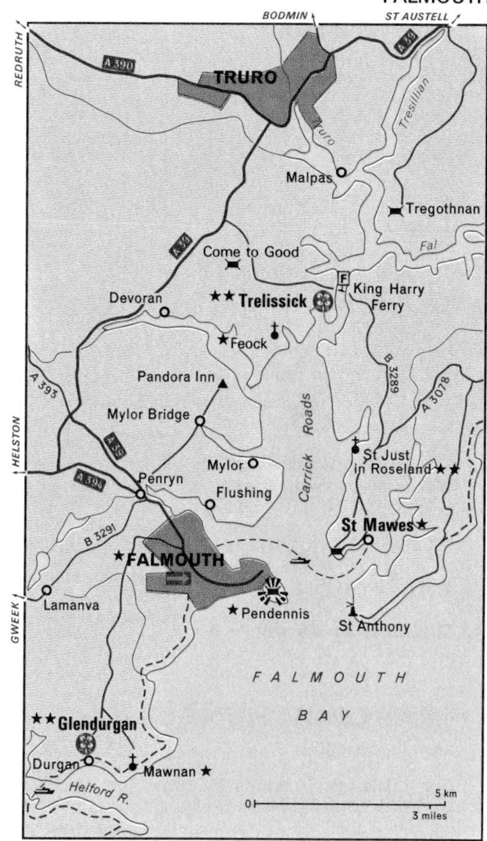

Arwenack Manor – *Grove Place.* Though redeveloped, Arwenack Manor incorporates the remains of Falmouth's oldest building : the 16C wall of the old Banqueting Hall is still visible *(left)* from the street, together with the manor's 16C possible gatehouse *(left wing)* and northwest corner *(right wing).* First records of Arwenack date back to the 14C when Jane, daughter of Robert of Arwenack, married a member of the Killigrew family. In 1544 John Killigrew became the first governor of Pendennis Castle *(see below)* and the house began to be enlarged. Sir Walter Raleigh was a guest at Arwenack.

Killigrew Monument – Although the **pyramid** *(opposite the house),* erected by a member of the Killigrew family, bears no inscription it is believed to be dedicated to the memory of the Killigrews.

Port Pendennis – *Behind Grove Place and Bar Road.*
The smart development consists of colour-washed houses surrounding an exclusive marina.

★ **Pendennis Castle** ⏱ – In the face of "pretensed invasion" in 1539-43, Henry VIII began to fortify the coastline, erecting two forts at Falmouth and St Mawes *(qv)* to safeguard the mile-wide entrance to the Carrick Roads. Crossfire overlapped and, as Carew *(qv)* put it, "St Mawes lieth lower and better to annoy shipping, but Pendennis standeth higher and stronger to defend itself". Elizabeth increased the defences against surprise Spanish raids. The challenge finally came in the Civil War : St Mawes yielded without a shot being fired but Pendennis withstood a 23 week siege before starvation brought submission in August 1546. Pendennis commands a superb **view**★★. Note over the entrance the royal arms with the Tudor lion and Welsh dragon supporters, also the splayed gun ports. In the keep are arms and an exhibition of coastal defence.

BOAT and FERRY TRIPS

★ **Cruises to Truro** – The banks are densely wooded with oak trees down to the water's edge where the birds *(qv)* include herons, cormorants and waders. Villages with a church, an old pub and half a dozen moored craft line the inlets : boathouses, slipways, laid-up ships of up to 30 000 tons and ships on the move mark the course; above are open fields, more woods, a church or two, houses in their own parkland.
Landmarks include :

★ **Pendennis Castle** – *See above.*

★ **St Mawes Castle** – *See St Mawes.*

St Anthony Lighthouse – *See Lighthouses (qv).*

Flushing – The village was founded in the 17C by Dutch settlers.

Penryn – The ancient, still-working quarry village lies far up the creek.

Mylor – The 16C-17C church has a gable turret, detached belltower and weather-boarded upper storey. The village, now a yacht and pleasure craft centre is a short distance further up the inlet which is straddled at its end by Mylor Bridge.

★★ **St Just-in-Roseland** – East bank : church and separate village. *See St Just-in Roseland.*

Pandora Inn – At the mouth of Restronguet Creek on the west bank lies the 17C whitewashed and thatched inn, possibly a former smugglers' hideaway.

Devoran – On the same creek, Devoran was once a tin and copper port.

★★ **Trelissick** – The house and grounds occupy a promontory where the Fal widens out into the Carrick Roads. *See Trelissick.*

King Harry Ferry – *See King Harry Ferry (qv).*

Tregothnan – The large 19C Georgian mansion was built from the proceeds of privateers *(qv);* it has a cluster of slim octagonal turrets and chimneys and can be seen on the point where the River Truro joins the Fal.

Malpas – The town lies at the junction of the Truro and Tresillian Rivers.

Truro – The town is two miles further upstream. *See Truro.*

★ **Cruises up the Helford River** – The scenery is predominantly pastoral. There are no stops, few houses, two landmarks : Durgan hamlet *(qv)* and Gweek Sea Sanctuary *(qv).*

★ **St Mawes** – *By ferry. See St Mawes.*

EXCURSION

★★ **Glendurgan Garden** – *4 miles southwest. See Glendurgan Garden.*

★ FARLEIGH HUNGERFORD CASTLE Somerset

Michelin Atlas p 17 or Map 403 – M, N30

The **castle ruin** ⏲ stands guard on the Wiltshire-Somerset-Avon border.
In 1369-70 Sir Thomas de Hungerford, a Wiltshire squire and onetime Speaker of the House of Commons, bought Farleigh manor house; he subsequently fortified it, transforming it into a rectangular walled castle with five-storey angle towers with conical roofs.
In 1420-30, Sir Thomas' son increased the castle to the south by the addition of an Outer Court enclosed by a new wall, towers and the two-storey East Gate which is still the entrance. Also enclosed by the new perimeter was the 14 St Leonard's Chapel, formerly the parish church.

★ **St Leonard's Chapel** – From the 16C west porch, steps lead down into the nave (1350) which contains a chaplain's funerary stone (*c*1480), a 12C font and a giant **wall painting** *(right of the east window)* of St George killing a now invisible dragon.
Under the wide semicircular arch in the chantry chapel, added by Sir Thomas in 1380-90, are the remarkable **Hungerford funeral monuments** of Sir Thomas (d 1398) in chain mail and his wife (d 1412) in cloak and mantle; beyond, beautifully carved in white marble, are the Parliamentarian, Sir Edward Hungerford (d 1648) and his wife.

★ FORDE ABBEY Dorset

Michelin Atlas p 7 and Map 403 – L31 – 4 miles southeast of Chard

The abbey is a synthesis of three major building phases and stands in garden which has taken owner-gardeners three centuries, notably the 20 to perfect.
The Cistercian monastery was 400 years old and still very much abuilding under its 32nd abbot, **Thomas Chard,** when it was dissolved in 1539; the following century of neglect ended in 1649 when the estate was bought by **Sir Edmund Prideaux** Cromwell's Attorney-General. In the next seven years he saved, knocked down and rebuilt Forde Abbey until it looked much as it does now. In the 19C the abbey was bought by ancestors of the present owners.

TOUR ⏲ *45min*

Exterior – The range extends from west to east with the main entrance at the centre beneath the Perpendicular **tower;** to the left lies the **Great Hall** with its t windows; beyond were the abbot's lodgings, remodelled by Prideaux in the 17 when he also castellated the front. Right of the entrance lay the cloisters which the north gallery remains, now glazed and surmounted by an upper storey; between the tower and cloister gallery Prideaux inserted, on the site the west cloister, a loggiaed and balconied two-storey block where he placed his **saloon.**
On the far right is the **chapel.**
Note the 16C tower's **two-storey oriel** with its mullioned and transomed window and friezes matching those above the Great Hall.

Interior – Just inside the entrance, the fan vault is visible above, still unfinished as at the Dissolution.

Great Hall – The hall has its original panelled ceiling but has lost its early proportions, the west end having been walled off in the 17C to create a separate dining room. Furnishings include an oak refectory table (1947), the royal arms, an 18C chandelier, 16C-17C chairs.

Grand Staircase – The staircase is spectacular, having an enriched plaster ceiling (1658) and a carved bannister, a mirror image of which has been painted on the surrounding walls.

Saloon – The room has a coved ceiling, moulded with fruit and flower garlands, small pendants and the Prideaux arms enriched with gold. The side panels portray *The Slaying of Abel* and *The Sacrifice of Isaac* with everyone in Commonwealth dress. The **Mortlake tapestries** are after the Raphael Cartoons now in the Victoria and Albert Museum, London.

Library – The former refectory was created as a second eating place in the 15C when the Cistercian order was permitted to eat meat; as not all the monks approved the concession, the community had two refectories. Note the recess for the reader's desk, and the 15C roof; the 19C Gothick windows and fireplace and the end screen made out of Breton box-bedsteads.

Monks' Dormitory – The dormitory range, above an 11-bay undercroft, is 160ft long with lancets along the outer wall. It was divided down the centre in the 19C when it was also given a new vaulted ceiling. The **gun** is an 18C French pinnace gun.

Return to the ground floor.

Chapel – The chapel, with Norman rib vaulting, round columns and scallop capitals, has been repeatedly remodelled, most vigorously in the 17C.

Consult the Map of Places to Stay at the beginning of the guide to choose a suitable location.

★★ FOWEY Cornwall — Pop 2 092

Michelin Atlas p 3 or Map 403 – G32 – Facilities

The attraction of Fowey (pronounced "Foye") lies in the exploration of its quay, houses, yards, church and museum; in the prospect of walks out towards Gribbin Head, or of boat trips round the harbour and the coast – where the cliffs rise dark and sheer from the water – or upriver between slopes densely wooded with oak, past small creeks and the china-clay quays with long tails of loaded railway wagons. Another pastime is just to watch the **river** while ships of up to 10 000 tons – British, French, Belgian, Swedish, Danish, Norwegian, Spanish, Italian, German – come in to load the clay; fishing boats set out in the evening; small yachts moored at Polruan swing with the tide; launches and rowing boats manoeuvre the waters; the pilot vessel comes and goes; the dredger keeps the channel clear; the ferries ply; fearsome rocks appear and disappear as the tide turns...

SIGHTS

Town Quay – Bordering the square, which marks the centre of the town and the waterfront, is an old inn, the **King of Prussia** *(qv)*, named after an 18C smuggler. The adjoining building was the fish or butter market with the counting house on the floor above.

Trafalgar Square and Lostwithiel Street – The second square is overlooked by the 18C granite ashlar **town hall** (*museum* ⊙), built over a 14C building, once the local prison – note the grilled window. **Toll Bar House** which dates back to the 14C, 15C and 18C and the **Ship Inn** opposite, built by the Rashleighs *(see below)* as a town house in the 15C, were linked by a bridge-room. Inside the inn are a carved ceiling and, above a fireplace, a marriage inscription : John Rashleigh – Ales Rashleigh 1570.

St Fimbarrus – *South St.* The 14C-15C church with a tall, pinnacled tower rising above the trees, a two-storey Decorated **porch,** a long south aisle and clerestory, is the last in a line of churches. The site was first occupied in the 7C by a chapel to St Goran which was succeeded by a wooden chapel to St Finn Barr; the Norman church was destroyed by a pirate raid in 1150. The new church, dedicated in 1336, was set alight by French seamen in 1456 in retaliation for raids by the **Fowey Gallants,** those "rich, proud and mischievous men", part traders, part privateers, part pure pirates; even today the carved pulpit, formerly a doubledecker, is Gallants' booty, made from panelling from the captain's cabin of a Spanish galleon taken in 1601.

Inside, beneath the 500 year old **wagon roof,** note the octagonal **piers** without capitals and the Norman **font** of dark Catacleuse stone; at the east end are portrait tombs, memorials and aged brasses and slates to two local families, the Rashleighs of Menabilly House (rebuilt 19C), which was used as the setting for *Rebecca* and *The King's General* by Daphne du Maurier, and the Treffrys of Place, a 19C house in the town centre enclosed by high walls with two thin, dissimilar castellated towers.

In the church tower is an 18C **ringer's rhyme.**

Fore Street – The narrow shopping street is lined by old houses with jettied gables or houses angled into corners as are the 17C Lugger Inn and Globe Posting House.

Post Office – The handsome Georgian house facing down Fore Street is entered through a shell-hooded doorway; adjoining is the Customs House of the same date.

Car Ferry – The vehicle ferry, known for the last 700 years as **The Passage,** links North and Passage Streets *(the continuation of Fore St)* to Bodinnick. Lining the street are houses built by prosperous 17C-19C townsmen overlooking their wharves and the river; the smaller houses with windows and balconies overhanging the water were built later on the former slips. At the ferry end, note **Captain's Row** (1816), a modest range complete with Captain Bates' own brass knocker.

WALKS

★★ Gribbin Head – *6 miles Rtn. Follow the Esplanade to its end (car park); then join the Cornwall South Coast Path.*

Fortifications at the water's edge – The 14C blockhouse and its pair opposite were the anchor points for the harbour chain across the river mouth (note the marks on the rocks); **St Catherine's Castle,** now a ruin, was a Henry VIII fortification.

Readymoney Cove – The small cove serves as the town beach; a stretch of sand is revealed at low tide. The Coast Path comes out on the cliff top and makes a gradual climb to the headland.

★★ Gribbin Head – The head, extending half a mile out to sea, 242ft high and topped by an 82ft waymark, affords **views★★** for miles in all directions.

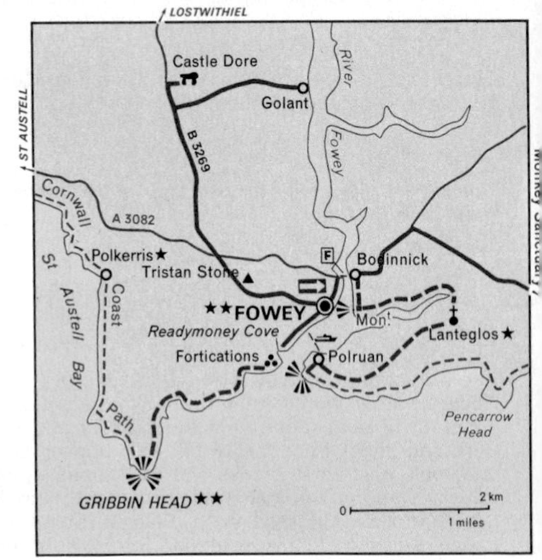

★ Lanteglos Church – *5 miles. Take The Passage or car ferry across the river.*

Bodinnick – The ferry lands at the foot of the steep main street. To the right is a former boatbuilders' yard, long since converted into a private house, and to the left, the medieval **Old Ferry Inn;** stone and slate houses with minute, flower filled gardens support each other up the hill.

Take Hall Walk (right) downstream past the 1939-45 War Memorial.

From the monolithic memorial to "Q" (Sir Arthur Quiller Couch) there is a **view★★** across to Fowey. Further on there is a shelter bearing a **plaque** which records that on 17 August 1644 **Charles I** narrowly escaped death from a sniper's bullet while surveying the Parliamentary forces occupying Fowey.

The path turns inland by Pont Pill creek and descends to the road bridge at Pont; start down south bank and where the road turns inland (beyond Carne), take the footpath (350yds) across the fields.

★ Lanteglos Church – The large 14C-15C parish church stands isolated on a wooded valley slope. It is built with old masonry which includes a Norman doorway incorporating a 7C-8C **XP stone** and medieval blocks of granite weighing up to 8 tons.
The interior, divided by unequally tall arcades of plain octagonal columns, is covered by the original carved **wagon roof.** The carved **font** of Pentewan stone is early 13C.
At the east end are **tombs** of the Grenvilles and the Mohuns; Thomas Mohun supervised the building of his own tomb (in a canopied recess) but, being still alive when the brass was finished, left the date of death incomplete.

The road leads west to Polruan.

Polruan – Before the descent to the old town at the water's edge, bear left to the coastguard station from which there is a **view★★** west to Gribbin Head, Dodman Point and the Lizard and east to Rame and Bolt Heads. Drop down to the harbour past the cliff and waterside houses, the pubs and boatyards to the passenger ferry.

EXCURSIONS

★ Polperro – Pop 1 192. *9 miles east by Bodinnick.*
The oldest cottages in this attractive and popular, vehicle-free, fishing village are at the bottom of the steep road which follows the stream down to the inner and outer harbour by the creek.
Twisting and stepped alleys are close-packed with cottages, millhouses, shops, forges and boathouses; from the headlands, views extend far out to sea.

★ **Monkey Sanctuary, Looe** – *27 miles east by Bodinnick.*

★ **Looe** – Facilities. Pop 4 279. The town, renowned for its safe, fine sand beaches, lies in the open valley on either side of the River Looe which divides almost immediately upstream into two tributaries. East and West Looe are linked by a 19C bridge.

Continue east by B3253.

★ **Monkey Sanctuary** ⊙ – In a 19C seaside villa and in an enclosure occupying much of the garden, dozens of Amazon woolley monkeys live and breed, perform effortless acrobatics and, when inclined, come out to meet their visitors.

Bear west, A387, to Sandplace station then right by a by-road to St Keyne station.

Paul Corin Mechanical Music Centre, St Keyne Station ⊙ – The rare assemblage of automatic music instruments includes pianolas, an orchestrion, street, fair and cinema organs.

Golant – *5 miles north. Leave Fowey by the Lostwithiel Rd, A3082.*

Tristan Stone – *1¼ miles from town centre, before Four Turnings, on right side of the road.* The stone, a relic of the Tristan *(qv)* legend, stands 8ft tall and was transferred from a nearby site where it was said to have been erected in AD 550.

Castle Dore – *3 miles by A3082 and B3269, 200yds north of Castledor crossroads, 15yds inside a field with a broken gate.* The second Tristan-Arthurian relic is an Iron Age lookout point which is said to have been one of King Mark's wooden halls of residence in the 6C AD *(now densely overgrown).*

Return to Castledor crossroads and take the left by-road (east) down to the river.

Golant – The riverside village has a 15C-16C landmark **church** with a low, embattled tower. Inside, a single arcade divides the nave and aisle beneath original wagon and cradle roofs; **bosses** and wall plates are beautifully carved as are the **pulpit** and **stalls** made from medieval bench-ends (apostles, St Sampson, a jester). The **sculpture** of Christ's head in chestnut is believed to be Spanish, possibly taken from one of the Armada ships.

FROME Somerset — Pop 19 678

Michelin Atlas p 17 or Map 403 – M, N30

The town, at a crossing on the river of the same name, was from AD 685 until the 19C an important market and wool cloth town.

Streets – Market Place and Bath Street, which lead up steeply from the bridge, are lined with shops beneath older 17C-19C upper floors and skylines punctuated by gables. The chief interest, however, lies in the side streets : 18C houses and two and three house terraces; a **Blue Coat School** and **almshouses** of 1726; the picturesque **Cheap Street** with 16C-17C shops, lamp standards, bay windows, oversailing upper floors, swinging iron signs lining either side of the cobbled pathway divided at the centre by a swift-running stream; the paved and winding Gentle Street with larger 17C-18C houses and a gabled 17C inn...

St John's – The church, overlooking Cheap Street and standing on a Saxon site, is 14C-15C restored in the 19C. The castellated tower and recessed octagonal spire are of the same date.

EXCURSION

★ **Farleigh Hungerford Castle** – *11 miles north. Take A361 going northeast; bear left into A36; turn right opposite the Red Lion, Woolverton.*

Tropical Bird Gardens, Rode ⊙ – The 17-acre park which includes ornamental trees, flower gardens and a clematis collection, lakes, a stream and a waterfall, provides the setting for strutting ornamental pheasants, free-flying macaws, penguins and flamingos and large aviaries containing more than 220 different species : there are eagles, owls and other birds of prey; finches and canaries; parrots, parakeets and cockatoos; birds from the jungle and from Pacific Islands... Throughout the summer the narrow-gauge **Woodland Steam Railway** runs through the grounds.

Return to Woolverton and take B3110.

Norton St Philip – *See Norton St Philip.*

Take A366 due east.

★ **Farleigh Hungerford Castle** – *See Farleigh Hungerford Castle.*

The development of "henge" architecture in England was probably due to the Bronze Age invaders from the Rhineland area: the Beaker Folk.
These physically strong, warlike people were well-equipped archers and had shapely stone battleaxes. The beakers and mugs found buried with them, and from which they derive their name, suggest that they were great drinkers of beer.

★ GAULDEN MANOR Somerset

Michelin Atlas p 7 or Map 403 – K30 – 9 miles northwest of Taunton

Gaulden Manor, a two-storey 16C red sandstone manor house with exceptional **plasterwork** inside, stands between the Brendon and the Quantock Hills. It is surrounded by tall trees, an immense old monastic fishpond bordered by poplars and by individual small gardens – quiet, secret, shaded, flower-filled or scented with herbs.

In the 1560s the house was chosen by **James Turberville,** Bishop of Exeter (d 1571), as the place to end his days after he had refused to take the oath of supremacy to Queen Elizabeth I and suffered a spell in the Tower of London.

In 1618 the house and farm were bought by a mercer from Wellington whose son, **Henry Wolcott,** emigrated to America in 1630 and founded a family which has since become so extensive that the members have formed a descendants' society.

In 1639 the bishop's great-nephew **John Turberville** repurchased the manor; although at first there was "scarce a chamber yet ready to lodge myselfe or my friends", he soon had it entirely refurbished and his arms implanted on the overmantels.

TOUR ⏲ *½ hour*

The porch and iron-studded oak door lead into the screens passage.

Dining Room – The former kitchen has a huge fireplace complete with a bread oven and salt niche.

Throughout the house choice pieces of **furniture** of all periods are on display, from 17C refectory tables to early ladder-back and Hepplewhite-style chairs, 16C-17C and late 18C oak chests, English and Meissen **porcelain,** modern **needlework...**

Great Hall – The hall has a splendid **plaster ceiling** of three garlanded roundels, the centre one descending in a solid ribbed pendant, the others showing reliefs of King David with his harp and an angel blowing the last trump. Round the room, a deep **frieze** continues the Biblical theme and, possibly in reference to Bishop Turberville's misfortunes, includes the scales of justice and a tower, from which it has been surmised that the ceiling and frieze and the considerable decoration over the Tudor fireplace date from the 16C; the decoration on the overmantel itself, however, showing the arms of John Turberville impaling those of his wife, must be 17C; possibly all the plasterwork is 17C, some of it achieved using older moulds.

At the far end of the room, 17C panelling and a line of lesser pendants screen a smaller room with its own 16C fireplace, known as the Chapel.

Stairs – The stairs have their original **oak treads;** note the old crooked **window** with bottle green glass which dates back to the 17C.

Turberville Bedroom – The room records the house's 17C associations through the **Turberville arms** over the fireplace and a **Wolcott window** and brass plate. The mirror is by Chippendale.

★★ GLASTONBURY Somerset — pop 6 751

Michelin Atlas p 8 and Map 403 – L30

Although there has only been a ruin on the site for the past four and a half centuries, the name immediately conjures up the great abbey, its existence for centuries as one of the richest houses owning vast amounts of land *(see Shaftesbury)* and as a centre of learning.

The town, which grew up round the abbey, has always centred on it.

★★ ABBEY

Legend and history – Glastonbury Tor and the Polden Hills were once islands rising out of the marshes which were connected by tidal channels to the open sea; by the Iron Age (450 BC) the hilltops were occupied by forts – the name Glastonbury means hillfort of the Glastings people – hut settlements being built above the waterline. Eventually timber trackways were laid across the "levels" *(qv).*

The abbey foundation appears most likely to have been as a 4C-5C Celtic monastery and church – a supposition which by the 12C had developed into a tale that it had been founded by St Patrick in person. Other legends developed : that Christ's disciples established the monastery and, most famous of all, that **Joseph of Arimathea** landed in Somerset one Christmas morning (some said returned, having come originally with the boy Jesus), bearing the Holy Grail. Joseph, according to the legend, set foot on a hill known as Avalon and later rested on a second hill, Wearyall, where he stood his staff upright in the ground; it promptly sprouted and flowered and has been known ever since as the **Glastonbury Thorn** – *Crateagus Praecox.* The original tree was cut down by the Puritans but descendants still bloom twice a year in December and May in the abbey grounds and in St John's churchyard *(see below).* Joseph was given land by the local ruler, Arviragus, and constructed a wattle and daub church on the site of the abbey Lady Chapel.

Another legend concerned **King Arthur** *(qv),* who, it was claimed, after being mortally wounded at the Battle of Camlann in 537, sailed away to the island of Avalon or Glastonbury, where his and Guinevere's bodies were "discovered" in the abbey cemetery in 1191 and re-interred in the chancel in 1278. The tomb survived until the Dissolution; the site is now marked by a plaque.

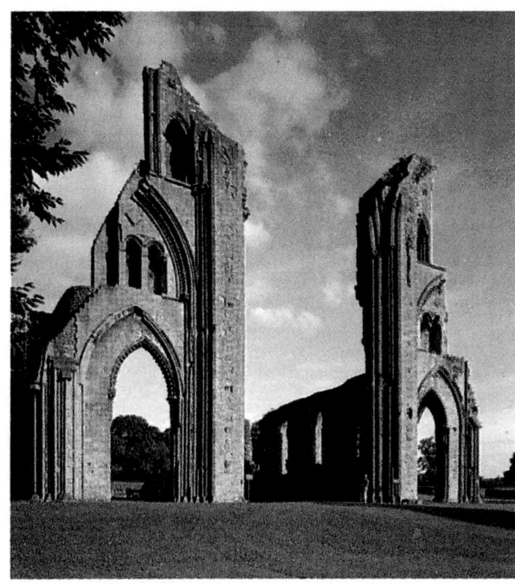
Transept piers, Glastonbury.

"Disputable matter", as **William of Malmesbury** *(qv)* termed the various theories of the abbey's foundation when he began to write its history in 1120, is replaced by "solid fact" from the 7C. In 688 **Ine,** King of the West Saxons – who had by then driven the Celts from Somerset – in consultation with **Aldhelm** *(qv),* built an additional church to that already on the site; in 943 Dunstan was appointed abbot. **Dunstan,** the son of a West Saxon noble, was born *c*910 near Glastonbury where he was educated before he entered the household of his kinsman, Athelstan (925-39), whose policy, in the tradition of Alfred, was the supremacy of Wessex against the Danes. When Dunstan lost favour at court, he went to Winchester where he became a Benedictine.

Successive kings recalled him to court; appointed him abbot of Glastonbury which he enlarged and rebuilt both spiritually and physically and which during his abbacy (943-59) became famous as a centre of learning. He was recalled as a political administrator, suffered royal displeasure and outlawry before Edgar appointed him Bishop of Worcester and London and, in 961, Archbishop of Canterbury in which capacity he crowned **Edgar** first King of all England in Bath Abbey (973). Edgar died two years later and was buried at Glastonbury.

The abbot appointed to Glastonbury after the Conquest considered the church inadequate for the richest abbey in the land and, in the manner of Norman prelates of the time, began to rebuild it. The task was completed by his successors only to be destroyed entirely in a fire in 1184. Rebuilding began immediately with the St Mary's or Lady Chapel, which was completed within two years, and then proceeded slowly over the next two centuries. It was at this period and immediately following that the abbacy was taken over by the ambitious Bishop Savaric (d 1205) of Bath and Wells and the abbey church declared to be a cathedral; it was also at this time that the abbey began to acquire vast manorial holdings and great riches and that **Abbot Richard Bere** (1493-1524), who was a great populariser as well as a great churchman and builder, developed the cult of Joseph of Arimathea.

The Dissolution in 1539 brought annihilation : the abbot, Richard Whiting, despite having taken the Oath of Supremacy, was brutally executed with two brothers on Glastonbury Tor, the other forty-five monks and 120-130 lay servants were dispersed, the manors were confiscated and the buildings allowed to fall into ruin.

TOUR ⏲ *½ hour*

The ruins, extending far across the lawns, stand tall amid majestic trees. The tower piers, arches, south nave wall, even the relatively complete shell of the Lady Chapel, give no idea of what the abbey church must have looked like during the short years of its prime – the remains in their glorious setting are, nevertheless, unforgettable.

St Mary or Lady Chapel – The chapel, in Doulting stone, has a **corner turret** and walls decorated with blind arcading and a modillioned cornice; the west end has three stepped lancets. The **doorways** are rounded, that to the north being enriched, possibly later, with **carved figures** of the Annunciation, the Magi and Herod.

The chapel stands on the site of the first wattle and daub church; all subsequent churches, including King Ine's (which measured 42ft), have been built to its east. Within the chapel are embrasures with zigzag decoration and arcading, the St Joseph Crypt (*c*1500) and a view east through the arch in the chapel wall *(see below).*

Nave – The distant chancel walls rise east of the transept piers, which supported the crossing tower, with the site of the Edgar Chapel beyond – the nave, chancel and retrochoir together measured 375ft, the full length of the abbey was 555ft – longer than Salisbury or Wells Cathedrals, shorter than Winchester.

Bishop Bere's rebuilding was completed in the early 15C with the construction of the **Galilee** which joined the main church to the Lady Chapel through the arch in the chapel wall.

The **Edgar Chapel,** a rebuilding of a mausoleum for the Saxon Kings, whom the abbey also claimed as founders, was undertaken early in the 16C.

Throughout, the style was Gothic which became slightly more ornamented with time. Each area would have been painted, directly on the stone, shortly after it was completed (a scale model in the museum gives an idea of the completed church).

★ **Abbot's Kitchen** – The 14C kitchen, the sole building to survive intact, is square with an eight-sided roof rising to superimposed lanterns which served to draw the smoke from the corner fires in the kitchen up the flues in the roof.

Glastonbury Thorn Tree – The large thorn tree *(labelled)* stands north of the abbey.

St Patrick's – The church was built in 1512 to serve no longer extant almshouses.

TOWN

The two principal streets, High Street and Magdalene Street, intersect at the Victorian-Gothic Market Cross.

Magdalene Street – The street contains a number of attractive small 17C-19C town houses. South of the abbey entrance are the pedimented town hall (*c*1814), the mid-18C Pumphouse *(private)* from the days when Glastonbury aspired to be a spa, a group of medieval almshouses (restored) and a 13C chapel.

St Benedict's – The pinnacled tower, glimpsed *(west)* at the top end of the street just before the market cross, belongs to a Perpendicular church of *c*1520. It was built on an older site by Bishop Bere, whose mitre and initials may be seen outside the north porch and whose rebus is carved on one of the roof corbels in the north aisle.

High Street – The street is overlooked by two buildings formerly connected with the abbey, the tribunal or old courthouse and a hotel, founded in the 14C and nobly rebuilt in the 15C by an abbot to ensure that there was suitable accommodation for the pilgrims, lawyers and other respected visitors to the abbey.

Tribunal ⊙ – The building dates from the 14C when it was timber fronted; the fine ashlar stone face, the canted bay, stone mullions and doorway were added by Bishop Bere in 1500; the latest additions were made in Elizabethan times when it had ceased to be abbey property.
Today it houses the Tourist Information Centre and a **museum** of excavated antiquities from the Iron Age **Lake Villages** *(qv)*.

George and Pilgrims Hotel – Interesting features of the hotel front include its actual height below the embattled roofline, the heavy string courses to emphasise the width of the building, the intricate, panel-style decoration and asymmetrically placed entrance decorated with the abbey arms, those of Edward IV and one blank. Inside are the original oak panelling, beams, doorways, an early fireplace and old Dutch tiles.

★★ **St John the Baptist** – The 134½ft church **tower** is one of the finest in Somerset with its "crown" of crocketed pinnacles which rise through buttresses and shafts from the lower stages to stand high above the battlements of two tiers of pierced arcading.
The church was rebuilt in the 15C in part because of the collapse of the earlier Norman, crossing tower. The **nave** of seven bays has a clerestory, making the interior "lightsome", as Leland declared, beneath its 15C Somerset oak **roof** on angel corbels.
Note especially the finely carved Charles II **royal arms,** the **chest** bought secondhand in 1421, the **domestic cupboard** of 1500, the **15C glass** *(chancel north window),* the 15C **tomb chests** of the wealthy cloth merchant Richard Atwell and his wife *(transepts)* and another with an alabaster effigy with angels and camels round the base.
In the churchyard is the **Glastonbury Thorn Tree** from which the Queen is sent a sprig in bloom each Christmas.

At the end of the High St turn right down A361 Shepton Mallet Rd Lambrook-Chilkwell St; turn off right into Bere Lane; 550yds in all.

★ **Somerset Rural Life Museum** ⊙ – The 14C "home" barn of Glastonbury Abbey is the outstanding exhibit of the museum, which illustrates 19C daily life on a Somerset farm, at work outside and in the home, and is appropriately housed in a 19C farmhouse and the adjoining farm buildings.

Farmhouse – The house (1896) illustrates domestic life : the original kitchen with its range, rag rugs, lead pump and sink; *(cellar)* cheese production – copper vat presses, awards; *(upstairs)* history of John Hodges who spent his life in the village of Butleigh working for the local squire.

Cowsheds – The cycle of activities in the farming year – including cider making and peat digging – are illustrated by hand tools and early machinery.

Barn – The modestly sized barn (93ft x 33ft) has an exceptional **roof** and **stonework**. The barn is cruciform with buttressed walls and two porches framing the massive double doors; the four gable ends are decorated with animal finials and roundels containing the symbols of the four evangelists; a carved head surmounts each corner buttress. During restoration in 1978 the original local roofing stone was replaced with shingles from the Cotswolds (80 tons). The dominant internal feature is the timber **roof,** composed mainly of oak with some elm and chestnut; the exceptional width is spanned by a skilful two-tier cruck structure.
The barn and the adjoining courtyard display the wagons, ploughs and other machinery which after centuries of slow development are now historic farm relics.

Return to Chilkwell St; turn right (250yds).

Chalice Well and Gardens ⊙ – The well, a natural spring pouring out 25 000 gallons of water a day at a constant temperature of 52°F – 11°C, has long been associated with the abbey legend of Joseph of Arimathea who is said to have hidden the Grail or Chalice beneath the spring waters, whereupon they flowed red.

Wellhouse Lane, which provides an outlet for the water just beyond the well, leads to the Tor. Park at the bottom and walk up the steep path or continue 250yds along the lane to a gentler path.

★ **Glastonbury Tor** – The Tor (521ft high) is a landmark visible for miles around and worth the climb. The tower at the summit is the last remnant of a Church to St Michael, built in the 14C on a hillfort and Saxon church site.
On a fine day, the **view**★★★ includes the Quantocks and Bristol Channel *(northwest);* the Mendips – Wells Cathedral, 5 miles, *(northeast);* the Marlborough Downs and possibly Salisbury *(east);* the Polden Hills *(southwest).*

EXCURSION

★ **Shoe Museum, Street** ⊙ – Pop 9 454. *2 miles southwest on A39.*
In a setting of lawns, trees, a clock tower and a Henry Moore bronze sculpture near the centre of the town stands Clark's Shoe Factory founded in 1825. In the oldest part of the factory are displayed hand-tools for making shoes, 19C machinery, fashion plates and showcards, tally books and a collection of shoes from Roman times to the present : button boots, dancing slippers, postilions' boots, children's shoes...
In the town *(between the shopping centre and car park)* is a modern stone mosaic-mural of familiar heights, towers and the landscape of central Somerset.

★ GLENDURGAN GARDEN Cornwall

Michelin Atlas p 2 or Map 403 – E33 – ½ mile southwest of Mawnan Smith

Dropping down to Durgan hamlet on the Helford River is the great sub-tropical **Glendurgan Garden** ⊙.
The valley garden is planted with English broad-leaved trees, conifers and ornamental foliage trees from all over the world (everything is unobtrusively labelled).
In spring and early summer the garden is a brilliant profusion of flowers : wild daffodils, bluebells, primulas; rhododendrons, camellias, azaleas, magnolias. Later come hydrangeas and later still, the blaze of autumn colour.

The Maze, Glendurgan Garden.

The garden also contains a **Giant's Stride** (maypole) and a famous **Maze;** all mazes, it is said, have the same solution, but it is nonetheless best to allow one hour to complete it...

★ **Mawnan Parish Church** – *½ mile east.* The 15C granite church stands on a spur at the mouth of the Helford River – walk round to see the **view**★★.
The church incorporates part of an Early English sanctuary and has massive granite piers; it is noted for its impressive modern needlework which gives colour and warmth to the interior.

★ GREAT CHALFIELD MANOR Wiltshire

Michelin Atlas p 17 and Map 403 – N29 – 2½ miles northeast of Bradford-on-Avon

The manor, surrounded on all sides by park and farmland, was originally fortified with a moat, curtain wall and bastion. In the 1430s Thomas Tropnall, steward to Lord Hungerford, MP and landowner, entered on thirty years of disputes and lawsuits to possess the house, which had been in his family since the Conquest but had passed to another branch; in 1467 Great Chalfield was his. Two years earlier he had purchased a stone quarry near Box, so that almost immediately he was able to begin work on the house, rebuilding and extending it and ordering the north face to its present attractive, mellow gold appearance of paired but dissimilar gables, finials, chimneys, buttresses and most particularly two oriels, one three-sided with a small pyramid roof surmounted by his coat of arms with supporters, the other semicircular, poised on corbels and a buttress and coroneted with a strawberry leaf decoration. To complete the forecourt, Tropnall erected a bellcote and added a crocketed spire to the parish church.

TOUR ⊙ *45min*

Porch – Note the vaulting, Tropnall's arms and the squint through which visitors were surveyed before being admitted through the wicket in the oak door.

Great Hall – In the Hall (40ft x 20ft x 20ft) it is unclear what is 15C-16C and what 20C; during those centuries the manor passed from owner to tenant farmer, from being a prize possession to a Parliamentary garrison. In 1836 the absentee owner had a survey and drawings made but then lost interest; in 1905, a new owner, using the meticulous 19C drawings, began removing accretions, rebuilding, putting in a carved oak screen and collecting stout examples of 16C-17C refectory tables, benches, stools, chests, Cromwellian chairs, court cupboards, Jacobean small tables, Caroline chairs...

Dining Room – The panelling and ceiling are of 1550. Note the squint to the porch, and the wall painting of a man with five fingers and a thumb, possibly Tropnall himself.

Bedroom – The bedroom, at the top of the stone staircase, includes the three-sided oriel window visible from the front of the house. It is adjoined by a closet built over the porch where a maid or page would have slept.

★ **All Saints** – The spire, the **panelled hood** which forms the porch and the wagon-roofed Tropnall chapel were added to the 14C church in 1470 by Tropnall, whose arms appear on the 15C crested **stone screen** although he is buried at Corsham; the chancel and vestry date from the 16C-18C. Other points of interest are the tub font, the 17C **three decker pulpit,** the 17C-18C chandeliers, the wall paintings of St Katherine (in the chapel) and the consecration crosses flanking the door.

GREAT TORRINGTON Devon — Pop 4 025

Michelin Atlas p 6 or Map 403 – H31

Great Torrington, or Torrington as it is known locally, was selected in 1966 by the Trust established at Dartington *(qv)* as the site for a glass factory which is now a leading manufacturer of plain lead crystal.

SIGHTS

★ **Dartington Crystal** ⊙ – *Left down School Lane, off New St opposite the church.* The factory now employs over 250 men and women, many of whom can be seen from gantry walks at work in small teams, gathering, blowing, shaping the glass, always keeping it turning to produce the well known lead crystal pieces.

Parish Church – "The church was blowen up with powder Febre ye 16 ano 1645 and rebuilt in 1651" – a matter of Royalists inadvertently setting off the 80 powder barrels they had been storing in the church when 200 of their men were packed into the building as prisoners of the Parliamentarians. How much of the 14C church, built on an older site – the town dates back to pre-Saxon times – was destroyed is not known but the pillars in the east arcade are decorated with detailed 14C carving while those opposite are square, solid and more utilitarian as though erected at speed in 1651.
The oak **pulpit** and **sounding board,** carved with cherubs and wreaths, are 17C; the **white ensign** (by the organ) flew at the Normandy Landing in 1944.
Note, among the lists of rectors and vicars, the name of Master, later Cardinal, **Thomas Wolsey.**

High Street – The High Street, which is also the market place, extends north from the **Pannier Market** (1842) between the twin-gabled **Black Horse Inn** (1681) and the Georgian-style **Town Hall** ⊙ (museum of bygones).

Castle Hill – *250yds south.* The 12C castle disappeared long ago but the site affords a good **view** south across the River Torridge towards Dartmoor.

EXCURSIONS

Holsworthy – *15 miles southwest on B3227 and A388.*
The town, with a lively pannier market (Wednesday), centres on the **square** which is lined by colour-washed and half-timbered shops and pubs. Streets lead off at the corners to the church with a tall ashlar tower and downhill to an old mill.

King's Nympton – *17 miles east by B3227, A377 and left turn before the station.*
The hilltop village, which retains a few thatched houses, has a Perpendicular church with a green copper octagonal spire.
The sill, between the porch and the interior, is probably the shaft of a Celtic cross. The carved bosses of the wagon roofs have been enriched above the screen. The box pews, pilastered reredos and communion rails with alternating balusters date from the 18C. The royal arms appear over the south door.

South Molton – *15 miles northeast on B3227.*

Atherington Church – The church, much restored in 1884 but with the original wagon roof, has a **rood screen** which at right angles becomes a **parclose screen** with a rare and beautifully decorated gallery.

Chittlehampton Church – The church overlooking the village square has a spectacular 115ft tower which rises by four stages, each underlined by a frieze and pinnacled buttresses, to a crest of pierced battlements, pinnacles and sub-pinnacles after the Somerset style *(qv)*.

South Molton – The old wool town, with colour-washed houses and a Georgian town centre, bustles with life particularly on market day (Thursday).
The guildhall, facing the town square, Broad Street, dates from 1743 and houses the town **museum** ⊙ (18C fire engine, minerals, an old cider press, pewter...). Note also the 19C pannier market next to it, the Medical Hall with an iron balcony supported on columns on an island site and the 15C church with pinnacled tower (107ft).

Quince Honey Farm ⊙ – *Off A361, Barnstaple Rd.* A walk-through gallery behind glass allows visitors to view the bees in the hive and the processing of honey from flower to table.

HARTLAND Devon — Pop 1 421

Michelin Atlas p 6 or Map 403 – G31

This most remote corner of Devon lies behind a ridge (750ft) which is the watershed for small, local streams which leap spectacularly from the cliffs into the sea, and for Devon's major western rivers the Torridge and the Tamar.
Beyond the ridge the wooded valleys give place to almost bare rock which rises as it approaches the sea and at Hartland Point reaches 350ft before plunging vertically into the ocean. The **Devon Coast Path,** as it follows every indentation of the rugged cliffs, affords breathtaking **views★★★** of the pointed offshore rocks projecting out of the swell as far as the eye can see.

SIGHTS

Hartland Village – The narrow streets of the village lead to a small square; in North Street a well-established local potter produces and sells his practical wares.

Hartland Church – *2 miles west at Stoke.* The 14C-15C church, the "Cathedral of North Devon", has a four-staged, buttressed and pinnacled tower, 128ft tall with a niche containing the figure of St Nectan. Like its predecessor, the tower serves as a landmark for ships at sea – the earlier tower, legend has it, was erected in the 11C by Gytha as a thank-offering for the safe passage in a storm of her husband, Godwin, Earl of the West Saxons and father of King Harold.

Interior – The tall nave with wide arcades is covered by ceiled, carved, painted and gilded **wagon roofs.** A 45ft carved **rood screen,** in typical Devon style, extends across the full width of the church, the nave arcades having had to be raised to accommodate its 13ft height and the 6ft wide gallery above the crested cornice and multi-ribbed coving.
Note also the square Norman **font** with zig-zag carving on the shaft, arcading on the bowl and faces at each angle, a small **brass** of 1610 and the late 14C carved tombchest in Cornish Catacleuse stone which came from the dissolved Hartland Abbey.

Hartland Quay – *1 mile west of Stoke.*
During fierce storms at the end of the 19C the Atlantic swept away the centuries-old quay which had been newly rebuilt. Today a row of cottages, a hotel and shipwreck museum mark the main street, while the quay foundations afford a **viewpoint★★** from which to look at the striated cliffs, inlets and offshore rocks which characterise the beautiful, wild length of coast.

HATCH COURT Somerset

Michelin Atlas p 7 or Map 403 – L31 – Hatch Beauchamp, 6 miles southeast of Taunton

The square Georgian house of Bath stone, graced by a tall arcade of columns at the top of a shallow flight of steps, small end pavilions with pyramid roofs and a pierced balustrade, dates from 1755. It was designed by Thomas Prowse, MP, a substantial landowner and amateur architect.
The house overlooks a small park with a herd of fallow deer. Though there is no association with Jane Austen, the house once proved a perfect setting in which to film one of her novels.

TOUR ⊙ ½ hour

Hall and Staircase – The hall is planned with great style to lead through a screen of fluted Ionic columns to the **staircase,** which rises to a half-landing where it divides and returns; the **landing** above, columned, triple-arched and with a groined vault, sweeps round behind a curved balustrade.
In the hall stand rare 17C **walnut benches** and an **oak table** of *c*1630 (9ft 6in).

Drawing Room – The room has its original **plasterwork ceiling.** The Japanese silk embroidery of peacocks is 19C.

Library – The **bookcases** follow the line of the walls in a graceful arc.

Orangery – The gallery is curved to enhance the house's exterior appearan

Museums – Two rooms, converted into small museums, contain **fine English ch** including a dark green set of Minton dessert plates with birds in white reli and mementoes of **Princess Pat's Regiment** (Princess Patricia's Canadian Lig Infantry) and of early aviation.

St John the Baptist's – The church behind the house was rebuilt on an old site in the 15C-16C when it was given its embattled tower of blue lias whi is overtopped by its stair turret and the surrounding trees.

HELSTON Cornwall

Pop 8 54

Michelin Atlas p 2 or Map fold 31 – E33

Helston is the home town of the famous Furry Dance; the other 364 days the year it is the market town for the Lizard Peninsula. Its 600 years' traditi as a stannary *(qv)* or tin assay town is recalled in the name Coinagehall Stre

★★ The FLORA DAY FURRY DANCE

Date : 8 May annually – or preceding Saturday if 8th falls on a Sunday or Mond
The town is closed to traffic.
Five processional dances are performed, at 0700, 0830, 1000, 1200 a 1700hrs, all except the Hal-an-Tow (0830) accompanied by the band. The 3-4m route has minor variations but all dances begin and end at the Guildhall a go up Meneage Street; all pass through houses, shops and banks, and the doo and lower windows along the route are decorated with bluebells and greene The most spectacular dances are at 1000hrs when 800 children aged 8-1 dressed all in white, set out, and at midday when on the first stroke from t Guildhall clock 130 couples start circling in the Invitation Dance – the men top hats and suits, the women in big hats and garden party dresses.

SIGHTS

Guildhall – The classical guildhall, surmounted by a striking clock, stands the junction of the major thoroughfares, Coinagehall, Wendron and Menea Streets.

Folk Museum ⊙ – *Church St.* In the old market halls, at the foot of the wi granite steps by the Guildhall, the local museum of trades and domestic bygon has well laid out exhibits on fishing (flat "maglans" for scooping fish from t sea), agriculture, mining and housekeeping.
Two Helston men are given pride of place : Bob Fitzsimmons (1863-191 prize-fighter, who was born in a 17C thatched cottage (61 Wendron Street), a Henry Trengrouse (1771-1854), inventor of the ship-to-shore rocket life-savi apparatus, whose tomb is in the churchyard.

St Michael's – The 18C church with Furry Dance angels in the east windo is lit by a 24 branch 18C chandelier.

Cross Street – Characterizing the street are the late Georgian **Great Office** w a columned porch, top floor bay window and iron balcony, the 18C vicara with an oriel window, neat doorway (no 10) and small-paned **bow windows.** Leadi off the street to the parallel Coinagehall Street are a number of "opes".

Coinagehall Street – The wide street is drained by ancient gutters, know as "kennels". Note the variety of old windows above the shop fronts, the pre-1 thatched Blue Anchor Inn with 18C horizontal sash windows, **Chymder House** (ea 19C), square and stuccoed, the 16C **Angel Inn,** with its own well, once an Exc Office (see the string course above the porticoed entrance), and a long coachi inn.

EXCURSIONS

★ **Flambards Village Theme Park, Culdrose** ⊙ – *3 miles southeast off A30*
To the constant whirr of the helicopters of Royal Navy station, Culdrose, ju a field away, a Concorde flight deck may be explored, or the gallery of Wo War II mementoes, worldwide satellite communications, a Westland Whirlwi and Widgeon...
By contrast the lamplit, cobbled street of houses in the **Victorian Village** reve crowded rooms, an inn and 19C shops with wooden counters and racks of ja drawers, boxes and barrels : an apothecary's, a milliner's, a butcher's, a baker's A variety of other attractions – "Britain in the Blitz", the Grand Canyon rides ar the "Hall of Miscellany", computer puzzles – provide entertainment to suit m tastes.

★ **Poldark Mine, Wendron** ⊙ – *3 miles north on B3297.*
One mine among the 50 in production from the 15C-20C in the Wendron distr has been reopened to allow visitors to see the underground workings a 18C-19C machinery in place.

Tour – On the surface are gardens, amusements and rides, steam locomotiv traction and beam engines...

Go to the mine entrance; put on a safety helmet. No smoking undergrou

There are 12 marked viewpoints in the mine from which can be seen a bright blue chloride "lode" or seam in the roof, an access-ventilation shaft of 1730, a tunnel showing early working space, waterfalls, exposed tin lodes, an underground postbox, rock drills, a stamping machine and water-wheel, the latter in a chamber hollowed out in 1493. The wheel now generates the mine's emergency electricity supply.

Seal Sanctuary, Gweek ⊙ – *5 miles east off A394.*
The sanctuary, in a beautiful **setting★** overlooking the Helford River, cares for pups separated from their mothers or injured against rocks. Once recovered in the hospital, the young seals disport themselves in the pools before being restored to the ocean. The sanctuary also has a penguin pool and an aquarium, exhibitions on the environment highlighting the threats to nature, and a woodland trail in its lovely grounds.

HIGH HAM Somerset — Pop 722

Michelin Atlas p 8 or Map 403 – L30

The village, which stands 300ft above the surrounding Sedgemoor levels, is reached by a series of short climbs; from the road and from the village itself there are **views★★** of the Polden and more distant Mendip Hills *(northeast)*, Bridgwater Bay and the Severn Estuary *(northwest)*, the Quantocks *(west)*, Taunton Vale *(southwest)* and even of Dunkery Beacon on Exmoor.
At the centre is the **village green**, shaded by tall trees and overlooked by a scattering of stonebuilt 17C-18C-19C houses and the parish church.

St Andrew's – The church is notable for its high **clerestory**, its wide Perpendicular windows above the battlements and the **gargoyles** which mark the aisle roofs – among them are a fiddler, a piper and a trumpeter, a listener with his hand to his ear, a stone thrower and a chained monkey nursing a baby.
The embattled tower is 14C whilst the remainder of the building "was builded anew from the foundation and finished within the space of one yeare, 1476".

Interior – With so many windows, the **roof** above the nave can be clearly seen with its tie-beams, king posts, bosses and arched braces rising from angel figures. The high **oak screen** which widens out into a panelled coving and ornate cornice was carved by Glastonbury monks in the early 16C.
Note also the Ham stone **pulpit** of 1632; the **lectern** with turned balusters and linenfold panelling; the 15C **poppyhead pews** and round Norman **font** with cable moulding.

Stembridge Tower Mill ⊙ – *½ mile east along Stembridge rd.*
The windmill of 1822, which worked until 1910, is unique in having a **thatched cap** at the summit of its blue lias tower. Inside, the rail on which the cap turned, enabling the sails to face into the wind, is visible at the top of the windmill *(qv)*. Among the outhouses, note the **bakehouse** with wooden gutters.

HONITON Devon — Pop 6 490

Michelin Atlas p 7 or Map 403 – K31

The **pottery** and **lace** which have for so long made Honiton a household name are both still made in the town. A new jabot made in 1983 for the Speaker of the House of Commons took 500 hours to complete.
Despite its 17C-18C Georgian appearance – the result of numerous fires which swept the wide main street from the Middle Ages to the 18C – the town dates back to the 12C when it was founded as a village settlement on either side of the London-Exeter road (A30 – now by-passed). By 1257 a pannier market and the annual July fair were in being; by Tudor times fine glove-making, a cottage industry, was complementing the important local sheep and wool industry, and by the early 17C pillow lacemaking, introduced by refugees from the continent, had also been established. In the 18C Honiton became a staging town with coaching inns flanking the wide High Street.

★ **All Hallows Museum** ⊙ – *High St, next to the 19C parish church.*
This local museum's major displays concentrate on lace : a fine wedding veil, a matronly overskirt with a 40in waist, handkerchiefs, flounces, a lacemaker's sampler with prices...
Other exhibits include Honiton pottery, Victorian scent and smelling bottles, bead purses, card and table games, a 19C kitchen-laundry with tub and washing line.

EXCURSIONS

★ **Ottery St Mary** – *7 miles southwest by A30 and B3177. See Ottery St Mary.*

Farway Countryside Park ⊙ – *6 miles south by A375 and B3174.*
The **views★** from the 189-acre hilltop park extend over the fertile east Devon landscape of fields, woodland and the Col River valley. Among the penned animals are rare breed sheep, a Brahman bull, Bagot and Pygmy goats, spotted pigs and small hogs bred back to resemble those of the Iron Age. In the paddocks are deer, ponies and Long Horned cattle.
Donkey cart rides, pony rides and pony trekking are available.

HORTON COURT Avon

Michelin Atlas p 17 or Map 403 – M29 – 3 miles northeast of Chipping Sodbury

This green valley on the northern edge of Horton village has been inhabited f centuries; the attractive group of Cotswold stone buildings which comprise t Court ⊙ consists of the church and manor house, both rebuilt in the 14C-15 and the hall (12C).
In the 16C William Knight was appointed prebendary of Horton; he becar protonotary of the Holy See and, in 1527, Henry VIII's envoy to Rome in t unsuccessful divorce negotiations. His advancement is reflected in the higl decorated **doorway** (16C). His **arms,** granted on the prebendaryship, are crown and flanked by the **protonotary's hat and tassels** (fewer than for a cardinal); the carv **Renaissance columns** recall his visit to Rome.

Hall – The building, a unique link between Saxon domestic halls and la medieval halls, dates from 1100-50. Despite strengthening and rebuilding, t introduction of a Tudor fireplace and conversion to other uses – RC chapel an inserted upper hall in the 18C when the house belonged to a descenda of the letterwriting **Pastons** – there remain, unscathed, the **south doorway** ar opposite, the **north door** in a wall of early dressed stone.

Ambulatory – The six-arched detached ambulatory, built by Knight in t manner of an Italian loggia, stands opposite a giant **tulip tree** on the south si of the house overlooking the valley garden, which was designed in the medie manner on several levels.

Church – St James', built in the 14C on the site of the Norman chur contemporary with the hall, has been repeatedly altered and restored. It has 14C arcade, wagon roofs, a re-cut Norman font with 17C cover, a Jacobe pulpit and several Paston memorial tablets.

EXCURSION

Badminton – *5 miles southeast by A46 and B4040.*
Badminton is well known on three counts : the original court dimensions a rules of the game of Badminton were established from the size of the hall Badminton House when bad weather compelled the younger members of t household to play battledore and shuttlecock indoors; the Three Day Event Hor Trials are held in the park in April; the Beaufort hounds are kennelled near t house.
The house *(private)* is a palatial mansion in biscuit coloured stone, set on t edge of the Cotswolds in a park landscaped by Capability Brown. It was bu in the 1670s and 1740s. There was already a "fair stone house" on the esta but in the eyes of its young owner it proved inadequate for entertaining Charles when he came on a visit in 1663. By 1682, therefore, when the king creat the man reputed to be his richest subject the first Duke of Beaufort, the hou had been rebuilt and taken on much of its present appearance. The second pha came after the third duke had returned from the Grand Tour with a gre enthusiasm for the Palladian style and commissioned William Kent to enlar the house accordingly.

ILFRACOMBE Devon

Pop 9 966

Michelin Atlas p 6 or Map 403 – H30 – Facilities

The town, long the most popular resort on the North Devon coast, achiev success in the 19C with the development of steamship day outings from Sou Wales and the arrival of the railway bringing visitors in their thousands fro the Midlands and the North Country.

SIGHTS

★ **Capstone Hill** – From the "summit" of the 156ft high hill there is a go bird's-eye **view**★ of the town, the harbour mouth, the rock-enclosed bays a beaches on either side.

Hillsborough – The hill on the town's eastern edge, at the centre of the pleasu ground, rises to 447ft and affords an even more extensive **view**★★ along t coast.

St Nicholas' Chapel ⊙ – *Lantern Hill.* In the early 14C the beacon set as marker on Lantern Hill was replaced by this mariners' chapel which, though mu altered, still shines a red bearing light at night to guide shipping in the Bris Channel.
From the rock platform on which the chapel stands there is good **view**★ out sea and of the almost land-locked harbour. A promenade (starting from the qua half circles the headland a few feet above sea-level.

Tunnels Beaches ⊙ – *Granville Rd.* The pools were an early 19C enterpri in which the hill between the road and the sea was tunnelled by Welsh mine and the rock cove, on the far side, made accessible. The cove was then equipp with a sea wall to prevent the tide running out and so provide all day bathir In the 19C water was pumped to the baths at the entrance and heated winter.
The pools, now surrounded by amenities, are still very popular today.

EXCURSIONS

Hele Corn Mill – *1 mile east by A399.* Deep in the valley stands a restored 16C watermill *(qv)* producing stone-ground flour. The machinery turns very quietly, driven by an overshot waterwheel (18ft) : detailed explanations of the mill and milling.

Chambercombe Manor ⏲ – *1 mile southeast by A399.* The white-painted stone house (15C-17C) lying in a wooded dell is slate-roofed where it was once thatched. Inside, features include 200-300 year old polished **lime ash floors,** hard as granite and said to be made of wood ash and scrumpy laid like cement; a 13C Peter's Pence **almschest; barrel vaulting,** a Tudor plaster frieze and the arms of Lady Jane Grey in the principal room. Upstairs, the robustly carved Elizabethan four-poster bed is made from Spanish oak timbers. A Cromwellian oak **cradle,** Jacobean chest of drawers, William and Mary yew **tallboy** and a Victorian room are also of note.

★ **Braunton** – *8 miles south by A361. See Braunton.*

★ ILMINSTER Somerset — Pop 3 681

Michelin Atlas p 7 or Map 403 – L31

The Ham stone town on the south side of the London-Exeter road (A303) originated in Saxon times, was listed in Domesday as possessing both a minster and a market, and grew to prosperity in the 15C-16C on wool – Ilminster was a named cloth. New houses were built, old houses refronted in Georgian times, the town's well-being depending, as it still does, on being at the heart of some of England's best agricultural land, both dairy and arable.

★★ **St Mary's** – The climax of the church exterior is its **crossing tower,** modelled on that of Wells Cathedral *(qv).* It rises through two stages of bell openings – paired and three abreast with intervening shafts, transoms, tracery and Somerset tracery; it continues to a crest of gargoyles, fountains of pinnacles and a spirelet on the stair turret.

Interior – Inside are a tie-beam and king-post **roof,** a **fan vault** at the crossing and the **Wadham Chapel.** This remarkable "glass lantern" was built in 1452 to contain the **tomb chests** (inlaid on the lids with large brasses) of Sir William Wadham (d 1452) and his wife, and Nicholas (d 1618) and his wife, the latter the founders of Wadham College, Oxford.

Market Square – The square is characterized at its centre by the single-storeyed Market House, open on all sides and last rebuilt in 1819.

EXCURSION

★ **Barrington Court Gardens** – *3 miles northeast by B3168. See Barrington Court Gardens.*

★★ KILLERTON Devon

Michelin Atlas p 7 or Map 403 – J31 – 7 miles north of Exeter

The house of 1778 stands at the foot of a wooded hillside in glorious parkland on a site purchased by the Aclands in the 17C. After successive remodellings it now houses Acland portraits, contemporary 18C-19C furniture including some pieces especially made for the house, and the National Trust's Collection of 18C-20C Costume.

HOUSE ⏲ *45min*

Music Room – The **chamber organ** dates from 1807, the late 18C **square piano** was made by Clementi, the grand piano is of 1870. The 18C mahogany **china cabinet** is from Exeter. Note the portrait and figurine of **Hannah More** *(qv)* who was supported in her work by Sir Thomas Acland, the then owner of the house.

Drawing Room – The mahogany **secretaire-bookcase** is late 18C, the giltwood **pier glasses** are after Chippendale.

Library and Dining Room – The walnut **bookcases** were especially designed for the house; note the **dumb-waiter, pier glasses** and marble **folio cabinets,** also custom-made.

Upstairs – The rooms, which serve as the setting for displays from the National Trust **Costume Collection,** are peopled with men, women and children in period tableaux : a 1930s cocktail party, a mid-18C musical or painting group, a 1920s nursery, a Victorian mourning group showing one of Queen Victoria's dresses, jet, crêpe, a child in funereal black, a line of 1900s bathing costumes. The displays, historic and sometimes amusing, change every year.

GARDEN ⏲

The garden near the house provides colour throughout early spring to late summer with bulbs, early flowering shrubs, clouds of rhododendrons banked along the hillside, magnolias and island beds. Later the wide herbaceous borders on the terrace come into their own and, lastly, the broad-leaved trees with their autumn tints against the silver grey, pale gold and dark green of the conifers. The stables house an exhibition on the history of the family and estate; the Markers cottage is a medieval cob house.

★ KINGSBRIDGE Devon — Pop 4 164

Michelin Atlas p 4 or Map 403 - I33

The old market town at the head of the estuary is the capital of the area known as South Hams. Fore Street descends very steeply to the quay where a weekly market, opened in 1217, is still going strong (Tuesday, Market Hall, Fore St).

SIGHTS

Quay - The Quay stands on land reclaimed from the once important harbour.
Circle the open square and, by way of Squeezebelly Passage, turn right into Fore St.

Fore Street - The street is bordered by slate-hung houses dating from the 15C-19C, between which run narrow passages leading to small, medieval courtyards.

Town Hall - The hall with a clock and arcaded front is 19C.

Shambles - The colonnaded walk known as the Shambles *(qv)* is fronted by eight Elizabethan granite pillars which support the 18C upper floor.

St Edmund, King and Martyr - The tower and spire are 13C but the church was rebuilt in the 15C when the town was prosperous, and restored in the 19C. Inside, note the variation in the chancel arches, the two squints and the 13C font.

King's Arms Hotel - The 17C-18C inn near the top of the street *(on the right)* became a stage in 1775 for the Exeter-Plymouth coaches.

Cookworthy Museum and Old Grammar School ⏲ - The long stone building on two floors was erected in 1670 by Thomas Crispin, a fuller, as a grammar school. The **panelled schoolroom** with a **master's seat** surmounted by the royal arms of Charles II contains a display on **William Cookworthy** (1705-80), born nearby, the Quaker apothecary who discovered kaolin (china-clay; *qv*) and petunze (china-stone) near St Austell in 1756. The one-time school kitchen which produced food for 60 boarders, a costume room, a turn of the century pharmacy, a special exhibitions room and a farm gallery complete the local museum.

★★ BOAT TRIP ⏲ to Salcombe

To sail down the estuary between the open downlands, past the mouths of the six wooded creeks and additional inlets headed by small waterside villages, to Salcombe *(qv)*, watching the tern and even buzzards overhead and, if the tide is falling, the waders *(qv)* including heron in the shallows, is a very enjoyable experience.

★★ KINGSTON LACY Dorset

Michelin Atlas p 8, 9 or Map 403 - N31 - 3 miles northwest of Wimborne Minster

Once a royal estate, Kingston Lacy was purchased between 1632-36 by Sir John Bankes (1589-1644); he also bought the Corfe Castle *(qv)* estate in 1635. The house was built by his son, Sir Ralph Bankes (*c*1631-1677), to designs drawn by Roger Pratt in 1663 and considerably altered by Robert Brettingham for Henry Bankes after the latter's marriage in 1784.
A major transformation was undertaken by his son, the eccentric William Bankes (1786-1855), who travelled extensively on the continent and in the Middle East; although he lived in exile in Italy after 1841, following a scandal, he continued to direct the work by letter. His architect was Charles Barry, who encased the red-brick mansion in Chilmark stone, installed a grand staircase and added a *porte cochère* to the new entrance at ground level on the north front. The family collection of paintings, one of the earliest made by a member of the gentry to survive, was enriched by William. He himself was responsible for much of the interior decoration; he commissioned many ornamental features, particularly in *biancone*, a hard stone-coloured marble from Bassano in Italy.
Further alterations were made at the turn of the century; in 1891 the whole estate was left to the National Trust which has carried out extensive restoration work.

HOUSE ⏲ *1 hour*

Entrance Hall - Although low and dark, the new entrance hall created at basement level by William Bankes is supported on Doric columns with a decorated ceiling. The carved marble tables are Italian, the bronze cranes 19C Japanese. Beyond the screen is a chimneypiece bearing the Bankes coat of arms, flanked by two Carrara marble radiator covers, with bronze insets, one of which *(right)* shows the original Kingston Hall.

Marble Staircase - Barry was delighted with the Carrara **marble staircase** which turned out "far beyond" what he had expected.
The **loggia** on the half-landing looks out over the "Dutch" parterre with its golden yews.
The **bronze figures** by Marochetti (1853) represent Sir John Bankes, Lady Mary Bankes and Charles I; below the king the siege of Corfe Castle is shown in relief.

Library – The room was designed after 1784 by Brettingham for Henry Bankes, whose portrait by **Batoni,** who painted many an Englishman on the Grand Tour in Rome, hangs on the window wall, near Sir John Bankes portrayed in his judge's robes. Above the shelves hangs a series of portraits of his children by **Sir Peter Lely.** Over the fireplace are the keys of Corfe Castle granted to Lady Mary Bankes in recognition of her courageous defence of the castle when it was besieged by the Parliamentary forces in the Civil War. The "Persian design" carpet (1819) is from Axminster *(qv).*

Drawing Room – This room, typically Edwardian in character, was refurnished by the late Mr Bankes' mother on her marriage in 1897; the walls were hung with rose damask. Some features remain from earlier years : the 18C chimneypiece and doors; the stencil for the Bankes motto on the frieze came from Venice in 1846. There are several family portraits : Sir John and Lady Borlase, who was Sir John Bankes' daughter, by **Van Dyck;** Mrs Henry Bankes by **Romney;** her daughter Lady Falmouth by **Lawrence;** Mrs Walter Bankes and her daughter Daphne painted in watercolour in 1902. Among the **enamel miniatures** painted on copper by Henry Bone (1755-1834) are portraits of Elizabeth I and several members of the Bankes family circle.

Dining Room – Owing to a fire in 1910 little has remained of Barry's work in this room : the ceiling, the crests above the windows, the walnut shutters and the **boxwood doors** which were carved in Venice (1849-1853) from original models selected and arranged by William Bankes. The room was repanelled in oak and cedar from the home park. The dominant feature is the painting of **The Judgement of Solomon** attributed to **Sebastiano del Piombo,** although William purchased it as by Giorgione. Below it stands a late 16C Italian cedarwood coffer. To the right of the organ, moved here from its original position in the Saloon over the doors to the Drawing Room, hangs an 18C English tapestry, probably made in Soho. Below it is the Bankes family silver displayed on a sideboard bought in Soho in 1786. The William IV dining chairs are made of mahogany and covered in giraffe hide.

Billiard Room – The important collection of ancient **Egyptian artefacts** amassed by William Bankes during his two expeditions to the Nile in 1815 and 1818 (the second with the seasoned tomb-robber Giovanni Belzoni) are largely housed here. Other monuments adorn the garden.

Spanish Room – William Bankes spent 17 years creating his "Golden Room" as a setting for the Spanish paintings he had collected during the Peninsular War : **Velasquez'** portrait of Cardinal Massimi. Although the paintings are uneven in quality, Bankes was ahead of fashion in his taste and devoted much thought to their framing and hanging. The **ceiling** (*c*1609) came from a Venetian palazzo, as did the **gilded leather** covering the walls; the skins have been cleaned and rearranged to restore the room to its original brilliance. The pearwood doors, painted with Seasons, are Bankes' own design. The carpet is an Axminster bought in 1820.

Saloon – The original flat ceiling and gallery at the southern end were removed in Henry Bankes' time when the **painted barrel vault** and cornice and frieze, then in fashion locally, were introduced. The room serves as gallery for the family collection of paintings : **The Holy Family with St John** by Giulio Romano, once in Charles I's collection and bearing the royal cipher on the back, in a frame designed by William portraying the four previous owners; **Rubens'** portraits of two Grimaldi sisters; *The Four Elements* by Jan Brueghel the Elder; portrait of Francesco Savorgnan delle Torre by **Titian :** portrait of the First Earl of Portland by **Van Dyck;** an Italianate landscape by Berchem, owned by Sir Ralph Bankes; Mr Altham (his uncle) as a Hermit which is attributed to Salvator Rosa. An oil sketch of William Bankes by Sir George Hayter stands on the table in the north window.
The lustre, the pelmets and the Savonnerie carpet were supplied by Henry Bankes; William provided most of the furniture : Anglo-Indian ebony seats covered with Berlin floral embroidery, four 18C colonial Dutch "burgomeister" chairs of ebony or satinwood, a pair of Louis XIV Boulle pedestals, a pair of Italian giltwood candelabra set in marble niches designed by William, the centre tables made in the 19C from 17C walnut cabinet doors; a Charles II marquetry box mounted in the 19C.

State Bedroom – Both the bed, carved in holly in Venice, and the ceiling, also Venetian, were incomplete when William died. Note the Dutch walnut seawood marquetry cabinet.

GARDENS ⊙

The terrace with its furnishings, which was introduced by William Bankes, leads down to smooth lawns and the pink granite **obelisk** discovered by William at Philae in Egypt in 1815. It was finally erected in 1829, the Duke of Wellington laying the foundation stone. The Greek inscription, which helped in the deciphering of the hieroglyphs, commemorates a decree exempting priests from taxation. The great **cedars** were planted by the Duke of Wellington, Edward VIII and the Kaiser. The landscaped park with a "wilderness", now the Fernery, was created in the 18C to replace the original 17C formal gardens.

Cider has been made in Britain for centuries – a cider press was basic equipment in many country houses – and often features in recipes of the Southwest of England.

★ KNIGHTSHAYES COURT Devon

Michelin Atlas p 7 or Map 403 – J31 – 2 miles north of Tiverton

The house, which is a fine example of Victorian Gothic architecture, is situated • the east bank of the Exe Valley facing south overlooking parkland and the town Tiverton in the distance. It was at Tiverton that **John Heathcoat,** a prosperous lace-m owner, born in Derbyshire in 1793, built a new mill in 1816 after his Midlands wor (where he had installed his own bobbin net (1808) and other machines) had be wrecked by Luddites. Philanthropist and man of liberal ideas, as well as an invent Heathcoat represented Tiverton in parliament from 1832-59.
His grandson, **John Heathcoat-Amory,** inherited the business, took over t parliamentary seat and, in the late 1860s, commissioned an architect to bu him a new house out of town.
William Burges was a skilled and inventive architect – there is a brilliantly balanc or compensating asymmetry about the house exterior which gives it life – but was dilatory and so in 1874 Heathcoat-Amory sacked him, employing in his ste **J D Crace** who was strongly influenced by the pre-Raphaelite movement. The res is a country house, complete with conservatory, which is a true period piece.

HOUSE ⏲ ½ hour

The furniture is 18C and 19C English with some 18C Dutch marquetry piec The interest throughout the rooms is to note the contributions of each archite also where the decoration is a combination of the work of both.
In the **hall** the corbels of men and animals are by Burges, the other decoration by Crace; the walls of the **bedroom corridor** are covered by Crace's original stencilled designs.
In the **boudoir,** the teak panelling, chimneypiece and repainted ceiling are all by Crace.
Downstairs in the **dining room** the decoration is by both architects; the walnut chairs were made in Wales in the early 19C.
The ceiling in the **morning room** is by Crace; the brass chandelier is after Pugin's Gothic style. Note the collection of 17C Italian majolica.

Knightshayes Court.

Beneath Burges' elaborate ceiling in the **library sitting room** are a *Madonna a Child* by Matteo di Giovanni (1435-95), a Flemish **Annunciation** of *c*1400 and Claude. The mahogany drum table is 18C; the bracket clock is French with English movement.
In the **drawing room,** the ceiling and chimneypiece are by Burges; among t pictures are a Constable *(Field Flowers and Poppies),* a Bonington, a Turner a a Rembrandt self-portrait.

GARDENS ⏲

The renowned gardens are not old – the transformation and expansion to t present 25 acres began in the 1950s when the then Sir John and Lady Amc began to transform the elaborate scheme of regular, stepped parterres, design by Burges, into **terraced gardens.**
They next incorporated the yew hedges, planted east of the house in the 188(into Pool and Formal Gardens with a brilliant Alpine terrace below. Note t **topiary fox and hounds** of the 1920s.
Finally, extending the cultivated area yet once more, they created the interesti **Garden in the Wood** and the **Willow Garden.**

★ LACOCK Wiltshire

Pop 1 28

Michelin Atlas p 17 or Map 403 – N29 – Facilities

The calm, attractive, stone and brick-built village has always been under spec patronage : first of the abbey, then the Talbots and now the National Tru

LACOCK VILLAGE

The village comprises four streets which form a hollow square.

★ **High Street** – The wide thoroughfare, often blocked in medieval times by t weekly wool and produce market and the three-day fair, leads to the abbey. (either side mellow roofs of tile and stone cover cottage-shops and houses various heights, sizes and designs.

Porch House – The gabled, black and white half-timbered house is 16C.

Inn – This old building was refaced with red brick in the 18C.

Tithe Barn – The barn with its timber roof, on the street corner, dates from the 14

West Street – The broad street at right angles marked the old village's perimeter.

George Inn – The George is the oldest inn in this village of at least one pub to each street.

The Brash – The high, up-raised **pavement** which turns the street corner is named after the loose broken rock used in its foundation.

Church Street – The street runs parallel to the High Street up to the church.

Cruck House – The house derives its name from the exposed beam which, following a 14C building method, supports both roof and wall.

Angel Inn – This 15C inn is named after the gold coin of the time (1480) bearing the figure of the Archangel Michael. The horse passage leads to the old coaching yard which gives access to the beamed interior.

Market Place – Church Street opens out into what was the village's original market place; Lacock's first market charter was obtained by Ela, Countess of Salisbury and abbess, in 1241 *(see below)*.

King John's Hunting Lodge – This so-called lodge dates from the 16C.

Tanyard – The yard includes a drying loft for skins and a gaunt 19C work-house.

East Street – The fourth of the village's four streets is narrowly enclosed by 16C and 18C houses and onetime shops.

★ **St Cyriac** – The Perpendicular church is a "wool church" from the time of Lacock's prosperity from the 14C-17C as a wool and cloth market on the London-Bath road.
Distinctive exterior features include the large embattled and pinnacled **porch** fronting an older **tower** which was crowned, in the early 18C, with a recessed, octagonal spire; the Perpendicular tracery of the north aisle west window; and, on the south side, which is decorated with amused gargoyles, a mullion-windowed **cottage,** added *c*1615.
Inside is the **Talbot** or **Lady Chapel** which has 15C lierne vaulting with rib encircled pendants and arches decorated with carved masks and small animals, all of rare craftsmanship. The **tombchest** in the chapel is also remarkable : dating from 1566 and set up for Sir William Sharington *(see below)*, it is ornamented with carved strapwork, cartouches, panels, vases of flowers, cherubs and a shell crest.
In the south transept is a brass to Robert Raynard (d 1501) in armour and heraldic tabard, his wife in a kennel headdress, and their 13 sons and 5 daughters.

★ **Fox Talbot Museum of Photography** ⊙ – The museum is housed in the 16C barn at the abbey gate. The ground floor is devoted to **William Henry Fox Talbot** (1800-77), the inventor of modern photography : his notes and letters, equipment, early cameras and collotypes and awards from all over the world. The upper floor (note the splendid roof timbers) celebrates the work of present-day photographers.

★ LACOCK ABBEY ⊙ *45min*

"A grand sacrifice to Bacchus" was held by **John Ivory Talbot** to celebrate the opening in 1755 of the new entrance hall to the abbey, constructed in the Gothick style recently made fashionable by Horace Walpole at Strawberry Hill, Twickenham. The house had been in the family for two centuries having been purchased at the Dissolution in 1539 from Henry VIII by Talbot's ancestor, **William Sharington** for £783 and repurchased by him from the crown for £8 000 in the 1550s, after unsuccessful political intrigues and coin-clipping at the Bristol mint had put him in the Tower. On Sharington's return to Lacock he built the tower on the south front and the Stable Court which includes domestic quarters, a bakehouse, dairy, brewhouse and hay lofts, beneath large dormered roofs, decorative chimneys and heraldic beasts.
As Talbot followed Talbot (Sharington's niece married the first), alterations followed in the style of the day : Ivory Talbot continued to add his Gothick embellishments, three oriels were added to the south front in 1827-30 by **William Henry Fox Talbot** whose first successful photograph was of the centre window.

House – Of particular interest inside are the Gothick entrance hall with "not expensive terracotta performances" in the niches and arms on the vault; a massive bronze **pestle and mortar** engraved with Sharington's name and scorpion crest; an exceptionally carved **stone fireplace** and a modern copy of a 1225 edition of *Magna Carta,* probably sent to William Longespée *(qv)* as Sheriff of Wiltshire and kept by his wife, **Ela, Countess of Salisbury,** when she succeeded him in the office – the only woman sheriff in the county's history.
In **Sharington's Tower,** built as a belvedere, is a **stone table** (*c*1550); its octagonal top is supported on the shoulders of four grinning satyrs.
In the South Gallery or Drawing Room note the prints from Fox Talbot's **original negatives** of the centre oriel, and the shelves of china.

Walk round to the south front to visit the cloisters.

Cloisters – The surviving conventual buildings date from the foundation of the abbey by Ela, Countess of Salisbury, in 1232; they include *(see plan beside south door)* : the sacristy, flanked by two chapels; the chapter-house, entered through double arches; the warming room with a cauldron made in Malines (1500).
The Countess' tomb was originally housed in the church which was demolished in 1540.
The **15C cloisters** are decorated with carved bosses of angels and animals, the pelican and lamb, a mermaid and a jester.
In the 16C the north gallery was converted by Sharington into offices and lodgings with decorated chimneys and dormer windows.

Brewhouse – The 16C building contains a mash tun and boiler, lead-lined cooler and fermenting vessel.

★ LAND'S END Cornwall

Michelin Atlas p 2 or Map 403 – C33

Access for vehicle-borne visitors to the famous stretch of coast is now via the **Land's End Visitor Centre** ⊙, though the Cornwall Coastal Path provides an impressive alternative approach for ramblers and walkers and overlooks some of the finest local **cliff scenery**★★★.
The attraction of Land's End itself *(illustration p 13)* is less its physical beauty than its position on the western tip of the mainland perpetually assailed by the Atlantic swell surging relentlessly against the cliffs. Inshore rocks, the **Armed Knight** and the holed **Enys Dodnan,** may be the mountain peaks of the lost land of **Lyonesse** *(qv)* submerged beneath the waves.
Offshore stands the Longships Lighthouse *(1½ miles; see lighthouses, qv)* among swirling currents and submerged reefs; further west lie the Isles of Scilly *(27 miles).*
The sense of magnificent isolation has been diluted somewhat by the complex which comprises a host of exhibitions, attractions and entertainments (the *Last Labyrinth,* Dollar Cove suspension bridge, land trains, a model village, the Lobster Pot Maze, *Man against the Sea,* the Shipwreck Play Area...) but the coastline itself remains largely unadulterated and just a short walk (RSPB Warden tours available) leads away from the crowds.
Early morning always provides a quiet, solitary view while sunset and nightfall, when the lighthouses come into their own, offer a more memorable experience.

LANGPORT Somerset

Pop 2 461

Michelin Atlas p 8 or Map 403 – L30

The town, at the tidal limit of the River Parrett, was for centuries a small but important centre for traffic sailing upstream into the heart of Somerset and down to Bridgwater and even overseas. Its main street, Bow Street which crosses the River Parrett by an iron bridge, follows the ancient course of a Roman causeway.
The town's architectural heyday was in the 18C-19C, the late Georgian period, when Palladian-styled, Tuscan-pillared houses were erected in Bow Street and Cheapside.

All Saints – The church was rebuilt in the late 15C; the **stone relief** *(over south door)* of a lamb and cross supported by twin angels and saints, carved *c*1200, was retained from the Norman church previously on the site.
The **tower,** buttressed, battlemented and pinnacled, with a taller stair turret, rises from the door and west window, through transomed windows with Somerset tracery and flanking niches, and a bell stage of three windows abreast, the outer ones blind, the centre traceried. Embattling marks the rooflines; pinnacles add to the height of the chancel which is enriched with tall windows and handsome tracery.
The **east window** contains largely medieval glass.
Buried in the churchyard is Langport's famous son, **Walter Bagehot** (1826-77), economist, banker and author of *The English Constitution.*
The Hill (A372) continues east, the road bridged at the town boundary by the **Hanging Chapel,** a 16C guild or corporation chapel, constructed over a vaulted gateway which effectively frames the view of the one mile distant Huish Episcopi *(see below).*

EXCURSIONS

★ **Muchelney** - *2 miles south by a by-road. See Muchelney.*

★ **Long Sutton** - *4 miles east by A372.*

Huish Episcopi - St Mary's church **tower★★** is one of the great jewels in the Somerset crown.
Built in the 15C of local blue lias and mellow Ham stone, it rises, supported by stepped and pinnacled buttresses, to pierced battlements and fountains of crocketed pinnacles.
Each stage is underlined by panel tracery or a quatrefoil frieze : the Somerset traceried and transomed three-light window is flanked by niches, the paired bell lights are divided and framed by shafted pinnacles... The height to the very top is 99ft.
The Norman **west doorway** (1150-1200) with zigzag decoration was "fired" to a dark rust-gold in a disaster in the early 1300s when much of the church perished.
The parish is said to have served Trollope as the model for Plumpstead Episcopi in *The Warden.*

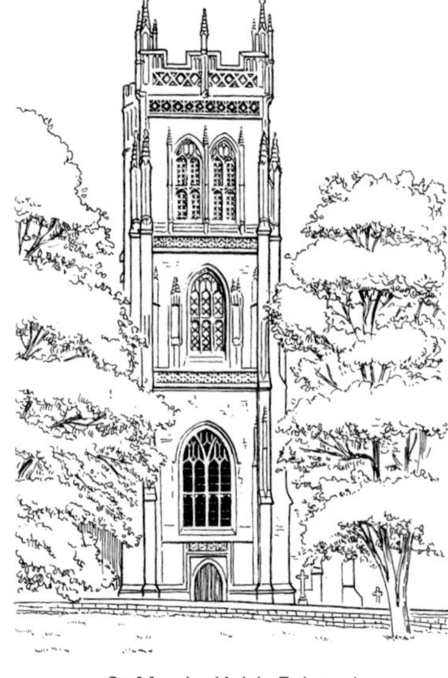
St Mary's, Huish Episcopi.

After 2 miles turn right off A372.

★ **Long Sutton** - The parish **church★★** at the village centre dates from 1490. The **tower,** with a taller stair turret, rises through three stages from the spandrelled door and west window with tangential arcs instead of transoms, to a window with framing niches, three belfry windows, the outer ones blank, the centre filled with Somerset tracery and, finally, an embattled crest with every feature ending in a pinnacle.
Inside are an outstanding **roof** of tie-beams, king posts and angel figures, a coloured **rood screen** with slender tracery between the mullions and a contemporary 16-sided, coloured **pulpit** with small 19C figures filling the original canopied niches.

★ **Midelney Manor** - *4½ miles west by A378 and a by-road.*

Curry Rivel - The Perpendicular **church** which incorporates earlier features within its walls has strangely banded **buttresses** and a tall tower with a taller stair turret built of blue lias with Ham stone dressings. Note the quatrefoil frieze and transomed, Somerset traceried bell openings.
The urn-crowned column, in the vicinity, is the **Burton Pynsent Monument.** Built of blue lias faced in Portland stone, it was designed by Capability Brown and erected in 1765 by William Pitt the Elder to Sir William Pynsent, who left the statesman his Elizabethan manor.

Turn round at Curry Rivel and bear right towards Drayton.

★ **Midelney Manor** ⓥ - The manor dates back to King Ine's charter of 693 under which he granted Muchelney, Midelney and Thorney - Great, Middle and Thorn Islands which rose above the surrounding marshlands - to the Benedictines. The abbot built a hunting lodge on Midelney which, by the 16C, was let to a John Trevilian whose sons built the present house which is still occupied by the family. The classic H plan of the grey stone house was disrupted by the brothers' quarrelling when it was under construction : no central porch but two separate entrances in opposite corners of the forecourt were built and, inside, a massive partition wall which was not pierced until 1926. Trevilians in the east wing enlarged and improved their range, notably in the 18C when the interior was remodelled in the Queen Anne style.
Inside are Georgian and Louis XV **furniture,** porcelain and **armorial china,** paintings and family portraits and **mementoes** including high sheriffs' banners and city freemen's presentation caskets - one of which, in silver, is a model of the house. The intertwined histories of the manor and the family are also explained.
In the flower-filled garden is an early 18C **falcons' mews.**

High Ham - *4 miles north. See High Ham.*

Admission times and charges for the sights described are listed at the end of the guide.

Every sight for which there are times and charges is identified by the symbol ⓥ in the middle section of the guide.

★★ LANHYDROCK Cornwall

Michelin Atlas p 3 or Map 403 – F32 – 3 miles south of Bodmin

The fascination of Lanhydrock lies in the incongruity of a fine mid-17C style granite exterior, with battlements and corner pinnacles, containing a Victorian-Edwardian interior.
In 1881 all but the entrance and one wing of the house was gutted by fire. After four years of reconstruction, the new exterior exactly matched the unscathed north wing, while the interior included all the latest in Victorian amenities including central heating, bathrooms and modern kitchens.

Gardens and grounds – In front of the three wings of the house, in place of the original forecourt, lies a **formal garden** leading towards an elegant Renaissance-style **gatehouse** and to the 450 acres of wooded parkland and rolling farmland in which the house and garden sit. To the rear are **terrace gardens,** planted with specimen and flowering trees, magnolias, azaleas, camellias, rhododendrons and hydrangeas.

TOUR ⏲ *1 hour*

Grand Hall – Inside the 17C porch, which was not consumed by the fire, the Grand Hall is Victorian-17C with family portraits on the walls and mementoes on the tables.

Inner Hall – The **wallpaper** is a William Morris design.

Dining Room – The stately 19C room, with its 19C panelling, has a **table** set with fine china and glass and a **centrepiece** made in shining Cornish tin; the owners, the Robartes, were tin mine-owners. Note, on a side-table, the hand painted dessert plates.

Lady Robartes' Room – The small room is cosy with family photographs, books, a desk, a small piano, armchairs, a needlework box and a bobble chenille cloth on the table.

Corridor and Billiard Room – The masculine area of the house is given character with game trophies on the walls, a fur-lined coat, hat and gloves ready for an outing...

Smoking Room – The panelled room is furnished with a Turkey carpet, Eton and Oxford favours, a mounted fish and half a dozen easy-chairs.

Bedrooms – The rooms reflect the owners' personalities : cane furniture and innumerable photographs for the last Miss Robartes; practicality for Lord Robartes; grace for Lady Robartes, from whose room there is a beautiful **view.**

Long Gallery – The gallery, 116ft in length and occupying the north wing, is roofed with an outstanding 17C **plaster barrel vault.** The surface is divided into 24 sections, each carved in deep relief with an Old Testament scene and separated from its neighbours by banding decorated with every conceivable bird and beast.

Servants' Quarters – The rooms on the second floor give a vivid insight into the contrast in lifestyles enjoyed by those above and below stairs at the turn of the century.

★ LAUNCESTON Cornwall

Pop 6 017

Michelin Atlas p 3 or Map 403 – G32 – Local Map p 49

Perched high on the Cornwall-Devon border, Launceston was Cornwall's chief town until 1835 when the assize court moved to Bodmin. Every age is represented in the buildings : a castle founded in the 11C by William I's brother, **Robert of Mortain** *(qv),* Earl of Cornwall; one of the four gates of the medieval walled town; narrow, twisting streets; a market; 18C-19C shop fronts; galleries; a church and chapel of ease; houses of all periods ranging from half-timbered Tudor, through 18C and 19C to 20C post-war anonymous styles.

SIGHTS

★ **Castle** ⏲ – Walk through the former bailey and up the motte steps to the shell keep; circle the wall before mounting the 13C centre tower for the **view★** of Dartmoor, Bodmin Moor (Brown Willy and Rough Tor) and the Tamar.
The castle's history is not adventurous : it was visited by the Black Prince, was seized by the rebels in the **Cornish Rebellion** *(qv)* of 1549, and changed hands twice during the Civil War. Until 1840 it served as an assize court and prison, being notorious for imprisoning or executing prisoners on the nod; **George Fox,** founder of the Society of Friends, was incarcerated in it for several months in 1656.

★ **St Mary Magdalene** – The Perpendicular church of 1511 gives the lie to the impossibility of carving **granite** : walls, buttresses, two-storey porch, gables are closely patterned with quatrefoils, coats of arms – Henry VII's on the east gable – fleurs-de-lis, roses, pomegranates and, below the east window, Mary Magdalene. The tower is 14C.
The interior with slender piers, pointed arches and **wagon roofs** contains a pre-Reformation painted **pulpit,** a brass on the south wall and the royal arms of George I.

South Gate – The medieval gateway rises through two floors to a castellated parapet; it has served as the former guardhouse and gaol.

Local History Museum ⏲ – *Lawrence House, Castle St.*
The museum presents a range of exhibitions on local life through the ages.

★ LITTLECOTE Wiltshire

Michelin Atlas p 18 or Map 403 - P29

"The Knight was brought to his tryall, and to be short this judge had this whole house, parks and manor, and (I thinke) more, for a bribe to save his life" – the knight was Sir John Dayrell; the crime, the murder of his newborn, bastard baby; the judge, the future Lord Chief Justice, Sir John Popham *(qv)*; the house, Littlecote; the date, the late 16C.

In those dark days a handmaid was delivered of a son by Dayrell by a local midwife; when she took the newborn baby to the father waiting by the fireplace in the corridor outside he put it on the fire; the mother remained masked throughout her travail. The midwife, after two years, told a justice of the crime and Dayrell was brought to trial before Sir John Popham.

In over 700 years Littlecote ⊙ has been owned by six families and received seven royal visits : Henry VIII in 1520 and 1536, Elizabeth I in 1601, Charles II in 1663, William of Orange in 1688, Queen Mary in 1928, George VI and Queen Elizabeth in 1941.

The medieval house was extended eastwards during the 16C to almost the full length of the present north (garden) front; it was built of flint relieved by brick courses, stone tiles and had a fine oriel window providing a good view of the gardens from the gallery. The south (park) front, in deep rose brick with stone dressings outlining the large windows and centre gables, was added by Sir John in 1590.

HOUSE *½ hour*

The **oldest rooms** in the house are arranged to recall events in July 1642 on the eve of the Civil War. Four cavalrymen with their kit occupy the Trooper's Room.

The austere Cromwellian **Chapel,** with a central pulpit and no altar, has survived unaltered since that period.

The rich **panelling** in the Brick Hall contrasts with the most unusual early 18C **wall paintings** in the Dutch Parlour.

The **Great Hall** (1590) displays the **arms and armour★** of the Littlecote contingent of the Parliamentary army : buffcoats, breastplates, helmets, gauntlets, pikes, pistols, carbines and muskets. Note also the magnificent panelling, the plasterwork ceiling and the prehistoric Irish elk antlers. The long 17C table (30ft) was built in situ and is netted at one end for the game of shuffle-board.

ROMAN MOSAIC FLOOR

Beside the river *(west of the house)* are the remains of a Roman villa (2C AD) and pseudo-religious precinct; the beautiful **mosaic floor** shows Orpheus surrounded by female representations of the four seasons. It was discovered in 1727 by an estate steward, whose wife embroidered a panel of the design; it was re-excavated and restored in 1977-80.

Roman Mosaic, Littlecote.

GARDENS

The area between the house and the river is divided by brick walls enclosing five knot gardens in front of the house, a rose garden with 4 000 trees, a medieval garden, a herb garden and a potager for vegetables.

PARK

Displays of **falconry** are held in the park *(south of the house)*.

VILLAGE

The outbuildings *(east of the house)* contain **mews** for the birds of prey, stabling, a traditional farmyard with old breeds of animals, craft workshops, an imaginative display of **classic cars** (1919-89) and an adventure playground; a narrow-gauge **railway** runs beside the river to the Roman villa.

The Cornish pasty is possibly the most famous dish to originate from Cornwall. It is a type of turnover made of shortcrust or, occasionally, puff pastry with a filling of meat, onions and potatoes. Pasties were first invented for the Cornish miners as a convenient way of taking a whole meal down the mines: the pastry, which served only as a container, held both sweet and savoury fillings, at opposite ends.

★ LIZARD PENINSULA Cornwall

Michelin Atlas p 2 or Map 403 - E33, 34

The Lizard, England's most southerly point and the source of **Serpentine roc** is known for the telecommunications dishes on windswept Goonhilly Dow and the coves and fishing villages strung like a necklace around its high-cliff shore.

VILLAGES and COVES on the Lizard

A tour of all the villages - 100 miles - about 5½ hours - is possible b indigestible.

Praa Sands - Praa Sands, just west of the Lizard peninsula, is known for three-mile beach.

The Loe - The freshwater **lagoon** known as The Loe (no bathing or fishing) is drowned valley, dammed at its mouth by the shingle bar swept up by t Atlantic.

Along the foreshore the sand extends from Gunwalloe Cove to **Porthleven,** resort, active fishing port and boat-building harbour, distinguished by a 19C clo tower.

★ **Gunwalloe Fishing Cove** - The thatch roofs of Berepper mark the descent to t even smaller village of fishermen's cottages crowded behind the minute **co** Pieces of eight (gold coins) have been washed up on the beach from a galle lost off the point.

★ **Cury** - The 14C **church★** of St Corentin of Brittany is distinguished by a **Cel cross** (9ft), a Norman **south door** framed by columns and a decorated tymp num, a rosette-carved font and a transept-chancel squint with an octagor column.

Poldhu Point - The **Marconi Memorial,** a granite obelisk at the cliff edge 200y south of the point, marks the site of the radio station from which signals we first sent out by Marconi and successfully received in Newfoundland 12 December 1901.

★★ **Mullion Cove** - The cove, which lies back from the line of cliffs, is framed by white sand beach, small harbour, a natural **rock arch,** pinnacles and an offshc island.

Nearly a mile inland in Mullion village stands the 15C-16C **church★**, dedicat to the Breton saint, Malo or Mellane of Rennes; it has a granite and serpenti tower, polished lime ash floor, the royal arms of Charles II, early 16C carv **bench-ends** and a 13C font decorated with a serpent. Sheep-dogs attending chur with their masters could leave by the "dog-door" in the nailed south door when nature called.

Kynance Cove.

★★ **Kynance Cove** - The high cliffs, sand beach uncovered at low tide and pinnacle rocks emerging from the brilliant blue-green sea on a clear day are a memorable sight. It is advisable to visit out of hours as up to 10 000 visitors have been counted on a fine summer's day.

The Lizard - The lighthouse *(qv)* is the only feature of interest on the point.

★ **Landewednack** - **Serpentine** is the hallmark of the pretty, old thatch-roofed village where the **church★** and its tower are made of the glossy green and black-velvet stone, the Norman **door** in the battlemented porch is framed with black serpentine columns and zig-zag and circle decorated *voussoirs,* and the pulpit and lectern entirely carved out of the stone. Today village craftsmen tu and polish the stone into ornaments.

Grade - The village's present church (1862) incorporates all that survived t ravages of wind and rain over the years : the early 14C two-storey **tower** square blocks of serpentine and granite with tall pinnacles, the **font** and 1 brass.

★ **Cadgwith** - The delightful **fishing village** of thatched and slate-roofed cottages w whitewashed walls overlooks the shingle beach of a minute cove.

Ruan Minor - The **church★**, once a Norman chapel, built of granite and local dark green serpentine stone, gained its serpentine tower (25ft) in t 14C.

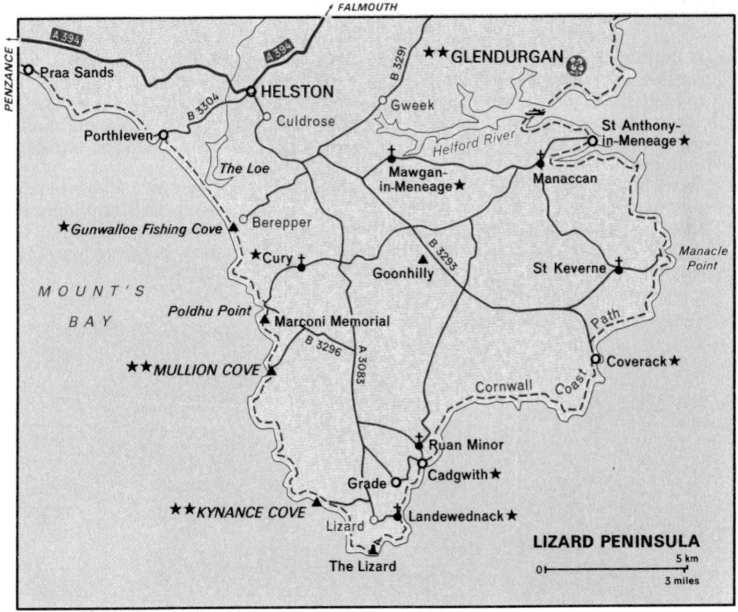

Goonhilly Satellite Earth Station ⏲ – *7 miles southeast of Helston by B3293.* The British Telecom Visitors' Centre explains the history and development of telecommunications through films, displays and working models of telephone exchanges and fax machines; a bus tour of the site includes a visit to the first aerial, the old Observation Tower and the Operation Control Area.

★ **Coverack** – A 1 : 6 descent leads to the old **fishing village** of thatched and slate-roofed cottages overlooking the harbour and wide cove. The village was famous for smuggling – even the name means "hideaway" in Cornish. In 1840, it is said, officers seized some 125 casks of spirits from a band who then undertook a "second wrecking" or raid to recapture the kegs so as not to disappoint their customers – spirits were usually bespoken. Three casks were left for the officers as consolation...

St Keverne – The original octagonal ribbed church **spire** had become so important as a landmark to shipping avoiding **The Manacles** underwater reefs that it was immediately rebuilt when struck by lightning in 1770.
The **church**★ was built in the 14C-15C by Cistercian monks but the **arcade** in green-grey-white-rose stone probably came from Brittany in the 13C.
Note the three sets of **rood-screen stairs,** carved **bench-ends,** a faded St Christopher **wall-painting,** the 15C font and Jacobean pulpit.

Manaccan – The Norman church, altered in the 13C-15C and restored in the 19C, is known locally for the fig-tree growing out of the 14C, slate tower wall.
Note the Norman door with three orders of columns and ribbed *voussoirs,* also the **squint** inside.

★ **St Anthony-in-Meneage** – St Anthony and Gillan lie on either side of a small creek. The church, to which Gillan parishioners come by boat at high tide, is 12C-15C.

Mawgan-in-Meneage – The village and its granite **church**★ stand by a creek on the Helford River.
The 15C **tower** rises through three stages to ribbed pinnacles on **angel corbels.** Coats of arms flank the door; angel capitals adorn the tower arch.
Note the **squint,** and the **sword** and **helmet** of the Royalist, Sir Richard Vyvyan.

★★★ LONGLEAT Wiltshire

Michelin Atlas p 8 or Map 403 – N30

A bend towards the end of the long drive through rolling woodland suddenly reveals the splendour of Longleat, the magnificent Elizabethan house of pale golden stone which rises from a glorious lakeside setting. The square building comprises three tiers of large mullioned and transomed windows surmounted by an animated skyline of balustrading, ornamental chimney-stacks, turrets and statues.
Close by the house, the formal flower gardens are bordered by a stable block, an orangery and the lake; at a distance flourish groups of azaleas and rhododendrons. Deeper within its extensive grounds, but largely hidden from view, are a safari park, a maze (the largest in the world), a butterfly garden, a narrow-gauge railway (15in), a two-acre adventure playground and numerous other attractions.

Longleat House.

LONGLEAT HOUSE

The house is over four centuries old; the contents – portraits, furniture, porcelain, books, embroideries, silver – range over the whole period, reflecting the diverse interests of the unbroken line of Thynns from Sir John, who in 1541 purchased the site of a 13C Augustinian priory from Henry VIII for £53, to the present Marquess of Bath; the family tree from 1215 is at the foot of the Grand Staircase.

Exterior – The house was completed in 1580. Sir John Thynn, "an ingenious man and a traveller", acted as his own architect, drawing on the many ideas he had gleaned during his life at court, as brother-in-law to Sir Thomas Gresham the financier and builder of Osterley Park, and as adjutant and steward to the Duke of Somerset in whose service he travelled abroad, served on the battlefield and observed the remodelling of Syon Park and the construction of the original Somerset House in London, a building in the Renaissance style. The result has been justly termed "the first great monument of Elizabethan architecture".

Interior – It was Sir John's idea that the rooms at Longleat should look not on to inner courts, as was 16C custom, but out over the park.
In the 19C seven rooms along the east front had their decoration radically altered to the Italianate style. The transformation was the achievement of the 4th Marquess, a traveller and connoisseur who visited Venetian, Florentine and Roman *palazzi* and returned with ideas, artefacts and craftsmen, with roundels, cameos and painted ceiling panels, Baroque plasterwork, wall hangings and furnishings.
Against this sumptuous background are set family portraits, master paintings, English, French, Portuguese furniture, ceramics from Europe and the Orient, silver and crystal, splendid centrepieces...

TOUR ⏲ *1½ hours*

Great Hall – The hall contains a splendid **fireplace** pillared by five terms, the Gresham golden **grasshopper crest** in the ceiling, galleries displaying the **arms** of Sir John Thynn and his patron, the Duke of Somerset, panelling hung with trophies and vast hunting scenes by the 18C painter John Wootton... Note also the 30ft **shuffle-board** table of *c*1600, the oak and steel treasure chests, 17C armchairs, inlaid writing-tables...

Ante-Library – The first of the transformed rooms, furnished in the French Empire style, contains a portrait of the 6th Marquess painted in 1971 by **Graham Sutherland** (1903-80).

Red Library – The long gallery, which houses some 6 000 of the 39 000 volumes in the Longleat collection, has Florentine inlaid walnut **bookcases,** a 17C inlaid secretaire, an 18C **writing desk** and a 20C laburnum, holly and robinia **table** made by John Makepeace *(qv)* for the house's 400th anniversary.

Breakfast Room – The room is hung with yellow damask and furnished with Chippendale-style chairs set round a table laid for breakfast. On the walls are family portraits including the 5th Marquess by William Orpen *(over the fireplace),* the 4th Marquess, who Italianised the house, his wife by G F Watts (full length in a dress to be seen in the collection displayed in the Corridor on an upper floor).

Lower Dining Room – The table below the gilded, coffered ceiling gleams with a gilt 17C **steeple-cup,** silver-gilt wine flagons, crystal, silver and Sèvres china. Chairs and furniture are of 17C Portuguese ebony and ebonised mahogany. On the panelled walls hang portraits of the 1st Marquess by Lawrence *(over the fireplace),* **Sir John Thynn,** the builder *(left)* and Thomas Thynn *(window alcove),* a friend of the Duke of Monmouth, known for his riches as Tom o' Ten Thousand and assassinated in Pall Mall in 1682.

State Dining Room – In the first of the state rooms the table is set with a silver **centrepiece** (1837) of 1 000oz, representing the last charge in the Civil War Battle of Landsdown Hill, silver **salt-cellars** of the *Cries of London* (1851) and 18C silver plates. The walls are covered with Cordoba leather and hung with 17C portraits.

Saloon – The 90ft Elizabethan Long Gallery with a wall of windows on to the park, a massive **marble fireplace** and alabaster doorcases contains fine small **furniture** : 17C and 18C Sicilian and French clocks and French tables – note the mirror pair of tortoise-shell and brass – James II chairs with their original rose brocade...

State Drawing Room – The end room in the series of those transformed overlooks the hall through an embrasure. It is richly decorated with ceiling panels after Titian and Veronese and 17C Genoese velvet from which the gold thread disappeared on the journey from Italy. The carpet of a curious green shade was originally red in colour; it was dyed to complement the grass outside by an impulsive marchioness. The fine **paintings** are Italian except for a portrait by Hans Eworth of *Master John,* son of Sir John the builder, at six months *(by the door).* Note among the furniture the French **inlaid tables** with gilt mounts by Boulle, a **writing-table** made for Louis XVI and acquired by Talleyrand, and an 18C galleried, marquetry **bonheur du jour.**

PARK and GARDENS ⏲

The park was landscaped in 1757 by **Capability Brown,** who planted specimen trees in the foreground and dense woods on the hillside; he also created the present tree-fringed Half Mile Pond out of the early 18C "canal" which had been contrived by combining the original ponds (long leat) in the valley.
The flower gardens, containing roses, hydrangeas and flowering trees graced by free-roaming peacocks and white doves, have been developed since Brown's day. They are enclosed by high yew hedges and wistaria covered walls. An orangery houses exotics amid pools.
Tucked away behind the house are the **Maze,** planted in 1975 and consisting of over 1½ miles of pathways bordered by yew hedges, the huge children's playground, the tropical greenhouse which is home to exotic butterflies, the narrow-gauge railway which runs through the woods and beside the lake (coarse fishing available)...

SAFARI PARK ⏲

The safari park is famous for its lions but also boasts white, golden tabby and Siberian tigers, African elephants, white rhinos, hippos, rhesus monkeys, gorillas, giraffes, zebras, eland, deer, buffaloes, camels, long horned cattle, Canadian timber wolves, Shetland ponies... Safari boats cruising the lake are accompanied by leaping, honking sea-lions.

★★ LUNDY ISLAND Devon Pop 17

Michelin Atlas p 6 or Map 403 – F, G30

Visiting Lundy ⏲ is a carefree adventure, starting with the boat trip from the mainland : there are no cars – except for a Landrover and a tractor – no telephones, no newspapers; there is a shop selling necessities and the island's own **puffin stamps,** a tea-house, a pub and a farm. The attraction of the island is its fascinating bird, marine and wild life, and the simple pleasure of a place undisturbed by modern attractions.
The island derives its name from the Icelandic word for puffin, *Lunde,* but together with the colony of these eye-catching birds there are also other sea birds : razorbill, guillemot, fulmar, Manx shearwater, shag, kittiwake, different species of gull...
Animals on Lundy include Devonshire cattle, wild **Soay sheep,** mountain goats, **Sika deer** and the free-roaming, handsome dun-coloured **Lundy ponies** (a New Forest-Welsh Mountain cross established in the 1930s).
In 1986 Lundy was established as a Marine Nature Reserve : grey seals, basking shark and porpoise have been seen. The clear waters and numerous wrecked ships in the area offer excellent diving.

GEOGRAPHY

The island is a triangular granite rock mass, three miles long, less than a mile wide, rising 400ft out of the Atlantic-Bristol Channel breakers. The west face mounts sheer from the sea, the cliffs advancing and retreating behind sharp offshore rocks and coves; to the north, the line of the cliffs appears to extend to the horizon. The east coast is less precipitous, descending in steps and by way of hanging valleys to wide bays and shingle beaches all covered by the sea at high tide.
The undulating land is clothed with turf, close-cropped at the south end by the farm stock and to the north by the wild goats, the dark Soay sheep brought over from St Kilda's in 1920 and now naturalised, and rabbits in whose burrows puffins sometimes nest in the spring. Gorse, bracken and peat bogs are to be found in the hanging valleys; sycamore in the sheltered hollow at the southeast end of the island. In the spring pink thrift covers the upland grass, rhododendron groves enliven the east cliff lower path.

HISTORY

The Mariscos, a Norman-Somerset family, came to Lundy in the 12C; they were a lawless, violent group who built a stronghold where Bronze and Iron Age man and Celts had previously settled. In the 13C, a Marisco plotted against Henry III who had him hanged, drawn and quartered before seizing the island, destroying his stronghold and appointing a royal constable who in 1243 completed the castle still confusingly known as Marisco's Castle.
The island's position in the Channel made it the perfect hideout for pirates throughout the centuries of Bristol's trade with Europe, America and the West Indies. In 1750 Thomas Benson, MP and High Sheriff of Devon, leased the island and became the biggest pirate of all, diverting prisoners he had undertaken to transport to America to work the quarries, preying on cargo ships and swindling insurance companies.
The modern era dates from the 19C when the quarries were worked industrially, the road built up from the beach and the church erected. The last private owners introduced the Lundy ponies, the rarely-seen deer, the Soay sheep, also the puffin stamps.

SIGHTS

A complete circuit of the island is 11 miles, a walk to the northwest point about 6 miles there and back. Flat shoes and outdoor clothing are advised.

Northwest Point Walk – The path, which runs along the island's spine, is lined by 2½ ton stones set by Trinity House as markers for the lighthousemen who had to find their way in fog and darkness to the northern light. There are constant changes of view : straight ahead, for example, where because of the space, the light and the lie of the land, the island appears to go to infinity..

Old Light – The original lighthouse of 1819 was erected on the island's highest point where, shining at 567ft into the mist and clouds, it was invisible from the sea. To one side the skeletal, winged aerogenerator harnesses the energy of the Atlantic winds to supplement the island's electricity supply.

Walled Enclosure – The ground is an early Christian burial ground.

Battery – *West coast.* The battery was built by Trinity House *(qv)* as a fog signal station in 1863 *(path down just south of Quarter Wall),* blank rounds being fired in bad weather every 10 minutes from the George III cannon.

Quarter, Halfway and Threequarter Walls – The cross walls date from the 18C.

Quarries – *East coast.* The quarries were worked in the 18C by Benson *(see above)* and industrially in the 19C – the Quarry Pool is inhabited by great orfe (fish).

Pondsbury and Punchbowl Valley – The large dewpond drains towards the west.

Jenny's Cove – The main habitat on the island of the puffin.

Tibbetts Point and Cottage – *East coast.* The Admiralty look-out and granite building were constructed in 1909 on the second highest point on the island.

Devil's Slide – The steep slip, which is far up the northwest coast, is a proving ground for rock climbers.

North Light – The now automatic lighthouse *(qv)* was built, with its pair, in 1896 to replace The Old Light. The stones in the fields are from Bronze and Iron Age hut circles.

East Cliff Lower Path – The path, noted for its rhododendrons, extends from just beyond the Battlements to below Quarter Wall.

Marisco Castle – The 12C-13C castle stands witness to the island's rugged history.

Millcombe House – The Classical-style granite house was built in the 1830s as the home of the island's then owners.

St Helena's – The large, strangely urban looking church, was erected in 1896.

South Light – Below the lighthouse divers explore offshore wrecks.

★★ LYDFORD Devon Pop 1 880

Michelin Atlas p 3 or Map 403 - H32 - Local map p 90

The long village on the western edge of Dartmoor *(qv)* straggles down from the main road towards the River Lyd and the gorge, the buildings getting ever older as far as the group of cottages and the rector's onetime house, built with stout oak timbers in the 16C; now an inn, it displays coins minted in the village between 978 and 1050, the time of Aethelred the Unready.

★★ LYDFORD GORGE ⊙

2 hours for the joint Upper and Lower Path walk.

First right over the road bridge or, for those not wishing to walk far, continue 1½ miles along the road to the Waterfall entrance.

The gorge is about 1½ miles long with rock walls in places 60ft high. The cleft narrows and widens by turns, the river swirling at the feet of tall beeches, sycamores and a dozen other varieties of tree. Among the birds to look out for are woodpeckers, dippers, possibly a heron.

Lydford Gorge.

The Paths - There are three marked paths from the main entrance - two interconnect, near the Waterfall, enabling a return by a different route.

Upper Path - *1¼ miles.* The path follows the northeast-southwest course of the gorge from above, affording bird's-eye **views** of the river and glimpses of Dartmoor.

Lower Path - *1½ miles.* The path at the water's edge skirts the northwest bank *(handrails in more difficult parts - liable to be wet and slippery after rain).*

Third Path - *1 mile Rtn.* The path leads in the opposite direction from the Pixie Glen to the Bell Cavern by way of the thundering whirlpool known as the **Devil's Cauldron.**

White Lady Waterfall - The fall, a 100ft single strand of water, is at the south end of the gorge.

ADDITIONAL SIGHTS

Lydford Castle - From the 7C-13C Lydford was of military importance as a Saxon outpost, first against the Celts and later against the Danes - Lydford was sacked in 997.
The present ruined **keep,** two storeys high on top of its mound, represents the remains of a stronghouse, erected in 1195 and rebuilt to hold prisoners and tinners awaiting trial before their own stannary court *(qv).* By the 14C the court was notorious, "Lydford law" being such, it was said, that "in the morn they hang and draw and sit in judgement after". The castle continued as a prison until the 17C and as a stannary court until 1800.

St Petroc's - The church, one of 30 possibly founded personally by St Petroc in the 6C, was rebuilt and enlarged on Norman foundations in the 13C, 15C and 19C - the south aisle and tower are 15C, note how the latter was mis-joined on to the earlier nave.
Inside, the plain **tub font** is Norman; the tower-nave arch is decorated with carved Gothic panelling; the **rood screen** in the traditional style is modern as are the 69 **bench-ends** carved in 1923-26 by two men, one for the figures, one for the borders. Outside, by the south porch, is the **tomb** with the entertaining epitaph "Here lies in horizontal position, The outside case of George Routleigh, Watchmaker..."

Walkers, campers, smokers...
please be careful!
Fire is the worst threat to woodland

Respect the life of the countryside
Drive carefully on country roads
Protect wildlife, plants and trees

LYDIARD PARK Wiltshire

Michelin Atlas p 17 or Map 403 – O29

House ⊙ – The mid-18C stone house, two storeys high, eleven bays wide with pyramid-roofed pavilions, overlooks spreading cedars and distant avenues. The rooms are notable for their proportions, moulded plaster and white-painted woodwork – note how funds ran out before the gold leaf highlighting the library ceiling was complete. 18C and 19C furniture and fine china have been assembled, together with family portraits of the St Johns, owners of the manor for 500 years, and works by the 2nd Viscountess Bolingbroke who was a talented 18C amateur artist.

★ **St Mary's** – The minute parish church is so full of **monuments** to St Johns that in the words of John Aubrey, the antiquary, it "exceeds all the churches of this countie". Eighteen figures are represented – recumbent in alabaster, kneeling or standing behind the original railings, beneath funeral helms, painted in a remarkable 17C triptych, or, in the case of Edward who died in the Civil War standing in gilded armour between parted curtains.
The church is older than the monuments, dating from the late 13C-15C. Note the traces of medieval wall paintings, Jacobean pulpit, 18C altarpiece and wrought-iron **communion rail**, and the **Jacobean screen** with the royal arms borne by robust supporters.

★ LYME REGIS Dorset

Pop 4 510

Michelin Atlas p 5 or Map 403 – L31 – Facilities

"The remarkable situation of the town, the principal street almost hurrying into the water, the walk to the Cobb skirting round the pleasant little bay... the Cobb itself, the very beautiful line of cliffs stretching out to the east of the town, are what the stranger's eye will seek", wrote Jane Austen in *Persuasion*.
The town's name dates from the 14C when Edward I gave the manor to his second queen.

Fossilling – The areas where fossils are found are west of the Cobb and **Monmouth Beach** (where the Duke landed in 1685), round the point and in Pinhay Bay, east *(2 miles)* of the town, below the 450ft high **Blue Venn Cliffs** (Charmouth; *2 miles*) **Stonebarrow** and **Golden Cap** *(4½ miles)*.

FIND OUT *(in Lyme or Charmouth)* the time of HIGH TIDE – the sea comes in fast to the foot of the cliffs and there are no getaway paths; DO NOT CLIMB THE CLIFFS or cut out fossils embedded in the cliff faces as the cliffs are not stable and rock falls are frequent, especially after rough weather. Do not enter closed areas; always be aware of the tide.

SIGHTS

Broad Street – The main street is lined along its steep sides by late Georgian houses with shops below, and inns of earlier date including the Royal Lion, bay windowed above a pillared porch. At the bottom are the sea and the **views**.

Bridge Street – The street, bearing left, crosses the outlet of the Lyme and before it turns uphill, overlooks a ledge known as the **Gun Cliff** from the days when the town was besieged by the Royalists (1644).

Museum ⊙ – The collection of **lace**, particularly point lace, and the 1710 Sun Insurance **fire engine** are overshadowed by the **fossils** found in this, the prime fossil area in England. The greatest "finder" ever was **Mary Anning** (1799-1846) whose father, a carpenter, imbued her with his skill and passion for fossilling. Early on she found a good ammonite which she sold for 2*s* 6*d;* at the age of 11, after a violent storm had brought down tons of cliff rock between Lyme and Charmouth, Mary Anning found the first complete fossil of the 180 million year old **ichthyosaurus.** In 1824 and 1828 she made further unique finds, first of a **plesiosaurus** then of a **pterodactyl.**

St Michael the Archangel – The church, truncated at its west end by the road and ever in danger at its east end of sea erosion and landslip, has nevertheless survived since Norman times – one of the bells is inscribed "O Sea spare me". The 58ft west **tower** was the crossing tower of the Norman church, the present porch that church's nave.
When the larger, Perpendicular church came to be built, the Norman chancel was demolished and replaced by a wide nave and aisles.
Note the difference in level from west to east, the **piers** with their shield and foliate carving in place of capitals, the plain, testered **Jacobean pulpit** presented by a Mercer and Merchant Adventurer in 1613, the **gallery** of 1611 with the borough arms and the **window** to Mary Anning *(see above)*.

Marine Parade – The houses lining the parade, pink washed, pantiled and many with upper observation window bays, date back to the 18C and early 19C; note on the house between the hotel and Library Cottage, the huge **ammonite fossil** embedded in the walls.

★ **The Cobb** – The Cobb is a breakwater, a curving 600ft long stone jetty, with its back braced against the Atlantic swell and a small harbour on its lee side. It lies half a mile west of the town, built of boulders and rocks at the end of the Marine Parade. Neither the origin of the name nor the date of the first wall of rocks, in which fossils can still be seen embedded, are known although it is recorded that repairs were being carried out in the 14C. It is Lyme's focal point and the dramatic setting used by novelists from Jane Austen to John Fowles.

Landslip – *See Landslip.*

★ LYNTON and LYNMOUTH Devon   Pop 2 075

Michelin Atlas p 6 or Map 403 – I30 – Facilities

Lynton and Lynmouth, complementary small towns in a hollow at the top and at the foot of 500ft North Devon-Exmoor cliffs, rejoice in glorious **views★** across the Bristol Channel to the distant Welsh coast, in sweeping moorland, cliff walks and wooded valley walks beside rushing torrents and waterfalls and, since 1890, in a **Cliff Railway.**

The architecture in **Lynton** is predominantly Victorian-Edwardian, the larger houses in their own gardens now largely converted into hotels; **Lynmouth** remains a traditional fishing village with small stone cottages and houses, a few still thatched, to which have been added seaside villas and more recent buildings following the flood disaster of 1952 when the River Lyn burst its banks, broke bridges and swept through the village, bringing down mud and 40 000 tons of boulders and broken tree trunks in its storm waters.

Cliff Railway ⏲ – The railway is 900ft long and rises at a gradient of 1:75 to connect the two resorts. The two cars operate by gravity, the top car taking on water to hoist the lower one and discharging as it reaches the bottom.

EXCURSIONS

★ **Valley of the Rocks** – *1 mile west along the Coastal Rd.*
The rocks, swathed in bracken, rise from the wide, grass-covered valley floor to crests of bare shale, spectacularly carved by the wind into fancifully named outlines...

★ **Watersmeet** – *1½ miles east by A39, then 200yds along a footpath – local map p 161.*
The spot is where the waters of the East Lyn and Farley rivers meet in a deep, wooded valley, dappled with sunlight and green with ferns; the river bed is strewn with great boulders around which the water swirls and falls in an unending cascade. A fishing lodge of 1832 stands on the far bank across a footbridge.

Lynmouth Foreland – *4 miles east by A39 and a by-road.*
Foreland and its lighthouse *(qv)* provide a **vantage point** from which to overlook the hogsback cliffs on either side. The Foreland itself, composed of ancient red and grey quartz grits and slate, is surprisingly bare of trees.

Heddon's Mouth – *5 miles east by the Coastal Rd to Hunter's Inn then 3 miles Rtn on foot through the woods.*
The road skirts three bays from above before coming to the village of Martinhoe and, just beyond, Hunter's Inn. The rift followed by the Heddon is spectacular with rock walls rising 700ft in places before it opens out into a small, sheltered, pebble bay.

Combe Martin – *16 miles west by A39 and A399.*
The village, between Exmoor and Ilfracombe, straggles the length of the combe, marked by a 19C folly, the **Pack of Cards Inn** and a pink sandstone **church** with a west tower 99ft tall, decorated with gargoyles. Lead and silver mines were worked locally from the 13C to the 19C.

Combe Martin Motorcycle Collection ⏲ – *Cross St.* The machines of early and late manufacture include a Brough Superior said to be that on which **T E Lawrence** *(qv)* met his death.

Ilfracombe – *21 miles west by A39 and A399. See Ilfracombe.*

★ LYTES CARY Somerset

Michelin Atlas p 8 or Map 403 – L30 – 4 miles southeast of Somerton

Two 16C oriels in Ham Hill stone beneath swan and gryphon finialled gables and an attached chapel distinguish the manor house which was occupied by fourteen generations of the Lyte family from the time when William Le Lyte, Sergeant-at-Law under Edward I, built the first house on the site in 1286.

The Lytes of the 16C-17C were interested in botany and genealogy : Henry made a garden at Lytes Cary and published (1578), as an enlarged translation from the Dutch, a work which became widely known as *Lyte's Herbal;* his son traced the genealogy of James I from Brutus, which earned him the king's pleasure and award of the Nicholas Hilliard miniature of the king set in gold and diamonds (now in the British Museum).

In the 18C the house was sold and fell into decay. In 1907 it was rescued by Sir Walter Jenner, son of the physician, who restored the fabric, furnished the interior with 17C-19C pieces and textiles in character, and laid out Elizabethan topiary gardens in the original forecourt, a parterre garden, a yew alley...

TOUR ⏲ *45min*

Hall – The hall, which was added to the original house *c*1453 has a typical Somerset roof of arch braces, cusped wind braces and an ornate cornice marked by supporting half-angels holding shields bearing the Lyte arms.

The 15C **fireplace** is original, the landscape above it is by Jan Wyck (17C).

Of especial note among the furniture and furnishings are two oak refectory tables, one with the massive turned legs of *c*1600, the second with the fluted frieze of the mid-17C, the pair of late 17C **delft tulip vases** and the late 18C **mahogany cheese coaster.**

Lytes Cary, Somerset.

Oriel Room – The room, which served as the family dining room, was heated by a miniature version of the hall fireplace.
The **oak bird cage** dates from the 18C. Note the copies of pages from the *Herba (see above).*

Great Parlour – The parlour, with the bay and other windows overlooking the garden almost filling one side, is notable for its original 17C **panelling** with fluted Ionic pilasters and pillared chimneypiece.
Among the wealth of beautiful 17C-18C oak and walnut furniture, note the laburnum oyster **parquetry sidetable** on six legs, a red tortoise-shell **bracket clock** (London, 1700) and, in contrast, a Chinese lacquer bureau cabinet (*c*1700).

Little Parlour – The small room, a carpenter's shop until restored by Sir Walter Jenner whose portrait hangs on the wall, was probably the study of the antiquarian-botanist Lytes of the 16C-17C.
Among the furnishings are a pair of 18C **jardinières,** 17C brass **lantern clock** (Taunton), 18C-19C glass and a semicircular mahogany **drinking table** with a wheeled decanter trolley, which enabled both wine and imbibers to be warmed by the fire.

Great Chamber – The great room at the top of the stone newel staircase is embellished by the upper part of the parlour bay window and a **plaster ceiling** coved and ribbed; on the end wall are the **arms** of Henry VIII.

Chapel – The detached chapel, dating from 1343, is the oldest feature of the house. The **frieze** of coats of arms was added by the genealogist member of the family in James I's reign.

MADRON Cornwall

Pop 1 269

Michelin Atlas p 2 or Map 403 – D33

★ **St Maddern** – The third church on the site overlooking Mount's Bay was constructed between the 14C and the 16C.
The 250 **bosses,** carved to 16 different patterns, and the **cornice angels** (retained when the roof was renewed) date from the 15C. The furnishings and monuments include an **inscribed stone** *(southwest wall)* thought to be 8C Celtic; an Early English sedilia *(Lady Chapel);* five pre-14C animal **bench-ends;** a 17C brass; several 17C slate memorials; a 14C English **alabaster panel** of ten angels, probably from a reredos or shrine. The wooden panel bearing the Tudor rose and the royal arms of Henry VII was carved in earnest of the loyalty of the vicar and the congregation after a lapse in support of Perkin Warbeck *(qv).*
The **rood-screen,** with faintly coloured original wainscot panels and crocketed gables, dates from 1450. The bell from the local **Ding Dong Tin Mine** (closed 1878) hangs by the south door; opposite is a panel of **tin marks,** in local use from 1189. The **Nelson banner** *(north wall)* was made in haste in 1805 to be carried before the major and burgesses of Penzance processing to Madron for the first Trafalgar Service; the procession and service are held annually on the Sunday nearest 21 October.

Well and Baptistery – *1 mile north (sign : Wishing Well); park; 10 mins on foot Rtn.*
The rag-tree beside the well shows that people still believe in the water's healing properties. St Maddern's baptistery (6C) has a circular basin and an altar stone.

In this guide
town plans show the main streets and the way to the sights;
local maps show the main roads and the roads recommended in a round tour.

★ MAIDEN CASTLE Dorset

Michelin Atlas p 8 or Map 403 – M31 – 2 miles southwest of Dorchester

The massive, grass-covered **earthwork ramparts** ⊙, the finest in Britain, are three miles long as they follow the hillside contours to enclose about a hundred acres on the saddleback down. They have commanded a **view★** of the surrounding countryside for more than 2 000 years.

Building periods – A Neolithic settlement was established on the site in *c*3000 BC. The existing fort was begun *c*800 BC when 16 acres on the east knoll were enclosed by a single rampart with entrances to east and west. At the end of the century the west knoll was added to the enclosure, now some 47 acres.

In *c*150 BC the rampart was rebuilt to twice its original size and augmented by a 50ft deep ditch; additional fortifications were constructed to north and south.

The **final phase** came in 100-60 BC when the appearance of the sling, with a range of 100yds, caused the outer ditches and ramparts to be remodelled and the gateways, always well protected by inner and outer walls, to be made even more of a chicane.

Inside, the walls, huts, storage barns and metalled streets were kept in good order, ammunition dumps of 20 000 beach pebbles for use as sling stones were kept prepared. In **AD 43,** however, the future Roman Emperor, Vespasian, besieged Maiden Castle as part of his campaign to subdue southern England. The Roman infantry advanced up the slopes, cutting their way through rampart after rampart until, in the innermost bay, they reached the huts which they fired. Under cover of the smoke, the entrance was forced, the inhabitants put to the sword.

At the end of the 4C a Romano-British **temple** and adjoining priest's house and hut were built (foundations uncovered on the east knoll), since when the site has been deserted. All the finds from the excavations are in the Dorset Museum, Dorchester *(qv).*

★ MALMESBURY Wiltshire

Pop 2 581

Michelin Atlas p 17 or Map 403 – N29

The centre of Malmesbury boasts one of England's finest market crosses, overlooked by the abbey which stands outlined against the sky, crowning a spur.

St Aldhelm (639-709) – The man (later canonised) who by his preaching, it is said, completed the conquest of Wessex, was a pupil at the school which was part of the religious community established in the town in the 7C by the Irish teacher, Maidulf; uniquely for the time, he went on to Canterbury, so becoming the first English scholar to combine the learning of Ireland and Europe. In 676 he returned to Malmesbury as teacher, **abbot,** builder of churches in the town at Bruton and Wareham, founder of monasteries at Frome and Bradford-on-Avon, and counsellor to his kinsman, the West Saxon King, Ine (r 688-726). In 705, when the See of Sherborne *(qv)* was founded, Aldhelm was appointed the first bishop. He is buried at Malmesbury.

The town's name is a combination-corruption of Maidulf and Aldhelm : Maelhelmsbury.

Other men associated with Malmesbury include Elmer, the **Flying Monk,** who launched himself from the old abbey tower in 1010 and "flew" 250yds before crashing but remained convinced that it was only lack of a tail which had brought him down; **William of Malmesbury** *(qv)* (1095-1143), monk, abbey librarian and great early historian, and the philosopher **Thomas Hobbes,** born in the town in 1588 (d 1679).

Three historic American families also have associations with the area : the **Washingtons** who in the 17C lived in Garadon *(3 miles east);* the Penns who originated in Minety *(6 miles northeast);* and **Abraham Lincoln's mother,** Nancy Hanks, who was a member of an old Malmesbury family.

West lunette, Malmesbury Abbey.

★ ABBEY ⏲ ¼ hour

The present church, an amazing conjuncture of gaunt ruin and living architecture was begun in the 12C. At its zenith, in the 14C, it extended 320ft from east to west, had a clerestory and vaulted roof, possessed a central crossing tower with a spire, and a west tower. It was surrounded by Benedictine conventual buildings.
In 1479 a fierce storm brought down the spire and tower, which in their fall destroyed the east end, transepts and crossing; one hundred years later the west tower fell, destroying three west bays of the nave. A majestic six bays remain. Between these cataclysmic events the monastery was suppressed by Henry VIII on 15 December 1539 and sold for £1 516 15*s* 2½*d* to William Stumpe, a local clothier, who used the stone to construct Abbey House. At first he set up looms in the nave of the old abbey church but in 1541 he presented the building to the people as their parish church.

Porch – The unique feature of the abbey is the **porch** : mid-12C Romanesque carving with trail and geometrical patterns on the eight orders, medallions of Biblical scenes (defaced), continuous banding and, in the **tympanum,** two angels supporting a mandorla with Christ in Glory at the centre – the figures are elongated like those in the lunettes on either side above the blind arcading.

Interior – The massive Norman pillars with scalloped capitals support just-pointed arches and a **triforium** of great rounded bays, crisply collared with zig-zag carving. On the south side note the **watching loft** from where the abbot or a monk could follow the service beyond the chancel screen.
The medieval stone screen at the end of the south aisle marks the chapel of St Aldhelm who was buried in an earlier abbey destroyed by fire in 1050; also buried in this earlier church (medieval tomb : *north aisle*) was **King Athelstan** (r 925-39), like his grandfather Alfred, a great admirer of Aldhelm.
A tombstone in the churchyard *(left of the path)* commemorates Hannah Twynnoy, mauled to death by a tiger from a travelling circus in 1703.

★★ MARKET CROSS

The cross was built of local stone in 1490 when the town was known for its tanning and felt making, silk weaving, lace making, spinning and of course its woollen weaving; it had a twice weekly market. More than a mere shelter, the cross rises 40ft high in a paeon of buttresses, crocketed pinnacles, castellations and flying arches to a spirelet, supreme pinnacle and cross. Note the carving and small, grinning masks – "a right faire costly peace of worke" as John Leland declared.

ADDITIONAL SIGHTS

St John's Bridge – The bridge *(on A429)* got its name from the hospital built by the Order of St John of Jerusalem on the town outskirts in the 13C. The hospital was dissolved, the knights banished; in 1694 the aged buildings were re-founded as almshouses. Through an archway is the Old Courthouse.

Bell Hotel – The hotel was built in the 16C to replace the guesthouse of the suppressed monastery using stone and timber from the conventual buildings.

High Street – The street and those behind it are lined with 16C-19C terrace houses with stone tiled roofs, many of which were refaced in the 18C with stone ashlar. The network of older streets and alleys is interconnected by a rare number of footbridges crossing tributaries of the Avon and Ingleburn Rivers which almost encircle the town.

★ MARLBOROUGH Wiltshire

Pop 5 330

Michelin Atlas p 17 or Map 403 – O29

The town, strategically placed on the London-Bath road *(A4),* has been known since the 19C for its school and in earlier centuries was famous as a market town; it was named by John Aubrey as "one of the greatest markets for cheese in the West of England". The main street, parallel to the River Kennet, developed westwards from a Saxon settlement (now The Green) to where the Normans soon after the Conquest, took over a prehistoric mound (60ft) as the site for a motte and bailey castle.
By the time the castle had fallen into ruin in the 14C, Marlborough had developed into a market : the long street was filled weekly with downland sheep and cattle and stalls of wool, meat, fresh produce and cheese. Room was needed to herd the animals; the cottages of the period were small and insubstantial and they were pushed further and further back until the street attained the extraordinary width which even permitted open stalls, or shambles *(qv),* to be pitched in a double line down the centre as they are still on market days.
The Civil War left scars but they were as nothing compared to the fire of 1653 when, it is recorded, "in the space of three or foure houres, there was burnt down to the ground about two hundred twentie foure dwelling Houses, besides many out-houses and stables, and most of the Household goods and Wares in the shops of many of the Inhabitants... The whole losse arising unto four score thousand pounds likewise there was burnt downe to the ground one of the Churches (St Mary's), and the Market House."

Marlborough Downs – The Downs, which extend in a wide semicircle north of the town, are traversed by the ages-old **Ridgeway Path** *(qv)*. The chalk slopes once grazed by the vast flocks of sheep, which make every town in Wiltshire a wool town in origin, are now scattered with small towns and villages, to the west especially, and threaded by local roads running between high hedges; to the east, the land folds in a quilt of large arable fields outlined by straggling files of trees, hedges and ditches, and, on the skyline, stalwart clumps of dark green deciduous broad-leaves.

SIGHTS

High Street – The wide High Street leads from The Green at the far east end of the town to the College at the west end. It is not the architecture which makes the street attractive but the up and down rooflines, the individuality of the houses with their ground-floor shopfronts, and at the east end "the pent houses", as Pepys called them when he stayed in the town in 1653, "supported on pillars which makes a good walk". In the same range are several shops which were "improved" in Georgian times by the insertion of first floor Venetian windows.

Town Hall – The hall in brick and stone, overlooking the High Street along its full length from the east end, was built to a Classical 17C-18C design on an island site by late Victorian craftsmen.

St Mary's – The church, also at the east end of the High Street in a network of small streets (Perrin's Lane, Patten Alley), was rebuilt after the fire during the Commonwealth, hence its Puritan austerity. The chancel is 19C.

Sun Inn – The inn and the modest brick range of which it is a part are timber-framed and date from the early 17C.

Castle and Ball – The inn, built in the 17C, was refronted after the fire and turned into a coaching inn in 1745. The house next door, which was pantiled in the 18C, was once an inn where Shakespeare is said to have played.

Sts Peter and Paul – The church on the green island site at the west end of the High Street is, like St Mary's, Norman in origin with Perpendicular remodelling, but was ferociously renewed in the 19C.

The Green – The Green, beyond the east end of the High Street, was the site of the Saxon settlement; the nearby Silverless and Kingsbury Streets are bordered by a variety of handsome 17C-19C houses : timber-framed, Classical 18C with pillared porches, ashlar-faced and weatherboarded and with windows from lattice to sash, oriel to Venetian.

Marlborough College – *Private.* The mound-site of the Norman castle *(see above)* was acquired in 1550 by Protector Somerset; in the 17C-18C both his grandson and the 6th Duke built separate mansions in the grounds, 1½ million bricks being required before the second was completed *c*1725.

In 1750 the house was let as a coaching inn, which flourished until the advent of the railway, when it was sold to become a school. At its foundation in 1843 the College numbered 200 boys; in the century and a half since, buildings have proliferated and pupils (now including girls) have increased in number to *c*900.

Marlborough White Horse – The **white horse** *(qv)* is cut into a low escarpment on the south side of the Bath road (A4) just west of the College.

EXCURSIONS

★★ **Savernake Forest** – *2 miles southeast. Entrances off A346 Andover and A4 London roads; parking and picnic places; hearths for open fires – otherwise NO FIRE; modestly equipped camping sites (c/o Forestry Commission).*

Savernake was a royal forest, hunted by Norman and Tudor kings alike, its woodland yielding boar and deer. In the 18C Capability Brown replanted the 4 000 acres, which it now comprises, with oak, ash, larch and thousands upon thousands of beech trees. Crossing the forest in a northwest-southeast line, passing halfway along its 3-mile course through the compass point intersection known as the Eight Walks, is the **Grand Avenue**★★★, palisaded with the superb grey-green trunks of 130ft beeches.

Round tour – *14 miles; leave Marlborough south by A346, bear left into A338.*

★ **Wilton Windmill** ⊙ – The mill (visible from A338 beyond East Grafton) was built in 1821 on top of the down behind the small village of Wilton, grouped around its duckpond.

The sweeps, two rigged with canvas sails, two with louvres, turn when corn is being ground but cannot be allowed to operate when visitors are in the mill owing to insufficient room in the cap. Inside the cap, the grinding machinery, similar to that of a watermill *(qv)*, can be seen together with the way in which the fantail, which never stops whirring, turns the sweeps into the wind.

Great Bedwyn – The old church is built of flint in the transitional Norman-Early English style with a square tower dating from the late 12C. The interior features arcades with dogtooth decoration supported on round columns with deeply undercut, all-different capitals, corbels carved with crowned heads and Seymour memorials : the tomb of Sir John (d 1536), father of Edward Seymour (Protector Somerset) and of Jane Seymour, a brass to John Seymour (d 1510) and a bust and gay cherubs on the tomb of a 17C duchess.

The unusual **stone museum** ⊙ presents a static display of worked stone and artefacts set in a working stonemason's yard.

★ **Crofton Beam Engines** ⏲ – The pumps were installed near the highest point on the Kennet and Avon Canal to supply water from underground sources to the locks descending in either direction. There are two engines, one an 1812 **Boulton and Watt** with 42in piston and cast-iron beam which is the oldest beam engine regularly in steam in the world. When the engines are in steam there are **boat trips** ⏲ *(1½ hrs)* through the tunnel.

Rejoin the A346 to Marlborough.

Pewsey – *7 miles south on A3455.*
The village of Pewsey, the chief feature of which, since 1911, has been a statue of King Alfred, gives its name to the **Vale of Pewsey★**, a beautiful stretch of country between Salisbury Plain and the Marlborough Downs. On the outskirts is the Pewsey **White Horse** *(qv).*

★ MARTOCK Somerset — Pop 3 712

Michelin Atlas p 8 or Map 403 – L31

The glory of Martock, a village built entirely in its older parts of Ham Hill stone, is the 15C-16C church and the glory of the church is its **angel roof.**

★★ **All Saints** – The west **tower** marked the completion of the church's reconstruction in the 15C-16C. It rises from a shafted door and five-light window, which starts below the string course and fills the second stage, and the elevation then continues through a bay and paired, transomed bell openings, all tracery-filled, to a typically pinnacled crest.

Interior – The **roof** presents an ordered arrangement of embattled tie-beams, purlins, king posts and braces, of carved pendants, tracery and pierced coffering – 768 panels in six different patterns. The 67 **lifesize angels** in wood and stone were added in 1513.
The paintings of the Apostles, in the niches above the arcades of Ham Hill stone, date from the early 17C; St James the Less is portrayed as James I and St Simon Zelotes as William Cecil, Lord Burghley (W on his cuff).
The clerestory was originally glazed with heraldic glass : ten shields to each window, "about 120 coats" a 17C diarist calculated; in July 1645 the Parliamentarians came to Martock, held a thanksgiving service for the capture of Bridgwater and smashed the lot.
The five stepped windows at the east end are relics of the Early English church on the site.

Main street – Among the houses lining the main street close to the church are the 13C-14C **Treasurer's House,** so-named because the rector of Martock was treasurer of Wells Cathedral; the 17C gabled manor house, much rebuilt after a fire in the 19C, and **Church House,** a long low building of two storeys with mullioned windows in which the door is surmounted by the date, 1661, and a composite inscription in English, Latin, Greek and Hebrew from the time when it was the local grammar school.
The main road also borders the **Market House,** a small Georgian building with a Venetian window, upraised upon arcades which once sheltered market stalls, and a market cross in the form of a Doric column.

MILTON ABBAS Dorset — Pop 433

Michelin Atlas p 8 or Map 403 – N31

Henry VIII dissolved Milton Abbey in 1539; Lord Milton, Earl of Dorchester, removed the village with similar autocracy two and a half centuries later.
The property was valuable and Henry sold it for £1 000 to his proctor, Sir John Tregonwell, who constructed a house amid the conventual buildings, while the village adopted the abbey as a parish church. **Lord Milton** in the 18C would have none of this : he rebuilt the village (1771-90) out of sight of the abbey, knocked down almost all the remaining conventual buildings and built himself the house (now a boys' school) at the centre of a park which he had planned by **Capability Brown.**

ABBEY ⏲ *½ hour*

Massive as it is (136ft long), the abbey was never completed. The first church was struck by lightning in 1309 and almost destroyed; building re-started in 1331 in the Early English – Decorated styles but virtually ended at the Black Death in 1348. As a consequence the abbey comprises an aisled presbytery, the crossing with its tower and the transepts.

Transepts – The contrasting tracery in the windows is late Decorated *(south)* and Perpendicular *(north).* The *Tree of Jesse* is by Pugin; the white marble funeral monument was designed by **Robert Adam.**

Presbytery – The height of the stone vaulting, the size of the presbytery or chancel recall that this was intended to be a great medieval abbey. In the 15C the monks erected the reredos of three tiers of canopied niches; Dissolution, Reformation and Puritanism have stripped it of brilliant colour and saintly figures, so that today it stands bone-white, like a piece of lace.

Furnishings – The mother-of-pearl **Crucifix,** the tall, hanging **tabernacle** with an octagonal spire of carved and once painted wood, the **panel painting** of King Athelstan, the founder of the abbey, are all 15C; the bust of the pilgrim St James is 16C.

HOUSE ⏲ ½ hour

Lord Milton, future Earl of Dorchester, commissioned **William Chambers,** future architect of Somerset House in London, to design his new mansion : the style outside was of the plainest to complement the abbey.

Staterooms – The most impressive of the typical 18C staterooms with their plasterwork **ceilings** and white **marble chimneypieces** are the **library,** where the bookcases are framed by paired pilasters, and the **ballroom,** covered by a tunnel vault with Adam-style moulding.

Abbot Middleton's Hall – The hall, the one part of the old monastery to remain, dates from 1498. Beginning with plain panelling, the walls rise through a clerestory, interspaced with angel-supported stone shafts, to a **hammerbeam roof** with panel tracery.

★ MILTON ABBAS VILLAGE

The village was rebuilt by Lord Milton as twin lines of identical **thatched cottages,** well spaced on either side of the grass-verged main street.
Marking the centre are the **church,** erected in 1786 with stone and timber from the abbey tithe barn, and the **Tregonwell Almshouses,** a rebuilding of the 16C houses of the original village.

★ MINEHEAD Somerset — Pop 8 449

Michelin Atlas p 7 or Map 403 – J30 – Facilities

Minehead was the chief port in the area from the 14C to the 17C, trading with Ireland (in wool), Virginia and the West Indies. In the 19C with the arrival of the railway the town became a "seaside watering place"; today Minehead's economy revolves around local light industry and the large summer holiday camp east of the town.
The town was the birthplace, in 1917, of the science and space writer Arthur C Clarke, author of *2001 : A Space Odyssey.*

SIGHTS

Esplanade and Quay Street – The wide roads follow the curving line of the sea wall round to the harbour jetty and the small harbour filled with pleasure-craft and rowing boats. Lining the side of the road, at the foot of the wooded slopes of North Hill, is a thread of colour-washed and stone seamen's cottages (17C-19C).

Higher Town – The community of houses on North Hill, many thatched and with round-cornered cob walls, is linked by steeply rising and turning roads, winding lanes and stepped alleys.

★ **Church Steps** – *Access : on foot, by Church Path, an opening off Quay St; by car, up Quay Lane, at the juncture of the Esplanade and Quay St. In both cases keep bearing right to lead into St Michael's Rd.* Church Steps are best explored from the top downwards.

★ **St Michael's** – The church of light grey sandstone with a buttressed and battlemented **tower** (87ft high) has stood on the hill since the 14C-15C when it replaced a Norman building in turn probably successor to a Saxon church. Inside is a 16C coved **rood screen** with a foliated crest which remained intact throughout the Commonwealth because, fortunately, the churchwardens were Parliamentarians.
The octagonal font with a kneeling figure, possibly the donor, dates from *c*1400; the brass of a young woman and effigy of a priest *(both east end)* are late 15C; the pulpit is 17C as is **Jack Hammer,** the clock jack; the **chandelier** is 18C.
The **royal arms** on the north wall and over the south door are of Queen Anne, George II and Charles II, at whose coronation the churchwardens, at a time when beer was less than 1*d* a pint, provided 16*s* for beer for the refreshment of the bellringers.
Outside, on the tower, note the figure of God holding a Crucifix *(north face)* and St Michael weighing souls with the Virgin tipping the scales in our favour *(east).*

★ WEST SOMERSET RAILWAY ⏲

The WSR, which owns the longest private line in Britain, operates diesel business and shopping services and, in the holiday season, services by **steam trains** which puff and whistle along the line *(illustration p 259).*
The line, which opened in 1862, was extended to Minehead in 1874; the track, originally the Great Western Broad Gauge of 7ft 0¼in, was converted within ten years to standard size. In 1922 the West Somerset became part of the Great Western Railway, in 1948 of British Rail and in 1971 the line was closed. This was not the end, however, for in March 1976, under "new management" the West Somerset Railway Company re-opened for business.

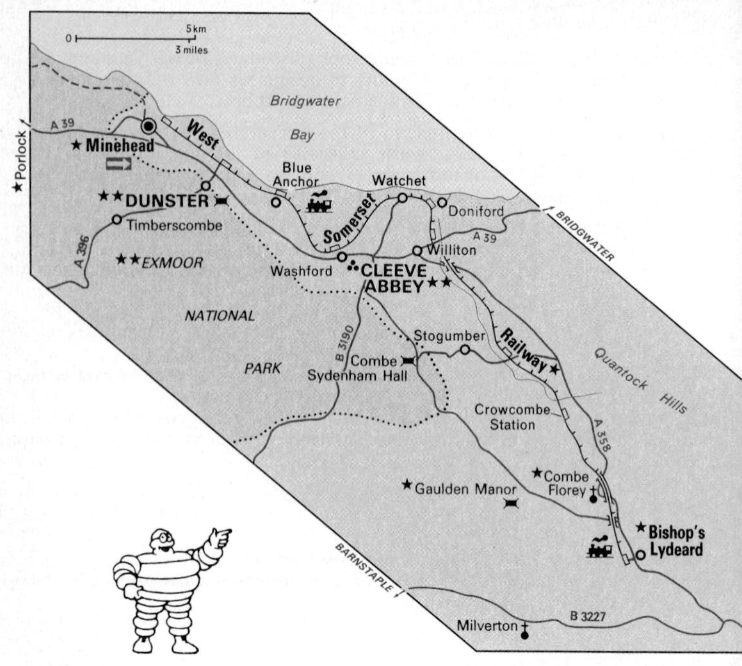

Minehead - Bishop's Lydeard - *1¼ hours*

The following stations and landmarks characterize the 20 mile journey :

★ **Minehead** – Platform long enough to take 16-coach train; signal box from Dunster and water tower from Pwllheli, N Wales; restoration depot. Holiday camp, sea on left.

Conygar Tower – *See Conygar Tower (qv).*

★★ **Dunster Castle** – *See Dunster.*

The line follows the shore round the bay – view of Hinkley Point Power Station and the Welsh coast on a clear day.

Blue Anchor – Signal box; seaside village with caravan site; sand and pebble beach.

Washford Bank – 1:65 gradient; Washford; restoration depot.

★★ **Cleeve Abbey** – *See Cleeve Abbey.*

Watchet – On the hilltop the 15C tower of St Decuman Church, below a large papermill at the entrance to the town. Watchet, home port of Coleridge's *Ancient Mariner (qv),* is the oldest commercial harbour along this part of the coast still in active trade. The line approaches to within feet of the cliff. Helwell Bay is popular with fossil-hunters.

Williton – Brick-built signal box, second water tower from Pwllheli (steam trains often take on water – halfway point), goods shed and siding. Views of the Quantocks *(east)* and Brendons *(west).*

Stogumber – Village with red sandstone church with 14C tower *(1 mile).*

Crowcombe Station – Village *(1¾ miles).* 400ft above sea-level, the topmost point of the line, beautiful countryside, walking centre for the Quantocks.

★ **Bishop's Lydeard** – Signal box, goods shed, renovation depot. *See Bishop's Lydeard.*

EXCURSIONS

★ **Porlock** – *10 miles west by A39.*

★ **Selworthy** – The white-walled thatched cottages and ancient stone tithe barn make a perfect setting for the small, embattled Church of All Saints.
The 15C-16C **church**★, white-walled with dark stone trims, is entered through a two-storey porch set between finely traceried windows. The door is linenfold panelled. The interior is light, with slender piers. The **south aisle** (1538) is known for its original wagon roof embellished with carved **bosses** and **angel wall plates**. Note the slender turned balusters of the **communion rail** (*c*1700).
Outside, there is a splendid **view**★★ of Dunkery Beacon *(qv)* to the southwest across Exmoor.

Allerford – The village of a few houses and a pub, nearly all built of local red sandstone, is known for its ancient **packhorse bridge.**

★ **Porlock** – *See Porlock.*

★★ MONTACUTE HOUSE Somerset

Michelin Atlas p 8 or Map 403 - L31

Montacute House, the village (pop 734) and its Perpendicular parish church were all built of Ham Hill stone; the tawny-ochre and grey-brown colour casts a warm glow upon the houses, large and small, and the inns and small bay-windowed shops which surround the Borough, or large village square.

House – The Elizabethan H shaped mansion of three storeys was built in 1597-1601 by Sir Edward Phelips, a successful lawyer, Speaker of the House of Commons (1604) and Master of the Rolls (1611). Nearly two centuries later, in 1786, Sir Edward's namesake and his wife attended a "Sale of the Materials of Clifton House then Pulling Down" and bought "The Porch, Arms, Pillars and all the Ornamental Stone of the Front to be Transferred to the Intended West Front of Montacute" *(illustration p 28)*.
The **early house,** true to the Elizabethan style, rose majestically and symmetrically on either side of a porched entrance front, through tiers of transomed windows to an open balustrade, obelisks and small, rounded gables. Flanking either side were taller, shaped gables and columnar chimneys; bay windows gave subtle relief to the lower walls. In deference to Renaissance fashion, there were a modest entablature and niches filled with nine roughly carved worthies in Roman armour. The rear, west face, between advanced wings, was plain with pointed gables and square chimney stacks.

The "Intended West Front" – The front was a key part of 18C Edward Phelips' plan to reverse the house : he determined that instead of entering from the east through the balustraded forecourt with its twin pavilions with ogee roofs crowned by open stone spheres, a new approach should be made from the west, which, however, needed to be dignified for the role – hence his attendance at the Clifton House sale.
The Ham stone from Clifton matched perfectly. Phelips used his purchase as a shallow infilling between the advanced wings to produce a new west front.
On the new **porch** at the centre he implanted his own arms, on either side fluted and spiral shafting, pierced balustrading, a Noah's ark of heraldic animal finials...
Land, farms, furniture and possessions were accumulated and sold as the Phelips family fortunes rose or declined. From 1911 Montacute was let – the most famous of the tenants being **Lord Curzon** (1915-25) who entrusted the redecoration to the novelist Elinor Glyn. In 1931, in a sad state of dereliction, the house was purchased by the National Trust.

TOUR ⏲ *1¼ hours*

Ground floor

Visitors enter through the original east doorway into the screens passage.

Dining Room – The room was created by Lord Curzon out of the old buttery from which dishes were once carried in ritualistic procession through the Great Hall and up the stairs to the formal dining room *(see Library below)*. The Elizabethan-style chimneypiece bears the **Phelips arms** of 1599; the **tapestry** of a knight against a *millefleurs* background is Flemish (Tournai); the walnut **refectory table,** 16C Italian. Among the **portraits** are Mary, Queen of Scots, and Robert Dudley, Earl of Leicester.

Great Hall – The hall, the communal living room until after the Restoration, retains from the 16C its **panelling,** the **stone screen** with rusticated archways and pillars with ram's head and acanthus leaf capitals and a roughly carved crest, and the **heraldic glass** in the window which includes the arms of Queen Elizabeth and Sir Edward Phelips.
The **Skimmington frieze,** a 17C plaster relief at the far end of the hall, shows a hen-pecked husband taking a drink while minding the baby and later being paraded around the village astride a pole.

The Skimmington Frieze, Montacute House.

Parlour – The room retains its original Ham stone **fireplace,** Elizabethan **panelling** and **frieze** of nursery animals. Among the 18C furniture are a Gobelins tapestry of 1788, *The Hunter,* a settee and chairs with needlework covers, a giltwood table, Gothick long-case clock and a centre table of beautiful simplicity by Thomas Chippendale the Younger.

Drawing Room – The room contains chairs covered in red damask made in 1753 by Walter Linnell for Sir Richard Hoare *(qv),* giltwood **side-tables** with eagle supports, a George I walnut **card-table,** a Boulle brass and tortoise-shell **chest,** and Chinese porcelain lion dogs and birds.

Staircase – The staircase, of which each **tread** is a single 7ft block of stone, rises by straight flights around a stone core – the intermediary stage between spiral stairs and Jacobean wooden staircases built around open wells. The tapestries are 15C-16C.

First Floor

Lord Curzon's Room – The room, besides his lordship's bath neatly stowed in a "Jacobean" cupboard, contains a 17C **overmantel** of *King David at Prayer,* an 18C bed, a Dutch oak drop-leaf table and an 18C japanned skeleton mirror.

Crimson Room – The room, so-called since the 19C when red flock wallpaper replaced the tapestries which once hung below the plaster frieze, is furnished with a sumptuous oak four-poster carved with the arms of James I.

Library – The library, formerly the dining room and the destination of the dishes brought in procession from the distant kitchens, is chiefly remarkable for its brilliant **heraldic glass** – a tourney of 42 shields displaying the Phelips arms, those of the sovereign and, by way of a compliment, those of Phelips' Somerset neighbours and friends at court. Other features from the time when this was a stateroom are the monumental Portland **stone mantelpiece** and **plaster frieze,** the Jacobean **inner porch,** the 19C moulded plaster ceiling and bookcases. The library steps date from 1770.

Top Floor

Long Gallery – The 172ft gallery with oriels at either end occupies the whole of the floor and is the longest in existence. Today it provides a perfect setting, through 90 **portraits** (on loan from the National Portrait Gallery), for a panoply of **Tudor England** and the early Jacobean Age.
In the main gallery contemporaries, friends and rivals stand together, kings and queens *(centre bay)* and full-length portraits of Lord Burghley, James I as a boy with a falcon, Prince Henry, Charles I as a boy, Francis Bacon, and Philip Herbert, 4th Earl of Pembroke, who was responsible for so much at Wilton House *(qv).* Five dependent rooms are filled with the personalities of the Reign of Henry VIII, Elizabeth and her Court, The Elizabethan Age, The Early Stuart Court and The Jacobean Age.

★★ MORTEHOE Devon — Pop 1 552

Michelin Atlas p 6 or Map 403 – H30

The point marks the western end of the spectacular Somerset-North Devon coast and offers good **views** over the coastline and the impressive landscape inland.

★ **St Mary's Church** – The late 13C **tower,** which was added to the original 12C Norman church, was saved from ruin in 1988 when a banker's draft for £25 000 was stuffed into the offertory box by an anonymous benefactor. In the 13C a chantry to St Catherine was added to the south side of the church by the then rector, Sir William Tracey; tradition claims, probably falsely, that it contains the bones of Sir William de Tracey *(qv),* who fled to Devon after murdering Thomas Becket in 1170.
The **font** is Norman or Early English; the finely carved 16C **bench-ends** show the Instruments of the Passion; the **angel mosaic** adorning the early chancel arch dates from 1903.

Morte Point – *½ mile Rtn on foot.*
From Mortehoe a walk over the close-cropped turf on the gently rising headland leads to the 200ft **vantage point**★ that is Morte Point, from which the coast and other headlands may be surveyed.

EXCURSIONS

To the south lie Devon's best known sand beaches, providing a contrast to the rocks and cliffs which characterize the rest of the north coast.

Woolacombe – Facilities. *1 mile south by B3343.*
The holiday village overlooking Morte Bay is known for its miles of yellow sands.

Croyde – *6 miles south by B3343 and B3231.*
The small village lies in a bay between Baggy Point and a lesser headland.

★ **Braunton** – *10 miles south by B3343 and B3231. See Braunton.*

★ MORWELLHAM Devon

Michelin Atlas p 3 or Map 403 – H32 – 4 miles southwest of Tavistock

Morwellham's heyday was the brief period between the Devon Great Consols *(qv)* copper strike of 1844 and the coming of the Great Western Railway to Tavistock in 1859. In those few years some 450 000 tons of mineral ore were shipped the 20 miles downstream to Plymouth in boats which, in most cases, carried only 50-100 tons a time. The industry and traffic were prodigious : the mined ore was brought from Tavistock by canal barges to a point 287ft above the river from where it descended by an inclined railway powered by a waterwheel, which was later supplemented by a second railway powered by steam; the quays, which had developed slowly since the river port came into existence in the 13C, had to be modified beyond recognition to provide tiled wharves to keep the ore and arsenic clean and a dock large enough to take six 300-ton schooners at a time. The number of villagers increased to 200; model cottages, houses, a shop, a school, a chapel, a butcher's shop, a pub, a hostelry, workshops and warehouses were built.
As rapidly as it had boomed Morwellham died : the canal was superseded by the railway; the mines became exhausted; Devon Great Consols declined; the population fell to 50.
Over twenty years ago the Morwellham Trust took over the area around the old port, which had remained virtually untouched since the last century, as part of a conservation project encompassing the Tamar Valley region; today Morwellham Quay is a bustling re-creation of its former self, complete with people in period costume.

MORWELLHAM QUAY ⊙

Riverside tramway – The electric tramway runs along above the river before entering the George and Charlotte copper mine, which was last worked in 1868; the working conditions are dramatically evoked.

Lime kilns – Lime to treat the local acid soil was produced by burning limestone.

Museums and Workshops – The mining and port museums describe the operation of the two enterprises. In the smithy, cooper's shop and assayer's laboratory the different skills are demonstrated by people in 19C costume. Quay Cottage recreates the domestic life of a 19C workman.

Waterwheels – Water power pumped drinking water for the villagers, drove the mill which ground manganese ore to powder, flushed silt from the docks and operated the first inclined plane railways, of which few traces remain.

Great Dock – The dock was built in 1858 to handle the rising output of the copper mines; the quays were covered with tiles which are visible in places.

Farmyard – The Victorian farm buildings contain a water-powered threshing machine, typical 19C farm animals and the stables of the shire horses which draw the carriage for rides along the Duke of Bedford's drive.

Canal Tunnel – Above the village (250ft) is the entrance to the tunnel, built by John Taylor from 1803 to 1817, which carried the canal under Morwell Down to Tavistock; in 1933 the water was diverted to the electricity generating station.

EXCURSION

★ **Cotehele** ⊙ – *6 miles southwest via Gulworthy, A390 west and by-roads.*
This old fortified manor house (built 1485-1627) overlooks the Tamar from a wooded hillside. The gardens boast yew hedges, a golden ash and large tulip tree; the walled garden contains a medieval dovecote and a fish stewpond. The gateway, tower **(views)** and great barn are late 15C.
The 16C **Great Hall** has a timbered roof, Tudor fireplace, 18C campaign chairs and crested pewter. The **Old Dining Room** is hung with tapestries and contains a restored 16C centre table and 17C-18C furniture.
The late 16C **Chapel** features the original barrel ceiling, 16C Flemish triptych and Crucifixion panel, a rare faceless pre-pendulum clock, unaltered since *c*1489. Bacchic Soho tapestries adorn the **Punch Room.** Upstairs, note the late 17C four-posters with original hangings.

Cotehele Mill and Quay ⊙ – Estate workshops by the river include a wheelwright's, a blacksmith's, a saddlery, cider house and mill. Cottages, a small maritime **museum** ⊙ and the *Shamrock*, a restored Tamar barge, give an idea of 18C-19C activity on the river.

★★ MUCHELNEY Somerset

Pop 161

Michelin Atlas p 8 or Map 403 – L30 – 2 miles southwest of Langport

The abbey ruins, the 15C parish church, the medieval priest's house and th village of attractive 17C-18C cottages – many obviously incorporating dresse stones from the abbey – make an attractive group.

Abbey ⊙ – Part of the abbot's lodging is all that remains of the Benedictin monastery which was founded in AD 693 on what was then an island *(se Glastonbury)* at the centre of the frequently flooded marshland. The abbey wa destroyed by the Danes in the 870s, refounded *c*950 and finally dissolved in 153 The abbey's annual income, recorded in Domesday as being £51 16*s*, had rise by the 16C to £447, an increase which contributed, at the expense of the spir to the brothers' temporal well-being : after a visitation in 1335 they were charge with living too well, leaving the church in disrepair, riding about the country an keeping unfit company, dining in private, owning costly utensils and ornate bed Whether the house reformed or not, the abbot's lodgings were rebuilt in th Tudor Gothic manner and remain as testimony to the grandeur of monastic li in the 15C-16C.

After the Dissolution, the domestic quarters were occupied as farmhouses f some 200 years while the church, which measured 247ft, and conventu buildings were ruined and looted for their fabric. Backing onto the south cloist walk, which remains, would have been the refectory and, in the corner, the abbot lodging.

Kitchen – The gabled and battlemented south front leads into the kitchen, a lon lofty room with a massive, double-sided **fireplace,** 17ft wide by 7ft deep.

Walk up the stairs at the far end.

Guestroom – The fine **door** *(right)* leads into the large guestroom which has coffered **oak ceiling,** mullioned windows and a stone fireplace.

Return to the ground floor and walk up the wide stone staircase.

Parlour – The **Abbot's Staircase** leads through a decorated **archway** to the parlou This room, which served as a waiting and meeting room, is lined with **linenfo** panelling and equipped with a large **panelled settle** before stone mullioned ar transomed windows. It also contains an impressive **stone fireplace,** ornamente with quatrefoils, friezes of fruit and foliage and, high on the framing shafts, pair of couched lions.

★★ **Parish Church** – The early 15C Perpendicular church on an older Norman even Saxon site stands within three feet of the north transept of the former abbe church.

The massive tower rises through three stages from the west door and window a window flanked by canopied niches, a belfry stage of two bays framed by shaf springing from lower buttresses and continuing like those at the centre through th battlemented crest to end as secondary pinnacles to those at the angles.

Inside, the wagon roof was transformed in 1600-25 by a local man into a fu colour, **painted ceiling** of smiling, bare bosomed angels in Tudor costume enjoyir the heavenly life.

Note also the panelled arch to the west tower, the 15C octagonal font with carvin of the Crucifixion, the 19C **barrel organ** still capable of playing 25 hymns and 3 doub chants, the 17C Netherlandish **stained-glass roundels** *(chancel windows)* and, in th chancel and around the font, 13C **tiles** from the abbey Lady Chapel.

Priest's House ⊙ – The thatched house dating from 1308 has a mediev two-storey hall and a 16C cinquefoil Gothic window; the interior is well preserve with much original masonry and timbers.

Muchelney Pottery ⊙ – *1 mile south of the village.*

At the pottery John Leach, son of David, grandson of Bernard Leach *(qv)*, produc the hand-thrown, wood-fired domestic stoneware to be seen in shops ar exhibitions in many parts of the country.

NEWQUAY Cornwall

Pop 13 905

Michelin Atlas p 2 or Map 403 – E32 – Facilities

Town plan in the current Michelin Red Guide Great Britain and Ireland

Newquay is a resort of golden sands backed by cliffs which advance in headlands and points – East Pentire, Towan and Porth Island – once settled b prehistoric man. In 1439 the villagers were building a "new quay". During th 18C and 19C Newquay was a pilchard port, exporting salted fish to Italy ar Spain; the **Huar's House** still stands on the clifftop where the huar sounded h long horn to summon the fishermen when a shoal of pilchards entered the ba When the railway arrived in the 1870s the town became a china-clay and mine port and then a resort.

EXCURSIONS

★ **Trerice** – *3 miles southeast by A392 and A3058. See Trerice.*

★ **Penhale Point and Kelsey Head** – From each of the headlands there is **view★★** north to Towan and Trevose Head, south to Godrevy Lighthouse *(q* and St Ives and, inland, from the St Austell china-clay pyramids to Camborr and Carn Brea.

The Coast Path turns away before the end of Penthale Point East but follov the cliff line of Penthale Point West and Kelsey Head. Roads lead out to bo Penthale Points stopping short about ½ mile from the cliff edges.

The Coast to Hell's Mouth – *26 miles south.*

Perranporth – Three miles of beach provided the setting, and the coming of the railway the opportunity, for Perranporth to turn itself, early this century, into the resort which it has been ever since. The time also was ripe : the pilchard, after 100 years, had vanished, smuggling had ended and the mines were ceasing to be profitable.

St Piran's Oratory – *2 miles on foot Rtn across the sand dunes.* St Piran's stood like a rock, appearing and disappearing in the tide of sand which surrounded it from its construction in the 6C-7C on the burial site of the saint who, according to legend, crossed the sea from Ireland on a millstone. In 1835 the sands, always shifting, blew away from the 7C oratory, revealing a building 29½ft long, 16½ft wide and 19ft high, of granite, porphyry, slate, quartz and rubble. In 1980 the ruins were reburied *(site marked by a plaque).*

★★ **St Agnes Beacon** – The beacon *(last 500yds up a field footpath)* at 628ft, between the village and the headland, affords a **panorama**★★ from Trevose Head to St Michael's Mount. In the foreground, between 300ft high Cligga Head, where the granite begins, and the beacon, there extends the typical north Cornwall landscape, short-turfed, undulating, windswept, speared by old mine stacks.

Porthtowan – The attractive small cove is known for its surfing.

★ **Portreath** – A 1:6 road descends the valley on either side to lead to the cove, the harbour with its stalwart breakwater and the small village resort.

Follow the coast road, B3301.

★ **Hell's Mouth** – *Car park beside the road.* From the cliff edge the blue-green-black sea breaks ceaselessly against the sheer, 200ft encircling **cliff-face;** the only sounds are the screaming of the sea-birds and the endless wash of the waves.

For historical information on the region consult the table and notes in the introduction.

NORTON ST PHILIP Somerset — Pop 781

Michelin Atlas p 17 or Map 403 – M, N30

The village, off the main road to Bath, was known for centuries to wool and cloth merchants who came twice a year to what were among the biggest cloth fairs of the West Country.

Charters to hold the fairs were obtained, originally, in the 13C by the Carthusian monks who had built a monastery nearby at Hinton, on land given them by Ela, Countess of Salisbury, the founder of Lacock Abbey *(qv).* The charterhouse which was called *Atrium Dei* was dedicated to the memory of her husband, William Longespée (d 1226; *qv*), natural son of Henry II and half-brother to Richard Lionheart.

By the 18C the local speciality, in Defoe's words, was "fine medley, or mixed cloths such as are usually worn in England by the better sort of people and are exported in great quantities to Holland, Hamburg, Sweden, Denmark, Spain, Italy etc".

At the centre of the main street, lined by old stone houses, stands the famous George Inn.

The George Inn, Norton St Philip.

★ **George Inn** – The building was erected *c*1223 as the monks' hostel while they were constructing Hinton Charterhouse. When the priory was complete the hostel became the priory guesthouse and inn and eventually a storehouse for wool from sheep raised on the priory lands. It was initially a single-storey building of local stone with a wide **central archway;** in the 15C two half-timbered, oversailing storeys were added, with three attractive **oriel windows.**
At the Dissolution, while the priory lands passed to the crown and the priory itself was encouraged to fall into ruin, the inn continued to provide hospitality to wool merchants and clothiers since Norton had become a weaving centre. Despite the decline of the industry in the early 18C, the village remained a welcome halt for travellers. Samuel Pepys, who stopped by with his wife on 12 June 1668, commented "dined very well, 10*s*".
Ten days before the Battle of Sedgemoor *(qv)*, **Monmouth's** men fought a running battle with the king's force in the fields outside the town. The duke, who had a price on his head, was surveying the scene from the inn, when a sniper fired but missed, at which, according to a local ballad, he "gaily turned him round and said : My man you've missed your mark and lost your thousand pound".
The arch leads to the old beamed rooms and the flowered **courtyard** at the back with a long **medieval gallery** along one side.

The length of time given in this guide
– for touring allows time to enjoy the views and the scenery
– for sightseeing is the average time required for a visit.

OKEHAMPTON Devon

Pop 4 113

Michelin Atlas p 4 or Map 403 – H, I31 – Local map pp 90-91

The market town, formerly on the main Exeter to Cornwall road (A30) but now by-passed, skirts the northern boundary of Dartmoor. Saxon in origin but abandoned, Okehampton was refounded as a strongpoint by the Normans. It became a medieval market town and prospered in the great wool period, only to tear itself apart during the Civil War; again it recovered, particularly after the improvements in communications of the 18C-19C.

SIGHTS

Chantry Chapel – *Fore St.* The chapel of ease on a near-island site at the east end of the main street was rebuilt in 1862 with many embellishments including obelisk pinnacles. The pulpit dates from 1626.
The old yard, through an arch behind the chapel, has been turned into professional craftsmen's studios and a shop.

Town Hall – *Fore St, on the corner with Market St.*
The town hall is in a former merchant's town house of 1685.

White Hart Inn – *Fore St.* The refronted inn, which was given an impressive portico in the 18C, has held a licence since the town gained its charter in 1623. In the 18C-19C it was a posting inn, the centre of local transport, where parliamentary candidates and their supporters schemed and celebrated in the manner described by Trollope and Dickens; Okehampton long boasted two members, including Pitt the Elder for a time.

Arcade – *Fore St – St James St (south side).*
The short, 19C shopping arcade is typical of the period with its overhead ironwork and black and white pavement.

Red Lion Yard – *Fore St – car park (north side).*
The small, open-air precinct with statuary and paved courtyard is surrounded by arcaded, two-storey gabled buildings.

Museum of Dartmoor Life – *White Hart Yard, West St.*
The collection is in two cottages, a mill, a warehouse and an old printer's workshop, grouped round a yard approached through a granite archway. It looks at the changing lifestyles, from prehistoric times to the present, of the people who have lived and worked on Dartmoor. Temporary exhibitions and craft demonstrations complement the collection.

Okehampton Castle – *Castle Lane.* The strategic site, the end of a spur beside the River Okement, was selected by the Normans for a motte and bailey castle, a wooden defence protected at the foot of the mound by a ditch. The Courtenays, Earls of Devon and the owners in the 13C, rebuilt the castle only for it all to be slighted when Henry III executed the Earl of Devon in 1538 and attainted his property. In the 18C-19C the ruined castle was purchased by a politician for the parliamentary benefits it bestowed.
There remain a two-storey **outer gatehouse,** a barbican with the outer bailey behind it, and the **gatehouse** proper with its attendant guardroom, forming part of the high inner wall. The diamond-shaped inner bailey is enclosed by the walls of the 13C residential buildings, notably the hall *(right)* which communicates with the guardroom by steps and, at the far end by means of a service room, with the kitchens. On the other side are lodgings, the chapel and another kitchen. The square **keep,** part 14C, part older, has a gaunt **stair turret** at the northeast corner leading to the upper rooms.

EXCURSIONS

Sticklepath – *4 miles east on A30 – local map p 91.*
The attractive village with its slate and thatch roofed houses – two dated 1661 and 1694 – gardens, old inn and bridge over the River Taw extends for half a mile along the main road. At the centre are the foundry and a Quaker Burying Ground (through an arch in a 17C-18C range of houses).
The **Museum of Water Power** ⊙ in the old foundry displays the variety of high-quality **agricultural hand-tools** produced there from 1814 to 1960 : scythes, billhooks, axes, cleavers, shovels. The machinery was powered by water from the river and still has working waterwheels : one waterwheel drove a pair of trip-hammers and ancillary machinery including shears, a second, the fan from which air passed through underground pipes to the forges, while a third turned the grinding mill where tools were sharpened and finished.

Spinsters' Rock – *9 miles east along A30 and A382; left turn by Drewsteignton.*
The megalithic tomb chamber or quoit, consisting of three large upright stones surmounted by a capstone, is visible over a gate to a field on Shilstone Farm.

South Zeal – *5 miles east, just north of A30.*
The village, which lies just within Dartmoor's northern boundary, was once a chartered borough. Several interesting buildings from that time still stand in the square and along the main street : the early 16C **Oxenham Arms** built of granite as the manor house, a house dated 1714, another **house** dated 1656 but much restored, a 15C house with a **tower porch.** The 15C church, in the centre, was built as the guildhouse of the local wool trade workers.

★ OTTERY ST MARY Devon — Pop 3 957

Michelin Atlas p 5 or Map 403 – K31

Ottery, standing on the River Otter, surrounded on all sides by lush green slopes and well away from the main road, avoided the arterial plan and developed gradually on a hillside site as a network of winding streets, small squares and hidden corners, each lined by 17C and Georgian houses. At the top of the hill is the twin-towered parish church, reminiscent, in miniature, of Exeter Cathedral.

★ ST MARY'S

The manor was given in 1061 by Edward the Confessor to a church foundation in Rouen and bought back in 1336 by **Bishop John de Grandisson** of Exeter in order that he might found a college or sanctuary for poetry and learning here, in this village only twelve miles from the cathedral. The college endured for 200 years before being dissolved in 1545 by Henry VIII. The manor was presented to Edward Seymour, future Duke of Somerset, but on his attainder reverted to the crown and was finally resold by Charles I.
The church in which the villagers had always worshipped became the property of the parish under the supervision of first four then twelve local residents or "Governors", a system which continues to this day.
Henry took "all the plate jewells ornaments goods and cattalles apperteigninge to the late surrendered College".

Exterior – The **towers** (64ft high) were built in the 14C when the existing church was remodelled in the Decorated style by Bishop Grandisson. The lead-covered **spire** (31ft), which was re-structured in 1908 using the old lead, resembles one which crowned the north tower of Exeter cathedral until 1752; the **weather vane,** one of the oldest in the country, is a **Whistling Cock,** so-called on account of the two tubes which run through its body and make it moan in the wind.

Interior – The high rib and panel vaulted nave contains the canopied tombs of Sir Otho de Grandisson, the bishop's younger brother, in full armour (d 1359) and his wife; at the **crossing** the bishop himself is portrayed on the centre boss.
Against the wooden gallery in the south transept is **Grandisson's clock,** dating from the collegiate period, cared for in 1437-38 at a cost of 3*s* 4*d* and more recently totally rebuilt so that, like its fellows at Exeter, Wells and Wimborne Minster, it still tells the time.
Note the 19C mosaic **wall tiling.**
In the **chancel** the coloured vaulting changes to a curvilinear pattern to complement the window tracery. The altarscreen is 19C-20C; the **sedilia** is pure 14C Decorated Gothic. The tomb is that of John Haydon (d 1587), sometime "governor" of the church and builder of Cadhay *(qv).*
In the ambulatory note the Elizabethan **brasses** *(south side)* and the stone minstrels' gallery. The **Lady Chapel** beyond contains the church's gilded wooden **eagle lectern** dating from Grandisson's time, one of the oldest and grandest in England, also medieval **choirstalls** and a **corbel portrait head** *(at the opening, south wall)* of Bishop Grandisson in a mitre.
The **Outer South or Dorset aisle,** added in 1520, is notable for its **fan vaulting** with large pendent bosses terminating in Tudor roses, its **corbels,** its owls on the piers at the west end and, on the second pier from the west end, an elephant's head (1520).

★ PADSTOW Cornwall Pop 2 256

Michelin Atlas p 2 or Map 403 – F32 – Facilities

Padstow was for centuries a major port, being the only safe harbour on the nort Cornwall coast, once the rocks, cross winds and currents at the mouth of th Camel Estuary had been negotiated. In the 6C St Petroc, landing from Wale founded a Celtic minster here before journeying on to Bodmin; in 981 minste and town were destroyed by the Vikings.
The town recovered, developing over the centuries into a fishing harbour an mineral and china-clay port and even a harbour from which trans-Atlanti emigrants set out in craft as small as 10 tons. As boats became bigger howeve fewer could make port owing to the sand or **Doom Bar** at the estuary mouth formed, according to legend, at the curse of a dying mermaid shot by a loc man.

PADSTOW 'OBBY 'OSS

The May Day celebrations, their origin lost in the mists of antiquity, begin a midnight in the square or Broad Street with the singing of the Morning Son – "let us all unite for summer is acome unto day". In the morning a children' horse, a **blue 'oss** and the original **red 'oss** make their appearance and pranc throughout the day to accordion and drum bands.

SIGHTS

Harbour – The harbour, filled with fishing boats and launches *(see below)*, surrounded on three sides by quays each backed by old houses, boathouse and pubs.

South Quay – Opposite the Harbour Master's Office is a group of 16C, two-store granite houses with slate roofs, comprising the **Old Court House** with a shell hoo over the door, **Raleigh Cottage,** where Sir Walter Raleigh *(qv)* as Warden of Cornwa collected dues, and the minute **Harbour Cottage.**

North Quay – The 15C **Abbey House,** once a nunnery, has a nun's head carvin dripstone.
A network of narrow streets runs back behind the quay, the alleys darkene by tall houses, many with exposed beams and oversailing upper floors abov small shop-fronts.

St Petroc Major – The church with its embattled west tower begun in th 13C contains an octagonal **font** of Catacleuse stone carved by the **Master St Endellion** *(qv).*
The cross-shaft in the churchyard is Celtic, the wrought-iron gates are 18

BOAT TRIPS ⏲

Despite what the boatmen say, to a landsman it is frequently quite choppy. Th cruises head beyond the estuary to view **Stepper Point, Pentire Point,** the **Rump** and, in Portquin Bay, the spectacular **cliffs,** caves and rocks, and possibly a mode wreck, caught on the rocks, her back broken by the waves.

EXCURSIONS

★ **Bedruthan Steps** – *8 miles southwest by B3276.*

Portcothnan – The tiny village lies at the back of a deep square cove.

★ **Bedruthan Steps** ⏲ – The 1½ mile arc of sand spectacularly scattered with gia rocks worn to the same angle by waves and wind is visible over the cliff ed – the rocks were the stepping stones, legend has it, of the giant Bedrutha

★ **Trevose Head** – *6 miles west by B3276 and by-roads; last ½ mile on foo*
The 243ft head stands halfway between Hartland Point, 40 miles to th northeast, and West Penwith – four lighthouses *(qv)* are visible at night. By day the **view★★** is of bay following bay, offshore rock islands, small sandy coves palisaded to seaward by towering rocks.

Trevone – *3 miles west by A3276.*
The village and chapel with a slate spire stand in a small sandy cove, guarded by fierce offshore rocks. The spectacular approach to the village from Padstow is by way of the **Cornwall Coast Path★★** *(5 miles on foot)* which circles 242ft **Stepper Point** with its white waymark and passes the natural rock arches of **Porthmissen Bridge.**

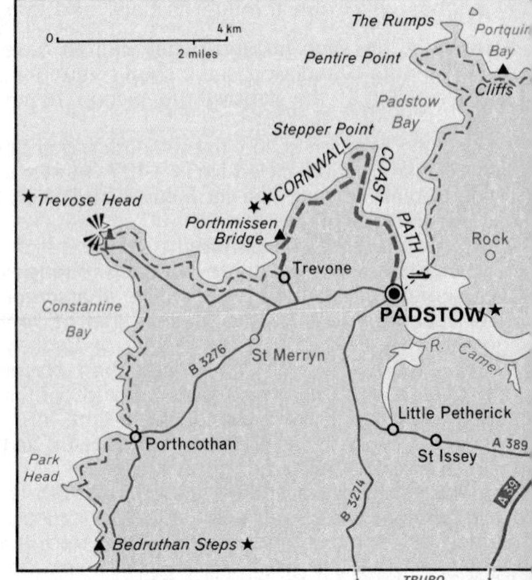

St Issey – *5 miles south by B3274. Turn left into A389 to Little Petherick.*

Little Petherick – The remodelled medieval church lies at the bottom of a steep-sided valley, its tower just visible in the trees; from the hilltops on either side there are **views** far across the Camel River.

St Issey – The medieval church tower collapsed in the 19C, necessitating a total rebuilding and meticulous repiecing of the Catacleuse stone altarpiece by the Master of St Endellion *(qv)*; a second carving is on the south altar.

★ PARNHAM HOUSE Dorset

Michelin Atlas p 8 or Map 403 – L31 – 5 miles north of Bridport

Parnham ⊙ combines a mellow stone house set in a wooded valley and beautiful furniture, each of their time : Elizabeth I and Elizabeth II. The E-shaped **house** of Ham stone is gabled, finialled and multiple chimneyed, and emblazoned on the oriel above the entrance. The handsome grounds include formal **gardens** bounded by stone walls and balustrades, courtyards, fountains, topiaried yews, a river and a lake.
The house was begun around a Great Hall built by Sir Robert Strode in the 16C. In the 17C the mansion was overrun by Cromwell's soldiers, who murdered Lady Anne Strode in that same Great Hall.
After centuries of neglect it was restored, enlarged and crenellated by John Nash. In 1976 it was purchased by John Makepeace, who set it to rights once more and established it as the **John Makepeace Furniture Workshops,** the School for Craftsmen in Wood, and an exhibition gallery for modern furniture and living art.

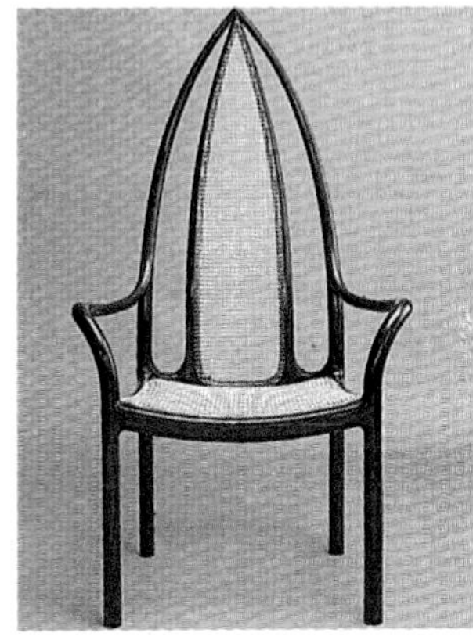

Chair by John Makepeace in ebony and nickel silver.

Makepeace is considered to be among the country's outstanding furniture designers; pieces are commissioned, a few may become prototypes of limited editions, most are unique pieces, often celebratory, as is the fourth centenary table at Longleat *(qv)*.

★ PENCARROW Cornwall

Michelin Atlas p 3 or Map 403 – F32 – 4 miles northwest of Bodmin

The Palladian-style house ⊙, with Delabole slate roofs and pediments at the roofline and above the first-floor windows, has been in the same family since it was built in the 1770s.

House – Inside, **Joshua Reynolds** family portraits, an **Arthur Devis** conversation piece with St Michael's Mount in the background *(anteroom)*, Continental, English and Oriental porcelain, Georgian wine glasses and several beautiful items of Georgian furniture grace the different rooms. Note a small Georgian **envelope table,** the giltwood **Adam furniture** *(Drawing Room)* upholstered in the same rose silk damask as the curtains – "treasure" from a Spanish ship captured by a relative off the Philippines in 1762. The portrait above the Louis XVI settee is of the "little Cornish baronet", Sir John St Aubyn *(qv)*.
On the walls enclosing the cantilevered staircase which leads to the bedrooms, with their William IV and George IV four-poster beds, are Samuel Scott paintings (1755) *The Tower and London Bridge* and one of the striking portraits of **Charles I** *(qv)* painted by Edward Bower from sketches he made in Westminster Hall at the trial.

Gardens – Pencarrow is known for its trees, conifers especially, from all over the world, planted in the 1830s and since diversified to include English broad-leaves. Superb specimens soar 75-100ft, line the mile long drive and continue beyond a Victorian rockery and a sunken Italian garden to a lake and American Gardens. Spring bulbs, rhododendrons, camellias, azaleas and vivid blue hydrangeas carpet the ground.

★★ PENWITH Cornwall

Michelin Atlas p 2 and Map 403 – C, D33

Penwith, the western tip of Cornwall, the most westerly headland in Englan with Land's End at its edge, has a windswept beauty all its own deriving fron its granite foundation, the blueness of the ocean, the small granite churches witl their individual, landmark towers, the Celtic wayside crosses.

Spiking the undulating hillsides along the north coast are the chimneys an derelict engine-houses of old mines; older still are the prehistoric villages an ancient hillforts which crown the hill tops. It is an area of legend and combine wide open space with lush, leafy vales.

The area described below is that west of the Hayle-Penzance road (A30).

SOUTH PENWITH

Penzance – Land's End

★ **Penzance** – *See Penzance.*

★ **Newlyn** – *See Newlyn.*

★ **Mousehole** – Mousehole (pronounced Mowzell) is an attractive – and ofte crowded – small village. The **harbour** is protected by a quay of Lamorna granit and a **breakwater** dating from 1393. Standing back from the fishermen's lov granite cottages at the water's edge is the half-timbered Keigwin Arms, the onl house left standing after the 16C Spanish raid.

Beyond the end of the harbour the beach extends past **Merlyn,** an offshore rocl the Battery Rocks – site of a gun emplacement until the 19C – and Th Mousehole, an old smuggler's cave, to **Spaniards' Point** where the raiders lande in 1595; they pillaged the countryside, burned **Paul Church** – the 15C pinnacle tower, a major seamark, survived – and sacked Mousehole, Newlyn and Penzanc before eventually being driven off.

Lamorna and Lamorna Cove – Half a mile separates the village from the cove below the Carn-du headland which marks the boundary of Land's End granite.

★ **The Merry Maidens and The Pipers Standing Stones** – The Pipers (13½ft tall), 15 in number, stand hauntingly in the field just north of the road; the Merry Maidens (4ft tall), 19 in number, squat and still, form a circle in the field to the south. The story goes that the maidens and pipers were turned to stone for dancing and making music on a Sunday.

★★ **St Buryan** – The village and surrounding landscape are dominated by the 14C granite **church tower**★★ (92ft) square and pinnacled, from which, it is claimed, the towers of 16 other Cornish churches can be seen. The ring of six bells is the second heaviest in Britain.

King Athelstan built the first St Buryan Church in AD 931, following his conquest of the Scilly Isles *(qv)*. The major features today are the **porch,** amazingly worked in granite; 15C **font** with three angels and a Latin cross; 17C **slate tombstone,** finely carved (*west wall;* other beautifully lettered 18C stones outside); 13C coffin-shaped tombstone *(northwest corner of the tower);* 15C **rood screen.** Note the **Celtic Crosses** outside.

Logan Rock – *Access on foot from the Coastal Path.*

The "logan", a 70-ton boulder which moved at the touch of a finger, was displaced by a Royal Navy party as a prank last century; although repositioned it has never been as keenly balanced.

★ **Porthcurno** – The road, which drops through the trees to the village, ends at the cove where the Atlantic laps the shelving shell-sand beach, protected on either side by bluff headlands.

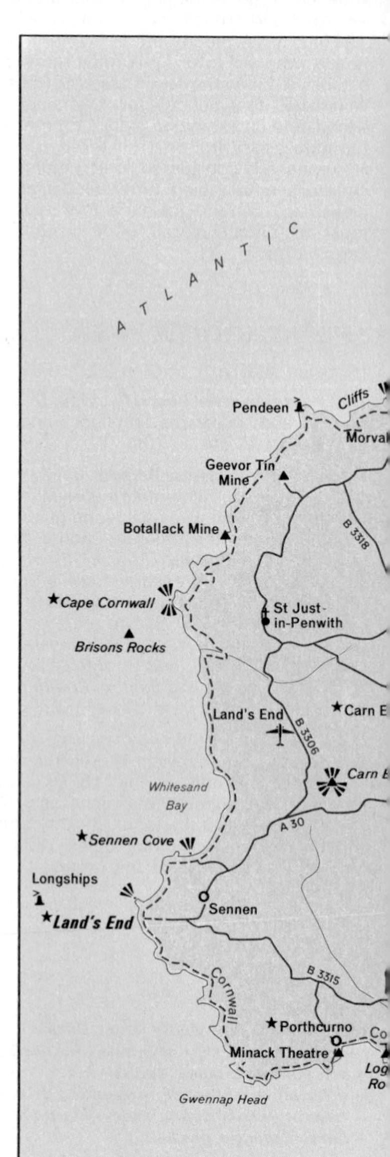

Minack Theatre ⏲ – *Access by road from the beach car park; also by a steep, uneven path up from the beach (20min Rtn).*
The history of the cliffside theatre which was created in 1929 by Miss Cade, with its stunning ocean back-drop, is told through photographs, models and audio-visual techniques in the **Rowena Cade Exhibition Centre.**

★ **Land's End** – *See Land's End.*

WEST PENWITH

Penzance – Land's End – Pendeen Light

Trereife Park – *See Trereife Park.*

Sancreed – The **church**★★ is a rebuilding dating from the 15C when the population of the village numbered less than 100 – it reached its maximum of 1 398 in 1851 when the local tin mines were in peak production.
The two stage granite **tower** of alternate deep and shallow courses is crowned by battlements and corner pinnacles. Inside, the arcade of five bays on solid granite columns, transept arching, a traceried window *(west end, south aisle),* 14C Norman **font** with crowned angels at the bowl corners remain from earlier sanctuaries. The **rood-screen** shows typical medieval human and animal figures half-hidden in the foliage on the lower panels.
Outside in the churchyard are 5 **Celtic Crosses**★★ – two of them (8C-11C) are outstanding, with carved shafts and, on the heads, Christ in a tunic with expanded sleeves.

★ **Carn Euny** ⏲ – *5min walk across the fields from Sancreed – St Just Rd.* The outstanding feature of this Iron Age village, inhabited from the 7C BC to mid-Roman times, is the **fougou** (Cornish for cave). This comprises a creep and 40ft long passage, drystone-walled and roofed with large granite slabs, which leads to the unique round chamber, some 10ft across, stone walled, corbel roofed and once domed.

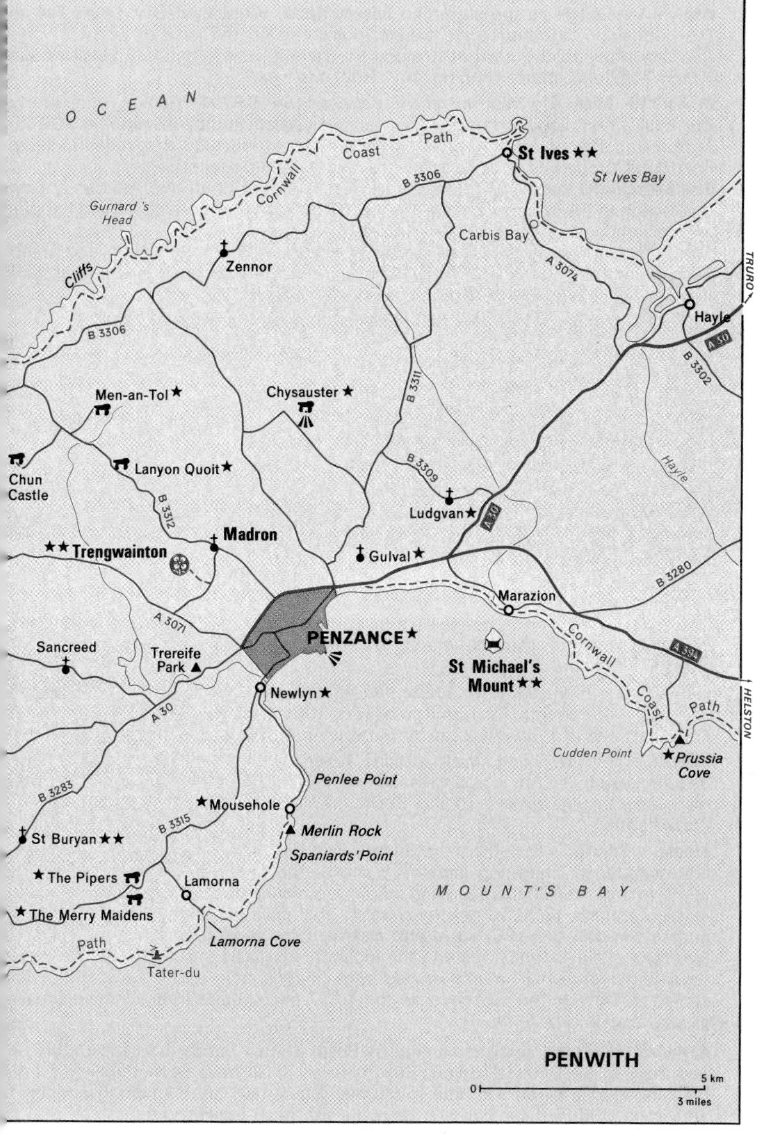

Carn Brea – *East of B3306.* The ground rises to 200ft in a rounded hillock, know since **John Wesley** *(qv)* preached there as Carn Brea Chapel.

Sennen – St Sennen on the cliff-top, the most westerly **church** in England, its thre stage, pinnacled, granite **tower** a marker for ships at sea, is an enlargement o a 13C chapel of which the chancel, transept and north wall remain. The sout aisle, granite arcade and the tower were completed by 1430 when a petitio was sent to the pope requesting a licence for a local burial ground, sinc experience showed that attendance at funeral services in St Buryan three mile away left the village open to local pirate raids. By the tower is a 7ft **wayside cross★**

Go down to the cove by road or by the footpath (20min Rtn on foot).

The footpath skirts a number of small standing stones in a field.

★ **Sennen Cove** – The cove, with the massive Pedn-men-du headland at its back the breakwater, fishermen's hard and small harbour, the beach, RNLI station an slip, houses and pub, offers a wide **view★** over Whitesand Bay, the Brisons Rock and Cape Cornwall.

Land's End Aerodrome ⓥ – *A30.* Short coastal flights and day excursions to th Isles of Scilly *(qv);* public viewing terrace.

St Just-in-Penwith – The prosperity enjoyed in the 19C by a tin mining town i reflected in the substantial buildings lining the triangular square.
The **church★** just off the square has a 15C pinnacled **tower,** walls of dressed granit and an elaborate 16C porch. Note two faded **paintings;** the *Christ of the Trades* i especially interesting for its illustration of 15C craftsmen's tools. Dating from th mid-5C, when St Just himself was alive, is a gravestone with a Chi-Rho (XF monogram, known from its inscription as the **Selus Stone** *(before north door).* In th churchyard are part of a wayside cross and a market cross bearing a Crucifixio

★ **Cape Cornwall** – *1½ miles from St Just, last 400yds on foot - 30min Rtn.* Th **view★★** opens out as the path climbs to the "summit", distinctively marked b a ruined mine chimney. During the walk, even on a fine day, all may b momentarily obscured as a wisp of cloud tangles with the 230ft hillock. Fror the vantage-point by the stack the **Brisons Rocks,** Whitesand Bay, **Land's End** an the Longships Lighthouse are visible, possibly also the Isles of Scilly.
A promontory to the northeast hides the ruined, now legendary **Botallack Min** which had long shafts running out under the sea.

Geevor Tin Mine ⓥ – *Northwest of Pendeen on B3306.* Geevor was one c Cornwall's last working mines. It consists of vertical shafts descending 200-25 fathoms to the underground workings which extend over 4sq miles includin horizontal tunnels (drifts) and inclines beneath the ocean bed.
The **underground tour** takes the cage down the Victory Shaft and the dandy dow the incline to the work face where the vertical system of Cornish mining (stopinc is explained.
The **surface tour** visits the tin treatment plant where tin, copper, iron and arseni were separated from the bedrock; the magnetic separator produces high (70 tin) and medium (25% tin) grade concentrates.

Pendeen Lighthouse – *See Lighthouses (qv).*

NORTH PENWITH

Penzance - Morvah - Hayle

★★ **Trengwainton Garden** – *See Trengwainton.*

Madron – *See Madron.*

★ **Lanyon Quoit** – The quoit of three upright stones supporting a massive capstor is immediately recognisable from the road *(climb the style for a close view* Dating from the Neolithic Age and therefore *c*4 000 years old, quoits (also know as cromlechs or dolmens) were burial chambers inside barrows or mounds c earth and stones.

★ **Men-an-Tol** – *On the moor, to the right of the lane.* The stone, once known a the Devil's Eye, stands between two upright boulders, a 5ft disc with a larg hole at the centre, through which, "to bracken" disease, one had to crawl nin times against the sun.

Chun Castle – *From the farm at the end of the road, walk ½ mile up the marke hill track – 45min Rtn.* The Iron Age hillfort, 100yds across, with gateway uprigh and scattered stone walls, can only be seen before the bracken grows.

Morvah – The tiny village with a **church tower** which long served as a seamen beacon is a place from which to make for the North Cornwall Coast Path (200yd for a spectacular **view★★** of the 300ft granite cliffs which drop vertically int the Atlantic.

Zennor – Zennor sits half a mile inland, in a dip in the rock-strewn, windswe countryside. Its charming **museum** ⓥ shows the evolution of implements fro stone to iron : in a kitchen, a wheelwright's, a blacksmith's, for quarrying, mining Inside Zennor's 12C-13C granite **church★**, built on a 6C site, enlarged in the 15 and restored in the 19C, are a **tithe measure** now serving as a holy water stou two **fonts** of Hayle limestone and the legendary **mermaid** – a small 16C seductre on a bench-end-chair, neatly carved with floating hair, a tiny waist and a lon scaly tail. Outside the church, note the 1737 sundial and three Cornish Crosse

★★ **St Ives** – *See St Ives.*

Hayle – The estuary town is flanked by Porth Kidney Sands *(west)* to Carbis Ba and the 3 miles of Hayle Towans Beach *(north)* to Godrevy Point; towan is Cornis for sand dune. In the 19C the foundries, which had been smelting copper, t and iron, produced the famous giant **Cornish beam engines** *(qv).*

The **Paradise Park** ⓥ *(B3302)* bird collection and centre for wildlife conservation is home to brightly coloured macaws, parrots and cockatoos, owls, eagles (flying demonstrations), flamingos, penguins and the near-extinct **Cornish chough,** among others. The otter breeding sanctuary (baby otters sometimes on view) and Victorian walled garden provide added interest.

★ **Ludgvan** – The village, straggling along the road, opens out on a corner with a small green bordered by the churchyard. The **church**★ is 14C; the granite **tower** with its gargoyles, battlements and pinnacles, is 15C.
Christianity is said to have been brought to the area by Ludewon, a 6C Irish missionary. A contemporary **Celtic Cross shaft** has been built into the tower steps while inside is a small wedge-shaped, **granite slab** with two incised crosses, believed to be a 7C Christian grave marker *(on a window sill).* The scalloped **font** is Norman.

★ **Chysauster** ⓥ – *100yds across a field.* This, the best preserved **prehistoric Cornish village,** never fortified, inhabited probably from 100 BC to AD 250, consists of eight houses in two lines of four, built below the crest across a hillside. The roughly circular houses are constructed of blocks of stone – the massive walls are up to 4ft high – with entrance passages to inner courtyards. At each house would have been a pole – post-holes evident in some cases – which would have supported a cone-shaped, thatched roof.
A stream flowed from the hilltop to the marsh below where thatching reeds grew. It was an agrarian community. Off to one side is a *fougou (see Carn Euny, above).* The **view** extends over towards Penzance and Mount's Bay.

★ **Gulval** – The village centre is marked by a vivid triangular flowerbed and by the parish **church**★ of 1440 with its three stage granite tower.
Inside the church are a 14C-15C **font** with an angel on one corner, angel-capitalled **pillars** stained where iron rings were attached by the Parliamentarians to tie up their horses when using the nave as stables, a **cross** *(south aisle window sill)* of mother-of-pearl inlaid in dark, ancient wood, said to be from a tree from the submerged Forest of **Lyonesse,** located, according to some, in Mount's Bay.

★ PENZANCE Cornwall — Pop 18 501

Michelin Atlas p 2 or Map 403 – D33 – Facilities
Town plan in the current Michelin Red Guide Great Britain and Ireland

Penzance with its wonderful **outlook**★★★ on Mount's Bay and St Michael's Mount *(qv),* has been a holiday resort for 150 years. Progress in communications brought about each successive stage in the town's development : from mineral and passenger port to spring vegetable and flower despatch point, fish market within easy reach by train of London and the Midlands, and now holiday resort accessible by train, coach, car, helicopter and aeroplane.
The town, which suffered badly in the Spanish raid of 1595 *(see Mousehole),* extends for a couple of miles in each direction around the bay. Within the overall area it divides into three distinct districts : Harbour-Quay, east of the Battery Rocks; the Western Promenade; Market Jew and Chapel Streets, the principal shopping areas at the centre of the town, and their surrounding streets.

HARBOUR – QUAY DISTRICT

Harbour – The MV **Scillonian III** ⓥ, the boat to the Isles of Scilly *(qv),* berths daily throughout the summer in the harbour which is crowded with pleasure craft, small cargo vessels, fishing boats and the pilot's launch.

★ **National Lighthouse Centre** ⓥ – *Wharf Road.* The museum is arranged in the old Trinity House *(qv)* buoy store and centres on a fascinating assortment of lighthouse artefacts, including the beautiful and ingenious lights themselves : it traces the development from the early days of lighted chandeliers through cut-glass prisms to a massive optic rotating in a bath of mercury. Displays of ship's lights and fog horns, model ships and the reconstruction of a room inside a lighthouse are among the exhibits. A short video tells of the dramatic construction of the surprisingly decorative Eddystone lighthouse *(illustration p 24).*

Quay – At the end of the quay, on the corner between the dock and the Battery Rocks, behind the typical massive Cornish sea wall and the large, turn-of-the-century open-air swimming pool, stands the **Barbican,** a mid-18C granite "cellar" or fish store now housing a craft centre *(upstairs)* and aquarium.
Behind the quay, a maze of alleys leads back to the main streets.

Penzance Heliport – *1 mile east off A30.* The heliport at the east end of the town is the take-off point for helicopters to the Isles of Scilly *(qv).*

WESTERN PROMENADE

The wide promenade and the Queen's Hotel, built in 1861, epitomise the confidence Penzance so rightly had that it would become a prime resort. Half a mile long and extended by the road to Newlyn *(see below),* it affords a **view**★★★ of St Michael's Mount and the headlands round to the Lizard.
Behind the wide road, inland at the town end, the network of short streets includes **Regent Terrace, Voundervour Lane** and **Regent Square,** lined by small, 18C-19C town houses. Further inland, the streets lead to **Morrab Gardens** ⓥ, the public gardens planted with tropical species and graced with a 19C bandstand.

MARKET JEW and CHAPEL STREETS

The heart of the town is 18C-19C, older buildings having perished in the Spanis raid of 1595.

Market Jew Street – The street rises from the station and harbour to a statu of **Humphry Davy** (1778-1829), chemist, physicist, inventor of the miner's safety lam

Market House – The granite building of 1837 is distinguished by a bright gree copper dome.

Museum and Art Gallery ⓥ – *Penlee House, west of the Market House.* fine collection of paintings from the **Newlyn School** (1880-1910; *qv*) is include among the art and decorative arts of West Cornwall; the **tin mining exhibit** include a rare, early **ingot** recovered from the bed of the River Fal. By the house entranc stands a 7ft inscribed Celtic Cross.

★ **Chapel Street** – The street cuts down from the side of the Market Hall to goose's foot of four lanes leading to the Battery Rocks, the Quay, the Dock an the Promenade; its distinctive character includes something of both the o harbour and the spacious 18C-19C days. Among notable landmarks are :

Egyptian House – The amazingly decorated house dates from *c*1835 and is th sole survivor of several designed in the style at the time.

Union Hotel – The hotel, refronted in 1810, was built twenty years before as the Tow Assembly Rooms; from the minstrels' gallery in the ballroom (now the dining room the news was first announced in England of the victory at **Trafalgar** *(qv)* and the dea of Nelson. The master of a Penzance fishing boat crossed the course of HMS *Pick* as she was making for Falmouth with Collingwood's despatch, heard the news an broke it to the mayor before their lordships received it in London.

No 44 and Abbey House – *Abbey St.* The 17C group of buildings is said to ha been associated with St Michael's Mount when it was a priory.

Turk's Head – The 13C inn with a "new" front added after the Spanish raid 1595 is probably the oldest building in the town.

Admiral Benbow – The 15C-16C Benbow was a smugglers' meeting place an is named after an 18C band, the Benbow Brandy Men, whose second command, during a raid, clambered on the roof and fired off his pistols to crea a diversion. The revenue men rushed out and shot him down but the inn an the band were saved and he recovered, to be raffishly commemorated in th figure lying along the roof ridge.

The inn has been restored with ships' timbers and decorated with vividly coloure coats of arms, figureheads and the gilded carving of a cherub's head from th *Colossus,* the man o' war from Nelson's fleet wrecked off the Isles of Scilly *(q* when bringing back Sir William Hamilton's collection from Sicily in 1798.

★ **Maritime Museum** ⓥ – *19 Chapel St.* The museum, smelling richly of rope and ta displays shipwrights' tools, sailor-made models and half-models, hanging churc ships, a model of a dockyard with two wooden-walled battleships und construction, a full size, walk through section of a four-decker, 95-gun, man o' w of *c*1750... There are cannon, an ancient handgun and telescope, flintlock pisto silver and pewter forks and spoons, keepsakes and medicine chests, treasur objects from the *Association* which, with three other men o' war, *Romney, Eag* and *Firebrand,* foundered in October 1707 off the Isles of Scilly *(qv).*

EXCURSIONS

★★ **St Michael's Mount** – *5 miles east by A30, A394 and Marazion. Se St Michael's Mount.*

★★ **St Ives** – *7 miles northeast by B3311. See St Ives.*

★ **Prussia Cove** – *9 miles east by A30 and A394.* The cove inside Cudden Poi is renowned for tales about its smugglers *(qv).* The hero of the most famo is John Carter, known like his inn as the **King of Prussia.**

Trereife Park ⓥ – The estate, in a lovely setting on the edge of a combe, includ the **Horse Stud**, farm animals, old bakery vehicles and agricultural tools, and th **National Museum of Gypsy Caravans,** comprising a collection of decorated carava with descriptions of the old gypsy lifestyle.

The handsome Queen Anne house of grey stone has views across the lawr and paddocks towards the woodland below. It was originally a farmhouse b was remodelled in the early 18C when the family's fortune increased; th adjoining buildings are later additions. The impressive yew hedge on the sou side of the house is *c*200 years old. The gardens and grounds offer croque putting and woodland walks.

★ **Land's End** – *10 miles west by A30. See Land's End.*

The Coast from Penzance to Mousehole – *3 miles south.*

★ **Newlyn** – Newlyn has always been and remains the major fishing harbour in Moun Bay and the west : it is noted for its mackerel and whitefish, lobster and crab. The village, with cottages clustered round the harbour and on the hillside, retai its individuality; in the 1880s this characteristic and the beautiful light attract painters who founded the **Newlyn School** (**Newlyn Art Gallery** ⓥ on the main road; s also Penzance Museum and Art Gallery, *above*).

Continue along the coast road.

Penlee Point – The old lifeboat house, from which the *Solomon Browne* set out on heroic rescue attempt and perished with all on board in December 1981, now shelte an auxiliary boat, RNLI memorabilia and "honour boards" of boats manned Mousehole men. Adjoining is a memorial garden to the men of the *Solomon Brow*

★ **Mousehole** – *See Mousehole.*

★ PLYMOUTH Devon — Pop 238 583

Michelin Atlas p 3 or Map 403 - H32 - Facilities - Local map p 114

The name Plymouth conjures up many famous names and events : the Hoe, Drake, Hawkins, Frobisher, Raleigh, Cooke, the Pilgrim Fathers, the Sound and, since the early 18C when William III laid down Devonport Dockyard, Royal Naval ships of the line.

The city developed from the amalgamation of three towns : Sutton, at the mouth of the Plym, Dock (renamed Devonport) on the Hamoaze and Stonehouse on the coast in between. In earlier times Sutton was "a mene thing, an inhabitation of fishars" (Leland) but trade with France under the Plantagenets and worldwide trade under the Tudors, particularly Elizabeth I, brought prosperity, so that for a time Plymouth was the fourth largest town in England after London, Bristol and York. Today the city, which has a spacious, airy feel to it, is arranged in three distinct areas : the Hoe and its environs, adorned with the splendour of Victorian and Edwardian buildings; the older, bustling Barbican region by the harbour with its fish market and narrow streets; the modern commercial centre, rebuilt after the Second World War, providing wide, shop-lined avenues.

PLYMOUTH SOUND

The Sound forms a natural harbour at the mouth of two rivers, the Plym *(east)* which gave its name to the growing port in the 14C and the Tamar *(west)* which flows into the Sound round **Drake's Island.**

Breakwater – The 19C breakwater, which marks the southern limit of the Sound two miles offshore, was constructed against the heavy sea swell which rolls in from the southwest. It is one mile in length; the engineer-designer was **John Rennie;** it took 4½ million tons of local limestone to build, 29 years to complete (1812-41) and cost £1½ million.

Beside it, on an island rock, stands the round **Breakwater Fort** (*c*1860).

At either end are beacon lights *(qv)* and, at the east end, a large iron lobster-pot refuge at the top of a 24ft pole, into which anyone wrecked can climb and await rescue, now by helicopter.

Eddystone Lighthouse – The lighthouse *(qv)* can be seen on the skyline, about 14 miles to the southwest.

Plymouth Hoe.

PLYMOUTH HOE

The hoe (the word meant hill) evokes the vision of Drake looking out to sea across the Sound in 1588 towards the approaching Armada and stooping to finish his game of bowls while he waited for the tide to turn so that his ships could leave harbour. Visitors still gaze out over the water, spotting the naval vessels, the pilot cutters, the daily ferries to Roscoff, the twice-weekly ships to Spain from Millbay Docks, the fishing and pleasure boats leaving or returning to their moorings.

The east side of the headland is occupied by the Royal Citadel overlooking the Barbican *(see below)* and across the mouth of Sutton Harbour to **Mount Batten,** now an RAF weather, rescue and marine craft repair station; facing The Sound are Millbay Docks (continental ferries); on the west side are Cremyll and Torpoint ferries, the Royal Naval Base in Devonport and the Tamar bridges : Brunel's Royal Albert Bridge *(qv)* and the impressive suspension bridge.

Monuments and buildings on the Hoe

3 Elliot Terrace (Z G) – The house was the home of Lord and Lady Astor wh were both MPs for Plymouth, one after the other : Waldorf between 1910 an 1919, Nancy until 1945.

Drake Statue (Z A) – The bronze statue by Boehm was erected in the 19C, wes of centre, on the inland side of the wide east-west Promenade.

Armada Memorial (Z B) – The memorial stands as a pendant on the east side c the Hoe.

Naval War Memorial (Z D) – The pillar memorial, surrounded by rose gardens, bear the names of 22 443 men. The anchor in Anchor Way is from the last Ark Roya

Royal Air Force Memorial – The bronze figure of a pilot pays tribute to the heroisr of over 2 000 men of the Commonwealth and Allied air forces.

Smeaton's Tower (Z) ⏲ – The white and red painted lighthouse replaced a beaco obelisk when it was re-erected on the Hoe in 1884 after its 123 storm-battere years on the Eddystone Rocks.
Climb up the steps and ladders *(93 steps)* in the ever narrowing cylinder – not how the two bunks are fitted round the walls – to the gallery and splendi **view★★**.

★ **Plymouth Dome** (Z) ⏲ – The large, modern centre tells the rich history of th city through tableaux, surprising guides in period costume and audio-visu shows, abetted by high technology (computers, radar). It follows the glory day of the Elizabethan era, through the Age of Piracy and the troubles of the Civ War to the town's rebirth as a seaside resort in the 19C and the devastatic of the Blitz.

Royal Citadel (Z) ⏲

The Royal Citadel, now garrisoned by the Royal Artillery, was built in the reig of Charles II between 1666 and 1671. Earlier forts on the site and its immedia predecessor, which was begun in 1590 by Sir Francis Drake but never complete were designed to protect Plymouth from sea-borne attack. The cannon on th 17C fort could be trained not only on enemy ships entering the Sound, at th time the Dutch, but also on the town, since Plymouth had supported th Parliamentarian cause during the Civil War.

Ramparts – The walls, which have a circumference of about three quarte of a mile and present a sheer face of 60ft in places (now used as a commanc scaling exercise) command **views★★** of the Barbican, the Sound and the mou of the Tamar.

Main Gate – The Portland stone gate (1670) originally contained a bust Charles II in the niche to complement the royal arms and inscription. It wa however, considered politic to remove the head and substitute four cannon ba when the citadel was surrendered personally to William III in 1688.

Chapel of St Katherine – The small chapel was rebuilt with walls 2ft 9in thi in 1688 and enlarged to twice its size in the 19C. The frescoes on the ea wall were painted by an NCO in the Royal Engineers who died in the First Wor War.

BARBICAN

Old, historic Plymouth survives in the Barbican, an area extending over a quart of a mile inland from the harbourside. The district combines modern interes and amenities – shops, restaurants, ships' chandlers, pubs, craft studios – wi medieval houses, Jacobean doorways, cobbled alleys, the harbour...

Begin at the waterfront.

Mayflower Stone (Z) – *West Pier.* The pier, adorned with stones and plaqu was the embarkation and alighting point for many famous voyages, includi the sailing of the **Pilgrim Fathers** on 6 September 1620 in their 90ft ship, *T Mayflower* (17C pavement stone); the *Tory* sailing to colonize **New Zealand** in M 1839; the *Sea Venture* voyaging to **Bermuda** in 1609; the return of the **Tolpud Martyrs** *(qv)* in 1838; the safe arrival of the American Seaplane, *NC4,* completion of the first **Transatlantic Flight** in 1919; the sailing of Sir Humphr Gilbert to Newfoundland in 1583.
On the far side of the road *(left, high on the wall by the flight of steps)* a plaq commemorates "10 Squadron **Royal Australian Air Force** stationed at Mt Batt 1939-45".

Turn north.

Fish Market (Z) – The market is a hive of activity in the early morning.

Island House (Z K) – The late 16C house (restored) is where the **Pilgrim Fath** (the names are listed on a board on the wall) may have spent their last nig before setting sail.

Turn right behind the house into New St.

Elizabethan House (Z) ⏲ – *32 New St.* The timber-framed and limestone hou and its neighbour *(opposite),* distinguished by **windows** which extend across t full width of the fronts on the ground and first floors, were built in the late 1 as part of a development of thirty houses for small merchants and ships' captai prosperous from the trade in wine, Newfoundland cod, tobacco and sugar a in booty captured at sea.

Inside, the house remains largely unadulterated : there is no electricity, no lights or fittings, just exposed **beams** and large **fireplaces.** The layout of the rooms is familiar, however, with kitchen and "living" area at ground level, bedrooms upstairs. The rooms are sparsely furnished with beautiful pieces of stout 16C-17C **oak furniture,** carved and patinaed with age – note the snug box bed on the top floor – and give an idea of the comforts of the time for a modestly wealthy household.
Note the **pole staircase** round a ship's mast; the worn wooden treads were mended by putting another on top until there were as many as four boards to a tread.

Continue up New St.

Elizabethan Gardens ⊙ – *left, narrow passage between houses.*
Aspects of a typical period garden of a ship's captain's house have been recreated : herbs and a knot garden.

Return to New St and take the first street opposite through to Southside St.

Coates Black Friars Gin Distillery (Z E) ⊙ – A low, wide granite doorway leads into a chamber containing the onion shaped, glass lined, steel vats in which today's Plymouth gin is prepared – a secret process by which 100% raw barley spirit produced in Scotland is transformed by distillation, flavouring and dilution with pure Dartmoor water.
The **Refectory Room** (now a restaurant) dates from 1425 when a Dominican (black friars) monastery stood on the site – note the plaque on the façade, above the low stone archway. Enter the main gateway to peer through the glass partition up at the **roof** built on arch braces and resembling an upturned keel, and to see prints of old Plymouth.

Cut through one of the "opes" on the opposite side of the street.

Parade (Z 26) – The quayside, lined by houses, warehouses and inns, takes its name from the days when the Royal Marines, established in Plymouth by the Board of Admiralty in 1755, used to parade on the cobbled pavement. Note the imposing Custom House.

PLYMOUTH

Street	Grid
Armada Way	YZ 2
Cornwall Street	Y
Drake Circus Centre	Y
New George Street	Y 24
Old Town Street	Y 25
Royal Parade	Z
Beaumont Road	Y 3
Buckwell Street	Z 4
Charles Cross	Y 6
Charles Street	Y 7
Derry's Cross	Z 9
Drake Circus	Y 10
Eastlake Street	Y 12
Elliot Street	Z 13
Gasking Street	Y 14
Great Western Road	Z 16
Hoe Road	Z 17
Kinterbury Street	Z 18
Lambhay Hill	Z 20
Mayflower Street	Y 22
Millbay Road	Z 23
Parade	Z 26
Princess Street	Z 27
Quay Road	Z 28
St. Andrew's Cross	Z 31
St. Andrew's Street	Z 32
San Sebastian Square	Z 33
Southside Street	Z 34
Woolster Street	Z 36

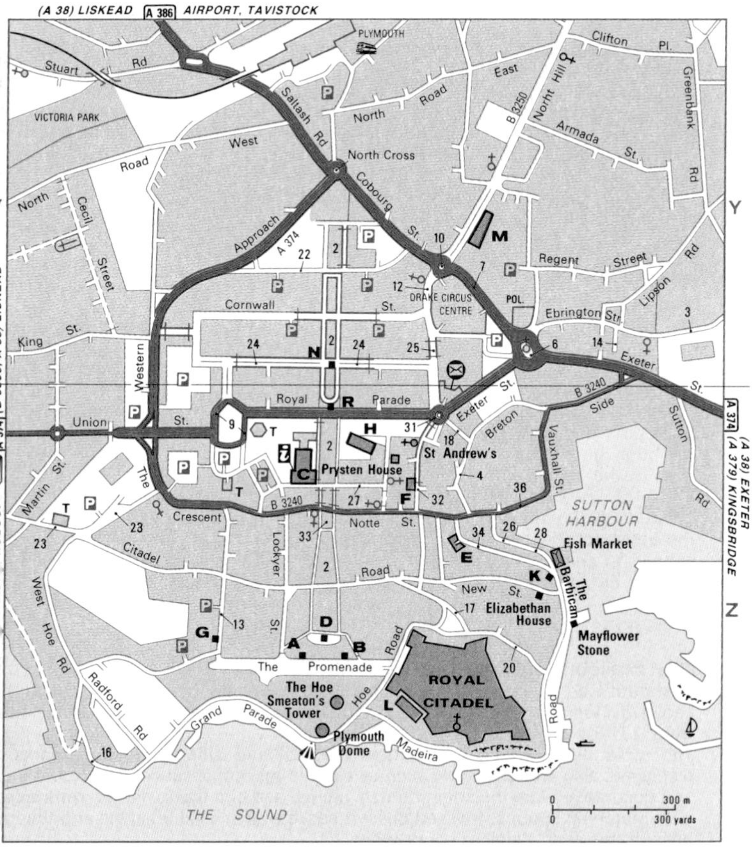

CITY CENTRE

New Buildings

Following the devastation of the Second World War, much of the city was rebu following designs by Sir Patrick Abercrombie (1879-1957), a pioneer of post-w urban planning. The result is wide streets and pedestrian areas, enlivened wi sculptures and carvings (note the figure of Drake on the corner of Armada W and Notte Street, for instance).

Civic Centre (Z) ⏲ – The 14 storey centre, the south wing of which hous the Tourist Information Centre, was opened in 1962.

Council House (Z C) ⏲ – Inside, **engraved glass panels** adorn the doors and t staircase by John Hulton. It is here that the **corporation plate** is housed.

City Flagstaff (Z R) – The mast at the juncture of Armada Way and Roy Parade is mounted on a replica of Drake's drum (the original is in Buckla Abbey, *qv*).

Armada Sundial (Y N) – The impressive monument stands proudly at t crossing of Armada Way and New George St.

Old Buildings

Guildhall (Z H) ⏲ – The building with a campanile-style tower dates from 187 the last in a line going back to the 15C; on the Hoe side the city's coat of arr is visible, transferred from the 17C poorhouse.

St Andrew's (Z) – The church, which was founded in 1050, was rebuilt in t 15C in the Perpendicular style. In 1941 a fire bomb exploded in the churc only the outer walls, fluted granite piers, chancel arch and tower (136ft) survive The church was rebuilt and reconsecrated in 1957.

Windows – The six distinctive windows were designed by **John Piper** (1904-9 in the 1950s. The tower window depicts the instruments of the Passion; no how the ladder, the lance and the reed are arranged to form St Andrev Cross. The vivid colours of the glass contrast with the patina of the flo surfaced in Delabole slate *(qv)*. Below each window is a complementa altar.
On a window ledge *(first window west of the south door)* is the so-called **Dra crest scratching** which shows the *Golden Hinde* with a cord from her bow par encircling a globe; the rough engraving is believed to have been made by a mas working in the church at the time of Drake's return on 3 November 1580 frc his circumnavigation of the world.
Among the **memorials** are a 12C-13C Purbeck marble effigy and a tablet to **Frobis** and **Drake** *(north transept)* and a tablet to William Cookworthy *(south wall; s below)*. Note the royal arms of Charles I, George III and George IV.

Prysten House (Z) ⏲ – The priests' house of stone, built three storeys hi round an inner courtyard, dates from the 15C and is thought to be the old house in Plymouth; it may have lodged the priests from Plympton Priory w came to officiate at St Andrew's. The courtyard probably served as a courtroc for cases tried before the prior, who held civil as well as ecclesiastical autho in the town.
Note the **window frames** and stone mullions, stone **fireplaces** and the bea – smoke-blackened from the time when, after the Dissolution, the house beca a bacon-curing store for a while.

Door of Unity – The door facing the church commemorates two US na officers killed in action in 1813 and buried in St Andrew's churchyard.

Merchant's House Museum (Z F) ⏲ – *33 St Andrew's St.*
The Museum of Old Plymouth is accommodated in the 16C Merchant's Hou The three-storey timber building has limestone walls and jettied upper flo supported on stone corbels; the windows extend almost the full width and hei of the front. The **pole staircase** is built round a shaft (35ft).
Each floor consisted of a principal front room and a back room; there were sn bedrooms on the upper floors.
Although built in the 16C the house was probably given much of its pres style in the 17C when it was bought by William Parker, mayor of Plymouth 1601-02. Parker was a sea-captain, merchant and typical adventurer a privateer *(qv)*, who had amassed enough gold to buy and improve the ho through buccaneering on the Spanish Main and possibly also as master of t victualling ship to Drake's fleet at the time of the Armada.
Among the exhibits is the reconstruction of one of Plymouth's old pharmaci

ADDITIONAL SIGHTS

★ **City Museum and Art Gallery** (Y M) ⏲ – *Drake Circus.*
Plymouth was the home of the adult **William Cookworthy,** discoverer of the Corn kaolin *(qv)* which made the production of **hard paste porcelain** a reality in this cour from 1768.
The rapid development of the new material and different factory marks displayed, also **domestic pieces** such as cider mugs, cups, sauceboats and teap and decorative ware including human, animal and bird **figures,** vases, centrepie with matching spoons, trellised dessert baskets all in vivid enamels and the m difficult, because flawless, pure white.

The gallery also boasts a unique collection of **Reynolds family portraits** – Joshua Reynolds was born in Plympton in 1723 (d 1792).
The **history gallery** is distinguished by the **Drake Cup**, a silver parcel-gilt globe with an astrolabe, presented to Drake by Queen Elizabeth in 1582.

Plymouth Aquarium (Z L) ⊙ – *Madeira Rd.* The fish, eels and flatfish and mackerel, the sea anemones, starfish, dog-fish, crabs and other crustacea swimming in the sea-water tanks around the gallery are almost all from local waters. The 50 kinds of fish and many hundred invertebrates are there primarily, in fact, for observation by the **Marine Biological Association of the UK** as part of their research on increasing the supply of food from the sea.

BOAT TRIPS ⊙

Dockyards and Warships – *1 hour.* From Phoenix Wharf past the Mayflower Steps round under the Hoe to Devonport Docks on the Tamar.

River Yealm – *2 hours.* From Phoenix Wharf past the Breakwater at the entrance to the Sound and east along the coast to Newton Ferrers at the mouth of the Yealm.

River Tamar – *4-5 hours; optional return by train from Calstock.*
From Phoenix Wharf up the Tamar to Calstock, Morwellham and Weir Head (Gunnislake). *See Tamar River.*

EXCURSIONS

★ **Saltram House** – *3½ miles east, just south of A38 (before Plympton). See Saltram House.*

★ **Buckland Abbey** – *11 miles northwest by A386 – bear left at Yelverton; signposted from Crapstone. See Buckland Abbey.*

★ **Yelverton Paperweight Centre** ⊙ – *9 miles north on A386 (200yds along a loop road just off the roundabout).*
A dazzling array of *c*800 paperweights, ranging from deep, resonant colours to misty pastel, reveal the rich variety of designs – marbled, floral, swirling – made in the 19C and 20C by English, Scots, French, German and Chinese craftsmen.

Mount Edgcumbe – *9 miles west by Torpoint car ferry, A374 and B3247 to Cremyll or 2 miles by Cremyll passenger ferry from Admiral's Hard, Stonehouse. See Mount Edgcumbe.*

Dartmoor Wild Life Park, Sparkwell ⊙ – *9 miles east on Plymouth-Cornwood by-road.*
The collection, in large paddocks, aviaries and shelters on the edge of Dartmoor, ranges from timber-wolves to chickens, from monkeys to owls and red deer.

Yealmpton – *9 miles southeast off A379.*

Kitley Caves, Yealmpton ⊙ – The caves, in a wooded setting beside the River Yealm, were discovered in the early 1800s by quarrymen blasting for limestone – a couple of ruined kilns stand near the entrance. The caves contain stalactites and stalagmites and a number of rock pools.

1 mile beyond Yealmpton turn right.

National Shire Horse Centre ⊙ – Though the large centre specializes mainly in shire horses, the complex also includes a falconry centre (flying displays) and other animals from butterflies to pigs.
The shires, between 15 and 20 of them, stallions, geldings, mares and foals, mostly black with blazes, white socks, characteristic feathered legs, and curved Roman noses, weigh up to one ton each. They work and dominate the 60-acre farm.
The old stone farm buildings date back to 1772 with the long main stable, its hayloft above, turning the corner opposite the house. The porch leads into the harness room, gleaming with brass and leather, and stable, where those horses not at work may be viewed.
There are daily parades of horses, mares and foals, and special pageants.

★ POOLE Dorset — Pop 122 815

Michelin Atlas p 9 or Map 403 – 031

Poole overlooks one of the largest natural harbours in the world.
The port, with ships sailing to foreign parts, appears to have been well established by the 12C-13C when it took the ascendancy over Wareham (to the west) where the channel was silting up. Warehouses such as the Town Cellars were built, Henry VI granted the town the status of a **Custom Port** and **Port of the Staple**, so licensing it to export wool and woollen cloth *(qv)*, at that time Dorset's and England's most valuable product.
As trade increased during the 16C-18C, particularly with Newfoundland, the town found even greater prosperity which resulted in the refacing or rebuilding of many houses in the Georgian style still evident in parts. It is at this period that a house *(private)* of Tudor origin in Market Street was divided : the owners were presumably of different fortunes as in the one case the frontage was kept unaltered with exposed beams; in the other the more prosperous owners had the frontage Classically refaced.

The **Poole fleet,** carrying cod and salt fish to Spain and Portugal, continued t expand until by 1802 it had 80 ships on the Newfoundland run and more tha 200 engaged elsewhere.
In the mid-19C trade shifted to Scandinavia (timber, coal and clay).
Today, in addition to bulk traffic in grain, fertilizer, timber and clay, it is developin into a major lorry and heavy vehicle **roll-on-roll-off port** with transporter park entrepot sheds and as many as three ferry sailings daily for the Continer (Cherbourg). **Yachting** and **powerboat racing** have also become popular.
On the landward side Poole has attracted big business, so that stacked behin the quay there are now the modern office blocks of national and multination enterprises. The human dimension is on the **Quay,** in the **Old Town** and in **Poo Park,** this last containing a saltwater lake and amusement facilities.

QUAY and OLD TOWN

Quay – The quayside is lined with yacht chandlers, inns and restaurants. The giant, dark blue steel sculpture entitled *Sea Music* (1992), by Sir Anthon Caro, is a landmark for ships entering the port. Viewing platforms around provide a panorama of the town, the harbour and out to sea.

Natural World ⊙ – The warm rooms of this combined aquarium and serpentariu contain tanks of sharks, exotic and local fish, frogs, iguanas, spiders, snake crocodiles and any number of other creepy, fascinating or usually dangerou reptiles, arachnids, insects, fish and amphibians.

Poole Pottery ⊙ – The tour of the huge shop and crafts centre, which incorporate Dartington Crystal, passes potters, glassblowers and engravers at work; i another part, old tiles decorate the walls and there are displays of commem ration pieces.

RNLI Museum ⊙ – Large models show developments in the design of lifeboa and the heroic deeds of the crews since the Institution's foundation in 182

Old Town – The district extends inland to the church and Old Guildhall. O the quay stand the handsome late 18C **Customs House** of red brick, with a doorwa at the top of twin stairways, and the old Town Cellars *(see below).*

Bear back from the quay to the church.

St James' Close – The close, a green and flowered triangle, frames the large **chur** of 1820 with high windows and a tall doorway in its west tower. All aroun are **18C town houses,** each in its own garden.

Guildhall – *Market Street.* The high cost of the building, £2 260 14*s* in 176 is justified by its **perfect proportions** and the contrasting curved and straight line the circular clock-face in the triangular pediment, the round-headed door beneat the square porch, the round and flat-topped windows, the **horseshoe staircase** wi plain iron railings. It was used by the corporation for meetings, as a quart sessions courtroom and by the court of admiralty, which determined prize mone and salvage dues.

★ MUSEUMS

Waterfront ⊙ – *High Street.* The old Oakley's Mill uses modern technique – videos and computer simulations – room sets and obsolete artefacts to illustra the history of Poole's maritime community. The fascinating displays encompas underwater archeology – Studland Bay Wreck; maritime trades; a Victorian stre scene with sound-effects; the first Scout Camp on Brownsea Island.
The **Town Cellars,** part of a 15C wool warehouse with a fine timber **roof,** is devote to temporary exhibitions.

Scaplen's Court ⊙ – *High Street.* The court is a Tudor house built around central courtyard and was discovered this century beneath years of accretion it now houses items portraying domestic life through the ages : 18C furnitur Poole pottery, 19C children's clothes and toys, Dorset buttons and crochetwor 17C-18C legal documents, a Victorian kitchen.

EXCURSIONS

★★ **Compton Acres** – *3 miles east by B3369. See Compton Acres.*

★ **Brownsea Island** – *See Brownsea Island.*

Sandbanks – Facilities. *2 miles southeast by B3369.*
The promontory runs like a mile-long, built-up breakwater to enclose Poo Harbour. At the point is a roll-on-roll-off chain ferry to Studland *(qv).* The boa which cross from Poole Quay to Brownsea Island call at Sandbanks.

FOLLOW THE COUNTRY CODE

Guard against all risk of fire.
Fasten all gates.
Keep dogs under proper control.
Keep to the paths across farmland.
Avoid damaging fences, hedges and walls.
Leave no litter.
Safeguard water supplies.
Protect wildlife, wild plants and trees.
Go carefully on country roads.
Respect the life of the countryside.

★ PORLOCK Somerset Pop 1 368

Michelin Atlas p 7 or Map 403 – J30 – Local map p 161

Porlock is an attractive village despite the crowds. It is surrounded on three sides by the Exmoor hills and has a narrow winding main street marked by a church with a lopped spire, and thatched and creeper-covered houses. **Porlock Hill** to the west with a superb **view★★** remains as notorious as ever with a 1:4 gradient; "the man from Porlock", who interrupted Coleridge as he began to write *Kubla Khan,* remains as unknown a character as ever.

★ **St Dubricius Church** – The church has a truncated, octagonal **spire** covered in oak shingles set on a solid 13C stone tower. It is not known whether the tower was ever completed and subsequently destroyed in a storm or whether it was abandoned halfway – one story has it that the workmen left to follow the hunt as it passed through the village and never returned from the moor. Inside, the **Early English arcade,** the **east window** of three tall lancets under one arch, the double piscina and arch at the west end of the nave are all 13C; the Perpendicular windows were inserted during the 15C reconstruction. Note the remarkable **canopied tomb** with alabaster effigies of John, 4th Lord Harington and his wife (dd 1417, 1461).
The dedication and tradition of foundation by St Dubricius or Dyffrig is a reminder of the work in the southwest of Celtic missionaries from Wales in the 5C-6C; Dubricius, a legendary figure who died aged 120 in *c*612, is said to have been a friend of King Arthur and present at the Battle of Bladon Hill in 517.

Porlock Weir – *Take the by-road on the right at the end of the village.*
The small harbour filled with pleasure-craft is overlooked by white-washed cottages and old inns.

EXCURSION

★ **St Beuno, Culbone** – *2 miles along the Ashley Combe Toll Rd; park at the old farm toll gate; 3 miles on foot Rtn : go armed with insect repellent or a fly whisk.*
The irregular path is through broad-leafed woods which extend back from 400ft cliffs towards the Exmoor hills – but always within sound of the sea.
Suddenly, in a dell with a rushing stream, there is the 12C-13C **church** of St Beuno, the smallest complete church in England (12ft 4in across by 35ft long). The walls of rubble stone are intended to be rendered and whitewashed; the roof is of slate, as is the spirelet added *c*1810. On the north side, the possibly **Saxon window** of two lights, cut out of a single block of sandstone, is decorated at the top of the mullion with a relief of a cat-like face.
Inside, the chancel has had a too-large east window inserted and a neo-Gothic reredos but the **rood screen** was carved with foils and cusps by 14C craftsmen. The family pew is 17C, the **benches** are pre-Reformation and the circular **font** is possibly Saxon.

★ PORTLAND Dorset Pop 10 915

Michelin Atlas p 8 or Map 403 – M32

The Isle of Portland is a peninsula 4½ miles long which in winter stands defiant amid the Channel storms, its name mentioned almost daily in gale warnings in the shipping forecasts; in summer it becomes a place where visitors head for **The Bill,** its southernmost tip, to stand in the sun on the springy turf and idly watch the horizon.
Portland stone has been quarried all over the island since the Middle Ages and the landscape is pockmarked with worked-out quarries. Everything on Portland is built of the pure white limestone which is durable yet soft enough to carve; Wren chose it for St Paul's Cathedral.

SIGHTS

Portland Bill – The Bill, in addition to being a splendid **vantage point★★**, is distinguished by three markers : **Portland Bill Lighthouse** *(qv),* the **Bird Observatory,** a former lighthouse, and the **Obelisk** of Portland stone, erected as a way-mark in 1844.

Portland Museum ⊙ – The museum, Avice's House in Thomas Hardy's *The Well-Beloved,* presents a history of the island with exhibits from 19C days when convicts worked the quarries, and built the prison (1848) and St Peter's Church.
The **Pulpit Rock** may be climbed to provide a perch high above the waves.

Portland Castle ⊙ – The castle was built in 1539-40 at the water's edge on a Saxon site as one of **Henry VIII's forts** along the south coast. The fabric is Portland stone, the cost was a colossal £4 964 19*s* 10¼*d,* it being the finest of all the castles erected. Additions were made in Elizabeth's reign, in the 17C and early in the 19C.

Portland Harbour – The harbour Henry VIII's castle was designed to defend was protected on three sides but wide open to the east. In the mid-19C work began on the system of breakwaters and channels which, after 20 years' construction by convicts, was to provide one of the largest and safest harbours in the world.
Today it is occupied by the **Admiralty Underwater Weapons Establishment.**

★★ The RIDGEWAY PATH Wiltshire

Michelin Atlas pp 17, 18 or Map 403 – O, P, Q29

Length, course, conditions – The modern Ridgeway Path extends 85 miles from Overton Hill near Avebury via the Uffington White Horse *(qv)* to the Ivinghoe Beacon near Tring; it passes through five counties, Wiltshire Berkshire, Oxfordshire, Buckinghamshire and Hertfordshire, combining the prehistoric ridgeway path across the chalk downs west of the Thames with the Roman Lower Icknield Way beyond the river crossing at Streatley. The modern path, opened in 1973, is waymarked by Countryside Commission acorns *(see below)*.

The west section is suitable for walking, horse riding and bicycling. There are car parks at intersections with main roads.

The going is straightforward; the grass and earth track, which occasionally rises to 900ft, is generally wide, passing along downland crests, beside fields, through woods and coppices. It is mostly out in the open, affording wide **views** across the downs – beware the ruts in the path and remember that chalk is muddy and slippery after heavy rain.

For those intending to walk a considerable distance or the full length, the 1:50 000 (1¼ inch) Ordnance Survey maps (nos 173, 174, 175 and 165) are recommended.

Wild flowers and **herbs, butterflies** – chalk-hill blues and many of the browns – and **birds** – particularly skylarks, and occasionally a kestrel or buzzard – may be seen along the way, particularly over the chalk.

History – Before the Uffington White Horse, Avebury or Stonehenge, before the sea broke through the chalk around 6000 BC to form the English Channel and make Britain an island, our prehistoric ancestors were already walking the Ridgeway Path.

The **Paleolithic** and **Mesolithic** peoples (600 000-2500 BC) were nomadic and able to wander freely to and from the continent, to hunt the forests and scrub that covered all but the chalk uplands which, because they were less overgrown and offered easier going, the nomads began very early to use as regular tracks. In time, the paths penetrated across country following the line of chalk which extends in a swathe from the Norfolk coast, through the Chilterns to the North Wessex and Hampshire Downs where tracks along the North and South Downs also converged. Finally, all led down to the Dorset coast and the sea.

In the **Neolithic** period (2500-1900 BC), by which time the Channel was in being the huntsmen and herdsmen began to settle, grazing the downlands with sheep and scratching the soil to grow grain. They made pottery and wove cloth; they buried their dead in long barrows and, as they began to come together in tribes constructed the prehistoric monuments in the Avebury area (Windmill Hill, *qv*). They also traded, bartering with early, itinerant traders who came along the track with fine axe and arrow heads from Cornwall, Cumbria and Wales.

The Bronze Age (1900-450 BC) saw the invasion of the east coast and of Dorset by **Beaker Folk**, who used the chalk upland tracks to penetrate far inland. They fashioned metals for their own use – copper, tin, bronze and gold (from Cornwall and Ireland) – exported bronze tools and weapons and obtained, in exchange the pottery and weapons from Brittany, Holland, the Mediterranean and central Europe discovered in their graves by modern archeologists. The constant traffic of traders and itinerant smiths, who cast tools and weapons and, resmelting the metal, exchanged new for old, meant that by 1700 BC the Ridgeway and Icknield Way had become regular trade routes.

The Beaker Folk were overcome by the **Urn People,** invading warriors from Brittany (1700 BC) who had a sophisticated taste for luxuries which were brought by new traders along the old upland routes : gold from Ireland, jet from Yorkshire, amber from the Baltic, blue pottery beads from Egypt. Their name derives from their practice of burying the cremated ashes of the dead in urns in the round barrows which may still be seen on the Wiltshire Downs.

The first wave of **Celts** came over in the 8C BC : their weapons were still of bronze although their agriculture was well advanced – their small rectangular field cultivation is even now visible from the air. In turn they fell before a second wave of Celts : the 5C BC men of the **Iron Age.** As invasion followed invasion, Celts already established defended themselves in the hillforts to be seen everywhere in the region.

The **animals** of the early herdsmen – cattle, sheep, horses, hogs – were leaf, tree bark and scrub eaters; the forests became so reduced that the nature of the countryside was changed for ever; the animals became herbivores. Man, however had reached the Iron Age : not only weapons but tools for clearing scrub and forest had become keener and agricultural implements had begun to evolve. With the **Romans** began settlement of the valleys and lowlands with paths and even made-up roads linking the towns. The Ridgeway was abandoned except by drovers who, until the advent of rail and road transport, continued to travel the tracks with their cattle and sheep, heading for London.

AVEBURY to the WILTSHIRE BORDER *17 miles*

The track, by its nature, does not progress from sight to sight, but skirts them by a mile or two.

★ **Avebury** – *See Avebury.*

White Horse – *Hackpen Hill. Ridgeway-Marlborough-Wootton Bassett road crossing.* Arriving at 892ft on the horse, the visitor cannot therefore get a good overall impression of it, though it can be examined from close to; the commanding **view** includes Windmill Hill *(qv)*.

Barbury Castle – The Iron Age hillfort crowning the down is a triple-embanked earthwork enclosing 11½ acres, with openings to west and east through which the modern path passes. The castle is named after an Anglo-Saxon chief, Bara, who fought a battle in 566 on the slopes to the north.

Liddington Castle – Iron Age hillfort.

Fox Hill and Charlbury Hill – The hills are marked respectively by a radio tower and an orange-flashing aircraft beacon.

The acorn sign which waymarks the Ridgeway Path.

ST AUSTELL Cornwall — Pop 20 267

Michelin Atlas p 3 or Map 403 – F32

The old market town of St Austell rose to importance in the mid-18C with the discovery in the area by **William Cookworthy** of **china-clay** which has been mined locally ever since. The residue, green-white slag pyramids have become a distinctive local landmark.

In the town, where the streets are steep and camellias bloom in the front gardens, are the 17C **Market House,** the White Hart, once a posting inn and, on an island site, the parish church.

★ **Holy Trinity Church** – The exterior is remarkable for its tall, late 15C **tower,** embattled, corner pinnacled and profusely decorated on all four sides with masks, angels and niches containing statues and groups of the Annunciation, the risen Christ and the Trinity.

Inside, beneath the old wagon roofs and 15C arcade, note how the **nave** is out of line with the tower and the older 13C chancel. The granite **font** (*c*1200), one of the most impressive in Cornwall, is carved with "gorgons, hydras and chimeras dire".

EXCURSIONS

★★ **Wheal Martyn Museum, Carthew** ⊙ – *2 miles north on A391.*

China clay (kaolin) is a constituent of many manufactured products as well as porcelain. The English China Clays Group, which works 26 pits, has the greatest production in the world at nearly 3 000 000 tons a year. Of this 15% goes into fine china, earthenware, tiles and sanitary ware, 75% into papermaking and the rest into plastics, rubber and synthetic rubber, paints, pharmaceuticals, cosmetics, fertilizers, textiles, leather goods... More than 70% (2 100 000 tons) is exported annually (this may be seen at Fowey, *qv*). A short film explains the old pumping and modern pressure jet extraction and the refining process which can be followed outside among the obsolete drags, settling tanks, waterwheels, drying kiln, horse wagons and steam engines. Operations in two modern clay pits can be viewed from the high point of the Nature Trail.

Roche Rock – *6 miles north on A391 and B3274.*

Above the man-made landscape of fields and distant china-clay pyramids there rises an age-old elemental outcrop of grey-green-black schorl on which an early 15C anchorite built a granite chapel.

★★ **St Austell Bay** – The wide bay circles west from **Gribbin Head**★★ *(qv)* to the line of cliffs terminating in **Dodman Point** (373ft) to the south.

★ **Polkerris** – The small village with a sand beach is sheltered to landward by steep cliffs, to seaward by a curving sea wall.

Par – The onetime pilchard harbour and processing town, tin port and smelting works is now powdered white from the clay loaded into ships in the dock.

Biscovey – In an old Victorian school *(north side of A390 by Par crossroads)* the **Mid-Cornwall Galleries** ⊙ present a brimming display of pottery, modern brasswork (fenders), textiles and knitting, painting and sculpture in wood and stone.

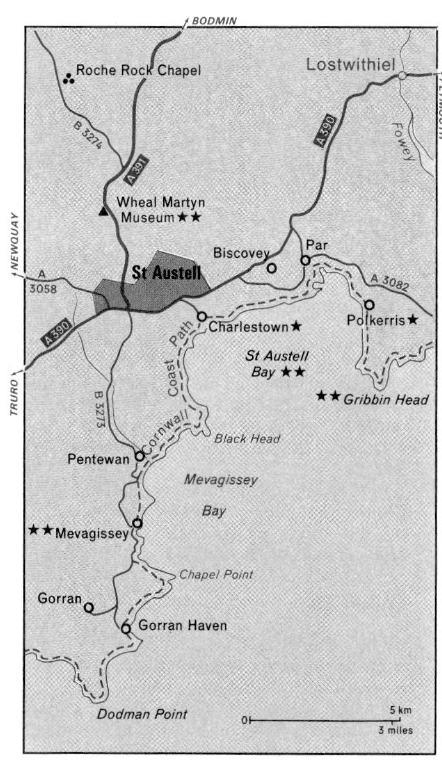

★ **Charlestown** – From 1792-98 Charles Rashleigh (after whom the village was subsequently renamed) began to turn the fishing village of West Polmear into a thriving port. The long, unspoilt main street of colour-washed houses leads to the dock (1798) designed by Charles Smeaton where china clay is loaded, the pier (1792) and outer basin (1794) from which emigrants sailed to America. On either side are beaches and small coves.
The **Shipwreck and Heritage Museum** ⓥ is entered through the tunnels of an old china-clay dry, now lined with tableaux of 19C life in Charlestown. The varied exhibits give a comprehensive survey of shipwrecks, their causes, sea rescue, laws of salvage, diving on wrecks, items recovered from famous ships (gold, leather, porcelain, pewter...).

Pentewan – Stone for many of Cornwall's churches and large houses was quarried nearby for centuries and shipped from the harbour, which lies sheltered between the promontories.

Mevagissey Harbour.

★★ **Mevagissey** – Facilities. A popular fishing port with houses irregularly terraced up the hillsides, colour-washed, half-timbered or weather-boarded with oversailing upper floors; an inner harbour with 1770s pier, old quayside boathouses and sail lofts (now shops and restaurants); a maze of twisting back streets and steps; nets drying on walls; slate everywhere, on roofs, as front doorsteps and window sills; a fisherman's loft with nets of every variety of mesh size, weight and colour – such is Mevagissey. The town is crowded with visitors all summer long but a few minutes' walk leads to one of the headlands for a gull's eye view.

Gorran Haven – The oldest **houses** are to be found in Church Street, Fox Lane and Rattle Alley. The tiny **church** of St Just was built as a seamen's chapel and lantern; the distinctive pentagonal **tower** is 15C.

Use Michelin Maps with a Michelin Guide.

★★ ST IVES Cornwall — Pop 9 439

Michelin Atlas p 2 or Map 403 – D33 – Facilities
Town plan in the current Michelin Red Guide Great Britain and Ireland

St Ives, a fishing harbour, home for several years of a group of famous artists (the St Ives School, *qv*) and still a working artists' centre, attracts great numbers of visitors. Areas of interest include the small headland known as the **Island,** a network of stepped and winding alleys, hillside terraces, archways, "back doubles", all lined by colour-washed fisherman's houses, crowded shoulder to shoulder. The curving quayside and main street are known as **The Wharf** and **Fore St.**
The town's prestige has increased with the opening of the **St Ives Tate** ⓥ, a West Country satellite of the London Tate Gallery, exhibiting a wide range of works by the many artists who loosely make up the St Ives School *(qv),* in a specially-designed building overlooking Porthmear beach.

SIGHTS

★ **St Ia** – The church with its pinnacled 85ft **tower** of Zennor granite, clearly visible from the harbour, dates – except for the 20C baptistery – from the 15C when it was built in a single phase.
Note the **wagon roof, bench-ends** and carved **font.**
The **Lady Chapel** is unique for the tender *Mother and Child* by **Barbara Hepworth** (1953) who also designed the stainless steel Christmas rose candlesticks.

★★ **Barbara Hepworth Museum** ⊙ – Barbara Hepworth (1903-75) came to St Ives during the Second World War and settled permanently.
The house, filled with a lifetime's **sculpture**, and the studio with unfinished blocks of stone contrast with the small, white-walled garden, dense with trees and vivid flowers, which provides an uncrowded setting for some twenty sculptures in bronze and stone *(see Art and Artists, qv)*.
Two Hepworths stand before the Guildhall and in Malakoff Gardens (bus station).

Barbara Hepworth garden sculpture.

Penwith Gallery ⊙ – *Back Road West.*
The gallery, in a converted pilchard factory, displays painting, sculpture and pottery by Penwith artists.

St Nicholas Chapel – The chapel on the "Island" is the traditional seamen's chapel built as a beacon. It commands a wide **view**★★ including Godrevy Lighthouse *(qv)* across the bay.

Smeaton Pier – The pier was constructed in 1767-70 by the builder of the then Eddystone lighthouse *(qv)*. At its shore end is the small St Leonard's sailors' chapel.

St Ives Museum ⊙ – The local museum is filled with everything to do with historic St Ives.

Sloop Market – The old market, with studio workshops and enamellers, leather workers, a potter or a silversmith at work, can be an interesting port of call.

★ ST MAWES Cornwall

Michelin Atlas p 2 or Map 403 – E, F33 – Facilities

The small low-lying stone houses, thatched, pink-washed or ivy-covered – one dated 1760, another with a Sun Life Insurance firemark – the hotels, pubs and small shops along the curving line of the waterfront continue up the steep road and tributary alleys behind the square. Flowers everywhere confirm that St Mawes has the mildest, sunniest of climates.

★ **St Mawes Castle** ⊙ – The clover-shaped castle, constructed as a pair to Pendennis *(qv)*, commands a **view**★ up the Carrick Roads and across to Falmouth. Unlike Pendennis which withstood many weeks of siege in 1646, St Mawes capitulated to the Parliamentarians; neither fort, in the event, defended the Roads, the purpose for which they were originally constructed with their overlapping gunfire.

★★ ST MICHAEL'S MOUNT Cornwall

Michelin Atlas p 2 or Map 403 – D33

St Michael's Mount is the focal point of every **view** across the bay and itself commands **views**★★ towards the Lizard and Land's End.
The castle is approached up a steep zig-zag path through the trees *(25min Rtn)*.

Legend, foundation, Dissolution – In the 4C BC ships came from the Mediterranean to the **Island of Ictis,** as they named it, to trade in tin, copper and gold; in AD 495, according to Cornish legend, fishermen saw St Michael standing on a westerly ledge of the granite rock which rises high out of the sea, whereupon the island became a place of pilgrimage. By the 8C, it is said, a Celtic monastery had been founded upon it which endured until the 11C.
At the same time, in 708 in France, St Michael appeared three times in a vision to Bishop Aubert of Avranches, who then built an oratory to the saint on the island from then known as Mont-St-Michel. By the time of the Battle of Hastings, the oratory in France had developed into an important Benedictine community to which St Michael's Mount passed as a dependency. The English house, always modest by comparison with the French monastery, was ultimately appropriated during the course of the Hundred Years War by Henry V as alien property and was finally suppressed in 1535.

Strongpoint – Even while it was a pilgrimage goal, the Mount suffered from French and Spanish raids on the coast. In the Middle Ages it became a strongpoint from which Perkin Warbeck *(qv)* set out in 1497, and the men of the **Cornish Rebellion** tried to resist the imposition by Edward IV in 1549 of the Book of Common Prayer in English which they claimed not to understand. In 1588 it was from the church on the summit that a beacon signalled the approach up the Channel of the 130 galleons of the Spanish Armada.

The 17C saw the Mount involved in the Civil War : the harbour became a port of entry for arms purchased with Cornish tin from the French in support of the Royalist cause; in April 1646 the island surrendered to the Parliamentary forces and a year later received its last military commander, Col John St Aubyn, who subsequently purchased the castle as a family residence. In times of war the island is still garrisoned.

The Mount's owners – Col John St Aubyn, who died in 1684, according to tradition by being swept off his horse by a mighty wave when riding along the causeway, began repairs to the fabric and positioned his arms over the entrance when he was still governor. His great-grandson (d 1744), the third baronet, became famous when in an age of corruption Sir Robert Walpole, as Prime Minister, declared in the House, "All these men have their price except the **little Cornish Baronet**".
He rebuilt the harbour and the causeway (1727) and altered and embellished the castle interior in the 18C style.
A third phase of alterations occured in 1873-78 when Piers St Aubyn, architect and cousin of the then Sir John St Aubyn, first Lord St Levan, added a Victorian domestic wing to the southeast which descends by as many as five storeys down the rock face to preserve the familiar medieval skyline.

Jack the Giant Killer – Giants once abounded in Cornwall, according to an old map still in the house. They sat on the hilltops, dressed in loose tunics and floppy hats. St Michael's Mount was even built by a giant, a black-beard named Cormoran who would wade ashore to capture sheep and cattle and then return to the rock to sleep.
Jack, a local boy, decided to kill the giant. One night he rowed to the island and halfway up the path he dug a very deep pit; as dawn was breaking, Jack sounded his horn; Cormoran woke, came rushing down the path with the sun in his eyes, fell into the pit and died – the **pit** into which he fell is halfway up the hill.

St Michael's Mount, Cornwall.

TOUR ⏲ *1½ hours*

Doorway – The doorway is Tudor with the St Aubyn arms above it *(see above)*.

Entrance Hall – The hall, guardroom and garrison room in the oldest part of the house are 14C and still much as they were in the priory-fortress period.

Armoury – The armoury, altered in the 19C, displays, among the trophies, sporting weapons, coat of arms and a silken banner, the **oak chest** of the first Col John St Aubyn and 1944 paratrooper **beret** of another member of the family. Note the first of many **paintings** of the Mount throughout the centuries; in the rooms which follow there are family **portraits** in oil, in silhouette and in miniature.

Library – The library, in the oldest part of the castle, was transformed in the 18C. Note the watercolours of Mont-St-Michel and views from the lancet windows.

Chevy Chase Room – The former monks' refectory was given the lively plaster **frieze** of men and animals in the field in the 17C. The main roof timbers date from the 15C, the **royal arms** from 1660 (the 1641 date is a mystery). The dado and doors are 18C Gothick.
The great **oak table** dates from the 1620s; the **chairs** were made by the estate carpenter in 1800 after the pre-Dissolution*Glastonbury model still in the room; the **triangular chair** is Elizabethan; the court cupboard 17C.

Church – The church at the island summit, dedicated in 1125, was rebuilt in the 14C following an earthquake. In the 15C the windows were enlarged to include the two roses.

Note the banners, the **alabaster panels** in the altarpiece – the smaller ones are 16C Flemish, the larger rare 15C work from Nottingham – also the late 15C Flemish gilt brass **chandelier** (similar to that in Bristol Cathedral, *qv*) with figures of the Virgin and Child and of St Michael killing the dragon.
At the church entrance is a restored Gothic **Lantern Cross** carved with the Crucifixion, the Virgin and Child and the heads of an unknown king and pilgrim.

Anteroom and Blue Drawing Rooms – The creation of the three rooms was the idea of the "little Cornish Baronet" in the 18C. Blue walls, deeper blue furnishings, **Chippendale chairs** and settee, a highly ornate Louis XVI **clock** on a marble-topped commode, two alabaster and jasper **vases** stand beneath fine **Rococo plasterwork.** On the walls are choice family portraits by Gainsborough and Opie, and an 18C conversation piece by Arthur Devis with two Misses St Aubyn before a distant outline of the Mount.
The **chairs** in the anteroom are Strawberry Hill Gothick.

Battery – The battery *(below the entrance on leaving)* is armed with guns from a French frigate driven aground by fire from the Mount during the Napoleonic Wars.

Dairy – The octagonal walled dairy was built in the 1870s when there were 9 cows on the island.

MARAZION Pop 1 366

Pilgrims, waiting for the ferry or for the tide to fall so that they could cross the sands to St Michael's Mount, gave Marazion an increased importance throughout the Middle Ages. Pillage by local raiders, the Dissolution of St Michael's Priory and finally the Spanish raid of 1595 on Mousehole *(qv)* and other towns around the bay so reduced the town that it never recovered.

★ ST NEOT Cornwall — Pop 810

Michelin Atlas p 3 or Map 403 – G32

The approach to the moorland village of houses of tawny stone and a Perpendicular church of 1425 is up a wooded valley, enclosed by sweeping hillsides.

★★ **Parish Church** – Outside, pinnacles and battlements line the aisle and west tower; the interior is lit by 12 **windows** of rare, medieval English glass.

The Creation *(east window, south aisle)* – The finest, the oldest and the least restored window has God measuring out the universe and, at the end, Noah doffing his cap, having received orders to build the Ark.

The Flood *(1st window east, south aisle)* – Noah builds the Ark, which is a real sailing ship of the period, and the story continues with it surmounting perilous seas.

St George *(west window, north aisle)*, **St Neot** *(5th window east, north aisle)* and **Robert Tubbe,** the vicar from 1508-44 who was responsible for obtaining the glass, all appear, as do the donors, the young men and the young wives of the village, in the lower sections of the aisle windows.

SALCOMBE Devon — Pop 1 968

Michelin Atlas p 4 or Map 403 – I33
Town plan in the current Michelin Red Guide Great Britain and Ireland

Devon's most southerly resort lies at the mouth of the Kingsbridge Estuary between Prawle Point to the east and Bolt Head to the west.
The town, a onetime fishing village overlooking the estuary, has small sand beaches and coves (North Sands, South Sands, Batson Creek) within minutes of the main street and, in the street itself, more ships' chandlers than grocers. Old houses, boat-yards, the custom house and its quay, ships and a pontoon-pier line the waterside; more modern houses sprawl back up the wooded hillside. The estuary harbour, which extends from the sand bar in line with Sharpitor Rocks and after which Tennyson is said to have written *Crossing the Bar,* teems all summer with small yachts – as many as 6 000 visiting craft have been counted in a single season.
Salcombe even has a castle, **Fort Charles,** built at the entrance to the harbour in 1544, rebuilt in 1643 and besieged by the Parliamentary troops from 15 January to 9 May 1646 when it surrendered. It is now a picturesque ruin.

Ferries ⊙ – Ferries ply the harbour estuary : across to **East Portlemouth** (sand beaches and paths to Prawle Point), seawards to **South Sands** and inland to **Kingsbridge** *(qv)*.

EXCURSIONS

★ **Kingsbridge** – *5 miles north by A381. See Kingsbridge.*

Bolt Head – *7 miles Rtn on foot, joining up with the South Devon Coast Path.* Go by the Cliff Road, North Sands, The Moult, South Sands, left by hotel, over 400ft Sharp Tor or Sharpitor Rocks to round Starhole Bay and on to the downland head.

Overbecks Museum and Garden, Sharpitor ⏲ – *2 miles southwest.*
The attraction of Sharpitor is the **view**★★ from different levels of the terraced garden, planted with magnolias, agapanthus, hydrangeas...
The last owner of the Edwardian-style **villa** of 1913 was a Dutchman, Otto Overbecks, who was a research chemist with numerous other interests. He left the property to serve as a youth hostel (72 beds), an open garden and as a **museum** for his own natural history and inventive collections. To these have been added displays on old Salcombe.

Prawle Point – *16 miles by A381 to Kingsbridge, A379 via Charleton to Chillington then south along by-roads via Chivelstone to East Prawle; continue due south to the end of the road then walk 200yds.*
The panoramic **views**★★★ from the point are breathtaking.

★★ SALISBURY Wiltshire — Pop 36 890

Michelin map fold 28 – 030 – Facilities
Town plan in the current Michelin Red Guide Great Britain and Ireland

The magnificent **cathedral,** with its spectacular great **spire,** is a building planned and executed in a single style; the town, equally, was planned and did not just grow – such order was the result of both town and church having been brought specifically to the site in the 13C.
The earlier city of **Old Sarum** *(qv)* was two miles away, an Iron Age hillfort, a Saxon, Roman and, finally, a Norman strongpoint where two successive cathedrals were built in the outer bailey : the first by Bishop, later **St Osmund,** nephew of the Conqueror, which was struck by lightning and largely destroyed only five days after its consecration; the second, a much larger, richer building, was designed by **Bishop Roger.** The bishop also converted the existing keep into an episcopal castle-palace which, on his fall from power in 1139, was garrisoned by the king's men. His immediate successor, Bishop Joscelin, built a new episcopal palace beside the cathedral but friction between the king's garrison and the clergy, want of water, the bleakness of the hilltop and the lack of fear of attack finally combined in the 13C to make the citizens and clergy of Old Sarum seek pastures new and undertake the construction of a third Cathedral Church to the Blessed Virgin.

★★★ CATHEDRAL

For many people Salisbury epitomises the Early English style at its best, medieval Gothic in its purest, most ascetic form. It is unique among England's older cathedrals as it is built in a single style, with the slimmest Purbeck marble columns and the tallest spire.
It was built in **two phases** : foundation stone to consecration and completion of the west screen (1220-58-65); heightening of the tower and construction of the spire (1334-80). The materials used were silver-grey limestone from Chilmark *(12 miles west),* Purbeck marble, cement (the vaulting is painted cast concrete), lead for the roofs, masses of timber for scaffolding, shuttering and supports for the spire.

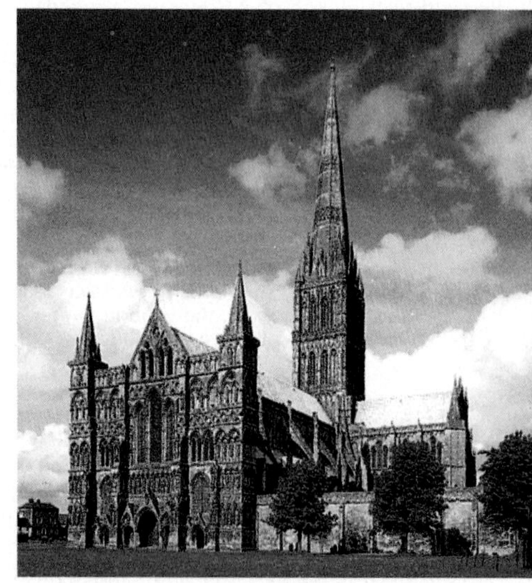

Salisbury Cathedral.

Exterior *floodlit nightly in summer*

West Screen – The decoration of the west screen extends from the gabled portals through lines of statue-filled niches, lancet windows and arcading to the pointed gable and corner towers with their miniature angel pinnacles and ribbed spires.

Tower – The upper stages of the tower, built a century later than the base, are complemented by the proportions of the lancets and two friezes of crested decoration; at the top of the corner, pinnacles and sub-pinnacles rise like fountains but fall just short of the first of the three carved bands encircling the spire itself.

Spire – From the heightened tower the spire (180ft) rises on walls 2ft thick at the base to its summit (404ft above ground level). *See Crossing below.*

Interior ⏲ *45min excluding roof tour*

The interior of the west screen exemplifies the beauty of pure line; nothing remains of the medieval colour – black, red and gold.

Nave – The nave extends for 229½ft out of a total length of 449ft, beneath an 84ft high vault. The **piers** of Purbeck marble, quatrefoils of grey, unpolished stone, canted by polished black shafts, are caught by slim, black, moulded capitals from which spring the pointed arches of the arcades, the galleries with their clusters of black colonnettes and the tall lancets of the clerestories.
Between the arcade pillars, tomb chests with recumbent figures recall the great of Old Sarum, Salisbury and the West Country : on the south side, **Bishops Roger** (d 1139) and **Joscelin** (d 1184), the shrine of **St Osmund** (d 1099) and the chain-mailed **William Longespée** (d 1226), half-brother of King John, husband of Ela, the founder of Lacock Abbey *(qv)*; opposite are Longespée the Younger (d 1250), warrior and crusader, Montacute (d 1390) and Hungerford (d 1449).

Crossing – Marking the crossing are **giant piers** of clustered black marble columns, intended to support the original low tower but, since the 14C, required to bear the extra 6 500 tons of the heightened tower and spire. Reinforcing internal and external buttresses and, since the 15C, massive tie-beam arches across the transepts and a Decorated stone vault over the crossing have relieved the strain in part but the piers have buckled by a clearly noticeable 3½in.

Pavement octagon – At the centre of the crossing pavement an octagon reflects the outline of the spire 45ft below its apex; in 1668 Sir Christopher Wren, when surveying the cathedral, dropped a plumbline from the spire point (brass plate) which shows that it has settled with a declination of 29½ins to the southwest.

North Aisle – The **medieval clock** (*c*1386) is the oldest working clock in England; in 1931 it was restored to its original condition with a verge and foliot balance instead of the later pendulum escapement. It was originally housed in the Bell Tower (demolished 1790) in the Close.

North Transept – Note the statue to Sir Richard Colt Hoare *(qv)* and the 13C cope chest.

South Transept – The Mothers' Union Chapel has an altar-frontal and hangings made from material from the 1953 Coronation.

South Chancel Aisle – The coloured tomb is of Sir Richard Mompesson (d 1627) and his wife, ancestors of the builder of the house in the Close *(see below)*; the window behind them is by Burne-Jones.
Note the inverted, 14C scissor arches in the sub-transepts.

Chancel – On either side of the choir are **chantry chapels,** monumental tombs and the ledger stone or plain lid of the coffin of **St Osmund** *(southeast corner)*.

Trinity Chapel – The **blue window,** *Prisoners of Conscience* (1980), is by Gabriel Loire, a stained-glass maker from Chartres who works in the medieval and modern tradition. For contrast look at the great **west window** which contains six medieval shields (once in the chapter-house) and 15C-16C figures. (The other glass is almost all monochrome or grisaille.)
Most beautiful of all in the Chapel are the slimmest of slim, black Purbeck marble **shafts** rising as ringed pilasters, columns and clustered piers to the groined vaulting.

Roof Tour ⏲ – *1 hour.* The tour ascends by spiral staircases *(120 steps)* to the Parvis Room (original medieval wooden roof and lead covering) and the triforium (full length **view** of the nave from the west end); it continues *(restoration work permitting)* up the tower through the clock and bell chambers to the external gallery at the base of the spire; otherwise to the gutters of the nave roof. **View** of the Close and Old Sarum.

CLOISTERS and CHAPTER-HOUSE

Work began on building the chapter-house and the cloisters in *c*1263, making the latter the earliest in any English cathedral; they are also among the longest (181ft). Both are in the Decorated Gothic style.

Chapter-House – The octagonal chamber (58ft across) rises from a single central column surrounded by eight ringed Purbeck shafts which ascend from the foliated capital as ribs to ceiling bosses, before dropping to clusters of slim columns which frame the eight giant windows. Below these a frieze of stories from the Old Testament (restored in the 19C) fills the spandrels between the niches which circumscribe the canon's seats.

★ CLOSE

The spacious and mellow Close with 16C-18C houses of ancient stone and terracotta brick was enclosed in the 1330s against the "riotous citizenry", using stone from the cathedral and castle of Old Sarum. **Choristers' Close** is a secondary enclosure in the northwest corner.
North of the cathedral a bronze *Walking Madonna* by **Elizabeth Frink** (1981) strides across the grass.
Four gates pierce the Close walls :

North or High Street Gate – The gate with a statue of Edward VII opens from the Choristers' Close into the town by way of an alley bordered by old houses and the **Matrons' College,** built in 1682 as almshouses for canons' widows;

Harnham or South Gate – The distant south gate leads to the suppressed De Vaux College and St Nicholas Hospital, the latter the source of Trollope's *The Warden.*

St Ann's and Bishop's Gates – The northern gate in the east wall (opening into St John's St) abuts Malmesbury House where Charles II took refuge in 1651; the southern gate *(private)* gives access to the Old Bishop's Palace, now the Cathedral School.

Three houses in the Close present rare collections in interesting settings :

★ **Salisbury and South Wiltshire Museum** ⊙ – *West side of the Close.*
The medieval house of stone, to which brick additions have been made throughout the centuries, has been known as the **King's House** ever since James I lodged there on a visit to the city.
The museum contains displays on Stonehenge; on excavations made in the 19C on Cranborne Chase by General Pitt-Rivers, who was a pioneer of scientific archeology; on local history including the Giant and Hob-Nob, 15C processional guild figures; local paintings and prints; local lace and costumes from the 1750s; several hundred pieces by Wedgwood; English glass and china enlivened by Bow and Chelsea figures, and a collection of tea-pots.

★ **Museum of the Duke of Edinburgh's Royal Regiment** ⊙ – *West side of the Close.*
The regiment was formed in 1959 by the amalgamation of the Royal Berkshire and Wiltshire Regiments. The museum is housed in a flint and brick building known as the **Wardrobe,** which was erected in 1254 as the Bishop's document storehouse; it was altered in the 15C and later converted into a dwelling.
Against the lime-yellow *papier maché* wall decoration in the hall, in the decorated 18C reception rooms and in the ancient cellar, epic moments in the regiments' histories are illustrated through displays of combat dress, weapons of the day, despatches, items of enemy uniform, maps, campaigns and medals, regimental silver, the overseas postings : William and Mary tankards (1691), snuffboxes, chased Indian silver claret jugs (1875) and centrepieces, including a long and scaly Chinese dragon.

★ **Mompesson House** ⊙ – *Choristers' Close.*
An 18C wrought-iron gateway leads to the Queen Anne House, built in 1701 by Sir Charles Mompesson whose initials appear in the cartouche over the door. At the rear a small **garden** shelters against the wall of the Close.

Staircase – The oak staircase, which was inserted in the 1740s beyond the wide arch at the back of the marble-paved hall, rises by shallow flights with three crisply turned banisters to each tread.

Baroque plasterwork – The staircase walls and ceiling are covered with a generous outpouring of swags, scrolls and cartouches. There is further notable plasterwork in the Drawing Room, Dining Room and Green Room *(upstairs)* where there is an eagle with spread wings.

Turnbull collection of 18C English drinking glasses – 370 different types of glass are displayed in period cabinets in the Dining and Little Drawing Rooms. The early examples of 1700-45 are characterized by thick glass and knobbed stems, the later glasses – after an excise tax of 1745 placed a levy on glass by weight – by lighter bowls and slender stems. Decoration as well as shape took all forms including air and opaque twist stems, enamelling and engraving, which was often commemorative or had a hidden or symbolic meaning as in Jacobite toasting glasses.

ADDITIONAL SIGHTS

Medieval streets – Between the cathedral and the 19C **Market Square** to the north lies a network of medieval streets and cut-throughs, lined by half-timbered houses with high oversailing upper floors and tall gables, dating from the 14C-17C with a few later insertions; the shops and stalls which once flourished along their length are recalled in the names : Fish Row, Butcher Row, Silver Street, Blue Boar Row, Ox Row, Oatmeal Row. At the centre in a small square is the **Poultry Cross,** a 15C hexagonal structure decorated with buttresses, pinnacles and a spirelet.

★ **Sarum St Thomas Church** – *Northeast end of the High St, overlooking St Thomas Sq and the medieval streets west of Market Sq.*
The low, castellated, square tower (1390) and the Perpendicular church are a rebuilding on the site of a wooden chapel of ease erected *c*1219 to provide a place of worship for the cathedral craftsmen.

Chancel Arch and Chancel – The arch is the setting for a *Doom Painting* (*c*1475) with, at the apex, Christ in Majesty in the New Jerusalem – 15C Salisbury ? The choir (1470, "modernized" in the 19C) has angel musician roof supports, the names and marks of contributing merchants on the south pillars, and a brass to the 16C wool merchant and mayor John Webbe, and his wife and six children.

Lady Chapel – The chapel, built by a wool merchant, master of the Tailors' Guild and mayor, is decorated with very small 15C frescoes and, since 1725, by splendid wrought-iron **railings** and finely carved **woodwork.**

South nave wall – Note the carved oak panel of 1671, "his own worke", by Humphrey Backham, the painted royal arms of Queen Elizabeth with the Welsh dragon supporter which preceded the Scots unicorn.

EXCURSIONS

★ **Old Sarum** ⊙ - *2 miles north on A345 (west side - signposted; car park through East Gate).*
Standing on the rubble walls of the castle's Norman inner bailey, visitors may view Salisbury Plain as did the guards of old. Two miles away to the south is the cathedral spire.
From the walls, which are those of Bishop Roger's 12C castle in the inner bailey - the first castle-keep on the site - can also be seen in the foreground, in the northwest corner of the outer bailey, the footings of Bishop St Osmund's **11C cathedral** and, superimposed, Bishop Roger's larger **12C church.** Models in Salisbury Museum.

★ **Heale House Garden, Woodford** ⊙ - *4 miles north by A360 and by-road to Lower, Middle and Upper Woodford; Heale House is between Middle and Upper Woodford.*
The 17C house of old rose brick with stone dressings, tall windows, pediments and a pitched roof, where Charles II sheltered after the Battle of Worcester in 1651, stands in a wooded valley at the end of a long avenue of poplars.
The garden of eight acres, secluded by clipped yew hedges, opens on to the River Avon; it is scented by a border-hedge of musk and sweet-smelling, old-fashioned roses and coloured by a long, wide and richly planted herbaceous border. A walled garden, part flowers, part vegetables, is quartered by a pergola of pleached apple trees; a water garden, planted with magnolia, a cherry tree, an acer, surrounds a Japanese tea-house approached over a red painted bridge.

Salisbury Plain - The Plain (10 x 20 miles) lies north of Salisbury and extends from the Wylye Valley in the south to the Vale of Pewsey *(qv)* in the north. Although known as a plain it is, in fact, gently undulating, clay-chalk downland with many of its knolls marked by prehistoric monuments - burial barrows, hillforts and Stonehenge *(qv).*
Prehistoric forts were succeeded by defended towns such as Old Sarum and Wilton and, eventually, by peaceful settlement.
Today the Plain is both an agricultural area of open pasture and arable farms, crossed by roads converging on Salisbury, and a military training ground; the Army, which arrived in the 19C, charges about in tanks (**road warning panels**) and is said to fire some 230 000 shells and bombs annually on designated ranges; the RAF, which arrived this century, performs airborne manoeuvres overhead.

Wylye Valley - *21 miles by A30 west and A36 north.*

In Wilton *(qv)* the road turns north into the Wylye Valley and follows the course of the river upstream along the southern edge of Salisbury Plain.
Attractive villages, usually comprising a church, a "big" 17C or 18C house, two or three lesser houses and several cottages, nearly all stone-built, mark the route every few miles.

Stapleford - The village is notable for its castle earthworks and a **church** with a square north tower, pinnacled, demi-pinnacled and balustraded, which makes it a landmark. Inside, the pillared arcade and font are both Norman.

Steeple Langford - The village is named after the small lead-covered **broach spire** crowning its Early English church.

Regimental Badge - *1 mile before Codford St Mary (right).* The emblem of the Australian Army, the Rising Sun behind a Crown, was cut into the chalk by Australian troops during the First World War.

Anzac War Graves - *On entering Codford St Mary, turn right by the church.* The tiny cemetery is maintained by the Imperial War Graves Commission.

Heytesbury - Note the 17C style **almshouses** of brick with a pedimented centre and lantern, the Hospital of St John and St Katherine *(left side of the road).*

Warminster - *See Warminster.*

★ **Wardour Castle** - *10 miles west by A30 and by-road. See Wardour Castle.*
The **Fovant** badges *(qv)* can be seen carved into the southern chalk hillside.

Newhouse, Redlynch ⊙ - *9 miles south by A338 and B3080.*
The three-storeyed Jacobean house of *c*1619, built of red brick to a Y or "Trinity" plan, has pitched roofs giving gables at the end of each wing and, in addition, three gables at the front. In the 18C the house was enlarged by flat-roofed, single-storey extensions to the two front wings.
In the 17C it was bought by the Eyres in whose family it has remained ever since; in the 19C a daughter of the house married Horatio Nelson's nephew, which explains the presence of various documents relating to Nelson, and period costumes.

The Romans first introduced wine into Britain over 2 000 years ago, though it remains a mystery when exactly the first vines were planted. Since the Second World War there has been a great revival in wine-making and many areas now offer local vineyard trails.

★★ SALTRAM HOUSE Devon

Michelin Atlas p 3 or Map 403 – H32 – 3 miles east of Plymouth

"The place is so gay, so riant, so comfortable and so everything that it ought to be" wrote the bride of 1809 of her new home. The house today is much as it was then.

In 1712, when Saltram House was purchased by the local Parker family, it was a Tudor mansion. In 1750 when John Parker inherited it his wife, **Lady Catherine Parker**, "a proud and wilful woman", set about aggrandising it. The extensions were all to her own designs in the Classical style with Baroque additions, particularly the interior plasterwork. Lady Catherine died in 1758.

In 1768 the house passed to her son, John Parker II, who was an MP and man about town. He was a lifelong friend of **Joshua Reynolds** *(qv)*, who was by then President of the Royal Academy. At Westminster he became acquainted with Lord Shelburne, statesman, patron of the arts and owner of Bowood House *(qv)* who introduced him to **Robert Adam**, the architect, who was working with **Thomas Chippendale**, the cabinet maker. Between 1768 and 1771 and again from 1780 to 1781, following a fire, Adam, Chippendale, Reynolds and Angelica Kauffmann all worked at Saltram.

Since the 18C there have been only two alterations, which were made in 1818 by the local architect, John Foulston. The library was extended by the addition of the music room; the entrance front was remodelled by the addition of a balustraded porch with Doric columns, the enlargement of the windows above and the addition to the pediment of the arms of John Parker III, newly created Earl of Morley.

Porcelain and china were bought in the fashion of the day but not "collected", the pictures, almost all family portraits, are closely hung as in a family album. The parkland and gardens surrounding the house include an octagonal summerhouse, an orangery, a temple and 18C stables.

TOUR ⏱ *1 hour*

Entrance Hall – Dominant in the hall decorated with **plasterwork** of 1750 and a great marble fireplace are the portraits of *Lady Catherine Parker* and *John Parker II, Lord Boringdon* (by Thomas Hudson). Note also the serpentine side-tables, 18C Chinese and Chinese-style delftware, the Louis XIV Boulle **clock** on its original bracket.

Morning Room – In the room hung with Genoa silk velvet are family portraits painted by Reynolds of *John Parker II, Lord Boringdon,* leaning against a gate, *Theresa Robinson, Lady Boringdon* – with her son, John Parker III the future Lord Morley, and the boy with his sister.

The **mahogany cabinets** on stands are Chippendale, the **black basalt vases** are Wedgwood (*c*1780), the Chinese-style cabinet is English. Note the *famille rose* punchbowl.

Velvet Drawing Room – The deep red and gold room with its original **stucco ceiling** was replanned by Adam with fluted Corinthian end pillars, giltwood tables and mirrors to serve as a prelude to the adjoining saloon. The Rococo **giltwood mirror** is mid-18C.

Saloon – The room, a double cube of 50 x 25 x 25ft, was designed throughout by Adam, from the ceiling to the complementary carpet (£126), the giltwood furniture upholstered in pale blue and silver silk damask like the walls, the pier glasses, the *torchères* which support ormolu-mounted tortoise-shell and blue-john "candle vases".

The chandeliers are 19C. The portrait of *Lady Boringdon* is by Reynolds.

Eating or Dining Room – Following the fire, the eating room and library were transposed and both entirely redesigned, including much of their furniture, by **Robert Adam.**

Note again the ceiling and complementary carpet, the picture frames, the marble-topped table and mirror between the windows, the curved **serving table** in the end bay.

Hall – The hall with its cantilevered **staircase** is a return to the pre-Adam house. The large **Boulle writing table** of tortoise-shell and brass is said to have been given by Louis XIV to Sarah, Duchess of Marlborough and by her granddaughter to Lady Catherine Parker. Note also the 18C **bracket clock** in an ormolu-mounted case; five 18C mahogany armchairs with their original needlepoint; *The Fall of Phaeton* by **Stubbs,** portraits of Joshua Reynolds and Parker by **Angelica Kauffmann.**

Blue Saloon, Saltram House.

Upper Rooms – Three rooms follow the fashion for 17C-18C Chinese painted wall hangings, figured, exotic, often formally comic and perfectly complemented by the slender posted 18C **bed** with feathered cresting, the Chinese-Chippendale **chairs,** the painted **mirrors.**

Boudoir – The olive-green and gold room became Lady Morley's sanctum on the death of her husband (John Parker III) in 1840. She selected the Regency centre table with a marble top, the 18C mahogany secretaire **bookcase** together with the family portraits.

Lord Morley's Room – Note the picture by Gardner of *Lord Morley as a Small Boy.*

Library – The room presents a gallery of portraits : by the American artist Gilbert Stuart (1755-1818), Reynolds *(Lord Boringdon* and *Sir John Chichester of Arlington, qv),* Northcote and Angelica Kauffmann *(Self-Portrait).*
The **tables** are functional as well as beautiful : the circular drum is a rent table with alphabetically labelled drawers, another is a writing table, another a games table and the Pembroke table opens into library steps.

Great Kitchen – The kitchen, built in 1779, was modernised a century later.

★ SANDFORD ORCAS MANOR HOUSE Dorset

Michelin Atlas p 8 or Map fold 27 – M31

The story of the house is as straightforward as the house is attractive in its setting amid the gently undulating countryside and a terraced garden with long, flowered borders. It was bought two centuries ago by the present owner's family as a farming property and leased to careful tenants. Since the 1870s the family has lived in it and returned it to life.

TOUR ⏲ *45min*

Exterior – The long and rambling house of the 1560s, which is built of brownish Ham Hill ashlar, is many gabled with every point the perch of a heraldic monkey, lion or other beast. The **windows** are hoodmoulded, stone mullioned and transomed, those to the Hall and Great Chamber above wide-bayed to let the light flood in through plain and armorial glass. Slim square **chimneys** crown the stone roofs.
The **entrance porch,** off-centre and advanced under its own small gable, is framed by slim octagonal shafts topped by minute obelisks.

Hall – The chamber is single storeyed with oak panelling, a **fireplace** with a Ham stone lintel and an overmantel displaying the full range of Jacobean carved fantasy.
On the walls are **Gainsborough** family portraits; among the furniture, examples of the periods represented in the house include Tudor, Jacobean, William and Mary and 18C.

Upper rooms – At the top of a **spiral stone staircase,** the Great Chamber, closets, landings, bedrooms are furnished with English and Dutch **marquetry chests** opening to reveal ever-smaller decorated drawers, cupboards and hidden recesses.
The **testered beds** range in date from Elizabethan to slender 18C; note the two **embroidered covers** : one in natural silk on silk *appliqué,* the other a William and Mary work, all glistening greens and brown.

★ Isles of SCILLY Cornwall — Pop 2 653

Michelin Atlas p 2 or Map 403 – inset – 28 miles southwest of Land's End
Access ⏲ from Penzance

Climate – There is an almost constant wind from the Atlantic and clouds, bowling in low over the ocean, hit the rocks and drop their moisture in short, soaking showers – windproof and waterproof clothing and shoes are, therefore, essential. On all the islands' leeward sides are long white sand beaches, coves, walks or flower-filled gardens. The water, clear, safe (except over the sandbars) and tempting, is icy.

The Archipelago – The islands have been variously identified as the mountain peaks of Atlantis, the lost land of **Lyonesse,** the westerly tin islands of the Phoenicians, known to Herodotus as the Cassiterides, or the Islands of the Blest where dead heroes were buried. The approach by sea (120 knots) or by air (500-2 000ft up) provides a **view★★★** of the archipelago of 5 inhabited, 40 uninhabited islands and 150 named rocks set in a close group in the clear, blue-green ocean. Headlands, reefs and saw-toothed needles stand ruffed in white spume, the larger islands lush and green.
What is certain is that the isles were Bronze and Iron Age settlements, the Roman outpost of Sylicancis, the Viking Syllanger; that from AD 400-1 000 there were Christian hermits on the isles, monks on Tresco; that Athelstan ejected the Danes from the islands in AD 930; that in 1114 Henry I granted Tresco to Tavistock Abbey for a Benedictine priory. In the 1830s **Squire Augustus Smith** became Lord Proprietor; in 1920 the Duchy of Cornwall took over all the inhabited islands except Tresco.

With the arrival of the Lord Proprietor, the islands knew 40 years of prosperity houses, churches and schools were built, five shipbuilding yards were established on St Mary's, the **flower industry** was begun. Prior to flowers, one of the island's main sources of income was derived from **kelp** : this was made by collecting and burning 22 tons of seaweed to produce 1 ton of kelp; each ton was then further reduced to 8lbs of iodine, which is vital to the glass and soapmaking industries.

Gig racing ⊙ – On Wednesday and Friday evenings throughout the summer the six-oared island gigs race in the St Mary's roadstead, usually starting off Samson and finishing at the Quay. The gigs of elm planking ¼in thick, 28-30ft long with 5ft beam and less than 2ft draught, were built as rival pilot launches and smuggling craft – they were banned from having more than six oars so as not to have an advantage over the excise cutters.

ST MARY'S

St Mary's (pop 2 106) is the largest island (3 miles across at its widest with a 9 mile coastline) where the majority of Scillonians live. At the Old Quay lie the excursion launches, one of the attractions for visitors who arrive by sea and air.

Hugh Town – The town runs the length of the sand bar between the main part of the island and a hill to the west, the **Garrison;** it overlooks the sea on two sides south across the silver **Porth Cressa Beach;** north over the harbour, **St Mary's Pool**.

Museum ⊙ – Local life is illustrated from prehistoric times to today by specimens, tools, coins, log-books, boats, posters, wrecks and treasure, including brooches found in *HMS Association (see below).* There is also an excellent **bird section** (native and migrant).

★ **Garrison Walk** – *Preferably an evening stroll; 1 hour.* Go through the **Guard Gate** built in the mid-18C when the defence was fortified with 18 batteries. Star Castle (now a hotel), eight-pointed on the brow of the hill, dates from the time of Queen Elizabeth's feud with Spain. Continue inside the rampart wall which circles the headland, scanning the **view★★**. The range of houses, one with a crest, at the walk's end, are the offices of the **Duchy of Cornwall** *(qv).*

Old Town and the eastern end – Roads and paths make it possible to follow the coastline, to cut across in any direction or even to start out on or, halfway round, to pick up the bus which makes regular circular tours. Features of interest include :

Porth Mellon – *West shore, just beyond the lifeboat.* The remains of a Henry VIII square fort are known as **Harry's Walls.**

Telegraph Tower – At 158ft the island's highest point.

Bants Carn – *15min walk Rtn from the tower.* 3C BC burial chamber of stones and capstones and the walls of an Iron Age village.

Porth Hellick – The large inlet is marked by a rough monument where Sir Cloudesley Shovell *(qv)* was washed ashore from the wreck of the *Association* in 1707. A gate close by opens the way to the top of the Down and the 4 000 year old passage grave.

Old Town Church – The church, rebuilt in the 19C on 12C foundations, is surmounted on its east gable by a 10C stone cross; in the churchyard are the graves of seamen from many lands.

★ **Peninnis Head** – The spectacular head has eroded granite rocks of majestic size.

★ TRESCO

Smith built himself, in the island stone and using wrecked ships' timbers, a Victorian-medieval castle mansion. Below the house, in the sheltered hollow around the old abbey ruins, he created the soon famous, subtropical gardens from seeds and plants brought back by Scillonian sailors and professional plant collectors.

★ **Abbey Gardens** ⊙ – The plants, despite the salt sea wind, burgeon and self-seed everywhere. The 12 acre garden, facing the sun, is divided by two long straight paths : the east-west **Long Walk**, and the north-south **Lighthouse Way** with flights of steps rising to a bust of Neptune, from where there is a **view★★** across to other islands and over the Tresco garden itself with its hundred and more varieties of trees and flowers.

Valhalla – Some fifty ships' figureheads, trailer and name boards, fiddles and carved ornaments from the thousand ships wrecked off the islands in the past two centuries stand gilded and boldly coloured, facing into the wind.

The isle's two tower forts, **King Charles'** and **Cromwell's Castles,** date from the 16C and 17C.

Ship's figurehead.

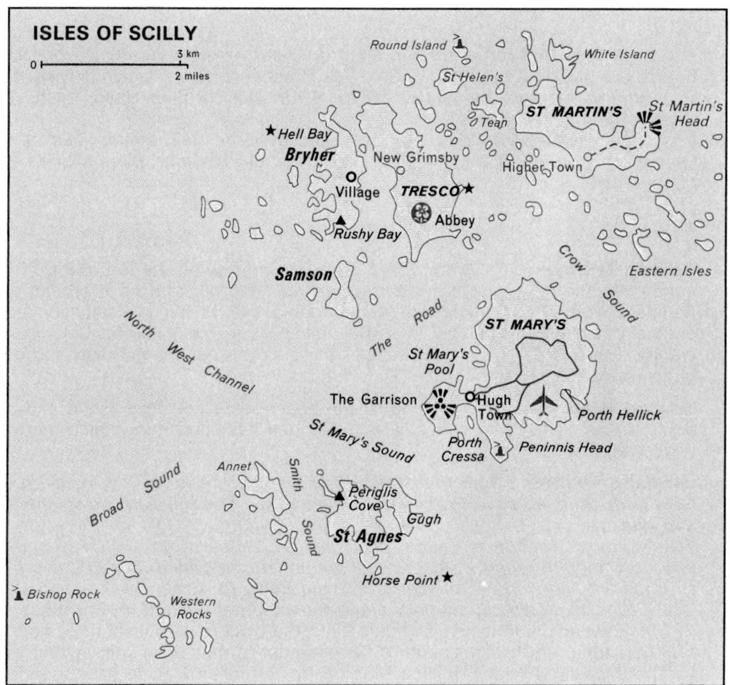

BRYHER

From the landing on the east shore a road leads past the 18C church to the **village** on Watch Hill and the **view★**. The path forks south to the sheltered beach at **Rushy Bay,** north to Shipman Head and **Hell Bay★** *(white-painted marker stones)* where the Atlantic thunders and pounds against rocks and cliffs. Incredibly from the minute fields on this and other islands, the islanders produce more than 1 000 tons of cut flowers a year – 12 daffodils weigh 5 oz...

ST AGNES

St Agnes and the islet of **Gugh** *(accessible across a sandbar at low water)* are separated from the other main islands by **St Mary's Sound,** a deepwater channel followed by the *Scillonian* at low tide. The channel is said to have made the islanders the most independent, the men the finest pilots, and the fiercest smugglers and wreckers.

Follow the road up to the 17C lighthouse (private house).

The right-hand path leads down to **Periglis Cove** and the small **church** built in the mid-19C from the proceeds of the wreck of a foreign frigate of 1781, the bell of which hangs in the turret. The **east window** dates from the 1960s.
Continue south by the footpath *(marked),* past the miniature pebble stone **maze** to the grandiose rock scenery of **Horse Point★**.
The path continues to the lighthouse.

ST MARTIN'S

The two mile long granite spine which is St Martin's presents a rugged shore to the northeast and fine sand beaches on all other fronts. Minute flower fields shelter in the hollows; tumuli or burial mounds crown the more exposed sites.
A path from Higher Town leads to the red and white waymark erected in 1683 on St Martin's Head, a 160ft high **viewpoint★★** from which to see the **Sevenstones Reef** *(7 miles north),* grave of the *Torrey Canyon* in 1967, and, two miles further off, the **Lightship,** on station since 1841. On a clear day the mainland coast is clearly visible.

SAMSON

The uninhabited island is characterized by twin hills joined by a narrow sand isthmus – a desert isle with megalithic remains and the ruins of 19C cottages.

SEATON Devon — Pop 6 157

Michelin Atlas p 5 or Map 403 – K31 – Facilities

The small seaside resort at the mouth of the River Axe close to the Devon-Dorset border lies behind a mile-long pebble beach between two headlands (**views★★**) : to westward are the dramatically white 400ft cliffs of Beer Head, to the east those of Lyme Regis *(qv)*.
An evening stroll east along the Esplanade past the tram station *(see below)*, over the bridge and along the path round the Old Harbour offers a good view of the sunset.

SIGHTS

Seaton Tramway ⌚ – *Harbour Rd.* The swaying ride on the top of the 2ft 9in gauge, electric tram with a great iron arm reaching back to the overhead wire, the hard seats, open guard-rail and sounding bell, is fun in itself. The track, originally laid for the railway in 1868, follows the Axe Valley to Colyton *(see below)*. The ride affords a good **view** of the countryside, the **waterfowl** and other birds *(qv)* on the river banks.

Seaton Hole – At the west end of the beach is Seaton Hole (sand and rock pools at low water) and above, a semi-wooded headland from which there are wide views out to sea.

Landslip – *Access : from the east side of the river make for the Axmouth Golf Course or Steppes Lane in Axmouth, then follow the cliff path down the face and into the slip.*
The signposted path is rough and can be slippery; it is NOT for those unaccustomed to rough walking; there are no intermediary exits and it is 5 miles to Underhill Farm on the outskirts of Lyme Regis (p 135).
Minor slips occur almost annually along the length of cliff but on Christmas Day 1839, between Bindon and Dowlands Cliffs, there opened a chasm three-quarters of a mile long, 400ft across and 150ft deep, which has been known ever since as The Landslip. About 8 million tons of rock are estimated to have foundered in the one night. The area is now a woodland nature reserve.

EXCURSIONS

★ **Colyton** – *3½ miles north by B3172, A3052 and B3161 or by the electric tram (see above; 8min walk up from the station).*
The village is dominated by its **church★** with pointed pyramid roof and lantern. It was built on a Saxon site when the Courtenays, Earls of Devon, were lords of the manor; it was enlarged during the 14C-18C. The pinnacled, octagonal **lantern** surmounting the roof was added in the 15C by a rich wool merchant, partly to serve as a beacon for his ships sailing up the then navigable River Axe. Inside, note the carved capitals at the east end, which was enlarged in the 14C; the great, Perpendicular west window (15C); the transept **screens** – one Perpendicular (16C) with lacelike stone tracery surrounding a canopied tomb, the other Jacobean (17C) with strapwork and surmounting obelisks.

★ **Branscombe** – *6 miles west along B3172, B3174 and A3052.*

Beer – Despite its huge popularity, Beer remains essentially a fishing village, with boats hauled up the shingle beach of the small cove between gleaming white rock headlands.
The rock is the **Beer stone** used by the Romans and since the 15C as a contrasting trim for cathedrals, churches and houses; the quality of the stone is such that it can be cut with a saw when newly quarried and hardens when exposed to wind and weather.
Note the spring which tumbles down the length of the main street into the sea.

Return to the Beer turning and bear west and south to skirt Beer Head.

★ **Branscombe** – The small village straggles in clusters of thatched cottages within small flowered gardens, along either side of a steep and winding road which at the end of two miles arrives at the beach and a group of old coastguard cottages. The village itself, which has a recorded history dating back to King Alfred, includes old and historic houses, a **forge** of 1580, an **inn** – the Mason's Arms – of 1360 and, on the valley side, the Norman **Church of St Winifred,** built on a Saxon site in the 12C. Inside, the oak-beamed roof and **Elizabethan gallery** with access from the outside staircase, the late 18C **three-decker pulpit** and box pews, the late 17C altar rail with twisted balusters, and a macabre monument of 1606 are all of particular interest.

Axmouth – *2 miles east along the Harbour Rd (B3172) or the Esplanade to the Old Harbour, over the river bridge (**views★**) then left upstream.*
Once a bustling riverport, the village is now a tranquil place with a winding main street overlooked by small houses, some still thatched, occasional 15C-16C larger houses on the hillside and two old thatched pubs, one half-timbered and 800 years old.
The **church** was rebuilt *c*1140 on what may have been a Saxon site and again in 1330 so that now it appears with Norman round columns marking the south aisle and a Norman north doorway, a Decorated chantry chapel and a Perpendicular tower. Note the Italian-style medieval paintings of an unknown saint and a Christ of Pity on the Norman pillars, also the 1667 Charles II hatchment.

Axminster – *8 miles northwest on B3172 through Axmouth and A358. See Axminster.*

SHAFTESBURY Dorset — Pop 4 831

Michelin Atlas p 8 or Map 403 - N30, 31

The town is built on the crest (700ft) of a spur which King Alfred fortified in his struggle against the Danes; little remains of his or earlier hillforts. There is an extensive **view★** south from Gold Hill and Park Walk across the Blackmore Vale, west into Somerset where Glastonbury Tor is visible on a clear day and north towards Salisbury Plain.

SIGHTS

★ **Gold Hill** - Behind the Town Hall the road descends in a steep cobbled curve into the valley below. It is bordered on the east side by small **16C, 17C and 18C houses,** thatched, tiled, built of stone or brick, each sitting on the shoulders of the one below; opposite stands a massive buttressed 13C ochre-coloured **wall.**

★ **Local History Museum** ⊙ - The garden path leads to the house which in the 19C was a barber's shop and before that a doss house. Inside is an interesting and amusing miscellany of bygones.

Abbey ⊙ - The Benedictine house of 100-140 nuns stood within a 4-acre precinct; today a walled garden not quite the extent of the great abbey church, which measured 240ft from east to west, encloses the excavated footings.
From its foundation in 888 the abbey was rich, as King Alfred endowed it with "100 hides of land" (9 000 acres). In 948 it was given the hinterland and the "right of wreck" along the coast west of St Aldhelm's Head *(qv);* thirty years later it became the centre of the cult of St Edward, King and Martyr, murdered at Corfe Castle *(qv).* In 1368 the abbess was granted a licence to crenellate the church and belltower; in the same period she took the rank of baron, keeping seven knights in fealty to protect the monarch and sending a representative to parliament.
Among the abbesses was **Marie de France,** the 12C Anglo-Norman lyric poet who was half-sister to Henry II, Plantagenet; among visitors was **Canute,** who died in the abbey in 1035.
It was said in the 15C-16C that if the Abbess of Shaston (Shaftesbury) were to marry the Abbot of Glaston (Glastonbury) their heirs would own more land than the king. In 1539 Henry VIII dissolved both abbeys.

★ SHELDON MANOR Wiltshire

Michelin Atlas p 17 or Map 403 - N29 - 1½ miles west of Chippenham

The stone exterior of the **manor house** ⊙ with its several additions was complete by the late 17C.
The oldest parts of the house, the sole survivor of a deserted medieval village, are the **Plantagenet porch** of 1282 and the massive wall behind it. Building phases in *c*1431 and 1659 added new fronts and the **detached chapel,** and introduced Tudor **fireplaces,** linenfold **panelling,** the Jacobean **staircase...**
Inside, among the splendid, massive 16C-17C **furniture** are refectory tables, 17C chests, a four-poster bed with a 17C embroidered cover, a **17C embroidery** of a Tree of Life with an elephant in the corner and a 15C plank chest in the Priest's Room, which has a **13C roof.**
In addition there are small collections of Nailsea glass *(qv),* Eltonware *(qv)* and William de Morgan ceramics, a Brueghel in the dining room, 19C sporting prints, cartoons and family mementoes from far and wide...
Outside, high yew hedges enclose a pond garden, a flower garden, an orchard and a garden filled with old fashioned and climbing roses.

★ SHEPTON MALLET Somerset — Pop 6 197

Michelin Atlas p 8 or Map 403 - M30 - 6 miles east of Wells - Facilities

Shepton Mallet, with Wells and Glastonbury, was a stocking knitting town in the 17C-18C, and a wool town producing pure wool cloth, serges, sailcloth and silk in the 18C-19C with as many as 4 000 people employed in the giant mills. The town, which is situated in the valley at the foot of the Mendip Hills, has always been and remains a livestock centre and market close to main highways including the Roman Fosse Way and the roads to Bristol, Frome and Ilchester.

SIGHTS

Market Place - The Market Place *(pedestrian precinct),* is bordered by 17C inns, 18C houses, shops and a modern public library.
The Market cross, a tall pinnacle (1500), is encircled by an 18C hexagonal arcade and by the Shamble.

Market Shamble - First built in Shepton in 1450, it is an obvious development from a little shed - the Anglo-Saxon meaning of the word. The shed developed into a permanent line of roofed stalls, which, in time, became a street of open fronted shops - mostly butchers', sometimes fishmongers' - from the disorder of whose backyards, slaughterhouses etc, the modern meaning evolved.

Walk through the modern buildings to the parish church.

★ **St Peter and St Paul** – The **west tower** with its stump of a spire is evidence of a change in architectural fashion. It was constructed on a Norman base in *c*1380 of local Doulting stone and, as it was intended to support a spire, it is a solid structure. It is also the earliest tower in the Somerset style *(qv)* : it is strengthened by pairs of set-back buttresses at the angles as it rises from the west door through stages marked by a big six-light window, statuary niches a clock bay and a bell tier of three paired openings, to reach the pierced balustrade and solid buttress pinnacles at the crest.
An eight-sided **spire** was begun, halted and capped; it was never completed, for what reason is unknown. The numbers of skilled masons and craftsmen had been seriously depleted by the Black Death (1348) and people may have grown used to the sight of a tower without a spire; some maintain that Shepton Mallet tower was so beautiful as to need no enhancement. It may also have been realised that a spire was a hazardous structure owing to human error and natural causes: countless Norman spires collapsed and all were at risk from lightning.
The interior reveals the church's Saxon origins, the Norman rebuilding, the 13C-17C enlargement, the Puritan depredations and the ardent Victorian remodelling. Note the circular **Saxon font,** the knights in chain mail and the **pulpit** of Doulting stone, richly carved in 1550 with niches, Renaissance cornucopias and flowers. The finest feature is the "richly wrought" **barrel vault** (1450); "the most glorious of all **wagon roofs** in England" consists of 350 carved panels and 1 400 leaves caught into nearly 400 bosses and half bosses.

Town Houses – It is worth strolling round the town to admire the pedimented doorways and well-proportioned windows of the **Georgian houses** and the **Strode Almshouses** of 1699 *(south of the church);* to explore the narrow, stone-walled lanes leading to **Leg Square** and the 18C clothiers' houses, **Eden Grove** and **The Hollies** with their columned doorways. The half-timbered **King's Arms** supplied ale to the prison opposite. **Peter Street** is lined with Georgian houses. In the lane to the left stands the old **Grammar School,** which was founded in 1627; the uncompromising Latin tag on the wall of the Georgian annexe reads *Disce aut discede* which means Learn or Leave *(north side of the church).*
On the far side of the Market Place and Town Street is **Great Ostry,** bordered by a 17C three-storey terrace of seven identical houses with mullioned windows. Further exploration of the lanes provides views of the old mills, the 17C gabled weavers' cottages and their handkerchief-sized gardens.

EXCURSIONS

★ **Downside Abbey** – *5 miles north off A37 and A367. See Downside Abbey.*

★ **Nunney** – *9 miles east on A361.*

East Somerset Railway, Cranmore ⊙ – *½ mile south of main road.*
The station has been restored to a modest Victorian appearance; the signal box converted into an exhibition gallery.
The depot, built in the tradition of Victorian train sheds, is a repair workshop for the stock which includes, as jewels of the collection, the locomotives Bluebell (P/0-6-OT/1910), Green Knight (4MT/4-6-0/1954) and Black Prince (9F/2-10-0/1959).
The East Somerset Railway opened in 1858, became part of the Great Western Railway and ultimately of British Rail, and was closed in 1967. The private line now extends for just under 2 miles.

Return to A361. Nunney is ½ mile north of the main road.

★ **Nunney** – The village of 17C-18C stone houses and cottages, with an inn sign spanning the main street, surrounds a moated castle and small church.
Dating back to 1393, **Nunney Castle,** which was slighted in 1645, remains as a picturesque ruin, its tall towers reflected in the waters of the moat.
The **church,** vigorously restored in the 19C, is 13C-16C. Note the spirally fluted Norman **font** with a Jacobean cover, 14C arcades with no capitals between the piers and arches.
Among the **tomb effigies** are Sir John Delamere (d 1390) who built the castle, Richard Prater and his wife who bought it in 1577 and their Cavalier grandson who lost it to the Parliamentarians. Note the castle model.

Evercreech – *4 miles southeast by A371 and B3081.*
Dominating the village square and medieval market cross, the **church tower**★ *(illustration p 149)* rises between shafted and pinnacled buttresses to immensely tall, twice-transomed bell-lights – the lower bays blind, those above tracery-filled. Pinnacles and sub-pinnacles continue the vertical lines ever higher above the crest. Inside is a tie-beam roof of angels and bosses richly gilt and coloured.

Batcombe – *7 miles southeast. After Evercreech, continue along by-roads 3 miles east.*
The tower of 87ft is a complete contrast to other church towers *(qv)* in the county, the profusion of pinnacles being all below the skyline.

Tithe means "tenth" and tithe barns date from the Middle Ages when farmers had to give a tenth of all crops grown to the Church. The grain was kept in tithe barns, which are noticeable now for being sturdy, handsome buildings which are much larger than ordinary farm barns.

★ SHERBORNE Dorset Pop 7 405

Michelin Atlas p 8 or Map 403 - M31 - Facilities

The town, in triumph, bought back the abbey as its parish church at the Dissolution, paying 100 marks for the fabric and 400 for the roof timbers, lead and bells, or £330 in all. It was a goodly sum but represented victory in the feud with the Benedictine community, and Sherborne, a prosperous market in a wool and sheep area, was about to become one of the principal cloth towns of the West Country.

★ ABBEY ⏲ *½ hour*

Construction – The abbey began as a **Saxon stone church,** which grew enormously in importance in 705 when Ine, King of Wessex, appointed as first bishop **St Aldhelm** *(qv),* of whom it was said that "by his preaching he completed the conquest of the West". Gradually the church was rebuilt by Aldhelm's 26 successors until by the Conquest a large Saxon cathedral stood on the site. In 998 a Benedictine community had replaced the earlier, secular canons and in 1121, 50 years after the see had removed to Old Sarum *(qv),* the church had become an independent abbey with the east end reserved for the monks, the west for the laity. During the 12C the church was rebuilt in the Norman style but west of the nave St Aldhelm's original church probably survived until it was replaced in the 15C by a chapel of ease, All Hallows.
In the century before the Dissolution, 1420-1504, the monastic church was again rebuilt, this time in the Perpendicular style but the Early English Lady Chapel and Norman porch, both of which survive in part, were left intact. As the chancel was nearing completion in 1437, a quarrel arose between the townsfolk and the monks over the narrowing of the doorway between All Hallows and the abbey. The townsfolk rioted and "a priest of All Hallows", according to Leland, "shott a shaft with fire into the top of that part that the monks used (the chancel) from that which the townsmen used (the nave); and the partition, chancing at the time to be thatched in the roof (while the rebuilding was going on), was set afire and consequently the whole church, the lead and the bells melted, was defaced". The chancel limestone walls remain to this day reddened by the heat of the fire. All Hallows was demolished in the 15C.

Exterior – The abbey is built of **Ham Hill stone :** deep honey-gold in sunlight, dark ochre on a grey day, old gold by floodlight. The Perpendicular windows rise in two tiers along the south front, divided midway by the great eight-light transept window. The **crossing tower,** on massive Saxon-Norman piers and walls, lifts to a final stage on thinner, recessed, 15C walls with bell openings in pairs below a parapet and twelve crocketed pinnacles. A parapet outlines the roofs; flying buttresses support the chancel.
Go through the porch and rounded **Norman doorway** with its zig-zag decoration.

Interior – The **fan vaulting** is magnificent and full of subtleties.

Choir – In the early 15C choir the **vaulting** is polychrome; the shafts shoot from the floor without a break, framing the arcade arches and clerestory windows directly above before breaking into fan ribs and the network at the crest. It is the earliest large-scale fan vault in the country, but is almost flat and, despite the flying buttresses, after 400 years the ridge had dropped 7ins and so vault and buttresses were rebuilt exactly in 1856.

Nave – The beautiful late 15C nave **vault** is slightly arched and so stands proud after 550 years.
The nave builders' problem was not the vault but a shortage of funds. The Norman aisle walls, Saxon west wall and arcade piers were, therefore, all retained; the piers were, however, neither opposite one another nor evenly spaced, the north file being 14ins to the west, making impossible a facsimile of the chancel fan vault with shafts rising from the ground to meet at the crest. Instead, a well-marked string course, emphasised by angel corbels, was inserted, a regular clerestory built above – the windows are out of line with the arcades – and the shafts sent from on high on their upward sweep to a cobweb of ribs in which only the bosses are coloured.

Chancel arch – A splendid, unadorned Norman tower arch divides the nave and chancel.

North aisle – The Saxon doorway to the original Saxon church can still be seen at the end of the aisle. In an open coffin, at the east end, is the skeleton of one of the **Saxon Kings,** Ethelbald or Ethelbert (850-60 or 860-66), elder brothers of King Alfred.

Lady Chapel – The chapel, with its engraved **glass reredos** by **Laurence Whistler** *(qv)* and its flanking chapels, was converted into a house for the Master of the School *(see below)* in 1560 and occupied as such for 300 years, hence the arms of Edward VI, the school's founder, on what is now the outside south wall of the abbey.

Choir – The stalls are modern with humorous medieval **misericords** and **arm-rests.**

South transept – The tomb by **John Nost** is of **John Digby,** 3rd Earl of Bristol (d 1698; *see below*), a man, according to the epitaph, "naturally inclined to avoid the hurry of public life, yet careful to keep up the port of his quality".

★ CASTLE

Raleigh and Elizabeth – The Old Castle *(½ mile east)* is a **ruin** standing proudly, if somewhat indecipherably erect *(see Museum below).* At the outbreak of the Civil War the Digbys, Earls of Bristol, moved into the old castle but in 1645, after being pounded by artillery fire and mined while under siege, it was ordered by Parliament to be slighted.
It was constructed in 1107-35 by Bishop Roger of Salisbury *(qv).* At the end of the 16C **Sir Walter Raleigh** saw it from the London-Plymouth road and, to persuade Elizabeth to buy it for him from the church, gave the queen a jewel

of the estimated value of the castle, namely £260. The jewel, or more probab a slightly smaller sum of money, was passed to the bishop, and the quee obtained the castle which she first leased and finally gave to her favourite. Th favourite, however, had committed the cardinal sin only a few weeks before marrying one of the queen's ladies-in-waiting, Bess Throckmorton. On discoverin the marriage Elizabeth, in a jealous rage, banned them from her court for ev – although Raleigh returned after five years – and threw them, separately, in the Tower. They were released after five weeks and journeyed to Sherborn By 1594 Raleigh had decided, after spending lavish sums, that the castle cou not be made into the type of house he wished to live in and he built Sherborr Lodge, the nucleus of the present castle, on the far bank of the River Yeo.

James I and the Digbys – James I, who repossessed Sherborne Castle 1608 when he imprisoned Raleigh, gave it to Prince Henry, then to his favourit Robert Carr, who, however, soon fell from grace; the king next offered it f £10 000 to **Sir John Digby,** long employed in trying to arrange a marriage betwee the future Charles I and the Spanish Infanta. Digby, created Earl of Bristo purchased the house, which had an intrinsic attraction and the sentimental lir of Digby's grandmother and Raleigh's wife both being Throckmortons. It h remained in the family ever since.

Castle Builders – When he came to build the new castle, **Sir Walter Ralei** created a four-storey house beneath a Dutch-style gable and balustrade; eac angle was marked by a hexagonal turret and each turret angle alternately b a tall, plain, square chimney or heraldic beast. The fabric was Ham stone wi rendered walls.

In 1620-30, between missions abroad, **Sir John Digby** enlarged the castle to th typical H-plan mansion of the time and its present appearance, using the san style and materials. The interior, by contrast, has rooms decorated in the styl and furniture of every period from the 16C-19C. "I imagined it to be one of tho fine old seats... but this is so peculiar," wrote Alexander Pope in 1722, "and i situation of so uncommon kind, that it merits a more particular descriptior

Grounds ⏲

The drive through the deer park to the house passes a 50-acre **lake,** inspire by a flash flood in 1757 which made the river overflow; the then Lord Digb determined to make the effect permanent and called upon **Capability Brown.** Th Adam-style stables and **dairy** constructed in stone from the Old Castle are als 18C.

Raleigh's Seat, a stone bench under the trees on the far side of the lake, is sa to be where Sir Walter was enjoying a quiet pipe when his servant, bringir him a drink, grew alarmed at seeing him apparently on fire and doused him wi ale. Among the trees are giant Virginia cedars grown from seed brought ba from the colony.

House ⏲ *45min*

The first three rooms epitomize the house's kaleidoscope of styles.

Library – The gallery was redecorated in the 18C in Strawberry Hill Gothi *(qv);* the furniture is Georgian. Note **Raleigh's** *History of the World* (1614) ar the portrait of *Sir Kenelm Digby* (1603-65), traveller, founder member of the Roy Society.

Solarium – The Raleigh parlour was converted in the 19C into a Victorian dinir room. The **heraldic chimneypiece,** installed at the time of the conversion, includ the ubiquitous family **ostrich,** adopted some 350 years ago for reasons unknov but present everywhere even on the weather-vanes in Sherborne town. Th **monkey supporters,** sometimes to be seen with the arms, originate from the tin when monkeys, kept as pets in the house, alerted a nursemaid of a fire in th children's rooms.

Red Drawing Room – The plaster **ceiling** is 17C, the furniture Georgian. Among the pictures are a portrait by **Cornelius Jansens** of *Sir John Digby,* first own of the present house, another of *Sir Kenelm Digby* with his wife and childre and a historic painting (1600) of Queen Elizabeth.

Sporting and Porcelain Rooms – Prints, trophies, Meissen and Chine figurines show the family's interest in the chase and as founders of the Blackmo Vale Hunt. In adjoining rooms pieces of 17C Chinese Transitional and 17C-18 K'ang-hsi periods make a proud display.

Green Drawing Room – Raleigh and Digby **arms** appear in the decoration Raleigh's five lozenges in shields on the ceiling; the Digby fleur-de-lis over th fireplace. The **walnut despatch** box is said to have held the would-be English-Spani marriage contract *(see above).* Note the French **kingwood writing-table,** the la Georgian commodes and a portrait of Col Stephen Digby, "Mr Fairly" in Fan Burney's diary.

Blue Drawing Room – The room, so-called from the original colour of th wallpaper, is crowded with fine English and French **18C furniture,** Chinese ar Japanese **lacquer** and **porcelain.** Among those portrayed are *Sir Jeffrey Hudso* Henrietta Maria's Dwarf; Henry, 1st Earl of Digby, by **Gainsborough**; John Digb 3rd Earl of Bristol, who received the future William III on the latter's journ from Brixham to London in 1688.

Hall – The hall, in the 16C part of the house, still has the **studded door** and **latti windows** from when the end wall was the outer wall of Raleigh's house.

The Procession of Queen Elizabeth.

Small Dining Room – Tudor and Stuart oak furniture are seen through the Elizabethan doorway.

Oak Room – The room with 1620 **panelling** contains two remarkable, draught proof **Jacobean inner porches,** decorated with fluted pilasters, pierced parapets and heraldic beasts (note the **wooden spring** on one of the door latches). The prehistoric antlers above the wide fireplace were found in Ireland; the medieval helmet is a tilting helm; the portrait is believed to be of Sir Walter Raleigh.

ADDITIONAL SIGHTS

Town centre – The abbey lies at the centre of the town west of the main, Cheap Street. This is marked at its start by an open square in which stands the **Conduit** *(left side),* the transposed lavatorium from the abbey cloister. On the same side *(corner of Abbey Rd)* are 17C **stone houses** and a combined wood-framed and stone house with three advanced, half-timbered gables.

Long Street. – The wide street leads off right to Sherborne Castle *(see above).*

Newland – The third road on the right curves southeast to join up with Long Street. It and the two before it are lined by 18C and early 19C **houses** built in irregular terraces in stone with period doors and windows.

St John's Almshouses – The 15C foundation comprises a **chapel** (medieval glass), a **hall,** two-storey houses and a cloister surrounding a low-walled courtyard. To the rear is the **Abbey Close,** ringed by modest 16C-18C houses.

Sherborne School – The school was granted a royal charter as a Free Grammar School by Edward VI in 1550 *(see above).*
It had grown to only 30 boys by 1850; 27 years later there were 278 and now *c*650. The buildings, including the Gatehouse and Great Court, are predominantly 19C-20C but follow the Jacobean style and are in the same Ham Stone where they abut such areas as the **Jacobean Schoolroom** (Old School Room) of *c*1625 and the **Library** (*c*1470).

Museum ⓥ – *Abbey Gate.* The museum's exhibits present life in the almshouses, a 15C wall painting, Victoriana, a model of the 12C castle which makes the ruins comprehensible *(see above),* and items on the local 17C-18C silk and present glass fibre industries.

EXCURSIONS

★ **Sandford Orcas Manor House** – *4 miles north by B3148. See Sandford Orcas.*

★ **Purse Caundle Manor** ⓥ – *5 miles east by A30.*
The silver-grey stone house, approached through courtyard gates, was L-shaped in the 15C-16C and extended to an Elizabethan E in the 17C. Its gables are crowned with the slim square chimneys known to be the hallmark of a group of local Dorset builders who flourished between 1600 and 1630.
Inside, the **Great Hall** boasts an arch-braced roof reinforced with tie-beams and built up with struts and king posts; there are massive 16C fireplaces and 17C panelling and gallery balustrading. The first floor **Great Chamber** has a barrel roof and is decorated with a Chinese painted wallpaper. Off the east end is the small, late 15C **oriel** seen from the lane.

Worldwide Butterflies, Over Compton ⓥ – *3 miles west off north carriageway, Sherborne-Yeovil Rd, A30.*

Butterflies – Tropical butterflies in brilliant velvet colours with wingspans of 6-9ins fly freely amid jungle plants growing in glass enclosures which each fill a whole room in the ancestral house; in high summer, in the Palm House, visitors walk among them. On the first floor are the silk-worms which, maintaining the traditi of the **Lullingstone Silk Farm** founded in 1932 and now at Compton, supply s for famous royal occasions.

Compton House – The setting for the butterflies is the part-19C, part-16C Tudor-sty mansion built on the foundations of houses dating back to pre-Domesday. In the garden are tall cedars of Lebanon and a small **church** with a high, pinnacl and embattled tower. Its several periods were "beautified" in 1882 by Robe Goodden, ancestor and namesake of the present owner, who had his **stat** sculpted from life and set inside the church three years before he died.

SIDMOUTH Devon — Pop 10 808

Michelin Atlas p 5 or Map 403 – K31

The town lies at the foot of wooded hills which descend to the sea where th sheer off exposing rock which is pinky-cream to the east (Salcombe Hill Cl and dark red to the west (Peak Hill, 500ft). The ebbing tide uncovers a bea of golden sand and, to the west, the **Chit Rocks** and further west still **Jacob's Ladc** or Western Beach – Jacob's Ladder itself comprises three flights of wooden ste to a fort-like building on the cliff top.

The **Esplanade** and several streets and terraces are lined by attractive Georgi and Regency houses from the time when Sidmouth had dreams of being fashionable watering-place.

EXCURSIONS

Ladram Bay – *2 miles west along South Devon Coast Path. Start from Pe Hill Rd.* From Peak Hill Cottage (thatched) the path goes through a glade beeches to follow the line of the cliff edge before eventually dropping down the small Ladram Bay (crowded in summer) with its spectacular eroded red cli and offshore stacks.

Donkey Sanctuary, Salcombe Regis ⊙ – *3 miles northeast by A3052; tu at signpost Dunscombe, Weston, Branscombe; entrance 300yds.* The fields a stables are full of rescued donkeys, gazing out of every corner, alert, inquisiti and enjoying life. In the **Slade Centre,** an indoor riding school, donkeys give rid each week to hundreds of handicapped children drawn from a wide area.

★ SOMERTON Somerset — Pop 4 339

Michelin Atlas p 8 or Map 403 – L30 – Facilities

The small town with an arcaded market cross boasts of having been the capi town of Wessex in the 10C and the county town in the 13C-14C; now it blissfully off all main routes and closely surrounded by rolling, wooded farmlan The houses and inns along the two main streets, which together form an L, a of the local blue lias or limestone with Ham stone trims, mullioned windo and stone tile roofs.

Houses and Inns – Around the **Market Place★** there stand the unique 17C arcaded **cross★**, the Town Hall of the same date but much altered, and the White Hart on the site of the town's early castle. East of the church are several **17C-18C houses,** a **16C house** with symmetrical oriels and dormers in the tiled roof, a **round-cornered house** with a Tuscan porch (now a bank), and, closing the street, the **Red Lion,** a 17C coaching inn with a rounded archway entrance surmounted by a pedimented Venetian window.

Market Cross, Somerton.

In contrast the tree-shaded **Broad Street** is lined by substantial 18C houses.

★ **St Michael's Church** – The octagonal south **tower,** which dates from the 13 is the oldest part of the church. The interior was transformed *c*1450 by t addition of a clerestory and a magnificent **tie-beam roof** with king posts a castellations, tracery, foliage, carved wall plates, 640 identical quatrefoil pane dragons and angels, all now highlighted in gold. Local beer and cider maki are said to be celebrated in the **barrel** (1ft long) which is shown bungho downwards *(north side of centre beam, 3rd oblong from west end).*

The **pulpit,** the **panelling** behind the altar and the **altar** itself, which has symb of mankind's fall and salvation carved on its legs, are all Jacobean; the **bisho chair** is said to be from Glastonbury *(qv)*; the brass **candelabra** are 18C.

EXCURSION

★ **Lytes Cary** – *4 miles south by B3151 and east from Kingsdon. See Lytes Ca*

★ STEEPLE ASHTON Wiltshire Pop 2 076

Michelin Atlas p 17 or Map 403 – N30 – 7 miles east of Trowbridge

Steeple Ashton gives the lie to the saying that lightning never strikes twice in the same place : the church possessed a "Famous and Lofty Steeple, Containing a height above the Tower 93 Foot" – it was breached on 25 July 1670 and had almost been rebuilt when "another terrible Storm of Thunder and Lightning happened October 15 the same year, which threw (it) down". The church, but not the steeple, was restored.
A local church had been in existence since 1252 and a weekly market and annual fair established since 1266. In the two centuries which followed, wool merchants and clothiers prospered, work people were attracted to the village, and many of the houses, forges and inns surrounding the green and lining the main street were built. Two clothiers and their wives added new north and south aisles to the church, the rest of the parish a new nave and the ill-fated steeple.
Decline came in the 16C-17C when a series of fires damaged and destroyed many houses and fulling was invented, a process in the manufacture of woollen cloth requiring running water which the village lacks. The people turned to agriculture and in the 19C many emigrated to America, Australia and New Zealand.

★ **The Green** – The **market cross** dates from 1714; the octagonal stone lock-up or **blind house** with a domed roof and no windows dates from 1773.

Houses on the Green and in adjoining streets – The two black and white half-timbered houses, one known as the **Old Wool Market**, are 16C and 17C; the timber-framed house with brick herringbone infilling on the upper floor, variously known as the Old Merchant's Hall and **Judge Jeffreys' House**, is 16C; **Ashton House** is early 16C with additions, extensions and a 1724 refronting; The Longs Arms is 17C. Blackburn Farmhouse *(by the telephone box)* was begun *c*1500; the cottage with three big brick chimneys, at the end of the High Street, is built on cruck beams *(qv)*; **The Sanctuary**, off Dark Lane, according to the records, was enlarged in 1500...

St Mary's Church – Gargoyles as opposed to a steeple decorate the Perpendicular exterior. Inside, it is the **roofs** which are chiefly of interest : the nave, even before the steeple fell upon it (possibly because an earlier stone roof had cracked), is covered with a lofty fan vault of oak and plaster; the aisles have intricate lierne vaulting in stone, the ribs descending to canopied niches supported on boldly carved half-figures. The chancel was added when the building was restored in the 19C.

The towns and sights described in this guide are indicated in black lettering on the local maps and town plans.

★ STOGURSEY PRIORY CHURCH Somerset

Michelin Atlas p 7 or Map 403 – K30

The outside of St Andrew's Church, with its octagonal, slate-covered spire rising from an early crossing tower, gives little indication of its interest.
The church, on land given by the Conqueror, was founded as a daughter house of the Abbey of Ste Marie de Lonlay in Normandy. By *c*1107 a priory church had been built; by *c*1180 the religious had so increased in number that the church had to be considerably enlarged. The community prospered but later declined to a prior, one monk and a few servants. In 1414 under the Alienation Act, Henry V sequestered the priory; in the 15C it became a **parish church.**

Interior – The **Norman doorway** leads through to the nave with its Perpendicular windows, 19C **Friendly Society boards** against the walls and 31 **benches** carved in 1524-30 with a pelican, a double-headed eagle, a spoonbill, a green man...

Crossing – At the crossing, wider than it is deep, the church's 11C date becomes apparent in the circular **Norman arches** with dog-tooth and zig-zag decoration, the arcade of great round pillars and remarkably carved **capitals** of Ham Hill stone. As completed *c*1107, the priory church comprised the crossing, a single-bay chancel with a rounded apse, transepts with round-apsed chapels and a minimal nave. In 1180 the chancel and transepts were extended eastwards converting the latter into three-bay, chancel aisles. Four medieval **angels** were retained at the corners of the nave at the time of the 19C restoration.

Furnishings – The **chandelier** was made in Bridgwater in 1732; the **tub font** *(north transept)*, decorated with cable moulding, four mysterious faces and St Andrew's crosses at the rim, is Norman; the encaustic **floor tiles** are medieval. The **sanctuary ring** was attached to the southeast crossing pier in the 13C when a murderer sought sanctuary in the church but absconded before his trial, leaving the priory liable for his fine (the provision of a ring was intended to enable any future miscreant to be chained to it while awaiting trial. The right of sanctuary was abolished in 1623).

Verney Chapel – Among the 18C wall monuments and tablets are memorials of William Verney (d 1333) who lies holding his heart, and John Verney (d 1472) the local squire, a rumbustious character who was summoned to Canterbury in 1442 to answer charges of interrupting the Latin service and preaching in and out of church in English. Seventy years after his death there is an entry in the accounts of 1540 for the purchase of a Great Bible (Cranmer's Bible) for 10*s* 6*d*, and 4*d* for a chain to secure it safely in the church.

★★★ STONEHENGE Wiltshire

Michelin Atlas p 9 or Map 403 – O30

Stonehenge is one of the world's classic sights – and a perpetual enigm It is perfectly oriented so that on Midsummer Day the sun, rising in its mo northerly position, appears exactly over the Heel Stone to anyone standing the centre. It can be assumed only that Stonehenge was considered a sacr place; little else is certain about it.

Stonehenge is 4 000 years old, dating from *c*2800-1550 BC (though some no put it 800-1000 years earlier). It is, therefore, several centuries later than t Great Pyramid in Egypt, contemporary with the Minoan culture in Crete, millennium earlier than the first Great Wall of China, 2 000 years earlier th the Aztec constructions (and carved stone calendars) of Mexico and 3 500 yea older than the figures on Easter Island.

The Druids, a Celtic priesthood, are a "modern" appendage : they arrived fro Europe in 250 BC.

The Stones – There are two types of stone at Stonehenge : **bluestones** fro the Preseli Mountains and the shores of Milford Haven in western South Wale and **sarsens** from the Marlborough Downs, 20 miles away.

The bluestones, so-called from their colour when first cleaved and weighing to 4 tons each, were transported, it is believed, along the South Wales coa to the Bristol Avon, along the River Frome, overland to the Wylye and Salisbu Avon and, finally, overland from West Amesbury to the site – a total distan of 240 miles on log rollers, sledges, rafts and lashed alongside small boats. Som at least, were brought to Wiltshire even before construction began Stonehenge, a large one having been discovered in a long barrow of *c*3000 E near Warminster.

The sarsens weigh up to 50 tons each; the journey was shorter but partly uph Motive power was human muscle.

The stones, blue and sarsen, were shaped on arrival with football-siz sarsen hammers : the **standing stones** were tapered at one end and tenon at the top to secure the curving, morticed **lintels** which were linked to ea other by tongues and grooves. To position the stones, holes were dug (wi red deer antler picks and cattle shoulder-blade spades) into which t stones were levered until they toppled upright and could be made fast wi rammed stones and earth. The trilithon lintels were next positioned at the ba and either gradually levered up on ever-rising log platforms, or perhaps lever up by means of ropes along greased and debarked oak beams angled again the uprights.

The period – Stonehenge was built in **three phases** between 2800 a 1550 BC, when its purpose in the life of the people of Wessex, of Britain a whole and probably nearby areas of Western Europe, must have be self-evident.

When work began the area was inhabited by nomadic hunters and their famili and by early farming settlers who had made the hazardous crossing of t Channel and North Sea in skin boats.

By 2000 BC the **Beaker Folk** *(qv)*, who had spread into Wessex along the cha upland tracks, had grown into a community of perhaps 12-15 000 people, rul by the powerful cattle barons of the Salisbury Plain who also controlled the me industry.

There was a growing priesthood, which at peak periods in the construction Stonehenge would call on the population to provide as many as 600 men one time to pull the heaviest sarsen stones up the south slope of the Vale Pewsey, or 200 to erect a sarsen upright...

Stonehenge.

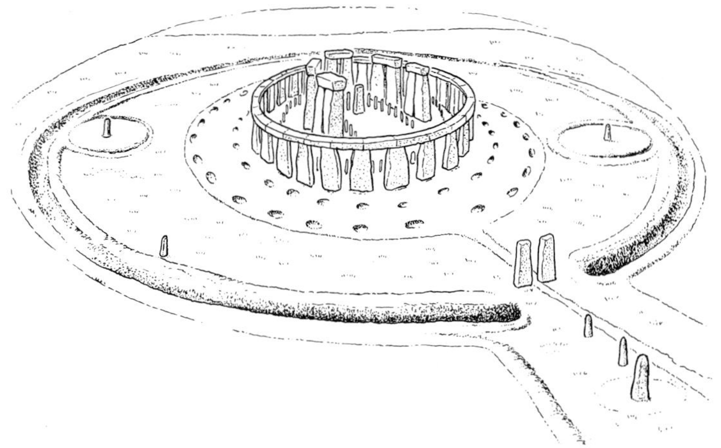

Stonehenge when complete.

The building design – In the **first phase** (*c*2800 BC) a ditch, an inner, chalk rubble bank 6ft high, and a ring of holes, known as the Aubrey Holes after a 17C antiquary, were dug to enclose an area 1 ½ acres in extent, 300ft in diameter. To the northeast the ditch and bank were cut to afford an entrance marked inside by two upright stones and, outside *(near the road)*, by the **Heel Stone** (and a timber gateway). Inside the enclosure, four **Station Sarsens** were set up at the cardinal points of the compass.
In the **second phase,** *c*2100 BC, a double ring of bluestones began to be set up at the centre and the **Avenue** was begun towards the River Avon at West Amesbury.
In around 2000 BC, during the **third phase,** the structure was transformed : the incomplete bluestone rings were replaced by a circle of tall sarsen trilithons, the lintels forming an upraised stone hoop; inside, five separate, giant trilithons rose in a horseshoe opening towards the Heel Stone. The entrance was marked by new uprights, one of which, the Slaughter Stone, now fallen, remains (names, now irrelevant, were given to many stones in the 18C); the bluestones were re-introduced to form an inner horseshoe. At the end of this phase, *c*1550 BC, Stonehenge appeared, it is believed, as illustrated.
Gradually the population and prosperity declined; Stonehenge, in use in 1100 BC, fell into ruin as stones tumbled and were removed. While it is certain that the axis of the sarsen stones points to where an observer at the centre would see the sunrise on midsummer's day, other original sightlines to the horizon have been largely destroyed and are less easy to verify. Lines joining the Station Stones may have marked the most northerly and southerly points on the horizon of sun and moon settings; the Aubrey Holes may represent a means of calculating the eclipses of the moon. It seems that Stonehenge may have been constructed as an observatory by a people who had a considerable knowledge of astronomy and were capable of erecting a monument the equal of the Seven Wonders of the Ancient World.

★ STOURHEAD Wiltshire

Michelin Atlas p 8 or Map 403 – N30 – 3 miles northwest of Mere

The garden is an example of an 18C "designed" English garden at its supreme best. In early spring the trees in bud present infinite shades of tender green, summer enriches the tones until in autumn the leaves turn to gold, scarlet, russet, brown, before abandoning the brown-black branches to winter.
Daffodils, bluebells, rhododendrons and azaleas provide brilliant background colour. The creator and first architect of these "pleasure grounds", which occupy some 400 acres, was Henry Hoare II (1705-85).
Henry Hoare I (1677-1725), son of the founder of Hoare's Bank (*c*1673) in the City of London, acquired the property in 1717 and built a new house on the site, designed by Colen Campbell, pioneer of English Palladianism. The house of 1721 comprised the present centre wing only; the flanking pavilions containing the library and picture gallery were added by Henry Hoare II's heir, Sir Richard Colt Hoare (1758-1838), antiquary, county historian and, like his grandfather, a traveller and collector.

GARDENS ⏲ *illustration p 33*

The short path, at the water's edge, is 1 ¼ miles easy going with benches at several vantange points.
Henry Hoare II was influenced in his garden design by the landscapes he saw on his travels and even more by the paintings of Claude and of Nicholas and Gaspard Poussin in which nature is presented in luminous shades, and focal points are provided by Classical buildings. In the same way as one viewed a picture, therefore, and in contrast to the preceding fashion of overlooking a formal parterre garden from the house, the grounds were laid out to be viewed from specific vantage points.

Hoare first formed the great triangular **lake;** then, as he began his plantings deciduous trees and conifers, "ranged in large masses as the shades in a painting he started, with his architect Henry Flitcroft, to build the Classical-style **focal poin** which, circling the lake in an anticlockwise direction, may be pinpointed fro across the water as the Temple of Flora, the Grotto, the Gothic Cottage, th Pantheon – originally known as the Temple of Hercules for which the statu was carved by Rysbrack after his earlier terracotta figurine in the Picture Galler In 1765 Hoare was given the Civic High **Cross** from Bristol which enabled hi to create an entirely English vista of the lake, the Turf Bridge, the Cross an in the background, Stourton church and village.
Colt Hoare laid the continuous paths, added new trees to increase the rang of colour and introduced the first rhododendron in 1791.

HOUSE ⊙ *45min*

The house suffered a grim sale of much of its contents in 1883 and a fire 1902 which destroyed the early 18C interiors although nearly all the conten of the ground-floor staterooms were saved.

Hall – In the cube-plan entrance hall are 18C **console tables** with fox suppor wheelback chairs, a gilded bronze **bust of Charles I** by Le Sueur, also **portraits** Sir Richard Hoare, founder of the bank, Henry Hoare I holding plans of the hous Henry Hoare II (figure by Michael Dahl, horse by Wootton) and Colt Hoare ar his son.

Library – The long gallery with a barrel vault contains fine furniture by **Thom Chippendale the Younger,** notably the mahogany library table for which he was pa £115. The two busts of Milton are by **Rysbrack,** the pen and wash drawings Venice by **Canaletto.** Note the carved wood chimneypiece and plaster relief the Apocryphal story of Tobit.

Music Room – The **square piano** of 1784 is by **Ganer** and the mahogany **card-tal** with lion legs and a bacchic frieze of 1740 by **William Linnell.**

Little Dining Room – The shellback **chairs** date from 1740. The 17C **silver-g centrepiece,** which was made in Germany, incorporates the double-headed eag of the Hapsburgs, adopted by the Hoares as their bank emblem.

Staircase Hall – The two Rococo gilt **pier-glasses** are by **John Linnell** (175

Cabinet Room – The mid-17C **cabinet** of ebony and gilt bronze with stone inla is Florentine; the 18C blue-john vase comes from Derbyshire.

Picture Gallery – On the walls hang the Claude and Poussin **landscapes** whic inspired Henry Hoare II in his garden design, also early Italian paintings. No especially the **Chippendale furniture,** the 18C **satinwood commode,** a beautiful ov inlaid **rent-table** and the **Rysbrack** Hercules figurine which served as the model f the sculpture in the Pantheon in the garden.

★ STURMINSTER NEWTON MILL Dorset

Michelin Atlas p 8 or Map 403 – N31

This lovely old **mill** ⊙ on the banks of the Stour, its weir over 250 yards upstrea rises in a picturesque setting overlooking meadows and the **15C bridge** in Sturminster Newton itself.
In 968 King Edgar granted Sturminster to Glastonbury Abbey *(qv);* the Domesda survey recorded the abbey as having three mills at that time and it is likely th one of them was on this site.
The present, largely 17C (stone) and 18C (brick) building dates in part back the 15C and was still in use commercially until recently. It rises over three floo and has the traditional layout of a corn mill *(qv)* : large wooden bins for stori grain at the top, **milling machinery** on the first floor with millstones, hopp winnower, crusher etc and ground floor for the bagging, weighing and stori of the finished meal and for controlling the machinery, all of which is no powered by a **water turbine** with a horizontal drive wheel (installed in 1904 ar still in working order) controlled by a sluice gate below the water level. The to shows different types of product achieved and ends with more modern equipme (20C hammer mills).

★ SWANAGE Dorset

Pop 8 411

Michelin Atlas p 9 or Map 403 – O32 – Facilities

The quarry town and harbour, from which stone and marble were shipped build Westminster Abbey and the Cathedrals of Exeter, Lincoln and Salisbu was transformed by the arrival of the railway into a "pleasant little watering pla with a good beach".
Some years before, **John Mowlem,** a native of Swanage, had begun to beaut the town. He had started as a local quarry boy before setting out for Lond where he founded a construction firm for which he imported stone from Purbe and granite from Cornwall, Aberdeen, Guernsey and Leicestershire, to accompli the massive Victorian rebuilding of the City and the resurfacing of roads a bridges with granite sets. The sailing ketches which brought the stone to Lond returned to Swanage with unwanted **street furniture,** dressed and carved ston even **monuments.**

SIGHTS

Mowlem Institute – *The Parade.* The modern complex on the front stands on the site of the institute presented to the town by John Mowlem in 1863.

Pier and **Wellington Clock Tower** – The small pier was built in 1896; the landmark-like tower stood at the south end of London Bridge until 1863 when it was pronounced an "unwarrantable obstruction". Mowlem offered to remove it and shipped it home. It never included a statue of the duke.

Turn inland up the High St.

Queen's Street – *Left.* Several City of London **bollards** are used as gate-posts.

Old Millpond – *Church Hill. Right off High St.*
The old millpond with a couple of ducks is surrounded by pretty 18C-19C cottages and houses with flowering creepers.

St Mary the Virgin – The church, rebuilt for the third time in 1859, has a **tower** which dates, in its lower half, from the 12C-13C when it served as a refuge for local townsfolk from marauding pirates – note the arrow slit windows.
Originally there was no door at ground level, entry being by means of a ladder to the first floor.

Return to the High St.

Town Hall – The ornate **17C stone front** of the hall originally stood in Cheapside in the City of London as the façade of the Mercers' Company; when Cheapside was widened, it was decided that it would be less costly to reproduce the stone front than to clean it of its "London black" and re-erect it.
London, therefore, has a 19C replica and Swanage Town Hall has the original 17C stone which Mowlem shipped home and which, for good measure, the sea air has gradually cleaned.

Our Lady of Mercy Convent – The Scottish baronial-style building, built by Mowlem's nephew George Burt *(see below)*, incorporates columns from London's old Billingsgate Market, statues from the Royal Exchange, tiles from the Houses of Parliament...

Durlston Country Park – *1 mile south by Lighthouse Rd.*
The headland, from which there is a panoramic **view★★**, the castle-folly-restaurant, Great Globe, London bollards and the lighthouse today make up the country park George Burt had in mind when he purchased 80 acres (now 260 acres) in 1862.

Castle – The folly is built of Purbeck stone with a full complement of towers, turrets, battlements and bastions; the stalwart granite bollards at the entrance are prototypes of those in Trafalgar Square. The interior is designed as a winter garden.

Take the path down towards the head. Note the London **bollards.**

★ **Great Globe** – Mowlem had the globe made in his yard at Greenwich. It is 10ft in diameter, 40 tons in weight and is made up of 15 segments of Portland stone held in position by granite dowels.

Anvil Point Lighthouse – *40min circular walk.*
The path to the all-white lighthouse *(qv)* passes the **Tilly Whim Caves,** a former cliffside quarry. The **view★★** extends from St Aldhelm's Head to Portland Bill *(west)* and from Hengistbury Head and The Needles *(east)*; inland are the Purbeck Hills.

EXCURSIONS

★ **St Aldhelm's Head** – *4½ miles southwest by B3069.*

Worth Matravers – This small village of stone houses round a duck pond once produced the finest-quality local marble; the slender shafts in Salisbury Cathedral were quarried here. In 1506 Swanage took precedence.
The **church** of rubble stone with ashlar dressings and 19C pyramid roof over its ancient square **tower** has several Norman features including, outside, the enriched south doorway and the **corbel table** which runs the length of the eaves, carved with grotesque heads of birds and beasts.
Inside, the **chancel arch** with its chevron moulding above round columns is mid-12C; the plain **tower arch** at the west end is earlier still.

Continue through the village 1½ miles southwest along surfaced roads and farm tracks.

St Aldhelm's Chapel – The chapel, dedicated to the local saint Aldhelm *(qv)*, stands squat and square on the windswept clifftop; the shallow, pyramid roof is surmounted by a turret which must once have held a fire cresset, or basket, as a sailors' lantern. It was built between 1150 and 1200. The rounded, Norman doorway leads into a 30ft sq chamber reminiscent of an undercroft with a square pillar supporting rib vaulting.

★ **St Aldhelm's Head** (or **St Alban's Head**) – The headland (352ft), one of the highest in the area, affords a grandiose **view★★★** north to the Purbeck Hills, east to the Old Harry Rocks, Hengistbury Head and The Needles, and west to Portland Bill. West along Kimmeridge Cliffs *(2½ miles on foot Rtn)* is **Chapman's Pool,** a dark circular pool eroded by the sea.

Studland – *5 miles north by Victoria Avenue and Northbrook Rd to B3351, bea right.*
Studland is the promontory closing Poole Harbour from the south. A **chain ferry** ⌚ runs from Shell Bay at the north end to Sandbanks *(qv)*.

Studland Beach – The two mile arc of sand below a narrow band of shingle i crowded in summer; the bay is wide and shallow; the **view★** vast across Pool Bay.

Studland Village – The village is small and scattered with houses half-hidden in gardens, and, not far from the water's edge, **St Nicholas Church★**, early Norman and fortress-solid with a low tower. Note the **corbel table** with grimacing heads, the lancets, the **leper squint** peering through the south chancel wal (glazed 1881). Inside are a **groined vault** and plain Norman arches on **cushion capitals.**

★★ **Old Harry Rocks** – The two stacks of gleaming chalk were once part of a continuous shoreline from The Needles but are now separated from the mainland and even from each other; Old Harry is the larger and three-legged, his wife the slimmer.

SWINDON Wiltshire

Pop 127 348

Michelin Atlas p 17 or Map 403 – O29

Swindon was the Mecca of the Great Western Railway from 1831, when it wa chosen as the line's main junction and site for its locomotive and carriage workshops, until 1948 brought about the demise of individual lines unde nationalisation.
In the early 19C Old Swindon was a typical hilltop market town of some 1 700 inhabitants; by the end of the century New Swindon, the railway town below numbered nearly 40 000 of whom 4 000 were directly employed by the GWR and most of the rest in growing and selling food, providing houses and lodgings. Today the town, still prosperous, is ringed by light industry estates, the centr stacked tall with 20C office blocks.

SIGHTS

★ **Great Western Railway Museum** ⌚ – *Farringdon Rd.* The museum is in the onetime "model lodging house" built by the company for its workers who came from all parts of England, particularly the North, Wales and Ireland. The hous was not popular and was remodelled as a Wesleyan Chapel – an appearance it maintains outside. Inside, it has been rebuilt and sparingly decorated with Victorian iron station furniture as a suitable hall of fame.
There stand a full-size replica of the **North Star** (which hauled the firs GW passenger train from Paddington to Maidenhead), the original **Lode Sta** a "Dean Goods", the 1903 **City of Truro,** the **King George V** – built in the town in 1927 – and an 0-6-0 1947 tank engine. Carriage doorlocks, signals working models, the prized gold disc railway pass, silver table centres and coffee urns modelled on famous locomotives, rattles, truncheons, lights headboards... give some indication of the array of equipment needed to run th line which, in its heyday, extended over 9 000 miles of track between London Bristol, Penzance, Fishguard and Liverpool, maintained 3 600 locomotives 9 000 passenger coaches, 82 000 freight wagons and employed more than 100 000 men.
Lining the corridor walls are posters, commands for royal trains and, in one gallery Brunel's signed drawings for the Clifton Suspension Bridge competition at Bristo *(qv)* after which he was appointed, in his own words, "Engineer to the fines work in England".

★ **Railway Village Museum** ⌚ – *34 Farringdon Rd.* To house its workers the company built not only the lodging house but also 300 one, two, three-up an three-down houses. The building material used was the limestone excavated from the nearby 3 212yd long Box Tunnel (1837-41).
In 1969-80 the cottages were cleaned to reveal from beneath soot and grim the original silver limestone; all were modernised save one, no 34, three-bedroomed house which was left with gas and oil lighting, a range, washin dolly, copper, mangle, brown-glazed sink and tin bath in the kitchen and flowered outside lavatory. It is furnished in 1880s style in the bedrooms, fron parlour and dining room – note the bowler hat on the peg in the hall : th unmistakable mark of a foreman's rank.

Civic Centre and Brunel Shopping Centre – The **Civic Centre** (lat 1950s-1980s), comprising administrative offices, the law courts, the Wyver Theatre, the College and monolithic commercial buildings, is constructed c diverse materials, from black brick to white marble, and remains strangel rudimentary. By comparison the **Brunel Centre** (mid-1970s), which adjoins an earlie shopping centre, is closely knit; the overhead arching above the mosaic pavemer and the peripheral arcading are airily reminiscent of the iron-work and glass c the great 19C railway termini. In one avenue stands a larger-than-life statue c Brunel.

Museum and Art Gallery ⌚ – *Bath Rd.* The museum, in a 19C house i Swindon Old Town, has a large and rare collection of **Prattware** – the mid-lat 19C pot-lids decorated with coloured landscapes, portraits, rural and dramati scenes to attract Victorian housewives into buying, possibly in inordinat quantities to complete a set of lids, commodities such as fish and meat pastes, pomades and cream. So popular were the decorations that they were later applied to table china. The museum also has sections on fossils and local history. A modern gallery displays a growing collection of paintings and ceramics by 20C artists.

Richard Jefferies Museum ⏲ – *Marlborough Rd, Coate. A345 before the roundabout, opposite a large garage and hotel.* In the farmhouse in which the naturalist and writer Jefferies was born in 1848 are early editions of his works and personal mementoes, also writings of Alfred Williams, the Hammerman or Railway Poet.

EXCURSION

Lydiard Park – *5 miles west off A420. See Lydiard Park.*

★ TAMAR RIVER

Michelin Atlas pp 3, 6 or Map 403 – G31, H32

Traditionally and physically, despite its many bridges, the Tamar marks the boundary between Devon and Cornwall – between Cornwall and the rest of the world, perhaps, since in conversation places are described as in the county or "beyond the Tamar". Although traders from the Mediterranean came to Cornwall by sea in the earliest times, the Roman legions never crossed the river; despite bridges and modern transport, it is still a dividing line.

Geographically the river rises away up in the far northeast corner of Cornwall, 60 miles from where it flows into its estuary, known as the **Hamoaze,** and Plymouth Sound. It is still navigable at high water as far as Calstock and even Morwellham and Gunnislake *(see below).* A thoroughfare in the Middle Ages and more importantly in the 19C for ships bringing down ore from the mines *(see below),* the river is now peaceful with woods, undulating fields and market gardens on either bank, the haunt of avocets, herons and other birds *(qv).* It is beautiful along almost its entire length.

LANDMARKS : PLYMOUTH SOUND to GUNNISLAKE

Mount Edgcumbe – Cornwall. *See Mount Edgcumbe.*

Cremyll Ferry – The old Cremyll Ferry *(qv)* was a rich source of revenue.

Mount Wise – Devon. The memorial is to **Scott of the Antarctic.**

Torpoint Ferry – Until the road bridge was built *(see below)* the chain ferry was the only vehicle link between Plymouth and Cornwall.

Royal Naval Base – Devonport. The base was developed as a dockyard and arsenal in the late 17C. In 1824 the name was changed from Dock to Devonport and in 1914 the town was merged with Plymouth.

River Lynher – Cornwall. The river, which rises on Bodmin Moor, widens out into a broad estuary where it flows into the **Hamoaze. Antony House★** *(qv)* overlooks the Lynher.

Tamar Bridges – The bridges, one rail, one road, connect Devonport with Saltash. The **Royal Albert** was built by Brunel *(qv)* in 1857-59 as part of the extension of the GWR into Cornwall. A combined suspension and arched bridge, supported by towering granite piers, it is an engineering feat even greater with its day-in day-out rail traffic than the more spectacular and graceful Clifton Bridge *(qv).*

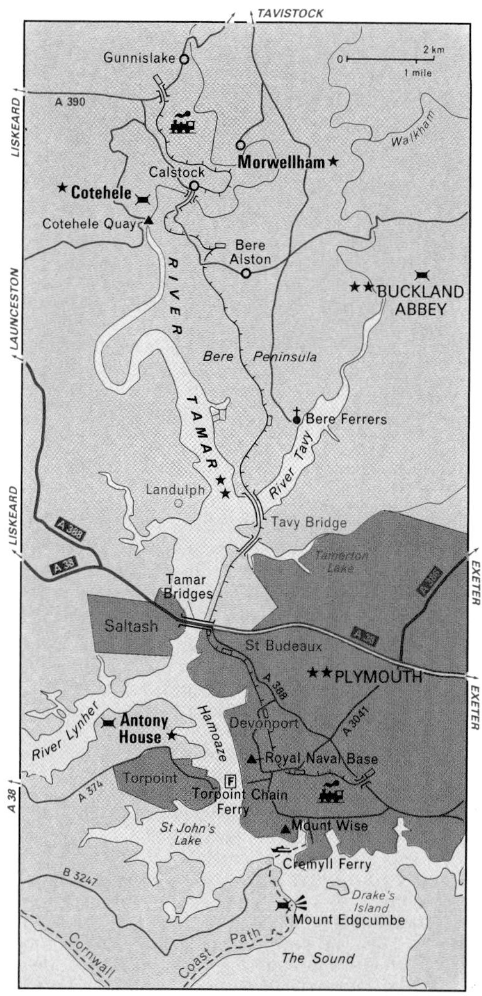

The **Tamar Road Bridge** was opened in 1962, replacing the centuries-old Saltash ferry. It was the model for the Forth and Severn Bridges and the Salazar Bridge in Lisbon.

Parson's Quay – Landulph, Cornwall. The quay is one of several marking the river banks on either side. Once used to embark the lead, silver, tin, copper and arsenic mined locally, the quays now serve as pleasure-craft moorings. Parson's Quay was, in addition, an embarkation point in the 15C for pilgrims setting out on the venturous journey to Santiago de Compostela in northern Spain.

River Tavy – Devon. The river, which rises on Dartmoor, is spanned by an eight-span railway bridge where it joins the Tamar.

Bere Peninsula – The tongue of land between the Tamar and the Tavy, with **Bere Alston** as its principal town and Bere Ferrers' 13C **church** overlooking the Tavy, as a local landmark, was an important silver and lead mining centre from the 13C-16C and again in the 19C, until the river burst its banks and flooded the workings in 1856.
On the double bend look out for avocets and other birds.

★ **Cotehele and Cotehele Quay** – Cornwall. *See Cotehele.*

Calstock – Cornwall. *Landing stage for most of the Tamar boat cruises.*
The small, once important river port was killed in 1908 when the spectacular 12-span railway viaduct was opened 120ft above the river.

★ **Morwellham** – Devon. *See Morwellham.*

Gunnislake – Cornwall. The minute village below rock heights tunnelled by old tin mines was famous for centuries as the most southerly bridge across the Tamar.
New Bridge (182ft long) was built in 1520 of large regular granite blocks; its seven arches are divided by cutwaters and refuges.

BOAT TRIPS

Boat trips up the Tamar depart from Plymouth *(qv).*

TRAIN EXCURSION

It is also possible to go up the Tamar Valley from Plymouth to Gunnislake by train and return from Calstock *(see above)* by boat. The train passes through Devonport, St Budeaux, under the Tamar bridges, over Tamerton Lake and the Tavy Bridge.

★ TAUNTON Somerset — Pop 47 793

Michelin Atlas p 7 or Map 403 – K30 – Facilities

Taunton's recognition as the county town in the 1850s when the Shire Hall was built was an acknowledgement that, after 1 000 years of steady development it had become the most important marketing and administrative centre in Somerset.
In the millennium it had progressed from being a battlefield where King Ine of Wessex won a victory against the English in 710 to an agricultural and livestock market at the heart of one of the nation's most fertile regions, the Vale of Taunton *(qv).* For more than six centuries it had also been an important cloth weaving town : it was the first to introduce the fulling mill to this country in 1218 and so start the shift from cottage industry to company mills; in 1702 Defoe described Taunton as a "large, wealthy, and exceedingly populous town (that had) so good a trade that they had 1 100 looms going for the weaving of sagathies and duroys" (fine wool and silk, and coarse woollen cloths).

SIGHTS

Castle – In 1497 **Perkin Warbeck** passed through Taunton on his rebellious expedition against Henry VII and was brought back to stand trial in the Great Hall of the castle. Nearly two centuries later the **Duke of Monmouth,** another rebel passed through the town, and in 1685 after the Battle of Sedgemoor *(qv)* many of his followers were brought before **Judge Jeffreys** at the **Bloody Assizes** in the same hall. Jeffreys condemned 508 to death but how many actually died is not known; estimates range from 300-500 with between 800 and 1000 transported to the West Indies; there was a brisk trade in pardons. The Bloody Assizes remain a raw memory in the southwest.
During the Civil War Taunton and the castle in particular were under siege three times, most notably in 1645 when the town, under Robert Blake *(qv),* resisted the Royalist forces for three months. In 1648 Parliament ordered the castle and manor to be sold; the sum realised was £9 210 17*s* 0½*d.* In 1662 the Royalist government ordered the castle to be slighted.
After the slighting the 11C-12C castle remained a ruin until it was rescued in the 18C. The east gatehouse is now incorporated into a hotel; the 15C **gateway** which leads through the south range into the inner ward, serves as the entrance to the museum *(below).*

★ **Somerset County Museum** ⊙ – A contemporary portrait of **Judge Jeffreys** by Kneller hangs in the **Great Hall.**

Displays in the section on early history include the **wooden trackways** laid in 2900 BC across the marshlands, the **Somerset Levels;** the prehistoric dug-out canoe and other finds from the **Lake Villages** around Glastonbury; the Roman mosaic of Dido and Aeneas. The **ceramics collection** contains pieces of Eltonware *(qv)*, Wrothamware, local Donyatt and 19C Martinware. There is a collection of Nailsea glass *(qv)*. The highlights of the Chinese pottery bequest are the Han dynasty vases (206 BC-AD 220) and a robust T'ang tomb figure (AD 618-906).

The **17C silver collection** displays a set of apostle and seal top spoons and beakers. A separate gallery recalls the Somerset Light Infantry with battle honours, uniforms and mementoes including a Stars and Stripes captured in 1813.

★ **St Mary Magdalene** – The church with its soaring tower closes perfectly the vista along Hammett Street.

Tower – The tower, which was completed in 1514 after 26 years of building, was the joy and climax to the 15C reconstruction of the parish church on its ancient Saxon site. At a period when the county was the third or fourth most densely populated in England and amongst the wealthiest, it represented the final flowering of what has remained Somerset's great contribution to church architecture *(illustration p 15)*.

It is of Ham Hill stone and is marked at every stage by crocketed pinnacles on set-back buttresses. From the door and a transomed west window it mounts to a frieze surmounted by the first of three similar sets of paired openings each of three lights with transoms, tracery and Somerset tracery, divided and framed by pinnacled shafts; the top pair, the bell openings, are taller, the pinnacles set diagonally, the walling above, panelled; higher still are a fourth frieze, spouting gargoyles, another frieze and the great **crown** of pierced battlements, pinnacles and, at the angles, four tiers of arcading and pierced, crocketed pinnacles flaunting iron wind-vanes – 163ft in all, the top pinnacles 32ft and pierced to minimise wind resistance. The vanes were added, as their 3½in numerals indicate, in 1682.

Interior – The interior is almost square with a narrow nave and double aisles; the outer aisle and arcade on the north side only were not rebuilt in the 15C and are Early English.

The roof is typical of Tudor Somerset with crested tie-beams, king posts, moulded arch braces, panelling, small oak-leaf bosses and **angels,** recently gilded and painted for the first time. Angels reappear in the arcade capitals, while amusing **medieval masks** decorate bosses above the light brackets, the inner aisles and the chancel arch *(north side possibly Henry VII)*; otherwise the statues are 19C replacements of those destroyed by the Puritans.

★ **St James'** – The church, except for the north arcade and aisle, is 14C-15C.

Tower – The 120ft tower of Quantock red sandstone with Ham stone decoration, which many believe to be the forerunner in design to St Mary's, rises from the doorway and six-light west window in stages marked by pinnacled buttresses and diagonally set pinnacles to a bell stage with transomed openings filled with Somerset tracery. Above are a **crest** of gargoyles, a pierced parapet, pinnacles and an overtopping **staircase tower** with a pyramid roof.

Nearby is **Vivary Park,** like St James', in the former priory grounds. Named after the monks' fishpond or vivarium, it has a striking Victorian fountain.

Public buildings and streets – Among the more notable buildings are the **Shire Hall** of 1855-58 in early Tudor style which brought county town status to Taunton *(see above)*; the **Tudor House** of 1578 (Fore Street) with its carved timbers and oversailing gable with multi-light oriel windows; the red-brick Market House of the 1770s with a pediment spanning its full width which stands at the centre crossroads.

The Bristol Road leads to two charitable institutions. **Gray's Almshouses** *(south side of East Street)*, two storeys built of brick with nine chimney stacks each comprising two diagonally set chimneys, date from 1635. **St Margaret's Leper Hospital** *(far end of East Reach, the continuation of East Street)* was founded in the 12C, rebuilt early in the 16C and converted into almshouses in 1612; the single-storey thatched building now houses the headquarters of the Community Council for Somerset. In 1977 the **Brewhouse Theatre** opened in a converted 19C warehouse by the river.

The most appealing streets are **Hammett Street**★ of 1788 with twin lines of dark brick **terrace houses** with attractive pillared and pedimented porches making the perfect frame for St Mary's at the street's end; The **Crescent**★ of 1807 *(westerly parallel to the High St)*, designed as a single undertaking; **Bath Alley**★ *(between the High St and the end of Corporation St)*, in which every house, cottage and shop was built in the 17C-18C to a different design; the wide High St *(pedestrian precinct)*, leisurely with late Georgian-early Victorian houses, shops and pubs...

EXCURSIONS

Trull – *3 miles south.* Pop 4 122. The **church**★, which is Perpendicular with a 13C tower, is known for its wooden pulpit which is carved all round with figures of saints and guardian angels wearing clothes in the style of the 1530s.

Hatch Court – *6 miles southeast on A358. See Hatch Court.*

TAUNTON DEANE Somerset

Michelin Atlas p 7 or Map 403 - K30

Taunton Deane or the Vale of Taunton lies west of the town, a beautiful diamond of fertile agricultural and cider apple country, watered by the River Tone and ringed by the moorlands and hills which characterize the county : the Quantocks to the northeast, the Brendons to the northwest and the Blackdowns to the south. At the foot of the hills are a number of small market towns, an old manor house and, on the Blackdowns, a monument.

TOWNS in the Vale

★ **Bishop's Lydeard** – The **houses,** some still thatched, the **almshouses** of 1616, with mullioned windows and curved doorway arches, and the church all in local **red sandstone** reflect the village's situation below the Quantock Hills.
The **church★** in true Somerset tradition is notable for its west **tower** of *c*1470 which rises from a transomed west window to the bell stage where the flourish begins with a three-light opening – transomed and traceried – flanked by buttress pinnacles; above are a collar of gargoyles, a pierced parapet and countless more pinnacles *(illustration p 149).*
Inside is an early 16C **rood screen** in which the elaborate tracery complements the fan vaulting and has a unique decoration of **lead stars;** note the finely carved **cornice.** The carved **bench-ends** of the same date are coloured the better to show the windmill and flying birds, the ships and symbols of the Passion. The pulpit is Jacobean.
In a wall cabinet *(light switch)* is the town's **market charter** of 1291 sealed by Edward I.

★ **Combe Florey** – The picturesque small village in a valley at the foot of the Brendon Hills is romantically named after a 12C knight, Hugh de Flori.
Almost every building is in the local pink-red, Quantock sandstone, most noticeably the **church** where a particularly deep-coloured stone has been employed for the embattled and pinnacled tower and for the trims and window tracery. Inside, note the **angels** at capital height *(tower arch and north arcade)* and the early 14C **tomb** with a lifesize effigy of a cross-legged knight and, presumably successive wives.

★ **Gaulden Manor** – *See Gaulden Manor.*

Milverton – The town, with the Brendon Hills to the northwest, surrounds a hillock crowned by the parish **church,** a 14C-15C building in the local red sandstone. The Perpendicular tower with a square stair turret rises to bell openings filled with Somerset tracery and a crest of battlements and pinnacles.
Inside, the **north arcade** is 14C, the **font** with cable moulding and a frieze of crosses is Norman, the **rood screen,** as can be seen from the date, was made in 1540.
The **stalls** and **benches** (15C-16C) are attractively carved with poppyheads, the twelve apostles, local characters, the arms of Henry VIII...
The **village** itself is a mixture of Georgian houses (North and Fore Streets and south Sand Street), small cottages and 19C houses, spiced with the occasional 17C house and, east of the church, the 15C-16C parsonage.

Wellington – The town had become a market and cloth centre by the 15C. In the 19C its communications were revolutionized by the construction of the Bridgwater-Tiverton Canal and in the 1840s by that of the Bristol-Exeter railway. The houses, the town hall of 1833, the Baptist Chapel, even the Friends' Meeting House, reflect the late Georgian–early 19C prosperity.
The 15C **church★** has a fortress-like **tower** of red sandstone which rises through three stages from a west door and four-light window to bell openings with Somerset tracery and a final flourish of gargoyles, battlements and pinnacles of which there are three to each angle and nine on the stair turret.
Inside are an Early English **east window** of three stepped lancets below encircled quatrefoils, a **lily crucifix** carved into the centre mullion of the east window of the south aisle, and the **funerary monument** of Chief Justice, Sir John Popham (d 1607; *qv*), who presided at the trials of Guy Fawkes, John Dayrell of Littlecote and Sir Walter Raleigh, and is shown recumbent on a chest beneath a canopy ornate with achievements and obelisks.

Wellington Monument – *2 miles south via by-roads.* The Duke of Wellington took the town's name for his title as it closely resembled his family name of Wellesley. Although he had no other connection with Wellington, the townspeople erected a grey stone monument in the form of a bayonet (175ft tall) in his honour on the Blackdown Hills; it is visible for several miles.
From its base there are **views★★** across Taunton Deane to the Polden Hills, the Quantocks, the Brendons and Exmoor and into Devon *(viewing table).*

Wiveliscombe – Wiveliscombe (pronounced wivvel-iss-cum) is the most westerly of the vale market towns and dates back to pre-Roman times when there was a fort on Castle Hill to the north. By the 14C-15C the village was prospering from occasional visits by the bishops of Bath and Wells to their manor house of which the gate still remains *(southeast of the church).*
Developments in cloth-weaving transformed the village : it became, with Frome, one of the most important in the county, its speciality by the late 18C being Penistones, the strong blue cloth popularly used for clothing slaves in the West Indies. The cloth was produced in such quantities that a Taunton carrier made £6 000 one year transporting it to London. More than 60 Quakers lived in the town in the 18C.
Prosperity brought rebuilding, so that houses and public buildings are almost all 19C. The red tile-hung public library in the **Market Square** was once the **Court House**

TAVISTOCK Devon

Pop 8 508

Michelin Atlas p 4 or Map 403 - H32

The modern market town constructed in the local volcanic, grey-green stone, retains many traces of its 19C days as a copper mining town and also of the monastic borough which it was from 980-1539. A bronze statue of **Sir Francis Drake** is a reminder that he was christened in the parish *c*1541.

The Benedictine abbey was the most resplendent house west of Glastonbury *(qv)*. The abbot obtained a charter for a weekly market in 1105, also an annual **Goose Fair**; at the same time **tin mining** was developing so that in 1281 Tavistock was named as a stannary town *(qv)*. Wool and cloth brought additional wealth which resulted in the parish church, already rebuilt in the 14C, being again rebuilt during 1425-50.

In 1539 the abbey was dissolved and the town was given by Henry VIII to **John Russell**, courtier, ambassador, counsellor and future Earl of Bedford.

With the start of the Napoleonic wars in the 1790s, **mining** became the most important local industry and when in 1844 one of the richest ever **copper lodes** or veins in Europe was discovered near the surface in a pheasant covert, Tavistock became a boom town. Five separate mines in an area of 167 acres were grouped into a company known as **Devon Great Consols** whose £1 shares, three years after being launched, were quoted on the Stock Exchange at £800. Production was at its peak from 1848-58 then slackened as the mines became exhausted (1901); in the half century 730 000 tons of copper ore and 72 000 tons of refined arsenic – used then in dyes, paints, glass-making, ink and insecticides – had been produced at a sale price of £4 000 000.

Bonuses from the new wealth were an increase in the population of the town to one and a half times its present size; the construction from 1803 to 1817, with French prisoners-of-war as navvies, of the 4 mile long **canal**, including 1½ mile tunnel, connecting Tavistock with the Tamar at Morwellham *(qv)*; the remodelling in neo-Gothic style of the **guildhall** and the Bedford Hotel (then a private house), and the construction of the **pannier market** and houses for the miners and townspeople.

St Eustachius Church – The embattled **tower** (106ft) was built in the 14C as one of the abbey gateways with doorways facing north and south. In the interior note : *(west end)* a 14C octagonal font, medieval chests, a brass **ophicleide** (an obsolete wind instrument from the 18C church band), carved organ case; *(northeast chapel)* early 17C **pewter flagons**, 15C bench-ends, window designed by William Morris (1876); *(south aisle)* **Clothworkers' Aisle**, bosses in the wagon roof.

TEIGNMOUTH Devon

Pop 11 995

Michelin Atlas p 4 or Map 403 - J32

The dark red cliffs and offshore rocks, which characterize Devon for so many holiday-makers, appear in an almost unbroken line between the Exe and Teign estuaries, the second distinguished by a huge red sandstone headland known as **The Ness**. *(Passenger ferries across both estuaries, also a bridge in the town across the Teign.)*

The **railway**, given pride of place as it travelled west in the mid-19C, runs at the foot of the cliffs, skirting the waterline, tunnelling through the headlands and rumbling in each resort, between the flower-decked esplanades and the beaches. Fishing for cod off the Newfoundland Grand Banks, shipbuilding and the export of dried fish brought prosperity to Teignmouth centuries ago; today its industries are offshore fishing and marketing, the handling of ball clay, and tourism.

EXCURSIONS

Powderham Castle ⏲ – *8 miles northeast by A379.*

The home of the Courtenay family, Earls of Devon, stands in its own deer park overlooking the Exe estuary. The rooms are hung with family portraits, many by Cosway (1742-1821), and a series of **coats of arms** tracing the family descent decorates the 19C Dining Hall, designed by the Devon-born architect Charles Fowler. The medieval Ante-Room contains a pair of rosewood **bookcases** (1740) and an unusual window, screened at night by a mirror, inserted over the fireplace. The library bookcases were made in Dawlish in the 1820s. James Wyatt designed the handsome **domed Music Room** (1794-96) which has a Carrara marble fireplace; Corinthian pilasters alternate with alcoves containing alabaster vases on marble stands; the gilt furniture incorporating the dolphin – the Courtenay family crest – and the Axminster carpet were made to order. The original Great Hall was converted into the staircase hall, which is decorated with magnificent **18C rococo plasterwork**, and the Marble Hall, which contains two 17C Brussels tapestries and a clock (1740) which plays tunes. The family **porcelain**, which is mostly French and was in daily use until 1935, is displayed in one of the medieval towers. The Chapel is now housed in a 15C barn with a timber roof.

Dawlish – *3 miles northeast by A379.*

With the arrival in the 19C of the railway along the coast, the village at the mouth of Dawlish Water developed into a fashionable resort. **Dawlish Warren**, a long spit of sand dunes obstructing the mouth of the Exe, is now a Nature Reserve.

Newton Abbot – *6 miles west by A381.*

The market town, which developed round a monastery (demolished) at the tidal limit of the River Teign, became the main South Devon **railway junction** in 1846 and trebled its population. It was at St Leonard's Tower (early 14C) in 1688 that William of Orange first proclaimed his intention to be king.

Ugbrooke House, Chudleigh – *8 miles northwest via Ideford by B3192 and by-roads.* *See Ugbrooke House.*

TINTAGEL Cornwall

Pop 1 566

Michelin Atlas p 3 or Map 403 – F32 – Facilities

Tintagel especially and the West Country in general have always been associate with the elusive legend of Arthur, "the once and future King". The tale has existe in the telling since the 8C and in written form since the 12C; it has been reto in the spirit of the time, with locations shifted, in the 12C by William Malmesbury *(qv)*, Geoffrey of Monmouth and the 12C chronicler **Wace** *(qv)*, wh added the Round Table, by Sir Thomas Malory, Spenser, Tennyson, Swinburr and T H White.
Tintagel is also known for having disclosed the largest find of 5C-6C easte Mediterranean pottery shards (more than in the rest of the British Isles p together), which suggests a healthy trade and that olive oil and wine were beir consumed in the area at that time.

ARTHURIAN LEGEND in Cornwall and the southwest

Arthur, son of Uther Pendragon, was born or washed ashore at Tintagel, whe he had his castle and lived with his queen, **Guinevere,** and the **Knights of the Rou Table** among whom was **Tristan,** nephew or son of King Mark whose fort w Castle Dore *(qv)*. **Merlin,** the magician, lived in a cave beneath Tintagel Cast and on a rock off Mousehole *(qv)*; the sword, **Excalibur,** forged in Avalon, w withdrawn by Arthur from the stone and finally thrown into **Dozmary Pool** *(q* **Camelot** is believed by some to be Cadbury Castle *(qv)*. The Battle of Mount Blad (*c*520), when Arthur defeated the pagan Saxons, was possibly fought Liddington Castle near Swindon or Badbury Rings, Dorset; the **Battle of Camlan** the last struggle against Mordred, the king's usurping stepson or bastard sc took place on the banks of the River Camel on Bodmin Moor. Mortally wounde Arthur sailed into the sunset, to the Islands of the Blest (the Isles of Scilly), to Avalon, held by some to be close to Glastonbury *(qv)* where his tomb w "discovered" with that of Guinevere in the 12C.

SIGHTS

Arthur's Castle ⊙ – *Access by a steep road from the main street; 30min R*
The **site**★★★ overlooking the sea from precipitous rocks is a greater feast to t eye than the fragmentary **castle ruin,** which includes walls from the 1145 chap and great hall, built on the site of a 6C Celtic monastery, and other walls dati from the 13C – all centuries later than Arthur's time...

★ **Tintagel Church** – Small and low-lying on the cliff, with its rough, early 1 granite **tower** standing four square against the wind, Tintagel church has lo been a sailors' landmark. It was first built between 1080 and 1150 and retai 12C features including the south door, the north doorway with tiny side windov crossing arches, the Early English triple lancet window in the north transept. T **font** is Norman with rudely carved heads and serpents; a second smaller fo has cable moulding.
There are also a 13C **memorial stone** with a carved foliated cross *(crossing, sou side)*, a medieval slate-topped **stone bench,** a **brass** of 1430. The new east windc is a recent addition (1991).

★ **Old Post Office** ⊙ – The small, rambling manor house, built with 3ft thi stone walls and undulating slate roofs at the centre of the village, dates frc the 14C.
Inside are a small, two storey, stone-paved medieval hall, with an ancie fireplace beneath exposed roof timbers, the postmistress' office and, up t narrow wooden staircase, two bedrooms beneath a maze of beams and col braces.

EXCURSIONS

★ **Boscastle** – *3 miles northeast off B3263.*
The village straggles downhill from the road to a long tongue of sea which po in at high tide between 300ft headlands. The picturesque inlet is the only **natu harbour** between Hartland Point and Padstow. The inner jetty dates from 15 the breakwater from the 19C; the onetime coaching inn is 15C; the cotta gardens are bright with flowers.

★ **Delabole Quarry** ⊙ – *4 miles southeast by B3263 and by-roads.*
Delabole, a name synonymous with slate in Cornwall and once much furt afield, is the oldest continuously worked slate quarry in Europe; Beaker Folk (on Bodmin Moor in 2000 BC used slate as baking shelves. The quarry, one the largest **man-made holes** in the world, has a perimeter of 1¾ miles and is 50 deep – *viewing terrace.*

Showroom – Demonstrations of slate splitting and a display of the old tools or used in quarrying. Roofing slates are sized down from queens and duchess to mere ladies.
The village is made of slate – church, houses, walls, steps, sills, gates and post

★ **Camelford** – *6 miles southeast by B3263 and B3266. See Camelford.*

Port Isaac – *9 miles southwest by B3263, B3314 and by-roads.*
The ancient fishing village with narrow streets and alleys and a small, protec harbour, from which Delabole slate was once shipped, stands in a designa area of outstanding natural beauty : cliffs drop to the sea in an almost unbrol line, any break being occupied by minute hamlets such as **Port Gaverne** and **Portq**

★ TINTINHULL HOUSE GARDEN Somerset

Michelin Atlas p 8 or Map 403 - L31

The **house,** comprising the present east front with a cross wing at the south end and only one room deep, was built as a farmhouse *c*1600. In 1630 Thomas Napper rebuilt the south wing, completing the gable with an **initialled datestone;** nearly a century later his grandson increased and reversed the house to its present appearance with a new **west front** and a **walled forecourt** which he intended to be the formal entrance.
This 18C pedimented front in Bath stone, dignified by giant pilasters and with a corresponding pedimented doorway, nevertheless retains such 17C touches as stone mullions and transoms in some of the windows.
The two-acre **garden** ⊙ is so planned that borders, flowering and foliage trees, and shrubs and colour schemes can be viewed from a number of angles and so planted that there is something to enjoy in all seasons.
The individually enclosed, formal gardens are laid out in line with the west front : the **Eagle Court** (named after the birds on the piers marking the 18C forecourt), the **Azalea Garden,** and the **Fountain Garden** where white flowers stand starlike against outlining yew hedges.
Off the view line are a Cedar Lawn, Pool and Kitchen Gardens.
The planting is arranged so that colours contrast, are massed or shade from the darkest to the palest tone, texture is varied with flowers and foliage, outlines with climbers, trees and shrubs, the exotic and the everyday...

TIVERTON Devon — Pop 14 745

Michelin map fold 25 - J31

The town between Dartmoor and Exmoor, at the confluence of the Rivers Lowman and Exe, grew rich in the 13C-17C on **wool.** In Tudor times merchants settled in the town, added an aisle and chapel to the church, endowed schools and almshouses.
By the 18C, in Defoe's words, Tiverton had become "Next to Excester, the greatest manufactoring town in the county and, of all the inland towns, next to it in wealth and in the numbers of people" : there were 55 fulling mills, 700 woolcombers. In the 19C the population grew to 10 500 and **lacemaking,** brought by **John Heathcoat** *(qv)* from the Midlands, had become the major industry, as it remains today having diversified into net-making and modernized its manufacture.
From its earliest days the town was defended by a castle; the Perpendicular church and mid-Victorian St Paul's Square are visible signs of its continuing affluence.

SIGHTS

Tiverton Castle ⊙ - *North Hill; just north of the church.*
In the 12C Henry I created the Norman, Richard de Redvers, Earl of Devon and presented him with a great swathe of land on which to build a ring of defensive forts : Tiverton, Exeter, Plympton, Christchurch and Carisbrooke. In the Civil War Tiverton castle was first besieged and then slighted; at the Restoration it was purchased by a rich wool merchant.
The massive 14C red sandstone **gatehouse,** vaulted in white Caen stone, gives access to a large grassed courtyard bounded by the curtain walls and towers above the River Exe (60ft below). Several rooms in the gatehouse and round tower now contain Civil War arms and armoury, items relating to the history of the castle, a panel from the New World Tapestry and a collection of historic clocks.

St Peter's Church - The 99ft **tower** in pink sandstone with corner pinnacles dates from *c*1400, when the **chancel** of the 11C church was also renewed. In 1517, after the nave and aisles had long been completed, the merchant John Greenway enlarged the south aisle and added the **porch** and **chapel** in the fashionable late Perpendicular style with larger windows, ornamented castellations, crocketed pinnacles. The additions were in contrasting white stone and the chapel decorated with reliefs including a line of **armed merchantmen** such as shipped their woollen cloth from Devon and brought home wine and raw wool.

Museum ⊙ - *National Schools, St Andrew St.*
The local museum has a great wealth of material : early bicycles, copy-books from old schools, trade tokens, a set of model soldiers depicting the Devon regiments from 1685-1975, Victorian laundry equipment, and galleries on the canal *(see below)* and local industry.

Grand Western Canal - *Canal Hill. Continuation of Gold St-Station Rd.*
The system was intended to connect the Bristol and English Channels by way of a 30-mile canal from Taunton to Topsham on the River Exe, with a spur coming off the mainstream to Tiverton. Although the Taunton-Tiverton reach was opened in 1814, no further building was undertaken and, when the Bristol-Exeter railway opened in the 1830s, the canal traffic decreased until only locally quarried stone and limestone were carried in the horse-drawn narrowboats.
In the 1960s 11½ miles of the canal course were reclaimed and repaired, wide boats and horses were found. Now it is possible to walk along or fish from the towpath or glide in the brightly painted *Tivertonian* drawn by amiable shires.

Old Blundells School – *Station Rd.*
The school *(private)*, which stands back from the road, can be seen through a gateway above which is a tablet announcing its name and foundation in 160· by the local clothier, Peter Blundell. The building, intended for the education c local boys, is a long single-storey range in dark gold stone with a slate covere pitched roof on the crest of which rides a small, colonnaded clock turret. Twi gables, each with a rounded doorway arch, divide the range.
The drive from the gate in the outer wall divides to approach each doorwa creating before the house a grass triangle, the scene of the fight between Joh Ridd and Robin Snell in *Lorna Doone (qv)*. Blackmore himself was a pupil at th school.

EXCURSIONS

★★ **Coldharbour Mill, Uffculme** ⊙ – *11 miles east by A373; after passing ove M5 turn right at the T-junction and left to Uffculme; the mill is at the end c the village.*
The working wool and worsted mill museum stands between a fast-flowin stream and leat which have provided power for paper, grist and woollen mill on the site since possibly as long ago as Domesday. The last, a wool mill, whic had run for nearly 200 years, flourishing at a time when the industry was movin north, closed in 1981.
The mill produces cloth and knitting yarn on sample machines, enabling the visitc to watch each process of combing, drawing, spinning, reducing, twisting, war and weft winding and weaving.

★ **Knightshayes Court** – *2 miles north on A396, turn right at Bolham. Se Knightshayes Court.*

Bampton – *7 miles north on A396.*
The small town, with Georgian stone houses bedecked with flowers lining th main street, is the gateway to Exmoor *(qv)* and famous for its annual Octobe **Pony Fair.**

TOLPUDDLE Dorset — Pop 280

Michelin Atlas p 8 or Map 403 – N31 – 8 miles northeast of Dorchester

The village of Tolpuddle, its name now a symbol of workers' rights to form trade union, lies at the centre of Dorset's farming country. In 1830 an agricultur labourer's wage was 9s a week; in the next two years it dropped to 8*s* the 7*s*... The villagers met, according to tradition, under the now-named **Martyrs' Tre** to form the Friendly Society of Agricultural Labourers.
Fear of militant trade unionism and riots brought arrest of the six ring-leader their trial at the Crown Court in Dorchester *(qv)* and the sentence of seven yea transportation. The cause of the Six Martyrs, as they soon became known, wa taken up by Robert Owen, by Cobbett in the House, and at mass rallies, un in 1839 the men were granted a free pardon, though not before they had worke in Australia in penal settlements and Hammett had been "sold like a slave f £1". Hammett was, in fact, the only one to return to the village, where he die in 1891.

TUC Memorial Cottages and Museum ⊙ – *North side of A35 just befo west end of the village.*
The line of six cottages was erected in 1934; at the centre, below the midd of the gables, is the **Tolpuddle Martyrs' Museum.**
In the centre of the village *(just beyond the garage)* is the **cottage** of one of th men, Thomas Standfield *(plaque)*.

Methodist Chapel ⊙ – Five of the six martyrs were Methodists *(exhibition* The **arch** to the chapel bears the affirmation handed to the judge immediate before sentence was passed. An annual service of commemoration is held i July.

St John's Church – The parish church of flint with stone trims retair elements of earlier sanctuaries, despite remodelling in 1855 : a Perpenc cular tower, Norman doorways, late 13C chancel and transept arches, Decorated north arcade and a 14C **tie-beam roof** with struts and crow posts.
Earliest of all, in the north transept, is the carved Purbeck **marble coffin-lid** of Phili a priest of AD 1100.

★ TORBAY Devon — Pop 93 995

Michelin Atlas p 4 or Map 403 – J32 – Facilities
Town plan in the current Michelin Red Guide Great Britain and Ireland

Torquay, Paignton and Brixham all began as fishing villages. In the 17C and 18C the Fleet would lie up in the bay, and wives, the first tourists, would come to visit their sailor husbands. By the early 19C the population of Torquay had grown to 2 000 and when the railway came to the town in 1842, the town resolved to profit from the natural advantages of a mild climate, exotic palm-tree vegetation, sea views and wide sand beaches. Hotels, a promenade, a pier and a pavilion were built, public gardens were laid out to make the town the "Queen of English watering-places". By the turn of the century Torquay was famous and the resident population, working largely for the tourists, had increased to 25 000. Fifty years later Paignton followed Torquay's example.
Brixham has remained a fishing village at heart with trawlers in the harbour and a live fish market on the quay. Also on the quay is the statue of William III who landed upon it in 1688 on his way to take the crown from James II.
In Torquay and Paignton – which market themselves as "The English Riviera" – the houses extend up the hill behind the shore; large pale Victorian and Edwardian hotels and villas set in lush gardens are now being replaced by modern apartment blocks and high-rise hotels, white by day, a spangle of lights by night.
In Brixham the brightly coloured fishermen's cottages and small houses, some dating back to the late 17C, wind their way uphill overlooking the harbour.

Ferry ⏲ – A ferry runs throughout the summer between Torquay and Brixham, providing a good view of the modern resort area curving round the bay.

TORQUAY

★ **Kents Cavern** ⏲ – *Wellswood, Ilsham Rd (right off Babbacombe Rd, B3199).*
The limestone caves run back 180yds into the hill. Excavations in the last two centuries have shown that they were inhabited by large prehistoric animals, by animals such as bears and hyenas and by humans for long periods from the Paleolithic era, 100 000 years ago, to Roman times.
The **tour** (½ mile) leads through galleries with rugged roofs and walls and contrasting chambers with beautiful crystal white, red-brown and green frozen water, pagoda and organ pipe **formations,** past **stalactites** and **stalagmites** – one 54ins tall is estimated to have been growing for over 50 000 years.

Torre Abbey ⏲ – *Torbay Rd.* The "Abbey", set in luxuriant gardens, consists of an 18C house, the so-called Spanish Barn and medieval abbey ruins.
The ivy-clad house, now a **local museum,** contains collections of **English pewter,** 18C-19C **glass** – wine-glasses, Nailsea flash glass *(qv),* old bottles, paperweights, jugs, and engraved and cut crystal – marine and topographical paintings, a rare set of proof copies of **William Blake's** illustrations for the *Book of Job,* and historical *tableaux* with costumed figures.
The **tithe barn**★ or "Spanish Barn", its great length (124ft) massively buttressed, dates from 1196; the 12 ribs of its original oak roof were increased to 17 during restoration in the 1930s. Its name dates from 1588 when the flagship of the Andalusian squadron of the Spanish Armada, *Nuestra Señora del Rosario,* was captured by Drake in Torbay and the 397 crew were imprisoned in the barn.
The **abbey** was unusually prosperous with an annual income of £396 (multiply by at least 30) when it was suppressed in 1539. It had been founded in 1196, in fulfilment of a vow made for the safe return of his son by William de Briwer, the lord of the manor and a justiciar in Richard Lionheart's absence on the Third Crusade. On the king's capture, de Briwer set out to raise the 150 000 marks demanded in ransom; he found 70 000, which were sent to Austria together with 67 hostages of whom one was his son. In the event the Austrian captor was fatally injured and, on his deathbed, released his royal prisoner without benefit of the ransom.
At the Dissolution the church was razed and the pink sandstone was incorporated in the "big house". Round the cloister garth are the ruins of the medieval **church** (168ft long) with undercrofts below, the **abbot's tower** and apartments, and the impressive east **wall** pierced by the entrance to the sacristy and chapter-house *(see also Cockington below).* The 14C **gatehouse** is better preserved because it was not slighted.

Babbacombe Model Village ⏲ – *off Babbacombe Rd, B3199.*
Minutely manicured gardens planted with bright flowers, dwarf conifers and bonsai trees form the backdrop to numerous miniature re-creations of scenes from English life, including weddings, bank robberies and car breakdowns, with appropriate sound effects : villages of thatched cottages, mineral oil drilling, waterskiing on the lake, a typical High Street...

PAIGNTON

★★ **Paignton Zoo** ⏲ – *½ mile west along A385.* The comprehensive collection of **wild animals** and a luxuriant **botanical garden** extend over 75 acres with wide paths and lawns shaded by tropical trees.
There are elephants, lions and tigers and a wolf, rhinoceroses and owls, penguins and giraffes, flamingos and porcupines, monkeys and orang-utans, camels, cranes, zebras, tortoises, reptiles and fish, exotic birds in the sub-tropical house and even a **miniature railway** (10¼in gauge) providing rides round the lake.

Oldway Mansion and Gardens ⏲ – *Torquay Rd.* The vast, Classical mansion (now council offices) with a giant portico, tall Georgian-style windows and balustraded terraces overlooking formal parterre **gardens** was built by the American sewing-machine magnate **Isaac Singer** (1811-75) when he retired to

Torquay in 1854. Inside, beyond displays on the mansion's history, is the imposing **hall** with its staircase rising to a gallery, heavily decorated with marble and *faux* marble, an Italianate painted ceiling, and squat brass balusters, oddly angled up the stairs.

Paignton Parish Church ⊙ – *Church St. Opposite Hyde Rd across Torquay Rd.* The Perpendicular church (1450-1500) of dark red sandstone, with a very tall landmark-style **tower** with pinnacles, stands amid houses all of the same colour. Inside, the **Kirkham Chantry Chapel,** with 15C-17C family tombs, is separated from the nave by a fine **stone screen** (mutilated at the Reformation).
Note, in the nave, the Norman sandstone **font** with honeysuckle decoration, the mutilated pre-Reformation **stone pulpit** and the **dog door** complete with latch *(north door).*

Paignton and Dartmouth Steam Railway ⊙ – *Queen's Park Station. For map see Dartmouth.* Steam locomotives provide a service on the former British Rail line (standard gauge) via Goodrington Stands to Kingswear *(6¾ miles – ferry to Dartmouth).* It is both an efficient and nostalgic ride with the old Victorian cast-iron furniture on the platforms, and the drivers and porters in period uniform.

BRIXHAM

★ **Berry Head** – *Car park on the south side of the headland.* An extensive **view**★★★ is visible from the headland. A **viewing table** announces "from this point 190ft above sea-level about 800 sq miles of sea are visible" and identifies every landmark round the sweep of Lyme Bay to Portland Bill *(42 miles east).* The headland attracts many seabirds – guillemots, kittiwakes and fulmars *(listed on notice board in car park).* There have been lookouts and fortifications on the headland since the Iron Age. The most obvious are the forts built in 1803; Napoleon never put them to the test but he did put in to Tor Bay on board the *Bellerophon* in 1815 on his way into exile on St Helena. The strange-looking modern construction is an aircraft navigational beacon.

EXCURSIONS

★ **Cockington** – *1 mile west from Torbay Rd along Cockington Lane.* The village is pure picture-postcard with all the **cottages** thatched above red sandstone or white-washed walls, an ancient (now modernized) **forge,** a mill pond, an inn, the Drum – a period pub by Sir Edwin Lutyens – and horse-drawn, open carriages plying between the village and the sea front.

Cockington Court ⊙ – The Classical 19C house, surrounded by 270 acres of wooded parkland and gardens full of rhododendrons, azaleas and camellias, contains the **Devon Rural Skills Trust.** Here the traditional rural skills are kept alive and demonstrated to visitors : wood turning, wheelwrighting, rush and cane seating, hurdlemaking, drystone walling, stained glass, patchwork...
The **parish church,** which dates from 1196, was given a tower when it was acquired by Torre Abbey *(see above)* in 1236. Note the 15C rood-screen, the old wicket door with its sanctuary ring *(qv),* the 15C font and the pulpit from Torre Abbey.

Compton Castle – *3 miles west. See Compton Castle.*

Berry Pomeroy Castle ⊙ – *5 miles west via by-roads; turn before Berry Pomeroy village.* The castle, erected soon after the Norman Conquest, is reputedly the most haunted in Devon. The remains of the medieval castle and of the 16C mansion have been falling into romantic ruin amid their verdant surroundings ever since the last Seymour left in 1703.

★ TOTNES Devon

Pop 6 133

Michelin Atlas p 4 or Map 403 – I, J32 – Facilities

The narrow main street at the centre of the town rises steeply between two and three-storey houses, half-timbered, Georgian or 19C, built of brick or stone, slate-hung, or colour-washed. It is divided into Fore Street and High Street by **East Gate,** also known as the Arch, a much-altered gateway dating back to Tudor times when Totnes was a walled town; the gate gives access to the old ramparts.

East Gate, Totnes.

SIGHTS

Start from the Bridge over the River Dart at the east end of the town (A385). Car park across the bridge, left, then right.

Bridge – The bridge, rebuilt in 1828, marks the tidal and navigable limit of the Dart. The quay below is still active.

Totnes Motor Museum ⊙ – *Steamer Quay.* The cars, motor-cycles and even the pedal and the motorised cycles, housed on two floors in the old cider warehouse, are all in working order and "exercised" at races, rallies and shows. Among the cars on display are an Austin 7, Talbot Martins, Voisins, Aston-Martins and Alfa-Romeos.

The Plains – *Sharp left on the town side. The open square is marked by an* **obelisk** in honour of **William John Wills,** native of Totnes, who was a member of the first party to cross the Australian continent in 1860. On one corner is an old coaching inn, the Royal Seven Stars, built in 1660.

Fore Street – The houses which line the street include **The Mansion** *(left)* in dark red brick, refronted in the 18C, which was originally the **King Edward VI Grammar School,** founded under royal charter in 1153; a late 18C Gothick house *(left in Bank Lane);* a 17C house (no 48), a 16C house with an oversailing upper floor (no 52) and, close by, the grandest Tudor house in the town, now a museum.

Totnes Elizabethan Museum ⊙ – *70 Fore St.* The museum displays items of local life from flint weapons to Great Western Railway bygones, 15C, Elizabethan and Jacobean furniture, Victoriana and a turn-of-the-century grocer's shop. One room is devoted to **Charles Babbage** (1791-1871), a mathematical genius, who was educated at the Grammar School; he designed the first computer, a cypher-breaking machine, a forerunner of the black box and an analytical machine using punched cards.
The most remarkable exhibit is the house itself, a rich Tudor **merchant's house** built *c*1575 when Totnes was enjoying the prosperity derived from the wool and cloth trade which had developed since the Middle Ages. The house has four floors with a half-timbered, jettied first floor, broad windows and a full-width gable pierced by the windows of the topmost small bedrooms. Inside the house note the **height** and lightness of the main rooms, the **timbering,** the unevenly-wide **floorboards,** 16C **fireplaces** and the number of small **closets** and corners, all now used for exhibits.

Continue up Fore St; just beyond the Arch turn right up a flight of steps.

Rampart Walk – The cobbled path of the old ramparts leads past cottages fronted with magnificent displays of flowers in tubs, troughs and pots.

Guildhall ⊙ – The hall's origins date from the 11C when it was part of a Benedictine Priory building until the Dissolution. It then became a cloth merchant's hall and finally the Guildhall with a council chamber, courtroom and mayor's parlour.
Among the exhibits relating to the town's history are Saxon coins pressed in the town mint in the reign of Edgar (958-75) and the cells of the town gaol.

Return to the main street, now the High St.

★ **St Mary's** – The parish and priory church, which dates from the 15C, has a massive tower built of red sandstone quarried at Duncannon adorned with gruesome gargoyles.

Pulpit – The pale stone pulpit (1460) was for centuries enclosed in mahogany cladding, hence its near-pristine condition.

Rood screen – The outstanding feature is the once coloured, now white, Beer stone rood screen of 1459 which, with paired lights, carved mullions, arched panels below, cusped tracery and fan coving above, extends across the full width of the church. Before the screen hangs an elegant **chandelier** (1701).
Note, halfway down the aisle, the 1636 Corporation pews.

Monuments – In the southeast chapel lies the **tomb** of Walter Smythe (d 1555), founder of Totnes Grammar School; against the north nave wall, the **memorial** to Christopher Blackhall (d 1633), seen kneeling at prayer above his four wives; against the west wall of the 19C north aisle, the large **terracotta plaque** to Walter Venning, born in Totnes in 1781, who became a London merchant and was the founder of the Prison Society of Russia where he himself died of gaol fever in 1821.

No 16 High St – The house, now a bank, was built in 1585 by a salted-pilchard merchant, Nicholas Ball (note the initials on the front). After his death in 1586 his widow married a second wealthy man, **Thomas Bodley** of Exeter, scholar, diplomat and founder of the Bodleian Library, Oxford.

Civic Hall – The modern hall has a large open forecourt on which, in summer, a pannier market is held, when Tudor fare is offered by sellers in Elizabethan costume.

★ **Butterwalk** – The granite pillared walk has protected shoppers from the rain since the 17C.

Devonshire Collection of Period Costume ⊙ – *Bogan House, 43 High St.* The old Tudor merchant's house, which has features from the Elizabethan to Georgian periods, makes a complementary setting for dramatic, changing displays of costume from the years 1740 to 1960. The collection includes meticulous details, from pressed pin tucks to accessories and underclothes.

Castle ⊙ – The castle walls command excellent **views**★★★ of the Dart River Valley, upstream towards Dartmoor where the high tors rise one behind the other and downstream along the line of the estuary towards Dartmouth *(qv).*
The ramparts which encircle the central mound are 14C, a rebuilding and strengthening in stone of the motte and bailey earthwork raised in the early 12C.

EXCURSIONS

★ **British Photographic Museum, Bowden House** – *½ mile southwest by A381; turn left (signposted).*
The purpose-built museum with small cinema (films shown) stands beyond a house with a handsome Queen Anne exterior, on the site of the old stableblock. It includes period reconstructions (Victorian studio, Edwardian darkroom) though the bulk is the enormous collection of cameras; the Exhibition Room alone contains over 400 Kodak cameras beneath changing photographic displays. Upstairs, every showcase is crammed with cameras and relevant paraphernalia ranging from the very earliest to the most modern, and features the big names in photographic equipment : Gandolfi, Leica, Ensign, Zeiss Ikon, Ilford, Agfa and many others.
The development of photography and cinematography is traced from the early ether, petrol or gas powered projectors and driers, mahogany plate cameras with brass fittings (1880s and '90s), box Brownies, a camera gun, coloured cameras (1930s), Bakelite models... There are press cameras, flash guns, miniature cameras, single and twin lens reflex cameras, more modest magic lanterns, cartoons and early hand-tinted photographs.

South Devon Railway – *See Buckfastleigh.*

Dartington – *2 miles northwest by A385 and A384. See Dartington.*

River Dart Boat Trips – *See Dartmouth.*

Berry Pomeroy Castle – *4 miles northeast by A381 and a by-road. See Berry Pomeroy.*

★★ TRELISSICK GARDEN Cornwall

Michelin Atlas p 2 or Map 403 – E33

The Classical, giant-porticoed, house (1825) set within **Trelissick Garden** ⏲ stands on a high promontory, superbly overlooking, and clearly visible from, the Carrick Roads *(qv)*. A walk around the house offers superb **views**★★ over the lush undulating countryside towards Falmouth and the open sea.
There are three gardens at Trelissick, surrounded by fine woodlands : the **Flower Garden;** the **East Lawn Garden,** where azaleas, rhododendrons and hydrangeas bloom luxuriantly in season and the beech tree trunks frame glimpses of the Roads; the woodland **Valley Garden,** which drops down towards the Fal (both sides of the road) with tall trees underplanted with foliage, exotics, bulbs, wood anemones and primulas.

★★ TRENGWAINTON GARDEN Cornwall

Michelin Atlas p 2 or Map 403 – D33 – 2 miles northwest of Penzance

The garden lies along the half mile drive to the house which is covered in wistaria and the New Zealand scarlet lobster claw plant. Beyond is a second garden of island beds of azaleas and rhododendrons, from which there is a **view**★★ of Mount's Bay.
An early owner, Sir Rose Price, who was a great tree planter, built the walled gardens to the right of the drive with beds banked up to face the sun, to produce early fruit and vegetables.
In the early 20C, with the owners of Trewithen *(qv)* and Hidcote in Gloucestershire, Sir Edward Bolitho financed Kingdon Ward's plant collecting expedition s of 1927-28 to bring back specimens from Burma, Assam and China from which the rhododendron and azalea collections have since been built up and hybridised. All the important and unusual plantings are fully labelled for easy identification.

GARDEN ⏲

A mass of rhododendron bushes, with blooms ranging from magenta to pale yellow to pure white, line the drive; overtopping them are the first of many tree ferns from Australia.

Stream Garden in spring, Trengwainton.

Two paths branch off the drive. The left-hand one makes for a stream and glades of rhododendrons beneath the trees, which include a maidenhair and the beautiful white ladies' handkerchief or *Davidia involucrata.* The right-hand path enters the series of five walled gardens, now particularly rich in tender magnolias – pink flushed, dark purple, narrow white, saucer-large and fragrant – besides a host of other flowering trees such as a Tasmanian cider gum, the small white flowered New Zealand tea, the Canary bird, the scarlet lobster claw, the passion flower, acacias, rhododendrons, camellias, fuchsias...

Beside the drive, the gurgling stream garden includes primulas, astilbes and wax-white arum lilies in front of a magnolia stellata, a tulip tree...

★ TRERICE Cornwall

Michelin map fold 32 – E32

The small, silver-grey, stone **manor house** stands in a wooded valley, framed by the walls and yew hedges of its flower gardens.

The house was rebuilt in 1572-73 to an E shaped plan with, on the east front, highly decorative scrolled gables and a hall with a beautiful window, stone mullioned and transomed with twenty-four lights and 576 small panes of 16C glass.

TOUR ⏲ *45min*

The interior is particularly notable for 16C **plasterwork.**

Great Hall – The fine **ceiling** which is ribbed and pendented, the scrolled **overmantel** and the miniature **arcade** which fronts the musicians' gallery demonstrate the plasterers' skill. Note also, from inside, the **great window** and among the furniture, a 20ft table made of oak from the estate in 19C, the mid-16C chest, late 17C travelling desk and 18C oak travelling case beneath an Aubusson tapestry.

Library – The library, with a faded green 19C Donegal carpet, is furnished with 18C-19C mahogany and walnut pieces among which are a domed **coffer** and a chiming, long-case **clock.**

Drawing Room – The room, the former solar, is also decorated with outstanding **plasterwork,** notably a barrel roof, with the family arms high on the wall at one end, and a decorated overmantel on telamons, dated with hybridised numerals.

Musicians' Gallery – The gallery offers an overview of the hall and a closer look at the plasterwork ceiling.

Court Chamber – Among the 17C-18C walnut furniture is a double dome **secretaire-bookcase.** Note also the long-case **clock** by Thomas Tompion (*c*1680).

North Chamber – The Georgian **mahogany furniture** is highlighted by a four-poster with clustered columns and a painted cornice. The ebonised bracket clock is by Joseph Knibb (1650-1711).

Lobby – The lobby contains a second Tompion long-case clock.

Mower Museum – In the barn is a collection of mowers which traces their development since the early 19C.

★★ TREWITHEN Cornwall

Michelin map fold 32 – F33

Trewithen is famous for the beautiful landscaping of its 20 acre garden.

GARDEN ⏲

Already in 1730 the ancestor of the present owners was reported as having "much improved the seat, new built a great part of the house, made good gardens". His successor planted trees to such good effect that, by 1904, a descendant decided "it was necessary to take an axe and claim air and light from amongst the trees, first for the house and those that should live in it and then for the plants". In 1905 there arrived 100 hybrids of *rhododendron arboretum* – precursors of the present 50 or more different varieties of rhododendron, 30 of camellia, 40 of magnolia, which give the garden its especial beauty. Planted in great bays at the edge of a lawn to frame a **vista,** beneath the trees, in alleys and dips, contrasting with the dark red feathered leaves of *acer palmatum atropurpureum,* they present an ever-changing billow of colour, a waxen stillness, a waving of white or pink against the sky... Of specialist interest are the **house hybrids** : rhododendron Trewithen Orange, Alison Johnstone, Jack Skilton, Elizabeth, camellia Trewithen pink, Glenn's Orbit and Donation.

HOUSE ⏲ *½ hour*

The 18C country house has all the classic features of proportion and panelling; the period furniture includes several lovely smaller pieces; in addition to portraits and paintings are Bristol glass, Chinese small bronzes and porcelain – notably blue and white ware – a collection of Japanese great plates and a collection of clocks.

TROWBRIDGE Wiltshire

Pop 27 299

Michelin Atlas p 17 or Map 403 - N30

Trowbridge, long established as a major wool and cloth town, became the county town only when the 1888 Local Government Act required councillors to be elected and it was found that Trowbridge, being on the railway, was accessible and convenient. Since the decline of the cloth trade it has turned to brewing and the manufacture of dairy products, bacon, pies, sausages and yogurt, in some cases, in the old mills. The earlier prosperity funded the multitude of 19C Nonconformist chapels and schools, the workers' terraced houses and Georgian houses.

TRURO Cornwall

Pop 17 852

Michelin Atlas p 2 or Map 403 - E33

In 1859 Truro seized the opportunity, rejected by Bodmin *(qv)*, of bringing the railway into the centre of the town.
By the 18C-19C Truro, once a river port, mining centre and stannary town *(qv)*, was known as the county "metropolis" with a theatre, assembly rooms, county library (1792), horticultural society, the Royal Institution of Cornwall and the cathedral (1850); it had developed into the most notable Georgian town west of Bath with 18C houses in Boscawen, Lemon and other streets. In 1980 the new County Court, designed by Evans and Shalev, was declared Building of the Year by the *Architects' Journal*.

SIGHTS

Truro Cathedral – Requests made over the centuries for Cornwall once more to become an independent see *(qv)* were finally acceded to and in 1850 the cathedral foundation stone was laid. Bishop Benson sought a church "exceeding magnifical", rural parishioners wanted "a proper job", the architect J-L Pearson, steeped in the last of Gothic Revivalism, proposed a "house of prayer" in the 13C Early English style. The approved design, an admixture of Normandy Gothic with upswept vaulting, space and vistas through tall arcades and, outside, three steeple towers which give the cathedral its characteristic outline, was completed by 1910.

★ **Royal Cornwall Museum** ⏲ – *River St.* The museum is the learned and colourful showplace of the Royal Institution of Cornwall (f 1818) with displays of English ceramics complementing an exhibit on **William Cookworthy** *(qv)*. There are also English pewter, **silver spoons** made in Truro in the 17C, works by **John Opie** (1761-1807), the "Cornish Wonder", the son of a St Agnes mine carpenter who found fame with his portraits, and a display on decorative arts.
The archeological department displays early Bronze Age **gold collars** and other objects made of Cornish and Irish gold, a fragment of a bronze dagger probably imported from Greece *c*1200 BC and Roman gold coins found in south coast harbours.
The tin and copper mining tools exhibit retraces the early streaming, or panning, done from *c*2000 BC for alluvial deposits, to the opencast mining of the Middle Ages and, finally, underground working. A 1C BC **tin ingot,** shaped in a knuckle or H form and weighing nearly 160lbs, found in the River Fal, is visible evidence of the age of the mining industry *(qv)*.

EXCURSIONS

★★★ **Trewithen** – *3 miles northeast by A39, A390. See Trewithen.*

★★ **Trelissick** – *8 miles south by A39 and B3289. Turn right at Four Turnings. Local map p 52.*

Come-to-Good – Come-to-Good, which appears from outside to be just a whitewashed, thatched cottage with linhay stables under the same roof, is a Quaker Meeting House. Built in 1710, it measures 27ft long by 20ft wide, cost £68 18*s* 3*d* to construct and is still in use.

Feock – The **church★**, standing above the village which overlooks the Carrick Roads, is distinguished by having a separate west **tower belfry** with a pyramid roof dating from the 13C. The church is 15C, restored in the 19C. Note the carved Catacleuse **font.**

★★ **Trelissick** – *See Trelissick.*

King Harry Ferry ⏲ – How the ferry, which has an 18ft tide rise and fall and is now a chain ferry, got its name and how long it has been operating across the picturesque valley no one knows, though the old **Ferry Boat Inn** on the bank is clearly several centuries old.

★★ **St Just-in-Roseland Church** – *23 miles south first by A39 east, then by A3078. Local map p 52.*
The church stands in the most perfect setting imaginable. The path leads steeply down from the lichgate, through the churchyard garden of rhododendrons, brooms, fuchsias, hydrangeas and a strawberry tree, to the church which stands so close to the creek that at high tide its mirror image is reflected in the water. The sanctuary, on a 6C Celtic site, is partly 13C, largely 15C but suffered a fierce restoration in the 19C.

Continue south to St Mawes.

★ **St Mawes** – *See St Mawes.*

St Anthony-in-Roseland – The forked peninsula between the Carrick Roads and the open sea is known as Roseland, meaning promontory. The headland points are marked respectively by St Mawes Castle *(qv)* and the lighthouse *(qv)* on St Anthony Head, from which the **view★★** extends up the Carrick Roads and, on a clear day, northeast towards Dartmoor.

★ **Veryan** – *13 miles southeast first by A39 east and then by A3078.*
The small village boasts five curious little white-walled **round houses** with Gothick windows and a conical thatched roof surmounted by a cross.

★ **Probus** – *9 miles northeast by A39 and A390.*
The granite church **tower★** (125ft 10in) is the tallest in Cornwall. Dating from 1523, it rises through three stages of niches, fenestration, carved string courses and gargoyles to a castellated crest complete with pinnacles. In the lofty interior, note the **tower screen** with its alphabet from the time when the room was used as a school, the royal arms of 1685, the two-figures **brass** of 1514 *(aisle, under the red carpet).*
The **County Demonstration Garden★** ⊙ is full of ideas and information for well-established and new gardens. Within its 54 different sections it displays shrubs, flowers, plants for shady and exposed positions, ornamental trees, herbs, hydrangeas in acid and alkaline soils, garden design for small spaces, vegetable growing...

Follow A390 to Grampound.

Grampound – The town, which boasts a high cross (12ft) in the market place, was once a parliamentary borough. In 1620 it returned John Hampden as its MP. In the 18C-19C it was a by-word for corruption : bribery was so rife that in 1821, eleven years before the Reform Act, Grampound was disenfranchised by special act of parliament.

UGBROOKE HOUSE Devon

Michelin Atlas p 4 or Map 403 – J32 – ½ mile east of Chudleigh

In 1750 the 4th Lord Clifford of Chudleigh employed Robert Adam to redesign the E-shaped Tudor manor house on the site and "Capability" Brown to design the park through which flowed the brook that gave the house its name. Adam demolished one wing and used the material to connect the other two around a courtyard, and added the solid, castellated towers at the angles.
The entrance is reached through an archway into the courtyard.

TOUR ⊙ *1¼ hours*

Entrance Hall – The small hall with an Adam cornice contains fine Brussels **tapestries** of *Romulus and Remus* – a present from Cosimo III of Tuscany to the 1st Lord Clifford in 1669 – and a tapestry by Francis Poyntz of Hatton Garden, London.

Staircase Hall – The domed hall has the christening present given by Charles II to his godson the 2nd Lord Clifford in 1671 : a magnificent **silver gilt ewer and salver.** Family portraits adorn the walls and an Epstein bronze bust of Lord Fisher of Kiverstone (grandfather of the present Lady Clifford) sits at the top.

Morning Room – This room was the site of the original Tudor entrance hall. It now contains family portraits, a fine William and Mary walnut **writing desk** (*c*1700), an 18C **breakfront bookcase** made (by Gillows of Lancaster) to a design by Chippendale. The Adam cornice includes a dragon and a lion (family crests). The Wilton carpet was made to a Persian design for the American magnate William Hearst and later bought by Lord Clifford.

Drawing Room – The room contains a notable collection of **portraits by Lely** and a portrait of Catherine of Braganza, by Huysman, in which the sitter is shown wearing the diamond earrings she later gave to her goddaughter Catherine Clifford. The very fine **Elizabethan tapestry** (now in three sections) with its rich colouring and vivid detail was rediscovered after centuries in store. The furniture includes a Georgian games table, a French Boulle table, a William and Mary cabinet (1685), a pair of Adam semicircular tables and a Victorian centre table with marquetry flowers.

Dining Room – The Adam room was originally hung with gold and silk damask. The Chinese armorial **porcelain dinner service** (*c*1740) on the mahogany Georgian **dining table** was a coming of age present for the 4th Lord Clifford. Other items include a fine George III mahogany spirit box (*c*1790) with its original bottles and glasses, and pieces of Worcester ware on the mantelpiece.

Cardinal's Room – Thomas Weld was a widower with one daughter when he decided to enter the Church; he subsequently became a bishop and then a cardinal. The room has various vestments, a patchwork bedspread (*c*1820) stitched by his daughter who married the 7th Lord Clifford, and an early 18C travelling medicine chest in laburnum veneer.

Tapestry Room – Adorning the walls are two Francis Poyntz **tapestries** (1670-71) after Raphael cartoons in the Victoria and Albert Museum; they were probably made for the chapel. The **George III bed** is hung with silk **embroidered hangings** from *c*1720. The tepoy is one of only six made commemorating the death of Lord Nelson.

Additional Rooms – Beyond the passages (coronation robes, 18C clothes etc) is the Victorian conservatory which leads to the oldest part of the house. Here the library and anterooms contain military uniforms, and matter relating to the **Secret Treaty of Dover** (*c*1670) which gave rise to the word "cabal" from the ministers who were in league with Charles II to unite with the French against the Austrians : Clifford, Arlington, Buckingham, Ashley and Lauderdale.

Chapel – The present chapel was designed by Adam in 1760; the Lady Chapel is a Victorian addition.

GARDEN ⏲

Amid the rolling parkland and woodland may be found formal designs, herbaceous borders, informal plantings and the three lakes which were created by Capability Brown by damming the Ug.
A Pets Corner includes sheep, rabbits and goats, and elsewhere beautiful species of pheasant (Golden, Silver, Lady Amherst) scratch in large pens.

★ WARDOUR CASTLE Wiltshire

Michelin Atlas p 8 or Map 403 – N30

The old castle stands on a spur, sheltered on three sides by wooded hills looking out west across a lake known as the Fish Pond. In May-June the lawns, where once the inner bailey was, are vividly outlined by rhododendrons.
The tower house, rock-like in its mass, hexagonal in form with corbel turrets marking the angles and a front advanced squarely as twin bastions to guard the entrance, has been falling into romantic ruin since the Civil War – its heroic hour.
The castle, a royal manor in King Alfred's reign, a Benedictine property from Domesday to the Dissolution, was purchased in 1547 by Sir Thomas Arundell. In the Civil War the castle's defences were put to the test : the Arundells were Royalists and in 1643, when Lord Arundell was at Oxford with the king, a Parliamentary force of 1 300 men laid siege to the castle which had a garrison of 25. On its surrender the house was looted, the contents sold, the park plundered. In 1644 the 3rd Lord Arundell besieged the place in his turn and again, after mining had wreaked further damage, the garrison surrendered.
In 1769-77 the then Lord Arundell commissioned the architect James Paine to build what turned out to be the largest Georgian mansion in the country. The stone house, **New Wardour Castle** *(private)*, has a circular, marble-floored hall, from which twin cantilevered staircases rise round the walls to a gallery ringed by Corinthian columns.

CASTLE ⏲

The ruins are those of a 15C-16C fortified tower house, built with accommodation for domestic living and lavish entertainment.
The house was constructed around a hexagonal courtyard. The Great Hall above the gateway had the chapel, solar and lord's chambers on one side and the screens passage, service rooms and kitchens on the other. The remaining rooms were guests' lodgings which were approached by spiral staircases built into the walls.
The 16C Renaissance entrance is decorated with the Arundell arms and a bust of Christ in a niche. Just inside the courtyard *(left)* are the stone stairs to the Great Hall, beautifully framed by a **Grand Entrance,** lion decorated, Tuscan pillared and with a contrasting, plain entablature.
In the gardens, note the ornate grotto and the Gothic pavilion.

★ WAREHAM Dorset

Pop 2 771

Michelin Atlas p 8 or Map 403 – N31 – Facilities

The attractive town is distinguished by its long main street which runs north-south from the River Piddle to the Frome and is lined by tightly packed Georgian and Victorian houses, most with shops below. Most earlier buildings were destroyed in 1762 when fire engulfed 133 houses in the town centre. In the 9C and 10C Wareham was often fired by the **Danes** as they retreated after making incursions inland from the port; **Canute,** who mounted his invasion of southern England in 1015 through Wareham, also fired the town. From the 10C Wareham was enclosed, except on the south side, by an earth rampart, pierced by three gates and later surmounted by a stone wall which was demolished by the Parliamentarians; these Saxon defences make an interesting **walk** *(½ hour).*
The town's prosperity, based on trade in wine, fruit, olive oil, wool and woollen cloth, cereals and foodstuffs, which developed in the Norman period, was marred in the 17C first by the Civil War, when the town changed hands a number of times, and then by the arrival of Judge Jeffreys *(qv)* to scourge those who had supported Monmouth in his Rebellion. By the 18C, when the fire occurred, trade was in decline as Poole Harbour and the River Frome had silted up, making Wareham inaccessible to shipping.

SIGHTS

★★ **St Martin's** – The church at the north end of the High Street appears as the epitome of an Anglo-Saxon church. It dates from *c*1030, the Danes having destroyed an earlier church which, if legend is to be believed, was built by St Aldhelm *(qv)* in AD 678.

Traces of **Anglo-Saxon building** remain in the "long and short" work in the external angles at the east end of the nave and chancel, the nucleus of the 11C church.

The **chancel arch** was rebuilt, the **north aisle** added by the Normans, the arcade rebuilt in the 13C, the south wall pierced and the elegant **window** inserted in the 14C; finally, in the 16C, although some hold that it dates from the 11C-12C, the **tower** was erected with its saddleback roof and round doorway. Decorating the walls are 11C-18C **paintings** *(timer switch)*, faint, faded, clear and indistinct by turns, of St Martin dividing his cloak, the arms of Queen Anne superimposed over those of Charles II, the Commandments... In the north aisle lies the posthumous marble effigy by **Eric Kennington** of Lawrence of Arabia *(qv)* in his desert robes, his hand on his dagger.

High Street – Three buildings in particular mark the street : the square **Red Lion Hotel** at the crossroads, typical of the rebuilding in brick after the 1762 fire; the **Manor House** (1712) in Purbeck stone which escaped the fire; and the **Black Bear** (*c*1800) with bow windows and a columned porch supporting its emblematic black bear.

Quay – The quay, where pleasure-craft now tie up, is lined to the east by an ancient russet-red brick **granary,** three storeys high (restaurant), and an adjoining **18C house** also of brick with tablet stones above the windows.

Local History Museum ⓥ – The collection includes a number of cuttings and photographs on T E Lawrence *(qv)* and his motor-cycles, notably the Broughs.

Lady St Mary Church – Rising behind the buildings at the east end of the quay is the battlemented tower of the parish church.

Adjoining it was one of England's oldest priories, a Benedictine nunnery reformed by St Aldhelm in the late 7C, destroyed by the Danes in 876, rebuilt by one of King Alfred's sisters in 915 and sacked by Canute in 1015. It was again rebuilt, only to be dissolved in the 16C (now a hotel).

The foundation of the church went back equally far, the first being built before AD 700. The erection of the second on the churchyard of the first resulted in the unearthing of the uniquely **engraved stones** of 6C-7C pre-Saxon, British chieftains and landholders *(north aisle)*.

This second church, unlike the priory, was not sacked by the Danes and survived more than 1 000 years as one of the largest and most magnificent **Saxon churches** in the land until 1842 when it was substantially rebuilt "on the grounds that the oratorical qualities of the then rector deserved a better setting"...

Interior – In the nave on a 13C Purbeck marble pedestal stands a very fine, late 12C **lead font,** one of only 29 surviving in England and unique in being hexagonal; in the aisle is the stone coffin traditionally associated with the murdered King Edward *(qv)*. In the chancel there are examples of bar tracery (12C-13C) to the north, reticulated (13C-14C) to the east. Among the memorials are **brasses** *(south wall)* and two 13C knights in chain mail and surcoats with crossed legs.

EXCURSIONS

★ **Corfe Castle** – *5 miles southeast by A351. See Corfe Castle.*

★ **Blue Pool** ⓥ – *3 miles south on A351 and right (west) at signpost.*

The heavenly blue-green lake (3 acres) is fringed by silver birch and pine woods and a circular path *(1 mile; 45min)*. The colour comes from the diffraction of light on minute particles of clay suspended in the water (36ft deep) which flooded in when the open-cast mine ceased production in 1880.

The **museum** explains the extraction of clay and its uses; tools, porcelain, pipes and pipe hair curlers used by wig makers in the 18C.

★ **Bovington** – *7 miles west on A352; after 6½ miles bear right and then second left.*

★ **Bovington Camp Tank Museum** ⓥ – The 140 and more tanks, massive, darkly camouflaged ironclads, which make up the museum, afford a crowded panorama of the historical and technical development of armoured fighting vehicles from 1915 to the mid-1970s.

The ranks of tanks on display include British, American, French, Russian, German, Japanese, South African, Italian and Swedish machines. In the adjoining Allan Jolly Hall are armoured cars, airborne light tanks and guided missiles and in odd corners and on the walls, souvenirs from the field, maps and field orders, models, insignia and battle honours, a T E Lawrence *(qv)* room and a costume exhibition featuring the Army Wife.

Return to the T-junction; turn right and right again.

★ **Woolbridge Manor** *(private)*, a three-storeyed house with a brick front and projecting porch, dates from the 17C when it was owned by the Turbervilles. As **Wellbridge Manor** it appears in *Tess of the d'Urbervilles* by Thomas Hardy as the setting for the ill-fated wedding night of Tess and Angel Clare. Beyond it the road crosses a medieval **packhorse bridge** with pointed cutwaters which rise to the parapet as pedestrian refuges.

Lulworth Cove.

★ **Lulworth Cove** – *11 miles southwest along A352, B3070 to West Lulworth.* The cove, which is circular, is almost enclosed by the downland cliffs.

Durdle Door – *Access : on foot from Lulworth Cove along the Dorset Coast Path, 2½ miles Rtn or continue on B3070 through West Lulworth to Toll Gate/Newlands Farm.* Durdle Door lies to the west, beyond Dungy Head, at the far end of St Oswald's Bay. The whole area of headlands and scalloped bays has been likened to a "crash course in geology" with Durdle the dramatic climax, for whereas elsewhere the geological material is mostly lias (at Lyme Regis), oolite, Purbeck stone, Portland limestone and chalk (Old Harry Rocks), at the Door impermeable folded strata were forced up on end to produce a striking **cliff archway.**

Arne – *4 miles east by by-roads.* This secret place on the peninsula at the mouth of the River Frome offers large amounts of peace and quiet : over 1 000 acres of the peninsula are a **nature reserve** owned by the RSPB. The woodland, heathland and saltmarshes teem with birdlife, wildlife and plantlife (nature trail, hide).
In the village, the one-room **Toy Museum** ⊙ is crammed full of endearing old favourites : dolls, teddy bears and particularly fine automata and wind-up toys. The Early English **church** (*c*1220) consists of nave and chancel under one roof with a porch and buttress on the south side; note the triplet east window hewn out of a single stone, and the remains of an early fresco above the door.

WARMINSTER Wiltshire — Pop 14 826

Michelin Atlas p 17 or Map 403 – N30

The former wool and cloth town boasts several Elizabethan and Georgian hostelries, some with galleried courtyards; off the main street, the tributary roads, with end-on views of the countryside, are marked by small Classical 18C houses. The small church of **St Lawrence** in the High Street was founded as a chapel of ease in the early 13C; since the 15C it has housed the town bell which rang the daily curfew at 4am and sounded feast and holy days. Closed by Edward VI, it was bought back by the townspeople for £38 6*s* 8*d* in 1675 and committed, uniquely, to the temporal care of local feoffees or trustees.

EXCURSIONS

Bratton Castle – *3½ miles east off B3098.*

White Horse – *See Chalk Hill Figures.*

Bratton Castle – A side road leads up to Bratton Castle and the horse's back and head (the view of the horse is too distorted to be comprehensible).
Bratton Castle, an Iron Age hillfort with earth mound ramparts enclosing some 25 acres, commands far-reaching **views★★** from its 300ft down.

Edington – *4 miles northeast on B3098. See Edington.*

Westbury – *8 miles north on A350.* The small town, its busy main street lined with 18C-20C shops and houses, has an old **market square** at one end overlooked by a Tuscan-pillared 19C town hall, a few houses, a few shops, three inns – one now Georgian, said to date back as an inn to the 14C. Nearby in its churchyard, surrounded by **Georgian houses,** is the 19C renewed Perpendicular Church of All Saints with a rare, oblong crossing tower and a lierne vaulted porch.

★ WELLS Somerset   Pop 9 252

Michelin Atlas p 16 or Map 403 – M30 – Facilities

In England's smallest cathedral city the streets and square bustle with shoppers and a twice-weekly market but within the precinct gates calm reigns where the Cathedral Green spreads out before the unique west front, that panoply of the church displayed through the famous of all ages, from Christ in Majesty, the apostles and saints, kings of the Bible and this land, queens, holy women, bishops, hermits and knights in armour.

★ CATHEDRAL

History and Construction – The cathedral is 800 years old, the bishopric of Bath and Wells 1 000 years, the foundation by Ine, King of Wessex 1 200 years old and the site as one of Christian worship possibly 1 600 years, being Roman or even Celtic. Of the early churches nothing remains above ground. In 1091 Bishop John de Villula (d 1122), having purchased the city and abbey of Bath, removed the throne; a successor, Bishop Savaric (d 1205), equally power-hungry, seized Glastonbury and omitted Wells from his title. Glastonbury, in time, regained its autonomy; the title of Bath and Wells was re-adopted and the throne returned to Wells.

The cathedral took more than three centuries to plan and build, from *c*1175 to 1508.

*c*1175	Building began – Wells was the first cathedral church in the Early English style. Three bays of the choir and most of the transepts were completed under Bishop Reginald de Bohun (d 1191).
1239	Cathedral consecrated. Nave completed, west front partly built and many statues carved under Bishop Jocelyn (1206-42).
Before 1250-1306	Chapter-house built in successive stages as finance allowed.
1315-22	Central crossing tower (182ft) constructed and separate Lady Chapel built beyond the east end.
1338-48	Scissor arches inserted to counteract tower subsidence on the west side.
*c*1320-40	Choir completed; retrochoir built to link east end and Lady Chapel, making the cathedral 415ft long from west to east. East, Golden Window glazed *c*1340.

The west towers (125ft) were added in 1384-94 and *c*1430; the cloisters rebuilt in stages *c*1420-1508.

TOUR

Exterior

West Front – Long ago it would have been blazingly dramatic, the figures coloured and gilded; it would have resembled an illuminated manuscript or a magnificent tapestry. Today it is more monochrome though tinted at sunset and gilded by floodlight. Despite much destruction by the Puritans, it is England's richest display of 13C sculpture.

The screen front is nearly 150ft across, twice as wide as it is tall, extending round the bases of the west towers – strange constructions which continue the gabled lines of the screen in slim and soaring pinnacled buttresses and tall paired lancets, only to stop abruptly. It may have been felt that elaborate cresting would detract from the screen with its near-300 statues, half of them life-size, which rises to a climax in the centre gable with a frieze of apostles and Our Lord. The figure of "Christ in Majesty" was sculpted by David Wynne as part of the 20C restoration.

Continue round to the north side of the cathedral.

North Porch – The porch leads to a twin doorway with a central pier of ringed shafts; on either side is a display of 13C delight in pure line, as exemplified in shallow tiers of subtly varied blind arcading.

Chain Gate – The "gate" (1459) is an opening in the two-storey covered way which links the oriclled Vicars' Hall *(see below)* to the Chapter-House and the north transept of the cathedral.

Quarter-Jack – *West wall of north transept.* 15C knights strike the bells with their pikes at the quarters.

Cathedral Roofs, Crossing Tower, Chapter-House – A good view of the pinnacled and balustraded **roofs** of the east end, of the **crossing tower** with paired lights, shafted buttresses, a pierced balustrade and fountains of pinnacles may be seen at this point, and of the octagonal **chapter-house** again buttressed, pinnacled, arcaded and balustraded above wide, foil-traceried windows. (Another beautiful view of the east end is from the Bishop's Palace garden – *see below.*)

Interior *1 hour*

Straight ahead is one of the **scissor arches** inserted to west, north and south when the west piers of the crossing tower sank; whether considered graceful or gaunt, they were an outstanding and successful solution to a nightmare problem and have become a hallmark of the cathedral.

Scissor Arch, Wells Cathedral.

The constant features, the **roof vaulting** and the **pier shafting,** are subtly varied in design in each cathedral sector – the vaulting reaches its climax in the star in the Lady Chapel, and the piers in the slender clustered column in the chapter-house...

Nave – The **piers** are topped by stiff leaf **capitals,** crisply carved and deeply undercut at the west end. At the top end of the nave, the stone **pulpit** dates from *c*1547 and the adjoining **Sugar Chantry** from 1489 – a pair in hexagonal plan with that opposite of Bishop Bubwith of 1424, but enriched with fan vaulting, angel figures in the frieze and an ogee-arched doorway.

Crossing – Pass under the scissor arch to see the **fan vaulting** which dates back to 1480.

South Transept – The **capitals,** less sharply carved, have men's heads and animal masks hidden among the leaves or digress to show a man with toothache or tell the tale of two caught in the act of robbing an orchard *(southwest pillar).* The **corbels** also portray figures including an angel.
The circular **font,** with a Jacobean cover, is the only relic of an earlier cathedral on an adjacent site.
Among the **tombs** note that of Bishop William de Marcia (d 1302), possibly a true portrait effigy, on a low chest encircled by a frieze of heads.

St Calixtus Chapel – The beautiful **tomb chest** of Thomas Boleyn (d 1472) is faced with several panels of Nottingham **alabaster** carved to represent God the Father and the Annunciation.

South Chancel Aisle – The chancel aisles are the resting place for **tombs** convincingly carved in 1220-30 to resemble seven early **Saxon bishops.**

Continue up the aisle to enter the choir.

Chancel – Immediately striking are the **vista** east through the three pointed arches behind the high altar to the retro-choir and Lady Chapel, and on high of the Jesse or **Golden Window** of medieval glass.
Note the **bishop's throne** made of stone, the tapestry bishops' banners and stall coverings of 1937-48 workmanship and the **Bekynton Chantry** of 1450, with the bishop, Keeper of the Privy Seal to Henry VI, both in full vestments and as a cadaver.

Return to the aisle.

Retro-Choir – The **piers,** few in number with shafts almost separated, produce a forest of ribs to support an intricate **tierceron vaulting.** Note a 13C cope chest and three of the cathedral's **misericords** which show respectively, a left-handed man killing a wyvern or dragon, Alexander the Great being lifted to heaven by two griffins, both medieval carvings, and a 17C illustration of a boy pulling a thorn from his foot.

Lady Chapel – The **star vault** meets in a finely **painted boss** above the unequal octagon which enters spatially into the retro-choir; most of the glass, smashed at the Reformation, has been replaced in its fragmentary state.

North Transept – The **lifesize carving** (1955) shows Christ rising from the tomb on Easter morning. The **astronomical clock** with the sun and a star revolving round the 24-hour dial dates from 1390; above is a **knights' tournament** which revolves eight times every quarter hour, one knight being struck down each time; also at the quarters, **Jack Blandiver,** the seated figure at gallery level, kicks his two quarter bells and, on the hour, strikes the bell in front of him (the mechanism is silent during services).

Chapter-House – A broad and graceful flight of **steps,** laid *c*1290 and since worn down by several million feet, curves up to the **chapter-house;** the octagonal structure is supported by a clustered **centre pier** from which 32 ribs fan out to meet those rising from each angle in an encircling octagonal rib. Below the traceried windows are the stalls, capped by crocketed and cusped gables resting on **figured corbels,** carved as portrait heads by medieval masons.

Vicars' Hall – The chapter-house steps were modified in the 15C when the Chain Gate *(see above)* was built; an exhibition on the building of the cathedral is housed in the covered way leading to the Vicars' Hall (1348).

Cathedral Precinct

Medieval Gates – Three 15C gates lead through from the city streets to the calm of the Green : **Brown's Gate,** a tall gatehouse (now a hotel) from the narrow Sadler Street, **Penniless Porch,** the towered gatehouse built by Bishop Bekynton in the 15C which affords access from the Square *(northeast corner)* and got its name from the medieval beggars who used to crowd it, and the **Bishop's Eye,** a polygonal towered archway from the centre of the east side of the Square.

Cathedral Green – The north side of the cathedral precinct is flanked by the Liberty, an area containing several 17C-18C houses; the Old Deanery, buttressed, battlemented and turreted in the 15C, was remodelled in the late 17C; the Chancellor's House, remodelled in the 18C, is now the home of the **Wells Museum** ⊙ containing statuary from the cathedral, archeological artefacts, silver, fossils...

★ **Vicars' Close** – East of the Chain Gate *(see above)* beneath the Vicars' Hall a gateway opens into the Vicars' Close, a long street (150yds) of **identical cottages** built *c*1360 for members of the cathedral in minor orders. The houses, to which the walled front gardens were added *c*1415, have been continuously occupied and altered except for **no 22,** which has retained its original outward appearance.
At the end – the street narrows for the sake of perspective – is a 15C chapel.

★ **Bishop's Palace** ⊙ – The palace, on the south side of the Green, stands stoutly walled and encircled by a moat visited by wildfowl and swans. The approach is through the Bishop's Eye *(see above)* and an inner, 14C gatehouse, square, castellated and formerly preceded by a drawbridge.
Inside are walled gardens, the springs or **wells** from which the town gets its name – 3 400 000 gallons a day or 40 gallons a second – the mellow ruin of the Great Hall, the present palace and a beautiful **view**★★ of the east end of the cathedral.
The **palace** itself is 700 years old. The walls with bastions and angle towers (rampart walk) and the moat were constructed in the 14C as a status symbol. The oldest part of the palace proper is the centre block with its undercroft of 1230-40, re-ordered and re-decorated inside in the 19C when a top storey was also added. The chapel dates from *c*1280.
At the end of the 13C, as a final embellishment, the **Great Hall** (115ft x 60ft) was built of red sandstone with corner turrets and great traceried windows. In 1552 the roof was stripped of its lead (the proceeds going to the king) whereupon the roof timbers rotted and fell in. Part of the remaining walls were removed in the 19C to make "a picturesque ruin".

ADDITIONAL SIGHTS

Market Place – The bustling town centre has been equipped since the Middle Ages with a **conduit** bringing water from the springs in the palace garden *(see above); the* **Gothick fountain** is a late 18C replacement of earlier fountain-heads.
Along the square's north side is a range of houses erected in 1453 by Bishop Bekynton and still known as the **New Works** (Nova Opera). There have been repairs but the range appears still much as described in a document of 1480. Marked on the pavement is Mary Rand's record long jump of over 22ft achieved at the 1964 Olympic Games.

High Street – The short High Street is lined above 20C shopfronts by houses with uneven rooflines which date from the 15C-17C; the King's Arms still has its 14C roof; the **City Arms,** a low, half-timbered building surrounding a small courtyard served as the city gaol from the 16C-19C.

St Cuthbert's – St Cuthbert's **tower** (122ft) is distinguished by its slender stepped buttresses framing enormously tall bell openings, a crest of blind arcading between corner buttresses and pinnacled turrets.
A Perpendicular church, it succeeds an Early English church (transept chapel window) and a Saxon building of which only the dedication remains; Cuthbert was an English monk and Bishop of Lindisfarne in 685-87.
Inside, the typical Somerset-style wooden **roof,** with tie-beams, cresting, coffering and a chorale of demi-angels, was vividly restored to its true medieval colouring in 1963. Note also the **piers,** elongated to take the clerestory and with differently carved capitals, the **royal arms** of Charles I and Charles II *(north aisle and north transept chapel),* the late Jacobean **pulpit,** exceptionally carved with scenes from the Old Testament (Jonah and the Whale, David and Goliath), two much mutilated **13C altarpieces** (transept chapels), also the **contract** for the altarpieces' erection in 1470.
Two massive **silver flagons,** presented *c*1639, make a gleaming display in their south pillar niche.
Outside, at the east end, stands **Priest Row,** a line of Victorian cottages on the site of former priests' lodgings, with neat porches and flowered gardens.

A number of Touring Programmes is given at the beginning of the guide.

Plan a trip with the help of the preceding Map of Principal Sights.

WESTON-SUPER-MARE Avon — Pop 60 821

Michelin Atlas p 16 or Map 403 - L29, 30 - Facilities
Town plan in the current Michelin Red Guide Great Britain and Ireland

The town is in the classic tradition of a large, popular English seaside resor donkeys, miles of dark gold sand scoured twice daily by the tide, hote restaurants, shops and stalls fringing the arc of the bay, public gardens, a museu of local history, the Tropicana Pleasure Beach with two water chutes and oth attractions... The popularity of Weston-super-Mare has developed since the tu of the century, since when its population has quadrupled; it also attracts ¼ milli visitors each year and 1½ million who come on day-trips.

★★ **The view** – Across the bay lie the islands of **Flat Holm** (lighthouse; *qv)* and **Ste Holm** (bird sanctuary); to the south is the square-towered **Uphill Church** (19C 1 000 year old site), further over, the long finger of Brean Down Point (Somers and, on the horizon, the Welsh hills.

★ WESTWOOD MANOR Wiltshire

Michelin Atlas p 17 or Map 403 - N30 - 1½ miles southwest of Bradfo on-Avon

It is the ensemble which counts in this small, two-storey house which has be continuously occupied and altered since construction began *c*1400.
Among the tenants of the manor ⊙, owned by Winchester Cathedral frc Saxon times to the mid-19C, were Thomas Horton, the clothier frc Bradford-on-Avon, who benefited the adjoining Perpendicular church by buildi the splendid **west tower,** crowned with a dome; note the initials TH in the dc spandrels.
Major alterations were made to the house in the first half of the 17C : the **po** and **staircase turret** were added, the Great Hall was divided horizontally to cre the **Great Parlour** above, **panelling,** including the frieze of landscape scenes, w installed in the Panelled Room, and the Biblical or symbolic **plaster overmant** (geese hanging a fox, a rose and thistle growing from the same stem) set i the Panelled, Oriel, Dining and King's Rooms.
By the 19C-20C neglect had almost brought the house to ruin before it w bought by a new owner who restored it to life and collected for it the 15 **Italian virginal,** late 17C-18C **spinet,** 17C English furniture and needlework cove for the chairs.

★ WEYMOUTH Dorset — Pop 38 38

Michelin Atlas p 8 or Map 403 - M32

Weymouth, a port with roll-on ferry services to Cherbourg and the Chan Islands, is a Georgian town associated with **George III** who was the first monar to stay in a seaside resort and chose Weymouth for the experiment : "T preparations of festive loyalty were universal," Fanny Burney wrote in her di in July 1789, "think but of the surprise of his Majesty when, the first time his bathing, he had no sooner popped his royal head under water, than a ba of music, concealed in a neighbouring machine, struck up God save great Geor our King".
The sovereign returned many times; in 1810, "the grateful inhabitants" erec the statue on the Esplanade which remains the town's major landmark.

Esplanade – The Esplanade beyond King George's statue, punctuated so 200yds further along by Queen Victoria's Jubilee Clock, follows the enormc sweep of the bay. Facing the sea are terrace houses of the late 18C–early 1 with first-floor iron balconies, sash windows (some with slender glazing ba canopies, copings and fine proportions, notably at the harbour end.

OLD TOWN

Situated close to the lively old harbour, now extended to 2 000ft and moori rows of smart sailing boats, is the heart of the old town which began on t far side of the inlet on **North Quay** and, as the town grew, spread to the mainla from the promontory on which Sandsfoot Castle had been erected in the 1 and Nothe Fort *(see below)* in the early 19C.

Custom House Quay, North Quay and Trinity Road – The quayside is lin with boat repair shops, inns and houses, and offers views of the inner harbc the town bridge and the old harbour, and the constant coming and going the yachts, sailing boats and ferry services.

Brewers Quay – *Hope Square.* This redevelopment of a large brewery and otl old buildings provides small and interesting shops, stalls and attractions.

Town Museum ⊙ – The display panels and showcases highlight aspects of t town's history.

★ **Timewalk** ⊙ – The entertaining *tableaux* and special effects lead through a tc of the town over the centuries : the grim horror of the plague, the looting a Spanish galleon, the Civil War, King George III taking the waters, smuggler The tour finishes with several large rooms devoted to the brewing process, frc the original huge copper-lined vats to the work of the coopers and farriers, the reconstruction of a small bar.

Discovery ⏲ – This friendly hands-on gallery explores laws and processes of science and technology (lasers, mirrors, water, sound, gravity) in an interesting and approachable way, appealing to all ages.

Nothe Fort ⏲ – The semicircular fort, built in 1860 as part of the defences of Portland Harbour and in active service until 1956, now houses the **Museum of Coastal Defence.** Perched on the edge of Weymouth's promontory, it offers panoramic **views**★ over Portland Harbour and Weymouth Bay. The numerous items on display include anti-aircraft guns, 19C cannons, 20C trucks, cases of guns and rifles, medals, model ships, photographs and Second World War newspapers, while scenes recreate aspects of life in the fort, from gun drill to ablutions : a quartermaster's store, an engineer's workshop, a barrack room, cells...

★ **Boat Trip** ⏲ – Weymouth Bay and Portland Harbour.

EXCURSIONS

★ **Abbotsbury** – *9 miles northwest along B3157. See Abbotsbury.*

Osmington White Horse – *6 miles east along A353.*
This white horse *(qv)*, which, with Uffington, is the only animal facing right, is unique in having a rider. The figure is popularly supposed to be George III, patron of Weymouth from 1789; an alternative version credits engineers, stationed at Weymouth in case of invasion in 1815, with the carving, whereupon the rider would be Wellington; Hardy, in *The Trumpet Major,* described it as a memorial to Trafalgar... The figure is the largest of all, being 323ft high by 280ft long.

WIDECOMBE IN THE MOOR Devon — Pop 603

Michelin Atlas p 4 or Map 403 – I32 – Local map p 91

The embattled **tower** with tall turreted pinnacles which soars high above Dartmoor *(qv)* makes the church a **landmark** for miles around; the traditional ballad, about Tom Pearse's grey mare and Old Uncle Tom Cobleigh and all riding to the **fair** (still held today – see Calendar of Events, *qv)*, has made Widecombe itself a popular legend.
The village, a cluster of white-walled, thatched cottages grouped round the church, stands in a shallow valley or wide combe – hence the name – surrounded by granite ridges which rise to 1 500ft.

The Cathedral of the Moor.

St Pancras – The 135ft-high tower of red ashlar was added, out of line, in the early 16C to the Perpendicular church which had been rebuilt in the late 14C-15C with money from the Dartmoor tin-miners.
Known as the **Cathedral of the Moor,** it is a vast building (104ft long) with monolithic arcades rising to plain **barrel roofs** decorated with a series of well-carved **bosses.**

Church House – The two-storey, long stone house, with its lean-to shelter outside, dates back to 1537 when it was the village alehouse. It was later converted into almshouses and, finally, the village school.

★★ WILTON HOUSE Wiltshire

Michelin Atlas p 9 or Map 403 – O30

William Herbert, the quick-witted favourite of Henry VIII, received from h sovereign – to whom he was related – the property of the dissolved Wiltc Benedictine Convent in 1544. Within ten years he had been created Lord Herbe of Cardiff and Earl of Pembroke, and had constructed a house on the old conve site worthy of receiving the new king, Edward VI.

The Palladian Bridge, Wilton House.

The idiosyncratic contributions of successive generations can still be clearly distinguished as they meld into the whole : 2nd Earl married "the greatest patronesse of wit and learning of any lady of her time", the sister of **Sir Philip Sidney** who, while staying at Wilton, composed his poem *Arcadia* – pictures in the Cube Room; 4th Earl, munificent patron who, in 1647, when all but the east front and most of the contents had been destroyed in a fire, commissioned **Inigo Jones** to design the house anew and incorporate within the plan a stateroom in which to hang his collection of royal and family portraits by **Van Dyck** : 8th Earl, founder of the Carpet Factory *(see below)*, traveller, connoisseur, collector, notably of the Wilto Diptych (since 1929 in the National Gallery, London), appointed agents to find ne pictures, and marbles to replace those sold to pay the debts of the spendthrift 7 Earl; 9th Earl, soldier, architect and friend of Lord Burlington and William Kent, bu the **Palladian Bridge** and redesigned the **garden;** 10th Earl, also a soldier and an authori on equitation, commissioned the **equestrian portraits** and 55 **Spanish Riding Scho gouaches** which hang in the two smoking rooms; 11th Earl employed **James Wyatt** 1801 to recast the house, demolish the old great hall, rebuild two fronts and bui the two-tier Gothic cloister in the original inner court to provide galleries for statua and historic mementoes such as Napoleon's despatch box, a lock of Queen Eliz beth's hair, verses by Sir Philip Sidney in his own hand...

TOUR ⏲ *1 hour*

Cloisters – The cloisters are a remodelling of the former inner courtyard.

State Apartments – The suite of apartments by **Inigo Jones** is characterized by classical wealth of enrichment, including giant Italian ceiling paintings, marb chimneypieces, superbly carved cornices, covings, doorways, overmantels, co umns, escutcheons at the centre of broken pediments, great carved drops... a picked out in gold leaf. The **furniture** ranges from the solid mass of marble and gi tables and red velvet and gilt sofas by William Kent to pieces by the young Chippendale, 18C French commodes and Boulle-style tortoiseshell brass table

Cube Room – The 30ft x 30ft x 30ft room is decorated in white and gold, th ornament delicate in keeping with the size of the room. The generations c portraits include Henriette de Querouaille, sister of Charles II's mistress and wi of the 7th Earl by Lely, and a portrait of *Van Dyck* by Charles Jervas.

Double Cube Room – The gallery of 60ft x 30ft x 30ft was especially designe by Inigo Jones as the sumptuously rich gold and white setting for the 4 Earl's unique collection of splendid **Van Dyck portraits** of the Herbert family an of Charles I, his Queen and their children.

Great Ante-Room – The seascapes are by **Van der Velde,** the **Rembrandt** portrait of his mother reading (*c*1629).

Colonnade Room – The family portraits are almost all by **Joshua Reynolds.**

Corner Room – A **Titian** portrait and religious and landscape paintings by **Andre del Sarto** and **Rubens** adorn the walls; the portrait over the fireplace is of Princ Rupert by von Horthorst.

Little Ante-Room – Among the pictures are a **Lucas van Leyden** and a **Mabuse** – not the view from the window.

Smoking Rooms – Besides the oil equestrian portraits and the Spanish Ridin School gouaches *(see above)*, note the typical Inigo Jones moulded detail i cornices, doorways and chimneypieces and the beautiful **furniture** including a lat 17C walnut table, a mirror and stands with ivory marquetry, the Chippenda Spanish mahogany bookcases and music cabinet (*c*1750), the walnut and leathe Regency chairs.

Hall – The 19C Gothic hall includes portrait busts of **Sidney Herbert** and **Florenc Nightingale** (Lord Herbert of Lea was Secretary of State for War in 1852 whe Florence Nightingale went to the Crimea).

East, Garden Front – The front is still reminiscent of the original Tudor mansio with angle pavilions and a central door beneath tall oriel windows. *Illustration p 12*

WILTON VILLAGE Pop 4 002

Wilton became the local fortified capital in the 7C-8C in the reign of Ine, King of Wessex, when "hundreds" were being grouped into "shires" which then, in many cases, took the name of their appointed centres – thus Wiltshire. In the 9C Alfred founded a Benedictine convent in the town; in 1033 Wilton was sacked by invading Danes and hardly had it recovered before it was devastated by the Black Death. Although nominally it remained the county town, it was eventually outstripped by Salisbury.

Market Place – At the centre, trees shade the ruined Perpendicular arcade and west window of the originally **Saxon church.** The Cross, nearby, is a composite of artefacts from an early Crucifixion to an 18C urn.

West Street – The wide Cotswold-style shopping street of 17C houses with later shopfronts is distinguished by the **Basilica of St Mary and St Nicholas,** a mid-19C feat of Italianate Romanesque by Thomas Wyatt, complete with 110ft high campanile and ornately decorated, gabled, west front.

★ **Royal Wilton Carpet Factory** ⊙ – *King St.* Carpet weaving began as a cottage industry but by the 17C had declined to so poor a standard that the much-travelled 8th Earl of Pembroke arranged for two skilled French Huguenot weavers, who were banned from leaving France on pain of death, to be smuggled over in wine barrels to set up a carpet factory. This succeeded so well that in 1699 it was granted "royal" status by William III.
Two rivers, the Wylye and the Nadder, flow through the mill which comprises buildings of the 17C-20C.

Tour – *45min.* Visitors see old carpet making crafts on original machinery, samples of carpets woven in the last 300 years and modern Wilton and Axminster looms at work.

★ WIMBORNE MINSTER Dorset Pop 14 193

Michelin Atlas p 9 or Map 403 – O31

Wimborne Minster, glimpsed across the water meadows, arouses curiosity about its size, its disparate towers, its extraordinary, chequered stonework.

★ MINSTER *½ hour*

The foundation dates from 1043, when Edward the Confessor established a college of secular canons on a site occupied by a Benedictine nunnery until it was sacked by the Danes in 1013. In 1318 Edward II declared the church a **royal peculiar;** in 1537, as a collegiate church, the community was suppressed by Henry VIII and the church given to the parish.

Exterior – The **stone** is local and varies in colour from grey to pinky-brown and cream; the **towers** are Norman (*c*1120-80) at the crossing, with round-headed and lancet windows, and Perpendicular at the west end, the latter being built in 1448-64, to take a peal of bells. The church had by then taken on its present appearance and size, there having been extensions in the 13C-14C.
The **quarter-jack** on the south wall of the west tower, installed in 1612, was originally a monk but since the Napoleonic wars, a grenadier, who strikes the two bells every quarter of an hour.

Interior – The Decorated outer walls of 1307-77 fit like a glove round the 12C Norman church which forms the core of the present 190ft long minster.

Crossing – The round columns with plainly **scalloped capitals** are Norman, as is the triforium with small rounded arches and Purbeck marble columns. The **eagle lectern** is 17C.

Nave – The **arcades** march west from the crossing, the first bays with rounded arches; above are the small round windows of the Norman clerestory although the actual **clerestory** is Perpendicular. In the north aisle are an **almsbox** set into the nearest pillar to the door, and a small tablet to a certain **Snodgrass,** who, with **Wardle** (in the tower), furnished Dickens with two famous names.

Tower – The octagonal black Purbeck **marble font** on marble shafts is late Norman (all decoration was stripped from it during the Commonwealth); the **astronomical clock** dates from 1320, pre-Copernican times when the earth was shown as the still centre of the universe with the sun (the hour hand) revolving round the outside of the dial face, and the moon also revolving to show the lunar phases. The present works are of 1792 – the model is modern. The **royal arms** on the wall are of Charles II – a relimning at the Restoration of those of Charles I which had been painted out.

East End – The east window of three tall lights surmounted by foiled circles dates from the *c*1220 extension of the church, the *Tree of Jesse* is 15C Flemish glass. In the **sanctuary,** adjoining **chapels** and the cusp-arched **crypt** are a **brass** of King Ethelred (d 871), elder brother of King Alfred, and a number of **tombs** including Sir Edmund Uvedale (d 1606), a coloured Renaissance figure, restored to have two left feet; the **Bankes** of Corfe Castle *(qv)* and Kingston Lacy *(qv);* **John de Beaufort,** Duke of Somerset and his duchess, the grandparents of Henry VII; Anthony Ettricke, 17C eccentric, who is buried in a wall recess so that he is neither within nor without the church and who had a final date of 1693 carved ready on his coffin but lived on, as the altered numbers show, to 1703. There are also old **chests,** one Saxon with a recess in the solid oak for relics...

TOWN

Bridges – The town is compact and still lies largely within the bounds of its three bridges : the **Canford** on the Poole road (A341), constructed of Portland stone with three bold arches in 1813, the **Juliana,** to the west (A31), over the River Stour with eight pointed arches and refuges in the brick parapet, which dates from 1636 (widened 1844), and the **Walford** to the north (B3078) which was originally a medieval packhorse bridge over the River Allen (widened in 1802).

High Street – The approach to the minster is one of the town's earliest streets.

★ **Priest's House Museum** ⏱ – This early 16C house is Wimborne's most complete medieval dwelling; additions were made in the 17C and 18C. The "front" room (an 18C addition) has mid 18C panelling and contains original stock from the onetime Victorian stationer's shop here. The rear parlour with a Tudor moulded **plaster ceiling** and *c*1700 panelling reveals its older wall treatment and carved stone fireplace. The cloth-hung hall, the main room originally, has its **timbering** still intact. Upstairs, note the dry storage space set into the chimney breast.
The **Victorian kitchen** and the Rural Life Gallery (wattle hurdle making, thatching) provide additional interest.
The long, narrow and peaceful **walled garden,** richly planted and boasting a very ancient mulberry tree, leads to a shallow mill stream. It offers a lovely view of the house's original **Tudor gables.**

Glass Studio ⏱ – *77 High St.* The fascinating and surprisingly quick process of glassblowing and shaping may be watched close up in this small studio workshop, where the wares are made entirely by hand using traditional tools.

Cornmarket and Square – The old street and former market square are overlooked by 17C-19C houses.

Westborough – The wide street leading north out of the Square was the principal area of expansion in the 18C and is therefore distinguished by Georgian houses.

EXCURSIONS

★★ **Kingston Lacy** – *1½ miles west by B3082. See Kingston Lacy.*

Cranborne Manor Gardens ⏱ – *18 miles north on B3078.*
The tall house, a former royal hunting lodge in Cranborne Chase, took on something of its present appearance in the early 17C when Robert Cecil, first Earl of Salisbury, received the manor from James I whose accession he had helped to secure.
The garden, including avenues of fine trees, was laid out by **John Tradescant** (1570-1638), designer and plantsman. Among the several areas enclosed by old walls and high hedges are an Elizabethan **knot garden** and a rare Jacobean **Mount Garden** where three low, circular grass tiers surround a central mound while outer beds with old-fashioned roses, peonies and foxgloves fill the spandrels.

★ WOOKEY HOLE Somerset

Michelin Atlas p 16 or Map 403 – L, M30

"Just under the hills, is the famous and so much talked of Wokey Hole" wrote Defoe in 1686. Since his day many more caves have been discovered but the stalactites he saw have grown only one inch apiece since then.
The approach is through wooded pastureland at the foot of the Mendip plateau.
Mill buildings in a wooded glen screen the hole in the cliffs (200ft) from which the River Axe gushes in a torrent at the rate of 12 million gallons a day. The river has no visible source : two miles away up on the plateau the soil composition alters from impervious shale to permeable carboniferous limestone through which rainwater percolates, collects in rock faults and wears a course which forms the passages and caves which comprise the Hole.

★ **Caves** ⏱ – The river is always present in the caves, in echoing, although mostly unseen, cascades and in deep green-blue-black pools, mirroring the walls which vary in colour from iron rust-red to leaden-grey and green-white. The caverns and narrow fissures of the tour (about 350yds) represent less than one tenth of the explored passages.
Stalactites, stalagmites, frozen falls, translucent pools, cliff faces of different-coloured rock, the stone outline of the witch – who one legend even claims was killed by King Arthur – ferns growing beside the arc lights, present an immutable world. During their 500 million year lifecycle the caves have been inhabited by Iron Age man in 300 BC and later by Romano-British and Celtic peoples.

★ **Papermill** ⏱ – Handmade rag paper with body, texture and a watermark has a unique quality of simple luxury; it looks deceptively easy to scoop exactly the right amount of raw material from the vat and distribute it evenly in the mould.

Paper was first made at Wookey Hole c1600; the mill supplied paper for the Confederate banknotes issued at Richmond, Virginia.

★ **Fairground Collection** ⏲ – The gloriously garish collection includes gallopers, spinners, old bioscope fronts, fascias, gods, deer, horses, dragons and peacocks... They were made for travelling fairgrounds (1870-1939); many were beautifully carved, painted and signed. The **Cabinet of Curiosities** is a re-creation of Madame Tussaud's original travelling show. The **Penny Pier Arcade** offers the chance to play on Edwardian slot machines or the possibility of dressing up in period costume for a sepia print photograph.

Museum – The display traces the geological formation of the caves, the source of the River Axe, the exploratory expeditions and the construction of the link tunnel in 1974. Note the **waterwheel** at the entrance.

Fairground galloper, Wookey Hole.

YEOVIL Somerset — Pop 36 114

Michelin Atlas p 8 or Map 403 – M31

The bustling town, the base of Westland Aircraft and the centre of the dairy farming industry, also remains the glove and leather centre which it has been since the 14C when gloving was a cottage industry, the skins then coming from sheep on the Polden and Quantock Hills – there is still a Glovers' Walk in the town.
Big increases in the population came after 1853, when the railway link with Taunton was opened. The **buildings,** therefore, are principally 19C-20C with a few, scattered 18C-19C, Georgian houses and older inns, most notably in **Princess Street,** the **High Street** (two old inns), **Silver Street** (inn sign on a fine wrought-iron bracket). **Church House,** in brick, west of the church, is Georgian.

★ **St John the Baptist** – The parish church stands tall upon the central hillock around which the town grew up, the 90ft **tower** a dominant landmark since it was erected in the late 14C. Severe and stoutly buttressed, it rises from a plain doorway and five-light window through an opening and a belfry bay to a high, pierced parapet. The church itself, an early Perpendicular, much pinnacled structure, was entirely constructed of grey lias, with Ham Hill stone dressings, between 1380 and 1400. All the **windows** – there are 18 – have five lights and measure 9ft wide by 20ft high, from which the church has come to be known as the "lantern of the west". Note also the dragon and other savage gargoyles.
Inside, the **roofs** above the tall, slim, clustered arcades have retained their original **bosses,** a strange collection of human faces and animal masks, many of the men, in the aisles especially, apparently in full African tribal warpaint, possibly inspired by the travellers' tales of returned crusaders.
Below the chancel is a **crypt** with rib vaulting resting on a central **octagonal pier;** it was once used as a charnel house and is approached from the chancel through an ogee-arched doorway decorated with a wreathed skull.
The **lectern** and **font** are both 15C, the former one of only four to remain from 1450. It stands 6ft 6in high, has lion feet and a triangular-section reading desk engraved with the figure of a friar, whose face was obliterated by the Puritans in 1565.

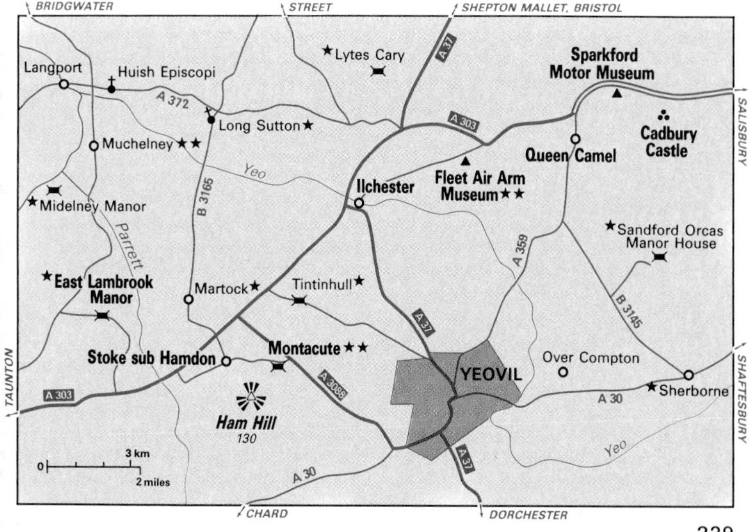

The Alfred Jewel, Yeovil.

Museum of South Somerset ⓥ – The museum is in an 18C coach house of mellow brick with Ham stone angle quoins and Venetian upper windows. The collections include **gloving tools** from when the industry was a local staple, a bequest of 18C-19C **glassware** with wine and cordial glasses and Nailsea glass *(qv)*, a special display of **firearms** and a **Petter oil engine,** the invention of a local man in 1895.
Also in the museum is a reproduction of the **Alfred Jewel,** discovered in 169 close to Athelney *(qv)*, believed to be the handle to a pointer, and depicting Chris in cloisonné enamel on gold plate, holding two gold sceptres. The finely-crafte letters in the filigree frame spell out, in Anglo-Saxon, the phrase "Alfred had m made".

EXCURSIONS

★★ **Montacute House** – *4 miles west on A3088. See Montacute.*

★★ **Fleet Air Arm Museum, Yeovilton** – *8 miles northwest by A37 and Ilchest by-road.*

Ilchester – The triangular **green** with its Tuscan column and ball finial erected i the 18C, the **square** overlooked by Georgian houses – among which is the **tow hall** – and by the **parish church** with a 13C fortress-like octagonal tower, hint a the town's long and varied fortunes.
Its importance began with the Romans who made it a cantonal capital, calle Lendinis, at the junction of the Fosse Way and the road from Dorchester; th Saxons maintained it as a centre and by 950 it had become a royal burgh. I the 11C-12C it possessed a flourishing market and a mint; by 1327 it had take over from Somerton as the county town, a position it maintained until the 19 when Taunton took its place.

Turn right in Ilchester. The airfield is beside the road (B3151).

★★ **Fleet Air Arm Museum** ⓥ – Royal Naval Air Station. Each year more than a quart of a million visitors come to see the 60 historic and present-day **aircraft,** the batt honours, paintings and photographs of famous actions, including the Falklanc War (1982) and the Gulf War (1991). There are also models, photographs auxiliary services, of training, reconnaissance and rescue, and flying displays routine and training most days, acrobatic and breathtaking on special displa days (local announcements).

★ **East Lambrook Manor** – *12 miles west. Take A3088 west out of Yeovil.*

Ham Hill – The hill (425ft) is a notable landmark and commands **views**★★ of th rolling countryside for miles around. It was once crowned by a prehistoric hillfo but its fame is due to the **quarry** from which limestone has been cut to bui churches, beautiful houses and small cottages throughout Somerset and th southwest. The stone varies in colour from creamy white and grey to yellov gold and brown ochre depending on the ferrous deposits in the ground. Aft more than a thousand years the quarries are exhausted and stone is now foun only for repairs.

Continue ½ mile along A3088; turn left and then right.

Stoke sub Hamdon – The village, which is in two parts and built almost entire of Ham Hill stone, has an attractive collection of 17C-18C houses an cottages.
The **parish church**★ stands amidst trees near a stream at the bottom of the hi A mixed building, it dates from the 12C-16C : the **tower,** on the north side, 13C at the base, 15C above, with battlements, a cornice and gargoyles; th chancel and nave in Ham stone, comprising the Norman church, were erecte *c*1100 – note the corbel tables along the chancel walls; the north transept wa added *c*1225, the south in 1300; the two-storey, north porch is *c*1325 thoug the doorway is Norman.
Inside, the **chancel arch** in dark Ham stone is carved with three orders of zig-za and lozenge decoration above small columns. Note the Norman **font** with cab mouldings and frieze, Jacobean pulpit and **hour-glass** and 17C **communion ra balusters.**

West of the village turn left into A303; at the roundabout turn right; in Sout Petherton bear right to Martock; after ½ mile turn left.

★ **East Lambrook Manor** ⓥ – The visit is primarily to the **garden** – a garden of "cottag mixtures", of exotic, old-fashioned, foliage and simple plants, lacking vistas b showing the close-up beauty of plants in separate gardens which extend roun two sides of the rambling, stone and brick house, once thatched and no Somerset-tiled.
When it was built *c*1470 the house probably belonged to a minor squire, merchant or a prosperous yeoman; in 1938, when discovered by Margery Fis and her husband, it was derelict and rat-infested; the garden, of course, wa a wilderness.
Before she died, Mrs Fish converted it into the **plantswoman's** garden which has remained. It is attractive throughout the year, modest in size (about 2½ acre and contains a mass of different species : hydrangeas, salvias, achilleas, alyssun primulas, lavender, ivies, vines, double daisies...

Cadbury Castle – *11 miles northeast by A359.*

Queen Camel – The small village possesses a parish church with a severe 14C west tower which rises to battlements and pinnacles, overtopped by the stair turret.

Continue along A359 to Sparkford.

Sparkford Motor Museum ⏲ – Over 200 vintage, veteran and classic cars and motorcyles, racing cars and bikes are exhibited here, and a theatre shows old motoring films. The international collection ranges from the more modest (Mini, Messerschmidt) to the most extravagant (Rolls Royce, Lanchester) by way of Italian sportscars, American models, British favourites...

Take the by-road east towards Chapel Cross and Cadbury Castle.

Cadbury Castle – The castle with commanding **views★★** crowned a hilltop 500ft above sea-level. Nothing remains on the 18-acre site, which was excavated in 1966-70.
Cadbury, which began as a prehistoric settlement, was converted in the Iron Age into a hillfort. It was still occupied at the time of the Roman invasion in AD 43 and was re-fortified in the late 5C.
The names of the River Cam to the west and Queen Camel have given rise to a belief that the Battle of Camlann was fought nearby, that the builder could only have been King Arthur *(qv)*, that Cadbury was, therefore, the fabled **Camelot.**

Celtic Cross, Sancreed.

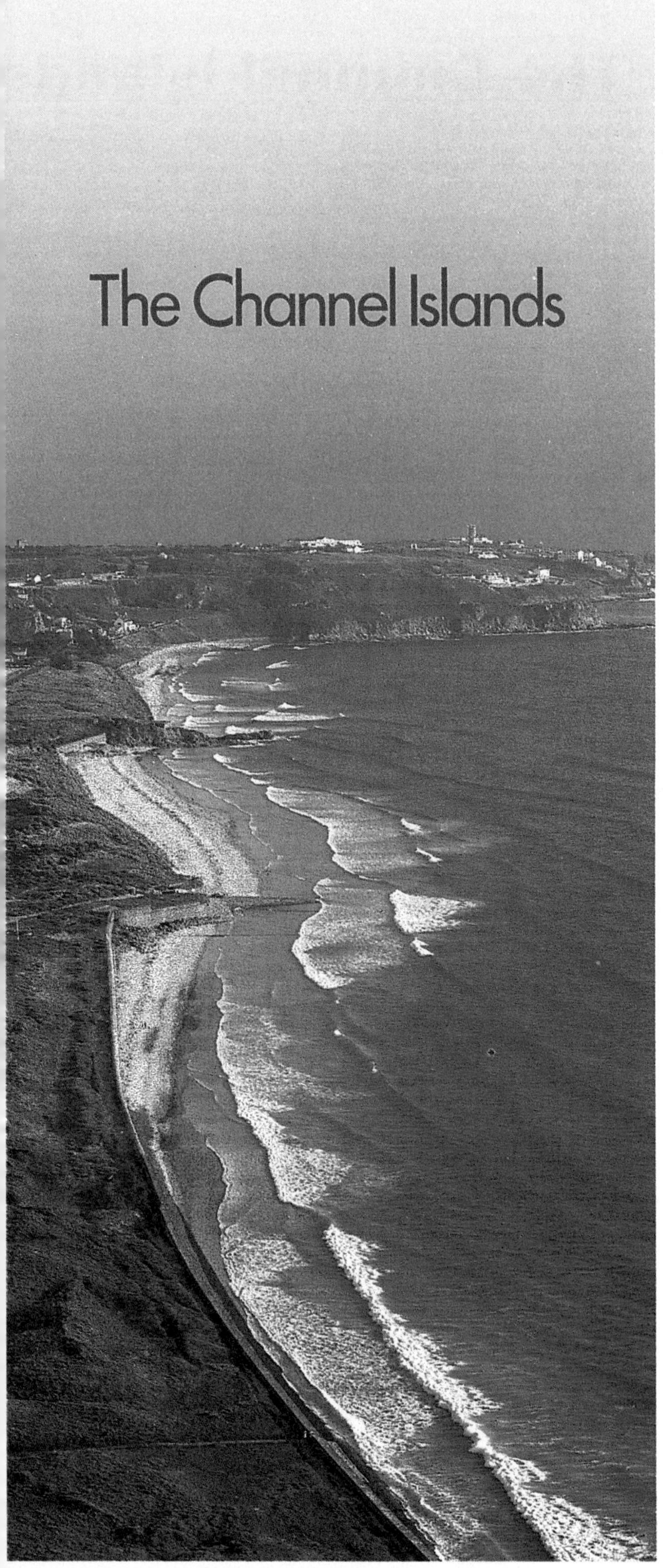

The Channel Islands

The Channel Islands

For many people the name of the Channel Islands conjures up a northern mini paradise providing a tax-free haven for the very rich or sun and sand for the holiday-maker.
A visit to the islands will reveal not only the mild climate, long sandy beaches, spring flowers and exotic semi-tropical plants but also wild cliffs and seascapes, quiet country lanes and traditional granite houses, excellent seafood and a fascinating history.
Although the Channel Islands have been attached to the English crown since 1066, they lie much nearer to the French coast and were largely French-speaking until this century. Under their apparent Englishness lie a thousand years of Norman tradition and sturdy independence.

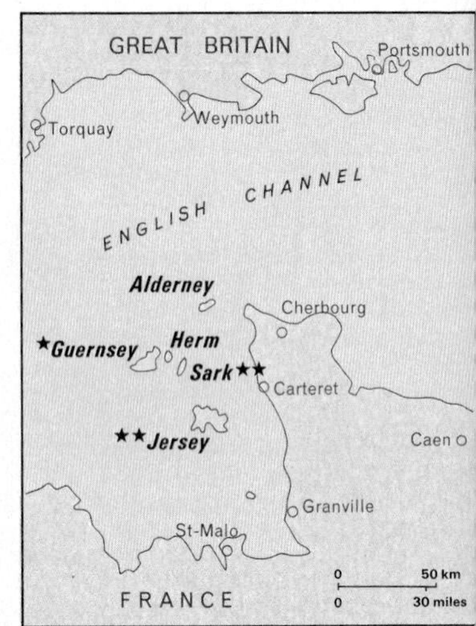

THREATS OF INVASION

Early invaders of the Channel Islands left impressive neolithic remains : **menhirs** and **dolmens.** The megalithic tombs consisting of one or several chambers were built of huge blocks of stone, sometimes with an entrance passage and heaped over with earth. Their excavation has contributed greatly to archeological knowledge of the period.
In 933 the islands were annexed by the Normans and attached to the English Crown by William the Conqueror. The loss of Normandy in 1204 did not break the link with England but over the centuries the French made repeated attempts to capture the islands. In 1483 a Papal Bull of Neutrality was issued which remained in force until 1689.
In the English Civil War Jersey was Royalist while Guernsey supported Cromwell; this is supposed to be the basis of the traditional rivalry between the two major islands.
Later, the rise of Napoleon brought the threat of invasion and so defensive towers, similar to the later Martello towers, were built along the coasts. In the mid 19C fresh fears of French invasion brought more fortifications, particularly in Alderney.

German Occupation – The Channel Islands were finally invaded in 1940 and occupied by the Germans for five years; they were the only British territory to fall to the enemy. The occupation brought hardships : lack of news except by clandestine radios, deportations to Germany, shortages of food and clothing; in 1945, when the islands were isolated, starvation threatened.
The massive concrete fortifications, built by the slave labour of the Todt Organisation as part of Hitler's impregnable Atlantic Wall, can still be seen in places; they were never tested, simply by-passed by the Normandy landings.

CONSTITUTION

The Channel Islands are divided into the Bailiwick of Jersey, which includes two rocky islets – the Minquiers and the Ecrehous – and the Bailiwick of Guernsey, which includes Alderney, Sark and Brecqhou, Herm and Jethou.
The original Norman laws and systems enshrined in the first charters granted by King John in the 13C have been renewed by subsequent monarchs, although modifications were introduced this century to separate the judiciary and legislature.
Each main island has its own parliament; tax is levied locally; no VAT is payable; coins and banknotes are issued locally but are not legal tender elsewhere; the islands print their own postage stamps.

Clameur de Haro – This is an ancient legal remedy which is still in force and is thought to invoke Rollo, a 10C Norse chieftain. A victim of wrongdoing must kneel down in the presence of two witnesses and say "Haro, haro, haro, à l'aide, mon Prince, on me fait tort" (Help, my Prince, someone is doing me wrong). This must be followed by the recital of the Lord's Prayer in French. The wrong-doer must then desist until a court ruling has been obtained.

RELIGION

Christianity seems to have been introduced in the 6C by Celtic saints from Brittany, Cornwall and Wales. Originally the parishes were attached to the diocese of Coutances in Normandy and remained so until Elizabeth I transferred them to the see of Winchester in 1568.

The form of worship adopted at the Reformation was Calvinism owing to the linguistic links with France and to the many Huguenot refugees who had fled to the Channel Islands. Anglicanism was eventually introduced at the Restoration in 1660 but the English language was not used for church services until this century.
Methodism was preached in the islands by John Wesley himself and has always had a strong influence, particularly in Guernsey.

LANGUAGE

Although English is now universal in the islands, the native tongue, a dialect of Norman-French, the language of William the Conqueror, is still spoken. In Jersey and Guernsey, societies for its preservation exist which trace the regional variations in vocabulary and pronunciation.

LIVELIHOOD

The Channel Islands (76 sq miles), which are composed of fertile granite plateaux sloping to open sand dunes, lie west of the Cherbourg peninsula and south of the main shipping lanes in the English Channel. The Gulf Stream and the southerly latitude ensure a mild climate.
Until the 18C fishing and agriculture were the main activities. In the Middle Ages large quantities of cod and conger eel were exported to England and Normandy to be eaten on the many days in the medieval church calendar when meat was forbidden. The fish were split and dried on small sticks *(perches)* in remote places, as the smell was unpleasant. The trade died when the Newfoundland fisheries were established in the 16C but the practice is recalled in eperquerie, a common place name in the Channel Islands. Seaweed (vraic – pronounced "rack") was used as fertilizer and also as fuel. Large flocks of sheep were kept on the rough ground and the words Jersey and Guernsey have entered the English language to mean woollen cloth or garments; in the 17C so many people were engaged in knitting that the harvest was neglected.
In the 18C huge fortunes were made from privateering under Letters of Marque; ship building and repairing flourished. In the 19C granite was exported in vast quantities for road-making and construction work. Cattle too, usually known as Alderneys, were in great demand owing to the high butter fat content of their milk; now only Jerseys and Guernseys are pure bred.
The Channel Islands' economy still relies on agriculture; the accent is on early vegetables – potatoes, tomatoes, grapes – and flowers. Tourism which began in the early 19C is an important source of revenue. In recent years many banks, insurance companies and finance houses have been attracted to the Channel Islands by their special tax status.

WRECKS AND LIGHTHOUSES

The Channel Islands are surrounded by extensive offshore reefs and rocky islets which are impressive at low tide or in rough seas. Together with the strong tides, treacherous currents and fog, they make these seas some of the most hazardous. Among the ships which have gone aground or foundered are a Roman galley, which sank off St Peter Port; the *White Ship,* carrying the heir to the English throne, which was caught on the Casquets in 1119; HMS *Victory,* which went down on the Casquets in 1774 with the loss of 1 000 men; the *Liverpool,* the largest sailing ship wrecked in the Channel Islands, which ran aground off Corblets Bay *(qv)* in a fog in 1902; the *Briseis,* which struck a reef off Vazon Bay in 1937 with 7 000 casks of wine on board; the *Orion,* an oil rig mounted on an ocean-going barge, which ran aground off Grand Rocques in Guernsey in 1978.
There are now four lighthouses owned by Trinity House in the Channel Islands. The earliest to be built was the Casquets (1723). Originally there were three towers, known as St Peter, St Thomas and Donjon, standing 30ft high and lit by coal fires. In 1770 oil lamps were introduced, and in 1818 revolving lights which had to be wound every two hours. There is now only one light, 120ft above sea-level, with a range of 17 miles in clear weather. The story of the lightkeeper's daughter, who found life on Alderney too noisy, is beautifully told by Swinburne in his poem *Les Casquettes.*
The Hanois Lighthouse was built in 1862 on the terrible Hanois Reef (qv). The first approaches for a light were made to Trinity House in 1816 but 43 years passed before the decision to build was taken. The tower of Cornish granite is 32ft in diameter at the base, rising to 117ft above sea-level.
Quesnard Light (1912) on Alderney and Point Robert (1913) on Sark are sited on land rather than offshore and can be visited. Point Robert is most unusual in that the light is mounted above the buildings for stores and accommodation which cling to the cliff face like a Greek monastery.

★★ JERSEY

Pop 72 970

Michelin Atlas p 5 or Map 403 – Local map below

Jersey is the largest of the Channel Islands (45sq miles); it measures 12½ by 5½ miles and lies only 15 miles from the coast of France. The visitor is greeted by a charming combination of Norman French tradition with English overtones. Local features echo not only Normandy but also Cornwall.
Owing to the Gulf Stream, Jersey enjoys an exceptionally mild climate and is thick with flowers in spring and summer.
Victor Hugo, who spent 3 years in Jersey before moving to Guernsey, was enchanted : "It possesses a unique and exquisite beauty. It is a garden of flowers cradled by the sea. Woods, meadows and gardens seem to mingle with the rocks and reefs in the sea".
The island is ringed by several circular defensive towers, built in the 18C ar 19C and similar to the Martello towers on the south coast of England.

GEOGRAPHICAL NOTES

Jersey is roughly rectangular in shape. The sparsely populated north coast formed of steep pink granite cliffs opening here and there into a sandy bay; alor the rest of the shoreline the retreating tide reveals great sandy ba (St Aubin, St Brelade, St Ouen, St Catherine, Grouville, St Clement).
The mild climate favours the growth of flowers and early vegetables : cabbage broccoli, potatoes, tomatoes, orchids, camellias, mimosa, daffodils and carnation these last appear on every restaurant table. Some crops are grown in the ope fields, others under glass. The pasture is grazed by the little Jersey cows, whic are protected from the winter cold by a sacking blanket and produce the deliciou thick Jersey cream. Unique to Jersey is the giant cabbage which grows up 10ft tall.
Fishing catches bring in crustaceans and other marine delicacies.

HISTORICAL NOTES

The tombs and prehistoric monuments found on the island indicate huma habitation between 7500 and 2500 BC. The Roman presence was brief but the 6C St Helier arrived and established Christianity. The dominant influence that of the Normans who invaded in the 10C. Customs and traditions datir from this time survive even today.
From 1204 when the French captured Normandy they made repeated attemp over the centuries to invade the Channel Islands. The last attempt occurre in 1781 when Baron de Rullecourt, a soldier of fortune, landed by night St Clement's Bay in the southeast corner of Jersey. Taken by surprise th Lt Governor surrendered but under Major Peirson, a young man of 24, the mili and British forces engaged the enemy and defeated them in the main squa in what came to be known as the Battle of Jersey; both leaders were morta wounded.

Constitution – Jersey is divided into 12 parishes, which together with th Minquiers and the Ecrehous, two groups of islets, make up the Bailiwick of Jerse it is attached to the English crown but has its own Parliament, the States Jersey. The Parliament, which is elected, consists of deputies, senators ar 12 parish constables. The Bailiff, who is appointed by the Crown, is the seni judge and President of the States. The Lt Governor, also appointed by the Crow a high-ranking military man, the Dean of Jersey, an Anglican clergyman, th Attorney-General and the Solicitor-General contribute to the debates in Parliame but in a consultative capacity only.

Famous Sons and Daughters – The most famous name connected with Jerse is Lillie Langtry *(qv)*, who became an actress and a close friend of Edward V and captivated British High Society with her beauty; she is buried in St Saviour churchyard. The fashionable 19C painter, Sir John Everett Millais (1829-96), gre up in Jersey and belonged to an old island family. So too did Elinor Gly (1864-1943), who became a novelist and Hollywood scriptwriter. The well-know French firm which makes Martell brandy was started by Jean Martell fro St Brelade; the trade mark is the old family seal. The de Carterets not on achieved importance locally in Jersey, Alderney and Sark but were granted lar in the new world by Charles II which they named New Jersey.

GOREY

This charming little port at the northern end of Grouville Bay is dominated by the proud walls of Mont Orgueil Castle set on its rocky promontory. Attractive old houses line the quay where yachts add colour to the scene in summer. In the days of the Jersey Eastern Railway *(see below)* there was a steamship service from Gorey to Normandy.

★ MONT ORGUEIL CASTLE ⏲ *45min*

Gorey castle received its present name in 1468; Henry V's brother, Thomas, Duke of Clarence, was so impressed by the castle's position and its defensive strength that he called it Mount Pride (Mont Orgueil in French). Over the centuries the castle has been the residence of the Lords and Governors of the island, including Sir Walter Raleigh (1600-03). The earliest buildings date back to the 13C although new fortifications have been added over the years. The castle is built on a concentric plan, each system of defence being independent of the others. The solid walls founded on the granite rocks are a formidable obstacle. It is like threading a maze to walk up the complex network of passages and steps to the summit.

The **view★★** from the top is extensive and varied : down into Port Gorey, south over the broad sweep of Grouville Bay, north to the rocks of Petit Portelet and west to the French coast.

A series of waxwork tableaux in the rooms of the castle illustrates significant events in the history of Mont Orgueil : Charles II during his exile in Jersey as the guest of the Governor George de Carteret *(qv)*, to whom he granted land in Virginia.

Mont Orgueil Castle, Jersey.

ADDITIONAL SIGHTS

★ **Jersey Pottery** ⏲ – A magnificent garden, hung with baskets of flowers and refreshed by fountains, surrounds the workshops where the distinctive pottery is produced. Each stage in the process is explained on large panels and the visitor can stand and watch the craftsmen at work at their various skills. The show room displays the full range of products for sale.

Faldouet Dolmen – A tree-lined path leads to this dolmen, which is 49ft long and dates from 2500 BC. The funeral chamber (20ft wide) is covered by a block of granite weighing 25 tonnes. Vases, stone pendants and polished stone axes were found when the site was excavated.

La HOUGUE BIE

Tall trees surround the tiny park, which is dominated by a high circular mound. The word Hougue, which is probably of Viking origin, means a barrow, while Bie may come from Hambye; in the Middle Ages the Lords of Hambye in Normandy owned land in this part of Jersey.

MUSEUMS ⏲ *1 hour*

To the left of the entrance gate stands a **wooden railway guard's van** from the Jersey Eastern Railway which ran from St Helier to Gorey between 1873 and 1929; within are photos, posters, notices, name plates and lamps etc connected with the railway.

Agricultural Museum – The museum illustrates country life in the 19C through a variety of agricultural and other implements used by different craftsmen and women : blacksmith, basket weaver, cooper, cobbler etc. Cider-making, which was an important activity until this century, required a circular granite trough for crushing the apples, a press, pulp shovels and barrels. Ploughs, scythes and threshing machines were used in the planting and harvesting of cereals; butter churns stand in the dairy.

Archeology and Geology Museum – Excavations have produced the many items on display : remains of mammoths, polished stone axes, flint tools, stone querns for grinding corn (belonging to neolithic settlers who were farmers), pottery, ornaments, metal objects (from the Bronze Age) found in St Lawrence etc. The section on geology presents samples of the various rocks and minerals found on the island.

★ **Neolithic Tomb** – The cruciform passage grave dates from 3000 BC. Similar tombs have been discovered in England and Brittany. The grave is covered by a 40ft mound of earth and rubble. A passage, 33ft long and roofed with granite slabs leads to the funeral chamber, which measures 10ft by 30ft and is covered with huge capstones (the heaviest weighs 25 tonnes); it opens into three smaller chambers.

★ **Chapels** – The mound is surmounted by two medieval chapels. The **Chapel of Our Lady of the Dawn** dates from the 12C; the altar (late medieval) came from Mont Orgueil Castle. The abutting Jerusalem Chapel was built in 1520 by Dean Richard Mabon after a pilgrimage to Jerusalem. The interior is decorated with frescoes of two archangels.

★ **German Occupation Museum** – A German bunker, built in 1942 as a communications centre, houses radio equipment, weapons, medals, original documents (orders and propaganda) and photographs of the period.

★★ JERSEY ZOO ⊙

The Jersey Wildlife Preservation Trust, often known as the Jersey Zoo, was founded by the naturalist Gerald Durrell in 1963 to preserve and breed threatened species. The symbol of the Trust is the dodo, the great non-flying bird of Mauritius which was first identified in 1599 and was totally extinct by 1693. The undulating park (10 acres) round Les Augrès Manor (16C) is home to over a thousand animals living in an environment similar to their natural habitat.

A special enclosure houses the whole gorilla family, including orang-utans from Borneo and Sumatra.

The zoo contains collections of rare lemurs from Madagascar, marmosets tamarins from Central America and spectacled bears (the only South American bear).

The night house enables visitors to observe the activities of fruit bats by artificial night light.

The park provides a safe environment for various species of birds in danger of extinction : pink pigeons from Mauritius have been bred in Jersey and reintroduced to their native island; the Rothschild Mynah birds and the Waldrapp Ibis are very rare in the wild and reproduce only occasionally in this zoo.

The Princess Royal Pavilion describes the history of the Trust and its work on wildlife and conservation (audio-visual presentation).

ST BRELADE

This seaside resort is situated in a sheltered bay which is perfect for water skiing. A waterfall tumbles over the rocks on the wooded slopes of the Winston Churchill Memorial Park which backs the bay.

At the western end of the beach, behind a screen of trees, the parish church and detached medieval chapel are surrounded by gravestones.

Parish Church – The church is built of granite from the cliffs of La Moye headland. The earliest parts of the structure – chancel, nave and belfry – date from the 11C. The church became cruciform in the 12C with the addition of a transept; the aisles were added in the 13C. The altar is a solid slab of stone marked with five crosses representing the five wounds of the Crucifixion. The 14C font is made of granite from the Chausey Islands, which lie south of Jersey and belong to France.

Fishermen's Chapel – The chapel, which is built of the same granite as the church, is decorated in the interior with some delicate medieval **frescoes**★ : The Annunciation *(east end)* is 14C; Adam and Eve *(right of the chancel)*, the Birth of Christ *(right of the nave)*, the Scenes from the Passion *(left of the nave and chancel)* and the Last Judgement *(chancel)* are 15C.

Behind the chapel a short flight of steps leads from the churchyard to the beach; this is the only surviving example of a **perquage** : as well as the right of sanctuary which was widespread in medieval Europe, all the churches of Jersey had a sanctuary path *(perquage)* leading to the shore by which fugitives could leave the island.

Traditional Cornish dishes include Muggety Pie (sheep's offal), the renowned Cornish pasty (qv), Kiddley Broth (the staple fare of poor tin-mining families : bread soaked in boiling water) and Stargazy Pie (so-named because of the pilchard heads poking through the crust).

ST HELIER

Pop 29 941

St Helier, the capital of the island, is named after the saint who landed on the island in the 6C and lived as a hermit for 15 years.

St Helier is a lively town, the main commercial centre on the island and the seat of government. Although the first market was established by 1299, the town hardly grew until the 19C when many new houses were built and the harbour was greatly extended. Many of the evocative Norman street names have been replaced by more sober English titles; thus Church Street was formerly called Rue Trousse Cotillon where women had to tuck up their skirts out of the mire. The shops in the pedestrian precinct formed by **King and Queen Streets** are a great attraction to tourists.

SIGHTS

Elizabeth Castle (Z) ⏲ – *Access on foot across a causeway at low tide (½ hour); otherwise by amphibious vehicle.*

The castle was built on an island, called St Helier's Isle after the hermit saint. In the 12C William Fitz-Hamon, one of Henry II's courtiers, founded an abbey on the site. The castle buildings were begun in the mid 16C and reinforced during the Civil War to withstand the repeated assaults of the Parliamentary forces; after a 50 day siege the Royalists surrendered. During the Second World War the Germans made their own additions to the fortifications : roving search-light, bunkers and gun batteries. The various stages in the construction of the castle are shown in the Guard room. The **Militia Museum** contains mementoes of the Royal Jersey Regiment : uniforms, weapons, flags and silver including an unusual snuff box in the shape of a ram's head. The former Governor's House contains waxwork tableaux of events in the history of the castle.

The Upper Ward encloses the keep, known as the Mount, where the Germans built a concrete fire control tower surmounted by an anti-aircraft position. There is a fine **view★** of the castle itself and also of St Aubin's Fort across the bay.

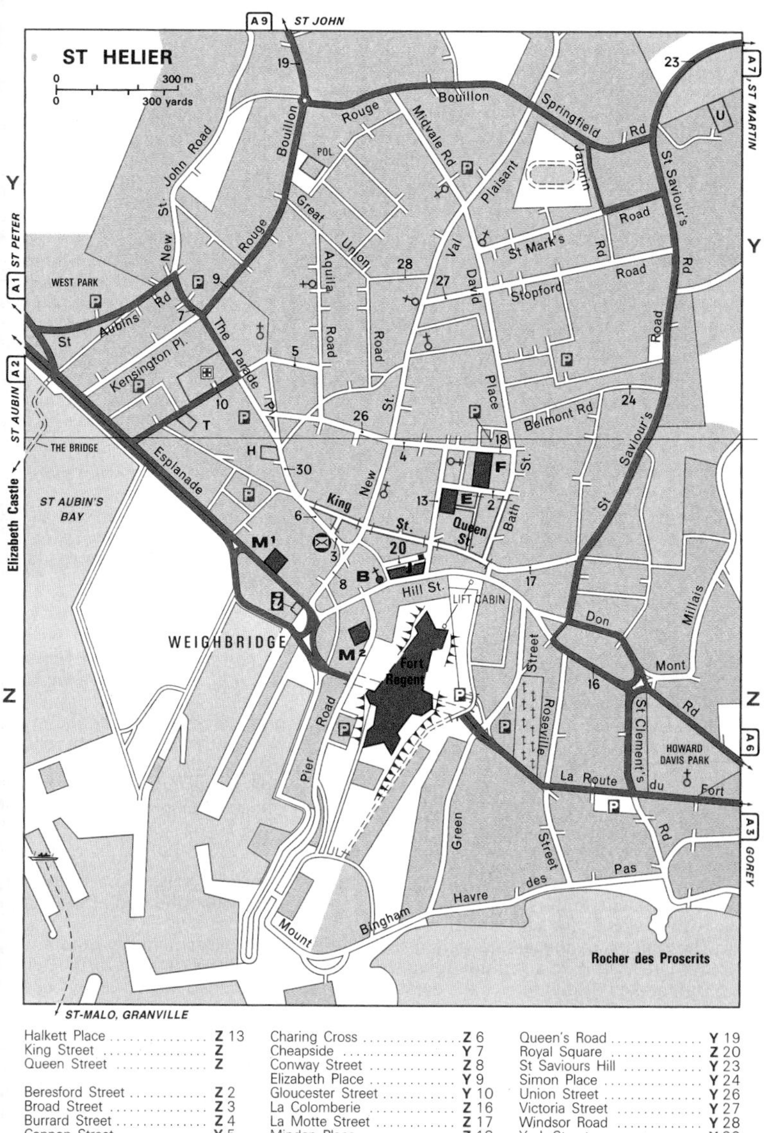

Halkett Place	Z 13	Charing Cross	Z 6	Queen's Road	Y 19
King Street	Z	Cheapside	Y 7	Royal Square	Z 20
Queen Street	Z	Conway Street	Z 8	St Saviours Hill	Y 23
		Elizabeth Place	Y 9	Simon Place	Y 24
Beresford Street	Z 2	Gloucester Street	Y 10	Union Street	Y 26
Broad Street	Z 3	La Colomberie	Z 16	Victoria Street	Y 27
Burrard Street	Z 4	La Motte Street	Z 17	Windsor Road	Y 28
Cannon Street	Y 5	Minden Place	Z 18	York Street	Y 30

South of the castle a breakwater extends past the chapel on the rock where according to legend, St Helier lived as a hermit *(procession on or about 16 July, St Helier's Day).*

★ **Jersey Museum** (Z M^2) ⊙ – The Jersey Museum is housed in an old merchant's house and an adjoining 18C warehouse.
On the ground floor, near the entrance, are historical maps of Jersey; further on is a display of the articles which accompanied Lillie Langtry *(qv)* on her travels. An audio-visual show provides a good introduction to the island.
The treadmill, which was turned by 12 men and operated a pepper mill, was used in St Helier prison during the 19C.
The first floor is devoted to the history of the island from the Stone Age to the present by means of reconstructions using authentic exhibits (working in the fields, the fisher folk, tourism). Further glimpses of the past can be gained through photos, films and two tactile and interactive screens.
The Barreau-Le Maistre art gallery, on the second floor, presents two centuries of paintings, drawings and water-colours by local artists or works on local subjects : Sir John Everett Millais, P J Ouless, J Le Capelain and the illustrator Edmond Blampied. There is also a collection of Chinese snuff boxes donated by Eric Young.
On the third floor there is a reconstruction of a 19C bedroom (1861).

St Helier Parish Church (Z B) – The pink granite church with its square tower dates from the 11C. In the south transept hangs a plan of the seating in 1868 showing the names of the pew-holders : the higher the rent the nearer the altar.

Royal Square (Z 20) – A statue of George II, dressed as a Roman emperor, looks down on this charming small square with its spreading chestnut trees. It was formerly the Market Place where malefactors were exposed in the pillory during market hours. Bordering the south side are the granite buildings of the **Royal Court House** ⊙. The public entrance bears the arms of George II, the Bailiff's entrance the arms of George VI. A plaque records the birth of the 12C Norman poet, **Wace** *(qv)*. At the east end of the range of buildings are the States Chambers *(entrance round the corner)* where the Jersey parliament sits in session.

Central Market (Z E) – The granite building is decorated with cast-iron grilles at the windows and entrances and covered with a glass roof supported on iron columns. A circular fountain stands at the centre of this lively and colourful scene. The fish market is round the corner in Beresford Street.

Fort Regent (Z) ⊙ – *Access by cable car or bus in Hill Street (summer only) or by escalators in Pier Road.*
The massive fortifications of Fort Regent were built to protect Jersey from invasion by Napoleon. Within, topped by a shallow white dome, is a modern leisure centre providing a variety of sports facilities and entertainment : swimming pool, Badminton, squash, table-tennis, snooker, play-area for children, puppet theatre, exhibitions, aquarium and audio-visual shows on the history and culture of the island.
The rampart walk provides splendid **views★** of the town and St Aubin's Bay *(west).*

Island Fortress Occupation Museum (Z M^1) ⊙ – Waxwork models in uniform, weapons and military equipment evoke this period in the island's history. Video of the occupation and liberation of Jersey (1940-45).

Le Rocher des Proscrits (Z) – *Take Pier Road going south, skirt Mount Bingham and continue along Havre des Pas to Dicq Corner (1¼ miles).*
The road follows the shoreline along the south coast. On the east side of the White Horse Inn, a slipway descends to the beach and a group of rocks. Le Rocher des Proscrits (The Rock of the Exiles), where **Victor Hugo** *(qv)* loved to meditate, is marked by a small plaque *(facing the road).*

EXCURSIONS

★ **Living Legend, St Peter's Valley** ⊙ – *4 miles northwest. Leave St Helier by A1 towards St Aubin; at Bel Royal turn right into A11, St Peter's Valley road and continue to C112 then follow signs.*
The granite buildings which house the Living Legend trace the history and myths of Jersey through an entertaining multi-sensory experience : the labyrinth of mysterious chambers, which incorporates castle towers and ships' decks, dramatically recounts various aspects of the islanders' lives and stories of heroes and villains with the aid of visual and sound effects (holograms, lasers, wind machines...).

Samarès Manor ⊙ – *1 mile east of St Helier.*
The name Samarès is probably derived from the Norman "salse marais" meaning a salt marsh. In the past the local salt production provided the lord of the manor with a significant part of his revenue.
The history of the estate began in the 11C when William Rufus granted the Samarès fief to his faithful servant Rodolph of St Hilaire. In the 17C Philippe Dumaresq decided to give the estate a new look; he drained the marsh by building a canal to St Helier and imported trees and vines from France. The gardens were created by Sir James Knott early in the 20C.
The estate *(plan available at the entrance)* comprises a herb garden where various plants used in cookery, dyeing, medicine and perfumery are grown, an 11C dovecote, a Norman crypt, the manor house including the dining room panelled in walnut, a farm with Jacob sheep, a walled garden, Japanese garden and water rock garden.

German Underground Hospital ⊙ – *3 miles west. Leave St Helier by A1 towards St Aubin; at Bel Royal turn right into A11 and right again into B89.*
The first men to work on excavating the underground hospital were Spanish republican prisoners captured in France. In 1942 hundreds of Russian prisoners arrived to swell the number of forced labourers. Only half the projected hospital was finished and used for only six weeks. In a granite labyrinth of tunnels, bordered by the unfinished sections, are the machine room, the officers' mess, a hospital ward, the telephone exchange, the Commandant's office, the operating theatre, the doctors' quarters etc. The occupation and liberation of the island are recorded on video films; display of weapons, photographs and posters.

Quetivel Mill ⊙ – *3 miles northwest. Leave St Helier by A1 towards St Aubin; at Bel Royal turn right into A11. Park by the mill pond; walk down through the wood; the tour begins on the top floor of the mill.*
The **mill,** which is charmingly situated between a herb garden and a shrubbery, on a bend in St Peter's Valley, is one of eight mills once operated by this stream. From the mill pond the water is channelled by the mill leat down through the wood (red squirrels and woodpeckers) to the mill wheel, a pitch-back overshot wheel. Quetivel Mill dates from pre-1309 and worked continuously for six hundred years until made obsolete by steam power. Plans were being made for its restoration in 1969 when fire destroyed all the machinery which had been brought back into temporary service during the German Occupation; only the walls were left. By 1979, however, re-equipped with parts from other disused Jersey mills, Quetivel was in operation grinding locally-grown grain and producing stone-ground flour for sale. The tour shows each stage of the process from the arrival of the grain by hoist in the loft to the production of stone-ground flour for sale on the ground floor. Most of the grinding stones are made of French burr, quarried near Paris; they are composed of segments set with plaster of Paris and will last a hundred years. A pair of stones will produce 25 tons of flour before needing to be dressed, when the grooves are recut to the required depth using a tool called a "bill" which has to be resharpened frequently owing to the hardness of the stone. This process would take a miller about a week.

Jersey Motor Museum, St Peter's Village ⊙ – *4 miles northwest. Leave St Helier by A1; at Beaumont turn right into A12.*
This collection of historic motor vehicles, all in working order and appearing at rallies in Jersey and elsewhere, includes the 1936 Rolls-Royce Phantom III used by General Montgomery in 1944 during D-Day preparations and the 1964 Hillman Husky which belonged to Sir Winston Churchill. Cars by Ford, Austin, Talbot, Bentley and Jaguar contrast with Allied and German military vehicles and motorbicycles. The museum also recalls the days of the Jersey steam railways.

TOUR OF THE ISLAND *local map below*

1 SOUTH COAST

From St Helier to Corbière Point *10 miles – about 2 hours*

St Helier – *See St Helier.*

Leave St Helier by A1 going west.

Millbrook – **St Matthew's Church** ⊙, also known as the **Glass Church,** was unexceptional until 1934 when **René Lalique** (1860-1945), the French specialist in moulded glass, was invited to decorate the interior. He designed and made all the **glasswork**★ : door panels, windows, lighting, font, altar reredos in the Lady Chapel, cross and pillars behind the high altar and the screens which are decorated with a lily motif. The luminescent and ethereal quality of the glasswork is most impressive when the lights are switched on at dusk. The work was commissioned by the widow of Lord Trent, who founded Boots the chemists; he lived at Villa Millbrook and was buried at St Brelade.

St Aubin – The little town, which faces east across St Aubin's Bay, is very popular in the summer for its long sandy beach and marina.
The fort on the island *(access at low tide)* was built in the reign of Henry VIII to protect the town. The steep, narrow streets and old houses cling to the cliffs along the shore.
The **Railway Walk** to Corbière follows the line of the old Jersey Railway *(qv)* which opened in 1870 from St Helier to St Aubin and was later extended.

Leave St Aubin by A13; bear left into B57.

★ **Noirmont Point** – The headland is still marked by the remains of German fortifications. The most advanced bastion gives a fine view of the rocks immediately below and round westwards to the Ile au Guerdain, surmounted by a defensive tower, in the centre of Portelet Bay.

Return to A13; bear left into B66.

Soon the road dips to St Brelade's Bay with its granite church among the pine trees.

St Brelade – *See St Brelade.*

Leave St Brelade by minor road west of the church; in La Moye bear left into B83.

Corbière Point – As the road descends, a magnificent view is steadily revealed of the rock-strewn point and the white lighthouse rising from its islet. The rock formation is dramatic with many reefs offshore; in rough weather the sea breaking on the shore is particularly impressive.
The lighthouse *(access on foot at low tide)* was built in 1874; in clear weather its beam carries 17 miles.

2 WEST COAST

From Corbière Point to Petit Etacquerel

8 miles - 1 hour

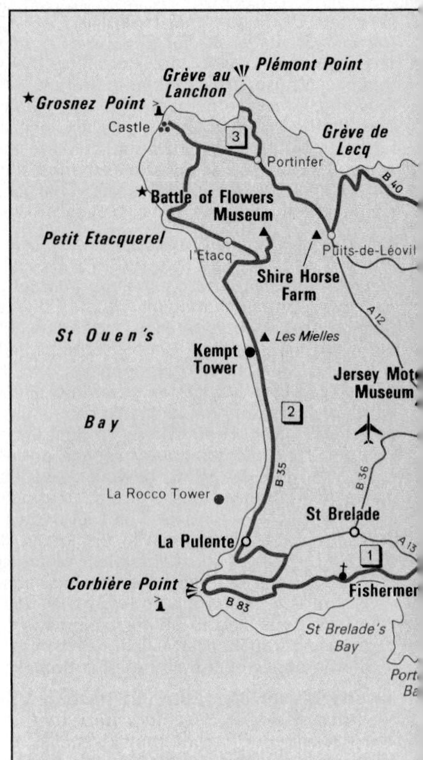

The major part of this coastline is taken up with St Ouen's Bay, a five mile stretch of sand backed by sand dunes. The landscape is wild and uncultivated, the vegetation sparse. A nature reserve, called Les Mielles (the Jersey dialect word for sand dunes), has been created to study and protect the local flora and fauna.

La Pulente – This small village is the main centre for gathering seaweed *(vraic)* which is used as fertilizer. Inland on the dunes is La Moye Golf Course. Offshore on a reef stands La Rocco Tower, built in 1880 *(accessible at low tide).*

St Ouen's Bay – The breakers which roll into the bay make it a favourite spot for windsurfers. The firm sand attracts motor and motorcycle racing fans.

Kempt Tower ⏲ – This defensive tower has been converted into an Interpretation Centre with maps, photographs and pamphlets about the region : geological features, archeological remains, flora and fauna.

Near L'Etacq bear east into B64 and left into C114.

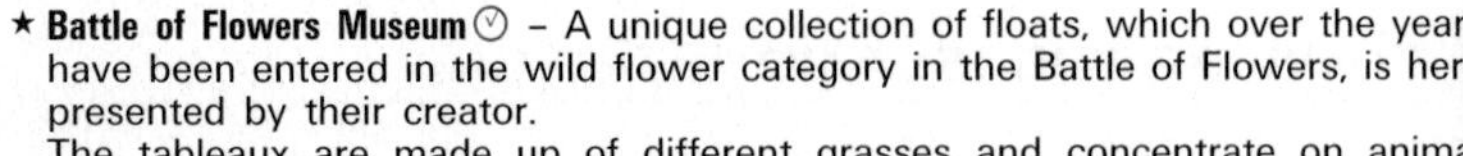

★ **Battle of Flowers Museum** ⏲ – A unique collection of floats, which over the years have been entered in the wild flower category in the Battle of Flowers, is here presented by their creator.
The tableaux are made up of different grasses and concentrate on animal subjects : the 101 Dalmatians are all there, the result of 1 400 hours of work; also Arctic, African and pastoral scenes.
The **Battle of Flowers** – held on the second Thursday in August along Victoria Avenue in St Helier *(see Calendar of Events, qv)* – was started in 1902 to celebrate the coronation of Edward VII; originally after the parade, the floats were broken up and the crowd pelted one another with the flowers, then mostly hydrangeas.

Return to L'Etacq and continue north along B35.

Petit Etacquerel – A defensive tower guards the point which marks the northern end of St Ouen's Bay. It is here that in 1651 Admiral Blake landed with the Parliamentary forces which forced the Royalists to surrender.

Continue north by B55 to Grosnez.

3 NORTH COAST

From Grosnez Point to Rozel Bay *17 miles - 2½ hours*

The north coast of the island is the least densely populated and consists of high rocky cliffs with an occasional small sandy bay. The cliff paths provide spectacular views of the uneven coastline. Early crop potatoes are grown on the steeply sloping hillsides (côtils).

★ **Grosnez Point** – An area of desolate heathland, covered with gorse and heather and known as Les Landes, extends from Etacquerel to Grosnez Point. Beyond the racecourse are the ruins of a medieval stronghold (*c*1373-1540); the high cliffs, the curtain wall with ditch, gateway and drawbridge, provided a place of temporary refuge against invasion. Magnificient view out to sea of Sark and the other islands (northwest).

Return to B55; in Portinfer turn left into C105.

The road skirts the holiday village to end in a car park.

Plémont Point – The rocky promontory projects into the sea providing a fine view of the cliffs.

From the car park a path descends to Grève au Lanchon.

Grève au Lanchon – Steep cliffs containing caves shelter this attractive small bay which has a sandy beach at low tide.

Return to B55; in Puits de Leoville turn right into C115 and right again into B34.

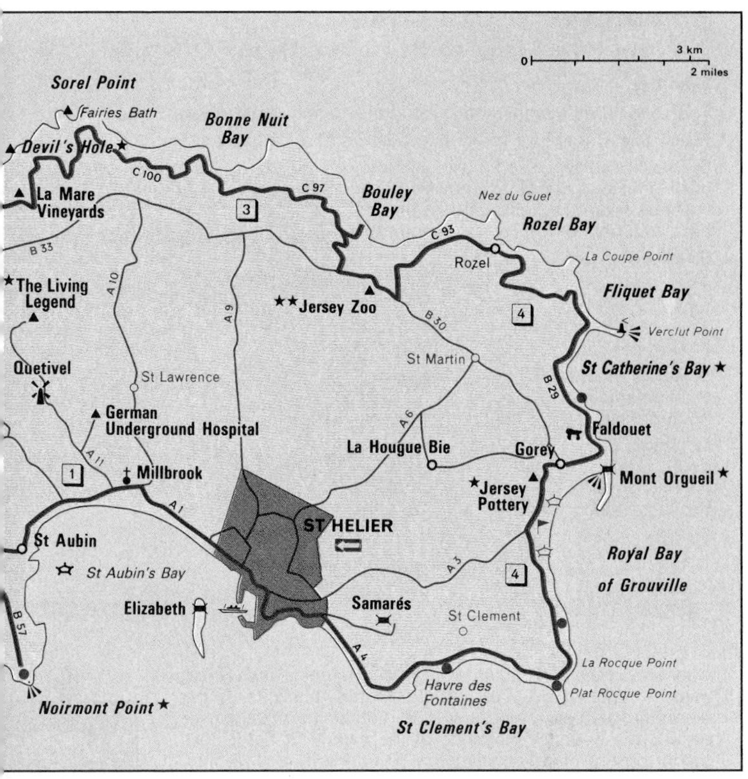

Shire Horse Farm ◷ – The chief attraction is the shire horses, their yearlings and foals which are bred on the farm, together with many other smaller animals and birds. Also on view are various horse-drawn vehicles, in which visitors may tour the neighbouring lanes at the leisurely speed of a shire horse. The circular stone trough in the farmyard was formerly used for crushing cider apples.

Return to Puits de Leoville. Take B65.

Grève de Lecq – This charming sandy bay with its stream and mill was defended against invasion most recently by the Germans in the Second World War and earlier against the French in the 18C-19C. The defensive tower was built in 1780.
The **barracks** were built between 1810 and 1815 to accommodate the 150 British soldiers who manned the gun batteries on the slopes around the bay. There were two blocks, each consisting of four rooms for the soldiers and two for the NCOs; the central building was for the officers. Behind stood the Ablutions block and two prison cells; to the south was the stabling.

Leave Grève de Lecq by B40, turn left into B33 and left again into C103.

La Mare Vineyards ◷ – The estate of an 18C farmhouse has been planted with the only vineyards and cider orchard in Jersey. An introductory video film, describing its history, the vineyards, the harvest and the wine-making process, adds to the interest of touring the vineyards and the gleaming modern vintry, where German-style white wines are produced and may be tasted : Clos de la Mare, Clos de Seyval and Blayney Special Reserve.

Continue along C103 to the inn.

★ **Devil's Hole** – *Park by the inn and take the concrete path down to the cliff.* The blow hole is an impressive sight; the noise of the sea entering the cave below rises up the chimney.

Take the minor roads east and north.

Sorel Point – When the tide goes out a man-made pool is revealed in the rocks *(right)* known as the Fairies' Bath (Lavoir des Dames).

Take C100 east along the cliffs.

Bonne Nuit Bay – Charles II is supposed to have returned from exile to England from this attractive bay where a stone jetty shelters the tiny harbour.

Bouley Bay – A sandy bay protected by a jetty and backed by high granite cliffs.

Leave by C102; turn left into B31.

★ **Jersey Zoo** – *See Jersey Zoo.*

Take C93 to Rozel Bay.

Rozel Bay – Part of the bay is taken up with a fishing port where the boats go aground at low tide. It is sheltered to the north by Nez du Guet where there are traces of a rampart built in 500 BC.

4 EAST AND SOUTH COAST

From Rozel Bay to St Helier *13 miles - 1½ hours*

Rozel Bay - *See above.*

The road turns inland before returning to the coast above Fliquet Bay.

Fliquet Bay - This is a rocky bay between La Coupe and Verclut Points.

★ **St Catherine's Bay** - The long breakwater (½ mile), which protects the bay to th north, was part of a British government scheme (1847-55) to create a huge nava harbour. From the lighthouse at the end there is a magnificent **view**★★ of sand bays alternating with rocky promontories along the coast southwards.

Gorey - *See Gorey.*

From Gorey to St Helier the coast road passes several defensive towers *(qv)* whic together with two 18C forts - Fort William and Fort Henry - seem to keep watc at regular intervals along the shore. This corner of the island is very popula in summer for its sandy beaches.

Royal Bay of Grouville - The prefix royal was bestowed by Queen Victoria, wh was greatly impressed by the magnificent crescent of sand stretching to L Rocque Point. Between the road and the shore lies the Royal Jersey golf course

St Clement's Bay - This sandy bay stretches from Plat Rocqe Point, past Le Hoc Point, marked by a defensive tower, to Le Nez Point *(2 miles)*. In 1781 Baro de Rullecourt landed with 600 French troops at the eastern end of the bay i the last French attempt to capture Jersey.

St Helier - *See St Helier.*

★ GUERNSEY

Pop 53 637

Michelin Atlas p 5 or Map 403 - Local map below

Guernsey is the second largest of the Channel Islands (24sq miles - 63sq km). Less sophisticated than its larger neighbour, Jersey, it has its own particular charm : a slower tempo, the Regency elegance of the capital St Peter Port, the proximity of other islands - Sark, Herm and Jethou. Since the Second World War its main sources of income have been tourism, tomatoes and offshore finance and insurance.

GEOGRAPHICAL NOTES

Guernsey is shaped like a right-angled triangle; the west coast forms the hypotenuse, the south coast the base and the east coast the perpendicular. There is little open country; from the air the whole island seems to be covered with glasshouses, small field and dwellings, linked by a network of narrow lanes. The only wild country i to be found along the southern cliffs, where flowers abound in spring, whil the sandy beaches and rocky promontories of the west and north coast ar excellent for bathing, surfing and exploring rock pools. The water lane, wher a stream runs in a channel in the middle of the road, is a special feature o Guernsey : Moulin Huet Valley, Petit Bot Valley.

As the island slopes from south to north away from the sun, most of the crop are grown under glass. The most famous export, the Guernsey tomato, was firs grown in 1893 among the grapes in the greenhouses, hence the name viner for a tomato farm. Grapes are still grown as well as melons, peas, potatoes anc of course, flowers. The pure-bred Guernsey cattle, famous for the rich crear content of their milk, are larger and hardier than the Jersey breed.

Fishing is still an important activity; in the past the ormer or sea ear *(oreille d mer)* was a local delicacy prepared by stewing or pickling after being well beate to make it tender. The shell is lined with mother-of-pearl and sometimes contain pearls. This mollusc is now rare and fishing is severely restricted in all the islands The abundant and varied supply of local granite, particularly from the Clos d Valle, has provided the islanders with an excellent and attractive building stone although it is hard to shape or carve : pink or brownish-red from Côbo and Albecc golden-yellow from L'Ancresse and grey, blue and black from other norther quarries.

HISTORICAL NOTES

Like its neighbours, Guernsey was inhabited in prehistoric times and is rich i Bronze and Iron Age monuments : dolmens. Traces of the Romans' presenc are slight; a Roman boat and amphora have been raised from the sea off S Peter Port. In the 6C St Sampson arrived from South Wales with his nephev St Magloire, although Christianity may have been introduced earlier; the ten islan parishes may date from this period or be based on earlier agricultural units In 933 Guernsey was annexed by the Duke of Normandy and after 1066 wa attached to the English Crown; all the charters granted to the island since 139 are housed in the Greffe in the Royal Court House in St Peter Port. Despite th loss of Normandy to the French in 1204, the link with the Crown was not severe until the Civil War when Guernseymen, angered by the exacting behaviour o the previous English Governor, declared for Parliament, although under th Constitution they had no right to do so. At the Restoration a petition wa presented to Charles II humbly begging a Royal Pardon, which was grantec

Although the Channel Islanders are not obliged to fight except to defend their islands and the monarch, many have served with the British forces; the Royal Guernsey Light Infantry suffered heavy casualties at Cambrai in 1917. Since 1939 201 Squadron of the RAF has been affiliated to the island, confirming the link established in the 1920s when it operated flying boats from Calshot.

Famous Guernseymen – Despite its size, Guernsey has nurtured several famous men : two Lord Mayors of London – Paul Le Mesurier (1793-94) and Peter Perchard of Hatton Garden (1804-05); Admiral Lord James de Saumarez (1757-1836) who fought against the French in the Napoleonic Wars; Major-General Sir Isaac Brock (1769-1812) who fought under Nelson and died in the defence of Canada against the Americans at Queenstown Heights; Thomas de la Rue (1773-1866) who made his fortune in London printing playing cards, postage stamps and currency notes.

La Chevauchée de St Michel – Until 1837 this medieval ceremony, which probably originated in pagan Normandy, took place every three years just before the feast of Corpus Christi with its procession of the blessed sacrament. The cavalcade (chevauchée) consisted of the Crown Officers and the officials of the feudal court of St Michel du Valle who made a tour of inspection of the island highways; they were dressed in costume and mounted on horseback, armed with a sword and attended by one or two footmen (pions). The pions were usually handsome bachelors as it was their privilege to kiss any young women they met. They lunched at Pezeries *(qv)*; dinner was provided out of the fines levied on the owners of any obstructions.

Constitution – The Bailiwick of Guernsey comprises the islands of Guernsey, Alderney, Sark, Herm and Jethou; Guernsey is wholly or partially responsible for the other four. The local parliament, known as the States of Deliberation, consists of 33 deputies, elected by public suffrage for three years, 10 Douzeniers, nominated by the Parish Councils for one year, 12 Conseillers, elected for 6 years by the States of Election, the Attorney-General and the Solicitor-General, and is presided over by the Bailiff. He is also president of the Royal Court which consists of 12 Jurats, appointed by the States of Election, and the Crown Officers. Proceedings are in English although French is still used for the formalities.

★ ST PETER PORT

The island capital is built on a most attractive site on a hillside on the east coast overlooking a safe anchorage protected from high seas by Herm and Sark. The medieval town by the shore was rebuilt after bombardment during the Civil War. Another building boom, financed by the profits earned from privateering in the late 18C, produced a delightful Regency town built in a variety of local granite embellished by elegant garden railings.

SIGHTS

★ **Castle Cornet** (Z) ⓥ – The castle suffered its greatest misfortune not in war but in a storm in 1672 when a lightning strike ignited the gunpowder store in the old tower keep. The explosion decapitated the castle, destroying not only the tower but the medieval banqueting hall and the Governor's house, and killed his wife and daughter. The original castle (*c*1206) was reinforced under Elizabeth I and again under Victoria. The Prisoners' Walk is the original barbican, an unusual and most effective piece of defence work. The castle was twice captured by the French – from 1338 to 1345 and briefly in 1356.

In the Civil War the island sided with Parliament while the Castle was loyal to the king and held out for eight years, being the last of the royalist strongholds to surrender. During those years the Castle fired 10 000 cannonballs into St Peter Port; young boys would gather them up and sell them back to the Castle.

On the Saluting Platform in the outer bailey the ceremony of the **noonday gun** is performed by two men dressed in the Guernsey Militia uniform; one trains a telescope on the town clock and the other fires the cannon.

From the Citadel there is a fine **view**★ of the harbour and town *(west)*, St Sampson, Vale Castle and Alderney *(north)*, Herm, Sark and the French coast *(east)* and Jersey *(south)*.

Maritime Museum – The museum relates the island's maritime history from the Gallo-Roman period to the present day. Exhibitions centre on the harbour, Roman and medieval trade, fish and fishing, smuggling, privateering, the Royal Navy; there is a gallery of marine art, a carpenter's workshop, displays on ship building and cross-Channel steamers, divers and lifeboats.

Militia Museum – Housed in the Hospital Building (1746) are two collections : the Spencer Collection *(lower floor)* of uniforms and insignia of the Channel Islands militias; *(upper floor)* regimental silver, musical instruments and mementoes of the Royal Guernsey Militia which was disbanded in 1939.

Armoury – Collection of weapons used by the Militia and other regiments connected with Guernsey; Civil War arms and armour.

Harbour (YZ) – The large modern harbour is a scene of constant activity : car and passenger ferries to the mainland and neighbouring islands, fishing boats and private yachts. The north pier was added in the 18C to the original 13C pier to form the Old Harbour. The Castle Pier and St Julian's Pier out to White Rock were built between 1835 and 1909, and the Jetty was added in the 1920s. The North Marina is destined to accommodate more private craft. It is worth strolling out to White Rock or visiting the Castle for a fine **view** of the town, the harbour and the neighbouring islands.

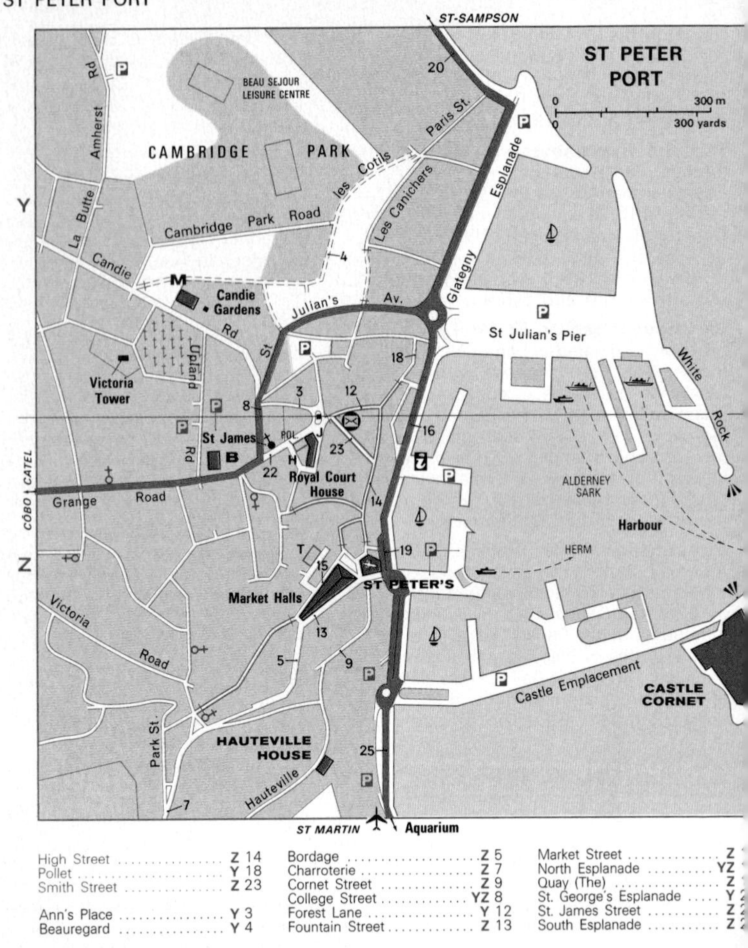

★ **St Peter's** – The Town Church, as it is known, was begun by William th Conqueror in 1048. The nave and west door are part of the original Norma structure. In those days it doubled as a fort and in the past it has housed th guns of the artillery, the fire engine, and the flower market on wet days.
The interior is furnished with an interesting range of stained glass and handsome collection of memorials and monuments commemorating famou Guernseymen.

★ **Hauteville House (Victor Hugo's House)** (Z) ⊙ – Victor Hugo *(qv)* was exiled fro his native France for political reasons in 1851. After a year in Brussels and thre in Jersey, from which he was expelled for disparaging remarks about Quee Victoria, he came to Guernsey. He bought this supposedly haunted house in 185 for a derisory sum. During his fourteen years' residence he re-decorated th interior, doing much of the work himself. The plain façade gives no hint of th incongruous and eccentric décor which reveals an unknown aspect of Hugo genius – interior design.
Every inch of wall and ceiling is covered with wood carvings or tiles (from Del or Rouen), tapestries or silk fabric. In the dining room a soup tureen serves a finger bowl and iron stands are incorporated into the "ancestors' armcha to give it a Gothic look; in the Red Drawing Room the torches of liberty he by the negro slaves are simply upturned candlesticks supporting copper sca pans. Mottoes and inscriptions abound and mirrors are placed so as to enhan the effect of various features.
Hugo used to work on his poems and novels standing at a small table in "th Glass Room" on the third floor overlooking the sea. From "the Look Out" whe he sometimes slept he could see the house of his mistress, Juliette Drou

Guernsey Museum and Art Gallery (Y M) ⊙ – A cluster of modern octagon structures, inspired by the adjoining Victorian bandstand (refreshments), hous the Lukis archeological collection and the Wilfred Carey collection of painting prints and ceramics. An excellent display traces the history of Guernse supplemented by videos of the island history and the "Clameur de Haro" *(q*

Candie Gardens – The beautiful gardens, descending from the Museum a the Priaulx Library (formerly Candie House), were laid out in 1898 with exo plants (maidenhair tree) and contain the first two experimental glasshouses bu in 1792. A dramatic statue of Victor Hugo *(see above)* dominates the slopi lawn.

Victoria Tower (Y) – The 100ft tower was designed by William Collings 1848 to celebrate the royal visit in 1846.

Elizabeth College (Z B) – The public school for boys was founded as a grammar school in 1563 by Elizabeth I to foster a supply of local English-speaking clergymen. The present building in pseudo-Tudor style by John Wilson dates from 1826-29.

St James' (Z) ⊙ – This elegant neo-Classical building, now converted into a concert hall, was formerly a church designed by John Wilson in 1818; the services were held in English for the British garrison.

Royal Court House (Z) ⊙ – The law courts and the States of Deliberation hold their sittings in this elegant building which was started in 1792. The island archives go back 400 years.

Market Halls (Z) – Both the architecture and the produce are a delight to the eye. On the right is the first covered market, Les Halles, with Assembly Rooms over, completed in 1782; opposite is the single-storey Doric-style meat market (1822); "Les Arcades, 1830" *(left)* is very handsome despite the loss of the final bay; next came the Fish Market, 1877, with its row of round windows like great port-holes and finally the Vegetable Market in 1879. All stand on the site of the Rectory Garden.

Aquarium ⊙ – A tank of writhing conger eels vies in fascination with brilliant tropical fish and local specimens from both fresh and salt water habitats. The tunnel housing them was excavated in 1860 to carry a tramway south along the coast but was abandoned after a rock fall. The Germans extended it in 1940-45.

EXCURSIONS

★ **Saumarez Park** – *2 miles by road to Côbo.*
The trees and shrubs of this beautiful park are matched by the formal rose gardens; the pond is alive with wildfowl. **The Battle of Flowers** is held here every year on the fourth Thursday in August; most of the floats which compete in the different classes are made of real flowers grown locally.
The house, now an old people's home known as the **Hostel of St John** ⊙, dates from 1721 and was the home of Admiral Lord James de Saumarez *(qv).*

Guernsey Folk Museum ⊙ – Housed in the outbuildings of Saumarez House, the museum is formed round an early 19C Guernsey kitchen and a Victorian bedroom : domestic utensils, cider apple crusher, farm implements, ploughs, carts and wagons.

Catel Church – The church of St Mary of the Castle (Ste Marie du Câtel) was built in the 12C on the site of a Viking castle. Outside the church entrance stands a granite statue menhir found inside the church in 1878. It represents a female figure, probably the mother-goddess of the Neolithic and Bronze Age cults. Inside *(north aisle)* are 13C frescoes of the Last Supper and the fable of the three living and the three dead.

German Underground Hospital ⊙ – *2 miles west of St Peter Port.* This complex of tunnels is kept as a memorial to the forced labourers who worked on its construction for 3½ years. It consists of an ammuniton store and a hospital comprising an operating theatre, 5 100-bed wards, X-ray room, mortuary, stores, kitchen, staff quarters etc. It was used briefly for D-Day German casualties.

★ **Little Chapel** – The unique miniature chapel, nestling in a shrubbery, sparkles in the sunshine; its clinker walls are faced both within and without with a brilliant mosaic of shells and fragments of glass and china. This unusual model of the grotto and shrine at Lourdes was built by Brother Deodat, a Salesian monk from Les Vauxbelets College, earlier this century.

ST SAMPSON

Guernsey's second port, which has taken all bulk cargoes since 1964, lies at the eastern end of the Braye du Valle *(see below).* Shipbuilding in the 18C was eclipsed in the 19C by the export of granite for road building; the first of the handsome granite quays was built in 1820.

The Bridge – Originally there was a bridge here across the Braye du Valle *(see below)* but when it was blocked in 1806 it was faced with stone to form a mooring. The reclaimed land west of the bridge is below sea-level at high tide.

St Sampson's – The oldest church in Guernsey was built where St Sampson came ashore in the 6C from Llantwit Major in South Wales. The oldest part of the church is the early Norman saddleback tower at the end of the nave. The attractive churchyard overlooks the disused Longue Hougue Quarry.

EXCURSIONS

Oatlands Craft Centre ⊙ – *1 mile west by Braye Road.* A set of old farm buildings with thatched roofs round a courtyard now houses a craft centre where individual artists and craftsmen exercise their skills in pottery, glass making and engraving, jewellery, patchwork, herbal cosmetics and bee-keeping. The two distinctive kilns produced bricks from 1800 to the 1930s for fortifications, chimneys and boiler pits for heating glasshouses, and clay pots for tomatoes.

Château des Marais (Castle in the Marshes) – *1 mile south by the coast road; turn right in Belle Greve Bay into Grand Bouet and then second right.* The ruined medieval castle crowns a low knoll which was first used in the Bronze Age and was protected by the surrounding marshy ground. It consists of an outer wall enclosing a ditch and inner fortification. Excavations in 1975-77 uncovered 13C coins in a chapel dedicated to Our Lady of the Marshes. The castle was refortified in the 18C and was later known as Ivy Castle owing to the creeper which covered it.

TOUR OF THE ISLAND *local map below*

1 CLOS DU VALLE

From St Peter Port to Vale Church *5 miles – ½ day*

Until the early 19C the northern part of Guernsey, known as Clos du Valle was cut off by a tidal channel, the Braye du Valle, from St Sampson to Gran Havre.

The channel was crossed by a bridge in St Sampson and by a causeway at lov water near Vale Church. For reasons of military security it was filled in by S John Doyle *(qv)*; the 300 acres of reclaimed salt pans and mud flats is nov covered in glasshouses. The Clos du Valle is densely populated owing to th many quarries which were worked in the area in the 19C.

★★ **St Peter Port** – *See St Peter Port.*

Leave St Peter Port by the coast road north.

St Sampson – *See St Sampson.*

★ **Vale Castle** – The medieval castle, now in ruins, was built on the site of an Iro Age hillfort (*c*600 BC) on the only high point in Clos du Valle, overlookin St Sampson harbour. There is a fine **view** inland, along the east coast and ou to sea to the Casquets reef, Alderney *(north)*, Herm and Sark *(west)* and Jerse *(south)*.

Bordeaux Harbour – The little bay provides mooring for fishing boats and the onl safe swimming in the area. It was the setting for Victor Hugo's novel *The Toiler of the Sea.*

Dehus Dolmen ⏲ – *Light switch on left inside the entrance.* This, the second larges passage grave in Guernsey, has four side chambers and is covered b 7 capstones; one of them bears the figure of an archer on its underside *(switc for spotlight)*.

It was first excavated in 1837 by Lukis whose finds are in the Guernsey Museu in St Peter Port.

Beaucette Quarry Marina – A breach was blasted in the side of this old diorite quarr to turn it into a perfect sheltered marina. Even at high tide only the tops of th masts can be seen.

★ **Fort Doyle** – From the fort there is an excellent **view** of the Casquets reef an Alderney *(north)*, the French coast, Herm and Sark *(west)*.

Fort Le Marchant – This promontory is the most northerly point in Guernse The fort is named after the founder of the Royal Military College at Sandhurs in England. Fine view, particularly of L'Ancresse Bay and L'Ancress Common.

L'Ancresse Bay – The bay is very popular for bathing and surfing particularly at the western end near Fort Pembroke.

L'Ancresse Common – This is the only extensive open space on the island and is much used for strolling, dog-walking, horse racing, cattle grazing, kite flying and as a golf course. The coastline is well defended by forts and 7 defensive towers.

The area is rich in archeological sites.

Les Fouaillages burial ground is 7 000 years old; excavations as recent as 1978-81 produced very interesting material.

La Varde Dolmen is the largest passage grave in Guernsey; human bones and limpet shells were found beneath the 6 capstones.

Vale Church – St Michel du Valle was consecrated in 1117 on the site of an earlier chapel to St Magloire who brought Christianity to Guernsey in the 6C with St Sampson. The church is very irregular in alignment, suggesting that it was built by the monks who lived in the neighbouring priory, which was in ruins by 1406 and finally demolished in 1928.

Outside stands a 7C monument unearthed in 1949 not far from the west door.

From the southeast corner of the Vale churchyard the Military Road, the first to be built by Sir John Doyle, runs straight across the island to the east coast north of St Peter Port.

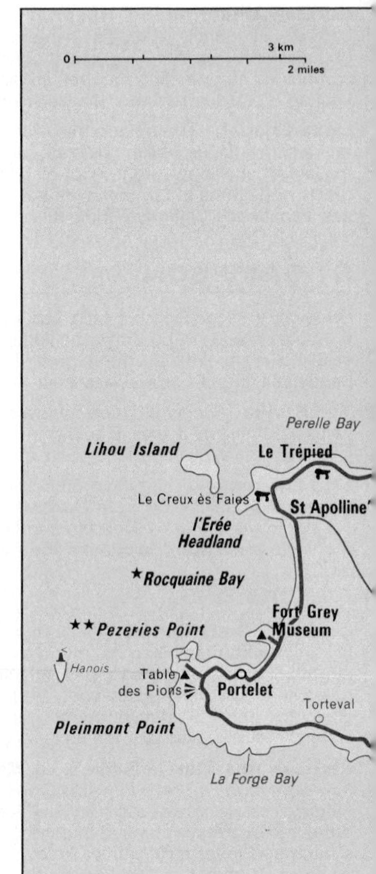

2 WEST COAST

From Grand Havre to Pezeries Point *10 miles - about ½ day*

Grand Havre – This ample inlet at the west end of the Braye du Valle *(see above)* is best admired from the Rousse headland with its tower and pier.

Grandes Rocques – From the German gun battery on the granite headland there is a fine view of the many sandy bays which scallop the west coast in both directions.

★★ **Côbo Bay** – The bay is a charming combination of sand for swimming and surfing and rocks for exploring marine life.

Vazon Bay – The huge beach between Fort Houmet *(north)* and Fort le Crocq *(south)* is excellent for swimming, sunbathing, surfing, horse riding and motor and motorcycle racing. Beneath the sands lie the remains of a submerged forest.

★ **St Apolline's Chapel** – In 1394 a charter was granted for a chantry chapel which is decorated with a **fresco** *(light switch)* of the Last Supper. The original dedication to St Marie de la Perelle was changed in 1452 to St Apolline, then very popular in Europe. She was an elderly deaconess who was burned to death in an anti-Christian riot in Alexandria in 249; as she was first struck repeatedly in the face and lost many teeth she is invoked against toothache and her emblem is forceps. After the Reformation the chapel became a barn but was restored in 1978.

Le Trépied Dolmen – This burial chamber at the southern end of Perelle Bay was excavated in 1840 by Frederic Lukis, whose finds are in the Guernsey Museum. In past centuries the site was used for witches' Sabbaths on Friday nights.

L'Erée Headland – The tall defensive tower on the headland is called Fort Saumarez. To the south stands **Le Creux ès Faies Dolmen**, a passage grave said locally to be the entrance to Fairyland. Excavation has produced items dating from 2000-1800 BC.

Lihou island – *Accessible by causeway at low tide.* The semi-detached character of the island is inviting to those seeking the contemplative life. In 1114 a priory was founded and dedicated to Our Lady of the Rock (now in ruins). Earlier this century there was a burst of activity from a factory making iodine *(qv)* from seaweed. The predecessor of the present lonely farmhouse was used by the Germans for target practice. On the west coast a 100ft rock pool provides excellent bathing.

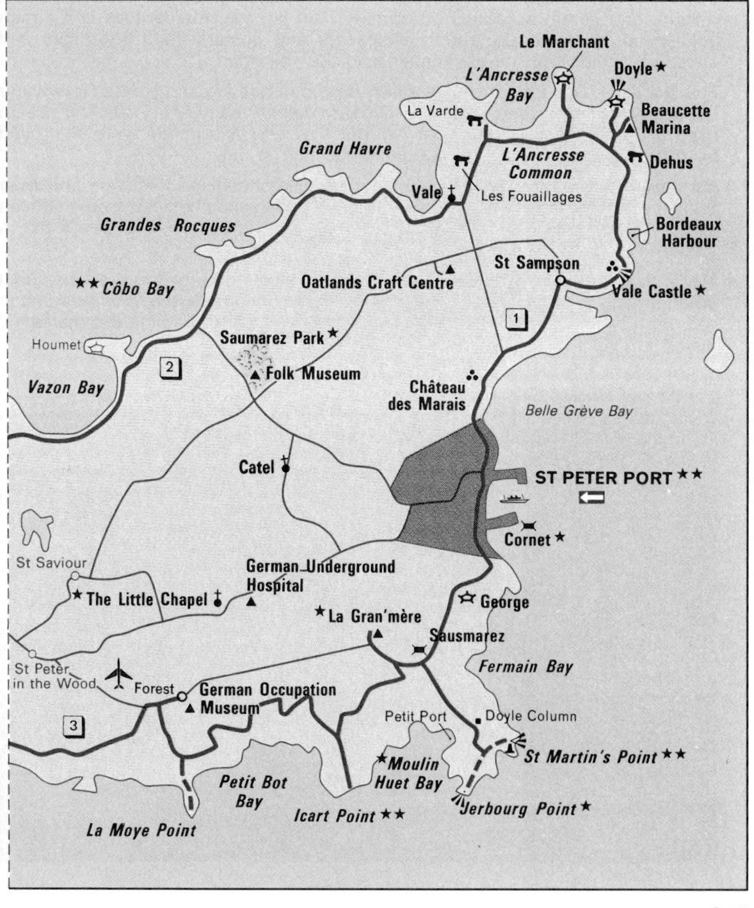

★ **Rocquaine Bay** – The grand sweep of the bay, which is protected from erosion by a high sea wall, is interrupted by the Cup and Saucer, originally a medieval fort to which a defensive tower was added in 1804. It is painted white as a navigation mark.

Fort Grey Maritime Museum ⊙ – The tower has been converted into a museum of west coast shipwrecks. The display covers the history of the fort, navigation and shipwrecks, the Hanois Reef and Lighthouse; *(downstairs)* relics from the 100 ships wrecked in this area between 1750 and 1978.

Portelet – The charming harbour full of fishing boats is backed by the houses of the Hanois Lighthouse keepers. Nearby is the **Table des Pions**, a circle of turf surrounded by a ditch and a ring of stones, where the pions of the Chevauchée de St Michel *(qv)* ate their lunch sitting at the grass table with their feet in the trench.

★★ **Pezeries Point** – This is the most westerly point in all the Channel Islands, a remote and unfrequented place. The fort was built in the Napoleonic era. The name Pezeries is a corruption of *eperquerie (qv)*.

3 SOUTHERN CLIFFS

From Pleinmont Point to St Peter Port *16 miles – ½ day*

These cliffs which extend along the south coast and round to St Peter Port provide some of the most wild and dramatic scenery in the island. The cliff face itself is often unstable and dangerous. A footpath, steep where it climbs in and out of the valleys and bays, runs from the western end to the town.

Pleinmont Point – The headland which is crowned by TV masts provides an extensive **view** : along the southern cliffs *(east)*, out to the Hanois Lighthouse and its surrounding reefs *(west)* and across Rocquaine Bay to Lihou Island *(north)*. From here to La Moye Point the cliffs are bare and rugged, indented by small bays and inlets and pierced by many caves. The roof of a cave in La Forge Bay has fallen in and formed a **blow-hole** *(souffleur)*; the best time to see and hear it in action is about 2 hours after low tide.

La Moye Point – The smallest of the three promontories on the south coast is wild and beautiful. Le Gouffre, a charming steep valley, flanks it on the west. On the east side precipitous steps lead down to a three-tiered mooring for fishing boats in the shelter of the headland.

German Occupation Museum ⊙ – *South of Forest Church.* This museum has grown out of a private collection of relics of the Nazi occupation of the Channel Islands: military and communications equipment, field kitchen, mementoes of German soldiers and forced labourers, newspapers and posters, food shortages and substitutes; video of the occupation and the liberation.

Petit Bot Bay – This attractive bay which has good bathing and sand at low water lies at the foot of a green valley guarded by a defensive tower (1780). The stream used to turn a corn and a paper mill but they and two hotels were destroyed by the Germans after a British Commando raid in July 1940.

★★ **Icart Point** – This is the highest and most southerly headland with very fine **views** of the coast. The view west reveals a string of quiet sandy beaches, some difficult of access, curving round to La Moye Point. On the east side is **Saint's Bay,** a favourite mooring for fishermen.

★ **Moulin Huet Bay** – A water lane runs down the valley, one of the most beautiful in Guernsey, to the bay where the stream plunges down the cliff face to the sea. Both this bay and its eastern neighbour are good for bathing but the sandy beach at **Petit Port** is superior.

Saint's Bay.

★ **La Gran'mère du Chimquière** – At the gate into St Martin's churchyard stands a Stone Age menhir carved to represent a female figure; her facial features were chiselled later. Known as the Grandmother of the Cemetery, she is supposed to guarantee fertility and receives gifts of coins and flowers. The statue was broken in two in the 19C by an over-zealous churchwarden but re-erected by the parishioners.

Return to the main road; turn right to Jerbourg.

The road passes the **Doyle Column** which commemorates Sir John Doyle, Lt Governor (1803-15); plaque showing distances to other islands.
The ramparts of a Bronze Age hillfort still crown the headland *(beyond the car park)* together with the remains of 20C German gun batteries.

★★ **St Martin's Point** – There is a magnificent **view** down to the lighthouse on the point, north up the coast to St Peter Port and seawards to the other islands.

★ **Jerbourg Point** – From the Pea Stacks rising from the sea just off the point the view swings northwest into the broad sweep of Moulin Huet Bay.

Sausmarez Manor ⊙ – The elegant Queen Anne house was built in 1714-18 by Sir Edmund Andros, onetime Governor of New York and the then Seigneur of Sausmarez. The roof-top "widow's walk" may be an original Guernsey feature, re-imported from America where it became popular; it provided a view far out to sea. The later Regency additions at the rear were largely rebuilt in the 1870s by General George de Sausmarez who served with the East India Company. The attractive interior displays portraits and souvenirs of the Seigneurs of Sausmarez's 750 years of occupation : the log of the round-the-world voyage of *HMS Centurion* in which Philip de Sausmarez served; the Inca silver from a captured Spanish treasure ship which was turned into coin of the realm; James II's wedding suit.
The extensive **grounds** contain some rare and exotic plants and a wild woodland garden, famous for its camellias; the park gates, with sculptures by Sir Henry Cheere, celebrate the return of the Manor to the de Sausmarez branch of the family in 1748.

Fermain Bay – *Access on foot from car park or by boat (summer only) from St Peter Port.* This charming bay, backed by densely wooded cliffs and an 18C defensive tower, offers a sandy beach and good bathing at low tide. The pepperpot tower is a Napoleonic sentry box.

Fort George – This modern luxury housing estate occupies the site of the British garrison, Fort George, built from 1782 to 1812 and destroyed by Allied bombers the day before D-Day. The garrison troops used to bathe in the sea below, hence the name Soldiers' Bay.

St Peter Port – *See St Peter Port.*

ALDERNEY

Pop 2 068

Michelin Atlas p 5 or Map 403 – Local map below

Alderney is ideal for a quiet holiday, where the natural beauty is unspoilt by more sophisticated attractions. It is the most northerly of the Channel Islands and lies 8 miles west of the tip of the Cotentin peninsula in Normandy. Three and a half miles long by no more than one and a half miles wide, the island slopes gently from a plateau (296ft - 90m) of farmland skirted by high cliffs in the southwest to a tongue of low-lying land in the northeast, fringed by rocky spits and sandy bays, and bristling with ruined fortifications. In spring and early summer the wild flowers are a delight : broom, thrift, sea campion and ox-eye daisies. There is plenty of interest for the bird-watcher : hoopoes and golden orioles, the occasional white stork or purple heron and several birds of prey; the main attraction, however, is the sea birds, especially the colonies of gannets and puffins. At low tide the rock pools reveal a variety of marine life; anemones, corals and ormers.

HISTORICAL NOTES

Island Fortress – Owing to its key position, nearest to England, France and the Channel shipping lanes, Alderney has frequently been fortified. The Romans seem to have used it as a naval base; there are traces of a late Roman fort at the Nunnery. The first English fortifications date from the reign of Henry VIII who started to construct a fort on the hill south of Longis Bay. Faced with the threat of invasion in the Napoleonic period, the British Government strengthened the existing defences and sent a garrison of 300 to assist the local militia.
The most impressive fortifications were built between 1847 and 1858. Alarmed by the development of a French naval base at Cherbourg, the British Government decided to create a safe harbour at Braye by constructing a huge breakwater and to defend the island by building a chain of 10 forts along the north coast from Clonque in the west round to Longis Bay in the east. There was also a plan to build another harbour at Longis and link it to Braye with a canal, thus strengthening the defence of the northeastern sector and providing a safe harbour whatever the wind. The forts were constructed of local stone with white quoins and dressings; several stood off-shore and were reached by causeways at low tide.

In June 1940 almost all the population left the island and the livestock was evacuated to Guernsey. During their five-year occupation the Germans re-fortified most of the Victorian forts and built masses of ugly concrete fortifications. When the islanders began to return late in 1945 they found their possessions gone and the houses derelict or destroyed. It took ten years and substantial government aid to make good the damage.

Constitution – Alderney is part of the Bailiwick of Guernsey. Since the introduction of the new constitution on 1 January 1949, the budget and other financial matters have to be approved by the States of Guernsey. Otherwise all island business is decided by the Committees of the States of Alderney, which consists of 12 elected members and an elected President, who serve for three years. The Court consists of six Jurats under a Chairman, who are appointed by the Home Office.
The pre-1949 constitution which had evolved down the centuries included two other bodies, the Douzaine, an assembly of 12 heads of families, and the Court of Chief Pleas. All offices were then elective. The feudal system under a seigneur was never established in Alderney and the later Governors, appointed by the Crown from the 16C to the 19C, often met with opposition from the independent-minded islanders.

Earning a Living – Two constants in the economy of Alderney are fishing and farming. Today the visitor can enjoy a delicious variety of fresh fish and crustaceans and the products of the local herd of Guernsey cows. Before the Second World War cattle and granite and gravel were important exports.
Tourism, which began after the defeat of Napoelon when people came to visit the many retired military personnel who settled in the island, was given a boost when Queen Victoria visited the fortifications in 1854. Since the building of the airport in 1935 the number of visitors has not diminished.

ST ANNE

The charm of St Anne lies in its cobbled streets and smart granite houses; its appearance is reminiscent of villages in Cornwall and Normandy. The Town, as it is called by the islanders, lies about ½ mile from the north coast on the edge of the best agricultural land, known as La Blaye.
The original settlement of farmhouses was centred on **Marais Square,** then unpaved with a stream running through it where the washing was done, and **Le Huret,** where the people gathered to decide when to gather seaweed *(vraic)* to fertilize the fields. In the 15C more houses were built to the east of the square, to accommodate settlers from Guernsey, and the Blaye was extended to support a population of 700. In the 18C the huge profits made from privateering led to a building boom; thatch was replaced by tiles, the first Court House was built and the Governor spent money on improving the communal buildings as well as his own residence. The northern part of the town – **Queen Elizabeth II Street, Victoria Street and Ollivier Street** – developed in the early Victorian era when the population of the island trebled with the introduction of a military garrison and many immigrant labourers. Workmen's cottages were built at Newtown and elsewhere. Many attractive houses and gardens line the green lanes, such as La Vallée, which run from St Anne down to the north coast.

SIGHTS

St Anne's – The church, consecrated in 1850, was designed by Sir Gilbert Scott in the transitional style from Norman to Early English cruciform and built in local granite dressed with white Caen stone. The cost was borne by Revd Canon John Le Mesurier, son of the last hereditary governor of Alderney, in memory of his parents. The church is unexpectedly large as it was intended to hold not only the local population, then swollen by immigrant labourers, but also the military garrison.
English was then replacing Norman French as the local language; the lectern holds two Bibles and the texts in the apse and near the door appear in both languages. Below the west window, which shows children of all races, are six brass plaques commemorating the Le Mesurier family which governed the island from 1721 to 1825. Queen Elizabeth II's visit to Alderney in 1957 is recalled in the window in the Lady Chapel.
During the war the church was damaged by being used as a store and the bells were removed; two were recovered on the island and the other four were found in Cherbourg. The churchyard gates in Victoria Street, erected as a memorial to Prince Albert, were removed by the Germans but replaced by a local resident.

Museum ⊙ – The Alderney Society's Museum presents a comprehensive view of the island : geology; flora and fauna; archeology, particularly finds from the Iron Age Settlement at Les Hughettes; domestic and military history, including the Victorian fortifications and the German Occupation.
The collections are displayed in the **old school** which was endowed in 1790 by the Governor *(inscription over the gate).*
The **Clock Tower** (1767) standing nearby is all that remains of the old church which was pulled down when the present one was built. The original dedication to St Mary, and the name of the town too, was changed to St Anne early in the 17C.

Royal Connaught Square – This elegant square, which was renamed in 1905 on the occasion of a visit by the Duke of Connaught, was the centre of the town in the 18C.

Island Hall *(north side)*, a handsome granite building which is now a community centre and library, was enlarged in 1763 by John Le Mesurier to become Government House. The first house on the site was built by Captain Nicholas Ling, who was appointed Lt Governor in 1657 and lived there until his death in 1679. **Mouriaux House** was completed in 1779 by the Governor as his private residence.

Court House ⊙ – The present building in Queen Elizabeth II Street (formerly New Street) dates from 1850. Both the Court and the States of Alderney hold their sessions in the first-floor Court Room which was restored in 1955.

Victoria Street – This, the main shopping street, runs north past the church gates and the war memorial, which records the dead of both world wars. Its name was changed from Rue du Grosnez to celebrate Queen Victoria's visit in 1854.

Butes – The recreation ground, formerly the Butts, provides fine views of Braye Bay *(northeast)* and across Crabby Bay and the Swinge to the Casquets *(northwest)* and the English Channel.

TOUR OF THE ISLAND *9 miles – 1 day – local map below*

It is possible to walk round the island following the cliff-top footpath or to drive round making detours on foot to places of interest.
In summer there are boat trips ⊙ round the island from Braye Harbour; tours ⊙ of the fortifications are organised once a week.

Braye – The harbour is protected by Fort Grosnez (1853) and the massive **breakwater** (1 000yds) which was begun in 1847 and was originally even longer. Although very exposed to Atlantic storms, it makes a pleasant promenade in fair weather. The first quay, the Old Jetty, was built in 1736 by the Governor; the concrete jetty dates from the turn of the century.

Alderney Railway ⊙ – Formed in 1978, the Alderney Railway Society operates the only standard-gauge railway to survive in the Channel Islands. The line was opened in 1847 to carry stone to the harbour; now steam and diesel trains run from Braye Road to Mannez Quarry.

★ **Braye Bay** – The largest bay on the island offers a sandy beach with good bathing and a fine view of the ferries, yachts and fishing boats in the harbour. Skirting the beach is a strip of grass, Le Banquage, where the seaweed *(vraic)* was left to dry.

Fort Albert – Mount Touraille, at the east end of Braye Bay, is crowned by Fort Albert (1853), the main element in the Victorian chain of forts and the German fortifications. From the seaward side there is a fine **view** inland to St Anne, westwards across Braye Bay to Fort Grosnez and the breakwater with Fort Tourgis in the background, and eastwards over the northern end of the island.

Hammond Memorial – *At the fork in the road east of Fort Albert.* The forced labourers of the Todt Organisation, who worked on the fortifications during the Nazi Occupation, are commemorated in a series of plaques inscribed in the languages of the prisoners. There were three camps on Alderney, each holding 1 500 men.

North Coast Bays – Three excellent sandy bathing bays cluster round the most northerly headland beneath the walls of Fort Chateau à l'Etoc (1854), now converted into private flats : **Saye Bay**, nearly symmetrical in shape; **Arch Bay**, named after the tunnel through which the carts collecting seaweed reached the shore; **Corblets Bay**, overlooked by Fort Corblets (1855), now a private house with a splendid view.

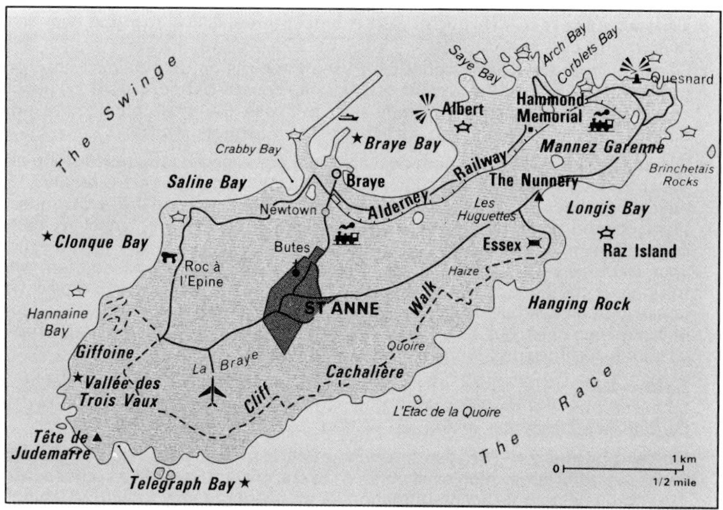

Mannez Garenne – The low-lying northern end of the island, known as Manne Garenne (Warren) is dominated by the remains of a German Observation Towe on the edge of the quarry.

Quesnard Lighthouse ⊙ (1912) stands 121ft high and casts its beam nearly 1 miles. From the lantern platform there is a magnificent **view★** of the coast an the Race and, on a clear day, of the nuclear power station on the French coas Many ships have come to grief on this rocky coast where the strong current of the Swinge and the Race (Raz) meet. The most famous was the *Liverpoo* which ran aground in a fog in February 1902.

Three forts command the coastline; Les Homeaux Florains (1858), now in ruins, wa approached by a causeway; Fort Quesnard, on the east side of Cats Bay, and For Houmet Herbe, another offshore fort reached by a causeway, were built in 1853

Raz Island – A causeway, which is covered at high tide, runs out to the islan in the centre of Longis Bay. The fort (1853) has been partially restored and ther is a fine **view** of Essex Castle and Hanging Rock *(southwest)*.

Longis Bay – The retreating tide reveals a broad stretch of sand, backed b a German tank trap, which provides excellent shelter for sunbathing. The ba was the island's natural harbour from prehistoric times until it silted up earl in the 18C. Traces of an Iron Age settlement were discovered at **Les Huguette** in 1968 when the golf course was being laid out on Longis Common; the find are displayed in the museum. Various relics (coins, tiles, pottery and brickwork suggest the existence of a Roman naval base protected by a fort (*c*2C-4C AD

The Nunnery – This building, which is thought to be the oldest on the islan stands on a rectangular site enclosed within a 16ft high wall. John Chamberlai converted it to his use when he became Governor in 1584. Its name was supplie by the British soldiers who were garrisoned there in the late 18C. It is now privat dwellings owned by the States of Alderney.

Essex Castle – The first fort on Essex Hill overlooking Longis Bay was begu in 1546 by Henry VIII but abandoned in 1553. It consisted of an outer baile to hold the islanders and their flocks, around a central fort divided into four keep All but the north and west sides of the outer wall were razed in 1840 whe the present structure was built, to be used first as a barracks and then as military hospital; it is now private property. The pepperpot gazebo was adde by the Governor, John Le Mesurier, who started a farm to feed the garrison a the Nunnery and called it Essex Farm; the name ascended the hill to the castl

Hanging Rock – The tilt of the 50ft column of rock projecting from the cli face is said to have been caused by the people of Guernsey hitching a rop to the rock and trying to tow Alderney away.

Cliff Walk – From Haize round to Giffoine there is a magnificent cliff walk serve by frequent paths running inland back to St Anne. The cliff edge is indente by a series of small valleys sloping seawards and a few narrow bays, difficu or impossible of access; bathing is not advisable owing to the swiftly-flowin currents in the Race. The view of the steep cliffs plunging into the rock-strew sea is magnificent.

Cachalière – A path leads down past the old quarry to a pier, built early this centur for loading granite but abandoned owing to the dangerous offshore current The name derives from Chicago where the Alderney man who paid for the pie had made his fortune. From here the rocks of **L'Etac de la Quoire** can be reache at low water.

★ **Telegraph Bay** – *Access by path and steps; beware of being cut off from the bas of the steps by the rising tide.* The Telegraph Tower (1811), which provide communication with Jersey and Guernsey via a repeating telegraph signal o Sark, has given its name to the bay below. Except at high tide there is exceller bathing, sheltered from all but a south wind, and a fine view of La Nache an Fourquie rocks.

Tête de Judemarre – The headland provides a fine **view** of the rock-bound coas and of the islands of Guernsey, Herm and Sark.

★ **Vallée des Trois Vaux** – This deep cleft is in fact three valleys meeting on a shingl beach.

Giffoine – From the cliff it is possible to see the birds on their nests in the gann colony on Les Etacs. The remains of a German coastal battery crown the headlan above Hannaine Bay, where sandy spits between the rocks provide reasonab bathing. Fine **view** of Burhou, Ortac and the Casquets *(north)*.

★ **Clonque Bay** – A zig-zag path descends the gorse and heather-clad slope abov the attractive sweep of the bay. A causeway runs out to Fort Clonque (185 which has been converted into flats for visitors. Seaweed from Clonque wa highly prized as fertilizer and two causeways enabled the "vraicing" carts descend to the beds of seaweed.

Just south of Fort Tourgis (1855), now largely derelict, at the northern end the bay, is the best preserved burial chamber on the island, **Roc à l'Epine,** whic consists of a capstone supported on two upright stones. Alderney was once ric in such megaliths but all the others seem to have been destroyed when th Victorian fortifications were built.

Saline Bay – The shore, which is exposed to heavy seas so that bathing ca be hazardous, is commanded by a gun battery and Fort Doyle, now a youth centr beyond lies **Crabby Bay** in the lee of Fort Grosnez.

Burhou Island ⊙ – The island, which lies across The Swinge (about 1½ miles 2km), supports large colonies of puffins and storm petrels as well as other sea bird A hut provides simple accommodation for an overnight stay for birdwatching.

★ SARK

Michelin Atlas p 5 or Map 403 – Local map below

The island of Sark is a haven of rural and maritime peace. No cars or aircraft pollute the air; the only approach is by sea. The island is 3½ miles long by 1½ wide, barely two square miles in area. It is divided into two parts, Great Sark and Little Sark, linked by La Coupée, a high narrow neck of land, which inspired Turner and Swinburne and figures in the climax of Mervyn Peake's novel, *Mr Pye*. Just off the west coast lies the island of Brecqhou across the Gouliot Passage.
Sark is the last feudal fief in Europe and also the smallest independent state in the Commonwealth; its traditions date from the reign of Elizabeth I. Of the 560 inhabitants, half are descended from the settlers who colonised the island 400 years ago.

GEOGRAPHICAL NOTES

The island of Sark is a green plateau bounded by high granite cliffs dropping sheer into the sea. The boat from St Peter Port passes south of Herm and Jethou before skirting the impressive cliffs at the north end of the island.
Among the farms are small houses with carefully tended gardens full of flowers; the pastureland, where the sheep graze, is bordered by uncultivated land along the cliffs; in spring and summer the granite plateau is clothed in wild flowers.

HISTORICAL NOTES

It seems that St Magloire from Brittany landed in Sark in the middle of the 6C with 62 companions and founded a monastery. In the 9C the island was prey to Viking raids but little is known of the island's history before it became part of the Duchy of Normandy. In 1042 Sark was given to the Abbey of Mont St Michel by William the Conqueror, the Duke of Normandy. A few years later the island was attached to the diocese of Coutances. In 1336 Sark was invaded by a party of Scotsmen under David Bruce, a king in exile. Two years later Sark was attacked by Frenchmen. In 1349 the monks abandoned the island and for several years it was a lawless place, the haunt of pirates. The French regained it in 1549 but were thrown out by an Anglo-Dutch force which returned it to England.
In 1565 Elizabeth I granted Sark to Helier de Carteret, Lord of the Manor of St Ouen in Jersey, on condition that he established a colony of 40 settlers prepared to defend the island. This Helier became the first Lord of Sark.
He divided the land into 40 holdings and attributed them one to each of the 40 families who had accompanied him from Jersey; each tenant had to build and maintain a house and provide an armed man to defend the island. The number of holdings has not changed since then nor hardly has the constitution. At its head is the hereditary Lord (seigneur) who holds the fief of Sark; the present holder is Michael Beaumont, grandson of Sybil Hathaway, the Dame of Sark, whose long reign from 1927 to 1974 saw the island through difficult and changing times. The Seigneur of Sark has retained a number of privileges from the feudal period : the right to keep pigeons and to own a bitch. He also receives one thirteenth of the sale price of all island property.
Sark has its own parliament, the Chief Pleas, composed of the 40 tenants and 12 deputies elected for three years. The Seneschal is responsible for justice, together with the Clerk of the Court (Greffier) and the Sherriff (Prévôt). Law and order are upheld by the Constable assisted by the Vingtenier. A person under arrest is held in the tiny prison (2 cells) for 48 hours. In summer the local force is supplemented by a policeman from Guernsey. Serious cases are heard by the Guernsey courts.

TOUR OF THE ISLAND *1 day – local map below*

One of the charms of Sark is the absence of cars. The only motor vehicles allowed are the farmers' tractors, one per landholding. In summer horse-drawn carriages and wagonettes provide transport for the visitors. There are also bicycles for hire or one can set out on foot to explore the road and tracks, the cliffs and bays and headlands with their stunning views.

Visiting Sark.

GREAT SARK

Maseline Harbour – After passing below the lighthouse (1912) which appears to grow out of the cliffs on Point Robert, the boat docks inside the modern concrete jetty which was inaugurated in 1949 by the Duke of Edinburgh when he and the then Princess Elizabeth visited Sark. A human chain passes up the baggage from hand to hand and arranges it on the tractor-drawn trailers. A short tunnel leads to the local "bus" which takes passengers up Harbour Hill *(½ mile)* to La Collinette crossroads.

★ **Creux Harbour** – Opposite the tunnel to Maseline Harbour is a second tunnel to Creux Harbour, an older and picturesque little harbour, which is dry at low tide and is now used only by the hovercraft from Jersey or when Maseline is inaccessible.

La Collinette – The crossroads at the top of Harbour Hill is called La Collinette. Straight ahead stretches The Avenue, once the drive to the original manor house and lined with trees but now the main street lined with shops. The small barrel-roofed building on the left at the far end is the island prison built in 1856.

St Peter's – The church dates from the 19C. The embroidered hassocks are the work of the island women; the designs incorporate the motifs and some of the names of the landholdings with which the seats are traditionally associated.

★ **La Seigneurie** – The present manor house, the residence of the Seigneur of Sark, stands on the site of St Magloire's 6C monastery; all that remains of the former buildings is the name La Moinerie. The house was begun in 1565 and considerably enlarged in 1730 by the Le Pelley family who then held the fief of Sark. The square tower, which provides a splendid view of the island, was built as a signalling tower in 1860 by the Revd William Collings, then Seigneur of Sark. The beautiful stone and granite house is sheltered from the wind by a screen of trees and high walls.
The dovecote in the garden behind the house is built of alternate bands of brick and stone.
The **gardens** ⊙, on which the Dame of Sark lavished so much attention, are luxuriant with flowers and shrubs, some brought from foreign parts, and maintained with undiminished care.

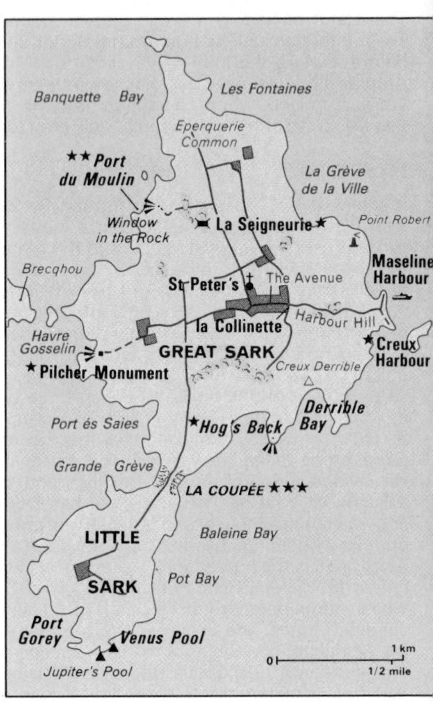

★★ **Port du Moulin** – A road along the north side of the Seigneurie grounds soon turns into a path following the windings of the clifftop. The sign "Window and Bay" marks the way to the **Window in the Rock**, which the Revd William Collings had made in the 1850s to provide an impressive **view** of Port du Moulin.

Return to the fork in the path and take the other branch to Port du Moulin.

The bay, which is popular with bathers in summer, is flanked by stark rocks in strange shapes; at low tide huge arches in the rock appear. On the right rise Les Autelets, three granite columns accessible as the sea retreats.

★ **Pilcher Monument** – This granite column was raised in memory of a London merchant, F Pilcher, who died at sea in 1868 with three companions while returning to Guernsey. From the plinth there is a fine **view** of the west coast and of Brecqhou, Herm, Jethou and Guernsey. A path runs down to Havre Gosselin where yachts moor in the summer months.

Derrible Bay – At Petit Dixcart turn left into a stony path, then right into a path beside a field. A left fork leads down through the trees to Derrible Bay. Part way down, a turning to the right leads to the **Creux Derrible**, an enormous hole in the granite cliffs. The retreating tide reveals a large sandy beach in Derrible Bay.

Return to the first fork and bear left.

★ **Hog's Back** – At the seaward end of this high ridge stands an ancient cannon. The **view** is magnificent : to the left Derrible Bay and Derrible Point; to the right Dixcart Bay with La Coupée and Little Sark in the background.

★★★ **La Coupée** – The narrow isthmus joining the two parts of Sark is a unique and impressive spectacle. On either side steep cliffs drop over 260ft into the sea. The view is magnificent : to the right lie Brecqhou, Jethou, Herm and Guernsey; to the left the coast of Jersey can just be seen; further left and more distant is the coast of France. At the foot of the cliff on the right is Grande Grève Bay, a good place for bathing in summer *(steps down to the beach)*.
The concrete roadway and the guard rails were constructed in 1945 by German prisoners of war working under the direction of the Royal Engineers.

Grande Grève Bay.

LITTLE SARK

On the southern headland are the chimneys of the old silver mines, now overgrown, which were started in the 19C but had to close because of the infiltration of water into the workings.

Venus Pool – A footpath to the left of the old mine chimney runs down to a pool which is visible at low tide. This circular pool under the cliffs has been formed by the action of the sea.

Port Gorey – At low tide visitors can walk from the Venus Pool westward round the headland via **Jupiter's Pool**, several caves and the rocks in Plat Rue Bay, to Port Gorey which served the silver mines; it is necessary to judge the tides and allow plenty of time.
The clifftop path is always open and provides a fine view down into Port Gorey.

HERM

Michelin Atlas p 5 or Map 403 – Local map below

Herm (1½ miles long by ½ mile wide) lies half-way between Guernsey and Sark. The broad sandy beaches on its north coast contrast with the steep cliffs at the southern end of the island. Herm is a haven of tranquillity having neither roads nor cars; there are however many footpaths across the dunes, through the woods and along the cliffs. The deep fringe of rocks which lies offshore is very impressive at low tide.
Southwest of Herm, across a narrow channel, the islet of Jethou *(private)* rises like a hillock in the sea, the home of many sea birds.

HISTORICAL NOTES

The prehistoric tombs made of granite slabs found in the north of the island are evidence of human settlement in 2000 BC. The Romans left a few traces of their passage : coins, pottery.
In the 6C Christianity was introduced by St Magloire who founded monasteries in Sark and Jersey. The monks of Sark built a small chapel on a reef between Herm and Jethou; it was engulfed in the 8C during a violent storm which separated the two islands.
In the 17C pirates used the island as a base from which to prey on the many shipwrecks in the area. For a period the island was deserted but in the 19C the quarrying and export of granite brought prosperity. The population reached 400. As Crown property the island was let to various tenants; in 1890 a German prince, Blucher von Wahlstatt, built the manor house and planted the pine and eucalyptus trees; in 1920 Herm was leased to Sir Compton Mackenzie, who wrote several novels on the island, including *Fairy Gold* which is set on Herm, before finally settling on Jethou. During the Second World War the island was occasionally occupied by German troops and appeared in a German propaganda film called *The Invasion of the Isle of Wight;* the British mounted a commando raid in February 1943; the island suffered chiefly from neglect. In 1947 Herm was sold by the Crown to the States of Guernsey and since 1949 the tenant has been Major Peter Wood, who has introduced basic services such as running water and electricity and a limited amount of commercialization consistent with the obligation to preserve Herm's natural attractions and peacefulness. There is a small permanent community of ten families living and working on Herm throughout the year.

TOUR OF THE ISLAND *3 hours - local map below*

At high tide the boat docks at the jetty in the only harbour, where an ancient crane is still in service; at low tide the boat docks by the landing steps at Rosière.

A footpath running right round the island leads to the sandy bays, the rocky coast and the outlying reefs, and the high cliffs. From Herm the other islands are visible : Jethou and Guernsey *(west)*, Alderney *(north)*, Sark *(east)*. Jersey lies twenty miles south and the French coast is usually in view to the east.

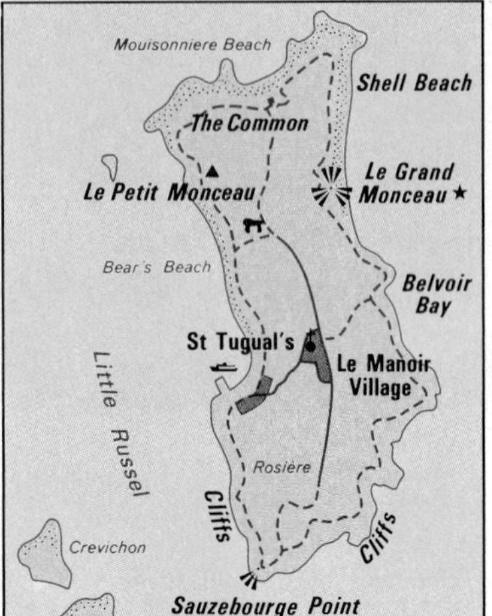

Le Manoir Village – A surfaced road climbs up to the farm and the handful of cottages which make up the hamlet next to the 18C manor house with its square tower.

St Tugual's Chapel – The chapel was built of island granite in the 11C when Robert the Magnificent was Duke of Normandy. There is a handsome stained-glass window depicting Christ stilling the Tempest.

The Common – The northern end of the island is composed of sand dunes, known as the Common, covered by prickly vegetation and fringed by sandy beaches which are very popular in summer (Bear's Beach, Mousonniere Beach, Shell Beach). Half-way along the north coast stands a stone obelisk; it replaces a menhir which mariners used as a landmark.

★ **Le Grand Monceau** – From this hillock there is a splendid panoramic **view** of the sands, the rocks and the islands. North on the horizon lies Alderney; to the east the French coast.

Le Petit Monceau – This is a smaller hillock, overlooking the Bear's Beach.

Shell Beach – The beach is composed of millions of shells deposited by the tides and currents.

The Cliffs – In contrast with the low land in the north, the southern end of the island is composed of steep granite cliffs dropping sheer into the sea.

Belvoir Bay – A small sheltered sandy bay, good for bathing.

Sauzebourge Point – The southern headland provides a view of Jethou *(southwest)* with Guernsey in the background *(west)* and Sark *(southeast)*.

Practical
Information
53808

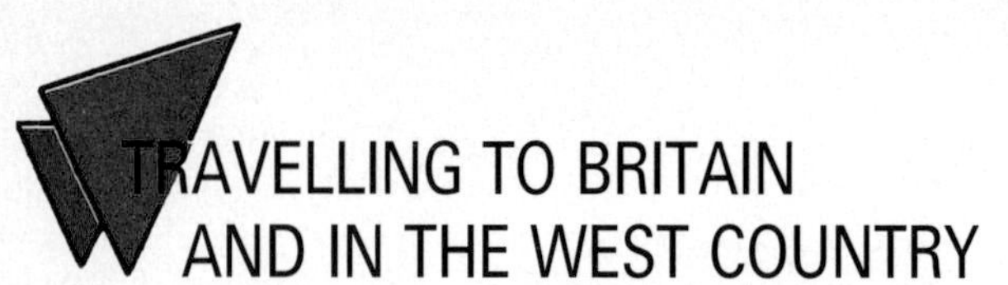

TRAVELLING TO BRITAIN AND IN THE WEST COUNTRY

Passport – Visitors entering Britain must be in possession of a valid national **passport.** In case of loss or theft report to the local police and the relevant embassy.

Visa – Visitors who require an **entry visa** should apply at least three weeks in advance to the British Embassy.
US citizens should obtain the booklet *"Your Trip Abroad"* ($1), which provides useful information on visa requirements, customs regulations, medical care etc for international travellers, available from the Superintendent of Documents, Government Printing Office, Washington DC 20402-9325.

Customs – The UK Customs Office produces a leaflet on customs regulations and the full range of "duty free" allowances (the Channel Islands have different regulations from England); available from HM Customs and Excise, Dorset House, Stamford Street, London SE1 9PS, ☎ (0171) 928 3344.
For US citizens *"Know before you go"* is available from the US Treasury Department (☎ 202 566 8195).

By air – There are no international flights direct to the West Country. Regular domestic services operate to Bournemouth, Plymouth, Exeter, Bristol and Newquay; enquire at local travel agents.
There are several airfields throughout the region; these are indicated on the **Michelin Atlas** to **Great Britain and Ireland** and on **Michelin Map 403**.

By sea – Details of passenger ferry and car ferry services to Poole, Weymouth and Plymouth from France or Spain can be obtained from travel agencies or from the main carriers : Brittany Ferries, ☎ (01752) 221321; Sealink UK Ltd, ☎ (01305) 770308; Truckline, ☎ (01202) 666466; Les Routiers (☎ Paris 43 87 61 68). For ferries to the **Channel Islands** see below. For the smaller islands – the Isles of Scilly, Lundy Island, Brownsea Island – see under Admission Times and Charges.

By rail – British Rail operates train services to many destinations in the West Country. A **Britrail Pass** allows unlimited travelling on the entire British Rail network.
Eurorail Pass, Flexipass and Saver Pass are options available in the US for travel in Europe and must be purchased in the US (☎ 212 308 3103 for information). Other versions exist for foreign visitors; they must be purchased in the visitors' home country. For further information on this and other regional rail passes consult the British Rail International office or sales agents.

By coach – National Express operates a regular service between the major towns in the UK including 30 destinations in the West Country. Special discount tickets available : Rambler Ticket, Tourist Trail Pass, Explorer Pass. Information and bookings from National Express, Victoria Coach Station, Buckingham Palace Road, London SW1, ☎ (0171) 730 0202, or contact local National Express agents.

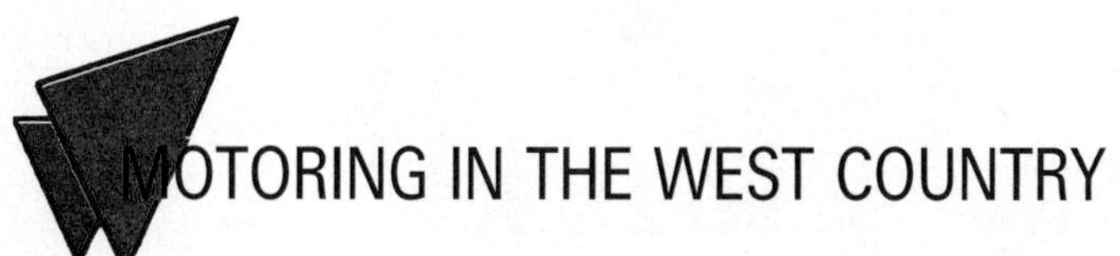

MOTORING IN THE WEST COUNTRY

Documents – Nationals of EC countries require a valid national **driving licence;** nationals of non-EC countries require an **international driving licence** (obtainable in the US from the American Automobile Club).
For vehicles registered abroad it is necessary to have the **registration papers** (log-book) and a **nationality plate** of the approved size.

Insurance – Insurance cover is compulsory; although no longer a legal requirement, the **International Insurance Certificate** (Green Card) is the most effective proof of insurance cover and is internationally recognised by the police and other authorities.
Certain motoring organisations run accident insurance and breakdown service schemes covering holiday periods. Europ-Assistance (252 High St, Croydon CR0 1NF; ☎ (0181) 680 1234) has special policies for motorists.
Members of the American Automobile Club should obtain the brochure *"Offices to serve you abroad"*.

Highway Code – The minimum driving age is 17 years old. Traffic drives on the left and overtakes on the right. Traffic on main roads and on roundabouts has priority. In the case of a **breakdown** a red warning triangle or hazard warning lights are obligatory.

Full or dipped headlights should be switched on in poor visibility and at night; use sidelights only when the vehicle is stationary in an area without street lighting.

It is compulsory for the driver and front-seat passengers to wear **seat belts.** Back-seat belts must be worn where they are fitted; children under the age of 14 must travel on the rear seats.

Drivers suspected of **speeding** or **drink-driving** are liable to prosecution.

Speed limits – The maximum permitted speed is 30mph-48km/h in built-up areas, 60mph-96km/h on single carriageways and 70mph-112km/h on motorways or dual carriageways.

Parking regulations – In towns there may be multi-storey car parks, parking meters, disc systems and paying parking zones; in the last case tickets must be obtained from the ticket machines (small change necessary) and displayed inside the windscreen; failure to display may result in a fine.

Route Planning – **Michelin Map 403** and the **Michelin Road Atlas** of **Great Britain and Ireland** show the major (A) roads and many of the minor (B) roads in the West Country.

Car Rental – There are car rental agencies at airports, railway stations and in large towns throughout Britain. European cars usually have manual transmission but automatic cars are available on demand. An **international driving licence** is required for non-EC nationals.

ACCOMMODATION

Places to stay – The map of Places to Stay *(qv)* indicates places for overnight stays.

The **Michelin Red Guide Great Britain and Ireland** provides a selection of hotels, guest-houses and restaurants.

The West Country Tourist Board publishes several free brochures and the local Tourist Information Centres also have lists and leaflets of hotels, bed and breakfast and other accommodation; many operate an accommodation booking service.

Youth Hostels – Britain's youth hostels are open to members of the Youth Hostel Association (Trevelyan House, St Albans, Herts AL1 2DY, ☎ (01727) 855215) or to those with an international membership card. Package holidays are available comprising youth hostel vouchers, rail and bus pass or hostel vouchers, return rail fare and cycle hire.

Camping and caravanning – The British Tourist Authority publishes *Camping and Caravanning in Britain* and local Tourist Information Centres supply lists of camping and caravan sites. The Caravan Holiday-Home Campaign publishes *Freedom,* a brochure of the holiday parks in the West Country, which is available from PO Box 26, Lowestoft, Norfolk NR32 3LM; ☎ (01452) 413 041.

Electricity – The electric current is 240 volts AC (50 HZ); 3-pin flat wall sockets are standard.

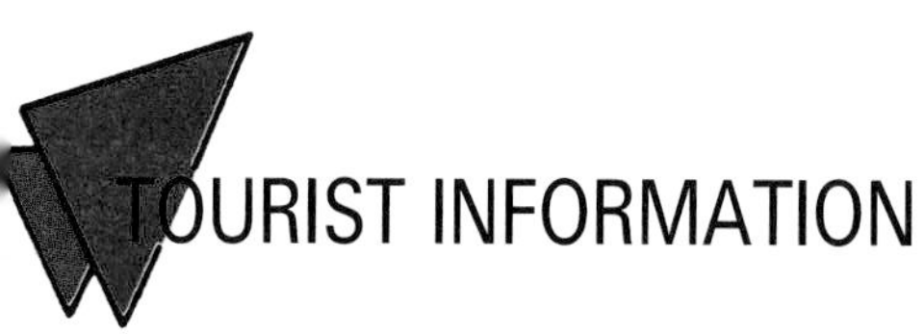

TOURIST INFORMATION

Tourist Boards – For information, brochures, maps and assistance in planning a trip to the West Country apply to the **British Tourist Authority (BTA),** the **English Tourist Board (ETB)** or the **West Country Tourist Board (WCTB)** *(addresses below).*

Tourist Information Centres – The addresses and telephone numbers of the Tourist Information Centres to be found in most large towns and many tourist resorts in the West Country are printed in the Admission Times and Charges. The centres can supply town plans, timetables and information on local entertainment facilities, sports and sightseeing.

Tourism for the Disabled – Some of the sights described in this guide are accessible to disabled people; see Admission Times and Charges. The **Michelin Red Guide Great Britain and Ireland** indicates hotels with facilities suitable for disabled people. The Royal Association for Disability and Rehabilitation (RADAR) publishes an annual guide with detailed information on hotels and holiday centres; apply to RADAR, 25 Mortimer Street, London W1N 8AB, ☎ (0171) 637 5400.

Great British Heritage Pass – This ticket (fifteen-day or one-month version), which gives access to over 500 stately homes, castles and gardens throughout Britain (including some owned by the National Trust), is available from ETB.

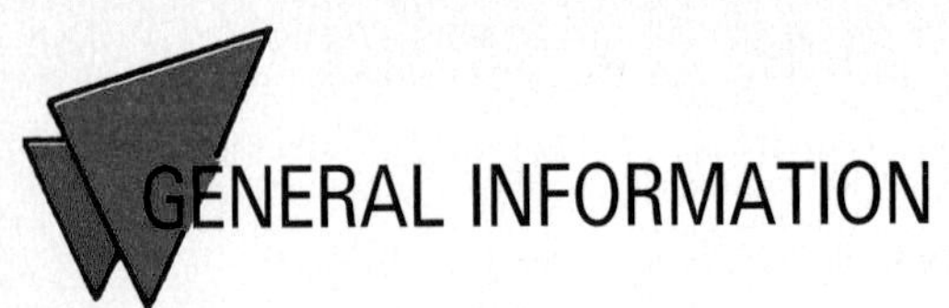

GENERAL INFORMATION

It is advisable to book well in advance for the holiday season.

Climate – Owing to the Gulf Stream, the West Country enjoys relatively mild weather throughout the year. The sunny and bright days of spring may be interspersed with sudden showers; in summer (especially in July and August) the warm weather and splendid beaches attract thousands of visitors, and in autumn the countryside mellows to mild days between cool mornings and evenings. Winter in the West Country can be dramatic, with gales and storms; calmer weather brings crisp mornings and invigorating days but temperatures in the far southwest are never extreme.

Time – In winter standard time throughout Britain, including the Channel Islands, is Greenwich Mean Time (GMT). In summer (mid-March to October) British clocks are advanced by one hour to give British Summer Time (BST) which is the same as Central European Time.

Medical treatment – Visitors from EC countries should apply to their own National Social Security Offices for Form E111 which entitles them to medical treatment under an EC Reciprocal Medical Treatment arrangement.
Nationals of non-EC countries should take out comprehensive insurance. American Express offers a service, "Global Assist", for any medical, legal or personal emergency – call collect from anywhere ☎ 202 554 2639.

Currency – The decimal system (£1 = 100 pence) is used throughout Britain although the Channel Islands have different notes and coins which are not legal tender outside the islands.

Banking – Banks are open from Monday to Friday (except public holidays, *see below*), 0930 to 1530 or 1630. Some banks offer a limited service on Saturday mornings, 0930 to 1230, and larger branches have cash dispensers which remain open most of the day.
Exchange facilities outside normal banking hours may be available at hotels, bureaux de change and travel agencies.
Some form of identification is necessary when cashing travellers cheques or Eurocheques in banks. Commission charges vary; hotels usually charge more than banks.

Credit Cards – The major credit cards – Visa/Barclaycard (Carte Bleue), Access (Mastercard/Eurocard), American Express and Diners Club – are widely accepted in shops, hotels and restaurants and petrol stations.
Most banks have cash dispensers which accept international credit cards.

Post – Postage stamps are available from Post Offices and some shops (newsagents, tobacconists etc).
Post Offices are generally open Monday to Friday, 0930 to 1730 and Saturday morning, 0930 to 1230; sub-post offices close at 1230 or 1300 on Wednesday or Thursday.

Telephone – In an **emergency** phone **999** – fire; police; ambulance; coastal, mountain and cave rescue.
Most countries can be dialled direct. Dialling codes are found at the front of telephone directories and in codebooks. For queries apply to the Operator (☎ 100), London Directory Enquiries (☎ 142), national Directory Enquiries (☎ 192) or the International Operator (☎ 155).
Pre-paid phonecards **(British Telecom, Mercury)** for national and international calls from public phones are available from Post Offices and some shops (newsagents, tobacconists etc). Some public phones also accept credit cards.

Public Houses – Pubs may open within the statutory licensing hours which are Mondays to Saturdays, 1100 to 2300 and Sundays, 1100 to 1500 and 1900 to 2230.
Young people under 18 years of age are subject to various restrictions.

Shopping – Shops in the towns are generally open Mondays to Saturdays from 0900 to 1730 or 1800; smaller stores may close for an hour in the middle of the day. Most towns have an early closing day (ECD) – usually Wednesday or Thursday – when shops close at midday (see the **Michelin Red Guide Great Britain and Ireland**).

Public and Bank Holidays – The following are days when banks, museums and other monuments may be closed or may vary their hours of admission :

New Year's Day (1 January)
Good Friday (Friday before Easter)
Easter Monday (Monday after Easter)
May Day (First Monday in May)
Spring Bank Holiday (Last Monday in May)
August Bank Holiday (Last Monday in August)
Christmas Day (25 December)
Boxing Day (26 December)

In addition to the usual school holidays at Christmas, Easter and in the summer there are mid-term breaks in February and late October.

mbassies

ustralia	Australia House, The Strand, London WC2B 4LA; ☎ (0171) 379 4334.
anada	Macdonald House, 1 Grosvenor Square, London W1X 0AB; ☎ (0171) 629 9492.
ance	21/23 Cromwell Road, London SW7 2EN; ☎ (0171) 581 5292
ermany	23 Belgrave Square, London SW1X 8PZ; ☎ (0171) 235 0282.
pan	101 Piccadilly, London W1V 9FB; ☎ (0171) 465 6500.
ew Zealand	New Zealand House, The Haymarket, London SW1Y 4TQ; ☎ (0171) 930 8422.
SA	24-31 Grosvenor Square, London W1A 1AL; ☎ (0171) 499 9000.

RECREATION

formation on the activities listed below is available from WCTB (which publishes booklet, *Activity and Leisure Holidays*), ETB or local Tourist Information Centres.

ational Trust – The Trust owns and conserves places of historic interest or natural eauty, including coast and countryside properties. There are reciprocal arrange-ents between NT and similar overseas organisations (Royal Oak Foundation etc). T Head Office, 36 Queen Anne's Gate, London SW1 9AS, ☎ (0171) 222 9251. ome properties host special events such as festivals, exhibitions, concerts or sheep og trials; enquire in advance for details.

nglish Heritage – EH restores, conserves and maintains over 350 properties presenting the wide range of England's architectural heritage : Fortress House, 3 Saville Row, London W1X 1AB, ☎ (0171) 973 3000. EH has reciprocal rrangements with Historic Scotland and Cadw.
or a diary of events (archery displays, battle re-enactments, medieval music etc) eld at English Heritage properties, apply to EH Special Events Unit *(address below)*, ☎ (0171) 973 3457. For details of summer concerts (often with firework displays) pply to EH Concerts Unit : Keysign House, 429 Oxford Street, London W1R 2HD, ☎ (0171) 937 3427 or 937 3428.

ational Gardens Scheme – The National Gardens Scheme publishes an annual uide to private gardens which open to the public for a limited time, in aid of charity; vailable through bookshops at £2.50 or by post at £3.00 (inc postage and packing) om Hatchlands Park, East Clandon, Guildford, Surrey GU4 7RT, ☎ (01483) 211535.

ational Parks – For details of guided walks and further information contact the elevant authorities : Dartmoor National Park, Bovey Tracey, Devon TQ13 9JQ, ☎ (01626) 832 093. Exmoor National Park, Exmoor House, Dulverton, Somerset A2 9HL, ☎ (01398) 23665.
arge parts of the West Country have been designated **Areas of Outstanding Natural eauty;** for information on parks and nature trails contact the Countryside ommission, John Dower House, Crescent Place, Cheltenham, Gloucestershire GL50 RA, ☎ (01242) 521381, or the Forestry Commission, 231 Corstorphine Road, dinburgh EH12 7AT.

ature Reserves – There are several nature reserves, bird sanctuaries and wildlife arks in the West Country as well as the bird colonies on Lundy Island and the les of Scilly, and the world-famous Jersey Wildlife Preservation Trust in the Channel lands. Apply to local Tourist Information Centres for details.
eaflets and booklets on **birdwatching** – there are many native and migrant birds to e seen in the West Country – and recommended sites are available from the Royal ociety for the Protection of Birds (RSPB), South-West Regional Office, 10 Richmond oad, Exeter, Devon EX4 4JA, ☎ (01392) 432691.

ambling – The many long-distance footpaths and countryside trails include the idgeway Path (Wiltshire), the Cotswold Way (Avon), the Two Moors Way (Devon), e West Mendip Way (Somerset) and the Leland Trail (Somerset). The well-known outh West Coast Path covers about 550 miles around the peninsula, and the owpath of the Kennet and Avon Canal meanders through Avon and Wiltshire. ontact WCTB for details.

iding and Pony Trekking – Details of private stables, residential centres and ail riding are available from local Tourist Information Centres.

ycling – Brochures indicating the designated cycle-ways in the West Country are vailable from WCTB. Ferry companies and the rail network will transport ccompanied bicycles; bicycles may also be hired locally.

Association of Railway Preservation Societies – The Association publishes an annual free guide to Steam Railways and Museums, available through Tourist Information Centres or by sending a stamped addressed envelope to Mr R Williams, 16 Woodbrook, Charing, Ashford, Kent TN27 ODN, ☎ (0123 371) 2130.

Boating and Sailing – There are marinas and yacht clubs, some with sailing schools, all round the coast of Dorset, Devon and Cornwall, and offshore racing throughout the season *(see Calendar of Events)*; details of local facilities and annual waterway rallies, regattas and festivals are available from local Tourist Information Centres or from the Royal Yachting Association, RYA House, Romsey Road, Eastleigh, Hampshire, ☎ (01703) 629 962.
Information and leaflets on boating, barging and cruising are also available from the Association of Pleasure Craft Operators, 35a High Street, Newport, Shropshire TF10 8JW; ☎ (01952) 813572.

Water Sports – Information on surfing (which is especially popular along the North Cornwall coast where the Atlantic rollers can provide ideal conditions), windsurfing, sail-boarding, water-skiing, canoeing and sub-aqua diving, and on tuition and equipment hire, is available from local Tourist Information Centres. The British Water Ski Federation, 390 City Road, London EC1V 2QA, ☎ (0171) 833 2855, can provide details of where to water-ski and where to learn the sport; for canoeing contact the British Canoe Union, Mapperley Hall, Kucknow Avenue, Nottingham NG3 5FA ☎ (01602) 821100.

Fishing – The West Country offers enormous variety for anglers, in its rivers, lakes, estuaries and harbours or in the sea itself. The WCTB publishes a *Guide to Angling in South West England* (£1.30), and information on seasons, fisheries, price of licences and permits may also be obtained from local Tourist Information Centres and tackle shops.

Golf – Golf courses which welcome visitors are marked on the **Michelin Atlas Great Britain and Ireland** and on **Michelin Map 403**. The WCTB publishes *Learn to Play Golf* and has details of golfing holidays and local courses.

Wine Trails – The English Vineyards Association publishes a leaflet, *Visit English Vineyards*, outlining the history of viticulture in England and giving details of vineyards open to the public (10 each in Somerset and Devon, 4 in Cornwall, 3 in Wiltshire, 2 each in Dorset and Avon, 1 in the Channel Islands). Apply to the English Vineyards Association Ltd, 38 West Park, London SE9 4RH, ☎ (0181) 857 0452.

Crafts – Many craft studios (pottery, weaving, lace, jewellery) are open to visitors in summer. There are demonstrations of obsolete crafts in some local museums.

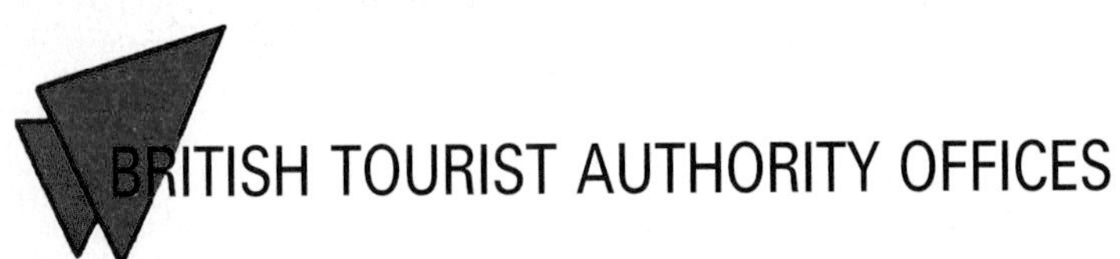

BRITISH TOURIST AUTHORITY OFFICES

British Tourist Authority (BTA) and the **English Tourist Board (ETB)** : Thames Tower, Black's Road, London W6 9EL, ☎ (0171) 824 8000. The **West Country Tourist Board (WCTB)** 60 St David's Hill, Exeter, Devon EX4 4SY, ☎ (01392) 76351.

Australia	Midland House, 171 Clarence Street, Sydney, NSW 2000. ☎ (02) 29 8627.
Canada	Suite 600, 994 Cumberland Street, Toronto, Ontario M5R 3N3. ☎ (416) 925 6326.
France	63 Rue Pierre Charon, 75008 Paris. ☎ (1) 42 89 11 11.
Germany	Taunusstrasse 52-60, 6000 Frankfurt 1. ☎ (069) 23 64 92.
Japan	246 Tokyo Club Building, 3-2-6 Kasumigaseki, Chiyoda-ku, Tokyo 100 ☎ (03) 581 3603.
New Zealand	Suite 305, 3rd Floor, Dilworth Building, Cnr Customs and Queen Streets, Auckland. ☎ (09) 31446.
USA	625 North Michigan Avenue, Suite 1510, Chicago, Illinois 60611 ☎ (312) 787 0490. Cedar Maple Plaza, Suite 210, 2305 Cedar Springs Road, Dallas TX 75201 1814. ☎ (212) 371 9052. World Trade Center, 350 South Figueroa Street, Suite 450, Los Angeles, CA 90071. ☎ (213) 628 3525. 40 West 57th Street, New York, NY 10019. ☎ (212) 581 4700.

There are also BTA offices in Belgium, Brazil, Denmark, Hong Kong, Ireland, Italy, Norway, Netherlands, Spain, Sweden and Switzerland.

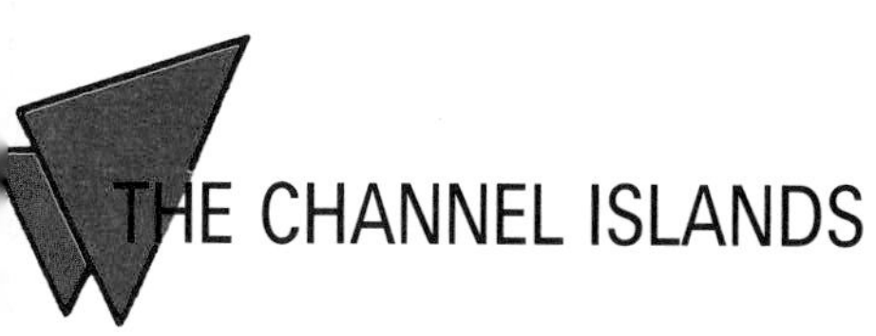

THE CHANNEL ISLANDS

ENERAL INFORMATION

ritish subjects do not need passports. There are no quarantine restrictions for nimals from the UK.

urrency – All the British clearing banks have branches in the Channel Islands. he local currency issued by the Banks of Jersey and Guernsey is not legal tender utside the islands.

RAVEL

y air – Direct to Jersey, Guernsey and Alderney from most airports in the UK by ir UK, Aurigny Air Services Ltd, British Air Ferries, British Airways, British Midland, rymon, Guernsey Airlines and Jersey European Airways.

y sea – To Jersey and Guernsey from Poole with British Channel Island Ferries, O Box 314, Poole, Dorset BH15 4DB, ☎ (01202) 681 155; or to Jersey and uernsey by SeaCat from Weymouth with Condor, Weymouth Quay, Weymouth, orset DT4 8DX, ☎ (01305) 761 551.

ee Admission Times and Charges at the end of this guide for details.

ransport – Private cars may be taken to Jersey and Guernsey. Hire cars are vailable in Jersey, Guernsey and Alderney. No cars are allowed on Sark and Herm. peed limits are 40mph in Jersey, 35mph in Guernsey; 20mph in the towns. Bicycle ire is available on all the islands except Herm.

CCOMMODATION

here is a wide range of hotels and guesthouses : see the **Michelin Red Guide Great ritain and Ireland.**

here are no caravan sites and caravans are forbidden.

here are camping sites in Jersey at St Aubin and St Brelade; in Guernsey in Torteval, ale, Castel, St Sampson's and St Peter Port; on Alderney at Saye Bay; on Herm t the Mermaid Site and the Little Seagull Camp Site.

OURIST INFORMATION CENTRES

ersey Tourism Office, 35 Albemarle Street, London W1X 3RP; ☎ (0171) 493 5278.

ersey Tourist Information Office, Weighbridge, St Helier, Jersey; ☎ (01534) 500 700.

uernsey Tourist Board, PO Box 23, White Rock, St Peter Port, Guernsey; ☎ (01481) 723 552.

lderney Tourist Board, St Anne, Alderney; ☎ (0148 182) 2994.

ark Tourist Board, Sark; ☎ (0148 183) 2345.

BOOKS TO READ

e Henge Monuments, G Wainwright, Thames and Hudson 1989

e Archaeology of South West Britain, S M Pearce, Collins 1981

omas Hardy : His Life and Landscape, Hawkins, National Trust 1990

essex – A Literary Celebration, Hawkins, Barrie and Jenkins 1991

ath, Sitwell, Century Hutchinson 1987

man Bath Discovered, B Cunliffe, Routledge and Kegan Paul 1984

glish Parish Churches as Works of Art, A Clifton-Taylor, Oxford University Press 1989

ational Trust Book of Long Walks, A Nicolson, Weidenfeld and Nicolson 1981

tional Trust Book of Ruins, B Bailey, Weidenfeld and Nicolson 1984

ue Guide : **Channel Islands,** P McGregor Eadie, A & C Black Ltd 1987

rka the Otter by H Williamson

e Arthurian Legends : by Thomas Malory, Spenser, Tennyson, Swinburne and T H White

maica Inn by Daphne du Maurier

e French Lieutenant's Woman by John Fowles

th Tangle by Georgette Heyer

e Alfoxden Journal : January-May 1798, Dorothy Wordsworth

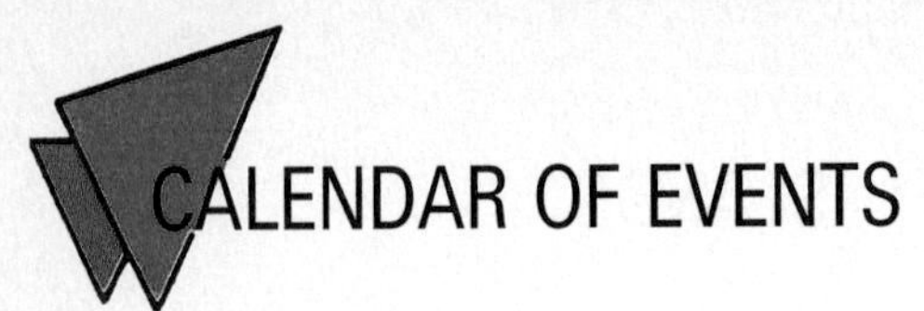

CALENDAR OF EVENTS

Horse Racing : Flat races and steeplechases are held throughout the year a racecourses in Wiltshire, Somerset and Devon.

1st and 3rd weekend in February

River Exe .... RSPB one-day birdwatching cruises.

Shrove Tuesday

St Columb Major
403 F32 .... Game of Hurling.

Mid-April

Devizes .... Devizes to Westminster International Canoe Race

One week in mid-April

St Endellion .... Music Festival.

Late April – early May

Minehead .... Hobby Horse Celebrations.

Newquay .... Great Cornwall Balloon Festival.

1 May

Padstow .... 'Obby 'Oss Celebrations.

8 May or preceding Saturday if 8th falls on a Sunday or Monday

Helston .... Flora Day Furry Dance.

Four days in early May

Badminton .... Badminton Horse Trials.

Three days in mid to late May

Chippenham .... Folk Festival.

Two weeks over late May and early June

Bath .... International Festival.

Late May to mid-September

Porthcurno .... Minack Theatre Summer Festival.

Early June

Bristol to Bournemouth .. Vintage Vehicle Run.

Mid-June

Brixham .... International Trawler Race and Quay Festival.

Two days in mid-June

Bath .... Steam and Vintage Vehicle Festival.

Two weeks in mid-June

Truro .... Three Spires Festival : Celebration of the Arts.

Late June

Glastonbury .... Glastonbury Pilgrimage.

July and August

Weymouth .... International Firework Festival.

Mid-July

St Helier .... St Helier's Day Procession.

Tolpuddle .... Tolpuddle Martyrs Rally.

Two days in mid-July

Devizes .... Kennet and Avon Canal Boat Rally.

our days in mid to late July

tourhead .... Summer Music Festival.

ast weekend in July

ristol .... Harbour Regatta.

ne week in late July – early August

idmouth .... International Festival of Folk Arts.

wo weeks in late July and early August

t Endellion .... Music Festival.

arly August

ewquay .... RAF St Mawgan International Air Day.

our days in early August

ruro .... International Festival of Music and Dance.

nd Thursday (Guernsey) and 4th Thursday (Jersey) in August

hannel Islands .... Battle of Flowers.

weekend in August or September

ristol .... International Balloon Fiesta.

lid-August

eymouth .... Weymouth Carnival.

hristchurch .... Regatta with fireworks and carnival procession.

ate August

artmouth .... Royal Regatta.

oole .... The Needles International Powerboat Race.

orbay .... Royal Regatta.

ugust Bank Holiday weekend

arrant Hinton 403 N31 ... Great Dorset Steam Fair.

wo days in early September

ong Ashton 403 L, M29 ... International Kite Festival.

ne day in early to mid-September

idecombe-in-the-Moor .. Widecombe Fair.

th November

eymouth .... Beach Bonfire and Fireworks.

n and around 5th November

hroughout the region ... Guy Fawkes Carnivals, with bonfires and fireworks.

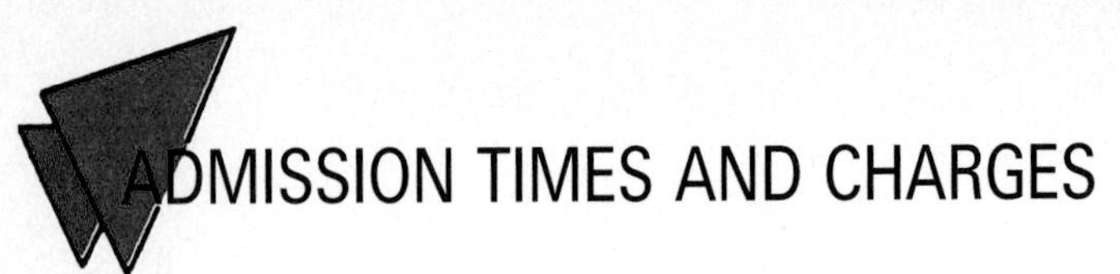

ADMISSION TIMES AND CHARGES

As admission times and charges are liable to alteration, the information printe below – valid for 1993 – is for guidance only.
⊙ : Every sight for which admission times and charges are listed is indicated b the symbol ⊙ after the title in the text.
Order : The information is printed in the same order as in the alphabetical sectio of the guide.
Dates : Dates given are inclusive. The term holidays means bank and public holiday
Last admission : Ticket offices usually close ½ hour before closing time; on exceptions are mentioned below.
Charge : The charge is for an individual adult; where appropriate the charge for family or child is given. Concessionary rates may be available for students and old-ag pensioners. Large parties should apply in advance.
Facilities for the disabled : As the range of possible facilities is great (for impaire mobility, sight and hearing) readers are advised to telephone in advance to chec
Tourist Information Centres : The addresses and telephone numbers are given f the local Tourist Information Centres, which provide information on local market day early closing days etc.
Abbreviations : NT indicates a property belonging to the National Trust; the Nation Trust in Scotland and in Northern Ireland have reciprocal arrangements. EH indicate English Heritage.

NB : From April 1995 all telephone dialling codes in Britain (including the Channel Islands) wi begin with 01 – eg (0305) 871 852 becomes (01305) 871 852. Please remember therefore t add the figure 1 after the initial 0 when dialling the numbers below, if necessary.

WEST COUNTRY

A

ABBOTSBURY

Swannery – Open April to October, daily, 0930 to 1700; otherwise, Sundays, 140 to dusk. £2.80. Guided tour (1½ hours). ☎ (0305) 871 852. Facilities for the disable

Sub-Tropical Gardens – Open mid-March to October, daily, 1000 to 170 otherwise, Tuesdays to Sundays, 1000 to 1700. £2.80. ☎ (0305) 871 852. Faciliti for the disabled.

Tithe Barn Country Museum – Open April to October, daily, 0930 to 180 otherwise, Sundays, 0930 to 1800. £1.50. Guided tour. ☎ (0305) 871 817. Limite facilities for the disabled.

St Catherine's Chapel – EH. Open all year, Mondays to Saturdays, 0930 to 183 (1600 mid-October to mid-March); Sundays, 1400 to 1600. Closed 1 January, Ma Day holiday, 24 to 26 December.

A LA RONDE

House – NT. Open April to October, Sundays to Thursdays, 1100 to 1730. £3. Guide tour. ☎ (0395) 265514. Parking; refreshments.

ANTONY HOUSE

House – NT. Open April to October, Tuesdays to Thursdays and holiday Monday also, June to August, Sundays, 1330 to 1730 (1645 last admission). £3.4 ☎ (0752) 812 191.

Mount Edgcumbe – **House and Earls Garden** : Open April to October, Wednesda to Sundays and holidays, 1100 to 1730. £3. ☎ (0752) 822 236. Parking. Faciliti for the disabled. **Country Park and Formal Gardens** : Open all year, daily, dawn to dus No charge. Parking; refreshments. Facilities for the disabled. **Visitor Centre** : Open Ap to October, daily, 1000 to 1730. No charge.

APPLEDORE

North Devon Maritime Museum – Open Easter to October, daily, 1400 to 173 (1630 last admission); also May bank holiday to September, Mondays to Friday 1100 to 1300 (1215 last admission). £1. Guided tour (1 hour) by appointmer ☎ (0237) 474 852. Limited facilities for the disabled.

ARLINGTON COURT

House and Carriage Collection – NT. Open April to October, Sundays to Frida and holiday Saturdays, 1100 to 1730. Guided tour (1 hour) by appointment. **Ground** Open as for house and also November to March, daily, dawn to dusk. £4.60 (hou and gardens). £2.40 (gardens). ☎ (0271) 850 296. Parking; refreshments. Faciliti for the disabled.

THELHAMPTON

ouse and Gardens – Open Easter to October, Tuesdays to Thursdays, Sundays, olidays, 1400 to 1800. £3.20. ☏ (0305) 848 363. Parking; refreshments. Limited cilities for the disabled.

VEBURY — The Great Barn; ☏ (06723) 425

lexander Keiller Museum – Open all year, daily, 1000 to 1800 (1600 October March). Closed 1 January, 24 to 26 December. £1.20 ☏ (06723) 250. Facilities r the disabled.

vebury Manor – Rooms subject to restoration, telephone to confirm. **Gardens** : Open pril to October, daily, 1100 to 1730. £2. ☏ (0672) 3388. Parking; refreshments.

luseum of Wiltshire Rural Life – Open late March to mid-November, daily, 1000 300 Saturdays, 1100 Sundays) to 1730 (1630 weekends); otherwise, weekends nly, 95p, family ticket £2.30. ☏ (06723) 555. Limited facilities for the disabled.

XBRIDGE

ing John's Hunting Lodge – Open April to September, daily, 1400 to 1700. No narge. Guided tour (½ hour). ☏ (0934) 732 012.

XMINSTER — Church Street; ☏ (0297) 34386

arpet Factory – Open all year, Mondays to Fridays, 0930 to 1200 and 1400 to 700 (1630 Fridays). Closed holidays, last week in July, first week in August, hristmas week. No charge. Parking.

ARNSTAPLE — Tuly Street; ☏ (0271) 47177

uildhall – Open third Friday in May to third Friday in September, Fridays, 1000 1230 and 1330 to 1530. No charge. Guided tour (40min). ☏ (0271) 73311.

luseum of North Devon – Open all year, Tuesdays to Saturdays, 1000 to 1630. losed holidays. No charge. Guided tour (1 hour) by appointment. ☏ (0271) 46747. acilities for the disabled.

t Anne's Chapel Museum – Open late May to October, Mondays to Saturdays, 000 to 1300 and 1400 to 1630; otherwise by appointment. No charge. Guided ur (½ hour) by appointment.

ARRINGTON COURT

ardens – NT. Open April to October, Sundays to Thursdays, 1200 to 1730. £3. **ouse** : Guided tour April to October, Wednesdays, 1330 to 1700. 50p. ☏ (0985) 47 777. Restaurant. Facilities for the disabled.

ATH — The Colonnades, Bath Street; ☏ (0225) 462 831

uided tours of the city – Walking tours depart from outside the Pump Room, undays to Fridays at 1030, Sundays also at 1430. No charge. Contact the Tourist formation Centre.

bbey – Open all year, Mondays to Saturdays, 0900 to 1800 (1900 June to August, 630 November to March); Sundays for services. Closed 1 January, 25 (afternoon), 6 December. Donation.

ump Room – Open March to October, daily, 0900 to 1800 (1900 July to August); therwise daily, 0900 (1000 Sundays) to 1700. Closed 25, 26 December. No charge. ☏ (0225) 461 111 ext 2782.

oman Baths : Museum – Open all year, daily, 0900 to 1800 (1700 November February). Closed 25, 26 December. £3.80, combined ticket with Museum of ostume £4.60. Guided tour (1 hour). ☏ (0225) 461 111 ext 2752. Refreshments. acilities for the disabled.

oyal Photographic Society – Open all year, daily, 0930 to 1730 (1645 last dmission). Closed 25, 26 December. £3. ☏ (0225) 462 841. Licensed restaurant. acilities for the disabled.

uilding of Bath Museum – Open March to mid-December, Tuesdays to Sundays, 130 to 1700. £2. ☏ (0225) 333 895.

luseum of English Naive Art – Open April to October, daily, 1030 (1400 Sundays October) to 1700. £2. ☏ (0225) 446 020.

ssembly Rooms – As for Museum of Costume (below) but closed occasionally r functions. No charge. Guided tour (½ hour). ☏ (0225) 461 111 ext 2752. acilities for the disabled.

luseum of Costume – Open March to October, daily, 0930 (1000 Sundays) to 800; otherwise, 1000 (1100 Sundays) to 1700. £2.40, combined ticket with oman Baths £4.60. Guided tour (1 hour). ☏ (0225) 461 111 ext 2752. Facilities r the disabled.

ath Industrial Heritage Centre – Open February to November, daily, 1000 to 1700; therwise, weekends, 1000 to 1700. Closed 24, 25, 26 December. £2.50, family cket £7. Guided tour (½ hour). ☏ (0225) 318 348. Refreshments. Limited facilities r the disabled.

BATH

No 1 Royal Crescent – Open April to September, daily, 1100 to 1700; March ar October to mid-December, Tuesdays to Sundays, 1100 to 1600. £3. ☏ (022 428 126.

Victoria Art Gallery – Open all year, Mondays to Saturdays, 1000 to 1730 (17C Saturdays). Closed holidays, 25, 26 December. No charge. ☏ (0225) 461 111 e 2772. Limited facilities for the disabled.

Bath Postal Museum – Open April to October, daily, 1100 (1400 Sundays) to 170 otherwise Mondays to Saturdays, 1100 to 1700. Closed 1 January, Good Frida 25, 26 December. £2. Guided tour (1 hour). ☏ (0225) 460 333. Refreshmen Limited facilities for the disabled.

Holburne Museum – Open all year, Mondays to Saturdays, 1100 to 1700, Sunday 1430 to 1800. Closed Mondays from November to Easter. £2.50. Guided to (1 hour). ☏ (0225) 466 669. Parking; restaurant; garden. Facilities for the disable

Herschel House Museum – Open March to October, daily, 1400 to 1700; otherwis weekends, 1400 to 1700. £2. Guided tour (1 hour) by appointment. ☏ (022 311 342.

Book Museum – Open all year, Mondays to Fridays, 0900 to 1300 and 1400 1730; Saturdays 0930 to 1300. Closed holidays. No charge. ☏ (0225) 466 00

Beckford Tower and Museum – Open April to October, weekends, holiday Monday 1400 to 1700. £1. Guided tour (½ hour). ☏ (0225) 312 917. Parking.

BICKLEIGH

Mill Craft Centre – Open April to 24 December, daily, 1000 to 1800 (1700 winte otherwise weekends, 1000 to 1700. £3.50. ☏ (088 485) 5419 or 5572. Parkin licensed restaurant. Facilities for the disabled.

Castle – Open Good Friday for one week, daily; Easter Friday to Spring bank holida Wednesdays, Sundays and holidays; Spring bank holiday to early October, Sunda to Fridays, 1400 to 1730. £2.80. Guided tour (1 ½ hours) except school holiday ☏ (0884) 855 363. Parking; refreshments. Limited facilities for the disabled.

BICTON

Gardens and Museum – Open April to September, daily, 1000 to 1800; Mar and October, daily, 1000 to 1600. £2.85. ☏ (0395) 68465.

BIDEFORD

ℹ The Quay; ☏ (02370) 477 6

Burton Art Gallery – Open all year, Mondays to Saturdays, 1000 to 1300 and 14(to 1700 (1600 winter); also summer Sundays, 1400 to 1700. No charge. ☏ (023 476 711 ext 315. Facilities for the disabled.

Tapeley Park, Instow – **Gardens** : Open Easter to September, Sundays to Frida and holidays, 1030 to 1800. Jousting and falconry displays most Sundays. Fro £2, child from £1. **House** : Guided tour (40min) Easter to September, as for garder £1.50, child £1. ☏ (0271) 860 528. Parking; tea room. Limited facilities for t disabled.

BLANDFORD FORUM

ℹ West Street; ☏ (02580) 454 7

Royal Signals Museum – Open all year, Mondays to Fridays, 1000 to 1700; Ju to September, weekends also, 1000 to 1600. Closed holidays and 10 days Christmas. No charge. ☏ (0258) 482 248. Parking.

Chettle House – Open April to October, Mondays, Wednesdays to Fridays a Sundays, 1100 to 1700. £1.80, children no charge. ☏ (025 889) 209. Parkin

BODMIN

ℹ Shire House, Mount Folly Square; ☏ (0208) 766

Museum – Open Easter to October, 1000 to 1600. No charge. Parking. Faciliti for the disabled.

BODMIN MOOR

North Cornwall Museum of Rural Life, Camelford – Open April to Septemb Mondays to Saturdays, 1000 to 1700. £1. Guided tour by appointment. ☏ (084 212 954. Limited facilities for the disabled.

Merlin Glass, Liskeard – **Showroom** : Open February to December, Mondays Saturdays, 1000 to 1700. **Workshop** : Open February to December; telephone f times. ☏ (0579) 342 399. Facilities for the disabled.

Restormel Castle – EH. Open Easter to September, daily, 1000 to 1800. Clos 1 January, 24 to 26 December. £1.10. ☏ (0208) 872 687. Parking; picnic are

BOURNEMOUTH

ℹ Westover Road; ☏ (0202) 789 7

Russell-Cotes Art Gallery and Museum – Open all year, Tuesdays to Sundays, 10(to 1700. Closed Good Friday, 25, 26 December. £1, no charge at weekends. Guid tour (1 hour). ☏ (0202) 551 009. Tea room. Facilities for the disabled.

Shelley Rooms – Open all year, Tuesdays to Sundays, 1400 to 1700. Closed Go Friday, 25, 26 December. No charge. ☏ (0202) 303 571. Parking. Limited faciliti for the disabled.

VEY TRACEY

von Guild of Craftsmen – Open all year, daily, 1000 to 1730. Closed winter lidays. £1. ☎ (0626) 832 223. Limited facilities for the disabled.

rke – NT parkland. **Rare breeds farm :** open April to October, daily, 1000 to 1700. .50. ☎ (0626) 833 909. Parking; refreshments.

use of Marbles and Teign Valley Glass – Open Easter to September, daily, 0900 1700. **Glassmaking :** Easter to September, Mondays to Fridays, 0900 to 1700, ndays and holidays, 1000 to 1500. No charge. Restaurant.

WOOD HOUSE

use and Grounds – Open April to October, daily, 1000 to 1800 or dusk. £4.30. (0249) 812 102. Parking; refreshments. Limited facilities for the disabled.

ododendron Walks – Open mid-May to mid-June, daily, 1000 to 1800. £1. No dogs.

ADFORD-ON-AVON — Bridge Street; ☎ (02216) 5797

xon Church of St Lawrence – Open all year, daily, 1000 to 1900 (1600 winter). charge. ☎ (0225) 865 797. Facilities for the disabled.

idge Chapel – Open all year, daily, 1000 to 1700; key available from the Tourist formation Centre, Waterlands, 34 Silver Street. ☎ (02216) 5797.

the Barn – EH. Open any reasonable time. No charge. ☎ (0272) 734472. Parking. cilities for the disabled.

AUNTON — Caen Street Car Park; ☎ (0271) 816 400

eat Field – For leaflets on Nature Trails etc, apply to the Tourist Information Centre.

rrows – ☎ (0271) 812 552 (warden). For leaflets on Nature Trails etc, apply the Tourist Information Centre.

IDGWATER — Town Hall, High Street; ☎ (0278) 427 652

dmiral Blake Museum – Open all year, daily, 1100 (1400 Sundays) to 1700. Closed , 26 December. Donation. Guided tour (2 hours). ☎ (0278) 456 127. Limited cilities for the disabled.

leridge Cottage, Nether Stowey – NT. Open April to September, Tuesdays to ursdays and Sundays, 1400 to 1700. £1.50. ☎ (0279) 732 662. Limited facilities the disabled.

arford Park – Open Easter weekend, and May to September, Wednesdays, ursdays, holidays, 1400 to 1730. £2. ☎ (027 867) 269.

illows and Wetlands, Stoke St Gregory – Open all year, Mondays to Fridays, 900 to 1300, 1400 to 1700. Guided tours (1 hour) Mondays to Fridays, every hour from 1000 to 1600. £1.75. **Showroom :** Open all year, Mondays to Saturdays, 900 (1000 Saturdays) to 1300, 1400 to 1700. No charge. ☎ (0823) 490 249.

IDPORT — 32 South Street; ☎ (0308) 24901

useum – Open Easter to October, daily, 1000 (1400 Sundays) to 1630; otherwise, ednesdays and weekends, 1000 (1400 Sundays) to 1630. Closed 24 to 6 December. 70p. Guided tour (45min) by appointment. ☎ (0308) 22116.

ISTOL — 14 Narrow Quay; ☎ (0117) 9260 767

uided tours of the town – Guided walks around the old city and harbour from d April to early September, Saturdays at 1430. Departure from Bridgehead. No arge. ☎ (0117) 9260 767.

athedral – Open all year, daily, 0800 to 1800. Donation. Guided tours by pointment. ☎ (0117) 9250 692. Refreshments.

rd Mayor's Chapel – Open all year, Tuesdays to Saturdays, 1000 to 1200 and 300 to 1600; Sundays, for services only. Donation. ☎ (0117) 9294 350.

arvey's Wine Museum – Open all year, Mondays to Fridays, 1000 to 1300 d 1400 to 1700; weekends 1400 to 1700. Closed holidays. £2.50 (including ass of sherry). Guided tour (2 ½ hours) by appointment. ☎ (0117) 9277 661. efreshments. Persons under 18 years of age not admitted.

eorgian House – Open all year, Mondays to Saturdays, 1000 to 1300 and 1400 1700. Closed 1 January, Good Friday, 25, 26 December. £2, combined ticket ith Red Lodge £2.50. ☎ (0117) 9211 362. Limited facilities for the disabled.

abot Tower – Open all year, daily, dawn to dusk; telephone to confirm. No charge. (0117) 9223 719.

ity Museum and Art Gallery – Open all year, daily, 1000 to 1700. Closed 1 January, ood Friday, May Day, Spring holiday, 25, 26 December. £2, children no charge. (0117) 9223 571. Café. Facilities for the disabled.

ed Lodge – Open all year, Mondays to Saturdays, 1000 to 1300 and 1400 to 700; may close without prior notice, telephone to confirm. Closed 1 January, Good iday, May Day, Spring holiday, 25, 26 December. £2, combined ticket with eorgian House £2.50. ☎ (0117) 9211 360.

t Stephen's City – Open all year, Mondays to Fridays, 0700 to 1700; weekends appointment. ☎ (0117) 9277 977.

BRISTOL

All Saints – Open term time only, Mondays to Fridays, 1000 to 1500. Close 2 weeks at Easter. No charge. ☎ (0117) 9277 454.

Christchurch – Open all year, Sundays to Fridays, 0700 to 1700; Saturdays b appointment. ☎ (0117) 9277 977.

St John the Baptist – Open all year, Tuesdays, Thursdays, 1200 to 1500. No charg ☎ (071) 936 2285.

John Wesley's New Room – Open all year, Mondays to Saturdays, 1000 to 130 and 1400 to 1600. Closed holidays, Wednesdays in winter. ☎ (0117) 9264 74

SS Great Britain – Open all year, daily, 1000 to 1800 (1700 winter). Closed 2 25 December. £2.80, child £1.90. Guided tour (1 hour) by appointment. ☎ (011 9260 680. Parking; refreshments. Limited facilities for the disabled.

Maritime Heritage Centre – Open all year, daily, 1000 to 1800 (1700 winte Closed 25 December. No charge. ☎ (0117) 9260 680. Parking. Limited faciliti for the disabled.

Industrial Museum – Open all year, Saturdays to Wednesdays, 1000 to 1300 ar 1400 to 1700. Closed 1 January, Good Friday, 25 to 27 December. £2, childre no charge. ☎ (0117) 9251 470. Limited facilities for the disabled.

Mayflower Steam Tug : Operates July to September, four days a month, 1200 to 180 £2, children £1. ☎ (0117) 9223 571.

St Mary Redcliffe – Open all year, daily, 0800 to 1800 (2000 June to Septembe Guided tour by appointment. ☎ (0117) 9291 487.

"Exploratory" – Open all year, daily, 1000 to 1700. Closed 1 week at Christma £3.75, child £2.50. ☎ (0117) 9225 944. Coffee shop. Facilities for the disable

Arnolfini – Open all year, Mondays to Saturdays, 1000 to 1900; Sundays, 12C to 1900; telephone to confirm holidays. No charge. Guided tour (45min). ☎ (011 9299 191. Café. Facilities for the disabled.

Zoological Gardens – Open all year, daily, 0900 to 1800 (1700 September to Ma Closed 25 December. £4.80, child £2.50. ☎ (0117) 9738 951. Parking; restaurar Facilities for the disabled.

Clifton RC Cathedral – Open all year, daily, 0700 to 2100 (2000 winter). ☎ (011 9738 411.

Blaise Castle House Museum – Open all year, Saturdays to Wednesdays, 10C to 1300, 1400 to 1700. Closed 1 January, Good Friday, 25, 26 December. N charge. ☎ (0117) 9506 789.

BROWNSEA ISLAND

Access – By ferry from Poole (the Quay) or Sandbanks, April to mid-October, dai services (½ hourly) 1000 to 1800 (1700 April, May). £3 from Poole, £1.95 fro Sandbanks.

Island and Nature Reserve – NT. Landing fee £2, family ticket £5. Open April mid-October, daily, 1000 to 2000 or dusk. ☎ (0202) 707 744. Guided ar self-guided tours available, ☎ (0202) 709 445. Refreshments. Facilities for th disabled.

BUCKFAST ABBEY

Abbey – Open all year, daily, 0530 to 2130. 75p (exhibition). Guided tour (40mi church; 1 ½ hours, site). ☎ (0364) 42519. Parking; refreshments. Facilities for th disabled.

BUCKLAND ABBEY

House – NT. Open April to November, Fridays to Wednesdays, 1030 to 173 otherwise, weekends, 1400 to 1700. £4 (house, grounds), £2 (grounds). ☎ (082 853 607. Parking; licensed restaurant. Facilities for the disabled.

BUDLEIGH SALTERTON — **i** Fore Street; ☎ (03950) 445 2

Otterton Mill – Open Easter to October, daily, 1030 to 1730; otherwise, 1130 1630. £1.50. Audio-visual presentation (hourly). ☎ (0395) 68521 or 6803 Restaurant.

C

CADHAY

House – Open July to August, Tuesdays to Thursdays, 1400 to 1730; also la spring, summer holidays, Sundays, Mondays, 1400 to 1730. £2. Guided to (1 ¼ hours). ☎ (0404) 812 432. Limited facilities for the disabled.

CAMBORNE AND REDRUTH

Camborne School of Mines, Pool : Museum of Minerals – Open all year, Monda to Fridays, 0900 to 1700. Closed holidays. No charge. ☎ (0209) 714 866. Parkin refreshments.

Cornish Pumping Engines and East Pool Whim – NT. Open April to October, dai 1100 to 1730 (1700 October). £1.80. ☎ (0209) 216 657.

CASTLE DROGO

Castle – NT. Open April to October, Saturdays to Thursdays, 1100 to 1700. **Garden** : open April to October, daily, 1030 to 1730. £4.60 (castle, garden, grounds), £2 (garden, grounds). ☎ (0647) 433 306. Parking; licensed restaurant. Limited facilities for the disabled.

CHARD

ℹ The Guildhall, Fore Street; ☎ (0460) 67463

Museum – Open early May to mid-October, Mondays to Saturdays, also Sundays from July to August, 1030 to 1630. £1.

Clapton Court Gardens – Open March to October, Mondays to Fridays and holidays, 1030 to 1700; Sundays, 1400 to 1700; otherwise by appointment. £3. ☎ (0460) 73220 or 72200. Parking; licensed restaurant.

CHEDDAR GORGE

ℹ The Gorge; ☎ (0934) 744 071

Cheddar Showcaves, Jacob's Ladder and Museum – Open all year, daily, 1000 to 1730 (1630 October to Easter). Closed 24, 25 December. £4.50 (Jacob's Ladder, Gough's Cave, Cox's Cave, Museum); family ticket (2A+2C) £13.50; tickets to individual attractions available. ☎ (0934) 742 343. Parking; refreshments. Limited facilities for the disabled.

Adventure Caving – Open all year, daily. Guided trip (1 ½ hours) by appointment. ☎ (0934) 742 343. Helmets, caving lamps and overalls provided; waterproof footwear advisable; basic English essential; minimum age 12 years.

Chewton Cheese Dairy – Open all year, daily, 0900 to 1700. **Cheese-making** : Mondays to Wednesdays, Fridays and Saturdays, 1130 to 1430. £1.50. Guided tour (45min). ☎ (0761) 21666. Parking; refreshments. Limited facilities for the disabled.

CHEW MAGNA

Stanton Drew Stone Circles – EH. Open all year, Mondays to Saturdays, 0930 to 1900 (1730 March to April, October, 1600 November to February). 50p. ☎ (0761) 490 563. Parking.

CHIPPENHAM

ℹ High Street; ☎ (0249) 657 733

Yelde Hall – Open mid-March to October, Mondays to Saturdays, 1000 to 1230 and 1400 to 1630. Closed holidays. No charge. ☎ (0249) 653 145 or 651 488.

CHRISTCHURCH

ℹ High Street; ☎ (0202) 471 780

Red House Museum – Open all year, Tuesdays to Sundays and holidays, 1000 (1400 Sundays) to 1700. Closed 25, 26 December. £1. Guided tour (1 hour). ☎ (0202) 482 860. Limited facilities for the disabled.

CLAVERTON

American Museum – Open April to October, Tuesdays to Sundays, 1400 to 1700; holiday Sundays, Mondays, 1100 to 1700. £3 (museum), £1.50 (grounds and gallery). Guided tour (1 hour). ☎ (0225) 460 503. Parking; refreshments. Limited facilities for the disabled.

Pumping Station – Open April to October, Sundays, 1030 to 1230 and 1400 to 1800; **pumps in steam** (river conditions permitting) May to September, telephone for times. £1, pumps in steam, £2.50. ☎ (0380) 721 279. Parking; refreshments.

CLEEVE ABBEY

Abbey – EH. Open April to September, daily, 1000 to 1800; otherwise, Tuesdays to Sundays, 1000 to 1600. Closed 1 January, 24 to 26 December. £1.50. ☎ (0984) 40377. Parking. Limited facilities for the disabled.

CLEVEDON COURT

House – NT. Open April to September, Wednesdays, Thursdays and Sundays, holiday Mondays, 1430 to 1730. £2.80 ☎ (0272) 872 257. Tea room.

CLOUDS HILL

Cottage – NT. Open April to September, Wednesdays to Fridays and Sundays, holidays, 1400 to 1700; otherwise, Sundays, 1300 to 1600. £2.20. ☎ (0985) 847 777. Parking.

CLOVELLY

Visitor Centre and village – Open July to September, daily, 0900 to 1800; otherwise, daily, 0930 to dusk. Closed 25 December. £1.50. ☎ (0237) 431288. Parking; refreshments. Facilities for the disabled.

Hobby Drive – Open Easter to mid-October, daily, 1000 to 1800. £1.25 per car. ☎ (0237) 431 000.

COMPTON ACRES

Gardens – Open March to October, daily, 1030 to 1830 (1745 last admission). £3.30. ☎ (0202) 700 778. Parking; café. Facilities for the disabled.

COMPTON CASTLE

Castle – NT. Open April to October, Mondays, Wednesdays, Thursdays, 1000 to 1215 and 1400 to 1700. £2.40. ☎ (0803) 872 112. Parking; refreshments. Limited facilities for the disabled.

CORFE CASTLE

Castle Ruins – NT. Open mid-February to October, daily, 1000 to 1730; otherwise, weekends, 1200 to 1530. £2.80, child £1.40. ☎ (0929) 481 294. Refreshments. Limited facilities for the disabled.

CORSHAM COURT

House – Open Good Friday to September, Tuesdays to Sundays and holidays, 1400 to 1800; otherwise, Tuesdays to Thursdays and weekends, 1400 to 1630. Closed December. £3. ☎ (0249) 712 214. Parking. Limited facilities for the disabled.

CRICKET ST THOMAS

Wildlife Park – Open April to October, daily, 1000 to 1800 (1700 or dusk, November to March). £5.50. ☎ (0460) 30755. Parking; restaurant; adventure playground. Limited facilities for the disabled.

D

DARTINGTON

Hall and Gardens – Open all year, dawn to dusk. Donation (£1.50). Guided tour (1 hour) £2. ☎ (0803) 862 271. Parking. Limited facilities for the disabled.

Cider Press Centre – Open all year, Mondays to Saturdays, 0930 to 1730; also mid-July to mid-September, Sundays, 0930 to 1730. Closed 1 January, 25, 26 December. ☎ (0803) 864 171. Parking; refreshments. Facilities for the disabled.

DARTMOOR

Becky Falls – Open Easter to November, daily, 1000 to 1800. £2.50 per car. ☎ (064 722) 259. Parking; licensed restaurant; picnic area.

South Devon Railway, Buckfastleigh – Open March to September, daily, 0930 (0900 holidays) to 1800. £5.20, family ticket (2A+2C) £15.90. Guided tour by appointment. ☎ (0364) 42338. Parking; café. Facilities for the disabled.

DARTMOUTH

ℹ Duke Street; ☎ (0803) 834 224

Newcomen Engine – Open Easter to October, Mondays to Fridays, 1200 to 1500. 20p. Guided tour (15min). ☎ (0803) 832 281.

Museum – Open all year, Mondays to Saturdays, 1100 to 1700 (1300 to 1600, November to March). 40p. Closed 24 to 26 December. ☎ (0803) 832 923.

Castle – EH. Open April to September, daily, 1000 to 1800; otherwise, Tuesdays to Sundays, 1000 to 1600. Closed 1 January, 24 to 26 December. £1.50. ☎ (0803) 833 588. Limited parking.

River Dart Boat Trips – Late March to October, daily; the river is tidal, times vary; telephone for timetable. ☎ (0803) 834 224.

Paignton and Dartmouth Steam Railway – Open April to October, daily; also early to late December. Trains depart at regular intervals from 1015. Telephone for timetable. £5.20 (Rtn). ☎ (0803) 555 872.

DEVIZES

ℹ St John's Street; ☎ (0380) 729 408

Museum – Open all year, Mondays to Saturdays, 1000 to 1700. Closed holidays. £1.50. ☎ (0380) 77369.

Canal Centre – Open all year, daily, 1000 to 1700 (1600 winter). Closed January. £1. ☎ (0380) 721279.

DORCHESTER

ℹ 1 Acland Road; ☎ (0305) 267 992

Old Crown Court – Open all year, Mondays to Fridays, 1000 to 1300, 1400 to 1700. Closed holiday Mondays and following Tuesdays. No charge. ☎ (0305) 252 408 or 267 992. **Cells** visited by appointment.

Dorset County Museum – Open all year, Mondays to Saturdays, 1000 to 1700. Closed Good Friday, 25, 26 December. £2. ☎ (0305) 267 992.

Dinosaur Museum – Open all year, daily, 0930 to 1730. Closed 24 to 26 December. £2.95, family ticket (2A+2C) £8.95. ☎ (0305) 269 880. Facilities for the disabled.

Dorset Military Museum – Open all year, Mondays to Saturdays and holidays, 0900 to 1700 (1300 Saturdays from October to June). Closed winter holidays. £1, child 50p. ☎ (0305) 264 066. Parking.

Tutankhamun Exhibition – Open all year, daily, 0930 to 1730. Closed 24 to 26 December. £2.95, family ticket (2A+2C) £8.95. ☎ (0305) 269 571. Facilities for the disabled.

Hardy's Cottage, Higher Bockhampton – NT. Open April to October, Fridays to Wednesdays, 1100 to 1800 or dusk, by appointment only. £2.30. ☎ (0305) 262 366. Parking. Limited facilities for the disabled.

Wolfeton House, Charminster – Open May to September, Tuesdays, Fridays and holidays, 1400 to 1800; otherwise by appointment. £2.50. ☎ (0305) 263 500. Parking.

DOWNSIDE ABBEY

Abbey Church – Open all year, daily, 0630 to 2030. No charge. Guided tour (45min) on written application to the Guestmaster, Downside Abbey, BA3 4RH. Parking. Facilities for the disabled.

DUNSTER

Castle – NT. Open April to October, Saturdays to Wednesdays, 1100 to 1700 (1600 October). **Garden and Park** : Open February to mid-December, daily, 1100 to 1700 (1600 February, March, October to December). £4.50, child £2.20 (castle, garden, park), £2.50, child £1.20 (garden, park). ☎ (0643) 821 314. Facilities for the disabled.

Water Mill – Open April to October, Sundays to Fridays, 1100 to 1700 (daily, July and August). £1.50, child 70p. ☎ (0643) 821 759. Tea room. Limited facilities for the disabled.

Molly Hardwick Doll Collection – Open April to October, daily, 1030 to 1630. 50p. ☎ (0642) 821 029. Parking.

Combe Sydenham Hall – Open Easter to October, Sundays to Fridays, 1000 to 1700; Saturdays, 0930 to 1200. £3 (house, garden, country park). ☎ (0984) 56284. Parking; refreshments. **Country park** : open Easter to October, Sundays to Fridays, 1000 to 1700; Saturdays, 0930 to 1200. Fly fishing ticket : £7 first hour (including hire of equipment); £3 subsequent hours; £1.50 per fish to retain.

DYRHAM PARK

House and Garden – NT. Open April to November, Saturdays to Wednesdays, 1200 to 1730 or dusk. £4.70 (house, garden, park). ☎ (027 582) 2501. Closed 25 December. Parking; refreshments. Facilities for the disabled. **Park** : open all year, daily, 1200 to 1730 or dusk. £1.50.

E

EXETER

i Paris Street; ☎ (0392) 265 700

Guided tours of the City – All year. For details apply to the Tourist Information Centre.

Cathedral – Open all year, daily, 0730 to 1815 (1700 Saturdays, 1930 Sundays). Donation (£1). ☎ (0392) 55573. Parking. Facilities for the disabled.

Maritime Museum – Open April to September, daily, 1000 to 1700; otherwise, weekends, 1000 to 1700, weekdays by appointment only. Closed 25, 26 December. £3.80, family £11.20. ☎ (0392) 58075. Parking; refreshments. Facilities for the disabled.

Quay House Interpretation Centre – Open all year, daily; summer, 1000 to 1700; winter, 1000 to 1300 and 1400 to 1600. Closed 25, 26 December. No charge. ☎ (0392) 265 213.

Royal Albert Memorial Museum – Open all year, Tuesdays to Saturdays, 1000 to 1730. No charge. ☎ (0392) 265 858. Limited facilities for the disabled.

Guidhall – Open all year, Tuesdays to Saturdays, 1000 to 1600 (1230 Saturdays). Closed holidays and for civic functions. No charge. Guided tour. ☎ (0392) 265 500.

Rougemont House Museum – Open all year, Mondays to Saturdays, 1000 to 1730. Closed Good Friday, 25, 26 December. £1.50, family ticket (2A+3C) £3.50. ☎ (0392) 265 858. Limited facilities for the disabled.

St Nicholas Priory – Open Easter to October, Tuesdays to Saturdays, 1000 to 1700. Closed Good Friday. 50p. ☎ (0392) 265 858. Limited facilities for the disabled.

Tucker's Hall – Open June to September, Tuesdays, Thursdays and Fridays, 1030 to 1230 (Civic functions permitting). No charge. ☎ (0392) 436 244.

Underground Passages – Open all year, Tuesdays to Saturdays, 1000 (1400 Tuesdays to Fridays from November to Easter). £1.50, family ticket £3.50. Guided tour (1 hour). ☎ (0392) 265 858.

Topsham Museum – Open February to November, Mondays, Wednesdays, 1400 to 1700; also August, September, weekends, 1400 to 1700. 60p. ☎ (0392) 873 244.

F

FALMOUTH

i 28 Killigrew Street; ☎ (0326) 312 300

Maritime Museum – Open all year, daily, 1000 to 1600 (1500 November to March). £1.10.

Art Gallery – Open all year, daily, Mondays to Fridays, 1000 to 1630. Closed 25, 26 December, 1 January and holidays. No charge. ☎ (0326) 313863.

Pendennis Castle – EH. Open April to September, daily, 1000 to 1800; otherwise, Tuesdays to Sundays, 1000 to 1600. Closed 1 January, 24 to 26 December. £1.80. ☎ (0326) 316 594. Parking; refreshments (summer). Limited facilities for the disabled.

FARLEIGH HUNGERFORD

Castle Ruin – EH. Open April to September, daily, 1000 to 1800; otherwise, Tuesdays to Sundays, 1000 to 1600. Closed 1 January, 24 to 26 December. £1.20. ☎ (0225) 754 026. Parking; refreshments (summer). Limited facilities for the disabled.

FORDE ABBEY

House – Open all year, Sundays, Wednesdays and holidays, 1300 to 1630. Guided tour (1 hour) by appointment. **Gardens** : open all year, daily 1000 to 1630. £4.30 (house, gardens), £3 (gardens), children no charge. ☎ (0460) 20231. Parking, refreshments. Facilities for the disabled.

FOWEY

4 Custom House Hill; ☎ (0726) 833 616

Town Hall Museum – Open Easter week, and Spring holiday to early October, Mondays to Fridays, 1030 to 1230 and 1430 to 1630. 50p.

Monkey Sanctuary, Looe – Open Palm Sunday to September, Sundays to Thursdays, 1030 to 1700. £3.50, child £1.50. Guided tour (2 hours). ☎ (0503) 262 532. Parking; refreshments. Limited facilities for the disabled.

Paul Corin's Mechanical Music Centre, St Keyne – Open Easter week, and early May to late October, daily, 1030 to 1700. £3. ☎ (0579) 343 108. Parking, refreshments; picnic area.

FROME

Tropical Bird Gardens, Rode – Open all year, daily, 1000 to 1830 or dusk (last admission 1 hour before closing). Closed 25 December. £3.50, child £1.75 ☎ (0373) 830 326. Parking; licensed cafeteria. Facilities for the disabled.

G

GAULDEN MANOR

Manor – Open Easter Sunday and Monday, and May to early September, Sundays, Thursdays and holidays 1400 to 1730. £2.80. Guided tour (½ hour). ☎ (09847) 213. Parking; refreshments. Facilities for the disabled.

GLASTONBURY

Northload Street; ☎ (0458) 832 954

Abbey – Open all year, daily, 0900 (0930 September to May) to 1800 or dusk Closed 25 December. £2. ☎ (0458) 32267. Limited facilities for the disabled.

Tribunal Museum – EH. Open Good Friday to September, daily, 1000 to 1300 and 1400 to 1800; otherwise, Tuesdays to Sundays, 1000 to 1300 and 1400 to 1600. Closed 1 January, 24 to 26 December. £1.10. ☎ (0458) 832 949. Parking.

Somerset Rural Life Museum – Open all year, Mondays to Fridays, 1000 to 1700 (1630 Fridays); April to October, weekends, 1400 to 1800; otherwise, Saturdays, 1100 to 1600. £1.20. ☎ (0458) 831 197. Parking; refreshments (summer). Facilities for the disabled.

Chalice Well and Gardens – Open March to October, daily, 1000 to 1800; otherwise, daily, 1300 to 1600. 60p. ☎ (0458) 831 154. Limited parking. Limited facilities for the disabled.

Shoe Museum, Street – Open Easter Monday to October, Mondays to Saturdays, 1000 to 1645 (1630 Saturdays). ☎ (0458) 43131 ext 2169. Facilities for the disabled.

GLENDURGAN

Garden – NT. Open March to October, Tuesdays to Saturdays and holiday Mondays, 1030 to 1730 (1630 last admission). Closed Good Friday. £2.50. ☎ (0326) 250 906.

GREAT CHALFIELD MANOR

Manor – NT. Open April to October, Tuesdays to Thursdays, 1215 to 1715. Closed holidays. Guided tours (45min) at 1215, 1415, 1500, 1545, 1630. £3.50. ☎ (0985) 847 777.

GREAT TORRINGTON

Dartington Crystal – **Factory** : Open all year, Mondays to Fridays, 0930 to 1530 Closed holidays. **Glass Centre** : Open all year, daily, 0930 (1000 Sundays) to 1700 Closed holidays. £2. ☎ (0805) 24233. Parking; licensed restaurant. Facilities for the disabled.

Town Hall Museum – Open May to September, Mondays to Fridays, 1015 to 1245 and 1415 to 1645; Saturdays, 1015 to 1245; otherwise by appointment. Closed holidays. No charge. Guided tour by appointment. ☎ (0805) 24324.

South Molton Museum – Open March to November, Tuesdays, Thursdays, Fridays 1030 to 1300, 1400 to 1600; Wednesdays, Saturdays, 1030 to 1230. No charge ☎ (0769) 574 122.

Quince Honey Farm, South Molton – Open Easter to October, daily, 0900 to 1800 (1700 October). £2.75. ☎ (0769) 572 401. Café; picnic area.

H

HATCH COURT

House – Open June to September, Thursdays, and August holiday Monday, 1430 to 1730. £2.50. Guided tour (1 ½ hours). ☏ (0823) 480 120. Parking; tea room. Limited facilities for the disabled.

HELSTON

ℹ Theme Park, Culdrose; ☏ (0326) 565 431

Folk Museum – Open all year, Mondays to Saturdays, 1030 to 1300 and 1400 to 1630 (Wednesdays, 1030 to 1200 only). ☏ (0326) 564 027.

Flambards Village Theme Park, Culdrose – Open Easter to October, daily, 1000 to 1730 (2000 end July, August). £7.50, child £6.50. ☏ (0326) 574 549. Parking; refreshments. Facilities for the disabled.

Poldark Mine, Wendron – Open April to October, daily, 1030 (1000 August) to 1730 (1800 August). £4.95, child £2.75. Guided tour (3 hours). ☏ (0326) 573 166. Parking; café. Limited facilities for the disabled.

Seal Sanctuary, Gweek – Open all year, daily, 0930 to 1800 (1600 winter). Closed 25 December. £4.50, child £2.50. Feeding time at 1100 and 1600. ☏ (032 622) 361. Parking; refreshments. Facilities for the disabled.

HIGH HAM

Stembridge Tower Mill – Open April to September, Sundays and Mondays, 1430 to 1700. £1.50. ☏ (0458) 250 818. Parking.

HONITON

ℹ Dowell Street Car Park; ☏ (0404) 43716

All Hallows Museum – Open April to October, Mondays to Saturdays, 1000 to 1700 (1600 October). **Lace-making demonstrations** : June to August. 60p. ☏ (0404) 44966.

Farway Countryside Park – Open Good Friday to September, daily, 1000 to 1700. £2. Guided tour (2 hours) by appointment. ☏ (040 487) 224. Parking; refreshments. Facilities for the disabled.

HORTON COURT

Hall and Ambulatory – NT. Open April to October, Wednesdays and Saturdays, 1400 to 1800 or dusk. £1.40. Guided tour (½ hour). Parking. Limited facilities for the disabled.

I

ILFRACOMBE

ℹ The Promenade; ☏ (0271) 863 001

St Nicholas' Chapel – Open late May to mid-October, daily, 1000 to 1300 and 1400 to 1700; also May to August, 1930 to dusk.

Tunnels Beach – Open May to September, daily, 0900 to dusk. 75p. Guided tour. Refreshments; picnic area. Facilities for the disabled.

Chambercombe Manor – Open Easter to September, Sundays to Fridays, 1000 to 1730. £3. Guided tour (1 hour). ☏ (0271) 862 624. Parking; refreshments.

K

KILLERTON

House – NT. Open April to October, Wednesdays to Mondays, 1100 to 1730. £4.60. ☏ (0392) 881 345. Parking; refreshments. Limited facilities for the disabled.

Garden – NT. Open all year, daily, 1030 to dusk. £2.80. ☏ (0392) 881345. Parking; refreshments. Facilities for the disabled.

KINGSBRIDGE

ℹ The Quay; ☏ (0548) 853 195

Cookworthy Museum – Open Easter to September, Mondays to Saturdays, 1000 to 1700; October, Mondays to Fridays, 1000 to 1700. £1.20, family ticket £3.20. ☏ (0548) 853 235. Limited facilities for the disabled.

Boat trip to Salcombe – Departure from **The Quay** May to August; Mondays to Saturdays, 3 to 4 trips daily (½ hour). £1.80 (single). Sundays, sea or river cruise (1 hour 45min). £3.50. ☏ (0548) 853 525 or 853 607.

KINGSTON LACY

House and Gardens – NT. Open April to October, Saturdays to Wednesdays, 1200 to 1630. Closed Good Friday. £5, child £2.50. **Park** : open as for house, 1130 to 1800. £2, child £1. ☏ (0202) 883 402. Parking; licensed restaurant. Limited facilities for the disabled.

KNIGHTSHAYES COURT

House – NT. Open April to October, Saturdays to Thursdays, 1330 to 1730. **Gardens** : open Good Friday to October, daily, 1030 to 1730. £4.80 (house, gardens), £2.80 (gardens). ☏ (0884) 257 381 or 254 665. Parking, refreshments. Facilities for the disabled.

L

LACOCK

Fox Talbot Museum – NT. Open March to October, daily, 1100 to 1700. Closed Good Friday. £2.20. ☎ (0249) 730 459. Parking. Limited facilities for the disabled.

Abbey, Cloisters and Grounds – NT. Open April to October, Wednesdays to Mondays, 1200 (1300 abbey) to 1730. Closed Good Friday. £4, child £2 (house, cloisters, grounds), £2, child £1 (cloisters, grounds). ☎ (0249) 730 227. Facilities for the disabled.

LAND'S END

Visitor Centre and Site – Open all year, daily, 1000 to dusk. Closed 24, 25 December. £5.50 (no charge to site before, after hours). Right of way for walkers over site. ☎ (0736) 871 501. Parking only, £3.50; restaurant. Facilities for the disabled.

LANGPORT

Midelney Manor – Guided tours May holiday to mid-September, Thursdays and holiday Mondays, 1430 to 1730 (1630 last tour). £2.50. ☎ (0458) 251 229. Parking.

LANHYDROCK

House – NT. Open April to October, Tuesdays to Sundays and holidays, 1100 to 1730 (1700 October). **Gardens** : as for house, daily. £5 (house, gardens), £2.60 (gardens). ☎ (0208) 73220. Parking; refreshments. Facilities for the disabled.

LAUNCESTON

ℹ Market Street; ☎ (0566) 772 321

Castle – EH. Open Easter to September, daily, 1000 to 1800; otherwise, Tuesdays to Sundays, 1000 to 1600. Closed 1 January, 24 to 26 December. 95p. ☎ (0566) 772 365. Limited facilities for the disabled.

Local History Museum – Open April to mid-October, daily, 1030 to 1630. Donation. Guided tour (1 hour) by appointment. ☎ (0566) 772 640 or 773 277.

LITTLECOTE

House, Grounds and Roman Mosaic – Open Easter to September, daily, 1030 to 1700. £4.95, child £3.95. Guided tour (2 hours). ☎ (0488) 684 000. Parking; refreshments. Limited facilities for the disabled.

LIZARD PENINSULA

ℹ Theme Park, Culdrose; ☎ (0326) 565431

Goonhilly Satellite Earth Station – Open Easter to October, daily, 1000 to 1800; otherwise by appointment. £3. ☎ (0326) 574 141. Visitor Centre; parking; licensed restaurant; adventure playground.

LONGLEAT

House – Open all year, daily, 1000 to 1800 (1600 October to Easter). Closed 25 December. £3.50. Guided tour (45min). ☎ (0985) 844 551. Parking; refreshments. Facilities for the disabled.

Safari Park – Open mid-March to October, daily, 1000 to 1800. £5 per car. ☎ (0985) 844 328. Parking; refreshments; butterfly garden; pets corner. Facilities for the disabled.

Maze : Allow 1 hour. 75p.

Narrow-Gauge Railway : £1.20. ☎ (0985) 844 579.

Coarse Fishing : Open mid-June to mid-March. Permits from water bailiff at lakeside; waters sometimes closed for contests. £4-£10. ☎ (0985) 215 082.

LUNDY ISLAND

Access – **Ship** from Bideford Quay all year, daily; from Ilfracombe Pier May to September, daily. £18.95. Time 2¼ hours. ☎ (0237) 423 365 (timetable), 470 422 (tickets). Parking; refreshments. **Helicopter** from Ilfracombe. ☎ (0271) 823 431.

Accommodation – Contact the Landmark Trust in advance; ☎ (0628) 825 925.

LYDFORD

Gorge – NT. Open April to October, daily, 1000 to 1730; otherwise 1030 to 1500 (waterfall entrance only). £2.80. Short walk (1 hour) 1 ½ miles; long walk (2 hours) 3 miles; the walk is arduous and suitable only for the able-bodied. ☎ (082 282) 441 or 320. Parking; refreshments. Limited facilities for the disabled.

LYDIARD PARK

House – Open all year, daily, 1000 to 1300, 1400 to 1730 (1600 November to February). Closed Sunday mornings, Good Friday, 25, 26 December. £1.40. ☎ (0793) 770 401. Parking; refreshments (summer). Facilities for the disabled.

Church – Key available from the house.

LYME REGIS — Church Street; ☎ (0297) 442 138

Museum – Open April to October, Mondays to Saturdays, 1030 to 1300, 1430 to 1700; Sundays, 1430 to 1700. 50p. ☎ (0297) 443 370.

LYNTON and LYNMOUTH — Town Hall, Lee Road; ☎ (0588) 52225

Cliff Railway – Open mid-March to 26 December, Mondays to Saturdays, 0800 to 1900; also Easter, holiday weekends and June to September, Sundays, 1000 to 1900. 30p. ☎ (0598) 52225. Parking. Facilities for the disabled.

Motorcycle Collection, Combe Martin – Open Easter, and end May to September, daily, 1000 to 1800. £1.50. ☎ (0271) 882 346. Facilities for the disabled.

LYTES CARY

Manor – NT. Open April to October, Wednesdays and Saturdays, 1400 to 1800 or dusk. £3.50, child £1.70. ☎ (0985) 847 770. Limited parking. Limited facilities for the disabled.

M

MAIDEN CASTLE

Earthwork ramparts – EH. Open all year, daily. No charge. ☎ (0272) 734 472. Parking.

MALMESBURY — Town Hall, Cross Hayes; ☎ (0666) 823 748

Abbey – Open all year, daily, 1000 to 1800 (1600 November to Easter).

MARLBOROUGH — George Lane; ☎ (0672) 513 989

Wilton Windmill – Open Easter to September, Sundays and holidays, 1400 to 1700; otherwise by appointment. 80p. Guided tour (weekends). ☎ (0672) 870 686. Parking. Limited facilities for the disabled.

Stone Museum, Great Bedwyn – Open all year, daily, 0800 to dusk. ☎ (0672) 870 234.

Crofton Beam Engines – Open April to September, Sundays, 1000 to 1630. £1. **Engines in steam** : April to September (confirm dates). £2.50. ☎ (0380) 721 279 (Canal Trust) or (0672) 870 300 (Crofton Pumping Station).
Boat trips; steaming weekends; private charter cruises. ☎ (081) 290 0031.

MILTON ABBAS

Abbey – Open all year, daily, 0930 to 1830. ☎ (0258) 880 207.

House – Open Easter week and school summer holidays, daily, 0930 to 1830. £1.20. ☎ (0258) 880 207. Parking; refreshments (summer).

MINEHEAD — 17 Friday Street; ☎ (0643) 702 624

West Somerset Railway – Open March to October, daily. £1 to £7, family ticket (2A+2C) £11 to £18. ☎ (0643) 704 996. Timetable at Minehead; bus connection Bishops Lydeard to Taunton. Parking; refreshments. Facilities for the disabled.

MONTACUTE

House – NT. Open April to October, Wednesdays to Mondays, 1200 to 1700. Closed Good Friday. **Garden and Park** : open all year, Wednesdays to Mondays, 1130 to 1730 or dusk. £4.60, child £2.30 (house, garden, park), £2.50, child £1.20, reductions November to March (garden, park). ☎ (0935) 823 289.

MORWELLHAM

Quay – Open all year, daily, 1000 to 1730 (1630 November to Easter, last admission 1530). Closed 24 December to 1 January. £6.25. ☎ (0822) 832 766 or 833 808. Parking; restaurant. Limited facilities for the disabled.

Cotehele – **Manor House and Mill** : NT. Open April to October, Saturdays to Thursdays, 1200 to 1730 (1700 October). **Garden** : open April to October, daily, 1100 to 1730 or dusk. Timed tickets : £5 (house, garden, mill), £2.60 (garden). ☎ (0579) 50434. Parking; refreshments. Limited facilities for the disabled.

MUCHELNEY

Abbey – EH. Open April to September, daily, 1000 to 1800. £1.10. ☎ (0458) 250 664. Parking. Limited facilities for the disabled.

Priest's House – NT. Closed for restoration work. ☎ (0985) 847 777.

Pottery – Open all year, Mondays to Fridays, 0900 to 1700; Saturdays, 0900 to 1300. £1 (demonstration). ☎ (0458) 250 324. Parking.

The Somerset Wine Trail links eight vineyards, including such well-known names as Wootton and Pilton Manor, Wraxall and Castle Cary. Somerset itself has about a dozen vineyards that are open to the public; there are eight in Devon, two in Dorset and three in Cornwall.

O

OKEHAMPTON

3 West Street; ☎ (0837) 53020

Museum of Dartmoor Life – Open Easter to November, Mondays to Saturdays, holidays, 1000 to 1700. £1. ☎ (0837) 52295. Parking; refreshments. Limited facilities for the disabled.

Castle – EH. Open April to September, daily, 1000 to 1800; otherwise, Tuesdays to Sundays, 1000 to 1600. Closed 1 January, 24 to 26 December. £1.50. ☎ (0837) 52844. Parking; picnic area.

Museum of Water Power, Sticklepath – Open March to November, Mondays to Saturdays, also Sundays June to September, 1000 to 1700. £1.60. Guided tour (½ hour) by appointment. ☎ (0837) 840 046. Parking; refreshments.

P

PADSTOW

☎ (0841) 533 449

Bedruthan Steps – **Cliff staircase** : NT. Closed temporarily; telephone for details. ☎ (0208) 74281.

Boat Trips – Contact Tourist Information Centre for details. ☎ (0841) 533 449.

PAIGNTON

See under Torbay.

PARNHAM HOUSE

House – Open April to October, Sundays, Wednesdays and holidays, 1000 to 1700. £2.50. ☎ (0308) 862 204.

PENCARROW

House – Guided tour (2 hours) Easter to mid-October, Sundays to Thursdays, 1330 (1100 June to early September) to 1700. **Gardens** : open as for house, daily. £3. ☎ (020 884) 449 or 369. Parking; refreshments. Facilities for the disabled.

PENWITH

Minack Theatre – **Box office** : Open for 1 ¼ hours before each performance. £4.50. ☎ (073 672) 810 471. Parking; refreshments.

Rowena Cade Exhibition Centre : Open April to October, 1000 to 1730 (1630 October). Closed 1200 to 1430 on matinée performance days. £1.40. Parking; refreshments.

Carn Euny – EH. Open all year, daily. No charge. ☎ (0272) 734 472. Parking.

Land's End Aerodrome – **Viewing terrace** : open all year, daily, 0800 to 1800. No charge. **Flights** : Sennen Cove £14; Porthcurno £19.50; Penwith (when available) £40. ☎ (0736) 788 771.

Geevor Tin Mine – Reopening June 1993; ring for details. ☎ (0736) 788 662.

Zennor Museum – Open 1 week before Easter to October, daily, 1000 to 1800. £1.50. ☎ (0736) 796 945. Parking; refreshments.

Paradise Park, Hayle – Open all year, daily, 1000 to 1800 (1600 November to March). **Flying demonstrations** (weather permitting) : Easter to September at 1200 and 1530. £4.25. ☎ (0736) 753 365. Parking; refreshments. Limited facilities for the disabled.

Chysauster Prehistoric Village – EH. Open April to September, daily, 1000 to 1800. Closed 1 January, 24 to 26 December. £1.20. ☎ (0736) 61889. Parking.

PENZANCE

Station Road; ☎ (0736) 62207

Cruises around the Cornish Coast – Apply to the Tourist Information Centre.

National Lighthouse Centre – Open March to October, daily, 1100 to 1700. £2, family ticket (2A+3C) £5. ☎ (0736) 60077.

Morrab Gardens – Open all year, daily, 1000 to 1800.

Museum and Art Gallery – Open all year, Mondays to Saturdays, 1030 to 1630. Closed 25, 26 December. 50p. ☎ (0736) 63625. Parking. Limited facilities for the disabled.

Maritime Museum – Open Easter to October, Mondays to Saturdays, 1000 to 1700. £1.50, family ticket (2A+4C) £4. ☎ (0736) 62476.

Trereife Park – Open April to October, daily, 1030 to 1730. Guided tours (25min) of house from 1200. **Horse demonstrations** : daily, at 1200 and 1530. ☎ (0736) 62750. Parking; licensed restaurant; picnic area. No charge, £1 for house. Facilities for the disabled.

Newlyn Art Gallery – Open all year, Mondays to Saturdays, 1000 to 1700. Closed Good Friday, 24 to 26 December. No charge. ☎ (0736) 63715. Refreshments.

.YMOUTH

ℹ Royal Parade; ☎ (0752) 264 849

meaton's Tower – Open Easter to October, daily, 1030 to 1700. 65p, combined ·ket with Dome, £3.45. ☎ (0752) 603 300.

ome – Open all year, daily, 0900 to dusk. Closed 25 December. £2.95, family ·ket (2A+4C) £8.40. ☎ (0752) 603 300 or 600 608. Café. Facilities for the sabled. Combined tickets to Smeaton's Tower and Citadel available.

oyal Citadel – Guided tours May to September, at 1200 and 1400. £2.50, ·mbined ticket with Dome, £4.50. ☎ (0752) 603 300.

izabethan House – Open Easter Saturday and Monday; May to September, ·esdays to Saturdays and holiday Mondays, 1000 to 1730 (1700 holidays). 80p. ☎ (0752) 264 878.

izabethan Gardens – Open all year, daily, 0900 to 1700 or dusk. No charge.

oates Black Friars Gin Distillery – Open Easter to September, Mondays to ·aturdays, 1030 to 1600. £1.50. Guided tour (45min). ☎ (0752) 667 062. Limited ·cilities for the disabled.

ivic Centre – **Roof Deck** : Open May to September, Mondays to Saturdays, 1000 · 1215 and 1300 to 1600. Closed holidays. Admission charge.

ouncil House – Open by appointment only. No charge. ☎ (0752) 264 858.

uildhall – Open all year, Mondays to Fridays, 1000 to 1600 when not in commercial ·e.

rysten House – Open April to October, Mondays to Saturdays, 1000 to 1600. 0p. ☎ (0752) 661 414.

lerchant's House Museum – Open Easter Saturday and Monday; May to ·eptember, Tuesdays to Saturdays and holiday Mondays, 1000 to 1730 (1700 ·olidays). 80p. ☎ (0752) 264 878.

ity Museum and Art Gallery – Open all year, Tuesdays to Saturdays and holiday ·ondays, 1000 to 1730 (1700 holidays). Closed Good Friday. No charge. ☎ (0752) 64 878. Refreshments. Limited facilities for the disabled.

quarium – Open all year, daily, 1000 to 1800 (1700 November to March). £1.50. ☎ (0752) 222 772.

oat Trips – Embark Phoenix Wharf or Mayflower Steps for cruises around the **ockyards and Warships,** from £2.80; **River Tamar,** from £3.50; **Looe and Weir Head,** from ·5; **River Yealm,** from £3.50. Contact Plymouth Boat Cruises Ltd, ☎ (0572) 822 797 · 822 202, or Tamar Cruising, ☎ (0572) 822 105.

elverton Paperweight Centre – Open end May to mid-September, daily, 1000 · 1700; otherwise, Wednesdays and Saturdays, 1000 (1300 Saturdays) to 1700. ·o charge. ☎ (0822) 854 250. Limited facilities for the disabled.

artmoor Wild Life Park, Sparkwell – Open all year, daily, 1000 to dusk. £4.95, ·hild £3.50. **Flying displays** : at 1200, 1600. ☎ (075 537) 209. Parking; licensed ·estaurant; picnic area; adventure playground.

itley Caves, Yealmpton – Open Easter to October, daily, 1000 to 1730. £2.80, ·hild £1.40. ☎ (0752) 880 202. Parking; refreshments.

ational Shire Horse Centre – Open all year, daily, 1000 to 1700 (1600 November · February). Closed 23 to 26 December. **Parade of Horses** at 1130, 1430 and 1615. **alconry displays** at 1300 and 1530. £4.95, child £3.30. ☎ (0752) 880 268. Parking; ·censed restaurant; picnic area. Facilities for the disabled.

OOLE

ℹ The Quay; ☎ (0202) 673 322

atural World – Open end May to August, daily, 0930 to 2100 (last admission); ·therwise, daily, 1000 to 1700 (last admission). Closed 24, 25 December. £2.95, ·amily ticket (2A+2C) £8.50. ☎ (0202) 686 712. Refreshments. Limited facilities ·r the disabled.

oole Pottery – Open March to 24 December, daily, 1000 to 1630 (1600 October · December). No charge. ☎ (0202) 668 681. Refreshments.

NLI Museum – Open all year, Mondays to Fridays, 0930 to 1630. Closed holidays. ☎ (0202) 671 133.

Vaterfront Museum – Open March to October, daily, 1000 (1400 Sundays) to 700; otherwise, Saturdays, 1000 to 1700, Sundays, 1400 to 1700. Closed · January, Good Friday, 24, 25 December. £2.95 (combined ticket with Scaplen's ·ourt Museum), family ticket (2A+2C) £7.25. ☎ (0202) 683 138. Refreshments ·ummer). Limited facilities for the disabled.

caplen's Court Museum – As for Waterfront Museum but closed for lunch 1300 · 1400. Closed 1 January, Good Friday, 24, 25 December. 75p. ☎ (0202) 683 138.

ORTLAND

Museum – Open Easter to September, daily, 1030 to 1300 and 1330 to 1745 2100 Fridays, holidays); otherwise, Tuesdays to Sundays, 1030 to 1300 and 1330 · 1645. Closed 1 January, Good Friday, 25, 26 December. £1. ☎ (0305) 821 804.

astle – EH. Open Easter to September, daily, 1000 to 1800. Closed 1 January, ·4 to 26 December. £1.10. ☎ (0305) 820 539. Parking. Limited facilities for the ·isabled.

S

ST AUSTELL

Wheal Martyn Museum, Carthew – Open April to October, daily, 1000 to 180(£3.80. ☎ (0726) 850 362. Parking; refreshments. Limited facilities for the disable

Mid-Cornwall Galleries, Biscovey – Open all year, Mondays to Saturdays, 100 to 1700. Closed Good Friday, 25 December to 1 January. No charge. ☎ (072 68 2131. Parking; refreshments. Facilities for the disabled.

Shipwreck and Heritage Museum, Charlestown – Open March to October, dai 1000 to 1900 (1700 winter). £2.50, family ticket (2A+2C) £5.50. Guided to (1 ½ hours) by appointment. Audio-visual presentation. ☎ (0726) 69897. Parkin refreshments. Facilities for the disabled.

ST IVES

i Street-an-Pol; ☎ (0736) 796 2

Tate Gallery – Open June to August, Mondays to Saturdays, 1100 to 1900 (210 Tuesdays and Thursdays), Sundays 1300 to 1900; otherwise, Tuesdays to Saturday 1100 to 1700 (2100 Tuesdays), Sundays, 1300 to 1700, holidays 1100 to 170 Closed 24-26 December, 1 January. £2.50, includes entry to Barbara Hepwor Museum. ☎ (0736) 796 226. Restaurant. Facilities for the disabled.

Barbara Hepworth Museum – Open June to August, same times as the Tate Galler otherwise, Tuesdays to Saturdays, 1100 to 1700, Sundays, 1300 to 1700, holida 1100 to 1700. Closed 24-26 December, 1 January. £2.50, includes entry to Ta Gallery. ☎ (0736) 796 226. Facilities for the disabled.

Penwith Gallery – Open all year, Tuesdays to Saturdays, 1000 to 1300, 1430 1700. 25p. ☎ (0736) 795 579.

St Ives Museum – Open end May to September, daily, 1000 to 1700. 50 ☎ (0736) 795 575.

ST MAWES

Castle – EH. Open April to September, daily, 1000 to 1800; otherwise, Tuesda to Sundays, 1000 to 1600. Closed 1 January, 24 to 26 December. £1.20. ☎ (032 270 526. Parking. Limited facilities for the disabled.

ST MICHAEL'S MOUNT

Castle – NT. Open April to October, Mondays to Fridays, 1030 to 1745 (1645 la admission); otherwise, guided tour by appointment only. £3, family ticket £ ☎ (0736) 69469. Restaurant.
Access by ferry : at high tide. 60p Rtn.

SALCOMBE

i ☎ (0548) 842 7

Ferries – Ferry to **Kingsbridge** : May to August; Mondays to Saturdays, 3 to 4 trip daily (½ hour). £1.80 (single). Sundays, sea or river cruise (1 hour 45min). £3.5 ☎ (0548) 853 525 or 853 607.

Ferry to **East Portlemouth** : all year, daily, 0800 (0830 holidays) to 1900. Close 25 December. 65p. ☎ (0548) 842 061 or 842 364.

Ferry to **South Sands** : all year, daily. ☎ (0548) 842 761.

Overbecks Museum, Sharpitor – **Museum** : Open April to October, Sundays to Friday 1100 to 1700. **Garden** : open all year, daily, 1000 to 2000 or dusk. £3 (museu garden), £2 (garden). ☎ (0548) 842 893. Parking; tea room. Limited facilities f the disabled.

SALISBURY

i Fish Row; ☎ (0722) 334 9

Cathedral – Open all year, daily, 0800 to 2015 (1830 September to April). Close Good Friday. Donation. Guided tour March to October, Mondays to Saturdays 093 to 1630, Sundays, 1600 to 1830; £1.50, family ticket £3. **Roof tour** : March to Octob and 26 December to 1 January at 1100 and 1400 (1200 and 1500 also, Ma to August); otherwise, Saturdays at 1100 and 1400. ☎ (0722) 328 726. Faciliti for the disabled.

Salisbury and South Wiltshire Museum – Open all year, Mondays to Saturday 1000 to 1700; also July to mid-September, Sundays, 1400 to 1700. Close Christmas. £2.25. ☎ (0722) 322 151. Facilities for the disabled.

Museum of the Duke of Edinburgh's Royal Regiment – Open February t November, daily, 1000 to 1630. Closed winter weekends. £1.50. ☎ (072 414 536. Limited parking; refreshments. Facilities for the disabled.

Mompesson House – NT. Open April to October, Saturdays to Wednesdays, 120 to 1730. £3, child £1.50. ☎ (0722) 335 659. Refreshments. Facilities for th disabled.

Old Sarum : Castle ruins – EH. Open all year, daily, 1000 to 1800 (1600 winter Closed 1 January, 24 to 26 December, £1.20. ☎ (0722) 335 398. Parking.

Heale House Garden, Woodford – **Garden** : open all year, daily, 1000 to 1700. £2.5 ☎ (072 273) 504. **House** : by appointment only. Parking.

Newhouse, Redlynch – Open August, Mondays to Saturdays, 1400 to 1730. £2.5 ☎ (0725) 20055.

SALTRAM HOUSE

House – NT. Open April to October, Sundays to Thursdays, 1230 to 1730. £4.80 including garden. ☎ (0752) 336 546. Licensed restaurant. Facilities for the disabled.

Garden – NT. Open April to October, daily, 1030 to 1730. £2.20. Facilities for the disabled.

SANDFORD ORCAS

Manor House – Open May to September, Sundays, 1400 to 1800; Easter Monday, Mondays, 1000 to 1800. £1.80. Guided tour (½ hour). ☎ (0963) 220 206. Parking.

Isles of SCILLY

ℹ Porthcressa Bank, St Mary's; ☎ (0720) 22536

Access – **Helicopter** from Penzance to St Mary's and Tresco; ☎ (0736) 63871. **Aeroplane;** ☎ (0720) 22677. **Skybus** from Land's End Aerodrome to St Mary's (15min). £36 single, £50 day trip; ☎ (0736) 787 017 or (0800) 243 723. **Skybus** from Exeter; ☎ (0736) 787017. **Boat** (the *Scillonian III*) from Penzance to St Mary's (4 ½ hours), April to October. £30 single. ☎ (0800) 373 307.

Gig Racing – April to September, Wednesdays and Fridays from 2000.

St Mary's Museum – Open Easter to October, daily, 1000 to 1200 and 1330 to 1630 (and 1900 to 2100, May to August); otherwise, Wednesdays, 1400 to 1600. 75p. ☎ (0720) 22337.

Tresco Abbey Gardens – Open all year, daily, 1000 to 1600. £3. Guided tour (1 hour). ☎ (0720) 22849 or 22566. Café. Limited facilities for the disabled.

SEATON

ℹ The Esplanade; ☎ (0297) 21660 or 21689

Tramway – Operates Easter to September, daily, 0940 to 1720; October, Mondays to Fridays, 0940 to 1720. £3.20 (Rtn). ☎ (0297) 21702. Facilities for the disabled.

SHAFTESBURY

ℹ 8 Bell Street; ☎ (0747) 53514

Local History Museum – Open Easter to September, daily, 1100 (1430 Sundays) to 1700; otherwise by appointment. 60p. ☎ (0747) 854 548. Limited facilities for the disabled.

Abbey – Open Easter to October, daily, 1000 to 1730. 80p. ☎ (0747) 852 910. Limited facilities for the disabled.

SHELDON MANOR

House and Gardens – Open Easter to early October, Sundays, Thursdays and holidays, 1400 (1230 gardens) to 1800; otherwise by appointment. £3. Guided tour (1 hour). ☎ (0249) 653 120. Parking; refreshments. Facilities for the disabled.

SHEPTON MALLET

East Somerset Railway, Cranmore – **Depot** : Open May to October, daily, 1000 to 1730 (1600 weekdays, September to October); November to December and March to April, weekends, 1 January, 1000 to 1600. £1.30. **Trains in operation** : May to October, Sundays and holidays, also some Wednesdays, Thursdays and Saturdays. £3.30. ☎ (0749) 880 417. Parking; licensed restaurant; picnic area. Facilities for the disabled.

SHERBORNE

ℹ Hound Street; ☎ (0935) 815 341

Abbey – Open all year, daily, 0830 to 1800 (1600 winter). No charge. Guided tour by appointment. ☎ (0935) 812 452. Limited facilities for the disabled.

Castle : **House and Grounds** – EH. Open Holy Saturday to September, Thursdays, weekends and holiday Mondays, 1400 (1200 grounds) to 1730. £3.60 (castle, grounds), £1.50 (grounds). ☎ (0935) 813 182. Parking; refreshments.

Museum – Open April to October, Tuesdays to Sundays and holidays, 1030 (1430 Sundays) to 1630; November to mid-December, Tuesdays, Fridays and Saturdays, 1030 to 1630. 50p. Guided tour (45min) by appointment. ☎ (0935) 812 252. Limited facilities for the disabled.

Purse Caundle Manor – Open May to September, Thursdays and Sundays, 1400 to 1700. £2. Guided tour (½ hour). ☎ (0923) 250 400. Parking. Limited facilities for the disabled.

Worldwide Butterflies, Over Compton – Open April to October, daily, 1000 to 1700. £3.99, family ticket (2A+2C) £8.99. ☎ (0935) 74608. Refreshments; picnic area.

SIDMOUTH

ℹ Ham Lane; ☎ (0395) 516 441

Donkey Sanctuary, Salcombe Regis – Open all year, daily, 0900 to dusk. No charge. Guided tour (2 hours) by appointment. ☎ (0395) 578 222. Parking; refreshments; picnic area. Facilities for the disabled.

STONEHENGE

Site – EH. Open all year, daily, 1000 to 1800 (1600 October to March). Closed 1 January, 24 to 26 December. £2.50. ☎ (0272) 734 472. Parking; refreshments. Limited facilities for the disabled.

STOURHEAD

Gardens – NT. Open all year, daily, 0800 to 1900 or dusk. £4, child £2 (Marc to October), £3, child £1.50 (November to February). ☎ (0747) 840 348. Parking restaurant. Facilities for the disabled.

House – NT. Open April to October, Saturdays to Wednesdays, 1200 to 1730 c dusk; otherwise by appointment. Closed Good Friday. £4, child £2. Guided tou (½ hour). ☎ (0747) 840 348. Parking. Limited facilities for the disabled.

STURMINSTER NEWTON MILL

Mill – Guided tour (20min) summer months, Thursdays, Fridays and Sundays, 110 to 1800. £1.

SWANAGE

The White House, Shore Road; ☎ (0929) 422 88

Studland Chain Ferry – Open all year, daily, 0710 to 2310 (last ferry); 25 Decembe 0800 to 1810. £1.80 (car), 40p (passenger). ☎ (0929) 44203.

SWINDON

32 The Arcade, Brunel Centre; ☎ (0793) 530 32

GWR Museum – Open all year, daily, 1000 (1400 Sundays) to 1700. Closed Goo Friday. £1.80. Guided tour (½ hour). ☎ (0793) 493 189. Limited facilities for th disabled.

Railway Village Museum – Open all year, daily, 1000 (1400 Sundays) to 1700 Closed Good Friday. 75p. ☎ (0793) 526 161 ext 4527.

Museum and Art Gallery – Open all year, daily, 1000 (1400 Sundays) to 173C Closed Good Friday, 25, 26 December. No charge. ☎ (0793) 493 188. Limite facilities for the disabled.

Richard Jefferies Museum – Limited opening; ring for details. ☎ (0793) 493 188

T

TAUNTON

Corporation Street; ☎ (0823) 274 78

Somerset County Museum – Open all year, Mondays to Saturdays, 1000 to 170C Closed 1 January, Good Friday, 25, 26 December. £1.20. ☎ (0823) 255 504 Facilities for the disabled.

TEIGNMOUTH

The Den, Sea Front; ☎ (0626) 779 76

Powderham Castle – Open Easter to October, Sundays to Fridays, 1030 to 1800 £3.95, family ticket £9.85. ☎ (0626) 890 243.

TINTAGEL

Arthur's Castle – EH. Open April to September, daily, 1000 to 1800; otherwise Tuesdays to Sundays, 1000 to 1600. Closed 1 January, 24 to 26 December. £1.80 ☎ (0840) 770 328.

Old Post Office – NT. Open April to October, daily, 1100 to 1730 (1700 October) Only 5 people at a time. £1.90.

Delabole Quarry – **Viewing Platform** : Open all year, daily. **Showroom** : Open all year Mondays to Fridays, 0800 to 1700. Closed 24 to 26 December. No charge. ☎ (0840) 212 242.

TINTINHULL HOUSE GARDEN

Garden – NT. Open April to September, Wednesdays to Thursdays, Saturdays anc holiday Mondays, 1400 to 1800. £3.20. ☎ (0747) 840 224. Parking; refreshments Limited facilities for the disabled.

TIVERTON

Phoenix Lane; ☎ (0884) 255 827

Castle – Open Good Friday to late September, Sundays to Thursdays, 1430 to 1730 Closed 25, 26 December. £2.75. Guided tour (1 ½ hours). ☎ (0884) 253 200 Parking. Limited facilities for the disabled.

Museum – Open February to December, Mondays to Saturdays, 1000 to 1630 Closed 1 January, 25, 26 December. £1. Guided tour by appointment. ☎ (0884 256 295.

Coldharbour Mill, Uffculme – Open Easter to October, daily, 1100 to 1700 otherwise, Mondays to Fridays and holidays, 1100 to 1700. £2.95, family ticket (2A+2C) £8. Guided tour (1 ½ hours). ☎ (0884) 840 960. Parking; licensed restaurant (Easter to October). Limited facilities for the disabled.

TOLPUDDLE

TUC Cottages and Martyrs' Museum – Open all year, Tuesdays to Sundays, 1000 to 1730 (1600 November to March). No charge. ☎ (0305) 848 237. Limited parking. Facilities for the disabled.

Methodist Chapel – Open Easter to September, Mondays to Saturdays, 0930 to 1800.

TORBAY

Ferry to Brixham – Open all year, daily. Telephone for timetable. ☏ (0803) 297 292. Rtn £3, single £1.70.

Torquay

ℹ Vaughan Parade; ☏ (0803) 297 428

Kents Cavern – Open April to October, daily, 1000 to 1800 (2100 July to August, except Saturdays); otherwise, daily, 1000 to 1700. Closed 25 December. £2.90, family ticket (2A+3C) £9. Guided tour (45min). ☏ (0803) 294 059. Parking; refreshments (summer). Facilities for the disabled.

Torre Abbey – Open April to October, daily, 0930 to 1800; otherwise, Mondays to Fridays, 1000 to 1700 by appointment. £2, family ticket (2A+3C) £4.50. Guided tour (1 hour) by appointment. ☏ (0803) 293 593. Tea room (summer).

Babbacombe Model Village – Open Easter to October, daily, 0900 to 2200; otherwise, daily, 1000 to dusk. Closed 25 December. £3.40, child £2.20 ☏ (0803) 328 669. Parking; refreshments. Facilities for the disabled.

Paignton

ℹ The Esplanade; ☏ (0803) 558 383

Zoo – Open all year, daily, 1000 to 1830 (1700 November to February). Closed 25 December. £3.95. Guided tour (45min). ☏ (0803) 527 936. Parking; restaurant. Facilities for the disabled.

Oldway Mansion and Gardens – Open May to September, Mondays to Saturdays, 0900 to 1700, Sundays, 1400 to 1700; otherwise, Mondays to Saturdays, 0900 to 1700 (1300 Saturdays). No charge. Guided tour (summer). ☏ (0803) 296 244 ext 2123. Parking. Facilities for the disabled.

Paignton Parish Church – Open all year, Mondays to Fridays, 1030 to 1230 and 1430 to 1630; otherwise by appointment. ☏ (0803) 559 059.

Paignton and Dartmouth Steam Railway – Open April to October, daily; also early to late December. Trains depart at regular intervals from 1015. Telephone for timetable. £5.20 (Rtn). ☏ (0803) 555 872.

Cockington Court : Rural Skills Trust – Open April to October, daily, 1030 to 1630. £1. ☏ (0803) 605 377.

Berry Pomeroy Castle – EH. Open April to September, daily, 1000 to 1800. £1.70, child 85p. ☏ (0803) 866 618. Parking. Limited facilities for the disabled.

TOTNES

ℹ The Plains; ☏ (0803) 863 168

Motor Museum – Open Easter to October, daily, 1000 to 1730. £2.50. ☏ (0803) 862 777. Parking. Limited facilities for the disabled.

Elizabethan Museum – Open mid-March to late October, Mondays to Saturdays, holidays, 1030 to 1700 (1230 Saturdays). 50p. Guided tour (45min) by appointment. ☏ (0803) 863 821.

Guildhall – Open Easter to October, Mondays to Fridays, 1000 to 1700. Closed holidays. 50p. Guided tour (20min). ☏ (0803) 862 147. Parking.

Devonshire Collection of Period Costume – Open Spring holiday Monday to September, Mondays to Fridays, 1100 to 1700, Sundays, 1400 to 1700. £1, family ticket £2.25. ☏ (0803) 862 827.

Castle – EH. Open Easter to September, daily, 1000 to 1800; otherwise, Tuesdays to Sundays, 1000 to 1600. Closed 1 January, 25, 26 December. £1.20, child 65p. Guided tour (½ hour). ☏ (0803) 864 406. Refreshments (summer).

British Photographic Museum, Bowden House – Open Easter Sunday to late September, Tuesdays to Thursdays, also holiday Sundays and Mondays, 1200 to 1730. £2.25. ☏ (0803) 863 664. Parking; licensed café.

TRELISSICK

Garden – NT. Open all year, daily, 1030 (1300 Sundays) to 1730 (1700 March, October). £3. ☏ (0872) 865 808. Parking; licensed restaurant. Facilities for the disabled.

TRENGWAINTON

Garden – NT. Open March to October, Wednesdays to Saturdays and holiday Mondays, 1030 to 1730 (1700 October). £2.40. ☏ (0208) 74281.

TRERICE

House – NT. Open April to October, daily, 1100 to 1730 (1700 October). £3.60. ☏ (0208) 74281.

TREWITHEN

Garden – Open March to September, Mondays to Saturdays and holidays, 1000 to 1630. £2 (April to June), £1.75 (July to September). **House** : open April to July, Mondays, Tuesdays and August holiday Monday, 1400 to 1600. £2.80. Guided tour (35min). ☏ (0726) 882 763 or 882 764. Parking; refreshments. Limited facilities for the disabled.

TRURO

Boscawen Street; ☎ (0872) 74555

Royal Cornwall Museum – Open all year, Mondays to Saturdays, 0900 to 1700. Closed holidays. £1. Guided tour (1 ½ hours). ☎ (0872) 72205. Refreshments. Facilities for the disabled.

King Harry Ferry – Operates from Feock to Philleigh (5min), April to September, daily; otherwise, Mondays to Saturdays. Telephone for timetable. Car £1.60 (single), £2.30 (Rtn). ☎ (0872) 72463.

County Demonstration Garden, Probus – Open April to September, Mondays to Fridays, 1000 to 1700; otherwise, daily, 1000 to 1600. £2. Guided tour (1 ½ hours). ☎ (0872) 74282. Parking; refreshments. Facilities for the disabled.

U

UGBROOKE HOUSE

House – Guided tour (1¼ hours) Spring holiday, and late July to August, Tuesdays to Thursdays and Sundays, at 1400 and 1545. **Garden** : open as for house, 1300 to 1730. £3.80, child £1.90. ☎ (0626) 852 179. Parking; refreshments. Facilities for the disabled.

W

WARDOUR CASTLE

Old Wardour Castle – EH. Open April to September, daily, 1000 to 1800; otherwise, weekends, 1000 to 1600. Closed 1 January, 24 to 26 December. £1.30. ☎ (0747) 870 487. Parking. Facilities for the disabled.

WAREHAM

Town Hall, East Street; ☎ (0929) 552 740

Local History Museum – Open Easter to mid-October, Mondays to Saturdays, 1000 to 1300 and 1400 to 1700. No charge. Guided tour (45min). ☎ (0929) 553 448. Limited facilities for the disabled.

Blue Pool – Grounds : Open March to November, daily, 0930 to 1800. **Museum** : open Easter to October, daily, 0930 to 1730. £1.60. ☎ (0929) 551 408. Parking; tea room; picnic area. Facilities for the disabled.

Bovington Camp Tank Museum – Open all year, daily, 1000 to 1700. Closed 10 days at Christmas and New Year. £4, family ticket (2A+2C) £8. Guided tour (2 hours) by appointment. ☎ (0929) 403 329 or 403 463. Parking; licensed restaurant. Facilities for the disabled.

Toy Museum, Arne – Open April or Easter to September, Tuesdays to Fridays, Sundays and holiday Mondays, 1330 to 1700 (1100 to 1730 July and August). £1.50, children 75p. Parking; tea room. Limited facilities for the disabled.

WELLS

Town Hall, Market Place; ☎ (0749) 672 552

Museum – Open April to October, daily, 1000 to 1730; otherwise, Wednesdays to Sundays, 1100 to 1600. Closed 24, 25 December. £1. ☎ (0749) 673 477. Limited facilities for the disabled.

Bishop's Palace – Open, August, daily, 1400 to 1800; Easter to October, Wednesdays, Sundays and holidays, 1400 to 1800. £1.50. ☎ (0749) 78691. Refreshments. Limited facilities for the disabled.

WESTWOOD MANOR

Manor – Open April to September, Tuesdays, Wednesdays and Sundays, 1400 to 1700. £2.80. ☎ (02216) 3374.

WEYMOUTH

The Esplanade; ☎ (0305) 772 444

Museum – Open April to December, daily, 0930 to 1730 (2200 school summer holidays); otherwise, Tuesdays to Sundays, 0930 to 1730. No charge. ☎ (0305) 777 622. Facilities for the disabled.

Timewalk – Open as for museum; last admission one hour before closing. £3.50. ☎ (0305) 777 622. Refreshments.

Discovery – Open April to December, daily, 0930 to 1730 (2200 school summer holidays); otherwise, Tuesdays to Sundays, 0930 to 1730. £2.70, family ticket £5.70 or £8. ☎ (0305) 789 007. Refreshments. Facilities for the disabled.

Nothe Fort – Open May to September, daily, 1100 to 1730; otherwise, Sundays, 1400 to 1700. £2. Parking; refreshments. Facilities for the disabled.

Boat Trips – Operate from the pier bandstand; cruise around **Portland harbour** (1 ½ hours), £2.25.

WILTON HOUSE

House – Open April to mid-October, daily, 1100 (1200 Sundays) to 1800 (1615 last admission). £5. ☎ (0722) 743 115. Parking; refreshments. Limited facilities for the disabled.

Royal Wilton Carpet Factory – Open February to November, Mondays to Saturdays, 1000 to 1515. Admission charge. ☎ (0722) 742 441.

WIMBORNE MINSTER

ℹ 29 High Street; ☎ (0202) 886 116

Priest's House Museum – Open April to October, daily; November to 24 December, weekends, 1030 (1430 Sundays) to 1630. £1. Guided tour (45min) by appointment. ☎ (0202) 882 533. Tea room. Limited facilities for the disabled.

Glass Studio – Open all year, Mondays to Saturdays, 0930 to 1700. Closed 1 January, 25, 26 December. No charge. ☎ (0202) 880940.

Cranborne Manor Gardens – Open March to September, Wednesdays, 0900 to 1700. £2.50. ☎ (07254) 248. Parking. Limited facilities for the disabled.

WOOKEY HOLE

Caves, Papermill and Fairground Collection – Open all year, daily. 0930 to 1730 (1630 November to February). £4.90. Guided tour (2 hours) of caves. Closed 17 to 25 December. ☎ (0749) 672 243. Parking; restaurant; picnic area. Facilities for the disabled.

Y

YEOVIL

ℹ Petter's Way; ☎ (0935) 71279

Museum of South Somerset – Open all year, Tuesdays to Saturdays, 1000 to 1600. No charge. ☎ (0935) 24774.

Fleet Air Arm Museum, Yeovilton – Open all year, daily, 1000 to 1730 (1630 November to March). Closed 24 to 26 December. £4.50, child £2.50. ☎ (0935) 840 565. Parking; refreshments. Limited facilities for the disabled.

East Lambrook Manor : Garden – Open March to October, Mondays to Saturdays, 1000 to 1700. £2, child 50p. ☎ (0460) 40328. Parking; refreshments.

Sparkford Motor Museum – Open all year, daily, 0930 to 1730. Closed 1 January, 25, 26 December. £2.95. ☎ (0963) 40804. Parking; cafeteria. Facilities for the disabled.

Clovelly harbour.

CHANNEL ISLANDS

JERSEY

ℹ Liberation Square, St Helier; ☎ (0534) 500 700

Mont Orgueil Castle – Open late March to late October, daily, 0930 to 1800. £1.

Jersey Pottery – Open all year, Mondays to Fridays, 0900 to 1730. Closed holidays. No charge. ☎ (0534) 51119. Parking; refreshments. Facilities for the disabled.

La Hougue Bie : Museums – Open March to October, daily, 1000 to 1700. Closed Good Friday. £1.50. Guided tour by appointment. ☎ (0534) 30511. Parking.

Jersey Zoo – Open all year, daily, 1000 to 1800 or dusk. Closed 25 December. £4.50, child £2.50. Guided tour (2 hours). ☎ (0534) 864 666. Parking; refreshments. Facilities for the disabled.

Elizabeth Castle – Open March to October, daily, 0930 to 1800 (1700 last admission). £2. Guided tour (1 ½ hours). ☎ (0534) 23971. Restaurant.

Jersey Museum – Open all year, daily, 1000 (1400 Sundays) to 1800 (1700 winter). Closed 25 December. £2. Guided tour by appointment. ☎ (0534) 30511. Restaurant. Facilities for the disabled.

Royal Court House – **States in session** : October to mid-July, Tuesdays, 1000 to close of business.

Fort Regent – Open all year, daily, 0845 to 2300. Closed 24 to 26 December. £3 (summer), £2 (Saturdays), £1.25 (winter), £1 (after 1700). Guided tour (1 hour) in summer. ☎ (0534) 73000. Parking; restaurant. Facilities for the disabled.

Island Fortress Occupation Museum – Open April to October, daily, 0900 to 2230; otherwise, 1000 to 1600. £2.50. ☎ (0534) 34306. Limited facilities for the disabled.

Living Legend – Open March to December, daily (not Tuesdays and Wednesdays in March and April), 0930 to 1630. £4. ☎ (0534) 485 496.

Samarés Manor – **Gardens** : Open April to October, daily, 1000 to 1700. £2.50. **House** : Guided tours (40min) Mondays to Saturdays, 1030 to 1200. £1.50. **Herb talks** : Mondays to Fridays, 1415. **Goat milking** : Daily, at 1600. ☎ (0534) 70551. Parking; refreshments. Facilities for the disabled.

German Underground Hospital – Open March to October, daily, 0930 to 1730 (1645 last admission); otherwise, Sundays, 1200 to 1730, Thursdays, 1400 to 1730. £3.65. ☎ (0534) 63734. Parking; café. Facilities for the disabled.

Quetivel Mill – NT. Open May to October, Tuesdays to Thursdays, 1000 to 1600. £1. ☎ (0534) 483 193. Parking. Limited facilities for the disabled.

Jersey Motor Museum – Open mid-March to October, daily, 1000 to 1700. £1.50. ☎ (0534) 482 966. Parking. Limited facilities for the disabled.

St Matthew's Church, Millbrook – Open all year, Mondays to Fridays, 0900 to 1800 (1700 in winter), Saturdays, 0900 to 1300, Sundays for services only.

Kempt Tower Interpretation Centre – Open June to September, Tuesdays to Sundays, 1400 to 1700; May, October, Thursdays, Sundays, holidays, 1400 to 1700. No charge. Guided tour (1 ½ hours) Thursdays at 1500. ☎ (0534) 483 651. Parking.

Battle of Flowers Museum – Open Easter to mid-November, daily, 1000 to 1700. £1.50. ☎ (0534) 482 408. Parking; refreshments. Limited facilities for the disabled.

Shire Horse Farm – Open March to November, Sundays to Fridays, 1000 to 1730. £2.50. ☎ (0534) 482 372. Parking; refreshments. Limited facilities for the disabled.

La Mare Vineyard – Open May to October, Mondays to Saturdays, holidays, 1000 to 1730. £2.50. Guided tour (1 hour) by appointment. ☎ (0534) 481 178. Parking; refreshments. Facilities for the disabled.

GUERNSEY

ℹ Crown Pier, St Peter Port; ☎ (0481) 723 552
ℹ The Airport, Forest; ☎ (0481) 37267

Castle Cornet – Open April to October, daily, 1030 to 1730. **Noonday gun** fired Mondays to Saturdays. £4, family ticket £9. Guided tour (1 hour). ☎ (0481) 726 518. Parking; refreshments.

Hauteville House – Guided tour April to September, Mondays to Saturdays, 1000 to 1130, 1400 to 1630. £3.50. ☎ (0481) 21911.

Guernsey Museum and Art Gallery – Open all year, daily, 1030 to 1730 (1630 winter). Closed 23 to 26 December. £2, family ticket £4.50. ☎ (0481) 726 518. Parking; refreshments. Facilities for the disabled.

St James' – Open all year, Mondays to Fridays, 0830 to 1800, Saturdays, 1000 to 1200. Closed holidays.

Royal Court House – **States in session** : September to July, last Wednesday of the month (earlier in December), 1000 to close of business. Details of debates available from the Greffe. ☎ (0481) 25277.

Aquarium – Open all year, daily, 1000 to 1700 (1600 October to May); summer weekends, 1000 to dusk. Closed 25, 26 December. £1.20. ☎ (0481) 23301.

Hostel of St John – Open all year, daily. Rooms on the ground floor only.

Guernsey Folk Museum – Open late March to late October, daily, 1000 to 1730. £2. ☎ (0481) 55384.

ierman Underground Hospital – Open May to September, daily, 1000 to 1200, 400 to 1700; April, October, daily, 1400 to 1600; March, November, Sundays nd Thursdays, 1400 to 1500. £1. ☎ (0481) 39100.

atlands Craft Centre – Open all year, daily, 1000 to 1700. Closed Sunday fternoons, November to March. No charge, **Shire Horse Centre** £1.50, **Bee Centre** 50p. ☎ (0481) 44282 or 49478. Parking; restaurant. Facilities for the disabled.

ehus Dolmen – Open all year, daily, dawn to dusk. ☎ (0481) 726 518.

ort Grey Maritime Museum – Open early April to early October, daily, 1030 to 730. £1.50, family ticket £3.25. ☎ (0481) 726 518. Parking.

ierman Occupation Museum – Open April to October, daily, 1030 to 1630; therwise, Sundays, Thursdays, 1400 to 1630. Closed January. £2. ☎ (0481) 8205. Parking; refreshments. Facilities for the disabled.

ausmarez Manor – House : Guided tour (40min) end May to September, Tuesdays ɔ Thursdays and holiday Mondays, 1030 to 1115 and 1430 to 1616. **Garden :** open ll year, daily, 1000 to 1700. £2. Doll's house collection and narrow-gauge railway. ☎ (0481) 35571. Parking; refreshments. Facilities for the disabled.

LDERNEY

Queen Elizabeth II Street; ☎ (048 182) 2994

luseum – Open Easter Saturday to October, daily, 1000 to 1200. £1, children no harge. ☎ (048 182) 3222.

ourt House – Open all year, Mondays to Fridays, 0930 to 1230, with permission om Clerk of the Court. **Court in session :** Thursdays, 1400. **States in session :** second Vednesday of the month, 1000 to 1230.

oat Trips – Ring the Harbour Office for details. ☎ (048 182) 2620.

orts Tour – Tour (3 hours) Easter to September, Wednesdays, 1400. Depart from utes. **Victorian or German forts tour;** booking daily from 1000. £8. ☎ (048 182) 3535.

lderney Railway – Open Easter to September, weekends and holidays, 1400 to 700. £1.30, £1.70 (steam trains).

uesnard Lighthouse – Open all year, daily, weather permitting. ☎ (048 182) 2522.

urhou Island – Open mid-July, to mid-March; otherwise closed for breeding season. 1 (daily), £2 (per night). Apply for permission from the Harbour Office, daily, 0800 ɔ 1800 (1700 winter, Mondays to Fridays). ☎ (048 182) 2620.

ARK

☎ (0481) 832 345

a Seigneurie Gardens – Open Easter to mid-October, Wednesdays, Fridays, 1000 ɔ 1700, Tuesdays, Thursdays, holidays, 1100 to 1500. 60p. ☎ (0481) 832 345.

INDEX

Names of places, houses, streets are in roman type : Avon, Tamar, Lanyon Quoi
Cheddar, Dartmoor, Lyme Bay, Longleat...

People, historical events, subjects are in italics : *Drake, Sir Francis, lighthouse*
Sedgemoor, Battle of, glass, military museums...

Where there are several page references the most important is in bold type : Adar
Robert 91, 152, **186**, 217-8.

A

B

C

D

E

F

G

H

I

J

K

L

M

N

O

T

U

V

W

Y - Z

NOTES

ACKNOWLEDGMENTS OF PHOTOGRAPHS AND ILLUSTRATIONS :

p 13 C Parker/BMV Picturebank, London
p 16 After Judges photo
p 18 A F Kersting, London
p 21 Beken of Cowes
p 24 Courtesy of Trinity House Lighthouse Service, London
p 25 JACANA: Antony 8/Boët 3, 4/CW 10/ Davenne 2/Ermie 6, 9/Ferrero 1/Mallet 11/ Nardin 7/Sailler 5
p 27 National Trust/John Bethell
p 28 National Trust Photo Library/Rupert Truman
p 29 N Duterque/Michelin
p 31 C Parker/BMV Picturebank, London
p 33 Vloo/J Alan Cash
p 35 BMV Picturebank, London
p 37 Courtesy of Penzance and District Museum and Art Gallery
p 38 Courtesy of the Tate Gallery, London
p 41 A F Kersting, London
p 43 A la Ronde
p 46 Vloo/J Alan Cash
p 55 BMV Picturebank, London
p 57 After A F Kersting photo
p 59 Vloo/J Alan Cash
p 65 After West Country Tourist Board/Mike Weaver
p 70 P Skinner/BMV Picturebank, London
p 76 Cosmos/Aspect/G Paxton
p 89 BMV Picturebank, London
p 91 Andy Williams Photo Library, Guildford
p 96 Ch Parker/BMV Picturebank, London
p 103 After J Salmon photo
p 105 National Trust/J Gibson
p 109 S Pitcher/BMV Picturebank, London
p 113 D Tucker/BMV Picturebank, London
p 123 Pitkin Pictorial
p 125 Vloo/J Alan Cash
p 134 Vloo/J Alan Cash
p 137 After A F Kersting photo
p 139 BTA
p 140 BMV Picturebank, London
p 142 M Stevens, Trowbridge
p 145 K Fletcher/BMV Picturebank, London
p 148 National Trust/John Bethell
p 149 After Zodiaque photo
p 155 After National Trust photo/Erik Pelham
p 159 A F Kersting, London
p 169 Trevor Burrows Photography, Plymouth
p 178 G Walden/BMV Picturebank, London
p 179 Hepworth Museum
p 180 Cosmos/Aspect/D Bayes
p 182 Everts/ZEFA
p 186 National Trust
p 188 After CEDRI photo/Gérard Sioen
p 195 Courtesy of Mr Simon Wingfield Digby, Sherborne Castle
p 196 After BTA photo
p 198 BMV Picturebank, London
p 199 With the permission of the Controller, HMSO
p 212 Vloo/J Alan Cash
p 214 National Trust/Tymn Lintell
p 220 BMV Picturebank, London
p 222 BTA
p 225 Vloo/J Alan Cash
p 226 BTA
p 229 West Country Tourist Board/Mike Weaver
p 230 After L C Hayward/Yeovil Council photo
p 231 After Murray King, St Ives/Penwith Council photo
p 233 Top/R Tixador
p 237 Top/R Tixador
p 250 Top/R Tixador
p 255 Top/R Tixador
p 257 Top/R Tixador
p 259 Courtesy of Richard Jones/West Somerset Railway
p 287 C Parker/BMV Picturebank, London
p 297 After BTA photo

MANUFACTURE FRANÇAISE DES PNEUMATIQUES MICHELIN

Société en commandite par actions au capital de 2 000 000 000 de francs

Place des Carmes-Déchaux – 63 Clermont-Ferrand (France)

R.C.S. Clermont-Fd B 855 200 507

Dépôt légal septembre 1993 – ISBN 2 06-156203-5– ISSN 0763-1383

Printed in the EC 12-94-13/1

Photocomposition et impression : MAURY Imprimeur S.A., Malesherbes

Brochage : MAME Imprimeurs, Tours